Wilma Austin

Nov 23-70

Brooklyn NY

2861 Fulton St
11233

The Lily Wallace
New American
Cook Book

THE LILY WALLACE
NEW AMERICAN
COOK BOOK

EDITOR-IN-CHIEF
Lily Haxworth Wallace
HOME ECONOMICS LECTURER AND WRITER
Instructor, Household Arts Department
The Ballard School, New York City

BOOKS, INC., Publishers

A Subsidiary of Publishers Co., Inc.
New York · Washington, D. C.

Color Plates Courtesy of
Campbell Soup Co.
Best Foods—Corn Products

Contents

CONTENTS

The New American

Index

A COOK BOOK is only as good as its index. The editors of the NEW AMERICAN COOK BOOK have developed an indexing system which makes every dish described readily and quickly available to the busy homemaker. The New American Index includes two major features.

1. The index numbers which appear opposite, at the left, of the title of every recipe.

2. The alphabetical list of all recipes, features, and other instructions contained in the book, the "Index," p. 923.

Following is a sample recipe from the section on egg dishes:

(220)   EGG CROQUETTES

1¼ cups very thick white   ½ teaspoon salt
   sauce (No. 2004)   1 tablespoon chopped parsley
4 hard-cooked eggs, chopped 1 cup dry bread crumbs
   fine (No. 202)   1 well-beaten egg

Combine sauce, cooked eggs, salt, and parsley. Chill. Mold into rounds or croquettes. Roll in crumbs. Dip in beaten egg, diluted with 2 tablespoons cold water. Roll again in crumbs. Fry in deep, hot fat (375° F.) about 2 minutes or until well browned. Serve hot with cheese (No. 2008) or tomato sauce (No. 2035). Serves 4.

Note the index number—(220). Every recipe in the book has a different number and these numbers run, consecutively, from

11

the front to the back of the book. No. 220 designates EGG CROQUETTES. Also the index number carries the information that Recipe No. 220 is an egg dish because every egg recipe is in the 200 block of numbers. Every section of the book has its own block of numbers which will become familiar to the user. Fruits are in the 100 block, canapés are in the 400 block, foreign recipes are in the 3500 block, etc. Every new class of dishes starts on a new one hundred. In some cases sections run through several hundreds as, for example, meats, the recipes for which run from 1301 to 1617. The next section—vegetables—starts with Recipe No. 1701. Thus, there are no recipes No. 1618 to 1700, inclusive.

How can you make use of these index numbers? Refer to the recipe for EGG CROQUETTES on the preceding page. When you are planning a menu, you can save time by simply jotting down dishes by number, rather than by name. This will eliminate mistakes because many dishes have similar-sounding titles and the wrong dish might be prepared if instructions are given by name. It will save time because the number will lead you directly to the proper recipe without any effort when you start to prepare the dish.

Now, read the recipe. The first item in the ingredients is *1¼ cups very thick white sauce (No. 2004)*. Turn to Recipe No. 2004 and there, before you, are complete instructions for making this item. Other cook books would refer you to some page in the book where you would waste valuable moments seeking exactly what you wanted.

The large index in the final section of this book is very complete. Everything is listed in alphabetical order and under every word which may be used in seeking it. Thus Recipe No. 220, EGG CROQUETTES, is listed as

Egg
    croquettes . . . . No. 220
and as
Croquettes
    egg . . . . No. 220

Accordingly, if you wish to plan a meal with an egg dish, turn to *egg* in the index and under it you will find all egg dishes.

Cooking Terms Explained

Baking

THIS is cooking in an oven. For best results the temperature of the oven should be regulated exactly as specified in all recipes for baked food. Following are the names given to the various temperature stages for baking:

Slow oven	250° to 325° F.
Moderately slow oven	326° to 349° F.
Moderate oven	350° to 375° F.
Moderately hot oven	376° to 399° F.
Hot oven	400° to 449° F.
Quick oven	450° to 500° F.
Very hot oven	501° to 575° F.

Barbecuing

The roasting of meats or other foods on a revolving spit before an open flame or glowing coals.

Basting

To pour fat, pan drippings, or other liquid over roasting, baking, or broiling foods either to prevent burning or to flavor.

Beating

Beating can be done manually or with any of several hand-operated or electrical devices on the market. Its purpose is to trap air within the food and, in general, the motion of food undergoing a beating should be from underneath to the top. Beating should always be vigorously done in order that the entire contents are kept constantly in motion.

Blanching

This is plunging into boiling water to either remove a skin or to whiten.

Boiling

This consists of heating water or other liquid until it bubbles rapidly. These bubbles rise to the surface of the liquid and leave it in the form of steam. A liqud, if the steam is permitted to escape freely, can never be heated to a higher temperature than its boiling point. At sea level water boils at 212° F. or 100° C. The temperatures at whch it will boil at higher altitudes are shown in the following table:

Altitude feet	Temperature of boiling water	
	°F.	°C.
1,025	210	99
2,063	208	98
3,115	206	97
4,169	204	95
5,225	202	94
6,304	200	93
7,381	198	92
8,481	196	91
9,031	195	90

The recipes in this book are all based on sea-level conditions. To boil food at 5,000 feet will require a slightly longer time than is stipulated herein.

Braising

Braising is browning meat in a hot receptacle in a small amount of fat, then cooking slowly in the meat juices or in added liquid (water, milk, cream, diluted lemon juice, juices from vegetables) in a covered utensil.

Broiling

This consists of cooking food by exposure to an open fire, coals, or a glowing heat unit.

Broiling, Oven

See *Oven Broiling.*

Broiling, Pan

See *Pan Broiling.*

Creaming

This is the softening of fat by means of pressure and beating at room temperature. Sugar or other ingredients are often added to the fat during the process of creaming.

Cutting In

This is a method for combining flour and shortening. They are combined in small, crumbly particles by blending them with the finger tips, two knives, or a pastry mixer.

Deep-Fat Frying

This consists of cooking food by immersing it in deep, hot fat. Food cooked by this method should always be placed on unglazed paper as soon as it is taken from the fat in order that as much fat as possible may be absorbed. If possible, the exact temperature of the fat should be determined by a thermometer. However, the temperature can be determined by dropping a small piece of bread in the fat and observing the length of time it takes to become golden brown. The temperature of the fat is denoted by the "bread tests" shown in the following table:

TIME FOR BROWNING BREAD	TEMPERATURE OF FAT
2 minutes	300°
1½ minutes	325°
1 minute	350°
50 seconds	365°
40 seconds	380°
35 seconds	390°

Dredging

This is the sprinkling of flour or some other dry, pulverized or granulated ingredient.

Drippings

The fat and juices which drop into the pan from roasting meats.

Fireless Cooking

Fireless cooking is done in an insulated container or oven, so constructed that it retains heat for a long time. The container or oven is first heated to the desired stage. All outside heat is removed and the food cooks in the long-lingering heat within. Instructions for cooking in this manner are always provided by the manufacturer of the equipment.

Folding In

This is the process of mixing foods without releasing the air bubbles which may have been beaten or cooked into any of the ingredients. It is done by lifting a part of the liquid from the very bottom of the bowl through the rest of the mixture to the top. This is continued until the foods are thoroughly blended.

Fricaseeing

Fricasseed food is food that has been browned and then simmered, in thick sauce or gravy.

Frying, Deep-Fat

See *Deep-Fat Frying*.

Frying, Pan

See *Pan Frying*.

Grilling

Same as *Broiling, Oven Broiling, or Pan Broiling*.

Kneading

This is the stretching and contraction of dough with the hands as more flour is worked into the mixture. Sometimes kneading is done only to smooth the texture of the dough.

Larding

This is the process of spacing small strips of fat salt pork or bacon (by means of a larding needle) throughout a less tender cut of beef, to add juiciness and flavor.

Measurements

All measurements in this book are *level*. Follow them exactly. See Table of Measures on page 20.

Oven Broiling

This consists of cooking foods in the oven of a gas or electric range. The food is placed in the broiler pan and cooked close to the heat.

Oven Poaching

This consists of baking with the dish or pan containing the food set in another dish containing hot or boiling water. It is a method used chiefly for custard or fluffy egg dishes.

Pan Broiling

This method calls for the cooking of food on a hot pan or griddle with only enough fat to prevent burning. Any excess fat which accumulates should be poured off at once or the food will fry instead of broil.

Pan Frying

This is frying in a hot pan in a small amount of fat. It differs from pan broiling in that the fat is allowed to accumulate and it differs from sautéing in that the food is not stirred frequently but is simply turned to cook both sides or, as in the case of fried eggs, the food may be cooked on one side only.

Parboiling

This consists of cooking foods partially by boiling. If the food is completely cooked in this manner, it is said to be *boiled*.

Poaching

To poach foods they are dropped into simmering water or other liquid and cooked for a short time. Poaching is usually used for eggs.

Poaching, Oven

See *Oven Poaching*.

Pressure Cooking

To cook by pressure it is necessary to have one of the several pressure cookers manufactured for the purpose. The food is cooked in trapped steam at pressures ranging up to 30 pounds per square inch with temperatures running up to 275° F. For most pressure cooking the pressure is kept from 10 to 15 pounds and temperature at 240° F. to 250° F.

Roasting

Modern cooking stoves have removed the difference between baking and roasting. In early times roasting consisted of cooking before an open fire. Today there is no technical distinction between baking and roasting but the latter term is usually applied to meats and some vegetable dishes.

Roux

A smooth mixture of flour and fat which is used to thicken gravies, sauces, and soups.

Sautéing

This is frying in a little fat in a hot pan. The food is stirred frequently so that the hot grease reaches all sides.

Scalding

This is to heat a liquid briefly to a point just below boiling or to briefly heat a solid food in liquid at the scalding point.

Searing

This is the very rapid cooking of the exterior of a food at high heat. It is usually done to seal in juices in foods to be cooked at lower temperatures for an extended period.

Shortening

This important ingredient in all kinds of batters, pastries, and doughs is synonymous with *fat*. It includes butter, all of the trademarked vegetable fats, margarine, lard, oil, or drippings. In most recipes any of these shortenings can be used, one for the other. Butter, because of its flavor, is recommended for cakes, butter icings, and fillings. For white cakes, a white shortening is preferred.

Simmering

This is heating water or other liquid to a temperature of above 175° F. but under the boiling point. Bubbles rise infrequently to the surface during simmering.

Steaming

Food is steamed when it is cooked in a bath of steam from boiling water.

Stewing

Stewing consists of either simmering or boiling food in a small amount of water or other liquid.

Stirring

Stirring is always done with a circular motion. Its purpose is to make certain that heat reaches every part of the food or to thoroughly mix or dissolve ingredients.

Sugars

Granulated sugar is intended wherever "sugar" is mentioned in recipes for breads, cakes, boiled frostings, and desserts. *A very fine granulated sugar* is recommended for cakes, or ordinary sugar sifted two or three times. *Powdered sugar* makes a fine cake but one that will dry out quickly. It does not make a perfectly smooth icing. *Confectioner's sugar* is used for uncooked icings and fillings because it combines readily with liquid to make a smooth, glossy icing. *Brown sugar* comes in both a light and dark variety. For Cakes and desserts, the light brown sugar is recommended.

Trying Out

This denotes the process of melting the fat from any scraps or small pieces of raw or smoked meats.

Whipping

Same as *Beating*.

TABLE OF MEASURES

(All measurements in this book are level.)

3 teaspoons	= 1 tablespoon		4 quarts	= 1 gallon
16 tablespoons	= 1 cup		2 tablespoons (liquid)	= 1 ounce
2 cups	= 1 pint or 1 pound		8 ounces	= 1 cup
2 pints	= 1 quart		16 ounces	= 1 pound

USEFUL EQUIVALENTS

4 tablespoons flour	= 1 ounce	1 square grated unsweet-	
1 cup flour	= 4 ounces	ened chocolate	= 5½ tbsps.
4 cups flour	= 1 pound	1 tumbler (common drink-	
3¼ cups whole wheat flour	= 1 pound	ing glass)	= 6 ounces
1 tablespoon butter	= ½ ounce	1 pound raisins	= 2⅔ cups
1 cup butter	= 8 ounces	1 pound dates	= 2½ cups
1 sq. unsweetened		1 pound figs (chopped)	= 3 cups
chocolate	= 1 ounce	1 pound walnuts (chopped)	= 3½ cups

HELPFUL SUBSTITUTIONS

1 teaspoon baking powder = ¼ teaspoon soda + ½ teaspoon cream of tartar
1 tablespoon cornstarch = 2 tablespoons flour, in thickening gravies or sauces
1 sq. bitter chocolate = 3 tablespoons cocoa + ½ tablespoon butter
1 cup milk = 1 tablespoon vinegar + 1 cup sweet milk

Fruits

~~~~~~

FRUITS add water, minerals, sugar, and vitamins to the diet, and bulk for the intestines. Some fresh fruit is required to be sure of getting Vitamin C, which increases resistance to infections and helps in the healing of sores and wounds. A deficiency of Vitamin C shows in disorders similar to rheumatism and an acute lack of it causes scurvy. This valuable vitamin is easily destroyed by cooking. In other respects cooked, canned, or dried fruits are equal in food value to fresh fruits.

Fruits to be eaten raw should be sound and ripe. It is best to select them personally at the market. They should be purchased in small quantities unless good storage space is available as ripe fruits spoil quickly. Before storing any fruits, examine them carefully. Use bruised or otherwise imperfect fruit first as they will spoil more easily than the rest.

The budget-wise homemaker can save money by selecting slightly imperfect fruits for cooking. She will also often be offered bargains by markets and peddlers with a surplus of fruit that is too ripe to keep. If such articles are bought in small quantities and are used at once, such purchases will turn out well.

BUYING GUIDES

Remember the largest is not always the best. Large-sized fruits and vegetables are not always of the best quality nor are they always economical to buy.

Avoid commodities that show decay. It is preferable to avoid commodities that show decay, particularly if they are not intended for immediate consumption. It may sometimes be desirable to buy such stock if it does not appear too wasty.

Do not buy merely because the price is low. It seldom pays to buy perishables just because the price is extremely low unless one's judgment of quality and condition can be relied upon.

Do not handle fruits and vegetables unnecessarily. Rough handling of fruits and vegetables when buying causes spoilage, for which the consumers ultimately pay, because the retailer must sell at a price that is high enough to cover such loss.

See that containers hold full measure. Small fruits and sometimes small vegetables are sold by measure in certain types of containers. Frequently these containers are repacked, sometimes so loosely that the container does not hold the quantity it should.

SELECTING FRUITS

Apples. Firm apples of good color and flavor are desirable. Usually apples that have a good color for their variety are full-flavored.

Apricots. They should be plump, fairly firm, and a uniformly golden-yellowish color. The flesh should be juicy.

Avocados or Alligator Pears. Heavy, medium-sized avocados which have a bright, fresh appearance and which are fairly firm or are just beginning to soften, usually are the most desirable. Avocados may have an irregular, light-brown marking known as scab. This does not affect the quality of the flesh.

Bananas. They should be plump and well filled out. Good eating quality is indicated when the solid red or yellow color of the fruit is flecked with small brown specks.

Blackberries, Dewberries, Loganberries, and Raspberries. Quality in this class of fruits is indicated by a bright, clean, fresh appearance combined with a solid, full color and plumpness.

Blueberries and Huckleberries. Quality is indicated as in blackberries, etc., above.

Cherries. Quality is indicated as in blackberries, etc., above.

Cranberries. Quality is indicated as in blackberries, etc., above.

Figs. They must be fully ripe to be of good quality. A ripe fig is fairly soft or soft to the touch, and will vary in color from a greenish yellow to purplish or almost a black, depending on variety.

Grapefruit. Grapefruits of good quality are firm, but springy to the touch; not soft, wilted, or flabby. They are well-shaped, and heavy for their size.

Grapes. Grapes should have a general appearance of freshness. They should be mature and the individual berries should be firmly attached to the stems. Mature grapes are usually plump.

Lemons. Lemons that have a fine-textured skin and are heavy for their size are generally of better quality than those that are coarse-skinned and light in weight. Deep yellow-colored lemons are usually relatively mature and are not so acid as those of the lighter or greenish-yellow color.

Limes. Limes that are green in color and heavy for their size are the most desirable.

Melons. Selection of melons for quality and flavor is not easy; it often tests the skill of the experienced buyer, who at times will have occasion to find fault with his own judgment. Sweetness and flavor in melons are not fully developed until the full-ripe stage of maturity is reached. Ripeness in almost all kinds of melons is indicated by the softening of the part of the fruit which surrounds the "eye" or "button" at the blossom end, and which yields to pressure of the finger.

Oranges. Oranges of the best quality are firm, heavy, have a fine-textured skin for the variety and are well-colored. Such fruits (even with a few surface blemishes, such as scars, scratches, and slight discolorations) are much to be preferred to oranges that have a badly creased skin, or are puffy or spongy, and light in weight. Puffy oranges are likely to be light in weight, lacking in juice, and of generally poor quality. Exceptions occur in the tangerines (of which Dancy is the principal variety), satsumas, King, and mandarin types and varieties.

Peaches. Quality in peaches is indicated by the general appearance and firmness of the flesh. A peach of fine quality should be free from blemishes, should have a fresh appearance, a ground color that is either whitish or yellowish and sometimes combined with a red color or blush depending on the variety. The red color or blush alone is not a true sign of maturity. The flesh should be firm or fairly firm.

Pears. Pears that are firm or fairly firm, but not hard, free from blemish and clean, and not misshapen, wilted, or shriveled, are generally of good quality. Some varieties are in prime condition while still a green or greenish-yellow color; others may be yellow and yet be too immature for eating.

Pineapples. Color and odor are the factors indicating quality in pineapples. A ripe pineapple in good condition has a fresk, clean appearance, and has a distinctive dark, orange-yellow color combined with a decidedly fragrant odor. The "eyes" are flat and almost hollow. Usually the heavier the fruit in proportion to its size the better the quality, provided the fruit is mature.

Plums and prunes. Plums and prunes of good quality are plump, clean, of fresh appearance, full colored for the variety, and soft enough to yield to slight pressure.

Quinces. They should be firm to hard, free from blemish, and of a greenish-yellow or golden-yellow color.

Rhubarb. It should be fresh, firm, crisp, tender, and either red or pink in color. The stalks should be fairly thick.

Strawberries. Strawberries should be of a fresh, clean, bright appearance, have a full solid red color, be free from moisture, dirt, and trash; and the cap should be attached.

(1) FRESH APPLES

Wash and dry for eating raw.

(2) FRESH APRICOTS

Wash and plunge in boiling water 30 seconds. Skins can then be removed. Apricots can be used as an alternate for peaches in almost any dish.

(3) AVOCADOS OR ALLIGATOR PEARS

Select ripe avocados. The flesh should be firm but should yield slightly to pressure. Wash and peel. Cut in half. Remove stone. Serve in halves, sliced, chopped, or diced with a slice of lemon. Or, the pulp may be mashed to a paste and served as a spread on toast with a seasoning of salt and grapefruit or lemon juice.

(4) BANANAS AND CREAM

Peel and slice bananas crosswise. Serve with milk, cream, or whipped cream and sugar. They are also delicious as a dessert with caramel sauce (No. 3109). Or, cut in half, lengthwise, and serve, sprinkled with sugar and lemon juice.

(5)   **BERRIES**

Remove imperfect fruit. Wash in a colander. Hull or remove stems. Sprinkle with powdered sugar. If fruit is too tart, let stand with sugar 1 to 2 hours. A sprinkling of lemon juice will neutralize excess tartness. Allow 1 quart berries for 4 servings.

(6)   **FRESH CANTALOUPE**

Wash and drain. Cut in halves, quarters, or sixths, according to the size of the fruit. Remove seeds. Chill but do not ice. Provide salt, sugar, and nutmeg and let each person season to taste. Or, the pulp may be cut out in small balls by a ball cutter and served in grapefruit glasses.

(7)   **CANTALOUPE RING**

Wash. Cut in 1-inch slices. Remove rind and seeds. Serve rings with fruit or vanilla ice cream (No. 2547) in center.

(8)   **CASABA MELONS**

Follow recipe for fresh cantaloupe (No. 6).

(9)   **FRESH WHOLE CHERRIES**

Wash and drain. Serve with stems on a doily-covered plate. Provide a spoon for the removal of the stones. Or, the stems may be removed and the cherries served in cocktail glasses, covered with water and cracked ice.

(10)   **CURRANTS**

Wash, drain, and remove stems. Serve, sprinkled with sugar. They are good mixed with raspberries.

(11)   **FRESH FIGS**

Remove skin. Serve whole or sliced with cream.

(12)   FRESH GRAPEFRUIT

Wash and drain. Cut in halves. Run a sharp blade, preferably of a grapefruit knife, inside the rind, separating it from the pulp. Cut out the center membrane. With knife separate pulp from the membrane dividing the segments. Grapefruit may be served without sugar or a teaspoon of sugar may be put in the center of each half several hours before serving. A small mound of any bright-colored fruit may be placed in the center as a garnish. Allow 1 half per serving.

(13)   GRAPES

Select firm fruit. Remove imperfect grapes. Wash and drain. Serve with a spoon for taking seeds from mouth. For salads, etc., cut grapes in half lengthwise, skin if desired, and remove seeds.

(14)   HONEYDEW MELON

Follow recipe for fresh cantaloupe (No. 6).

(15)   KING OF SIAM ORANGES

Serve same as oranges (No. 23).

(16)   FRESH KUMQUATS

Wash, drain, slice, and remove seeds. The entire fruit can be eaten, including the rind.

(17)   FRESH LEMON

For lemon-slice garnishes, wash, dry, slice crosswise ¼ inch thick and remove seeds. Serve slices in halves or quarters. For lemon juice, soften lemon by rolling or drop in boiling water for 10 seconds before cutting in half and squeezing.

(18)   FRESH LIMES

Select green limes. Treat same as fresh lemons (No. 17).

(19)   **MANDARINS**

Serve same as oranges (No. 23).

(20)   **MANGOES**

Select ones with soft, juicy fruit. Wash and drain. Make slit in skin and two slits joining and at right angles to first slit. Turn back skin and eat with a spoon.

(21)   **MUSKMELONS**

Follow recipe for fresh cantaloupe (No. 6).

(22)   **NECTARINES**

Serve as peaches (No. 25).

(23)   **FRESH ORANGE**

Wash and drain fruit. Cut in half, crosswise. Run a sharp blade inside rind, separating it from the pulp. Remove seeds, if any, and hard membrane from center. The center may be garnished with sugar or small pieces of any bright-colored fruit. They may also be served whole, with or without skins, or in segments, surrounding a mound of powdered sugar. Orange ambrosia is made by sprinkling orange slices with powdered sugar and shredded coconut.

(24)   **PAPAYA OR PAPAW**

Select fully ripened fruit. Wash, drain, and chill. Cut in half, lengthwise and then into wedges. Remove seeds. Serve with lemon or orange slices and some of the seeds.

(25)   **FRESH PEACHES**

Select large, firm peaches that yield slightly to finger pressure. Cut in halves. Peel. Remove stones. Slice. Sprinkle with sugar and serve with cream. Drop in boiling water 30 seconds if skins are hard to remove.

(26)   PERSIMMONS

Select ripe fruit. Wash. Drain. Cut off flower end. Cut in halves. Eat flesh with spoon.

(27)   FRESH PINEAPPLE

Select fully ripe fruit. Wash and drain. Cut out crown or twist leaves until crown comes off. Pare rind with sharp knife. Cut out "eyes." Remove spine. Slice, dice, shred, or cut into pieces of any desired size. Sprinkle with sugar. Chill and serve.

(28)   FRESH PLUMS

Wash, dry, and serve.

(29)   POMEGRANATES

Wash. Drain. Cut in halves. Serve with spoon. Seeds, as well as pulp and juice are eaten.

(30)   SATSUMA ORANGES

Serve same as oranges (No. 23).

(31)   TANGERINES

Serve same as oranges (No. 23).

(32)   FRESH WATERMELON

Wash, drain, and chill. Cut in slices 3 to 4 inches thick and serve ¼ of each slice per portion. Or, the pulp may be served without rind by scooping out balls with an ice cream scoop or by rotating a spoon in the pulp. Save remainder of the fruit for salads and the rind for preserving.

(33)   SIRUP FOR STEWED FRUITS

2 cups water   1 tablespoon lemon juice
1 cup sugar

Boil ingredients for 5 minutes.

(34)   APPLESAUCE

| 12 tart cooking apples | ⅛ teaspoon salt |
| 5 tablespoons sugar | |

Wash, peel, core, and quarter apples. Put them in saucepan. Half cover with cold water. Bring to boil. Cover. Reduce heat and let simmer until tender. Stir in sugar and salt. Cook 5 minutes more. Mash apples with a spoon or force through a sieve. Chill. If desired a little lemon juice, cinnamon, or nutmeg may be added after cooking. Serves 6.

(35)   BAKED APPLESAUCE

| 12 tart cooking apples | ⅛ teaspoon salt |
| ½ cup sugar | ½ teaspoon nutmeg |

Wash, peel, core, and divide apples into eighths. Place in greased baking dish. Half cover with water. Sprinkle with seasonings. Cover tightly and bake in moderate oven (350° F.) 2½ to 3 hours. Remove and scrape through a sieve or mash. Serves 6.

(36)   BAKED APPLES

| 6 apples | 6 tablespoons brown sugar |

Select smooth apples of uniform size. Wash and remove cores. Fill the center of each with 1 tablespoon brown sugar. Put in baking dish. Add enough boiling water to cover bottom of dish. Bake in moderate oven (350° F.), basting frequently with dish liquor, until tender, about 20 to 40 minutes, depending on size and variety of apple. A little lemon juice or cinnamon may be added to the water if desired. There are several alternates for brown sugar as a filling, among which are strips of bananas, marmalade, jelly, preserves, honey and lemon juice, corn sirup and lemon juice, hard cinnamon candy, canned or fresh berries, chopped orange, candied orange peel, chopped pineapple, chopped peach, marshmallow, preserved ginger, or nuts. Baked apples are usually served with the dish liquor or cream, but they may be served with whipped cream, marshmallow sauce (No. 3136), or meringue (No. 3205).

(37)   **APPLE FRITTERS**

    1 cup flour   ½ cup milk
1½ teaspoons baking powder   1 egg
    2 tablespoons sugar   5 or 6 tart apples
    ½ teaspoon salt

Mix and sift flour, baking powder, sugar, and salt. Add milk and well-beaten egg. Mix well. Pare and core apples. Cut in sections. Dip each piece of apple in the batter and fry in deep hot fat (340° to 375° F.) until brown. Drain on unglazed paper and sprinkle with powdered sugar.

(38)   **APPLE COMPOTE**

  3 uniform-size eating apples   3 cups sirup for stewed fruits
                              (No. 33)

Wash, peel, core, and quarter apples. Simmer in sirup until tender. Chill and serve. If desired, the apples may be sliced into rings before cooking. This compote is delicious if the sirup is flavored with cinnamon candy. Chopped ginger and cloves are also appropriate when added to sirup.

(39)   **FRIED APPLES**

Wash apples. Slice ½ inch thick. Remove cores. Sauté in melted butter until soft, turning occasionally to brown evenly. Or, they may be cored, quartered, and then sautéed as above.

(40)   **DEEP-FRIED APPLE RINGS**

Wash and core tart apple. Slice crosswise ¼ inch thick. Fry in deep, hot fat (340° to 390° F.) until brown, about 2 to 3 minutes. Drain on brown paper. Sprinkle with sugar. This is an excellent garnish for pork dishes.

(41)   **STEWED APPLES**

  6 tart cooking apples   ½ teaspoon vanilla
  6 tablespoons sugar   ½ teaspoon nutmeg

Wash apples. Put in saucepan. Half cover with water. Sprinkle with sugar, vanilla, and nutmeg. Bring to a boil and boil until skins are broken and apples are tender. Season with more sugar if too tart. Serve hot or cold with pan sirup and cream.

(42)   STEWED DRIED APRICOTS

Wash in warm water. Soak in cold water until fruit is as soft as fresh fruit, at least 24 hours. Heat gradually in same water. Do not bring to boiling point but simmer 30 minutes. Serve hot or cold.

(43)   APRICOT COMPOTE

<table>
<tr><td>8 almost-ripe apricots</td><td>3 cups sirup for stewed fruits
(No. 33)</td></tr>
</table>

Wash apricots. Puncture them in several places. Plunge into boiling sirup. Boil until tender. Chill and serve. Serves 4.

(44)   BAKED BANANAS I

Wipe bananas. Loosen 1 section of skin on each for entire length. Replace skin. Put bananas in baking dish. Cover and bake in hot oven (400° F.) until skins are dark. Remove skins and serve bananas with powdered sugar or lemon sauce (No. 3129).

(45)   BAKED BANANAS II

Wipe bananas. Remove skins. Place whole in greased baking pan. Cover with lemon sauce (No. 3129). Bake in moderate oven (350° F.) until tender and slightly brown.

(46)   SAUTÉED BANANAS

<table>
<tr><td>4 firm, ripe bananas</td><td>½ cup corn-flake crumbs</td></tr>
<tr><td>¼ cup lemon juice</td><td>2 tablespoons butter</td></tr>
</table>

Peel bananas. Cut in quarters. Dip in lemon juice. Roll in crumbs. Melt butter in pan and sauté bananas until well browned. Serve on lettuce. A well-beaten egg may be substituted for lemon juice and bread or cracker crumbs or corn meal may be used instead of corn flakes. Serves 4.

(47)   FRIED BANANAS

Remove skins from 3 bananas. Cut in halves, lengthwise and crosswise. Sprinkle with salt and lemon juice. Dip in flour, then in slightly beaten egg, diluted with 2 tablespoons water. Roll in fine crumbs and fry in deep hot fat (340° to 375° F.) 3 or 4 minutes or until brown. Drain on unglazed paper. Serve with roast meats. Serves 6.

(48)   BANANA FRITTERS

Peel bananas. Cut through lengthwise and again in pieces 1½ to 2 inches long. Follow recipe for apple fritters (No. 37).

(49)   STEWED BERRIES

1 quart berries   1 cup sugar

Pick over, wash, and drain berries. Put in saucepan. Add 1 cup cold water. Bring to boil. Cover. Reduce heat and let simmer 10 minutes. Stir in sugar. Bring to boil. Reduce heat. Let simmer 2 minutes. Serves 4.

(50)   STEWED BLUEBERRIES

1 cup sugar   1 quart blueberries

Mix sugar and 1 cup water. Bring to boil and boil 3 minutes. Pick, wash, hull, and drain berries. Add to sirup. Let simmer 5 minutes. Serves 4.

(51)   CHERRY COMPOTE

2 cups cherries   3 cups sirup for stewed fruits
                                (No. 33)

Wash and remove stones from cherries. Boil cherries in sirup 10 minutes. Chill and serve. Serves 4.

(52)   CHERRY FRITTERS

Remove stones if fresh cherries. Drain if preserved, pitted cherries are used. Follow recipe for apple fritters (No. 37).

(53)   **STEWED CHERRIES**

Wash and remove stems from cherries. Put in saucepan. Cover with cold water. Bring to a boil. Reduce heat and let simmer until soft.

(54)   **CRANBERRY SAUCE**

1 quart cranberries   1¾ cups sugar

Bring 2 cups water to a boil. Add berries. Cover and cook until outer skins have burst. Add sugar and let simmer 8 minutes. Pour into mold. Chill. For strained cranberry sauce, cook cranberries as above. Then strain through a sieve, scraping berries to force pulp through. Return strained liquid to fire. Add sugar. Simmer 8 minutes. Pour into mold. Chill.

(55)   **STEWED DRIED FIGS**

Wash thoroughly. Cover with water and let soak 12 hours. Heat them in water in which they have soaked and simmer slowly 2½ hours.

(56)   **ORANGE FRITTERS**

Separate sections of orange. Follow recipe for apple fritters (No. 37).

(57)   **PEACH OR APRICOT FRITTERS**

Cut halves of peach or apricot in quarters. Follow recipe for apple fritters (No. 37).

(58)   **BAKED PEACHES**

6 halves canned peaches   ½ tablespoon lemon juice
2 tablespoons brown sugar

Drain peaches, reserving sirup for fruit drinks. Put peaches, kernel side down, in a baking pan, being careful that they do not touch one another. Sprinkle with sugar and lemon juice. Bake in hot oven (400° F.) until brown, adding a little sirup if they seem too dry.

(59)   **PEACH COMPOTE**

4 peaches   3 cups sirup for stewed fruits
                             (No. 33)

Bring some water to a boil. Add peaches and boil 2 minutes. Remove peaches and plunge them into cold water. Remove skins. Boil peaches in sirup 10 minutes. Chill and serve. Serves 4.

(60)   **STEWED DRIED PEACHES**

Wash carefully. Cover with warm water and let stand 12 to 15 hours. Slip off skins. Put in fresh water. Let stand another 6 hours until flesh is soft as in fresh peaches. Warm water. Do not boil but let simmer 30 minutes. Serve hot or cold, sweetened with sugar, according to taste.

(61)   **PEAR COMPOTE**

4 pears   3 cups sirup for stewed fruits
                             (No. 33)

Wash and peel pears. Let simmer in sirup until tender. Chill and serve. Serves 4.

(62)   **BAKED FRESH PEARS**

1 quart Sheldon or Seckel   ½ cup maple sugar
    pears   ¼ teaspoon ginger
½ cup brown sugar

Wash pears and put in earthen bean pot, whole and unpeeled. Add other ingredients and ½ cup hot water. Cover and bake in slow oven (300° F.) 1½ hours. Add water as needed to prevent burning and to make a sirup at bottom of pot.

(63)   **BAKED PEARS**

Follow recipe for baked peaches (No. 58), using canned pear halves instead of peaches.

(64) ## STEWED DRIED PEARS

Wash. Put in saucepan. Cover with water and soak 12 hours. Heat in same water and simmer slowly 2 hours. Add ¾ cup sugar per pound of pears. Simmer 30 minutes more.

(65) ## PEAR FRITTERS

Cut pear in suitable-sized pieces. Follow recipe for apple fritters (No. 37).

(66) ## PINEAPPLE FRITTERS

Cut pineapple in suitable-sized pieces. Follow recipe for apple fritters (No. 37).

(67) ## GLAZED PINEAPPLE RINGS

1-pound can pineapple slices   8 tablespoons cranberry sauce
(No. 54)

Drain pineapple and place on broiling rack. Beat cranberry until smooth and spreadable, adding a little of the pineapple sirup to make it spread more easily. Top pineapple with cranberry. Place under a preheated broiling rack and broil until warm and glazed, about 10 to 20 minutes. Serve hot as a garnish for left-over slices of cold turkey or other poultry. Serves 8.

(68) ## FRIED PLANTAINS

Follow recipe for fried bananas (No. 46 and 47).

(69) ## STEWED PLUMS

Wash plums. Put in saucepan. Cover with cold water. Bring to a boil. Reduce heat. Let simmer until soft. Serve with juice.

(70) ## PLUM COMPOTE

8 plums   3 cups sirup for stewed fruits
(No. 33)

Wash plums. Boil them for 5 minutes in sirup. Chill and serve. Serves 4.

(71)   STEWED PRUNES

Wash. Put in water. Soak 12 hours. Heat slowly in water in which they have soaked. Cover closely and let simmer until skins are tender and liquid is of desired consistency. A dash of lemon juice may be added to water during cooking if desired.

(72)   BAKED QUINCES

6 quinces	¼ cup macaroon crumbs
3 tablespoons sugar	2 tablespoons butter
12 orange slices, ¼ inch thick	

Select ripe fruit. Wash, pare, halve, and remove cores. Put, cut side up, in greased baking pan. Put skins and cores in saucepan. Cover with boiling water. Boil 20 minutes. Strain. Put sugar in each half quince. Put orange slice on each half. Pour 2 tablespoons of the peeling liquor over halves. Cover. Bake in moderate oven (350° F.) until soft and red, about 2 to 2½ hours. Sprinkle with crumbs. Dot with butter. Bake, uncovered, in hot oven (425° F.) about 5 minutes or until brown. Serves 6.

(73)   RASPBERRY COMPOTE

1 pint raspberries	3 cups sirup for stewed fruits (No. 33)

Wash and hull berries. Bring sirup to a boil. Drop in raspberries and boil 1 minute. Chill and serve. Serves 4.

(74)   BAKED RHUBARB

1 pound rhubarb	¾ cup sugar

Wash rhubarb. Do not peel unless skin is very tough. Cut in 1-inch pieces. Put in baking dish. Add 1 cup boiling water and sugar. Cover and bake in moderate oven (350° F.) until tender, about 2½ hours. If desired, seedless raisins or chopped, pitted prunes may be added to dish before cooking. Serves 4.

(75) RHUBARB SAUCE

1 pound rhubarb   ¼ cup sugar

Wash. Peel if skin is tough. Cut in 1-inch pieces. Put in saucepan. Sprinkle with sugar. Cover bottom of pan with water. Cook slowly until soft. Serves 4.

(76) STRAWBERRY COMPOTE

Follow recipe for raspberry compote (No. 73), using strawberries in place of raspberries.

(77) TAFFY APPLES

1 cup granulated sugar   2 tablespoons butter
½ cup boiling water   6 apples
1 cup brown sugar   6 wooden skewers
½ cup cream

Melt one-half cup of the granulated sugar over a direct flame. Add the boiling water and cook to a smooth sirup. In a separate pan, cook the cream with remaining sugar and butter to the soft ball stage or to 236° F. Combine the two sirups and cook until drops of sirup will form a hard ball when dropped into cold water or to a temperature of 250° F. Cool the sirup to lukewarm. Place apples on skewers and twirl them in the caramel sirup. Dip them immediately in ice water to harden the caramel.

(78) APPLE CRISP

4 cups sliced apples   ½ cup flour
¼ cup hot water   ½ cup sugar
½ cup butter

Arrange apples in buttered baking dish. Pour water over apples. Cream the butter, add flour and sugar, and blend to form crumbs. Sprinkle over apples. Bake in hot oven (400° F.) 40 to 45 minutes or until apples are tender and top is browned. Serves 4.

(79)   APPLE PORCUPINE

1¼ cups sugar   ½ teaspoon cinnamon
1½ cups water   Blanched almonds
6 medium-sized apples   Cream
1 tablespoon butter

Boil sugar and water five minutes. Pare and core apples and cook in sirup until soft but not broken. Remove and place in baking dish. Add butter and cinnamon to sirup and boil until thick. Fill openings in apples with sirup. Slice almonds in thin strips and stick halfway into apples. Bake in moderate oven (350° F.) until nuts are brown. Cool. Serve with plain or whipped cream.

(80)   BANANA MIXED GRILL

4 hamburg patties, 1 inch   4 firm bananas, peeled
   thick   Melted butter
2 slices canned pineapple,   Salt
   halved

Arrange meat on preheated broiler rack. Place about 5 inches below heat. Broil 6 to 8 minutes until brown. Turn meat. Brush bananas and pineapple with butter. Sprinkle bananas with salt. Place fruit in broiler rack. Continue broiling until bananas are tender, about 8 minutes. Serves 4.

(81)   APPLE SLICES WITH CHEESE

Wash, core, and slice into rings a bright red eating apple. Spread with Camembert or cream cheese.

(82)   SPICED APPLES WITH CIDER

6 tart cooking apples   12 whole cloves
4 cups cider   6 whole allspice
2½ cups sugar   ¼ teaspoon ginger
1 stick cinnamon   Juice of 1 lemon

Wash, peel, core, and quarter apples. Mix other ingredients. Bring to a boil. Boil 10 minutes. Add apples. Simmer slowly until soft. Remove to hot platter. Boil sirup until thick. Strain and pour over apples. Serves 6.

(83) BANANA CREAM TOAST

1 cup milk	⅛ teaspoon salt
1 tablespoon flour	¼ cup cream
1 tablespoon sugar	2 sliced bananas

4 slices toast

Mix flour to a smooth paste with an equal quantity of milk. Heat remaining milk to boiling point. Stir in flour paste. Let simmer 10 minutes. Remove from heat. Add other ingredients except toast. Mix well. Warm up. Serve on toast. Honey may be substituted for sugar and evaporated milk may be used in place of cream. This can also be made with almost any other fruit or combination of fruits. Serves 4.

(84) FROZEN CANTALOUPE

Scoop out the pulp of a ripe cantaloupe. Sweeten to taste. Put in a tightly closed metal container and bury in a mixture of equal parts rock salt and crushed ice for 3 to 4 hours. Or, put pulp in freezing tray of a mechanical refrigerator until frozen. Any fruit juice or combination of fruit juices may be frozen the same way. Similarly, the pulp of watermelon or any other melon can be so frozen.

(85) CRANBERRY FRITTERS

Slice and cut cranberry sauce (No. 54) into 1-inch squares, ½ inch thick. Dust with flour. Then follow recipe for apple fritters (No. 37).

(86) CRANBERRY COLD CAKE

4 tablespoons butter	2½ cups cranberry sauce
2 cups graham cracker crumbs	(No. 54)

Melt butter. Mix with crumbs. Line a square mold with wax paper. Place alternate layers of crumbs and sauce in mold, with crumbs on top. Pack solid. Chill in refrigerator 3 hours. Unmold. Slice and serve with whipped or any desired ice cream. Serves 6.

87) BROILED GRAPEFRUIT

2 grapefruits   2 teaspoons butter
4 teaspoons sugar   4 maraschino cherries

Wash and drain grapefruit. Cut in halves. Run a sharp blade, preferably of a grapefruit knife, inside the rind, separating it from the pulp. Sprinkle each half with sugar and dot with butter. Broil at moderate heat until heated through and skin is slightly brown. Serve hot. Brown sugar and wine can be used in place of granulated sugar and butter. Garnish each half with a cherry. Baked grapefruit is prepared as above but is baked in a hot oven (450° F.) until the sugar has melted and the fruit lightly browned. Serves 4.

(88) BAKED GINGER PEACHES

3½ cups preserved peach   2 teaspoons diced preserved
    halves   ginger
¼ cup brown sugar   2 tablespoons butter

Put peaches, cut side up, in shallow baking dish. Add peach sirup. Sprinkle with sugar and ginger. Dot with butter. Bake in moderate oven (350° F.) until brown, 15 to 20 minutes. Serves 6.

(89) BAKED PEACHES ON FRENCH TOAST

2 large peaches   4 slices bread, ¼ inch thick
¾ cup sugar   1 well-beaten egg
Juice of ½ lemon   ¼ cup milk
Rind of 1 lemon, chopped   1 tablespoon honey
2 tablespoons butter   ⅛ teaspoon salt

Peel, halve, and remove stones from peaches. Dissolve sugar in ¾ cup water. Add peaches and simmer gently until tender, but not mushy. Remove peaches from sirup to a greased baking dish. To sirup, add lemon juice and lemon rind and boil 5 minutes. Pour sirup over peaches. Dot peaches with butter. Bake in hot oven (425° F.) 30 minutes, basting frequently with sirup. Cut bread in halves, diagonally. Mix egg, milk, honey, and salt. Dip bread in mixture. Sauté bread on both sides in greased pan. Put on hot platter. Put peaches on top of bread. Add pan sirup. Serves 4.

(90)   BAKED GINGER PEARS

Follow recipe for baked ginger peaches (No. 88), using pear
halves instead of peaches.

(91)   PEARS AND RICE

    2½ cups canned pears   1 cup rice
    Piece of ginger root   1 cup milk
    3 tablespoons sugar

Put pears and their own juice in saucepan. Add ginger root
and sprinkle with sugar. Cook slowly until juice has thickened.
Remove ginger root. Let pears cool. Boil rice 25 minutes in
slightly salted water. Drain. Rinse with cold water. Drain. Rinse
with hot water. Put rice in a mound on shallow dish. Arrange
pears around rice. Pour milk over rice. Serves 6.

(92)   PRUNE TOAST

    2 cups stewed prunes (No.   Liquor in which prunes were
        71)   stewed
              4 slices hard toast

Rub prunes through a sieve. Mix with prune liquor to consistency of soft butter. Cut toast in halves, diagonally. Dip in
prune liquor to soften. Put on platter. Cover with prune pulp.
The toast may be dipped in milk instead of prune liquor, if
desired. Serves 4.

(93)   RAISIN TOAST

    2 cups seedless raisins   4 slices hard toast
    2 tablespoons cornstarch

Wash raisins. Cover with cold water. Mix cornstarch into a
smooth paste with cold water. Bring raisins to a boil. Add cornstarch paste. Reduce heat and let simmer 35 minutes. Cut toast
in half diagonally. Soften in raisin liquid. Put on platter and
cover with stewed fruit and juice. If preferred, the toast may be
softened in milk instead of raisin juice. Serves 4.

(94)   **RASPBERRY MELON CUP**

   1½ cups fresh raspberries   3 cups watermelon, diced
   1 cup granulated sugar

Wash raspberries, cover with sugar, and let stand in refrigerator for one hour. Mash through a coarse sieve. Pile high in cocktail glasses the chilled watermelon cut in cubes and pour raspberry purée over each glass of melon. Serves 6.

(95)   **RHUBARB COMPOTE**

   1 pound rhubarb   3 cups sirup for stewed
                      fruits (No. 33)

Wash rhubarb. Do not remove skin unless it is tough. Cut in small pieces. Bring sirup to a boil. Add rhubarb. Cover and simmer until tender. Chill and serve. Serves 4.

(96)   **STRAWBERRY TOAST**

   4 cups fresh strawberries   4 pieces hard toast
   ½ cup sugar

Rinse berries and put in pot. Add sugar. Cover with cold water. Bring slowly to a boil. Remove strawberries to warm dish. Cut toast in halves, diagonally. Dip in pot liquor to soften. Put toast on plate. Cover with strawberries and sirup from pot. Serves 4.

(97)   **FROZEN WATERMELON**

Follow recipe for frozen cantaloupe (No. 84), using watermelon pulp or a mixture of watermelon and cantaloupe pulp.

(98)   **GEM RHUBARB SAUCE**

   4 cups diced rhubarb   1-14 ounce can pineapple
   ¾ cup light brown sugar   gems or cubes
   ¾ cup granulated sugar   2 tablespoons orange juice

Place rhubarb in a saucepan, add sugars and sirup drained from pineapple. Bring to a boil, reduce heat and simmer until rhubarb is tender. Stir in orange juice and pour sauce over pineapple gems which have been placed in a bowl. Chill well before serving. Serves 6.

(99) PINEAPPLE GEM APRICOT KABOBS

Arrange on skewers in order given, half a maraschino cherry, pineapple cubes, half of a canned apricot. Repeat. Brush with melted butter and broil until fruit is lightly browned. Serve as a garnish with meat. Vary the fruit combination according to your whim. Pineapple cubes, inch slices of bananas, orange cubes and cherries for color make a pleasing combination.

(100) BANANA SCALLOPS

1½ teaspoons salt	6 bananas
1 egg, slightly beaten	¾ cup corn flake crumbs

Combine salt and egg. Slice bananas, crosswise, into pieces ¾ to 1 inch thick. Dip in egg. Drain. Roll in crumbs. Fry in deep, hot fat (375° F.) until brown and tender, about 1½ to 2 minutes. Drain well on unglazed paper. Serve hot. If desired, ¼ cup evaporated milk may be substituted for egg and corn meal or bread or cracker crumbs may be used in place of corn flakes. Serves 6.

(100A) CANDIED ORANGE PEEL

Remove peel in quarters from 3 oranges. Cover with water and boil ½ hour. Drain. Cover again with water. Boil ½ hour longer or until tender. Drain. Cut peel in strips. Bring 1 cup sugar, 2 tablespoons light corn sirup and ½ cup water to boil. Add the peel and cook gently in sirup to cover until peel is clear. Cool in sirup several hours or overnight. Reheat. Drain. Roll in granulated sugar.

Cereals

~~~~~~

THE cereals—barley, buckwheat, corn, popcorn, oats, rice, rye, tapioca, and wheat—are the chief articles of food of most of the people of the world. Indeed, some races live almost exclusively on cereals. Down through recorded history, many great wars and campaigns have been waged for cereals or for valuable lands where they could be raised. Probably the first humans to inhabit the earth fed themselves largely by chewing cereal grasses.

Raw cereals should be purchased in quantities which will be used within a reasonably short time. In long hot spells there is a danger that the fats will turn rancid or that they will become wormy. They should be stored in airtight containers and be kept cool and dry. Prepared cereals, the proportionate cost of which is much higher than for raw cereals, keep well in their own containers.

Cereals should be thoroughly cooked. It is important in order to make their large starch content digestible. Long cooking also improves the flavor of cereals. In the case of most of the quickly prepared raw breakfast foods on the market, it would be well to cook slightly longer than is called for in the instructions of the manufacturer.

Do not waste uneaten remainders of cooked cereals. They can be used to advantage in a great variety of left-over dishes. They can be formed into patties or croquettes. Sometimes they can be used in place of some of the flour called for in bread recipes. They add bulk to meat and vegetable hashes and mixtures and can often be turned into delicious puddings.

44

(101)   GENERAL DIRECTIONS FOR COOKING CEREALS

Use a double boiler or 2 saucepans, one a trifle larger than the other. Fill the larger saucepan or lower part of double boiler ⅓ full of water and put the water needed for the cereal in the other vessel. When the water boils, add the salt and cereal slowly so that the water does not stop boiling, and let boil for 10 minutes. Place the pot with cereal into the double boiler and cover and let steam. If the cereal seems to be too thick, add boiling water. The oatmeal, hominy and other coarse grain cereals are improved by soaking overnight in water. They should be cooked in the water in which they have been soaked.

TIMETABLE AND DIRECTIONS FOR COOKING CEREAL

	Water	Cereal	Salt (teaspoon)	Steaming time
Oatmeal	4 cups	to 1 cup	1½	3 hours
Rolled Oats	2½ cups	to 1 cup	1	½ to 1 hour
Rice (boiled)	8 cups	to 1 cup	1	25 to 30 minutes
Rice (steamed)	3 cups	to 1 cup	1	1 hour
Wheat (rolled)	1½ cups	to 1 cup	1	1 hour
Wheat (granular)	4 cups	to 1 cup	1	1 to 3 hours
Corn Meal	6 cups	to 1 cup	1	3 to 6 hours
Cracked Wheat	6 cups	to 1 cup	1	3 to 6 hours
Hominy	4 cups	to 1 cup	1	1 hour

(By using the fireless cooker, the cereal can be boiled 10 minutes over the fire in the evening, and then cooked overnight in the fireless cooker.)

Any of the above cereals may be cooked with milk instead of water. In that case put in ⅓ the amount of water required at start of cooking. Boil 10 minutes. Add milk to make up the required amount of liquid. Almost any fruits can be cooked with the above cereals. Fresh, raw fruits should be added at time cereal is put in double boiler. Dried fruits should be soaked several hours before cooking. The water in which they were soaked should be used as the liquid for cereal. They should be cut in small pieces and added to the cereal at start of cooking. *Baked cereals*—Any of the above cereals may be baked. Use ¼ less liquid. After boiling, as above, transfer to a baking dish, instead of double boiler, cover tightly and bake in slow oven overnight. To reheat cereals pour a little boiling water over them, put in pan, set in another pan of water, cover tightly, and warm through, stirring occasionally. Breakfast cereals are delicious when served with canned or cooked fruits with the fruit sirup as sauce.

(102)   READY-TO-SERVE CEREALS

The ready-to-serve cereals are all pre-cooked, trade-marked products and many suggestions for cooking and serving are given with them. They should be fresh and crisp. If they are limp, heat for five minutes in a moderate oven (350° F.). If desired, fruits may be served with these cereals.

(103)   FRIED CEREALS

Any cooked, left-over cereals (No. 101) can be fried. Mold them into patties, dip in flour, and sauté until brown on both sides.

(104)   CEREAL RAREBIT

1 cup milk	3 cups mild, grated cheese
¼ cup butter	½ teaspoon pepper
3 cups any cooked cereal (No. 101)	2 well-beaten eggs
1 teaspoon prepared mustard	1 tablespoon Worcestershire sauce

Bring milk to a boil. Add butter. Add cereal and beat well. Add cheese, mustard, pepper, and eggs. Heat thoroughly. Stir in Worcestershire sauce and serve, piping hot, on toast. Serves 6.

(105)   BRAN

Bran is often used, mixed with other cereals. The mixture should be ¼ bran to ¾ other cereal. The bran should be added before start of cooking.

(106)   STEAMED RICE

1 cup rice	3 cups boiling water or milk
1 teaspoon salt	

Cook as other cereals (No. 101), steaming 45 minutes, stirring occasionally to prevent sticking. Put in colander. Rinse with cold water. Put colander over lower part of boiler and let steam dry rice thoroughly.

(107)   **BOILED RICE**

Soak 1 cup rice in 1 quart water 12 hours. Drain. Bring 1½ quarts slightly salted water to a boil. Add rice slowly so that water keeps boiling. Boil 30 minutes or until rice is soft, stirring occasionally. Drain in a colander. Pour boiling water over rice. Drain. Put rice in pan in which it was cooked. Cover and let stand over hot water 5 minutes. Serves 4.

(108)   **BOILED WILD RICE**

½ cup wild rice   2 teaspoons butter
½ teaspoon salt

Wash and rinse rice in cold water several times. Boil 3 cups water. Add salt. Pour rice in slowly while water continues to boil. Boil, shaking occasionally, until water is entirely absorbed, about 40 minutes. Add butter and serve hot. To steep wild rice, cover ½ cup rice with 4 cups boiling water and let stand 20 minutes. Drain. Repeat 4 times, using fresh water each time. Sprinkle with salt and add butter. Serves 6.

(109)   **BROWNED RICE**

Put rice in frying pan. Cook, stirring constantly, until brown. Then boil (No. 107) or steam (No. 106), same as for natural rice. This imparts a dark color to the finished dish.

(110)   **BUTTERED RICE**

Pour melted butter over freshly cooked boiled rice (No. 107) and let stand 5 minutes.

(111)   **CURRIED RICE**

Add 1 teaspoon curry powder, blended into 3 tablespoons butter, to rice and cook according to recipe for boiled rice (No. 107).

(112)   RICE CROQUETTES

2 cups steamed rice   1 tablespoon chopped
  (No. 106)   parsley
1 egg yolk   1 cup bread crumbs
              White of one egg

Mix rice, egg yolk, and parsley. Form into balls or croquettes. Roll in crumbs. Brush with white of egg. Roll again in crumbs. Fry in deep, hot fat (375° F.) 2 to 3 minutes, or until brown. Drain on unglazed paper. Chopped onion or celery will add to these croquettes. Serves 6.

(113)   SPANISH RICE

½ cup raw rice   ⅛ teaspoon sage
3½ tablespoons butter   ¼ teaspoon salt
3 tablespoons chopped onion   1½ tablespoons flour
2 tablespoons chopped green   1½ cups tomato pulp
  pepper

Sauté rice to a light brown in 1 tablespoon butter. Add 1½ cups hot water. Boil until dry. Cover and steam slowly 10 minutes. Put remaining butter, onion, pepper, sage, and salt in another pan and brown lightly. Add flour and ½ cup tomato pulp. Blend well. Add remaining pulp and boil 5 minutes. Pour over rice. Let steam until sauce has desired consistency. Serves 6.

'114)   RICE AU GRATIN

3 cups cooked rice   1½ cups thin white sauce
  (No. 106 or 107)   (No. 2004)
1 cup mild grated cheese

Put a layer of rice in greased baking dish. Sprinkle with cheese. Cover with layer of sauce. Keep alternating ingredients until all are used, having a layer of cheese on top. Bake in hot oven (425° F.) 20 minutes. Serves 6.

(115)   BAKED RICE AND CHEESE

3 cups steamed rice   1 cup milk
  (No. 106)   ½ teaspoon salt
2 tablespoons butter   ¼ cup bread crumbs
1½ cups mild grated cheese

Line bottom of greased baking dish with rice. Dot with butter. Alternate layers of rice and cheese, dotting each layer with butter, until rice and cheese are all used. Sprinkle with salt. Add milk. Spread top with crumbs. Bake in moderate oven (350° F.) until cheese has melted and crumbs are brown, about 20 minutes. Serves 6.

(116)   RICE WITH SLICED ALMONDS

3 cups fluffy boiled rice
  (No. 107)
Chopped parsley

½ cup blanched almonds,
  sliced thin
Paprika

Combine hot cooked rice with the sliced almonds. Place on serving dish and sprinkle with paprika; garnish with parsley. Serves 6.

(117)   RICE AND PINEAPPLE

2 cups cooked rice
  (No. 106 or 107)
1 teaspoon salt

3 tablespoons butter
1 cup diced pineapple
2 tablespoons sugar

Put layer of rice in greased baking dish. Season with salt and dot with butter. Add layer of pineapple. Sprinkle with sugar. Keep alternating layers until all ingredients are used, having a layer of pineapple on top. Bake in hot oven (425° F.) 20 minutes. Almost any fresh fruit can be substituted for pineapple. Serves 6.

(118)   RICE AND NUT PATTIES

4 tablespoons chopped onion
½ teaspoon sage
1 tablespoon butter
¾ cup milk
½ teaspoon salt

1 cup bread or cracker
  crumbs
1 cup chopped walnuts
2 cups steamed rice
  (No. 106)

Put onion, sage, and butter in pan. Heat slowly to soften but not brown onion. Add milk and salt. Bring to a boil. Put crumbs in a dish. Add cooked onion and milk sauce. Let stand 10 minutes. Add walnuts and rice and mix well. Form into patties and brown lightly on both sides in a hot broiler or oven. The mixture may also be formed into a loaf and baked in a hot oven (425° F.) until browned. Serves 6.

(119)　　CREAMY RICE EN CASSEROLE

3 cups hot cooked rice
(No. 106 or 107)
1 cup boiled peas
(No. 1823)

½ lb. fresh shrimp, boiled
(No. 1272)
2 cups medium white
sauce (No. 2004)

Grated cheese

Combine ingredients lightly. Turn into greased casserole, sprinkle with cheese and bake in hot oven (400° F.) until cheese is melted and slightly browned. Serves 4.

(120)　　ITALIAN BAKED RICE

1 cup raw rice
3 tablespoons olive oil
1½ teaspoons salt
½ cup broken macaroni
2 tablespoons chopped green
pepper

2 tablespoons chopped
onion
1 clove of garlic
¼ teaspoon powdered thyme
1½ cups tomato pulp
1 tablespoon butter

Sauté the rice with 1 tablespoon oil until lightly browned. Add ½ teaspoon salt and 2½ cups water. Cover and simmer until dry. Put macaroni in another pan. Cover with water. Add ½ teaspoon salt. Boil until soft. Strain in a colander. Sauté pepper, onion, garlic, and thyme in the remaining oil until brown, stirring constantly. Add tomato and remaining salt. Heat thoroughly and pour over rice. Put half of rice mixture in a greased baking dish. Add the macaroni and put remaining rice on top. Dot with butter. Bake in moderate oven (350° F.) 30 to 40 minutes. Serves 6.

(121)　　RICE AND PEAS

2 tablespoons butter
2 tablespoons flour
⅓ cup milk

3 cups boiled rice
(No. 107)
3 cups boiled peas
(No. 1823)

Mix butter and flour to a smooth paste in pan. Add milk. Heat and stir until smooth. Add rice and peas. Mix lightly. Put in greased baking dish. Cover and bake in moderate oven (350° F.) 20 minutes. Serves 6.

(122)   **RICE, LENTILS, AND FISH**

¾ cup raw rice	6 cloves
½ cup lentils	6 whole white peppers
2 onions, sliced	1-inch cinnamon stick
4 tablespoons butter	½ teaspoon powdered ginger
½ teaspoon salt	½ pound boiled fish

Mix rice and lentils. Cover with cold water. Let soak 30 minutes. Drain in a colander. Sauté onion in butter until crisp and well browned. Remove onion and sauté the rice and lentils in same pan until all the butter has been absorbed. Add salt, cloves, peppers, cinnamon, and ginger. Mix well and transfer to saucepan. Cover with hot water. Cover and simmer over a slow fire until water is all absorbed. Add fish and cook until heated through. Serve hot, garnished with the onion slices. Serves 6.

(123)   **RICE AND APPLE DUMPLING**

3 cups boiled rice (No. 107)	4 apples

Spread rice on a pudding cloth. Peel, core, and quarter apples. Heap apples on center of rice. Gather cloth so that apples are surrounded by rice. Tie tightly. Plunge into boiling water and boil 45 minutes. Serve hot with brown sugar and cream. Serves 6.

(124)   **RICE AND BACON**

1 slice bacon, chopped	1 cup boiled rice (No. 107)
3 cups canned or strained stewed tomatoes (No. 1893)	1 onion, sliced
	1 teaspoon salt

Fry bacon until crisp. Add onion, tomatoes, and rice. Cook to desired consistency. Add salt. Serve hot. Serves 6.

(125)   RICE AND EGGS

1 chopped onion
4 tablespoons butter
1 cup boiled rice (No. 107)
2 hard-cooked eggs,
   chopped (No. 202)
½ cup thick white sauce
   (No. 2004)

1 egg yolk
½ teaspoon salt
¼ teaspoon pepper
1 cup tomato sauce
   (No. 2035)
1 tablespoon chopped
   parsley

Sauté onion in butter until well browned. Add rice, eggs, white sauce, egg yolk, salt, and pepper. Cook and stir until very hot. Put in hot dish. Cover with tomato sauce. Sprinkle with parsley. Serves 4.

(126)   BROWNED HOMINY

Brown cooked hominy (No. 101) in a little fat, just enough to prevent sticking.

(127)   BAKED HOMINY

2 cups steamed hominy
   (No. 101)

2 well-beaten eggs
½ teaspoon salt

Mix ingredients. Put in baking dish. Bake in moderate oven (350° F.) 40 minutes. Serves 6.

(128)   FRIED HOMINY

2 cups steamed hominy
   (No. 101)

1 well-beaten egg
½ cup flour

Pack hominy in a greased mold. Chill. Cut in thin slices. Dip slices in egg, diluted with a little cold water. Dip in flour. Fry slices in little fat until brown. Serves 4.

(129)   HOMINY CROQUETTES

Follow recipe for rice croquettes (No. 112), using hominy in place of rice.

(130) HOMINY OMELET

2 tablespoons fat	⅛ teaspoon pepper
2 cups steamed hominy	1 tablespoon chopped
(No. 101)	parsley
½ teaspoon salt	1 tablespoon chopped onion

Melt fat in frying pan. Mix other ingredients. Put mixture flat in pan. When well browned on bottom, fold as an omelet and serve hot. Serves 6.

(131) BAKED HOMINY AND CHEESE

2 cups canned or strained stewed tomatoes (No. 1893)	⅛ teaspoon cayenne
	3 tablespoons butter or fat
	2 tablespoons flour
2 tablespoons chopped onion	2½ cups cooked hominy
2 cloves	(No. 101)
½ teaspoon salt	½ cup mild grated cheese
1 tablespoon sugar	½ cup bread crumbs

Simmer tomatoes, onion, cloves, salt, sugar, and cayenne 20 minutes. Strain. Melt 2 tablespoons butter or fat and blend with flour. Add strained tomato juice and bring slowly to a boil, stirring constantly. Put layer of hominy in greased baking dish. Add layer of cheese. Add layer of the tomato sauce. Repeat until all are used. Spread top with crumbs. Dot with butter or fat. Bake in hot oven (425° F.) 20 minutes, or until crumbs are brown. Serves 6.

(132) BROWNED CORN MEAL MUSH

Pack cooked corn meal (No. 101) in a greased baking pan. Chill. Cut in slices ½ inch thick and broil or bake at high heat until browned. Serve with maple sirup or honey.

(133) CORN MEAL FILETS

2 cups milk	¼ cup flour
½ cup corn meal	1 beaten egg
¼ cup salt	½ cup bread crumbs
1 tablespoon butter	

Bring milk to a boil. Sift in corn meal slowly, stirring constantly. Add salt and butter. Cover and let simmer slowly 20 minutes. Pour into greased mold. Cool. Cut into filets. Dip in flour. Dip in egg, diluted with a little water. Dip in bread crumbs. Put in greased baking pan and bake in moderate oven (350° F.) until brown. Serves 6.

(134)   BAKED CORN MEAL

2 cups corn meal   ⅛ teaspoon pepper
2 tablespoons butter   1½ cups sour milk or but-
2 well-beaten eggs   termilk
½ teaspoon salt   1 teaspoon soda

Sift corn meal slowly into 2½ cups boiling water. Cool. Add other ingredients, diluting soda in a tablespoon of hot water. Beat well. Turn into greased baking dish. Bake in moderate oven (350° F.) 30 minutes. This can replace potatoes with meat dishes. Serves 6.

(135)   CORN MEAL WITH CHEESE

2 cups steamed corn meal   ¼ cup bread crumbs
   (No. 101)   ½ teaspoon salt
1 cup mild grated cheese   ⅛ teaspoon pepper
1 tablespoon butter

Have corn meal hot. Put half on bottom of greased baking dish. Add cheese in a layer. Put remaining corn meal on top. Dot with butter. Sprinkle with crumbs, salt, and pepper. Bake in moderate oven (350° F.) 20 minutes. Serves 6.

(136)   BAKED CORN TAMALE

1 cup milk   2 tablespoons butter
1 teaspoon salt   2 tablespoons chopped onion
¾ cup corn meal   ½ cup chopped green pepper
1½ cups stewed corn   2 cups canned or strained
   (No. 1769)   stewed tomatoes
10 ripe olives, stoned and   (No. 1893)
   sliced   1 tablespoon sugar
1 slightly beaten egg

Bring milk to a boil. Add salt and sift in corn meal slowly. Stir smooth. Add corn, olives, and egg. Mix thoroughly. Melt butter in frying pan. Add onion and pepper. Sauté until lightly browned. Add tomatoes and bring to a boil. Sprinkle with sugar. Mix both mixtures. Pour into greased baking pan. Bake in slow oven (325° F.) until firm and nicely browned. It can be served hot or cold. Serves 6.

(137)   FRIED FARINA BALLS

½ cup farina	1 well-beaten egg yolk
2 cups milk	¼ cup flour
½ teaspoon salt	1 well-beaten egg
⅛ teaspoon pepper	½ cup bread crumbs
1 teaspoon onion juice	

Simmer farina and milk 15 minutes. Add salt, pepper, and onion juice. Simmer until milk is all absorbed. Remove from heat and mix with egg yolk. Cool. Form into little balls. Roll in flour. Dip in egg, diluted with a little water. Roll in bread crumbs. Fry in deep, hot fat (375° F.) 1 minute. Drain on unglazed paper. Use as garnish for roast meats. Serves 6.

(138)   POPCORN

If there is a suspicion that the corn is old, put it in a colander and run cold water over it 2 minutes before popping. Put ½ cup corn in popper. Shake over hot fire until all kernels have popped. Transfer to bowl. Sprinkle with salt. Pour melted butter over it, if desired. To pop in kettle or skillet, melt 2 tablespoons of butter in pan or kettle and turn to coat entire inside with grease. Add ½ cup corn. Stir until each kernel is coated with butter. Cover and shake or stir through a small opening until popping is completed. Turn into a bowl and sprinkle with salt.

(139)   POPCORN BALLS

1 cup popcorn (No. 138)	¼ cup mayonnaise
1 cup grated mild cheese	(No. 701)

Put popcorn through meat chopper. Mix all ingredients and form into small balls. Roll balls in ground popcorn. These can be used as a garnish with salads.

(140)   CHEESE POPCORN

Sprinkle hot buttered popcorn (No. 138) with finely grated cheese. Stir and mix thoroughly. Bake in moderate oven (350° F.) 2 to 3 minutes to melt cheese.

(141) RICE RING WITH CREAMED DRIED BEEF

Pack boiled rice (No. 107) in ring mold. Keep hot. Turn out onto large chop plate. Fill center with creamed dried beef (No. 1359) and slices of hard-cooked egg (No. 202). Garnish with canned apricot halves, grilled slightly in a broiler.

(142) SCRAPPLE

1 onion, chopped	Salt—Pepper
1 carrot chopped	1 cup chopped roasted pea-
1 cup corn meal	nuts
1 teaspoon sugar	

Mix onion, carrot, corn meal and sugar with 2 cups water. Season to taste with salt and pepper. Cook slowly until thick, about one hour. Beat in peanuts. Pack into an oiled pan or baking powder tin. Cool. Slice and fry in little fat. Two and one half cups stewed tomatoes (No. 1893) can be substituted for the water. Serves 8.

CEREALS IN COMBINATION

Cereals are used widely in combination with other foods, fruits, vegetables, meat, fish, etc. Throughout this book are many more dishes in which cereals play a major or minor role. Consult the index and these other cereal treasures will be found, listed under the names of each of the cereals.

Egg Dishes

EGGS may be served at any meal and in a variety of ways. Probably no other single article of food can be utilized in a greater number of dishes. Whether alone or with ham or bacon, or in omelets, soufflés, or croquettes, eggs may appear in the main dish of any meal. Many quick breads, cakes, salad dressings, sauces, desserts, and beverages not only taste better and look more attractive when made with a liberal proportion of eggs, but they are also higher in food value. In whatever way they are served, eggs are a good source of efficient protein and some of the minerals and vitamins needed for building the body and keeping it healthy.

The secret of success in cooking eggs and dishes in which eggs predominate, is to cook slowly at moderate, even heat.

TESTING FOR FRESHNESS

Eggs should not be stored near strongly scented foods.

There are two methods for home-testing eggs for freshness. (1) Hold egg before a light in a dark room. If the center is clear, the egg is fresh. (2) Drop egg in cold water. If fresh, it will sink to bottom and lie on its side. Old eggs lose part of their contents by evaporation and will not lie flat in this test.

(201) "PUTTING DOWN" EGGS

By far the best method of preserving eggs is to "put them down" in water glass, potassium and sodium silicate. Mix 1 part water glass, which may be purchased in any drug store, with 9 parts water, mixing thoroughly. Put liquid in an earthenware, enameled, or glass container. Clean eggs, but do not wash. Put eggs in liquid. Cover tightly. Keep in cool place but do not let freeze. The eggs will keep indefinitely and may be used in all recipes. If, however, preserved eggs are boiled, prick the small end with a pin or they will pop open. A less satisfactory method for preserving eggs is to plunge them in violently boiling water 5 seconds. This cooks the skin on the inside of the shell and keeps out air and prevents evaporation. Thoroughly dry eggs and pack in containers, standing them on the small ends. Keep in cool place. Grandmother used to preserve eggs by packing them in common salt or sand, small end down, being careful not to let the eggs touch one another.

(202)   SOFT- OR HARD-COOKED EGGS

For soft-cooked eggs or for hard-cooked eggs with tender whites, start the eggs in cold water to cover, supported on a rack. Heat the water gradually to simmering, but do not let it boil. Boiling temperature toughens white of egg. The temperature of the water should not be allowed to go higher than 185° F. For soft-cooked eggs, remove from the fire when the water simmers (or is 185° F.), cover the pan, and let stand for a few minutes. The length of time required must be found by experience. The number of eggs cooked at a time, the size of the pan, and the quantity and temperature of the water all affect the rate at which eggs cook. For hard-cooked eggs, continue the cooking over a low fire for 30 minutes after the water simmers, and keep it below boiling.

(203)   FRIED EGGS

Heat an iron frying pan and cover bottom of pan generously with butter or fat. Drop eggs into it. Fry slowly until white is set. If a harder yolk is desired the eggs may be turned and cooked on the other side. Serve hot. Allow 1 or 2 eggs per serving. For lyonnaise fried eggs, sauté chopped onion in butter or fat until brown. Remove onion and fry eggs in same fat. Serve with onion.

(204)   FRENCH FRIED EGGS

Melt butter in frying pan. Break eggs on saucer and slip carefully into pan. Tilt pan so fat is deep. Curl up egg white with knife, making a nest around the yolk. Allow 1 egg per serving.

(205)   **CODDLED EGGS**

Bring pan of water to a boil. Remove from heat. Drop in eggs. Cover and let stand 8 to 10 minutes.

(206)   **BOILED EGGS**

Put eggs in boiling water and boil for 3 to 5 minutes, depending on personal preference. Three-minute eggs are very soft and 5-minute eggs are quite firm. Hard-boiled eggs should remain in water 20 minutes.

(207)   **POACHED (DROPPED) EGGS**

Fill frying pan ⅔ full of water. Add ½ teaspoon salt for each quart water. Bring to boil. Break eggs and drop carefully on-to saucer. Transfer without breaking yolk to water. Do not let water boil after eggs are in it. Cook until white is firm and there is a film over yolk. Or, use milk instead of water and pour milk and a little melted butter over egg when serving. Poached eggs are good when served on corned beef hash (No. 1357), on any chopped cooked meat heaped on buttered toast (No. 988), on toast spread with pâté de foie gras, or when served with to-mato (No. 2035) or cream sauce (No. 2005).

(208)   **OMELETS**

Omelets fluffy and omelets flat are made of the same in-gredients: One or two eggs for each person, 1 tablespoon of milk for each egg, and salt to taste. Beat the egg yolks and whites separately for a fluffy omelet; beat them together for a flat omelet. To make a fluffy omelet for an average family use 6 eggs. Beat the yolks thoroughly and add 6 tablespoons of milk. If preferred, the milk may be heated; it will then cook the yolks slightly when it is added and give the mixture a smoother consistency. Or, one-half cup of hot medium white sauce (No. 2004) added to the yolks will make a larger omelet with more body. Fold the yolk mixture gradually into the stiffly beaten whites containing one-half teaspoon of salt. Have ready and hot a smooth heavy omelet pan containing 1 tablespoon melted butter or other fat, and pour the egg mixture into the pan. The omelet may be cooked in three different ways, but in any case start it on top of the stove at moderate heat. If a small-sized gas or oil burner is used, move the pan about so that the omelet will cook around the edge at the same rate as in the center. As soon as the omelet has browned slightly on the bottom, place it in a moderate oven (350° F.) and bake for 10 minutes. Or, continue the cooking on top of the stove until the mixture sets, and then place under a low broiler flame for 2 or 3 minutes. Or, if preferred, cover the pan during the whole period and so cook the top of the omelet with steam. When the omelet is done, crease it through the center, fold it over with a spatula, and roll it onto a hot platter without attempting to lift it from the pan. Pour over the omelet melted butter or other fat containing finely cut parsley, and serve at once. For a flat omelet beat the eggs with 1 tablespoon of milk for each egg and salt to taste. Pour a thin layer of the mixture into a hot greased omelet pan and cook slowly and evenly. When brown on the bottom, roll the omelet in the pan and turn it onto a hot platter. Chopped fried ham or bacon, cooked rice, any cooked meat or fish, cooked oysters, cooked chicken livers, sliced fresh strawberries, canned pineapple, grated cheese, or a cooked vegetable such as peas, mushrooms, or asparagus, or a combination of chopped onion, green pepper, celery, and parsley delicately fried in butter or other fat may be added to the egg mixture before it is cooked or may be spread over half of the cooked omelet before it is folded and turned on to the platter.

(209)   SCRAMBLED EGGS

6 eggs	1/8 teaspoon pepper
1/2 cup milk	1 tablespoon butter or fat
3/4 teaspoon salt	

Beat eggs slightly and combine with milk, salt, and pepper. Melt butter in iron frying pan. Pour in egg mixture. Cook slowly, stirring constantly, until creamy. Serves 4 to 6.

Alternates for Scrambled Eggs

Use canned or strained stewed tomatoes (No. 1893) in place of milk.

Cook with 1 tablespoon chopped parsley and 1/4 teaspoon onion juice.

Add chopped cooked chicken livers (No. 1508), chopped sautéed mushrooms (No. 1801), grated mild cheese, any chopped cooked meat, vegetables, or fish, diced broiled bacon (No. 1464), or chopped pimiento during cooking.

Add any cooked cereal before cooking.

Any form of scrambled eggs may be cooked over hot water, in which case reduce milk or other liquid one-sixth.

(210)   BAKED EGGS

6 slices bread	⅛ teaspoon pepper
6 eggs	1 tablespoon butter
½ teaspoon salt	½ cup milk

Cut bread in rounds. Cut out piece in center of each. Toast lightly. Place in a greased baking dish. Break eggs and drop each into center of toast slices. Sprinkle with salt and pepper. Dot with butter. Pour on milk. Bake in moderate oven (350° F.) 15 to 20 minutes or until whites have set. Serves 6.

(211)   SHIRRED EGGS

2 tablespoons butter	½ teaspoon salt
½ cup dry bread crumbs	⅛ teaspoon pepper
6 eggs	

Grease 6 individual custard cups with butter. Cover bottom and sides of cup with crumbs. Break eggs on saucer. Slip carefully into cups. Sprinkle with salt and pepper. Cover with crumbs. Bake in slow oven (275° F.) 15 to 20 minutes until white is set. Serve plain or with brown butter sauce (No. 2026). If desired, 2 tablespoons cream may be poured over eggs before cooking. They are also delicious if sprinkled with any mild, grated cheese. Excellent fancy shirred eggs may be produced by shirring eggs on top medium white sauce (No. 2004), mixed with chopped fried scallops (No. 1269), lobster meat (No. 1236), shrimps (No. 1272), fish, or creamed potatoes (No. 1844). In other styles of shirred eggs they may be baked in cups made by halving and scooping some of the pulp out of tomatoes, green peppers, or baked potatoes (No. 1837). If raw vegetables are used, bake in moderate oven (350° F.) until vegetables are tender. Allow 1 egg per serving.

(212)   STEAMED EGGS

Break eggs in buttered pan. Add 1½ tablespoons water for each egg. Season with salt. Cover tightly. Cook slowly until white is firm and there is a film over yolk. Serve hot.

(213)   EGG CUSTARD

Allow 1 cup milk and ½ teaspoon salt to 4 eggs. Beat eggs thoroughly with salt. Add milk, mixing well. Pour into greased cups or molds and steam in double boiler until set, from 30 minutes to 1 hour, depending on size. Or bake by setting molds in hot water, covering, and baking in moderate oven (350° F.) 30 minutes to 1 hour. Cool. Unmold. Serve with any desired sauce. Grated cheese, cooked corn, or diced cooked asparagus may be added to custard before cooking. Canned or strained stewed tomatoes (No. 1893) or any meat or vegetable stock can be substituted for milk. Allow 1 egg per serving.

(214)   PICKLED EGGS

12 hard-cooked eggs	1 teaspoon dry mustard
(No. 202)	1 teaspoon salt
1 quart vinegar	1 teaspoon pepper

Remove shells from eggs. Boil vinegar and add seasonings. Pour in glass jar. Drop in eggs. Cover and let stand at least 10 days before serving. If desired, several cloves may be stuck in each egg before they are put in vinegar.

(215)   STUFFED EGGS

5 hard-cooked eggs	⅛ teaspoon cayenne
(No. 202)	1 tablespoon melted butter
3 tablespoons grated Ameri-	1 cup medium white sauce
can cheese	(No. 2004)
1 teaspoon vinegar	¼ cup buttered bread
¼ teaspoon mustard	crumbs
1 teaspoon salt	

Cut eggs in half, lengthwise. Remove whites, keeping whole. Mash yolks. Add cheese, vinegar, mustard, salt, cayenne, and butter. Mold into shapes like whole yolks. Replace whites around mixtures. Put in baking dish. Add sauce. Sprinkle with bread crumbs. Bake in moderate oven (350° F.) 15 to 20 minutes or until crumbs are browned. They may be served with medium white sauce (No. 2004) or cheese sauce (No. 2008). Serves 4.

(216) DEVILED EGGS

6 hard-cooked eggs	½ teaspoon vinegar
(No. 202)	1 tablespoon chopped
2 teaspoons mustard	parsley
¼ teaspoon pepper	½ teaspoon paprika
¼ teaspoon salt	

Remove shells from eggs. Take thin slice off of whites at each end of eggs. Cut eggs in halves, crosswise. Remove yolks and mash, adding other ingredients and mixing well. Refill whites with mixture. Sprinkle with paprika. Arrange on lettuce. Serves 6.

Suggested Stuffings for Deviled Eggs

1—Mashed yolks, 2 tablespoons grated cheese, ¼ teaspoon mustard, 1 teaspoon vinegar, 1 tablespoon butter, salt, and pepper.

2—Mashed yolks, 2 tablespoons anchovy paste, 2 tablespoons mayonnaise (No. 701), 2 tablespoons lemon juice, 2 tablespoons chopped olives, 2 tablespoons chopped nuts, salt, and cayenne.

3—Mashed yolks, 2 tablespoons diced, crisp bacon (No. 1464), ½ tablespoon Worcestershire sauce, ½ teaspoon mustard, salt, and pepper.

4—Mashed yolks, 2 tablespoons sautéed chopped onion (No. 1811), ¼ cup chopped, sautéed mushrooms (No. 1801), 2 tablespoons tomato catchup, salt, and cayenne.

5—Mashed yolks, 1 teaspoon horseradish, juice of ½ lemon, 1 tablespoon French dressing (No. 716), salt, and pepper.

(217) RUSSIAN STUFFED EGGS

Remove shells from hard-cooked eggs (No. 202). Take thin slices from whites at both ends. Cut in halves, crosswise. Remove yolks and fill with caviar or chopped anchovies, sardines, or tuna fish. Mash egg yolks with mayonnaise (No. 701) or other salad dressing. Put a little of this mixture on each egg filling. Arrange rounds of buttered bread on a dish. Place one tomato slice on each. Set stuffed egg white on top. Allow 1 egg per serving.

(218)   EGGS WITH ANCHOVY

Follow recipe for deviled eggs (No. 216), mashing yolks with ¼ teaspoon salt, ⅛ teaspoon pepper, ⅛ teaspoon vinegar, ⅛ teaspoon olive oil, and 2 teaspoons anchovy paste.

(219)   MOLDED EGGS

Chop hard-cooked eggs (No. 202). Mix with 1 tablespoon melted butter per egg. Season with salt and pepper. Pack in mold and press. Chill. Allow 1 egg per serving.

(220)   EGG CROQUETTES

1¼ cups very thick white sauce (No. 2004)	½ teaspoon salt
	1 tablespoon chopped parsley
4 hard-cooked eggs, chopped fine (No. 202)	1 cup dry bread crumbs
	1 well-beaten egg

Combine sauce, cooked eggs, salt, and parsley. Chill. Mold into rounds or croquettes. Roll in crumbs. Dip in beaten egg, diluted with 2 tablespoons cold water. Roll again in crumbs. Fry in deep, hot fat (375° F.) about 2 minutes or until well browned. Serve hot with cheese (No. 2008) or tomato sauce (No. 2035). Serves 4.

(221)   EGG BALLS

6 hard-cooked egg yolks (No. 202)	¼ teaspoon pepper
	1 beaten egg
1½ tablespoons melted butter	½ cup dry bread crumbs
1 teaspoon salt	

Mash all ingredients except crumbs into a smooth paste. Form into little balls. Roll in bread crumbs. Sauté in little fat until browned. Serves 6.

(222)   GOLDEN EGGS

6 hard-cooked eggs (No. 202)	12 toast points
	2 teaspoons chopped parsley
1½ cups thin white sauce (No. 2004)	

Separate yolks and whites of eggs. Chop whites fine and add to hot sauce. Pour sauce on hot platter and arrange toast around edge. Force yolks through a sieve over the sauce. Sprinkle with parsley. Serve hot. Serves 6.

(223)　　　　FRENCH EGGS

6 hard-cooked eggs, quartered (No. 202)	1 tablespoon flour
1 tablespoon lemon juice	1 pint milk
¼ pound butter	1 tablespoon chopped parsley

Arrange egg quarters on dish. Sprinkle with lemon juice. Melt half of butter in pan. Add flour and cook slowly, stirring constantly, until thickened. Bring milk to a boil and add slowly to butter. Add remaining butter and parsley. Heat well. Pour sauce over eggs. Serves 6.

(224)　　　　SCOTCH EGGS

½ cup bread crumbs	¼ teaspoon pepper
½ cup milk	1 beaten egg
1 cup chopped, cooked ham	6 hard-cooked eggs
½ teaspoon mustard	(No. 202)

Mix crumbs and milk in saucepan. Heat slowly and stir into a smooth paste. Add ham, mustard, pepper, and beaten egg, mixing well. Take shells from hard-cooked eggs. Cover each thoroughly with mixture. Fry in deep hot fat (375° F.) 2 minutes. Drain on unglazed paper. Serve hot with tomato sauce (No. 2035) or cold. Serves 6.

(225)　　EGGS WITH CARROT SAUCE

6 hard-cooked eggs (No. 202)	1 tablespoon butter
1½ cups medium white sauce (No. 2004)	6 boiled carrots, sliced (No. 1745)

Halve eggs. Arrange on plate. Dot with butter. Mix sauce and carrots. Heat thoroughly. Pour over eggs. Serves 6.

(226)   LYONNAISE EGGS

2 tablespoons butter   1 cup hot milk
2 tablespoons chopped onion   4 hard-cooked eggs, sliced
1 tablespoon chopped parsley   (No. 202)
1 tablespoon flour

Melt butter in pan. Sauté onion and parsley to light brown.
Stir in flour. Add milk. Bring to boil, blending thoroughly. Add
eggs. Heat thoroughly. Serve on buttered toast (No. 988).
Serves 6.

(227)   EGGS À LA KING

2 cups medium white sauce   ½ cup boiled peas
   (No. 2004)   (No. 1823)
1 cup sliced, sautéed mush-   6 hard-cooked eggs
   rooms (No. 1801)   (No. 202)
              2 tablespoons chopped parsley

Mix sauce, mushrooms, parsley, and peas. Cut eggs in eighths
and add to sauce. Heat thoroughly and serve on buttered toast
(No. 988). Serves 6.

(228)   EGG CUTLETS

2 tablespoons butter   2 tablespoons chopped
½ cup flour   parsley
1 cup hot milk   6 hard-cooked eggs
1 teaspoon salt   (No. 202)
¼ teaspoon pepper   1 well-beaten egg
2 tablespoons chopped onion   ½ cup bread crumbs

Melt butter. Add ¼ cup flour. Blend. Add milk slowly, stirring constantly, and bring to a boil. Cook 5 minutes. Chop hard-
cooked eggs and add with onion and parsley to sauce. Season to
taste with salt and pepper. Chill. Mold into cutlets. Dip in remaining flour. Dip in egg, diluted with a little water. Dip in
crumbs. Fry in deep, hot fat (375° F.) 2 minutes. Drain on
unglazed paper. Serve with white (No. 2004) or Béchamel sauce
(No. 2033). Serves 6. If desired, the cutlets may be sautéed in
a little fat in frying pan.

(229)   EGGS AND MUSHROOMS

½ pound mushrooms	Few grains cayenne
1½ cups water	1 cup milk
1 tablespoon butter or fat	6 hard-cooked eggs, sliced
4 tablespoons flour	(No. 202)
1 teaspoon salt	2 tablespoons dried bread
Few grains pepper	crumbs

Wash mushrooms, drain and peel, and remove stems. Cook stems and peelings together in the water 15 minutes. Strain liquid into a cup. Slice mushrooms and fry slowly in the butter until tender. Mix flour, salt, pepper and cayenne together and add milk slowly to make a smooth paste. Add the cup of mushroom stock and cook over a slow fire, stirring constantly until thick. Add mushrooms. Put a layer of eggs in a casserole, then a layer of the mushroom mixture. Repeat this process until all the ingredients are used. Sprinkle top with crumbs. Bake in a moderate oven (350° F.) 20 minutes or until crumbs are brown. Serves 6.

(230)   SCALLOPED EGGS

6 hard-cooked eggs	1½ cups soft bread crumbs
(No. 202)	2 cups thin white sauce
¼ teaspoon salt	(No. 2004)

Chop eggs and season with salt. Put layer of crumbs in bottom of greased baking dish. Add a layer of egg. Add layer of sauce. Repeat until all ingredients are used, having a layer of crumbs on top. Bake in moderate oven (350° F.) 20 minutes or until crumbs are brown. Layers of chopped ham, other cooked meats, poultry, or fish can be added to this dish. Serves 6.

(231)   EGGS AU GRATIN

4 hard-cooked eggs	½ cup grated mild cheese
(No. 202)	¼ cup bread crumbs
2 cups medium white sauce	½ tablespoon butter
(No. 2004)	

Quarter eggs and put in greased baking dish. Mix sauce and cheese. Pour over eggs. Mix crumbs and butter. Sprinkle on top of sauce. Bake in slow oven (325° F.) until brown. Tomato sauce (No. 2035) can be used in place of medium white sauce. Serves 6.

(232)   CURRIED EGGS

6 eggs	1 teaspoon curry
4 tablespoons butter or other fat	1 teaspoon salt
	3 drops Tabasco sauce
1 tablespoon chopped green pepper	3 tablespoons flour
	2 cups milk
2 tablespoons chopped onion	3 cups cooked rice
2 tablespoons chopped celery	(No. 106)

Cook the eggs hard (No. 202). Make a sauce as follows: Melt the fat in a skillet, add the green pepper, onion, and celery and cook for 2 or 3 minutes. Stir into this the seasoning and the flour, mix well, and add the cold milk. Cook for 3 or 4 minutes, stirring constantly. Make a bed of the hot flaky cooked rice on a hot platter. Arrange over it the hard-cooked eggs, cut in quarters, and pour the hot sauce over the eggs and rice. Sprinkle the top with chopped parsley, and serve at once. Serves 6.

(233)   BAKED EGGS WITH ONION

2 small onions, sliced	2 tablespoons lemon juice
½ teaspoon salt	6 poached eggs (No. 207)
⅛ teaspoon pepper	¼ cup mild grated cheese
3 tablespoons butter	

Season onions and sauté in butter until tender. Do not brown. Put onion in greased baking dish. Add lemon juice and butter from pan. Place eggs on top. Sprinkle with cheese. Bake in moderate oven (350° F.) to melt cheese. Serves 6.

(234)   PLANKED EGGS

2 cups chopped, cooked meat	1 tablespoon melted butter
1 cup medium white sauce (No. 2004)	4 poached eggs (No. 207)
2 cups mashed potatoes (No. 1835)	

Mix meat and sauce. Spread on buttered plank. Make border with mashed potatoes, using pastry tube. Brush with butter. Put eggs on top of meat mixture. Bake in moderate oven (350° F.) 10 minutes. Serves 4

(235) POACHED EGGS WITH TOMATOES

6 slices buttered toast
  (No. 988)
6 slices fried tomatoes
  (No. 1894)
6 poached eggs (No. 207)
3 tablespoons butter

1 tablespoon chopped onion
1 tablespoon chopped
  pimiento
1 tablespoon chopped
  parsley

Arrange toast on platter. Put 1 slice tomato on each piece of toast. Put 1 poached egg on each. Brown onion, pimiento, and parsley in butter and pour over eggs. Serves 6.

(236) ANCHOVY POACHED EGGS

Spread anchovy paste on buttered toast (No. 988). Put poached egg (No. 207) on each. Serve with tomato sauce (No. 2035), to which has been added 1 teaspoon mustard and 1 tablespoon Worcestershire sauce. Deviled ham may be substituted for anchovy paste.

(237) POACHED EGGS WITH ASPARAGUS

Serve poached eggs (No. 207) on buttered toast (No. 988) and cover with 2 cups hot béchamel sauce (No. 2033) to which has been added 1 cup boiled asparagus tips (No. 1704) and ¼ cup grated Parmesan cheese.

(238) POACHED EGGS WITH CHEESE

Poach 6 eggs (No. 207). Place on slices of buttered toast (No. 988). Put 1 tablespoon cheese sauce (No. 2008) on each.

(239) EGGS FLORENTINE

Arrange poached eggs (No. 207) on nests of boiled and seasoned spinach (No. 1870). Pour over medium white sauce (No. 2004) and sprinkle with grated Parmesan cheese.

(240) EGGS À LA FINLAND

Serve poached eggs (No. 207) on nests of boiled rice (No. 107), covered with tomato sauce (No. 2035).

(241)   EGGS BENEDICT

Toast slices of bread, or split and toast English muffins (No. 1053). Place on each piece of toast a thin slice of fried ham (No. 1451) or crisp cooked bacon (No. 1464), and on top of this a poached egg (No. 207). Cover with hot hollandaise sauce (No. 2022) and serve at once.

(242)   EGGS WITH CREAMED CELERY AND BACON

Put creamed celery (No. 1762) on slices of buttered toast (No. 988). Put poached eggs (No. 207) on top. Garnish with broiled bacon slices (No. 1464).

(243)   MEXICAN POACHED EGGS

Add 1½ tablespoons sliced green olives, 1 shredded pimiento, and 2 tablespoons chopped green pepper to 1 cup hot tomato sauce (No. 2035) and pour over 6 slices buttered toast (No. 988). Put poached eggs (No. 207) on top and garnish with parsley.

(244)   CREAMY OMELET

Cook same as flat (No. 208) or fluffy omelet (No. 208), using ½ cup medium white sauce (No. 2004) instead of water or milk for liquid. Serve hot with additional sauce.

(245)   JELLY OMELET

Follow recipe for fluffy omelet (No. 208). Beat ½ cup jelly with a fork to the right consistency for spreading. As soon as the omelet is baked, spread quickly with the jelly and fold. Serve immediately. Serves 4.

(246)   CHEESE OMELET

Follow recipe for flat omelet (No. 208). Sprinkle ½ cup grated cheese on the omelet and put in a very hot oven (475° F.) until cheese melts. Fold and turn out on hot platter. Serves 6.

(247) SPANISH OMELET

4 thin slices bacon, minced	3 tablespoons milk
1 tomato, diced	½ teaspoon salt
1 onion, chopped	⅛ teaspoon red pepper
5 mushrooms, chopped	1 tablespoon butter
6 eggs	

Brown bacon. Add tomato, onion, and mushrooms. Cook slowly 15 minutes, stirring occasionally. Beat eggs with milk, salt, and pepper. Melt butter in another pan and pour eggs in. Fry slowly until eggs are set. Pour sauce from first pan over eggs. Fold omelet and turn onto a hot platter. Cover with remaining sauce from both pans. If desired, chopped green pepper may be substituted for mushrooms. Serves 6.

(248) CHICKEN OMELET

Warm 1 cup chopped, cooked chicken with 1 cup milk, 1 tablespoon flour, 1 tablespoon butter, salt, and pepper. Make omelet (No. 208). Pour chicken mixture over it just before folding. Serves 6.

(249) BANANA OMELET

4 eggs	1 tablespoon sugar
2 tablespoons cream	½ teaspoon salt
2 bananas, peeled and mashed	2 tablespoons powdered sugar

Beat eggs until light. Add other ingredients except powdered sugar and mix well. Fry slowly in greased frying pan until set. Fold and turn into hot platter. Sprinkle with sugar. Serves 6.

(250) CORN OMELET

6 eggs	1 cup canned corn
1 teaspoon salt	

Beat egg yolks until thick. Add salt and pepper. Fold into egg whites. Fold corn into egg mixture. Put in buttered pan and cook slowly until browned on bottom. Transfer to moderate oven (350° F.) and bake until dry. Fold and remove to hot platter. Spaghetti (No. 2302) and tomato sauce (No. 2035) may be substituted for corn. Serves 6.

(251)   BREAD OMELET

¾ cup bread crumbs	½ teaspoon salt
½ cup milk	1 tablespoon butter
3 eggs	

Put crumbs in cup. Fill cup with milk. Let stand 5 minutes. Beat lightly the egg yolks. Beat the whites stiff with a fork. Drain excess milk from crumbs. Beat crumbs and yolks together. Add salt. Fold in the whites. Melt butter in pan. Put in mixture and cook at high heat 1 minute. Reduce heat. Cover and let cook slowly 20 minutes. Remove to hot platter and fold. Serves 4.

(252)   SCRAMBLED EGGS WITH TOMATO

2 medium-sized tomatoes	1½ tablespoons butter
½ teaspoon salt	4 eggs

Peel tomatoes. Cut in eighths. Put in saucepan with juice. Sprinkle with salt. Bring to boil and boil 1 minute. Drain off juice in a colander. Dot with half of butter. Melt remaining butter in pan. Break eggs and drop in pan. Stir quickly. When partly cooked, add tomatoes. Stir to mix well and serve hot. One half cup of canned corn, enriched with 1 tablespoon butter, can be substituted for tomatoes. Serves 4.

(253)   SCRAMBLED EGGS AND BACON

Beat the eggs slightly with 1 tablespoon of cream or top milk for each egg, and season with salt and pepper. Pour the mixture into a pan containing 1 tablespoon of melted butter or other fat. Cook over hot water, stirring constantly until thickened. Remove and serve at once with crisp bacon (No. 1464).

(254)   EGG FRIZZLE

¼ pound chipped beef	½ teaspoon salt
4 teaspoons butter	⅛ teaspoon pepper
4 eggs	¼ cup milk

Cover beef with boiling water and let stand for five minutes. Drain and dry. Melt butter in skillet, add beef and heat thoroughly. Beat the eggs, add the seasonings and milk and mix well. Pour over the beef and stir frequently until eggs have cooked. Serve garnished with sprigs of parsley. Serves 4.

(255) BAKED FRENCH EGGS

⅛ pound butter
6 eggs
Salt—Pepper

1 tablespoon chopped parsley

Butter a baking dish. Heat to melt butter. Break eggs in dish. Lay slice of butter on each egg. Season with salt and pepper. Bake in moderate oven (350° F.) until whites are set. Remove to hot platter. Sprinkle with parsley. Serves 6.

(256) BAKED EGGS IN TOMATO SAUCE

2 cups canned or strained, stewed tomatoes (No. 1893)
1 slice onion
½ teaspoon salt
2 teaspoons sugar

Few grains pepper
2 tablespoons butter or fat
3 tablespoons flour
6 eggs
½ cup grated American cheese

Cook tomatoes, onion, salt, sugar and pepper together 20 minutes. Press the pulp through a sieve, discarding seeds. Melt butter. Add flour and mix well. Add the tomato juice slowly and bring to the boiling point, stirring constantly. Pour the sauce into six individual baking dishes. Break eggs, one at a time, into a cup and slip carefully into each dish. Sprinkle with cheese. Bake in a moderate oven (325° F.) 15 minutes or until eggs are firm. Serves 6.

(257) BAKED EGGS WITH CHEESE SAUCE

Put a thin layer of cheese sauce (No. 2008) in the bottom of a greased baking dish or individual baking dishes. Break eggs, one at a time, into a cup and drop carefully on the sauce. Cover them with another layer of cheese sauce. Sprinkle top with well-seasoned soft bread crumbs. Bake in a moderate oven (325° F.) 15 to 20 minutes or until the egg whites are firm and the crumbs are brown. Allow 1 egg and ½ cup sauce per serving.

(258)   BAKED EGGS WITH MACARONI

2 cups boiled macaroni (No. 2302)	½ cup mild, grated cheese
1 cup medium white sauce (No. 2004)	1 teaspoon salt
	⅛ teaspoon pepper
	4 eggs

Heat macaroni and place in greased baking dish. Mix sauce, cheese, salt, and pepper. Pour over macaroni. Drop eggs on top. Bake in moderate oven (350° F.) until eggs are set. Hot, steamed rice (No. 106) can be substituted for macaroni. Serves 4.

(259)   BAKED EGGS AND CHEESE

Break the desired number of eggs in a shallow, greased baking dish, add a few tablespoons of cream and salt enough to season, and sprinkle with a mixture of grated cheese and fine dry bread crumbs. Set this dish in a pan containing hot water and bake in a moderate oven (350° F.) until the eggs are set and the crumbs are brown. Just before serving add a few dashes of paprika to suit taste.

(260)   EGGS IN BACON RINGS

Half broil thin slices of bacon (No. 1464). Slip each slice in custard cups, lining the cup. Drop eggs into cups individually. Bake in moderate oven (350° F.) until eggs are set. Allow 1 egg per serving.

(261)   EGGS AND SPINACH EN CASSEROLE

1½ cups cold, chopped, boiled spinach (No. 1870)	1 cup cheese sauce (No. 2008)
6 eggs	Paprika

Put 4 tablespoons well-seasoned spinach in bottom of individual baking dishes. Drop a raw egg on top of each. Sprinkle with salt and pepper. Cover with sauce. Cook in a moderate oven (325° F.) 15 to 20 minutes or until eggs are set. Sprinkle with paprika. Serves 6.

(262) ITALIAN STYLE EGGS

2 tablespoons butter	1 tablespoon mustard
1 tablespoon Worcestershire sauce	1 teaspoon paprika
	1 teaspoon salt
3 tablespoons tomato catchup	6 eggs

Mix all ingredients but eggs in saucepan. Bring to boil. Break and drop in eggs. Cook slowly until set. Serve on buttered toast (No. 988) with sauce. Serves 6.

(263) BAKED EGG AND TOMATO

4 slices tomato   4 eggs

Salt—Pepper

Put tomato slices in separate greased custard cups. Sprinkle with salt and pepper. Drop egg in each. Bake in moderate oven (350° F.) until eggs are set. Serve on buttered toast (No. 988). Serves 4.

(264) BAKED EGGS IN TOMATO CUPS

Scoop out the centers of large, firm, ripe tomatoes. Sprinkle the tomato cups lightly on the inside with salt and dot with butter. Break an egg into each tomato, sprinkle with salt, pepper, and fine dry bread crumbs, and dot with butter. Bake in a moderate oven (350° F.) until the tomato skins are slightly wrinkled.

(265) EGG SOUFFLÉ

3 egg yolks	1 tablespoon chopped
1 cup hot, medium white sauce (No. 2004)	parsley
	3 egg whites

Combine beaten egg yolks, sauce, and parsley. Fold in the stiffly beaten egg whites. Put in greased baking dish. Set in pan of hot water and bake in moderate oven (350° F.) 35 to 40 minutes. Serve hot. Grated cheese, diced boiled shrimps (No. 1272), diced boiled lobster meat (No. 1236), any chopped, cooked meat or poultry, chopped cooked oysters or clams, any style, may be added to the sauce before it is combined with the egg yolks. Serves 4.

(266)   **EGG FLUFF**

1 slice bread	4 eggs
¾ cup milk	½ teaspoon salt
1 tablespoon melted butter	⅛ teaspoon pepper
or fat	

Break bread in pieces and put in cup. Fill cup with milk. Pour into a bowl and add beaten eggs, butter, salt, and pepper. Grease custard cups and fill each ¾ full with mixture. Bake in moderate oven (350° F.) 25 minutes. Serve hot. Serves 4.

(267)   **TOMATO-CHEESE SOUFFLÉ**

2 tablespoons butter	¾ cup milk, hot
3 tablespoons flour	1½ cups grated cheese
½ cup condensed tomato	¼ teaspoon dry mustard
soup, canned	4 eggs, separated

Melt butter, add flour, and cook until frothy. Then add milk and cook until thoroughly thickened. Stir in soup and cheese and heat until cheese is melted. Remove from fire and add mustard and egg yolks, adding one yolk at a time and beating thoroughly after the addition of each yolk. Beat the egg whites until stiff, but not dry, and fold them into the mixture. Pour into a well-greased casserole and bake in a moderate oven (350° F.) 50 to 60 minutes or until firm in the center. Serves 6. Put in pan of hot water while baking.

Beverages

BEVERAGES probably furnish more pleasure at meals or between meals than any other single course. The early-morning aroma of fine coffee makes a day start right. Beautifully colored and delightfully flavored cold drinks bring joy and happiness to meals served in hot weather. It is the punch bowl that forms one of the chief attractions at parties. The large numbers of men and women—old and young—who swarm into the soda bars in every part of the world provide ample testimony to the craving of everyone for fine drinks. The clever homemaker can serve in her home as delicious and refreshing drinks as can be found at the best-equipped fountains.

A good general rule to follow in serving beverages is, "Serve hot drinks hot and cold drinks cold." Never serve lukewarm hot drinks nor slightly cool cold drinks.

Make all beverages as lovely and colorful as possible. Select garnishes and ingredients in beverages for color as well as taste. Your critical guests will remember the beauty of your punch bowl long after the flavor of the punch is forgotten. Particularly study the possibilities of gaily-colored and garnished ice cubes (No. 333) as an accompaniment of cold drinks.

(301)   COFFEE

Coffee should be purchased in small quantities for home use as it quickly loses its aroma and flavor after exposure to the air. The refrigerator is considered the best place to keep coffee once it has been ground. After being made coffee should be served at once or it suffers greatly in loss of flavor. If it is necessary to let coffee stand, seal the lid of the pot and the spout to preserve aroma. There is no definite rule for the proper proportions of coffee and water. The strength of coffee is entirely a matter of personal preference. If weak coffee is desired, 1 tablespoon coffee to 1 cup water will suffice. Medium coffee would require 2 tablespoons coffee per cup of water and for strong coffee use 3 tablespoons coffee per cup of water. There are three usual methods of making coffee: (1) the drip or filter method; (2) the percolator method; (3) the boiled method. For drip or filtered coffee, put coffee in basket. Pour boiling water over it and let it drip or filter through. If the coffee lacks sufficient strength the liquid may again be put through the filter. Keep pot warm during dripping but do not boil. For percolated coffee put cold water in pot. Put coffee in basket. Bring water, by medium heat, to the percolating stage. Reduce heat to a point where percolation barely continues. Judge the strength of the coffee by its depth of color shown in the glass top. The cooking should continue for about 10 minutes after percolation starts. For boiled coffee, put coffee, a little cold water, and the white of an egg or some eggshells in a pot and stir thoroughly. Pour in boiling water and simmer 3 to 5 minutes with the spout sealed to keep in the flavor and aroma.

(302)   ICED COFFEE

Prepare strong coffee (No. 301). Fill tumblers half full of cracked ice or ice cubes. Pour in coffee. Add sugar and cream as desired.

(303)   CAFÉ AU LAIT

Scald milk while preparing coffee (No. 301). Pour equal amounts of hot milk and coffee into cup at the same time, a pot in each hand.

(304)   VIENNA COFFEE

This is very strong, black coffee (No. 301) served with whipped cream and sugar if desired. It is usually served at afternoon teas or as an after-dinner demi-tasse.

(305)   COFFEE SUBSTITUTES

Unless specific instructions are given for its preparation by the manufacturer, make according to directions for coffee (No. 301).

(306) TEA

The various kinds and grades of tea differ so materially that it is impossible to tell the exact amount of tea to use per cup of water. In using any particular tea for the first time, the safest method is to put in 1 teaspoon tea for each cup of water. Experience and personal preference will establish the proper amount after a few tries. Tea should never be made in a metal pan or kettle, but always in a glass or earthenware container. Put tea in the pot. Add freshly boiling water. Cover pot and let stand for 3 minutes. Strain liquid into another warm pot and serve at once. If a tea-ball or tea-bag is used, use same proportions of tea and water. Place tea-ball in pot. Pour in boiling water. Let stand, covered, for 1 to 3 minutes, according to taste. Remove tea-ball and serve at once. Tea-bags should be only half filled with tea in order that water may circulate freely among leaves. Good tea cannot be made by placing a tea-ball in a cup, as much of the aroma is lost. Serve with sugar and milk, lemon or orange slice.

(307) ICED TEA

Make strong tea (No. 306). Put ice in tumbler. Pour tea over ice. Serve with sugar and slice of orange or lemon.

(308) FLAXSEED TEA

Rinse ¼ cup flaxseed with cold water in a colander. Drain. Boil gently in 3 cups water 1½ hours. Drain. Serve with lemon juice, salt, or sugar. Serves 2.

(309) ICED GINGER TEA

Boil ginger root in water 3 to 5 minutes, according to taste desired. Strain and pour hot over cracked ice or ice cubes.

(310) COCOA

The general rule for cocoa is 2 teaspoons cocoa, ¼ cup cold water, 1 teaspoon sugar and ¾ cup milk for each cup cocoa desired. Cook the water and cocoa together until thick; add the sugar; stir until dissolved; add milk and boil 1 minute. If desired use all milk instead of any water.

(311)   ICED COCOA

Add ½ cup whipped cream to ordinary cocoa (No. 310).
Beat well. Chill.

(312)   COCOA SHELLS

Boil 1 cup cocoa shells in 6 cups water 3 hours, adding more
water when necessary. Strain. Serve with milk and sugar.

(313)   CRACKED COCOA

Simmer ½ cup cracked cocoa in 6 cups boiling water 3 hours,
adding more water when necessary. Strain. Serve with milk and
sugar.

(314)   COFFEE AND COCOA

Mix equal parts hot coffee (No. 301) and hot cocoa (No.
310). Flavor to taste with vanilla. Garnish with whipped cream.

(315)   CHOCOLATE

Use ½ square of chocolate, 1 tablespoon sugar and 2 tablespoons hot water for each cup of chocolate desired. Break chocolate into pieces, add hot water, cook together until smooth; add
sugar; stir until dissolved; add 1 cup scalded milk. Flavor with
vanilla. Let cook about 5 minutes in a double boiler. It may be
served with whipped cream.

(316)   ICED CHOCOLATE

Prepare hot chocolate (No. 315). Chill. Pour over cracked
ice or ice cubes. Sweeten to taste. Garnish with whipped cream.

(317)   MILK

In spending the food money, milk should be considered first,
as it is necessary for every one and is the best building food for
children. It also supplies the body with fuel, minerals, and Vitamins A, B and G.

Pasteurized milk is safer than raw milk, because complete
pasteurization kills germs that might be present, such as those

that cause tuberculosis, infantile diarrhea, septic sore throat, typhoid fever, diphtheria and scarlet fever. If raw milk is used or advised, it should, of course, be certified.

Milk should be covered and kept cold; that will keep it clean, sweet, and free from strange flavors and odors.

If there is no ice in the home, it may be necessary in hot weather to buy milk twice a day, letting the dealer keep it cold. A temperature between 45-50° F. keeps milk from spoiling.

Dried and evaporated milk have the same food value as pasteurized milk and, in some places, cost less. Dried milk can be used in small quantities as needed and need not be kept on ice. After the can is opened, evaporated milk must have the same care as fresh milk. Sweetened condensed milk has had sugar added as a preservative. It can be used in cooking, or in place of cream. It, too, must have the same care as fresh milk after the can is opened. These are all prepared by the addition of water. Use milk in soups, puddings and creamed dishes as well as to drink.

(318)   HOT MALTED MILK

Blend 1¼ tablespoons malted milk to a smooth paste with warm water. Add 1 cup boiling water. Stir and serve at once.

(319)   EGG MALTED MILK

Add 2 teaspoons malted milk to egg before adding other ingredients and then proceed as for eggnog (No. 323). A teaspoon of cocoa or sweetened chocolate may also be added if desired.

(320)   MILK SHAKE

Flavor cold milk to taste with any fruit or sweet sirup. Add a little cracked ice. Shake or stir well. If desired, 1 egg can be added before shaking or stirring. Cold coffee, chocolate, or cocoa can also be used to flavor milk shakes.

(321)   MILK PUNCH

Add 2 teaspoons brandy, sherry, or rum to 1 cup hot or cold milk. Sweeten to taste. Serve at once.

(322)   PEPTONIZED MILK

1 tube peptonizing powder   1 pint milk

Dissolve powder in ½ cup cold water. Add milk. Mix well. Chill.

(323)   EGGNOG

1 egg	Salt—Nutmeg
1 tablespoon sugar	¾ cup milk

Beat egg yolk. Add sugar, salt, and milk. Strain. Add egg white, stiffly beaten. Add pinch of nutmeg. Serve cold. If desired, 1 teaspoon cocoa can be added to mixture.

(324)   HOT PINEAPPLE EGGNOG

8 eggs	1 pint cream
6½ cups pineapple or other fruit juice	1 cup sugar
	¼ cup chopped orange peel

Separate egg yolks and whites. Beat yolks thoroughly in half the sugar. Beat whites thoroughly in remaining half sugar. Bring pineapple juice to a boil. Add cream. Reheat and pour over egg yolk mixture. Fold egg whites into hot mixture. Sprinkle with orange peel. Serves 12.

(325)   ICED COFFEE NOG

½ cup brown sugar	⅛ teaspoon salt
½ cup double-strength coffee (No. 301)	1 teaspoon vanilla
2 egg yolks, beaten	2 egg whites
	1 cup heavy cream, whipped

Combine sugar and the ½ cup freshly made coffee in top of double boiler, place over direct heat, and stir until sugar is dissolved and mixture boils. Pour slowly into the beaten egg yolks, stirring constantly. Cook over boiling water until thickened. Remove from heat, add salt and flavoring, chill. Beat egg whites until stiff, and fold into the mixture, with the whipped cream. Pour into a tray of automatic refrigerator, freeze until firm. Stir once during freezing. To serve, fill tall glasses half full of the frozen mixture, add rest of coffee chilled to fill glasses. Stir. Serves 6.

(326)   MINT JELLY COBBLER

½ cup fresh mint jelly   ¼ cup water
½ cup lemon juice   Shaved ice

Break up jelly slightly with fork. Add lemon juice and water. Fill glasses ⅔ full of shaved ice. Pour lemon mixture over ice, letting bits of jelly serve as garnish. Serve at once with short straws. Serves 4.

(327)   CREAM FLOAT

1 quart ginger ale   1 pint pineapple ice cream
                                   (No. 2567)

Pour ginger ale into tall glasses and drop into each several spoonfuls of pineapple ice cream. Serve at once. Serves 6.

(328)   GINGER ALE FLOAT

Fill tall beverage glasses two-thirds full of ginger ale and add a scoop of pineapple sherbet. Garnish with sprigs of mint.

(329)   SODA AND ICES

Bottled carbonated beverages combine pleasingly with ices or sherbets. Put small servings in iced tea glasses; then pour beverage over them. The following are palatable combinations:

(a) Apricot sherbet with ginger ale, grape, lemon, lime, orange, or raspberry carbonated beverage.
(b) Grape sherbet with root beer, or "cream" carbonated beverage.
(c) Orange sherbet with grape, orange, or "cream" carbonated beverage.
(d) Pineapple sherbet with grape carbonated beverage.
(e) Pineapple milk sherbet with lemon, lime, or "cream" carbonated beverage.
(f) Raspberry sherbet with lime, or raspberry carbonated beverage.
(g) Banana—Lemon—Orange sherbet with ginger ale, grape, lime and lemon, lime, pineapple, or raspberry carbonated beverage.
(h) Grape sherbet with ginger ale, or grape carbonated beverage.

(330)   SIMPLE SIRUP FOR BEVERAGES

Boil 2 cups sugar in 2 cups water 5 minutes. Store in cool place and use to sweeten fruit drinks.

(331)   CHOCOLATE SIRUP

8 squares unsweetened   3 1/2 cups sugar
    chocolate   1/2 teaspoon salt

Put chocolate in saucepan. Set that pan in large pan of boiling water. Cook until chocolate melts. Add sugar and salt. Blend well. Add 3 cups boiling water slowly. Boil until a thin sirup is formed, about 6 minutes. Pour into a jar. Cover and keep cool.

(332)   CHOCOLATE ICE CREAM SODA

3 tablespoons chocolate   2 tablespoons vanilla ice
    sirup (No. 331)   cream (No. 2547)
1 tablespoon cream   Soda water

Mix sirup and cream in tall glass. Add ice cream. Add soda water. Stir well.

(333)   FLAVORED ICE FOR COLD DRINKS

Tea, coffee, or fruit sirups and juices can be frozen in the trays of a mechanical refrigerator. The cubes can be used to chill drinks. Cubes may be garnished by placing cherries or mint leaves in their centers when half frozen.

(334)   LEMONADE

2 cups sugar   2/3 cup lemon juice

Boil sugar in 1 quart water 15 minutes. Add lemon juice. Cool and serve. Serves 4. Crushed or chopped fresh fruits or berries make a pleasing garnish and impart a wide choice of delightful flavors to lemonade.

(335)   EGG LEMONADE

1 egg   1/8 teaspoon salt
1 1/2 tablespoons sugar   2 tablespoons lemon juice

Beat egg thoroughly. Add other ingredients. Add 1 cup cold water slowly, stirring steadily. Serves 1.

(336)   GLORIFIED LEMONADE

2 cups sugar
3 cups water
3 lemons, juice
2 limes, juice

2 cups orange or lemon carbonated beverage, or
ginger ale

Boil sugar and water ten minutes. Cool. Add juice of lemons
and lime, and the orange or lemon beverage, or ginger ale. Serves
6.

(337)   GRAPE-JUICE LEMONADE

Juice of 3 lemons
⅓ cup sugar
2 cups grape juice

Enough ice-water to make 1
quart

Combine ingredients in the order given. Chill for ½ hour.
Serve in each glass a thin slice of lemon from which the seeds
have been removed. This quantity will serve 6 water glasses or
18 punch glasses.

(338)   SUPERB LEMONADE

1 cup lemon juice
2 cups sugar

1 orange, halved and sliced
1 cup pineapple cubes

Boil 2 quarts water. Add all ingredients. Chill. Pour over
cracked ice or ice cubes. Serves 8.

(339)   FLAXSEED LEMONADE

2 tablespoons flaxseed
1 cup sugar

3 lemons

Pour 1 quart boiling water over flaxseed. Simmer 45 minutes.
Add sugar and the rinds of the lemons, grated. Let stand 15
minutes. Add juice of lemons. Strain and serve hot or cold.
Serves 2.

(340)   ORANGEADE

5 oranges
1 lemon

½ cup sugar

Dissolve sugar in 4 cups water. Add juice of 4 oranges and
the lemon. Halve and slice remaining orange thin. Pour liquid
over cracked ice or ice cubes. Garnish with orange slices. Serves 4.

(341)   APPLEADE

Peel and quarter a sour apple. Cover with water and simmer until tender. Mash to a pulp in the water. Sweeten with sugar to taste. Cool. Add enough water to make 1 glassful.

(342)   LIMEADE

Mix ½ cup lime juice, ½ cup simple sirup for beverages (No. 330), and 2 cups water. Chill. Serves 4.

(343) GINGER ALE AND GRAPEFRUIT JUICE

Mix 1 quart ginger ale and 1 pint grapefruit juice. Pour over cracked ice or ice cubes. Serves 6.

(344)   MINTED GRAPE JUICE

Mix equal parts of grape juice and orange juice. Add fresh mint, crush well. Chill. Pour over ice cubes when serving. Garnish with sprig of fresh mint.

(345)   PINEAPPLE LIME FROST

Drop an egg white, 2 teaspoons of powdered sugar, and one tablespoon of lime juice into a clean mason jar. Stir a few seconds with a long spoon. Add one cup unsweetened pineapple juice which has been allowed to chill in the can before opening. Adjust screw cap to jar and shake vigorously until ingredients are well blended and frothy. Pour over ice in glass and serve at once. This amount will make 1 tall glass.

(346)   MULLED GRAPE JUICE

2 eggs	1 tablespoon sugar
⅛ teaspoon cinnamon	2 cups grape juice

Beat egg yolks lightly. Add cinnamon, sugar, and grape juice. Simmer over hot water until slightly thickened. Beat egg whites stiffly and fold into mixture. Turn off heat but keep over hot water 2 minutes. Serve hot. It may be cooled and reheated for serving. Serves 2.

(347) GRAPE GINGER

1 cup grape juice   4 cups ginger ale

Blend well and serve at once. Serves 4.

(348) FRUIT PUNCH I

4 quarts water
2 cups shredded pineapple
2 quarts strong tea
   (No. 306) or grape juice

2 pounds sugar
3 cups orange juice
1 cup lemon juice

Boil 1 quart water and sugar 1 minute. Cool. Add all other ingredients. Serve in a punch bowl with ice cubes. Garnish with orange and lemon slices, maraschino cherries, and sprigs of mint. Serves 50.

(349) FRUIT PUNCH II

4 cups hot water
2 cups sugar
1 small can chopped pine-
   apple

Juice of 3 lemons
Juice of 4 oranges
1 quart carbonated water

Prepare a sirup of the water and sugar and boil 15 minutes. Cool. Add fruit, juices, and carbonated water. Serve ice-cold. Serves 12.

(350) BLENDED FRUIT PUNCH

27 ounces canned apricot
   nectar
27 ounces canned pineapple
   juice

27 ounces canned pear nectar
13½ ounces orange juice
1 cup ginger ale

Mix first 4 ingredients. Chill. Pour over crushed ice or ice cubes. Add ginger ale just before serving. Serves 25.

(351) WHITE GRAPE JUICE PUNCH

Mix equal parts soda water and white grape juice. Serve cold.

(352)   LOGANBERRY PUNCH

45 ounces canned loganberry   13½ ounces orange juice
    juice   13½ ounces canned apricot
20 ounces grapefruit juice   nectar

Mix all ingredients. Chill and serve. Serves 25.

(353)   SPICED PINEAPPLE PUNCH

3 cups sugar   1 teaspoon whole cloves
3 cinnamon sticks, broken   8 cups pineapple juice

Boil sugar, cinnamon, and cloves in 2 cups water 10 minutes.
Strain and mix with pineapple juice. Chill and pour over crushed
ice or ice cubes. Serves 25.

(354)   RHUBARB PUNCH

4 cups rhubarb, cut in small   ⅓ cup lemon juice
    pieces   ⅛ teaspoon salt
2 cups sugar   Soda water or ginger ale
½ cup orange juice

Cover rhubarb with 1 quart water and cook until very soft.
Strain through a cloth. Add sugar. Bring to a boil, stirring constantly. Add orange juice, lemon juice, and salt. Chill. When
ready to serve mix with equal quantity of soda water or ginger
ale and pour over ice. Serves 10.

(355)   PRESIDENTIAL PUNCH

Mint sprigs   1 bottle orange carbonated
2 tablespoons sugar   beverage
1 pint strong lemonade   1 bottle ginger ale
    (No. 334)   1 pint plain or charged
1 bottle grape carbonated   water
    beverage

Select long stemmed sprays of mint, pinch the stems between
the fingers until the bruised sprigs give out their utmost flavor,
then thrust the stems into a deep pitcher half filled with ice.
If preferred the sprays may be arranged in a punch bowl with
the ice upon them. Over these sprinkle sugar and let stand half
an hour. Pour in the lemonade, water, grape carbonated beverage, orange carbonated beverage and ginger ale. Serves 20.

(356)   INDIAN FRUIT PUNCH

1 cup sugar
1 pint water
1 small can pineapple
1 small bottle maraschino
    cherries
3 oranges, cut into pieces

2 cups grape carbonated
    beverage
2 cups lime carbonated
    beverage
1 cup strawberry carbonated
    beverage

Make a sirup of the sugar and water, boiling for five minutes. Cool. Add the fruits. Thoroughly chill. When ready to serve add the carbonated beverages thoroughly chilled; ice cubes may be made of lemon carbonated beverage or fruit juices (No. 333). Serves 6.

(357)   BUFFET PUNCH

1 cup water
2 cups sugar
1 cup orange pekoe tea
    (No. 306)
5 lemons

6 oranges
2 cups crushed pineapple
    and sirup
1 cup maraschino cherries
4 cups ginger ale

Boil water and sugar for 10 minutes. Add cup of tea, juice of lemons, oranges, crushed pineapple, and sirup. Strain. Add one cup ice, cherries, and ginger ale. More water may be added if desired. For ice, cubes made of fruit juices (No. 333) may be used. Serves 8.

(358)   SPICE FRUIT PUNCH

2½ cups orange juice
1 cup pineapple juice
2 cups water
½ cup sugar
Grated rind of 1 lemon

1 tablespoon strained honey
6 whole cloves
½ teaspoon grated nutmeg
½ teaspoon cinnamon
3 pints ginger ale

Combine orange juice, pineapple juice, water, and sugar. Add grated rind of lemon, honey, cloves, nutmeg, and cinnamon. Mix and let stand 3 hours. Strain through cheesecloth and add the ginger ale. Stir briskly and serve in glasses containing ice cubes. The cubes may be made of carbonated beverages or fruit juices (No. 333). Serves 8.

(359)   COFFEE CREAM PUNCH

1 quart freshly brewed
    coffee (No. 301)
1 quart chocolate ice cream
    (No. 2549)

Nutmeg
¼ teaspoon almond flavoring
½ pint whipping cream

Chill the coffee and pour into punch bowl. Add ½ the chocolate ice cream and stir until it is partially melted. Add almond flavoring to the cream and whip until stiff. Place whipped cream and remaining ice cream alternately on top of first mixture. Sprinkle the cream lightly with nutmeg. Serves 12 to 15.

(360)   RUBY FRUIT PUNCH

1½ cups sugar
2 cups boiling water
3 cups cranberry juice
⅓ cup lemon juice

2 cups orange juice
1 quart ginger ale
Mint sprigs
Orange and lemon slices

Dissolve sugar in hot water. Add cranberry juice, lemon and orange juice. Chill. Just before serving turn into punch bowl, add ginger ale and orange and lemon slices. Serve decorated with mint sprigs. Serves 10.

(361)   CIDER PUNCH

3 cups water
1 cup sugar
½ teaspoon grated nutmeg
2 cups grape juice
1 cup grapefruit juice

2 cups cider
4 cups ginger ale, pale dry
    or golden
3 sliced lemons

Boil water, sugar, and nutmeg together 5 minutes. Cool. Add other ingredients. Put in punch bowl with cracked ice or ice cubes. Serves 12.

(362)   ALCOHOLIC PUNCHES

Almost any wines or liquors can be added to any punch if desired. Personal preference determines the quantity.

(363)   MULLED CIDER

1 gallon sweet cider
6 sticks cinnamon, broken
    in 1-inch pieces
1 tablespoon whole cloves
1 tablespoon whole allspice

2 pieces whole mace
3 cups brown sugar
2½ cups canned, spiced crab-
    apples

Put cider in kettle. Add cinnamon. Tie the other spices in
cheesecloth bag and drop in cider. Stir in sugar. Heat slowly
and simmer 20 minutes. Add apples 5 minutes before serving.
Remove spice bag before serving. Serve hot with an apple in
each cup. Yield: 3½ quarts.

(364)   PEPPERMINT ALE FIZZ

½ pound peppermint stick
    candy

2 cups whipping cream
1 quart ginger ale

Put the candy through a food chopper or roll with rolling
pin. Whip cream to custard-like consistency and fold in candy
crumbs, then place in freezing tray of refrigerator to freeze.
To serve: Place serving of frozen peppermint cream in tall
frosted glass and fill with cold ginger ale. Stir slightly with
spoon to make it fizz and serve with spoon and straw. Serves 6.

(365)   GINGER-MINT JULEP

1½ cups sugar
½ cup water
Juice of 6 lemons

½ cup fresh mint leaves
1 quart bottle ginger ale

Boil sugar and water 3 minutes. Pour over lemon juice and
crushed mint leaves. Let stand till cold. Add ice cold ginger ale
and serve immediately with a sprig of mint in each tall glass.
Serves 6.

(366)   ORANGE JULEP

1 quart orange juice
Juice 6 limes
1 cup powdered sugar

½ cup chopped mint leaves
Carbonated water

Combine the fruit juices, sugar, and chopped mint leaves. Chill
one hour and strain. Pour over crushed ice in tall glasses. Fill
with carbonated water and stir gently. Garnish with mint and
orange slices. Serves 4.

(367)   WHEY

Heat 1 pint milk slightly. Add 1 teaspoon pepsin essence or ½ junket tablet, dissolved in a little cold water. Let stand in warm place until curdled. Break curds and strain.

(368)   LEMON WHEY

Blend 1 cup milk and ¼ cup lemon juice. Let stand until it curdles, about 10 minutes. Strain and serve.

(369)   WINE WHEY

Bring 2 cups milk to a boil. Add 1 cup sherry wine. Bring again to a boil. Strain and serve.

(370)   ALBUMEN BEVERAGES

Beat 1 egg white to a froth. Add ⅓ cup orange or lemon juice. Sweeten to taste with a sirup made by boiling 1 cup sugar in 1 cup water 12 minutes. Albumen water is made by mixing beaten egg white with ½ cup water. Albumenized milk is prepared by mixing beaten egg white with ½ cup milk.

(371)   OATMEAL WATER

Boil 2 tablespoons oatmeal in 1 quart cold water about 2 hours or until quantity is reduced to 1 pint. Add 1 pint cold boiled water. Cool in covered pan.

(372)   RICE WATER

Rinse 2 tablespoons rice with cold water in a colander. Soak 30 minutes in 3 cups cold water. Bring to a boil and cook until rice is soft. Strain. Discard rice. Reheat water, season to taste, and serve with milk or cream.

(373)   BARLEY WATER

Rinse 2 tablespoons barley with cold water in colander. Soak in 1 quart cold water 4 hours. Boil in same water until it is reduced to 1 pint for infant feeding or to ½ pint for adults. Season to taste with salt, cream, lemon juice, or sugar.

(374) TOAST WATER

Toast thoroughly two slices bread. Break in pieces. Cover with 1 cup boiling water. Let stand 1 hour. Strain. Season and serve hot or cold.

(375) BEEF TEA

Cut 2 pounds raw beef in small pieces. Put in bottle or earthenware jar with a broken knuckle of veal. Cover tightly. Set bottle deep in pan of boiling water. Simmer 8 hours. Strain juice and cool to a jelly. Keep it in a cool place. To make tea add a little hot water to some of jelly. In a refrigerator this jelly will remain fresh for a week.

(376) RAW BEEF TEA

Make fresh for each meal. Shred ¼ cup raw beef. Fill cup with hot water. Let stand 15 minutes. Strain and serve at once.

(377) COOKED RAW BEEF TEA

Cut 1 pound raw beef in small pieces. Put in saucepan over low heat. Cook 6 minutes, stirring often to prevent sticking. Add 2 cups cold water and bring to a boil. Reduce heat and let simmer 10 minutes. Drain and serve at once, seasoned with a little salt.

(378) BROILED BEEF JUICE

Season with salt and broil 1 pound raw beef 4 minutes. Cut in pieces and squeeze all juice into a hot cup. Serve liquid at once.

(379) ELDERBERRY WINE

Put only enough water with the berries to keep them from burning and cook but a few minutes; just long enough to scald thoroughly. Strain through a cheesecloth, add eight cups of sugar to 10 cups of berry juice. Set away in a cool place to ferment and skim daily until clear. When bubbles cease to rise on top of the liquid, it is ready to bottle. Use only white sugar and you will have some of the richest flavored wine you ever tasted. Yeast is apt to sour the wine and it is a mistake to hurry the fermenting process. The addition of other liquor spoils the fine natural flavor.

(380)   PINEAPPLE FIZZ

1½ cups canned unsweetened
    pineapple juice
2 tablespoons lemon juice
3 drops Worcestershire
    sauce

1 egg white
Crushed ice
2 12-ounce bottles dry
    ginger ale

Place all ingredients except ginger ale in a shaker or screw cap jar, leaving room enough for a thorough shaking. Shake 20 times. Add chilled ginger ale and serve in cocktail glasses. Serves 12.

(381)   MINTED CHOCOLATE

1 cup chilled milk
2 tablespoons chocolate sirup
    (No. 331)
Sprig of mint

2 to 3 drops peppermint
    extract
2 tablespoons whipped
    cream

Add milk slowly to sirup, stirring constantly. Add flavoring, and beat or shake well. Pour into tall glass. Top with cream. Garnish with sprig of mint, if desired. Serves 1.

(382)   CHOCOLATE HIGHBALL

½ cup chilled milk
2 tablespoons chocolate sirup
    (No. 331)

½ cup cold ginger ale
Vanilla ice cream
    (No. 2547)

Add milk slowly to sirup, stirring constantly. Pour into tall glass. Add ginger ale and stir enough to mix. Add ice cream and serve at once. Serves 1.

(383)   FROSTED COFFEE

Pour freshly made, hot, strong coffee (No. 301) over cracked ice or ice cubes into tall glass. Top with chocolate ice cream (No. 2549). Stir well and serve at once. Or place a spoonful of chocolate ice cream in tall glass, add chilled coffee, and top with chocolate ice cream. Stir well and serve at once.

(384)   ICED COFFOLATE

¼ cup ground coffee	2 ounces unsweetened
6 cloves	chocolate
1 4-inch piece stick cinnamon	¾ cup sugar
Dash of salt	1 tablespoon flour
4 cups milk	1 egg, well-beaten

Add coffee, cloves, cinnamon, and salt to milk, and heat in double boiler until milk is scalded. Strain and return to double boiler. Add chocolate and heat until chocolate is melted. Beat with rotary egg beater until blended. Combine sugar and flour and add gradually to chocolate mixture and cook until thickened, stirring constantly. Then continue cooking 5 minutes, stirring occasionally. Cool slightly. Pour over egg and blend. Chill. Pour over cracked ice in tall glasses. Top with whipped cream, if desired. Makes 1 quart coffolate.

(385)   TWO-TONE FRUIT DRINKS

Two-tone fruit drinks in tall ice-filled glasses are the latest beverage innovations from sunny Hawaii. They are as pretty as a picture and taste just as good as they look. They have an expensive, sophisticated appearance that makes them suitable for elaborate entertaining, but in reality they will never tax a modest budget and are easily prepared for every day service. Favorite combinations include canned unsweetened pineapple juice and Concord grape juice or pineapple and canned red cherry juice. The two-toned effect is accomplished very easily. Fill a tall glass with crushed ice. Then fill glass to top with pineapple juice and grape or cherry juice by pouring the two fruit juices simultaneously—one on each side of the glass—over the ice. The juices should be well-chilled in the can before pouring. Serve at once with a long spoon before the juices have an opportunity to blend.

(386)   PINEAPPLE-BANANA MILK SHAKE

Peel and scrape one ripe banana. Mash well with a fork. Add 1 cup canned unsweetened pineapple juice. Blend with a rotary egg beater, pour in 1 cup milk, and continue to beat for a few seconds or until ingredients are blended. To serve pour over ice cubes in tall glasses. Dust with grated nutmeg. Serves 2.

(387)   FRAPPÉED PINEAPPLE JUICE

Prepare simply by filling a tall slender glass ⅔ full of crushed ice and pour in canned unsweetened pineapple juice which has been well-chilled. Garnish with a sprig of mint and pineapple gems and maraschino cherries placed alternately on a long cocktail pick.

(388)   CHERRY PUNCH

1 package cherry-flavored gelatin	⅛ teaspoon salt
	3 cups water
1 pint hot water	6 tablespoons lemon juice
4 tablespoons sugar	½ bottle ginger ale

Dissolve gelatin in hot water. Add sugar and salt and stir until dissolved. Add water, lemon juice, and ginger ale. Pour over cracked ice. Serves 6.

(389)   CURRANT JELLY HIGHBALL

½ cup red currant jelly	½ cup orange juice
3 to 4 tablespoons sugar	2 cups water
1 cup lemon juice	1 pint carbonated water

Combine jelly, sugar, juices, and water by beating with rotary egg beater. Pour over ice cubes or cracked ice in tall glasses. Add carbonated water. Garnish with thin slices of orange and mint leaves. Serves 8. Ginger ale may be substituted for carbonated water and sugar omitted.

Hors D'Oeuvres

Canapés, Cocktails, Appetizers

HORS D'OEUVRES, canapés; cocktails and savory appetizers furnish a small touch that transforms an ordinary meal into a party affair. The homemaker, who aims at distinction, finds this a fertile field for an ingenious display of her talent.

Some appetizers are served almost entirely as an introduction to meals. Others, however, are widely used as snacks late at night or as an accompaniment to beverages. At formal or informal parties, at which a meal is not a feature, a buffet of hors d'oeuvres and canapés will compete with the punch bowl as a center of interest.

Every ambitious housewife or homemaker can, with the guideposts set up here, produce many original gems of tasty artistry, both in appearance and savor.

(401) CANAPÉS

Slice bread thin. Cut into small rounds, triangles, or other dainty shapes. Toast or sauté on one side. Mix any of the combinations listed on pages 98 and 99, spread in layers, or use as garnishes, always aiming towards an interesting appearance. Place spreads on bread leaving a small place bare so that canapés can be picked up and eaten without soiling the fingers. Personal preference will determine the proportions of ingredients to be used in each mixture:

Spreads for Canapés

Chopped chicken, almonds, mayonnaise (No. 701).

Peanut butter, chopped pickle.

Mashed liverwurst, mayonnaise (No. 701).

Chopped corned beef, horseradish.

Cream cheese, jelly.

Chopped shrimp (No. 1272), celery, mayonnaise (No. 701).

Grated carrot with mayonnaise (No. 701).

Chopped celery, Roquefort cheese.

Chopped bacon (No. 1464) and hard-cooked egg (No. 202), mayonnaise (No. 701).

Anchovy butter—butter softened and mixed with anchovy paste.

Chopped egg (No. 202), sardine, mayonnaise (No. 701).

Cream cheese, chopped olives, chopped nuts.

Lobster butter (butter creamed with flaked lobster), lettuce.

Cottage cheese, chopped chives.

Crab meat, seasoned, chopped olives, hard-cooked eggs (No. 202).

Baked beans (No. 1708), mashed, with catchup.

Salmon, flaked; lemon juice, minced onion, mayonnaise (No. 701).

Orange marmalade, cream cheese.

Minced ham, chopped celery, mayonnaise (No. 701).

Deviled ham, chopped pickle, mayonnaise (No. 701).

Anchovy paste, cream cheese.

Sardine butter—sardines flaked and formed to a paste with butter.

Flaked salmon, chopped hard-cooked eggs (No. 202), chopped celery, chopped green pepper, mayonnaise (No. 701).

Tuna fish, flaked, capers, chowchow chopped celery, mayonnaise (No. 701).

Chopped shrimp (No. 1272), celery, chili sauce.

Chopped ripe olives, chopped onion, chopped celery, cream cheese, chopped pimiento.

Cream cheese, tomato catchup.

Fruit jams, cream cheese.

Jellies and butter blended.

Chopped dried beef, cream cheese.

Cooked codfish, French mustard, tartar sauce (No. 2044), grated Parmesan cheese.

Crab meat, cream sauce (No. 2005), grated Parmesan cheese, butter, pepper, curry powder, salt.

Flaked crab meat, chopped pickled onions, French dressing (No. 716), mayonnaise (No. 701).

Shredded crab meat, butter, lemon juice, paprika, salt.

Flaked, broiled finnan haddie (No. 1145) or boiled haddock (No. 1154), curry powder, grated Parmesan cheese.

Kippered herring, lemon juice, mayonnaise (No. 701), hard-cooked egg (No. 202).

Flaked lobster, mayonnaise (No. 701), lemon juice, chopped green pepper, cayenne, salt.

Sautéed, diced, pre-cooked lobster meat (No. 1236), sherry, Tabasco sauce, grated Parmesan cheese, cream sauce (No. 2005).

Chopped cooked oysters, any style, Hollandaise sauce (No. 2022), chopped parsley, butter.

Mashed shad or herring roe, mayonnaise (No. 701), lemon juice, paprika, grated onion.

Peanut butter, cottage cheese, chili sauce.

Melted cheese, paprika.

Mashed avocado pear, cream cheese.

Minced sardines, lemon juice, tomato catchup, butter.

Chopped hard-cooked egg (No. 202), chowchow mayonnaise (No. 701), minced boiled shrimp (No. 1272), lemon juice.

Peanut butter, minced crisp bacon (No. 1464), butter, chili sauce.

Sautéed liverwurst and chopped onion.

Chopped cooked frankfurter (No. 1476) or sausage meat (No. 1468), butter.

Chopped mild cheese, minced onion, mustard.

(402)   CAVIAR CANAPÉ

Cut bread in ¼ inch slices and cut in oblong pieces 1½ inches wide and 4 inches long. Toast on one side and spread other side with caviar mixed with a little finely chopped onion. Around the edge put a ¼ inch border of yolks of hard-cooked eggs (No. 202) pressed through a sieve. Lay a ⅛ inch strip of green pepper in the center. Either black or red American as well as imported caviar may be used.

(403)   OTHER CAVIAR CANAPÉS

Spread pieces of toast 3½ inches long and ½ inch wide with caviar. Divide diagonally into 3 sections, having end ones half a square. Sprinkle center with pickle, ends with peppers, and divide sections by pieces of anchovy.

Sauté rounds of bread until delicately brown on 1 side only. Spread plain side with watercress butter, and with pastry bag pipe border of butter around circumference. Fill centers with caviar and finely chopped yolks of hard-cooked egg (No. 202), used in equal proportions.

Cut hard-cooked eggs (No. 202) lengthwise and replace yolks of half of them with caviar. Arrange eggs on platter with lettuce, alternating light and dark halves. Mash yolks, mix with a little anchovy paste, chopped capers, vinegar and olive oil. Serve as sauce to eggs.

Cut bread in crescents. Toast on one side. Edge untoasted side with strips of pimiento. Next to pimiento place row of tiny onions. Fill center with caviar slightly cut with lemon juice.

Cut caviar slightly with lemon juice. Mix chopped onions with enough olive oil to make stick. Sauté small rounds of bread in olive oil. Cover ½ of each round with caviar, other half with onion. Separate with a little strip of green pepper or red pimiento.

Spread crackers with caviar mixed with lemon juice. Cover with whipped cream seasoned with white pepper. Garnish with a line of capers and serve immediately.

Spread small rounds of toast with caviar, mixed with finely chopped onion. Place small raw oyster on each.

Spread small rounds of toast with grated onion mixed with butter. Place onion rings on top. Fill centers with caviar.

Toast 4 slices graham bread, cut not more than ¼ inch thick and spread with horseradish butter while toast is still warm. Over this arrange in alternating rows—first row, sliced smoked salmon; second row, caviar; third row, filet of herring. Cut as desired. Garnish with parsley, sliced onion.

(404)   TURNOVER CANAPÉS

Roll plain pastry (No. 2701) ⅛ inch thick. Cut in 2-inch squares. Pile with any canapé (No. 401) or caviar spread (No. 403). Fold over pastry and press edges together. Fry in deep, hot fat (375° F.) 4 minutes. Drain on unglazed paper.

(405)   TOMATO CANAPÉS AND RELISHES

For a summer appetizer try chilled slices of marinated tomato garnished in various ways with slices of cucumber, radishes, olives, pickled onion, whole anchovies or a spoonful of savory salad. Serve them along with crisp celery, radishes and scallions.

(406)   POTATO CHIP CANAPÉS

Potato chips (No. 1862), crisped by reheating in an oven, can be used in place of crackers or toast in canapés. Some suggested potato-chip spreads are:

Two parts chopped ham with 1 part butter.
Equal parts cream and Roquefort cheese.
Two parts cream cheese and 1 part anchovy paste.

(407)   CLAM CANAPÉ

Spread toast round with pâté de foie gras. Edge with hard-cooked egg (No. 202) yolk creamed with butter. Arrange ring of chopped hard-cooked egg (No. 202) white inside yolk border. In center place a small, raw clam seasoned with tomato catchup, lemon juice, salt, Worcestershire sauce, Tabasco sauce, and horseradish.

(408)   FRIED SARDINE CANAPÉS

Drain, wipe, skin, and bone sardines. Brush with mustard. Sprinkle with lemon juice. Dip in well-beaten egg, diluted with a little cold water. Roll in bread crumbs. Fry in deep, hot fat (375° F.) 2 minutes. Place on buttered toast fingers.

(409)   BROILED CRAB MEAT CANAPÉS

Heap deviled crab meat (No. 1229) on thin crackers. Sprinkle with bread crumbs. Dot with butter. Broil golden brown.

(410)   SHRIMP CANAPÉ

Spread anchovy paste on toast cut into fancy shapes. Mince boiled shrimp (No. 1272), green and red pepper, and some apple, very finely; mix with a little mayonnaise (No. 701). Spread on thin slices tomato. Lay on toast. Decorate with chopped eggs (No. 202), bits of shrimp, and peppers.

(411)   ANCHOVY TOAST ROUNDS

Slice bread thin. Cut in small rounds. Toast on one side. Curl an anchovy on slice. Add a bit of chutney

(412) TOMATO AND ANCHOVY CANAPÉ

Cut bread same size as tomato slices. Sauté bread on one side in olive oil. Spread with creamed butter. Put thin slice of tomato on bread. Put 4 strips of anchovy on top. Garnish with chopped hard-cooked egg (No. 202) whites and mashed yolk, sprinkled on separately.

(413)   CANAPÉ CREPES

½ cup sifted flour   2 egg yolks
½ teaspoon salt

Sift flour and salt together. Beat yolks and mix with 1 cup
water. Gradually add to flour, beating smooth. Grill on both
sides on hot, greased griddle or frying pan. Cool. Pile with any
canapé (No. 401) or caviar (No. 403) spread. Roll. Any preferred griddle-cake batter may be used.

(414)   FRUIT CUPS

Various combinations of fruits may be used. The fruit should
be ripe and solid. All imperfect pieces should be discarded. The
fruits should be well mingled, care being taken not to bruise
them. Fruit cups should be well chilled but not iced. They
should be served in fruit cups or in a coupé glass, set in an ice
bed in a larger glass. In arranging a fruit cup it is important to
remember that appearance is very important. Every hostess will
be able to develop many unusual combinations which will
please her guests. Following are some proven and tasty fruit
cup combinations:

Segments of 1 orange, 2 sliced bananas, ½ cup crushed pineapple, ½ cup peeled
and seeded grapes, ½ cup sugar.

Two sliced bananas, 1 cup grated coconut, 1 cup pineapple cubes, 1 pear, cut in
cubes, segments of 1 orange, ½ cup sugar.

Chopped nut meats, chopped marshmallows, chopped pineapple, whipped cream,
cherries or strawberries.

Crushed pineapple, strawberries, dash of lemon juice.

Red raspberries, diced apple, diced pear, sliced peaches.

Stoned cherries, diced pears, sliced peaches.

Crushed pineapple, cubed watermelon, cantaloupe balls.

Blackberries, orange segments.

Grapefruit segments, crushed pineapple.

Orange segments, halved strawberries, white grapes.

Apricot halves, sliced banana, cranberry sauce (No. 54).

Cubed avocado, canned grapefruit, whipped cream.

Cantaloupe cubes, broken after-dinner mints.

Cantaloupe balls, diced pineapple.

Seedless grapes, cantaloupe balls, orange sections.

Diced watermelon, raspberries.

Watermelon balls, lime juice, crushed mint.

Strawberries, orange juice, sugar.

Halved strawberries, pineapple wedges.

(415)   FROZEN FRUIT COCKTAIL

½ cup crushed pineapple
2 cups orange pulp
¾ cup grapefruit pulp
¼ cup powdered sugar

1 cup lemon or lime carbonated beverage or ginger
ale

Add the sugar to the fruits and stir gently until sugar is dissolved. Add carbonated beverage. Set into freezing tray of automatic refrigerator. Freeze to slush. Serve as an appetizer. Serves 6.

(416)   GINGER ALE COCKTAIL

1 grapefruit, segments
halved
1 cup crushed pineapple
(fresh or canned)

3 tablespoons powdered
sugar
1 cup ginger ale
6 green cherries

Put a layer of grapefruit and one of pineapple in sherbet glasses. Sprinkle with powdered sugar and chill. When ready to serve, fill glasses with chilled ginger ale and crushed ice. Garnish with cherries, cut in small pieces, and mint leaves. Serves 6.

(417)   JUICE COCKTAILS

Serve juice cocktails in small glasses, ice cold, and garnished with bits of green. Suggestions for fruit juice cocktails are:

Orange juice.
Grapefruit juice.
Grape juice.
Orange and grape juice.
Strawberry and lemon juice.
Pineapple and rhubarb sauce (No. 75).
Cranberry juice, sugar, lemon juice.
Grapefruit juice, orange juice, lemon juice, carbonated water, sugar.
Orange juice, pineapple juice, sugar, nutmeg, cinnamon, cloves.
Liquor made by boiling pomegranate seeds and lemon slices 20 minutes, sugar.
Cider, pineapple juice, orange juice.
Tomato juice, flavored with onion and lemon juice.
Juice from canned beets, lemon juice.
Sauerkraut juice, lemon juice.
Tomato juice, Worcestershire sauce.
Clam broth (No. 582), lemon juice, catchup, Worcestershire sauce.
Clam broth (No. 582), tomato juice.

(418)   SPICED TOMATO JUICE

2 cups tomato juice
1 cup sugar
¼ teaspoon cinnamon

⅛ teaspoon nutmeg
½ cup lemon juice

Bring tomato juice, sugar, cinnamon, and nutmeg to boil. Strain. Chill. Add lemon juice and 1 pint ice water. Serves 6.

(419)   FROZEN FRUIT JUICE COCKTAIL

1½ cups loganberry juice
1 cup grapefruit juice

1 cup pineapple juice
3 tablespoons sugar

Combine ingredients, stirring until sugar is dissolved. Pour into freezing tray of refrigerator. When frozen around edges, remove and stir. Return to refrigerator and freeze to mushy stage. Serve in cocktail glasses, garnished with mint leaves. Other combinations of fruit juices can be used. Serves 8.

(420)   SPICED GRAPE JUICE COCKTAIL

1 pint bottled grape juice
¼ teaspoon cinnamon

¼ teaspoon nutmeg
Speck ground clove

Combine the grape juice, cinnamon, nutmeg, and ground clove in a saucepan and simmer for five minutes. Strain through fine cheesecloth and chill. Pour into cocktail or sherbet glasses and serve as a first course. Serves 6.

(421)   PINEAPPLE AND STRAWBERRY COCKTAIL

¼ cup lemon juice
1 cup orange juice
1 cup pineapple chunks

1 cup strawberries, hulled
and halved
Sugar to taste

Mix juices and sweeten with sugar. Combine fruits lightly and put in cocktail glasses. Add juice and sugar to taste. Top each serving with a whole strawberry. Serves 6.

(422) OYSTER COCKTAIL

36 small oysters
6 tablespoons tomato
   catchup
2 tablespoons horseradish

4 tablespoons lemon juice
$\frac{1}{4}$ teaspoon celery salt
$\frac{1}{8}$ teaspoon Tabasco sauce

Open oysters. Discard shallow half of shells. Put deep part of shells, containing oysters, on beds of cracked ice in deep dishes. Mix other ingredients for sauce. Serve 6 oysters on each plate with sauce in small cups in the center of each dish. Serves 6. Or, put 5 or 6 oysters in each of 6 shallow paper cups. Arrange on tray with horseradish, lemon slices, and sauce.

(423) SEA FOOD COCKTAIL

Combine any fish or shellfish, cooked or raw, according to taste, and serve on nests of lettuce in cocktail glasses with oyster cocktail sauce (No. 422). Or, serve various varieties of fish or shellfish in separate lettuce nests on plate, using same sauce.

(424) CLAM COCKTAIL

Follow recipe for oyster cocktail (No. 422), using small (cherrystone) clams instead of oysters.

(425) LOBSTER COCKTAIL

Arrange boiled lobster meat (No. 1236) on nests of lettuce in cocktail glasses. Serve with oyster cocktail sauce (No. 422).

(426) SCALLOP COCKTAIL

Cut fried scallops (No. 1269) in halves. Serve on nests of lettuce in cocktail glasses with oyster cocktail sauce (No. 422).

(427) SALMON COCKTAIL

Cut canned salmon into small pieces. Serve on nest of lettuce in cocktail glass with oyster cocktail sauce (No. 422).

(428)   SHRIMP COCKTAIL

Serve boiled shrimp (No. 1272) on bed of lettuce in cocktail glass with oyster cocktail sauce (No. 422). Allow 1 pound shrimp for 6 servings.

(429)   CRAB MEAT COCKTAIL

Serve boiled crab meat (No. 1227) on nest of lettuce in cocktail glass with oyster cocktail sauce (No. 422).

(430)   FROZEN FISH COCKTAILS

Any fish or shellfish cocktail may be served frozen. Mix fish with oyster cocktail sauce (No. 422). Put in closed container. Bury in equal parts rock salt and cracked ice 2 hours for a pint, 4 hours for a quart. Or, freeze in freezing compartment of mechanical refrigerator 1½ hours. Serve in cocktail glasses, garnished with parsley, olives, and lemon slices.

(431)   STUFFED CELERY

Thoroughly wash celery. Remove all tough strings. Chill. After filling with mixture, cut in 2-inch lengths and chill again. Some suggested fillings for celery are:

Equal parts of Roquefort and cream cheese, beaten together, with enough cooked (No. 737), French (No. 716), or mayonnaise dressing (No. 701) to moisten.

Two parts chopped sardines or anchovies, mixed with one part mayonnaise (No. 701).

Cottage cheese and chopped stuffed olives, moistened with cooked (No. 737), French (No. 716), or mayonnaise dressing (No. 701).

Cream cheese, minced parsley, paprika, chopped olives, chopped celery, French dressing (No. 716).

Chopped hard-cooked egg (No. 202), mayonnaise (No. 701).

Chopped hard-cooked egg (No. 202), chopped olives, chopped pimiento, chopped celery, mayonnaise (No. 701).

Cream cheese, finely chopped nut meats.

(432)   PIGS IN BLANKETS

Wrap raw oysters in thin slices of bacon. Fasten with toothpicks. Broil in high heat until bacon is crisp. Garnish with tartar sauce (No. 2044).

(433)   ONIONS IN BLANKETS

Wrap small slices of bacon around small, pickled onions. Fasten with toothpicks. Broil at high heat, turning occasionally, until bacon is crisp.

(434)   CHEESE IN BLANKETS

Wrap slices of bacon around 1-inch cubes of American cheese. Fasten with toothpicks. Broil at high heat until bacon is crisp, turning frequently to prevent cheese from melting.

(435)   CHICKEN LIVERS IN BLANKETS

Wash chicken livers. Cut in halves. Spread with mixture of equal parts mustard and chopped olives. Wrap slice of bacon around each liver half. Fasten with toothpicks. Roll in bread crumbs. Bake in hot oven (450° F.) 12 minutes.

(436)   SHRIMPS IN BLANKETS

Soak broiled shrimp (No. 1272) in seasoned milk. Wrap in thin slices of bacon or salt pork. Lay in broiler and brown on both sides. Serve on toasted wafers with quartered lemons.

(437)   OLIVES IN BLANKETS

Wrap slice of bacon around each olive. Fasten with toothpicks. Broil at moderate temperature until bacon is crisp. Serve hot.

(438)   STUFFED PRUNES IN BLANKETS

Remove pits from stewed prunes (No. 71). Place stuffed olive in each. Wrap slices of bacon around each prune. Fasten with toothpicks. Broil at high heat until bacon is crisp, turning occasionally.

(439)   STUFFED PRUNES

Remove stones from stewed prunes (No. 71). Insert cocktail sausage. Put in greased baking dish and bake in very hot oven (450° F.) until sausage is lightly browned. Serve on toothpicks.

(440)   CHEESE STUFFED OLIVES

Remove pimiento stuffing from olives. Fill with soft, mild cheese. Wrap a small, thin slice of bacon around each olive. Skewer with a toothpick. Bake in hot oven (425° F.) until bacon is crisp. Serve on crackers or toast rounds.

(441)   STUFFED PIMIENTOS

Cover pimiento with a layer of chopped, cooked ham, seasoned with a dash of Worcestershire sauce and moistened with cooked (No. 737) or mayonnaise dressing (No. 701). Form into a roll. Serve on lettuce, garnished with parsley.

(442)   SALT STURGEON BOATS

Halve 3-inch sour pickles lengthwise. Scoop out centers. Fill with cream cheese. Slice enough from unfilled side of pickle to make boat stand. Place small rectangle of salt sturgeon, sliced paper thin, on a toothpick to make a sail. Stick toothpick into pickle vertically and arrange on tray.

(443)   STUFFED BEETS

Marinate small, boiled beets (No. 1726) several hours in French dressing (No. 716). Cut slice off top and scoop out some pulp in center. Stuff with any canapé spread (No. 401).

(444)   STUFFED GRAPES

Slit, but do not separate Tokay or Malaga grapes. Remove seeds. Stuff with equal parts cream and Roquefort cheese, seasoned with onion juice and Worcestershire sauce.

(445)   STUFFED CUCUMBER

1 cucumber	Pepper-Paprika
⅛ teaspoon salt	Worcestershire sauce
½ cup cream cheese	¼ cup French dressing
¼ cup chopped green pepper	(No. 716)
2 tablespoons chopped onion	

Peel cucumber. Cut in half, lengthwise. Dig out seeds and some of pulp. Sprinkle with salt. Mix cheese, green pepper, and onion. Season with pepper, paprika, and Worcestershire sauce. Pack mixture in cucumber. Pour over French dressing. Chill. Cut in ¼-inch slices. Serve on lettuce leaves, garnished with pimiento and mayonnaise (No. 701).

(446)   CHEESE BALLS

¼ cup butter	⅛ teaspoon paprika
½ cup flour	1½ cups grated mild cheese
1 cup milk	1 well-beaten egg
¼ teaspoon salt	½ cup bread crumbs
2 tablespoons chopped green pepper	1 slightly beaten egg

Melt butter. Stir in flour. Add milk gradually, stirring constantly. Add salt, paprika, and green pepper. Beat cheese into well-beaten egg. Add cheese and egg mixture to sauce. Cook over hot water, stirring constantly, until cheese is melted. Chill. Mold into little balls. Roll in crumbs. Dip in slightly beaten egg, diluted with 2 tablespoons cold water. Roll again in crumbs. Fry in deep hot fat (375° F.) 1½ minutes. Drain on unglazed paper. Serve hot on tomato slices or in nests of lettuce or watercress.

(447)   BROILED CHEESE SARDINES

Toast bread fingers on one side. Butter other side and spread lightly with mustard. Roll sardines in grated Parmesan cheese. Put 1 on each toast finger. Season with salt. Broil at high heat until brown. Serve hot.

(448)   COCKTAIL CROQUETTES

Make any kind of croquettes very small. Serve, impaled on toothpicks.

(449)   COCKTAIL FISH BALLS

Make and cook tiny codfish balls (No. 1139). Impale on toothpicks.

(450)   BISMARCK HERRING

Cut in cubes. Serve on Norwegian flat bread, garnished with pieces of onion.

(451)   **ARTICHOKE HEARTS**

Drain canned artichoke hearts. Impale on toothpicks. Serve around bowl of mayonnaise (No. 701).

(452)   **CAULIFLOWER FLOWERETS**

Rinse flowerets. Drain. Remove imperfections. Sprinkle with salt. Chill 30 minutes in ice water. Drain. Impale on toothpicks and serve around bowl of mayonnaise (No. 701).

(453)   **PICKLED SHRIMP**

Boil shrimps (No. 1272). Pour over French dressing (No. 716) and let stand in refrigerator 4 hours. Stick toothpick in each shrimp and stick other ends of toothpicks in a grapefruit or head of cabbage.

(454)   **SAUTÉED ANCHOVIES**

Roll anchovies in flour. Dip in egg, diluted with a little water. Roll in cracker meal. Sauté to light brown in a little olive oil. Serve on toothpicks.

(455)   **COCKTAIL FRANKFURTERS**

Broil or pan-broil in little butter until brown on both sides. Or, they may be split lengthwise, without separating, and spread with a mixture of 1 part horseradish to 6 parts mustard. Fasten together with a toothpick and broil or pan-broil as above.

(456)   **COCKTAIL SAUSAGES**

Broil or fry until well-browned. Put on toothpick and stick free end of toothpick in an apple, orange, or grapefruit.

(457)   **ROLLMOPS**

Slice. Serve with a toothpick in each piece.

(458)   GRILLED SARDINES

1 can sardines	1 tablespoon tarragon
½ teaspoon paprika	vinegar
¼ teaspoon salt	Lemon slices
¼ teaspoon Worcestershire	Parsley
sauce	Hard-cooked egg
3 tablespoons sardine oil	(No. 202), sliced

Skin sardines. Mix other ingredients. Pour over sardines and let stand 3 minutes. Pour liquid into pan and heat. Add sardines and grill 1 minute on each side. Serve on toast fingers, garnished with slices of lemon, parsley, and hard-cooked egg (No. 202) slices.

(459)   DEVILED SARDINES

Skin sardines. Split and bone. Spread mustard on inside with few grains cayenne. Put together again. Roll in crumbs. Dip in well-beaten egg, diluted with a little cold water. Roll again in crumbs. Fry in deep, hot fat (375° F.) 2 minutes. Serve hot on toast fingers.

(460)   CHEESE AND ONION SNACKS

Put a cube of American cheese on a toothpick with a small onion. Stick toothpicks in rind of a large grapefruit.

(461)   CELERY AND CHEESE BALLS

Mix equal parts chopped celery and cream cheese. Season with salt and pepper. Mold into small balls. Roll balls in chopped parsley.

(462)   FINNAN HADDIE SHELLS

Mix 1 part chopped stuffed olives with 4 parts chopped, cold, broiled finnan haddie (No. 1145), moistened with mayonnaise (No. 701). Serve in clam shells, garnished with parsley and additional mayonnaise.

(463)   COTTAGE CHEESE ROLLS

1 cup cottage cheese
½ teaspoon Worcestershire
    sauce

2 tablespoons chili sauce
Salt-Pepper
12 slices dried beef

Mix cheese, sauces, and seasonings. Spread on beef. Roll and fasten with toothpicks.

(464)   CHEESE AND BEEF ROLLS

Spread small squares of thinly sliced bread with mayonnaise (No. 701). Add layer of pimento cheese. Cover with dried beef. Roll. Fasten with toothpicks. Broil until bread is well browned on all sides.

(465)   TOMATO CUPS

Cut off stem ends of small tomatoes. Scoop out centers. Turn upside down and drain thoroughly. Stuff with any canapé spread (No. 401).

(466)   SALMON AND CAVIAR ROLLS

Mix equal parts caviar and chopped ripe olives. Spread a layer on thin slices of smoked salmon. Roll. Chill. Serve, garnished with sliced lemon.

(467)   CHEESE AND NUT STICKS

Add grated American cheese to shortening before it is worked into plain pastry (No. 2701). Roll ¼ inch thick. Cut in narrow strips. Roll in ground nuts. Bake in hot oven (400° F.) 12 minutes. Or the pastry and cheese mixture can be formed in small balls before rolling in nuts.

(468)   JELLIED ANCHOVY

1 cup chopped anchovies
½ cup minced celery
2 tablespoons chopped onion
1 chopped green pepper
1 tablespoon gelatin
1 cup aspic jelly (No. 877)

2 sliced, stuffed olives
24 capers
1 hard-cooked egg
    (No. 202), chopped
8 sprigs parsley
2 sliced radishes

Mix anchovies, celery, onion, and pepper. Soften gelatin in enough cold water to cover. Melt gelatin over hot water. Stir gelatin into mixture. Pack in greased mold ½ inch thick. Chill. Cut into 8 pieces. Dip each in aspic. Garnish with olives, capers, egg, parsley, and radish. Chill again. Serves 8.

(469)   SARDINES IN ASPIC

Drain, skin, and bone sardines. Wrap each in thin slice of smoked salmon. Place on layer of set aspic jelly (No. 877). Pour over thick, liquid aspic. Chill. When set, cut neatly. Serve, garnished with slices of tomato, cucumber, or boiled beets (No. 1726).

(470)   LEI FRAPPÉ

¾ cup sugar	2 cups canned unsweetened
1 cup water	pineapple juice
1 cup orange juice	2 tablespoons lime juice

Boil sugar and water together 5 minutes. Add orange, pineapple, and lime juices. Cool, strain, and freeze to a mush. Serve in sherbet glasses. Garnish with a sprig of fresh mint leaves or a single berry or red maraschino cherry. Serves 6.

(471)   HAWAIIAN FRUIT PLATE

An attractive combination of colors and flavors includes nippy cheese balls (cream and Roquefort cheese and finely chopped celery with a dash of onion juice and Tabasco sauce) sprinkled with paprika arranged on geranium leaves or small greens in the center of a platter. Surround this with well-drained canned pineapple gems rolled in chopped mint leaves, ½-inch slices of bananas, dipped in lemon juice and rolled in chopped salted nutmeats, and strawberries sprinkled with powdered sugar. Avocado cubes dipped in lime or lemon juice make an interesting addition to this combination. Lift hors d'oeuvres from plate with cocktail toothpicks.

Soups

SOUPS are served for two purposes. The clear soups—bouillons and consommés—belong to the appetizer class and, in purpose, are allied to cocktails. The heavy soups—bisques, gumbos, purées, cream soups, chowders, and vegetable soups—have considerable nutritive value and they form an integral part of a meal and often serve as the main course.

Most American homemakers throw away the water in which fish, meat, vegetables, or cereals are boiled or simmered. These waters contain much of the mineral matters and vitamins from the cooked food. When this water runs down the sink, some of the most valuable part of the food goes with it. Save all pot and pan liquors and use instead of water in many other dishes.

Also all scraps of raw or cooked vegetables, meats, fish, and bones should be reserved for later use. They can all be thrown together with the water in which any or several of them were cooked and, with few additions, will make appetizing and nourishing soup. Truly, soups form one of the most valuable places for left-overs.

The toughest and least expensive of meat cuts make the finest soups because those often-overlooked or discarded remnants are the best-flavored. As a further aid to getting the best flavors, always simmer or boil soups in closely-covered kettles or saucepans.

TO CLEAR SOUP STOCK

To clear soup stock, add 1 beaten egg white and crushed egg shell to stock in saucepan. Stir and boil for 2 minutes. Then cover and simmer 15 minutes. Strain through 3 thicknesses of cheesecloth.

(501)   SOUP STOCK

1 pound bone	6 peppercorns
1 pound meat	1 teaspoon sweet herbs
½ cup minced onion	1 bay leaf
½ cup diced carrot	1 sprig parsley
½ cup diced turnip	1 piece celery root
1 teaspoon salt	4 whole cloves

Use cheap cuts or small scraps of raw meat and bone. Cut meat in small pieces. Put meat and bone in 1 quart slightly salted, cold water. Let soak 1 hour. Cover and simmer gently 2 hours. Add vegetables and salt. Tie remaining ingredients in a cheesecloth bag and put in liquid. Simmer 1 more hour. Remove bag of spices. Froth should be skimmed off frequently during cooking. This makes 3 cups stock. If stock is cooked in fireless cooker, add vegetables at start of cooking.

(502)   WHITE STOCK

3-pound fowl	1 turnip
1 knuckle of veal	1 carrot
2 stalks celery	2 teaspoons salt
1 onion	

Cut veal from bone. Dress, wipe, and disjoint fowl. Put veal, veal bone, and fowl in kettle. Add 1 quart water for each pound of meat and bone. Add other ingredients. Cover and simmer 5 hours. Strain and cool. The veal and chicken meat can be used for loaves, croquettes, or any left-over dishes.

(503)   COMMON SOUP STOCK

This can be made with any combination of left-over scraps or bones of raw or cooked meat, poultry, or vegetables and the water in which any meats, vegetables, macaroni, etc., have been cooked. Put it all together cold. Simmer, covered, 6 hours. Strain. It can be used as stock for many soups, gravies, and stews.

(504) ## FISH STOCK

2 tablespoons butter
1 tablespoon chopped onion
1 tablespoon chopped carrot
1 tablespoon chopped turnip
Bones, head, and trimmings
from fish
1 tablespoon chopped celery

1 bay leaf
1 tomato, quartered
1 slice lemon
1 1/2 teaspoons salt
1/4 teaspoon pepper
1 cup milk or cream
1 tablespoon flour

Melt 1 tablespoon butter in saucepan. Add onion, carrot, and turnip. Fry, but do not brown. Add bones, head, and trimmings from fish, celery, bay leaf, tomato, and lemon. Cover with cold water. Cover and simmer 2 hours. Add salt and pepper. Strain. Add 1 cup milk or cream to pint of stock. Blend flour to a smooth paste with a little cold water and add gradually to mixture. Heat, stirring constantly, until thickened. Makes 3 cups stock.

(505) ## BOUILLON

3 1/2 pounds beef, chopped
3 1/2 quarts water
1 onion
1 carrot
1 sprig parsley

2 stalks celery
1/2 bay leaf
2 cloves
6 peppercorns
1 teaspoon salt

Use beef from lower round. Put it in saucepan with water and let stand 1 hour. Place over the fire in covered pot and bring to boiling point. Skim. Reduce heat and simmer 3 hours. Chop onion, carrot, parsley, celery and add to soup. Add bay leaf, cloves, peppercorns, and salt. Let simmer 1 more hour. Strain into a bowl and cool quickly. When ready to serve, remove fat and clarify by method used in consommé (No. 507). Serves 10.

(506) ## WHITE SOUP

1 tablespoon butter
1 tablespoon flour
1 pint white stock (No. 502)
1 pint milk

Salt-Pepper
2 tablespoons chopped, cooked chicken
2 hard-cooked egg yolks (No. 202)

Melt butter in saucepan. Add flour, blending well. Gradually add stock and milk, stirring constantly. Season to taste with salt and pepper. Add chicken. Heat thoroughly. Serve hot, garnished with egg yolks, pressed through a sieve. Cooked veal, chopped celery, or steamed rice (No. 106) may be substituted for chicken. Serves 4.

(507)   CONSOMMÉ

4 pounds fowl	2 whole cloves
2 pounds knuckle veal	1 allspice berry
2 pounds beef	1 small bay leaf
4 quarts water	2 sprigs parsley
1 tablespoon salt	1 sprig thyme
½ cup carrots, cut in pieces	1 sprig savory
½ cup onions, cut in pieces	1 sprig marjoram
½ cup celery, cut in pieces	2 slightly beaten egg whites
1 teaspoon peppercorns	

Clean, disjoint, and cut up fowl. Saw knuckle bone in pieces and cut up veal and beef in small pieces. Put in a covered soup kettle and add water. Let stand 1 hour to draw out juices. Put over the fire and bring quickly to the boiling point. Reduce heat at once to simmering and cook 6 or 7 hours. Add salt, vegetables, and seasonings the last hour of cooking. Strain. Remove any fat when cold. Season more if necessary and clear by the following method: Put cold stock in a saucepan and add 2 slightly beaten egg whites. Put over fire and stir constantly until it boils. Boil 5 minutes. Let stand until it settles. Strain through 2 thicknesses of cheesecloth. Heat thoroughly and serve with toasted crackers. Serves 10.

Variations of Consommé

With asparagus tips and croutons.—Allow 4 boiled asparagus tips (No. 1704) and a tablespoon of diced croutons (No. 2105) to each serving.

Consommé Indienne.—Allow ½ tablespoon diced, cooked artichoke bottoms (No. 1701), ½ tablespoon diced, fried egg-plant (No. 1786), 1 tablespoon boiled rice (No. 107), and a few strips of cooked chicken to each serving.

Consommé à la Rita.—Allow 1 tablespoon boiled rice (No. 107), 1 tablespoon stewed, diced mushrooms (No. 1803), 1 tablespoon boiled peas (No. 1823), and a few strips of cooked chicken white meat per serving. Sprinkle with grated Parmesan cheese.

Garnished Consommé.—Sprinkle each serving with shredded lettuce or chopped parsley.

A la Royal.—Garnish with royal custard (No. 2102) cubes at time of serving.

Consommé Pimiento.—Add ½ cup of canned pimiento, forced through a sieve, ½ cup of sherry, and ⅛ teaspoon cayenne before clearing.

Princess Consommé.—Add ¼ cup boiled peas (No. 1823) and ½ cup chopped, cooked chicken before serving.

Macaroni Consommé.—Add 1 cup boiled macaroni (No. 2302) just before serving.

Consommé with olives and mushrooms.—Garnish with sliced stuffed olives, sliced, stewed mushrooms (No. 1803), and diced, cooked chicken.

(508)   JELLIED SOUPS

1 pint any clear soup or soup stock	1 tablespoon gelatin

Bring soup or stock to a boil. Cover gelatin with cold water and let soak 5 minutes. Stir into soup. Dissolve thoroughly. Pour into greased pan, tray of mechanical refrigerator, or bouillon cups. Chill until set. Two tablespoons tapioca may be used in place of gelatin, in which case soak tapioca in cold water 1 hour and cook stock, after tapioca is added, until tapioca is clear. Serves 4. Chopped celery, chopped green pepper, or chopped parsley can be mixed into jelly. Two-toned jellied soups can be made by preparing 2 consommés of different shades. Pour one to make a 1-inch layer. When set, cover with 1-inch layer of other. Chill until firm.

(509)   VERMICELLI SOUP

6 cups weak soup stock (No. 501)	1 teaspoon salt
⅔ cup vermicelli, in small pieces	½ teaspoon paprika
	1 tablespoon chopped parsley

Boil stock. Add vermicelli, salt, and paprika. Serve hot, sprinkled with parsley.

(510)   NOODLE SOUP

4 well-beaten eggs
10 chopped beet leaves and
   stems
½ cup cottage cheese
½ cup grated Parmesan
   cheese

½ cup bread crumbs
1 quart beet bouillon
   (No. 539) or stock
   (No. 501)
Salt-Pepper
Nutmeg

Thoroughly mix eggs, beet leaves and stems, cottage cheese, Parmesan cheese, and crumbs. Roll ¼ inch thick on floured board. Cut in narrow 2-inch lengths. Bring bouillon or stock to boil. Season to taste with salt, pepper, and nutmeg. Drop in noodles. Simmer until they float. Serve hot with grated Parmesan cheese. Serves 4.

(511)   CHICKEN BROTH

Dress, wipe, and disjoint 2-pound chicken. Put in saucepan. Cover with 2 pints cold water. Simmer until meat is tender, about 3 hours. Remove meat. Cool stock. Skim off fat. Reheat. Add ¾ cup boiled rice (No. 107). Season to taste and serve.

(512)   CHICKEN BOUILLON AND TAPIOCA

5 cups chicken broth
   (No. 511)

6 tablespoons tapioca

Bring broth to a boil. Add tapioca. Simmer gently until slightly thickened. Continue cooking over hot water until tapioca is clear. Serves 4.

(513)   CHICKEN NOODLE SOUP

3-pound chicken
2 pounds beef
1⅛ teaspoons salt
½ cup canned or strained,
   stewed tomatoes
   (No. 1893)

6 lettuce leaves
1 bay leaf
⅛ teaspoon celery seeds
⅛ teaspoon mustard seeds
Noodles (No. 2301)

Dress chicken. Wipe chicken and beef with cold, damp cloth. Disjoint chicken. Put chicken and beef in saucepan. Cover with cold water. Bring to a boil. Skim off fat. Add 1 teaspoon salt, tomatoes, lettuce leaves, bay leaf, celery seeds, and mustard seeds. Cover and simmer gently 4 hours. Cool. Strain. Let stand over night. Skim off fat. Heat slowly to boiling point. Drop in noodles (see below) and simmer until they are tender.

(514)   VELVET SOUP

1 quart chicken stock (No. 502)	¼ teaspoon pepper
2 whole cloves	1 cup chopped, cooked chicken
2 stalks celery	1 cup bread crumbs
2 sprigs parsley	2 tablespoons butter
1 onion	1 quart milk or cream
1 teaspoon salt	

Add seasonings and onion to stock. Heat until well blended. Strain. Add chicken. Sauté crumbs in butter. Add to stock. Add milk or cream. Bring to boil, stirring constantly. Serves 6.

(515) CREAM OF CHICKEN SOUP WITH CURRY

3 tablespoons butter	5 cups white stock (No. 502)
1 tablespoon chopped onion	½ cup chopped cooked chicken
1 teaspoon curry powder	
5 tablespoons flour	
Salt and pepper	

Melt butter in the top of a double boiler placed directly over the heat. Add onion and cook over low heat for about 5 minutes or until soft, stirring occasionally. Place over hot water. Add curry powder, flour, and stock and mix well. Cook, stirring constantly, until thickened. Add chicken and season with salt and pepper. Reheat. Serves 6.

(516)   CHICKEN GUMBO

1 disjointed 3½-pound fowl	2 tablespoons chopped onion
2 tablespoons butter	2 quarts okra, sliced and chopped
1 tablespoon flour	Salt—Pepper

Sauté chicken, onion, and flour until well browned. Add okra and 1 quart water. Bring to boil. Reduce heat. Cover and simmer until okra is dissolved, about 2½ hours, adding water to keep quantity the same. Remove fowl. Strip meat from bones. Return meat to soup. Season to taste. Serves 6. If desired, 2 quarts peeled and diced tomatoes may be added with okra, in which case reduce water by half.

(517)   **MULLIGATAWNY**

¼ cup butter	1 blade mace
¼ cup sliced onion	4 whole cloves
¼ cup sliced carrot	1 tablespoon chopped parsley
¼ cup chopped celery	1 cup canned or strained,
¼ cup chopped green pepper	stewed tomatoes
1 apple, pared, cored, and	(No. 1893)
sliced	Salt—Pepper
1 cup chopped raw chicken	1 cup boiled rice (No. 107)
¼ cup flour	5 cups white stock
1 teaspoon curry powder	(No. 502)

Melt butter in saucepan. Add onion, carrot, celery, green pepper, apple, and chicken. Cook until brown. Add flour, curry powder, mace, cloves, parsley, and tomatoes. Cover and simmer 1½ hours. Strain, reserving chicken. Add chicken to soup. Press other ingredients through sieve into soup. Season to taste with salt and pepper. Add rice and boiling white stock. Serves 6.

(518)   **GIBLET SOUP**

2 sets chicken or turkey	1 teaspoon mixed pickle
giblets	spice
4 tablespoons butter	Salt—Pepper
4 tablespoons flour	Dumplings (No. 954)
½ cup diced celery	2 sliced, hard-cooked eggs
1 tablespoon chopped onion	(No. 202)

Sauté giblets in butter until browned on all sides. Stir in flour, blending thoroughly. Add 4 cups cold water, celery, and onion. Tie spice in cheesecloth and drop in. Cover and simmer slowly until giblets are tender, about 1½ hours. Remove spice. Season with salt and pepper. Add dumplings. Cover tightly and simmer until dumplings are light. Serve with garnish of eggs. Serves 4.

(519)   **TURKEY SOUP**

Place the remains of a roast turkey (No. 1560), meat, bones, stuffing, gravy, etc., in a kettle. Cover with cold water. Cover and simmer 4 hours. Let stand 10 hours. Skim off fat. Remove bones. Reheat soup. Bring to boil. Add 1 tablespoon flour, well blended in a cup of cream or milk. Add meat from bones. Season to taste. Bring to boil. Serve hot. Serves 6.

(520)   PHILADELPHIA PEPPER POT

Put a knuckle of veal and a shin of beef and 1 slice of ham in a large saucepan. Cover with cold water and bring gently to boiling point. Skim and simmer 3 or 4 hours. Strain off liquid, return to pot, and add 6 diced potatoes, 2 sliced onions, ½ chopped hot red pepper, 6 cloves, 1 bay leaf, a bit of marjoram and, if desired, 1 tablespoon parsley. Cut the beef, veal and ham into small pieces and add to the other ingredients. Add ½ pound shredded cooked honeycomb tripe (No. 1480) and bring to boiling point. Add 2 dozen small dumplings (No. 954). Cover closely and simmer for ½ hour. Serve immediately. Serves 8.

(521)   POT AU FEU

2 pounds lean round steak	1 stalk celery
3 diced carrots	Bit of garlic
2 sliced leeks	Piece of red pepper
1 small onion	2 tomatoes
1 piece cabbage	

Wipe meat with cold, damp cloth. Cut in pieces. Cover with cold water. Cover and simmer until tender. Add other ingredients. Simmer until vegetables are tender. Serves 6. If vegetables are omitted, this can be served as bouillon, in which case rice, vermicelli, macaroni, or croutons may be added. Or, the bouillon can be served with a poached egg (No. 207) in each dish.

(522)   FRENCH BEEF SOUP

1 medium-sized soup bone	¼ cup stewed (No. 1769) or canned corn
2 teaspoons salt	
1 cup shredded cabbage	2 cups canned or strained, stewed tomatoes
1 chopped onion	(No. 1893)
2 diced potatoes	
1 sliced carrot	½ teaspoon pepper
2 tablespoons butter	

Wipe bone with cold, damp cloth. Place in kettle. Cover with water. Bring to boiling point. Reduce heat. Cover and simmer 1 hour. Add 1 teaspoon salt and simmer until meat is tender. Remove bone and leave 2 quarts stock in kettle. One hour before serving add the meat from the bone, shredded fine, and the other ingredients. Bring to a boil and simmer, covered, 30 minutes. Serve hot. Serves 6.

(523) SCOTCH BROTH

4 tablespoons barley	1 sliced carrot
3 pounds neck mutton	2 sliced onions
2 tablespoons salt	4 stalks celery

Soak barley in cold water 10 hours. Drain. Wipe meat with cold, damp cloth. Remove skin and fat. Cut in small pieces. Put in kettle and add 2 quarts cold water. Bring to boil. Skim. Cover and let simmer 2 hours, adding vegetables for last hour of cooking. Strain, cool, and remove fat. Reheat to boiling point. Add barley and simmer until barley is soft. Serves 8. The meat can be used in stews, croquettes, or meat cakes.

(524) CHINESE SOUP

1 pork bone	Dash of pepper
¼ pound pork meat	1 quart water
½ teaspoon salt	¼ pound fresh spinach

Simmer pork bone, meat, salt, pepper, and water in a covered pan about 1 hour. Remove pork bone and discard. Cut the pork meat into tiny strips. Bring the broth to a rapid boil, add meat strips and spinach, and cook until spinach is tender but has not lost its green color, about 10 minutes. Serve in Chinese bowls. Serves 6.

(525) OXTAIL SOUP

Wash 2 or 3 oxtails and disjoint into short lengths. Brown the pieces in fat, put them into a large kettle, cover with water, add a bay leaf and salt, and simmer until the meat is tender enough to fall off the bones. Strain off the broth, and to it add about 1 quart of diced vegetables, such as onions, carrots, turnips, and potatoes, and cook slowly until the vegetables are tender but not broken. Chop up the meat and serve in the soup. Season to taste with salt and pepper, and, if desired, Worcestershire sauce. Serves 6.

(526)   LIVER SOUP

3 tablespoons butter
½ pound chopped calf's liver
1 cup peeled, chopped mushrooms
1 teaspoon salt

1 tablespoon chopped parsley
4 cups bouillon (No. 505)
1 tablespoon flour
1 cup milk or light cream

Melt 2 tablespoons butter in saucepan. Add liver, mushrooms, and parsley. Sauté 5 minutes. Add salt and bouillon. Cover and simmer until tender, about 20 minutes. Mix flour to a smooth paste with remaining butter. Stir into soup until smooth. Add cream. Cover and simmer 5 minutes more, stirring frequently. Serves 6 to 8.

(527)   MOCK TURTLE SOUP

Stock in which calf's head has been cooked (No. 1492)
¼ cup butter
½ cup flour
2 cups stock (No. 501)

1 cup canned or strained, stewed tomatoes (No. 1893)
1 cup cooked calf's head meat (No. 1492)
2 tablespoons lemon juice

Boil calf's head stock down to 1 quart. Strain. Cool. Melt butter in another pan. Brown. Add flour and cook, stirring constantly, until well browned. Add 2 cups stock slowly. Bring to boil. Add head stock, tomatoes, calf's head meat, and lemon juice. Serve hot, garnished with royal custard (No. 2102). Serves 6.

(528)   BEEF EXTRACT

½ pound beefsteak, from round

Salt

Remove fat from meat. Wipe with cold, damp cloth. Broil at high heat 4 minutes, turning often to sear both sides. Cut in size to fit lemon squeezer. Make slashes in each piece. Put in squeezer and press out juice. Put juice in cup. Heat over hot water. Season with salt. Serve at once.

(529)   BEEF BROTH

2 pounds shoulder or shin beef

2 pounds bone
1½ teaspoons salt

Wipe meat with cold, damp cloth. Cut into small pieces. Crack bone. Put meat and bone in kettle. Add 3 quarts cold water. Put in slow oven (275° F.). Cook 10 hours. Strain through colander. Add salt. Cool quickly. Remove fat. Serve cold as a jelly or reheat in double boiler to simmering point, but do not boil. Serves 4.

(530) CREAM OF ASPARAGUS SOUP

1 bunch asparagus
2 tablespoons chopped onion
½ teaspoon salt

2 cups thin white sauce (No. 2004)

Brush asparagus to remove sand. Rinse in cold water. Drain. Put in saucepan with onion and salt. Cover with boiling water. Simmer until tips are tender. Strain, reserving 1½ cups stock. Cut off tips and press through sieve into stock. Add hot white sauce. Mix well. Serves 4.

(531) BAKED OR RED KIDNEY BEAN SOUP

2½ cups baked pea or red kidney beans (No. 1708)
1 stalk celery
4 cups water

1 slice onion
1 carrot
Salt—Pepper—Paprika

Boil the water, beans, onion, celery, and carrot until they are tender. A ham bone or bacon rind adds flavor. Add seasonings. Strain and serve with croutons (No. 2105). Serves 6.

(532) BEAN OR PEA SOUP WITH CURED PORK

Wash ½ pound dried beans or peas and soak overnight in 1 quart water. Wash and scrape a ham hock, put into a kettle, and add water to cover. If the meat is very salty, change the water several times. Simmer until the meat is tender. If convenient, allow the hock to cool in the pot liquor. Skim off the fat. Cook the soaked beans or peas in the pot liquor which has been diluted with water until it does not taste too salty. Add a chopped onion. When the vegetables are soft, press them through a sieve. To the soup stock add the purée, together with some of the pork, chopped, and mix thoroughly. To give the right consistency, add a little flour mixed with cold water and cook for a few minutes, stirring constantly. Add salt if needed. Serves 6.

(533)   BEAN SOUP WITH STOCK

2½ cups boiled lima beans (No. 1717)	2 quarts soup stock (No. 501)
2½ cups boiled string beans (No. 1712)	Salt—Pepper

Mix and simmer ingredients 1 hour. Season to taste with salt and pepper. Serves 6 to 8.

(534)   BEAN SOUP

1 cup navy beans	½ cup chopped onion
1 teaspoon salt	2 tablespoons chopped pars-
1 tablespoon butter	ley
½ cup sliced carrot	

Wash beans thoroughly. Drain. Put in saucepan. Add 2 quarts cold water. Bring to a boil. Reduce heat. Cover and let simmer until tender, adding salt when about half cooked. Melt butter in another pan. Add carrot, onion, and ¼ cup water. Simmer until water is gone, stirring frequently. Add two cups of liquor in which beans were cooked and let simmer, covered, until carrots and onion are tender. Add this mixture to the bean soup. Bring to a boil. Serve hot, garnished with parsley and croutons (No. 2105). Serves 6.

(535)   BEAN PURÉE

1 cup brown beans	1½ teaspoons salt
1 sliced onion	1 stale bread crust
2 small carrots	1 sliced tomato
3 stalks celery	1 cup cream
1½ tablespoons butter	

Wash beans. Put beans, onion, carrots, celery, butter, and salt in saucepan. Add 2 quarts cold water. Bring to boil and keep boiling until beans are soft. Add crust and tomato. Boil 15 minutes longer. Remove carrots. Press rest of mixture through a sieve. Add cream. Reheat. Serves 6. Any other shell or dried beans may be used for this soup. Let dried beans soak 12 hours in cold water before cooking.

(536)   BLACK BEAN SOUP

2 cups black beans	⅛ teaspoon pepper
3 tablespoons butter	⅛ teaspoon cayenne
1 onion	2 tablespoons flour
1 carrot	1 hard-cooked egg
2 stalks celery	(No. 202)
2 sprigs parsley	1 lemon
1 teaspoon salt	

Soak beans 12 hours. Drain. Melt butter in pan. Slice onion into it and sauté 5 minutes. Add beans, 2 quarts water, sliced carrot, celery, parsley, salt, pepper, and cayenne. Cover and simmer 3 to 4 hours, adding more water if necessary. Press through a sieve. Reheat over boiling water. Mix flour to a smooth paste with 3 tablespoons cold water. Add flour paste to soup. Stir until thick and smooth. Add seasonings if needed. Chop egg and add to soup. Serve with a slice of lemon at each plate. Serves 6.

(537)   LIMA BEAN SOUP

2½ cups boiled lima beans	3 tablespoons butter
(No. 1717)	2 tablespoons flour
2 cups milk	1½ teaspoons salt
1 slice onion, chopped	¼ teaspoon pepper
3 slices carrot, chopped	

Simmer beans 20 minutes in 2 cups water. Rub through sieve. Add milk. Sauté onion and carrot 5 minutes in butter. Strain, discarding vegetables. Blend flour in butter. Add salt and pepper. Stir into hot soup. Serves 6.

(538)   CREAM OF LIMA BEAN SOUP

2½ cups boiled lima beans	1 teaspoon salt
(No. 1717)	½ teaspoon paprika
2 slices onion	⅛ teaspoon Tabasco sauce
4 slices carrot	2 cups medium white sauce
½ teaspoon pepper	(No. 2004)

Simmer lima beans, onion, and carrot in 1 quart water until very soft. Rub through sieve. Add seasonings. Add hot white sauce. Mix well. Serves 6.

(539) BEET BOUILLON

6 beets
¼ cup chopped onion
1 potato

1 sprig parsley
Salt—Pepper

Wash and peel beets. Cut them in cubes. Put in saucepan. Scrub and dice potatoes, without peeling. Add to beets with onion, parsley, and 8 cups cold water. Bring to boil. Reduce heat. Cover and simmer until vegetables are tender, about 2 hours, adding water to keep about 1 quart in pan. Strain. Season to taste with salt and pepper. Serves 4.

(540) BEET AND CABBAGE SOUP

2½ cups diced, boiled beets
(No. 1726)
2 quarts soup stock
(No. 501)
1 chopped onion

1 small head cabbage,
shredded
Salt—Pepper
8 thick slices bread
½ cup grated cheese

Simmer beets, stock, cabbage, onion, and seasonings until cabbage is tender. Put bread slice in each dish. Pour soup over. Sprinkle with grated cheese. Serves 8.

(541) CREAM OF CARROT SOUP

2½ cups diced carrot
1 chopped onion
Salt—Pepper

2 cups medium white sauce
(No. 2004)

Simmer carrots and onion in 2 cups water until tender. Rub through sieve. Season. Add to hot white sauce. Mix well. Serves 4.

(542) CREAM OF CAULIFLOWER SOUP

1 small head cauliflower
1 stalk celery, sliced
1 slice onion

½ teaspoon salt
2 cups thin white sauce
(No. 2004)

Break cauliflower into small pieces. Soak in cold, slightly salted water 20 minutes. Drain. Put in saucepan with celery, onion, and salt. Cover with water. Simmer until cauliflower is tender.

Strain, reserving 1½ cups stock. Press cauliflower through sieve into stock. Add hot white sauce. Mix well. Serves 4.

(543) ESSENCE OF CELERY SOUP

5 cups white stock (No. 502)

1 cup chopped celery tops

Mix ingredients. Cover and simmer 20 minutes. Strain through cheesecloth. Serves 4.

(544) CREAM OF CELERY SOUP

1 small bunch celery
½ teaspoon salt
1 slice onion

2 cups medium white sauce (No. 2004)

Cut tops and stalks of celery into small pieces. Put in saucepan. Add salt, onion, and 5 cups cold water. Bring to boiling point. Reduce heat and let simmer until celery is very tender. Strain, reserving 2 cups stock. Press celery through sieve into stock. Add hot white sauce. Mix well. Serves 4.

(545) CREAM OF CORN SOUP

2 cups stewed (No. 1769) or canned corn
1 slice onion
1 teaspoon sugar
¼ teaspoon salt

2 cups thin white sauce (No. 2004)
1½ tablespoons chopped parsley

Simmer corn, onion, sugar, and salt in 1 cup water 20 minutes. Press through a sieve. Add hot white sauce and mix well. Add parsley. Serves 4.

(546) CORN SOUP

9 ears corn
12 tomatoes
2 cups milk

2 tablespoons butter
1 teaspoon salt
¼ teaspoon pepper

Rinse corn in cold water. Cut corn from cob. Plunge tomatoes in boiling water, then in cold water. Peel. Add to corn and put through a food chopper. Put in saucepan. Cover with 2 quarts cold water. Cover and simmer slowly 2 hours. Add other ingredients. Simmer 10 minutes longer. Serves 6.

(547)   CORN CHOWDER

4 tablespoons chopped onion	2 cups stewed (No. 1769)
3 tablespoons butter	or canned corn
4 cups milk	1 ½ teaspoons salt
3 cups boiled potatoes	⅛ teaspoon pepper
(No. 1834), cut in ¼-	Few grains cayenne
inch slices	6 small pilot crackers

Fry onion in butter until a delicate brown. Strain butter into a saucepan. Add potatoes, corn, milk, salt, pepper and cayenne. Bring to the boiling point. Serve a cracker in each portion of soup. Serves 6.

(548)   CREAM OF CUCUMBER SOUP

3 cucumbers	1 blade mace
2 tablespoons butter	2 cups thin white sauce
3 cups milk	(No. 2004)
1 slice onion	2 well-beaten egg yolks

Peel and slice cucumbers. Remove seeds. Sauté in butter 10 minutes. Add milk, onion, and mace. Bring to boil. Cover and simmer 5 minutes. Rub through sieve into hot white sauce. Put egg yolks in tureen. Pour in soup. Garnish with chopped parsley. Serves 6.

(549)   CRÈME VICHYSOISSE

6 leeks	¾ pound diced potatoes
2 medium-size onions	Salt—Pepper
½ cup butter	½ cup unsalted butter
2 quarts strained chicken	1 cup cream
broth (No. 511)	¼ cup chopped chives

Clean leeks. Chop leeks and onions and simmer slowly in butter, taking care that they do not brown. As soon as vegetables are soft, add chicken broth and potatoes. Season to taste with salt and pepper and cook gently until potatoes are soft. Press through a sieve. Add unsalted butter and cream and heat over hot water. Chill in the refrigerator. Serve with a sprinkling of finely chopped chives. Serves 6.

(550) LENTIL PURÉE

Follow recipe for bean purée (No. 535), using lentils in place of brown beans.

(551) CREAM OF MUSHROOM SOUP

¾ pound mushrooms
½ teaspoon salt
½ cup cream

2 cups medium white sauce (No. 2004)

Wash and peel mushrooms. Slice caps and stems and put in saucepan. Add salt and 3 cups boiling water. Simmer 20 minutes. Press through a sieve. Reserve 2½ cups liquid and pulp. Add cream and hot white sauce. Mix well. Serves 4.

(552) CLEAR MUSHROOM SOUP

Wash and peel mushrooms. Slice stems and break caps in pieces. Simmer, covered, in 6 cups consommé (No. 507) ½ hour. Serves 6.

(553) ONION SOUP

1 pound onions
2 tablespoons butter
1 tablespoon flour

1½ quarts rich chicken stock (No. 502)
Salt—Pepper

Parmesan cheese

Slice and sauté onions in butter until brown. Sprinkle with flour and stir. Add to chicken stock, adding slowly and stirring until smooth. Season with salt and pepper. If made in the morning and allowed to stand several hours before serving the flavor improves. Serve with a piece of French bread sprinkled with Parmesan cheese and toast in the oven at the last moment. Serve extra cheese to be sprinkled over soup at the table. Serves 6.

(554) ESSENCE OF ONION SOUP

5 cups white (No. 502) or fish stock (No. 504)

1 cup sliced onions

Mix ingredients. Cover. Simmer 20 minutes. Strain. Serves 4

(555)   CREAM OF ONION SOUP

4 sliced, medium-size   Dash of pepper
    onions   2 cups medium white sauce
½ teaspoon salt   (No. 2004)

Simmer onions, salt, pepper, and 2 cups water until onions
are tender. Press through sieve. Add hot white sauce. Mix well.
Serves 4.

(556)   PARSNIP CHOWDER

2 tablespoons diced bacon or   Salt—Pepper
    salt pork   1 quart milk, scalded
1 small onion, chopped   ½ cup butter
2 cups parsnips, diced   ½ cup fine corn flake crumbs
1 cup potatoes, diced   1 tablespoon minced parsley
2 cups boiling water

Fry the bacon or salt pork. Add onion and sauté until tender
but not brown. Add parsnips, potatoes, boiling water, and seasonings and simmer until vegetables are tender. Add remaining
ingredients and continue cooking until chowder is very hot.
Serves 6.

(557)   SPLIT PEA SOUP

1½ cups dried split peas   2 cups scalded milk
3 quarts water   2 tablespoons butter
Ham bone   ⅛ teaspoon pepper
1 onion, sliced

Wash and pick over peas and soak over night. Drain. Add
water, ham bone and onion. Cover and cook slowly 3 hours or
until peas are soft. Press through a sieve. Add milk, butter, and
pepper and heat thoroughly. Serves 6.

(558)   CREAM OF PEA SOUP

2 cups boiled (No. 1823) or   1 slice onion
    canned peas   2 cups thin white sauce
½ teaspoon sugar   (No. 2004)
¼ teaspoon salt

Simmer peas, sugar, salt, and onion in 1½ cups water 15 minutes. Press through a sieve. Add hot white sauce and mix well. Serves 4.

(559)   PEA SOUP

1¼ cups boiled peas	2 smoked sausages
(No. 1823)	2 teaspoons salt
1 cup chopped celery	½ teaspoon pepper
1 chopped onion	

Simmer peas, celery, and onion in 4 cups water until soft. Rub through sieve. In another pan cover sausages with boiling water and boil 10 minutes. Drain. Slice into soup. Add salt and pepper. Serves 6.

(560)   GREEN PEA SOUP WITH MINT

1 quart fresh peas	1 teaspoon sugar
1 onion	4 tablespoons butter
1 large sprig mint	2 egg yolks
1 teaspoon salt	½ cup cream

Shell the peas and break up the pods. Wash the pods and boil for two or three hours in the water in which other vegetables have been cooked, if possible. Strain and add the peas, the onion, mint, salt, and sugar, and three pints of water in which the pods were cooked. Cook until peas are tender, then rub through a sieve. Add butter and bring to boiling point. Season more if needed, and just before serving add the egg yolk diluted with the cream. Cook, stirring constantly for five minutes, but do not allow the liquid to boil. Strain and serve with croutons (No. 2105). Serves 6.

(561)   PEPPER AND TOMATO CONSOMMÉ

3 green peppers	1 teaspoon salt
2 tomatoes	3 cloves
1 onion	

Slice peppers, tomatoes, and onion. Put in kettle. Add 2 quarts boiling water, salt, and cloves. Boil 5 minutes. Reduce heat. Cover and simmer 2 hours. Strain and serve hot. Serves 6.

(562) PIMIENTO BISQUE

¼ cup rice	1 teaspoon salt
5 cups white stock	Few drops Tabasco sauce
(No. 502)	2 beaten egg yolks
3 canned pimientos	⅓ cup cream

Soak rice in cold water 1 hour. Drain. Put stock in saucepan. Bring to a boil. Add rice gradually. Cover and simmer until tender. Add pimientos and cook 5 minutes more. Press through a sieve. Add salt and Tabasco. Mix yolks and cream. Put in tureen. Add soup. Serves 4.

(563) CREAM OF POTATO SOUP

3 medium-size potatoes	2 cups thin white sauce
1 slice onion	(No. 2004)
1 sliced stalk celery	3 tablespoons chopped
½ teaspoon salt	parsley

Wash and cut potatoes in halves. Put in saucepan with onion, celery, salt, and 3 cups boiling water. Simmer until potatoes are tender. Strain, reserving 2 cups stock. Press potatoes through a sieve into stock. Add hot white sauce. Mix well. Sprinkle with parsley. Serves 4.

(564) BAKED POTATO SOUP

Bake three or four medium-sized potatoes (No. 1837) and meanwhile prepare a quart of well seasoned soup stock (No. 501). Force freshly baked potatoes through a sieve into the stock. Thicken with the yolk of an egg. When serving, place a half cup cream and a tablespoon of chopped parsley in the bottom of a warmed soup tureen and pour soup over it. Sprinkle paprika on top and serve at once. Serves 6.

(565) PUMPKIN SOUP

2½ cups canned pumpkin	2 tablespoons butter
3 cups milk	1 teaspoon chopped parsley
⅓ cup boiled rice (No. 107)	Salt—Pepper

Mix pumpkin with 1½ cups water. Bring almost to boiling point. Add milk. Reheat. Add other ingredients. Cook 15 minutes in double boiler. Serves 6 to 8.

(566)   MOCK OYSTER SOUP

12 roots oyster or salsify plants	2 tablespoons butter
1 quart milk	Salt—Pepper

Scrape roots. Cut in thin slices. Cover with water. Simmer until tender. Add milk and butter. Season to taste with salt and pepper. Bring to boil and serve hot. Serves 6.

(567)   CREAM OF SPINACH SOUP

1 quart spinach	2 cups thin white sauce
½ teaspoon salt	(No. 2004)

Wash and pick over spinach. Put in saucepan with salt and 3 cups boiling water. Simmer 20 minutes. Press through sieve. Add 2½ cups of the liquid and pulp to hot white sauce. Mix well. Serves 4.

(568)   SQUASH SOUP

Follow recipe for pumpkin soup (No. 565), using baked squash (No. 1878) in place of canned pumpkin.

(569)   CREAM OF STRING BEAN SOUP

2½ cups boiled string beans (No. 1712)	1 teaspoon salt
2 slices onion	½ teaspoon pepper
4 slices carrot	2 cups medium white sauce (No. 2004)

Simmer beans, onion, and carrot in 1 quart water until very soft. Rub through sieve. Season. Add to hot white sauce. Serves 6. Wax beans may also be used for this.

(570)   CREAM OF TOMATO SOUP

2 cups canned or strained stewed tomatoes (No. 1893)	½ teaspoon salt
	1 tablespoon chopped onion
2 teaspoons sugar	⅛ teaspoon soda
2 whole cloves	2 cups medium white sauce (No. 2004)

Simmer tomatoes, sugar, cloves, salt, onion, and ½ cup water 20 minutes. Strain. Add soda. Pour into hot white sauce. Mix well. Serves 4.

(571)   CLEAR TOMATO SOUP

3 ½ cups canned or strained   ½ teaspoon salt
     stewed tomatoes   ¼ teaspoon pepper
     (No. 1893)   ¼ teaspoon paprika
1 slice onion   1 teaspoon Worcestershire
1 cup chopped celery   sauce
1 teaspoon tapioca   1 teaspoon sugar

Simmer tomatoes, onion, and celery 20 minutes. Rub through
a sieve. Pour 1 pint boiling water through sieve into mixture.
Soak tapioca in cold water 10 minutes. Add to soup. Simmer
until tapioca is clear. Add salt, pepper, paprika, Worcestershire
sauce, and sugar. Combine thoroughly. Garnish with croutons
(No. 2105). Serves 6.

(572)   RUBY CONSOMMÉ

1 pint tomato juice   3 peppercorns
2 cups chicken stock   Salt—Pepper
     (No. 502)   Lemon slices
Basil leaves

Mix tomato juice with chicken stock and add seasonings. Let
simmer gently about 15 minutes. Then strain out basil leaves and
peppercorns. Float a thin slice of lemon on each serving. Serves
4.

(573)   GREEN TOMATO SOUP

3 cups chopped green tomato   3 tablespoons butter
3 cups boiling water   3 tablespoons flour
2 tablespoons minced onion   4 cups milk
1 ½ teaspoons salt   Salt—Pepper
¼ teaspoon soda

Simmer tomato in boiling water with onion and salt for about
20 minutes or until tender, adding more water if necessary. Add
soda. Melt butter in a double boiler. Add flour and mix well.
Add milk gradually and cook, stirring constantly, until thickened. Stir in tomato mixture and season with salt and pepper.
Serves 6.

(574) TOMATO OKRA

¼ cup rice	1 diced bell pepper
3½ tablespoons butter	¼ cup diced onion
2 stalks chopped celery	1½ teaspoons salt
3 cups canned or strained stewed tomatoes (No. 1893)	2 cups sliced okra pods
	3 tablespoons chopped parsley

Brown rice to light golden with 2 tablespoons melted butter in saucepan. Add 5 cups water. Bring to a boil. Sauté celery, bell pepper, and onion in another pan with remaining butter for 6 minutes. Add tomatoes. Bring to boil. Pour into rice. Add salt. Simmer, covered, until rice is tender. Add okra pods and simmer 15 minutes more. Serve hot, sprinkled with parsley. Serves 6.

(575) CREOLE SOUP

2 tablespoons butter	2 cups soup stock (No. 501)
¼ chopped green pepper	½ teaspoon salt
1 small chopped onion	⅛ teaspoon pepper
2 tablespoons flour	2 tablespoons boiled maca- roni rings (No. 2302)
1½ cups canned or strained stewed tomatoes (No. 1893)	1 tablespoon grated horse- radish
⅛ teaspoon cayenne	

Melt butter in saucepan. Add green pepper and onion. Sauté 5 minutes. Add flour, blending well. Add tomatoes slowly, stirring constantly. Cover and simmer slowly 15 minutes. Add stock, salt, pepper, and cayenne. Strain. At time of serving add macaroni and horseradish. Serves 4.

(576) VEGETABLE BROTH I

2 cups diced potatoes	1 cup chopped cabbage or spinach
1 chopped tomato	3 stalks celery, chopped
1 chopped onion	2 sprigs parsley, chopped
2 cups sliced carrots	1½ teaspoons salt
2 cups diced turnips	

Mix all ingredients. Add 3 quarts cold water. Cover and simmer 3 hours. Strain and serve hot. Serves 6.

(577)   **VEGETABLE BROTH II**

Add a little cream or evaporated milk to water in which spinach, asparagus, or peas were cooked.

(578)   **VEGETABLE SOUP**

½ cup dried lima beans	2 onions, sliced
½ cup dried peas	1 white turnip, diced
2 tablespoons barley	1 cup stewed (No. 1893) or
2 tablespoons rice	canned tomatoes
2 tablespoons kidney beans	1 teaspoon salt
2 quarts cold water	¼ teaspoon pepper
½ cup celery, cut in pieces	1 ham bone or 1 frankfurter
2 potatoes, sliced	

Wash beans, peas, barley, rice, and kidney beans and soak over night in cold water. Bring to boiling point. Add celery, potatoes, onions, turnip, tomatoes, salt, and pepper. Simmer slowly 2 hours. Add water as it cooks away. About half hour before serving add ham bone and more seasoning if necessary. Remove bone before serving. This soup should be quite thick and is a meal in itself. Serves 6.

(579)   **VEGETABLE CHOWDER**

Fry 1 cup diced salt pork until crisp. Chop an onion fine and cook it in the fat. In the meantime boil 2 cups diced raw potatoes and 1 cup each chopped cabbage, turnips, and carrots in 1 pint unsalted water. As soon as the vegetables are tender, add 1 pint milk and the cooked salt pork and onions. When heated, season to taste with pepper and salt if needed. Serves 6.

(580)   **SOUP JULIENNE**

2 small carrots	1 sliced onion
2 small turnips	1 tablespoon butter
¼ head of cabbage	4 cups soup stock
1 stalk celery	(No. 501)
½ teaspoon salt	

Wash and cut into narrow strips the carrots, turnips, cabbage, and celery. Cover with cold water. Add salt. Bring to a boil. Reduce heat. Cover and simmer until vegetables are tender. Sauté onion in butter in another pan until soft but not browned. Add stock and cooked vegetables, from which water has been drained. Bring to a boil and serve hot. Serves 4.

(581)   CREAM OF WATERCRESS SOUP

| 1 bunch watercress | 2 cups medium white sauce |
| 1/2 teaspoon salt | (No. 2004) |

Wash watercress. Chop leaves fine, reserving 2 tablespoons for garnish. Put remaining watercress in saucepan. Add salt and 2 cups water. Simmer 10 minutes. Add hot white sauce. Mix well. Serve, garnished with reserved watercress. Serves 4.

(582)   CLAM BROTH

| 12 large clams | 1 tablespoon butter |
| 1/2 teaspoon pepper | |

Pry open shells of clams, reserving juice in saucepan. Add clams in shells to juice. Boil 20 minutes. Strain. Let settle. Strain again through cheesecloth into saucepan. Bring to boil. Add pepper and butter. Serve hot in cups. Serves 4.

(583)   CLAM CHOWDER

1 dozen clams	1 1/2 teaspoons salt
4 tablespoons chopped onion	1/8 teaspoon pepper
2 tablespoons butter	4 cups scalded milk
3 cups boiled potatoes	2 tablespoons flour
(No. 1834), cut in cubes	

Strain liquor from clams and set it aside. Clean and pick over clams, removing all particles of shell. Chop fine and put into a saucepan with the liquor. Cook 10 minutes. Fry onion in butter until a delicate brown and strain butter into the clams. Add potatoes, salt, pepper, and milk and bring to the boiling point. Mix flour with a little cold water to make a smooth paste and add to the chowder. Stir gently until it thickens. Serve at once. Serves 6.

(584)   CLAM BISQUE

2 dozen clams	5 tablespoons flour
Liquor from clams	1 teaspoon salt
½ cup celery, cut in pieces	⅛ teaspoon pepper
2 tablespoons parsley, chopped	1 cup thin cream
2 tablespoons butter	1 cup milk

Strain liquor from clams through cheesecloth and add enough water to make 2 cups liquid. Remove all particles of shell and chop clams fine. Simmer clams, celery, parsley, and liquid together 10 minutes. Press through a sieve and keep hot. Melt butter, add flour, salt, and pepper, and mix to a smooth paste. Add cream and milk and bring to boiling point, stirring constantly. Add the strained clam liquid. Serve immediately. Serves 6.

(585)   CLAM AND CORN CHOWDER

Follow recipe for corn chowder (No. 547), using 1½ cups cooked, minced clams, any style, in place of an equal quantity of milk.

(586)   OYSTER STEW

1 pint oysters	2 tablespoons butter
1 quart milk	Salt—Pepper

Drain liquor from oysters and put in saucepan. Bring to boil and skim. Add oysters and simmer until edges begin to curl. Heat milk almost to boiling point. Add butter and seasonings, to taste, to oysters. Add milk. Serves 2.

(587)   OYSTER SOUP

3 pints milk	2 tablespoons butter
¼ teaspoon pepper	1 quart oysters
⅛ teaspoon cayenne	2 tablespoons flour
1 teaspoon salt	

Heat milk. Add pepper, cayenne, salt, and butter. Wash and drain oysters. Put in hot pan and boil, shaking constantly, until gills curl. Add to milk. Add flour, mixed to a smooth paste with cold water. Bring to boil, stirring constantly. Serves 6.

(588) OYSTER CHOWDER

Prepare same as clam chowder (No. 583), using oysters instead of clams.

(589) CORN AND OYSTER CHOWDER

Simmer 1½ cups oysters and oyster liquor until edges begin to curl and substitute for an equal amount of milk in corn chowder (No. 547).

(590) CLAM AND OYSTER STEW

Follow recipe for oyster stew (No. 586), using equal parts of soft parts of small clams and oysters.

(591) LOBSTER STEW

1 pound diced, boiled lobster meat (No. 1236)	1½ tablespoons butter
1 pint milk	1½ teaspoons salt

Heat the milk to the scalding point and add lobster meat. Heat thoroughly, add butter, salt and stir well. Serves 4.

(592) LOBSTER BISQUE

Remove meat from a 2-pound boiled lobster (No. 1236). Add 2½ cups cold water to the shell and claws and cook 25 minutes. Drain and reserve 2 cups stock. Cut lobster meat in small pieces. Add lobster and stock to 2 cups medium white sauce (No. 2004). Heat and serve immediately. Serves 4.

(593) FISH CHOWDER

2 tablespoons butter	1 quart milk
1 sliced onion	1 tablespoon salt
6 cubed potatoes	⅛ teaspoon pepper
2 cups chopped fresh fish	

Melt butter and sauté onion to a light brown. Strain butter into a saucepan. Add potatoes and 1 pint boiling water. Simmer 10 minutes. Add fish and simmer 20 minutes. Add milk, salt, and pepper. Heat to boiling point. Serves 6.

(594)   CONEY ISLAND CHOWDER

To recipe for fish chowder (No. 593) add 2 cups canned or strained, stewed tomatoes (No. 1893), ¼ cup chopped green peppers, and ¼ cup chopped celery, adding them with milk.

(595)   SALMON SOUP

1 cup canned salmon	1 quart milk
2 tablespoons butter	1 teaspoon salt
2 tablespoons flour	¼ teaspoon pepper

Drain oil and remove skin from salmon. Melt butter in saucepan. Add flour. Blend well. Press salmon through a sieve into butter and flour mixture. Add milk, salt, and pepper. Heat thoroughly. Serves 4.

(596)   CORNED FISH STEW

1½ cups dried lima beans	1 quart milk
3 cups flaked, corned fish of white variety	1 tablespoon butter
	⅛ teaspoon pepper

Soak beans in cold water 10 hours. Boil in same water until tender. Add fish and mix without breaking beans. Add milk, butter, and pepper. Mix well. Serves 6.

(597)   MOCK LOBSTER BISQUE

1½ cups thin cream	Small piece bay leaf
½ cup shredded codfish	Bit of thyme
2½ cups chicken broth (No. 511)	2 sprigs parsley
	½ teaspoon paprika
2½ cups canned or strained stewed tomatoes (No. 1893)	⅛ teaspoon soda
	4 tablespoons butter
	2 tablespoons flour
2 slices onion, chopped	

Scald thin cream and codfish in double boiler. Cook 20 minutes. Strain and discard fish. Add broth to stock. In a saucepan simmer tomatoes, onion, bay leaf, thyme, parsley, and paprika 10 minutes. Strain. Add soda. Melt 2 tablespoons butter in another pan. Add flour and blend. Add milk and bouillon mixture. Heat, stirring constantly, to boiling point. Remove from

heat. Add tomato mixture and remaining butter. Reheat. Serve
hot, garnished with whipped cream and paprika. Serves 6.

(598) SCALLOP STEW

1 quart scallops	1 quart milk
¼ cup butter	Salt—Pepper

Rinse scallops in cold water. Drain. Melt 2 tablespoons butter
in saucepan. Add scallops and sauté 8 minutes. Add milk. Season to taste with salt and pepper. Add rest of butter. Serves 6.

(599) COLD BUTTERMILK SOUP

1 quart buttermilk	1 tablespoon chopped dill
½ pound chopped, boiled	pickle
shrimps (No. 1272)	1 tablespoon mustard
½ diced cucumber	1 teaspoon salt
1 tablespoon sugar	

Mix all ingredients thoroughly. Chill. Serves 6.

(600) SHRIMP BISQUE

Follow recipe for lobster bisque (No. 592), substituting
canned or boiled shrimp (No. 1272), for lobster.

(601) CRAB BISQUE

Follow recipe for lobster bisque (No. 592), substituting
boiled crab meat (No. 1227) for lobster.

(602) OLD-FASHIONED SOUTHERN CRAB SOUP

Simmer 1 dozen "she" crabs until tender in boiling salted
water. This will require about 20 minutes. Pick the meat from
the shells and put the crab flakes and the crab eggs in a double
boiler. Add 1 tablespoon butter, 1 minced onion, and a few
grains freshly ground black pepper. Simmer gently for 5 minutes. Scald 1 pint milk and add to the mixture. Thicken with
1 teaspoon flour, blended with a little of the milk. Add ½ cup
rich cream, ½ teaspoon Worcestershire sauce, 1 tablespoon
sherry, and salt to taste. Reheat. Serve immediately. Serves 4.

(603) CHESTNUT SOUP

1 quart chestnuts	1 quart white stock
1 tablespoon chopped lemon	(No. 502)
rind	1 tablespoon butter
1 teaspoon chopped parsley	1 tablespoon flour
1 teaspoon salt	2 beaten egg yolks

Croutons (N. 2105)

Boil chestnuts 15 minutes. Shell, remove skins, and chop fine. Put in saucepan. Add 4 cups water, lemon rind, parsley, and salt. Bring to a boil. Cover and simmer ½ hour. Press through a sieve. Add stock. Bring to a boil. Add butter and flour, blended to a smooth paste. Cover and simmer 30 minutes, stirring occasionally. Put egg yolks in tureen. Pour in soup. Garnish with croutons. Serves 4.

(604) CREAM OF ALMOND SOUP

½ cup shelled almonds	1 quart thin white sauce
1 pint light cream	(No. 2004)
1 lemon rind	3 tablespoons butter

Chop almonds and pound into a paste with 1 tablespoon cold water. Put cream and lemon rind in saucepan. Bring to a boil. Pour hot white sauce into cream gradually. Bring to boil and simmer 5 minutes, stirring frequently. Add nut paste and cook over hot water 15 minutes. Remove lemon rind and serve hot. Serves 6.

(605) PEACH SOUP

2 cups sliced peaches	2 cloves
2 cups white wine	Sugar to taste
⅛ teaspoon cinnamon	

Put a pint of water with spices on the range. Add peaches. Cook until tender. Press through colander. Put back with the juice and boil for a few minutes. Stir in the wine and add sugar to taste. Heat just under boiling point and serve in hot plates garnished with croutons (No. 2105). Cider or grape juice can be used in place of wine. Serves 6.

(606)   CRANBERRY SOUP

½ cup cranberry sauce
   (No. 54)
1 sliced onion
1 cup chopped cabbage
½ cup beet bouillon
   (No. 539)

1 cup chopped, boiled beets
   (No. 1726)
1 teaspoon salt
1 tablespoon sugar
¾ cup sour cream
3 hard-cooked eggs
   (No. 202)

Mix cranberry sauce, onion, cabbage, and 6 cups cold water. Put in saucepan and boil 20 minutes, stirring occasionally. Add beet bouillon, beets, salt, and sugar. Put 2 tablespoons sour cream in each plate. Pour in soup. Garnish each plate with ½ hard-cooked egg. This may be also served cold, in which case chill thoroughly. Serves 6.

(607)   LEMON SOUP

⅓ cup lemon juice
3 well-beaten eggs

1 teaspoon salt
6 cups bouillon (No. 505)

Mix lemon juice, eggs, and salt. Add ¼ cup cold water. Sti' in boiling bouillon. Serves 6.

(608)   MACARONI SOUP

10 sticks macaroni, broken
2 quarts broth (No. 511),
   milk, or stock
   (No. 501)

1 tablespoon butter
1 sliced onion
¼ cup grated Parmesan
   cheese

Melt butter in saucepan. Add macaroni and onion. Cover with water. Boil until tender. Add broth, milk, or stock. Cover and simmer 10 minutes. Serve hot, sprinkled with cheese. Serves 6. Spaghetti, noodles, or rice can be substituted for macaroni. A thick soup with noodles, macaroni, spaghetti, or vermicelli can be made by combining boiled paste (No. 2302) with hot white sauce (No. 2004), 2 tablespoons chopped onion, ¼ cup grated Parmesan cheese, and milk to bring the soup to desired consistency. Serve additional cheese on side to be sprinkled on soup.

(609)   SOUR CREAM SOUP

¾ cup sour cream
½ cup sliced carrot
1 chopped onion
1 chopped stalk celery
1½ cups diced potatoes

1 teaspoon salt
½ cup macaroni, broken
2 tablespoons chopped
 parsley

Put cream in pan. Heat slowly, stirring constantly, until the oil and albumen have separated and the albumen is slightly browned. Add carrot, onion, and celery. Cook slowly for a short while but do not brown. Add 4 cups warm water, potatoes, and salt. Simmer until vegetables are tender. Boil macaroni in 3 cups water until soft. Drain macaroni water into soup. Cut macaroni into tiny pieces. Drop into soup. Bring to a boil. Serve hot, garnished with parsley. Serves 6. If desired, canned or strained, stewed tomatoes (No. 1893) can be substituted for all or part of the water. If preferred, spaghetti, noodles, or vermicelli can be used in place of macaroni.

(610)   EGG SOUP

4 cups of milk
1 tablespoon flour
4 eggs
1 teaspoon salt

¼ teaspoon pepper
2 chopped hard-cooked
 eggs (No. 202)

Put milk in double boiler. When hot, stir in flour, blended to a smooth paste with a little cold milk. Cook 20 minutes, stirring frequently. Beat eggs until light and stir into milk. Cook rapidly 2 minutes. Add salt and pepper. Serve hot, garnished with hard-cooked eggs. Serves 4.

(611)   EGG BOUILLON

2 well-beaten egg yolks
1½ cups soup stock
 (No. 501)

Pinch of nutmeg
1 tablespoon chopped
 parsley

Add yolks, seasoned with nutmeg, to boiling stock. Serve hot in cups, garnished with parsley. Strained stewed tomatoes can be substituted for the stock. Serves 4.

(612)   CHEESE SOUP

½ cup butter
6 tablespoons flour
1 quart rich milk
2 cups grated American
    cheese
½ cup chopped celery

½ cup chopped green
    peppers
½ cup chopped onion
½ cup chopped carrot
2 cups chicken stock
    (No. 502)

Melt 6 tablespoons butter. Add flour, blending well. Pour in milk gradually, stirring constantly. Bring to boil. Add cheese. Remove from heat but keep warm. Melt remaining butter in another pan. Add celery, green peppers, onion, and carrot. Sauté a light brown. Add stock. Mix well. Combine two mixtures. Reheat. Serves 6.

(613)   HOMINY SOUP

Boil 2½ cups steamed hominy (No. 101) in 3 quarts soup stock (No. 501) 5 minutes. Season to taste with salt and pepper. Serve and sprinkle with grated cheese. Serves 6.

(614)   CREAM OF BARLEY SOUP

½ cup pearl barley
1 onion
1 carrot
2 stalks celery

1 teaspoon salt
2 cups thin white sauce
    (No. 2004)

Soak barley in cold water 10 hours. Drain. Put in saucepan. Add 1½ quarts cold water, onion, carrot, celery, and salt. Bring to a boil. Reduce heat. Cover and let simmer until barley is tender, adding more water if necessary. Remove vegetables and press remaining mixture through a sieve. Add hot white sauce. Serves 6.

(615)   WHOLE-WHEAT CHOWDER

For whole-wheat chowder follow the recipe for vegetable chowder (No. 579), but in place of the vegetables called for, use 2 cups of cooked whole wheat (No. 101) and 2 cups of diced raw carrots. Add more milk if needed. Serves 6.

(616)   CANNED SOUP COMBINATIONS

1—Heat the contents of a can of condensed cream of mushroom soup, stirring until smooth. Add a can of ready-to-serve onion soup. Heat. Sprinkle Parmesan cheese on toast rounds; place a round in the bottom of each soup bowl and pour hot soup over it.

2—Combine a can of condensed vegetable soup with a cup and a half of milk and a can of cocktail sausages, including the liquid. Add salt to suit taste. Heat thoroughly and serve. Garnish with croutons (No. 2105).

3—Combine a can of black bean soup with a can of mushroom broth. Heat and serve garnished with chopped hard-cooked egg (No. 202).

4—Add a 7-ounce can minced clams to a pound can of oyster stew. Add a cup of milk, 2 tablespoons butter, a half teaspoon Worcestershire sauce, dash cayenne, and salt to suit taste. Serve piping hot.

5—Mix together one-half cup water and one-half cup cream; scald. Add a cup of cream-style corn, one-half teaspoon salt, a dash cayenne and a can of ready-to-serve tomato soup. Heat well. Serve garnished with croutons (No. 2105).

6—Combine a can of ready-to-serve consommé with a can of condensed pea soup, one-half cup water and one-eighth teaspoon thyme. Simmer gently for a few minutes before serving. Sprinkle with paprika.

7—Mix a can of ready-to-serve cream of asparagus or cream of spinach soup with a can of condensed chicken soup. Heat. Sprinkle chopped parsley on top of each serving and garnish with croutons (No. 2105).

(617)   THREE VARIETY SOUP

1 can cream of celery soup	1 can consommé
1 can turtle or mock turtle soup	1 hard-cooked egg (No. 202), grated

Empty can of celery soup into a saucepan; heat gradually, stirring in the other two soups, making certain they are thoroughly combined. (If condensed soups are used, add water according to directions on can.) Then heat quickly to boiling. Serve immediately garnishing the top of each serving with finely grated, hard-cooked egg. Serves 6 to 8.

(618)   **OATMEAL GRUEL**

¼ cup rolled oats   ¼ teaspoon salt
1½ cups boiled water

Add rolled oats, mixed with salt, to boiling water. Boil 2 minutes. Cook in double boiler 1 hour. Strain, bring to boiling point and add milk or cream to thin.

(619)   **RICE GRUEL**

1 tablespoon rice   1 cup milk

Rinse rice. Cover with cold water. Let stand 2 hours. Drain. Add milk. Cook 1½ hours in double boiler. Strain and season to taste with salt and pepper. Serve hot or cold.

(620)   **CORN MEAL GRUEL**

Follow recipe for oatmeal gruel (No. 618), using corn meal instead of rolled oats.

(621)   **CORN FLAKE GRUEL**

Follow recipe for oatmeal gruel (No. 618), using toasted corn flakes instead of rolled oats.

(622)   **CRACKER GRUEL**

Mix 3 tablespoons cracker meal to a smooth paste with ¼ cup cold milk. Add ¾ cup boiling milk. Stir thoroughly. Serves 1.

(623)   **BARLEY BROTH**

2 pounds shin of beef   3 sliced potatoes
1 cup pearl barley   Dash of thyme
3 sliced onions   2 teaspoons salt
2 tablespoons chopped   ¼ teaspoon pepper
    parsley

Wipe meat with cold, damp cloth. Put in kettle. Add 1 gallon water and other ingredients. Simmer, covered, 3 hours, stirring occasionally. Serves 6.

(624)   **HEARTY SOUP**

2 frankfurters, sliced	1 can condensed pea soup
1 teaspoon butter	1 can milk
1 can condensed bean with bacon soup	1 can water

Cut frankfurters in ⅛ inch slices and cook them in butter. Add soups, milk, and water. Heat and serve immediately. Serves 5 to 7.

(625)   **WINE SOUP**

1 pint any white wine	2 tablespoons sugar
1 small stick cinnamon candy	1 teaspoon cornstarch
Rind of 1 lemon, chopped	2 egg yolks, beaten
	Macaroons, small

Combine wine with 1 pint water. Add cinnamon, lemon rind, and sugar. Mix well and let simmer, covered, 10 minutes. Dissolve cornstarch in 1 tablespoon water and add to wine. Bring to a boil. Remove from heat. Add egg yolks, mixing thoroughly. Strain. Put macaroons in soup bowls and pour soup over them. Serves 6.

Salads

~~~~~~~~~~~~~~~~~~~~~~~~~~~~~~~~~~~~~~~

THE food value of salads, especially those served with vegetable-oil dressings, can hardly be overestimated. The oil furnishes heat and energy and the raw vegetables add much-needed vitamins and mineral elements to the diet. Salads also include a large proportion of water and mild acids which are beneficial to the digestive tract. In addition to food value, salads also provide economical meals and can be combined in such a wide variety of color and taste that they can be made the most attractive part of many meals.

The efficient and clever homemaker will produce better salad menus by observing the following few rules:

1. Serve at least one salad every day.

2. Never wash a wooden salad bowl. Simply wipe it clean with a cold, damp cloth.

3. Keep a constant supply of assorted **salad greens** in an oil silk bag or in the hydrator in the refrigerator.

4. Put dressing on salad at serving time. Otherwise it will wilt the greens.

5. Many fruits turn dark when cut. Accordingly, slice them at the latest possible moment or sprinkle them with lemon juice to preserve natural color.

6. Chill all salad ingredients thoroughly before combining them.

7. Many standard salads can be varied by serving on shredded cabbage instead of lettuce.

8. Use taste and care in arranging salads. The eye is as important as taste in keen enjoyment of food.

9. Use originality in the selection of dressings. The "same old salad" will give new pleasure with a different dressing.

10. Do not discard outer leaves of salad greens. Shred them and use in other salads.

It is not necessary to make salad dressings for each new salad. Almost any of the dressings in this chapter, except those containing whipped cream, will keep for a considerable period of time in the refrigerator.

(701) MAYONNAISE

1 egg yolk
2 tablespoons vinegar
¼ teaspoon mustard

¾ teaspoon salt
⅛ teaspoon pepper
1 cup salad oil

Beat egg yolk and add 1 tablespoon vinegar. Add mustard, salt and pepper and mix well. Drop oil a teaspoonful at a time into the egg mixture, beating constantly until ¼ cup oil is added. Then add it in larger quantities, beating thoroughly after each addition. As the mixture thickens, add the remaining vinegar a little at a time. (Half lemon juice and half vinegar may be used.) Keep in a cool place.

(702) FRUIT SALAD MAYONNAISE

Fold ⅓ cup whipped cream lightly into mayonnaise (No. 701).

(703) RUSSIAN MAYONNAISE

Add ⅓ cup chili sauce and 2 tablespoons chopped green pepper to mayonnaise (No. 701).

(704) PIQUANTE MAYONNAISE

Add ¼ cup chopped, sour pickle and 2 tablespoons chopped, pickled onions to mayonnaise (No. 701).

(705) TARTAR MAYONNAISE

Add 2 tablespoons chopped, sour pickle, 2 tablespoons chopped, stuffed olives, 1 teaspoon capers, and 2 tablespoons chopped parsley to mayonnaise (No. 701).

(706)   **RED MAYONNAISE**

Add ¼ teaspoon paprika and ¼ cup catchup to mayonnaise (No. 701).

(707)   **CUCUMBER MAYONNAISE**

Add ½ cup grated, well-drained cucumber to mayonnaise (No. 701).

(708)   **HORSERADISH MAYONNAISE**

Add 2 tablespoons grated horseradish to recipe for mayonnaise (No. 701).

(709)   **JELLIED MAYONNAISE**

Use 1 cup slightly liquid aspic jelly (No. 877) in place of egg yolk in recipe for mayonnaise (No. 701). Keep in cold place.

(710)   **MARSHMALLOW MAYONNAISE**

Substitute marshmallow whip for whipped cream in fruit salad mayonnaise (No. 702).

(711)   **BANANA NUT MAYONNAISE**

Add 1 mashed banana and 2 tablespoons peanut butter to recipe for mayonnaise (No. 701).

(712)   **CHEESE MAYONNAISE**

Add ¼ cup grated American cheese to recipe for mayonnaise (No. 701).

(713)   **MARMALADE MAYONNAISE**

Add ¼ cup orange marmalade to recipe for mayonnaise (No. 701).

(714)   POTATO MAYONNAISE

½ cup mashed potato (No. 1835)	½ teaspoon Worcestershire sauce
2 tablespoons olive oil	¼ teaspoon salt
3 tablespoons vinegar	¼ teaspoon mustard
1 teaspoon horseradish	¼ teaspoon sugar

Mix in order given and serve with cold meat.

(715)   SAVORY SALAD DRESSING

¼ cup liver sausage	½ cup mayonnaise
1 teaspoon chives	(No. 701)
¼ cup stuffed olives	

Crumble sausage. Chop chives and olives and blend with mayonnaise. Add sausage. To be served over fresh vegetable salad.

(716)   FRENCH DRESSING

1 cup olive oil	1 teaspoon sugar
3 tablespoons vinegar	⅛ teaspoon pepper
1 teaspoon salt	⅛ teaspoon paprika

Mix ingredients and beat or shake until thoroughly mixed.

(717)   LEMON FRENCH DRESSING

Substitute 3 tablespoons lemon juice for 2 tablespoons vinegar in French dressing (No. 716).

(718)   CHIFFONADE FRENCH DRESSING

Add ⅓ cup chopped, boiled beets (No. 1726) and 1 chopped, hard-cooked egg (No. 202) to French dressing (No. 716).

(719)   THOUSAND ISLAND FRENCH DRESSING

Add ¼ cup chopped green pepper, 2 tablespoons chopped, stuffed olives, 1 tablespoon chopped parsley, and 2 tablespoons chopped onion to French dressing (No. 716).

(720)   CURRY FRENCH DRESSING

Add ⅛ teaspoon curry powder to French dressing (No. 716).

(721)   SARDINE DRESSING

Add ½ cup sardines, mashed to a paste, to French dressing (No. 716).

(722)   BRESLIN FRENCH DRESSING

Add 2 tablespoons chopped pistachio nuts and 1 teaspoon chopped, sautéed mushrooms (No. 1801) to recipe for French dressing (No. 716).

(723)   GRAPEFRUIT FRENCH DRESSING

Substitute grapefruit juice for vinegar in recipe for French dressing (No. 716).

(724)   GINGER FRENCH DRESSING

Add 2 tablespoons chopped, preserved ginger to recipe for French dressing (No. 716).

(725)   RUSSIAN FRENCH DRESSING

Add 2 tablespoons chili sauce, 2 tablespoons chopped, red or green pepper, and 1 tablespoon chopped onion to recipe for French dressing (No. 716).

(726)   RED FRENCH DRESSING

Add ¼ cup chili sauce and 2 tablespoons horseradish to French dressing (No. 716).

(727)   CHILI DRESSING

Add 12 drops Tabasco sauce, 4 tablespoons chili sauce, and 1 tablespoon chopped onion to recipe for French dressing (No. 716).

(728)   PIMIENTO DRESSING

Add ¼ cup chopped pimiento to French dressing (No. 716).

(729)   MINTED FRENCH DRESSING

Add 3 tablespoons minced mint and 1 tablespoon sugar to recipe for French dressing (No. 716).

(730)   CREAM CHEESE DRESSING

Add ¼ cup cream cheese to recipe for French dressing (No. 716), beating it in thoroughly.

(731)   ANCHOVY DRESSING

Beat 2 teaspoons anchovy paste into recipe for French dressing (No. 716).

(732)   CHUTNEY FRENCH DRESSING

Add 2 tablespoons chutney to recipe for French dressing (No. 716).

(733)   ALL-PURPOSE FRENCH DRESSING

1 teaspoon salt	⅔ cup orange juice
2 tablespoons tomato catchup	¼ cup lemon juice
	½ cup salad oil
2½ teaspoons powdered sugar	2 tablespoons olive oil

Combine the salt, catchup, and sugar. Add alternately the remaining ingredients, beating well after each addition.

(734)   ROQUEFORT FRENCH DRESSING

2 teaspoons salt	½ cup vinegar
½ teaspoon black pepper	Dash red pepper sauce
1 teaspoon paprika	1 cup salad or olive oil
½ teaspoon dry mustard	1 clove garlic, cut in half
½ teaspoon confectioner's sugar	2-ounce package Roquefort cheese

Combine all ingredients except the cheese and let stand overnight. Then remove garlic from dressing and add the cheese, mashed fairly smooth.

(735)   HONEY FRENCH DRESSING

⅓ cup salad oil   ½ teaspoon salt
3 tablespoons lemon juice   ⅓ cup strained honey

Beat together the oil, lemon juice, and salt. Add honey slowly while beating. Serve with fruit salad.

(736)   TOMATO FRENCH DRESSING

1 can tomato soup   ¼ cup sugar
½ cup vinegar   1 tablespoon grated onion
½ cup salad oil   1 teaspoon salt
1 tablespoon of Worcester-   1 teaspoon paprika
    shire sauce   1 teaspoon dry mustard

Mix all together in jar and shake well.

(737)   COOKED SALAD DRESSING

½ teaspoon mustard   Few grains cayenne
1½ teaspoons salt   1 beaten egg
1½ teaspoons sugar   1 cup milk
1½ tablespoons flour   4 tablespoons vinegar
⅛ teaspoon paprika   1½ tablespoons butter

Mix mustard, salt, sugar, flour, paprika, and cayenne. Add egg and mix thoroughly. Add milk and vinegar. Cook over hot water, stirring frequently, until thick. Add butter. Cook and stir until melted.

(738)   WHIPPED CREAM DRESSING

Fold ½ cup whipped cream lightly into cooked salad dress-ing (No. 737).

(739)   TARRAGON DRESSING

Substitute 2 tablespoons tarragon vinegar for 2 tablespoons vinegar in cooked salad dressing (No. 737) and add 2 table-spoons chopped onion and 2 tablespoons chopped parsley.

(740)   HORSERADISH DRESSING

Add 3 tablespoons prepared horseradish to cooked salad dressing (No. 737).

(741)   CELERY DRESSING

Add ¼ cup chopped celery, 2 tablespoons chopped green pepper, and 2 tablespoons chopped red pepper to cooked salad dressing (No. 737). If preferred, chopped pimiento or chopped parsley may be substituted for peppers.

(742)   HAM SALAD DRESSING

Add ½ cup minced, cooked ham to recipe for cooked salad dressing (No. 737).

(743)   PEANUT BUTTER SALAD DRESSING

Beat ¼ cup peanut butter into cooked salad dressing (No. 737).

(744)   CREAM DRESSING

½ cup thick cream   1 tablespoon sugar
3 tablespoons lemon juice   Salt

Whip the cream thick. Add other ingredients, beating in thoroughly.

(745)   SOUR CREAM DRESSING

½ cup sour cream   1 tablespoon chopped chives
1 tablespoon tarragon   or onions
      vinegar   ½ teaspoon salt
              Pepper—Paprika

Mix and beat ingredients together with an egg beater, beating until light.

(746)   VINAIGRETTE DRESSING

1 teaspoon salt
⅛ teaspoon paprika
⅛ teaspoon pepper
1 tablespoon tarragon
    vinegar
2 tablespoons cider vinegar
⅓ cup olive oil

1 chopped pickle
2 tablespoons chopped
    green pepper
1 tablespoon chopped
    parsley
1 chopped, hard-cooked
    egg yolk (No. 202)

Mix all ingredients. Chill.

(747)   CUCUMBER SAUCE

1 cucumber
½ cup heavy cream
⅛ teaspoon salt

Few grains pepper
2 tablespoons vinegar

Pare cucumbers and chop fine. Chill well. Beat cream until stiff. Add salt and pepper. Fold in vinegar and finally the cucumber.

(748)   PINEAPPLE DRESSING

4 tablespoons flour
3 tablespoons sugar
Juice from 1 can sliced pine-
    apple

1 tablespoon butter
2 eggs
1 cup cream, whipped

Mix flour and sugar, adding pineapple juice a little at a time, until the mixture will pour. Heat remaining juice and add flour mixture. Cook directly over fire, stirring until slightly thickened. Place over hot water, add butter and well-beaten eggs. Cook again until quite thick, stirring constantly. Chill. Fold in whipped cream just before serving.

(749) GRAPEFRUIT SALAD DRESSING

¼ cup butter
¼ cup sugar
⅛ teaspoon salt
1 tablespoon cornstarch

1 cup grapefruit juice
2 slightly beaten egg
    yolks
½ cup whipped cream

Melt butter over hot water. Add sugar, salt, and cornstarch. Mix thoroughly. Add grapefruit juice. Stir in egg yolks. Cook and stir until mixture thickens. Chill. Fold in whipped cream when ready to serve

(750)   SLAW DRESSING

3 egg yolks	1 cup cream or milk
½ cup sugar	1 cup vinegar
2 tablespoons butter	⅛ teaspoon cayenne
1 tablespoon salt	3 egg whites

Mix egg yolks, sugar, butter, salt, cream or milk, vinegar, and cayenne. Beat well. Beat egg whites stiff and fold in. Cook in double boiler until thickened.

(751) MEAT SAUCE FOR VEGETABLE SALAD

¾ pound chopped beef	3 tablespoons tomato
1 onion, chopped fine	paste
4 stalks celery, diced	¾ teaspoon baking powder
2 tablespoons butter	1 teaspoon parsley, minced
½ pound mushrooms, sliced	Salt, pepper, and paprika

Rub skillet with garlic. Cook onion and celery in two tablespoons butter. Add mushrooms and parsley and cook a little longer. Sauté meat and baking powder in butter in another skillet. Combine mixtures. Add tomato paste and mix thoroughly. Season to taste with salt, pepper, and paprika. Add enough water to make sauce liquid, but not thin. Simmer very slowly about 20 minutes.

(752)   INDIAN SALAD DRESSING

Yolks 2 hard-cooked eggs (No. 202)	½ cup olive oil
¾ teaspoon salt	1 tablespoon red pepper, finely chopped
½ teaspoon powdered sugar	1 tablespoon green pepper, finely chopped
¼ teaspoon paprika	1 tablespoon pickled beets, cut in small cubes
Few grains cayenne	
Few grains white pepper	1 teaspoon finely chopped parsley
1 tablespoon lemon juice	
2 tablespoons vinegar	

Force egg yolks through a strainer and add salt, sugar, paprika, cayenne, white pepper, lemon juice, vinegar and olive oil. Shake thoroughly and add remaining ingredients.

(753)   GERMAN SALAD DRESSING

1 pint milk
2 tablespoons flour
2 tablespoons sugar
1 teaspoon butter
½ teaspoon celery salt

Salt—Pepper
1 well-beaten egg
3 tablespoons mustard
2 tablespoons vinegar

Bring milk to a boil in double boiler. Mix flour to a smooth paste with 2 tablespoons cold water and add to milk, blending well. Add sugar, butter, celery salt, salt and pepper as desired, and egg. Cool. Add mustard and vinegar. Beat thoroughly.

(754)   MELTED BUTTER DRESSING

2 egg yolks
6 tablespoons butter
Salt—Pepper

1 teaspoon lemon juice
3 chopped tarragon leaves

Melt 2 tablespoons butter over hot water. Add egg yolks. Stir constantly until slightly thickened. Gradually add remaining butter. Beat to a cream. Season with salt and pepper to taste. Add lemon juice and taragon leaves. One cup whipped cream may be folded into this at time of serving.

(755)   BACON SALAD DRESSING

Mix 1 part vinegar to 2 parts bacon fat and add chopped bacon which was fried crisp (No. 1464) in the fat.

(756)   MINERAL OIL DRESSING

2 egg yolks
¼ teaspoon salt

2 tablespoons lemon juice
1 cup mineral oil

Beat egg yolks with salt. Add lemon juice. Add oil, a tablespoon at a time, blending thoroughly before adding more.

(757)   MAPLE SIRUP DRESSING

1 beaten egg
1 cup maple sirup

Juice of ½ lemon

Mix ingredients and cook in double boiler until thick. Use 3 tablespoons of this as flavoring for 1 cup whipped cream.

(758)   **LETTUCE SALAD**

Wash leaves and let stand 30 minutes in cold water. Drain. Pour over French dressing (No. 716) and toss to coat leaves thoroughly. They may be sprinkled with chopped nasturtium blossoms, radishes, hard-cooked egg (No. 202), or a mixture of tarragon leaves, parsley, and chives, chopped together.

(759)   **LETTUCE AND TOMATO SALAD**

Chill lettuce leaves and tomatoes. Arrange lettuce on platter or individual dishes. Top with tomato slices or quarters. Serve with French dressing (No. 716) or mayonnaise (No. 701).

(760)   **MIXED GREEN SALAD**

6 lettuce leaves	1 cup thinly sliced Chinese
6 romaine leaves	cabbage
6 escarole leaves	1 tablespoon minced onion

French dressing (No. 716)

Rub bowl with garlic. Arrange the greens in layers and sprinkle with minced onion. Add dressing and toss. Serves 6. Other suitable combinations for mixed greens are:

Chicory, dandelion greens, garlic, diced broiled bacon (No. 1464).
Chicory, endive, escarole, garlic, lettuce, chopped onion, romaine.
Chicory, endive, tomato quarters.
Chicory, sliced green pepper, lettuce, romaine, watercress.
Chicory, lettuce, romaine.
Cucumber slices, garlic slices, green pepper slices, lettuce, sliced radishes, chopped scallions.
Cucumber slices, radish slices, romaine.
Curly endive, lettuce, spinach.
Curly endive, chopped pimiento.
Dandelion greens, sliced radishes, romaine, chopped scallions, watercress.
Green pepper, green and ripe olives, diced pimiento, romaine.

(761)   **WATERCRESS SALAD**

Prepare and serve same as lettuce salad (No. 758).

(762)   **ENDIVE SALAD**

Wash endives. Drain. Separate leaves or slice into halves or quarters. Let stand 30 minutes in cold water. Serve with French dressing (No. 716).

(763)   DANDELION SALAD

1 quart dandelion greens	3 cold boiled potatoes
3 hard-cooked eggs	(No. 1834)
(No. 202)	½ cup French dressing
3 onions	(No. 716)

Chop greens, eggs, potatoes, and onions and mix well with dressing. Serve on lettuce leaves. Serves 6.

(764)   RAW SPINACH SALAD

Wash the tender inside leaves of spinach. Let stand 1 hour in ice cold water. Serve with French dressing (No. 716), Russian mayonnaise (No. 703), or Thousand Island dressing (No. 719).

(765)   COMBINATION SALAD

Arrange crisp lettuce leaves on plate. Add quartered or sliced tomatoes, sliced cucumbers, sliced onion, and sprigs of parsley. Garnish with mayonnaise (No. 701). Sliced radishes or any other fresh greens or vegetables may be added. Or, the ingredients can be sliced thin, tossed lightly in a garlic-rubbed salad bowl, and sprinkled with French dressing (No. 716).

(766)   SLICED CUCUMBERS

Chill cucumbers. Wash, dry, pare, and slice thin. Sprinkle with French dressing (No. 716) a few minutes before serving. Or, they may be seasoned to taste at the table with lemon juice, salt, and sugar.

(767)   CARROT SALAD

2 cups chopped carrots	1 tablespoon chopped
1 cup chopped celery	parsley
1 cup chopped walnuts	½ cup mayonnaise
1 tablespoon chopped	(No. 701)
onion	

Mix thoroughly. Chill. Serves 6.

(768)   SPANISH SALAD

Arrange watercress on salad plates. On each plate put 3 slices tomato and 3 pickled onions. Garnish with mayonnaise (No. 701).

(769)   RADISH ROSES

Choose round, bright-red radishes without blemishes. From the root end cut 5 or 6 thin slices about ⅓ down the radishes. Turn back the red skin so pared to form petals. Make 2 slashes in radish below bottom of petals and let stand 2 hours in cold water.

(770)   TOMATO WITH MAYONNAISE

Cut slice from stem end of tomato. Scoop out some of pulp. Stuff with mayonnaise (No. 701). Chill. Allow 1 tomato per serving.

(771)   STUFFED TOMATO SALAD

6 medium-sized tomatoes	1 teaspoon chopped parsley
2 cups boiled shrimps	½ teaspoon salt
(No. 1272)	⅛ teaspoon pepper
1 cup celery, cut in pieces	Mayonnaise (No. 701)

Put tomatoes in boiling water for a moment to loosen skins. Peel and chill. Cut slices from the stem end and scoop out some of the pulp. Cut shrimps in pieces and add celery, parsley, salt and pepper. Moisten with mayonnaise. Fill the tomatoes with the shrimp mixture. Garnish with a spoonful of mayonnaise and a whole shrimp. Serve on crisp lettuce leaves. Crab meat may be used in place of shrimps. Serves 6. Other suggestions for tomato stuffings are:

Mixture of chopped celery, diced cucumber, tomato pulp, chopped parsley, mayonnaise (No. 701).

Mixture of chopped celery, chopped walnuts, tomato pulp, chopped parsley, mayonnaise (No. 701).

Boiled asparagus tips (No. 1704) and mayonnaise (No. 701).

(772)   POINSETTIA TOMATO

Make 8 slits through the skin of a tomato with a sharp-pointed knife from the stem end. Put tomato on plate. Insert knife under skin at stem and pull down until the skin lays flat, resembling leaves. Cut across middle of tomato, nearly cutting it in two, lengthwise. Then cut at right angle, form quarters, attached at the base. Garnish center with mayonnaise (No. 701).

(773) TOMATO AND THYME SALAD

Heap romaine, that has been pulled apart, in the salad bowl rubbed with garlic. Slice in two peeled tomatoes and add several paper-thin slices of onion separated into rings. Bruise about 10 thyme tips. Cut them up and add. Serve with French dressing (No. 716). Serves 4.

(774) TOMATO WITH CHEESE BALL

Cut slice from stem end of tomato. Scoop out some of pulp. Put in a little mayonnaise (No. 701). Drop in a small ball of cottage cheese. Cover with additional mayonnaise. Allow 1 tomato per serving.

(775) TOMATO AND ONION SALAD

1 head lettuce	6 thick tomato slices
½ cup mayonnaise	1 chopped Spanish onion
(No. 701)	½ teaspoon paprika

Make 6 nests with lettuce leaves. Put tomato slice in each. Top with mayonnaise. Sprinkle with onion and paprika. Serves 6.

(776) DEVILED EGG SALAD IN TOMATO CUPS

8 medium tomatoes	½ cup lemon juice
16 hard-cooked eggs	4 teaspoons prepared
(No. 202)	mustard
1 cup minced celery	½ cup mayonnaise
8 teaspoons minced onion	(No. 701)
8 teaspoons French dressing	Dash of cayenne
(No. 716)	1 head lettuce
2 teaspoons salt	

Wash and remove the stem end of the tomatoes. Then cut each tomato into fourths without cutting all the way through. Press back the petals and sprinkle on the inside with salt, cayenne, and some of the French dressing. Chill. Meanwhile chop the shelled hard-cooked eggs and add the remaining ingredients. Mix well and heap some of this mixture in the center of the tomatoes which have been arranged on individual beds of lettuce. Serves 8.

(777)   TOMATO AND FIG SALAD

3 ½ cups canned whole
    tomatoes
1 ¼ cups canned figs
2 tablespoons chopped
    pecans

1 head lettuce
½ cup mayonnaise
    (No. 701)
1 tablespoon chopped
    pimiento

Quarter tomatoes and figs and arrange attractively on nests of lettuce. Sprinkle with pecans. Garnish with mayonnaise, topped with pimiento. Serves 6.

(778)   CHEF SALAD

1 cut clove garlic
½ head lettuce, broken in
    pieces
½ bunch watercress
¼ thinly sliced cucumber
2 chopped hard-cooked
    eggs (No. 202)

¼ cup chopped celery
6 sprigs chicory
12 rolled anchovy filets
¼ cup thinly sliced Ameri-
    can or Swiss cheese
¼ cup French dressing
    (No. 716)

Rub wooden salad bowl with cut side of garlic. Arrange other ingredients in bowl, sprinkled with dressing. Toss lightly with wooden fork and spoon. Serves 6.

(779)   CELERY SALAD

Use 2 or 3 tender celery hearts on a bed of lettuce per serving. Serve with any salad dressing. Or, serve 4 or 5 inch-long pieces of stuffed celery (No. 431) on individual lettuce nests with preferred salad dressing.

(780)   POTATO SALAD

5 diced, cold, boiled po-
    tatoes (No. 1834)
½ cup French dressing
    (No. 716)
1 ½ cups sliced celery
½ teaspoon chopped onion

2 tablespoons chopped
    parsley
1 teaspoon salt
⅛ teaspoon paprika
½ cup mayonnaise
    (No. 701)

Marinate potatoes in French dressing (No. 716). Chill. Mix all ingredients. Garnish with lettuce, hard-cooked egg (No. 202) slices, and olives. Serves 6.

(781)   HOT GERMAN POTATO SALAD

3 pounds hot, boiled, sliced   2 tablespoons olive oil
   potatoes (No. 1834)   1 tablespoon flour
1 chopped onion   ⅓ cup sugar
1 tablespoon chopped   ⅓ cup white vinegar
   parsley   Salt—Pepper

Mix potatoes with ½ onion and parsley. Sauté remaining
onion in oil until soft and yellow. Add flour and blend well.
Add sugar, vinegar, and ⅔ cup water. Bring to boil, stirring
constantly. Add potatoes piece by piece, mixing well. Season
with salt and pepper. Serve hot or cold. Serves 6.

(782)   BEET AND POTATO SALAD

Add 2½ cups diced, boiled beets (No. 1726) to potato salad
(No. 780).

(783)   POTATO AND OLIVE SALAD

6 small, diced, cold, boiled   18 stuffed olives
   potatoes (No. 1834)   Mayonnaise (No. 701)
½ head of lettuce

Form potatoes in a mound on a bed of lettuce leaves. Put 1
olive on top and arrange others around mound. Garnish with
mayonnaise. Serves 6.

(784)   APPLE POTATO SALAD

Add 1 small, chopped apple to recipe for potato salad (No.
780).

(785)   SWEET POTATO SALAD

2 cups diced, cold, boiled   1 tablespoon chopped onion
   sweet potatoes   1 tablespoon chopped
   (No. 1881)   parsley
1 cup chopped celery   ½ cup French dressing
1 tablespoon chopped bell   (No. 716) or mayon-
   pepper   naise (No. 701)

Mix thoroughly. Chill. Serves 6.

(786)   SLAW

1 young cabbage	½ cup vinegar
½ cup cream	1 teaspoon salt
½ cup sugar	

Beat cream, sugar, vinegar, and salt together thoroughly until the dressing is like whipped cream. Discard outer leaves of cabbage. Shred rest finely and combine with dressing just before it is ready to serve. This is often used as a relish with meat and fish dishes. Serves 6.

(787)   HOT SLAW

Shred cabbage finely. Boil in slightly salted water until tender. Drain. Serve hot, thoroughly mixed with warm cooked salad dressing (No. 737).

(788)   CABBAGE AND APPLE COLESLAW

Mix 2 cups crisped and dried shredded cabbage, 1 cup diced apples with ⅓ cup cooked salad dressing (No. 737), adding salt and pepper to taste. Serves 6.

(789)   CELERY AND CARROT SALAD

2 cups chopped carrots	1 chopped onion
1 cup chopped celery	½ cup mayonnaise
2 tablespoons chopped parsley	(No. 701)

Mix and chill. Serves 6.

(790)   CABBAGE AND CARROT SALAD

1 cup chopped carrots	¼ cup chopped parsley
2 cups shredded cabbage	½ cup mayonnaise
2 sliced onions	(No. 701)

Mix and chill. Serves 6.

(791)   CARROT AND BELL PEPPER SALAD

1 chopped bell pepper
1 cup chopped carrots
3 cups chopped cabbage
¼ cup chopped onion

2 tablespoons chopped
   parsley
¾ cup mayonnaise
   (No. 701)

Mix thoroughly. Chill. Serves 6.

(792)   BEAN AND CABBAGE SALAD

1 cup boiled (No. 1721) or
   baked beans (No. 1708)
1 cup chopped cabbage
1 tablespoon chopped
   parsley

1 tablespoon chopped onion
½ cup cooked dressing
   (No. 737) or mayon-
   naise (No. 701)

Mix thoroughly. Chill. Serves 4.

(793) CABBAGE AND CUCUMBER PICKLE SALAD

2 cups shredded cabbage
½ cup chopped green
   pepper
1 tablespoon finely chopped
   onion
1 teaspoon sugar

⅓ cup chopped, fresh cu-
   cumber pickle
½ teaspoon salt
4 tablespoons mayonnaise
   (No. 701)

Combine and mix thoroughly. Serve in cups of lettuce and
arrange on a salad platter or on individual salad plates, garnished
with mayonnaise. Serves 6.

(794)   CABBAGE AND FRUIT SALAD

2 cups shredded cabbage
½ cup diced apricots
½ cup cubed oranges
⅓ teaspoon salt

¼ teaspoon celery seed
⅓ cup French dressing
   (No. 716)

Chill ingredients. Combine and serve in salad bowl. Many
other combinations of fruits, apples, pears, peaches, or berries,
may be used. Serves 6.

(795)   MACÉDOINE SALAD

1 cup boiled peas   1 cup diced, boiled string
   (No. 1823)   beans (No. 1712)
1 cup cubed, boiled carrots 1 small, boiled cauliflower
   (No. 1745)   (No. 1755)
1 cup sliced celery   1 cup French dressing
                                (No. 716)

Marinate peas, carrots, celery, and string beans in French
dressing (No. 716). Chill. Separate cauliflower flowerets and
marinate separately in French dressing (No. 716). Arrange
nests of lettuce on a platter and pile vegetables in them lightly.
Use cauliflower for a border around platter. Garnish with strips
of red and green pepper. Serves 6.

(796)   LUNCHEON SALAD PLATTER

2 ½ cups sliced, boiled beets   2 cups cottage cheese
   (No. 1726)   ½ cup crushed pineapple
2 ½ cups boiled string beans   2 tablespoons mayonnaise
   (No. 1712)   (No. 701)
½ cup French dressing   Head of lettuce
   (No. 716)

Chill beets and beans. Marinate each separately for 1 hour in
French dressing. Combine cheese, pineapple, and mayonnaise.
Pile cheese mixture on lettuce bed in center of platter. Surround
with shredded lettuce. Arrange beets and beans in individual
mounds on either side of cheese mound. Other cooked vegetables,
such as artichoke hearts (No. 1701), asparagus tips (No. 1704),
wax (No. 1712), lima (No. 1717) or kidney beans (No. 1721),
carrots (No. 1745), celery (No. 1761), or peas (No. 1823),
may be substituted for beets and string beans. Serves 6.

(797)   ASPARAGUS SALAD

Cook 1 bunch of asparagus in boiling salted water 25 to 35
minutes or until tender. Drain and cool. Cut off the stalky ends
leaving the tender tips. Marinate tips in French dressing (No.
716). Chill. Serve on crisp lettuce leaves with Thousand Island
French dressing (No. 719). Serves 4.

(798) BAKED BEAN SALAD

2 cups baked beans
(No. 1708)
½ cup French dressing
(No. 716) or mayon-
naise (No. 701)

1 cup diced, boiled beets
(No. 1726)
2 tablespoons chopped
onion
2 tablespoons chopped
dill pickle

Mix beans, beets, and salad dressing. Chill. Add the onion
and pickle. Arrange on lettuce or cabbage leaves. Garnish with
mayonnaise, dusted with paprika. Serves 6. Boiled kidney beans
(No. 1721) may be used in place of baked beans. A little diced,
crisp bacon (No. 1464) makes a tasty addition to this dish.

(799) PEA SALAD

2½ cups boiled peas
(No. 1823)
1 chopped onion
¼ cup chopped celery

¼ cup chopped nuts
¼ cup French dressing
(No. 716)
Head of lettuce

Drain peas. Mix with onion, celery, nuts, and French dressing. Arrange on lettuce leaves. Garnish with pimiento strips.
Serves 6.

(800) SPINACH SALAD

4 cups boiled spinach
(No. 1870)
½ cup cooked salad dressing
(No. 737)

1 sliced, hard-cooked egg
(No. 202)

Chop spinach. Mix with salad dressing. Form into mounds
with an egg slice on each. Serves 6.

(801) LIMA BEAN SALAD, ITALIAN STYLE

2 cups boiled lima beans
(No. 1717)
2 tablespoons chopped
parsley
1 chopped clove garlic

1 chopped Spanish onion
¼ cup olive oil
1 tablespoon vinegar
½ teaspoon salt

Mix beans, parsley, garlic, and onion with a fork. Gradually
add oil. Add vinegar drop by drop. Chill. Add salt. Serve in
salad bowl with a border of sliced tomatoes and onion rings.
Garnish with paprika. Serves 6.

(802)   STRING BEANS AND PIMIENTO SALAD

2 cups cold, boiled string
    beans (No. 1712)
1 cup chopped celery
3 pieces canned pimiento,
    diced

1 tablespoon chopped onion
1 tablespoon chopped
    parsley
½ cup mayonnaise
    (No. 701)

Mix thoroughly. Chill. Serves 6.

(803)   BEET AND EGG SALAD

1 cup diced, cold, boiled
    beets (No. 1726)
1 diced, hard-cooked egg
    (No. 202)

2 teaspoons chopped
    onion
3 tablespoons mayonnaise
    (No. 701)

Mix thoroughly. Chill. Serves 4.

(804)   LIMA AND GREEN BEAN SALAD

2½ cups boiled lima beans
    (No. 1717)
1 cup French dressing
    (No. 716) or mayon-
    naise (No. 701)

2½ cups boiled string beans
    (No. 1712)
1 head lettuce
2 sliced, hard-cooked eggs
    (No. 202)

Mix beans and string beans with ½ salad dressing. Arrange
lettuce leaves in salad bowl. Put in beans. Top with remaining
salad dressing. Garnish with egg slices. Serves 6.

(805)   ASPARAGUS PIQUANTE SALAD

½ cup sliced celery
2 tablespoons chopped chives
2 tablespoons chopped
    pimiento
2 cups boiled asparagus
    tips (No. 1704)

1 head lettuce
¼ cup French dressing
    (No. 716)
½ cup mayonnaise
    (No. 701)

Mix celery, chives, and pimiento. Arrange chilled asparagus
tips on lettuce. Sprinkle with French dressing. Top with mayonnaise, sprinkled with celery mixture. Boiled string beans (No.
1712) can be used in place of asparagus. Serves 6.

(806)   MOLDED SPINACH SALAD

Pack seasoned, boiled spinach (No. 1870) in small cups or molds. Chill. Unmold on beds of lettuce or cold cooked meats. Serve with French (No. 716) or chiffonade dressing (No. 718). Any other cooked greens may be used in place of spinach.

(807) CHEESE, NUT, AND PEPPER SALAD

4½ ounces cream cheese	2 teaspoons lemon juice
¼ cup chopped green pepper	¼ cup heavy cream
¼ cup toasted salted almonds	18 thin tomato slices
⅛ teaspoon paprika	1 head lettuce
⅛ teaspoon salt	Mayonnaise (No. 701)

Cream the cheese with a fork until soft. Add the green pepper, almonds, paprika, salt, and lemon juice. Add the cream, beaten stiff. Pack solidly in freezing tray of an automatic refrigerator and spread until smooth to a thickness of ¾ inch. Chill until firm enough to cut. Cut into small squares and serve on the slices of tomato arranged on lettuce. Garnish with mayonnaise. Serves 6. To toast almonds bake until a light golden brown in the oven.

(808)   ITALIAN SALAD

1 cup sliced, boiled maca- roni (No. 2302)	1 tablespoon chopped onion
½ cup diced celery	½ cup cooked dressing
½ cup diced carrots	(No. 737) or mayon-
½ cup boiled, green peas (No. 1823)	naise (No. 701)

Mix thoroughly. Chill. Serves 6.

(809)   CHEESE PEPPER SALAD

1 cup cottage cheese	2 tablespoons chopped
4 tablespoons cream	nuts
1 green pepper, sliced into rings	½ teaspoon paprika

Blend cheese and cream. Put mounds of cheese in center of pepper rings. Sprinkle with nuts and paprika. Serves 6.

(810)   BEET AND EGG SALAD

2½ cups diced, boiled beets (No. 1726)
1 chopped onion
¼ cup French dressing (No. 716)

6 deviled eggs (No. 216)
Shredded cabbage or lettuce
½ cup mayonnaise (No. 701)

Mix beets, onion, and dressing. Chill 1 hour. Alternate eggs and beet mixture on bed of greens. Garnish with mayonnaise. Serves 6.

(811)   SPANISH CORN SALAD

2½ cups canned whole grain corn
8 tomatoes
1 chopped pimiento
1 chopped onion
1 chopped green pepper
1 cup diced cucumber

Salt—Pepper
Cayenne
Tabasco sauce
French dressing (No. 716) or mayonnaise (No. 701)
Paprika

Drain the corn, saving the juice for soup. Scoop out the center of the tomatoes, making shells. Mix the tomato centers with the corn, pimiento, onion, green peppers, cucumber and seasonings. Blend with salad dressing, either French or mayonnaise. Fill tomato cups with the mixture, top with mayonnaise and a dash of paprika. Serve on lettuce. Serves 8.

(812)   ARTICHOKE HEART SALAD

5 cups canned artichoke hearts
Head of lettuce

¼ cup piquante mayonnaise (No. 704)

Drain the artichoke hearts, saving the juice for soup. Chill thoroughly. Arrange on crisp lettuce and serve with mayonnaise. Dust mayonnaise with paprika. Serves 6 to 8. To use fresh artichoke, remove stem and outside leaves. Discard thistle-like center or "choke." Soak in salted water ½ hour. Boil 25 minutes in salted water.

(813)   **MARBLED LETTUCE**

1 head lettuce
3 ounces cream cheese
1 tablespoon minced green
   pepper
2 tablespoons diced
   tomatoes

2 tablespoons carrots, grated
¼ tablespoon salt
⅛ teaspoon Worcestershire
   sauce
⅛ teaspoon pepper
1 teaspoon minced onion

Remove loose outer leaves from head of lettuce, and with sharp knife core it as you would an apple and remove entire heart. Cream cheese, add vegetables and seasonings, and pack tightly in center of lettuce. Wrap in damp cloth and waxed paper and chill in refrigerator until ready to use. Slice head in quarters. Serves 4.

(814)   **JELLIED VEGETABLE SALAD**

2¼ tablespoons gelatin
¼ cup cold water
1 cup boiling water
3 tablespoons vinegar
3 tablespoons lemon juice

¼ cup sugar
1 teaspoon salt
1 cup celery, cut in pieces
1 cup shredded cabbage
1 cup boiled peas (No. 1823)

Soak gelatin in cold water 10 minutes and dissolve in boiling water. Add vinegar, lemon juice, sugar and salt. Stir in the vegetables and mix thoroughly. Turn into a mold (or individual molds) dipped in cold water. Chill. Remove from mold to a bed of crisp lettuce leaves. Serve with cooked salad dressing (No. 737) and garnish with celery and radish roses (No. 769). Serves 6.

(815)   **TOMATO JELLY SALAD**

3 tablespoons gelatin
⅓ cup cold water
2½ cups canned tomatoes
2 whole cloves

¾ teaspoon salt
2 teaspoons sugar
1 small onion, sliced
Few grains cayenne

Soak gelatin in cold water 10 minutes. Cook tomatoes, cloves, salt, sugar, onion and cayenne together 15 minutes. Add gelatin and stir until dissolved. Strain. Turn into individual molds which have been dipped in cold water. Chill. Remove from molds to cups of crisp lettuce leaves arranged on individual salad plates. Garnish with cucumber mayonnaise (No. 707). Serves 6.

(816)   VEGETABLES IN TOMATO JELLY

1½ tablespoons gelatin
2 cups tomato juice
¼ cup vinegar
1 tablespoon sugar
½ bay leaf
½ teaspoon salt
⅛ teaspoon cayenne
1 small onion, minced

½ cup chopped cabbage
½ cup chopped celery
1 tablespoon minced green pepper
1 tablespoon minced pimiento
Juice of 1 lemon

Soak gelatin in cold water 5 minutes. Heat tomato juice, vinegar, sugar, bay leaf, salt, and cayenne together. Strain. Add to gelatin. Stir until dissolved. When partially set, add remaining ingredients. Pour into a lightly oiled mold. Chill until set. Serves 6.

(817)   BEET ASPIC

1 box aspic gelatin
1 cup hot water
1 bay leaf
2 whole peppers
1 clove
1 teaspoon tarragon vinegar
1 teaspoon chopped chives

1 can consommé
4 hard-cooked eggs (No. 202), cut in quarters lengthwise
1 small jar caviar
1 small cucumber, sliced
½ cup sliced beets

Let beets, bay leaf, peppers, clove, tarragon vinegar, and chopped chives stand in the hot water. Rinse a melon mold with cold water. Arrange caviar in center grooves, then arrange eggs and cucumbers, and lastly the beets. Strain spices from hot water and dissolve gelatin in it. Add consommé. Pour liquid into mold and chill in refrigerator for at least 12 hours. Unmold, decorate the divisions with cold Hollandaise sauce (No. 2022) put through pastry tube, and do not serve on a bed of lettuce. Serves 6.

(818)   VEGETABLE SALAD SUPREME

1 tablespoon gelatin
1 teaspoon salt
¼ cup sugar
2½ cups lemon carbonated beverage or ginger ale

1½ cups of fine chopped celery or diced, cooked vegetables, beets (No. 1726), peas (No. 1823), carrots (No. 1745), string beans (No. 1712), either alone or in combination

Soak gelatin in ½ cup cold water and dissolve over boiling water. Add all ingredients. Pour into individual molds and chill. Serve with mayonnaise (No. 701) on lettuce or watercress. A slice of hard-cooked egg (No. 202) placed in the bottom of each mold adds to the appearance. Serves 6.

(819)   FRUIT SALAD

1 grapefruit	3 slices pineapple
3 oranges	½ pound Malaga grapes
1 banana	

Peel grapefruit and oranges. Separate segments, discarding white membrane. Cut banana and pineapple in small cubes. Skin and seed grapes. Mix all ingredients. Drain. Pile lightly on lettuce leaves. Serve with pineapple dressing (No. 748). Serves 6.

(820)   WALDORF SALAD

3 cups diced apples	1 cup celery, cut in pieces
½ cup walnuts, cut in pieces	¾ cup mayonnaise (No. 701)

Mix apple, celery and nuts and moisten with mayonnaise. Arrange on crisp leaves of lettuce and garnish with whole nuts and candied cherries. Serves 6.

(821)   PEAR WALDORF SALAD

Prepare same as Waldorf salad (No. 820), using pear in place of apple.

(822)   BANANA AND PINEAPPLE SALAD

Make bed of fresh lettuce leaves on each plate. Put a slice of pineapple on top. Arrange slices of banana around pineapple and 1 slice on top. Put a maraschino cherry on top. Serve with pineapple dressing (No. 748), whipped cream dressing (No. 738), cream dressing (No. 744), or grapefruit salad dressing (No. 749).

(823)   PINEAPPLE AND CHEESE SALAD

1 head lettuce   ½ cup mayonnaise
6 slices pineapple   (No. 701)
¼ cup grated mild cheese

Arrange nest of lettuce on each plate. Put pineapple slice on each. Top with mayonnaise. Sprinkle with cheese. Serves 6.

(824)   FRUIT AND NUT SALAD

1 cup diced pineapple   1 cup sliced bananas
1 cup diced oranges   ¼ cup chopped walnuts

Mix fruits. Put on bed of lettuce leaves. Pour over pineapple dressing (No. 748). Sprinkle with nuts. Garnish with whipped cream. Serves 6.

(825)   ORANGE AND DATE SALAD

Head of lettuce   3 tablespoons chopped dates
36 orange segments   6 maraschino cherries
2 tablespoons chopped   1 cup Italian meringue
   walnuts   (No. 3207)

Arrange beds of lettuce on 6 plates. Put 6 orange segments on each, like the spokes of a wheel. Mix dates and walnuts and put in center as hub. Set a cherry on mixture. Pass Italian meringue. Serves 6.

(826)   BUTTERFLY SALAD

1 slice pineapple   ½ Malaga or Tokay grape,
1 slice apple, cored but   seeded
   unpeeled   1 strip pimiento
1 orange slice   Few leaves lettuce
1 teaspoon sugar   1 teaspoon chopped nuts
               Mayonnaise (No. 701)

Cut pineapple slice in half and place round edges together. Place apple slice on top. Top with orange slice, which has stood 20 minutes sprinkled with sugar. Form butterfly body with grape and pimiento. Garnish with lettuce. Sprinkle with nuts. Pass mayonnaise. Serves 1.

(827) ORANGE SALAD IN APPLE CUPS

6 tart red apples
2 cups sirup for stewed fruits (No. 33)
2 tablespoons gelatin
1½ cups orange carbonated beverage

1 cup diced celery
¾ cup lemon or lime carbonated beverage
½ cup chopped pecans
⅓ teaspoon salt

Scoop out apple centers. Put in saucepan. Add sirup for stewed fruits. Cover and cook slowly until tender. Cool. Soak gelatin in ¼ cup cold water 5 minutes. Dissolve over hot water. Add other ingredients. Mix well. Pour in apples. Chill until firm. Serve on nests of salad greens, garnished with strips of green pepper and pimiento and mayonnaise (No. 701). Serves 6.

(828) GRAPEFRUIT AND PEAR SALAD

1¼ cups canned grapefruit slices
1¼ cups canned pear halves
Endive

French dressing (No. 716) or mayonnaise (No. 701)

Cut pears in two, lengthwise. Arrange them alternately with grapefruit and endive. Serve with dressing. Serves 4.

(829) APPLE AND RAISIN SALAD

2 cups diced apple
1 cup raisins

½ cup fruit salad mayonnaise (No. 702)

Mix ingredients. Chill. Serve on lettuce leaves. Serves 6.

(830) STUFFED DATE SALAD

Wash dates. Remove stones. Stuff with chopped walnuts. Sprinkle with lemon juice. Serve on lettuce leaves. Allow 4 dates per serving.

(831) APPLE AND PIMIENTO SALAD

1 cup chopped apple
½ cup sliced celery
¼ cup chopped pimiento

½ cup fruit salad mayonnaise (No. 702)

Mix ingredients. Chill. Serve on lettuce leaves. Serves 4.

(832)   PRINCESS SALAD

1 cup crushed pineapple
1 cup chopped marshmal-
   lows
1 cup stoned cherries

½ cup pineapple dressing
   (No. 748)
1 cup chopped walnuts

Mix pineapple, marshmallows, cherries, and dressing. Chill.
Top with walnuts. Serve on lettuce leaves. Serves 6.

(833)   APPLE AND BANANA SALAD

1 cup chopped dates
2 cups diced apple
1 sliced banana

½ cup pineapple dressing
   (No. 748)

Mix ingredients. Chill. Serve on lettuce beds. Serves 6.

(834)   SUMMER SUNSET SALAD

1 small head lettuce
2 oranges
1 cup cottage cheese

1 cup blueberries
Lemon French dressing
   (No. 717)

Arrange lettuce on 4 individual salad plates. Peel oranges.
Slice thin. Cut each slice in half. Mound cottage cheese in center
of each salad plate. Surround with circle of blueberries. Edge
with half slices of orange. Serve with French dressing. Serves 4.

(835) PEACH OLIVE SALAD WITH CREAM CHEESE

⅔ cup chopped or sliced ripe
   olives
3 ounces cream cheese
1 tablespoon mayonnaise
   (No. 701)

4 large fresh peach halves
Shredded lettuce
Chopped almonds
Paprika

Blend together olives, cheese, and mayonnaise. Arrange fruit
halves, cut-side up, on beds of shredded lettuce, allowing one-
half to a serving. Cover tops generously with cheese and olive
filling. Sprinkle with chopped almonds and a dash of paprika.
Serves 4.

(836)   SUNFLOWER SALAD

Take sliced peaches and arrange on lettuce so as to form the petals of the flower. Place a scoop of chocolate ice cream (No. 2549) in the center. For the stem use a thin slice of pepper and for the leaves bits of lettuce. This is very attractive and can be served with any one of the many brands of dainty crackers. Allow 2 slices peaches per serving.

(837)   FRUIT CHEESE SALAD BOWL

3 oranges	1 cup cottage cheese
3 slices pineapple	French dressing (No. 716)
1 head lettuce	

Peel oranges and cut in sections, removing membrane. Cut sliced pineapple into large pieces. Put fruit in salad bowl with the lettuce. Add cottage cheese and a little French dressing and toss together lightly. Serves 6.

(838)   AVOCADO SALAD

1 large avocado	3 tablespoons olive oil
2 cups finely chopped fresh tomatoes	1 tablespoon lemon juice or vinegar
1 small onion, chopped	1 teaspoon salt
⅓ cup cottage cheese	Pepper

Peel avocado, remove seed and chop meat very fine. Toss with remaining ingredients in a salad bowl until thoroughly combined with oil and seasonings. Serves 6.

(839)   STUFFED AVOCADO IDEALE

2 cups boiled crab meat (No. 1227)	2 tablespoons lemon juice
1 cup celery, cut into small matchlike sticks	1 teaspoon finely chopped chives
¼ cup salad oil	4 anchovies
Salt—Pepper	¼ cup Russian dressing (No. 703)

2 avocados, cut in half lengthwise

Separate crab meat into large pieces. Marinate crab meat and celery separately for 15 minutes in seasoned salad oil. Scoop out balls from avocado, being careful not to break shell. Scrape out remaining pulp, mix with chives, and reserve. Sprinkle a few drops lemon juice over balls and pulp mixture to prevent darkening. Place crab meat in centers of empty shells; surround with avocado balls. Group celery sticks at each end of avocados and place one anchovy ring on top of each serving. Serve on crisp lettuce, in a bowl of cracked ice, with Russian dressing mixed with remaining avocado pulp and chives. Serves 4.

(840)   PRUNE SALAD

Remove stones from stewed prunes (No. 71) and fill with cream cheese. Allow 3 stuffed prunes per serving and serve on lettuce beds. Canned pears, apricots, or peaches may be substituted for prunes.

(841)   MOLDED FRUIT

2 tablespoons lemon gelatin	½ cup white grapes, halved
2 tablespoons sugar	1 cup orange carbonated
½ cup pineapple, cubed	beverage
½ cup maraschino cherries, halved	1 cup cherry carbonated beverage

Soak gelatin in ⅓ cup cold water. Dissolve over boiling water. Add sugar. Cool. Add beverages. When slightly stiffened add fruits. Pour into mold. Chill. Serves 8.

(842)   GINGER ALE FRUIT SALAD

2 tablespoons gelatin	1 cup grapes
¼ cup cold water	1 banana
½ cup boiling water	1 apple
¼ cup lemon juice	2 oranges
2 tablespoons sugar	¼ cup chopped nut meats
1 cup ginger ale	

Soak gelatin in cold water five minutes and dissolve in boiling water. Add lemon juice, sugar, and ginger ale. Cut grapes in halves and remove seeds. Slice banana. Peel and chop apple. Separate oranges into sections and remove membranes. When ginger ale mixture begins to thicken, fold in fruit and nuts. Turn into molds and chill. Serve on crisp lettuce leaves with fruit salad dressing (No. 702). Serves 6.

(843) CIDER GELATIN SALAD

2½ cups cider
2 tablespoons gelatin
1 cup chopped apples
½ cup chopped celery

¼ teaspoon salt
1 tablespoon chopped parsley
¼ cup chopped nuts

Soak gelatin in ½ cup cold cider 5 minutes. Bring remaining cider to boiling point. Pour into gelatin mixture, stirring until dissolved. Cool until congealing starts. Stir in other ingredients and pour into individual molds. Chill until firm. Unmold on beds of lettuce or watercress. Serve with French dressing (No. 716), mayonnaise (No. 701), or cooked salad dressing (No. 737). Serves 6.

(844) CRANBERRY SALAD

1 cup strained, unsweetened cranberry sauce (No. 54)
⅓ cup sugar
1 cup ginger ale
1 package gelatin

1 cup crushed drained pineapple
1 cup diced celery
2 tablespoons lemon juice
½ cup chopped walnut meats

Dissolve gelatin and sugar in hot cranberry sauce. When cool add lemon juice, ginger ale, and pineapple. When slightly congealed, stir in chopped celery and nut meats and turn into molds. When firm unmold and serve on lettuce with mayonnaise. (No. 701). A teaspoon of horseradish added to the salad dressing gives a delightful piquancy. Serves 6.

(845) ORANGE TOMATO ASPIC

1 tablespoon gelatin
1 cup orange juice
¾ cup canned condensed tomato soup

¼ teaspoon salt
Dash of cayenne
½ cup chopped celery

Soak gelatin in ½ cup orange juice 5 minutes. Dissolve over hot water. Add remaining orange juice. Mix well. Add soup, salt, and cayenne. Chill. When congealing starts, add celery. Pour into greased molds and chill. Serves 6.

(846) GRAPEFRUIT AND CHEESE JELLIED SALAD

1 cup grapefruit juice
1 cup cherry juice
1 package lemon-flavored
    gelatin

2½ cups grapefruit seg-
    ments
2 cups cottage cheese
8 melon slices

Mix juices and heat to boiling point. Remove from heat. Add gelatin and stir until dissolved. Cool until it starts to congeal. Add grapefruit and pour into a greased ring mold. Chill until firm. Unmold on bed of salad greens and fill center with cheese. Garnish with melon slices. Orange sections, or a combination of grapefruit and orange sections, may be used in this salad. Any raw fruit may be substituted for melon slices. Serves 8.

(847) FROZEN PEACH AND PECAN SALAD

8 peach halves
1 cup mayonnaise
    (No. 701)

1 cup cottage cheese
1 cup cream, whipped
1 cup pecans, chopped

Place the peach halves, hollow side up, in the freezing tray of refrigerator. Mix the cottage cheese, mayonnaise, cream and pecans together and pour over the peaches. Freeze about three to four hours. Serve on crisp lettuce. Serves 8.

(848)   COOL MELON MOLD

1 package lime-flavored
    gelatin
1 pint hot water

1½ cups cantaloupe or
    honey-dew melon cut
    in half-inch balls

Dissolve gelatin in hot water. Chill. When slightly thickened, fold in melon balls. Turn into mold. Chill until firm. Unmold on crisp lettuce and garnish with mayonnaise (No. 701), if for salad. Or, garnish with melon balls and mint and serve plain as dessert. Use only firm, ripe sweet melon. Serves 6.

(849)   FROZEN FRUIT SALAD

6 ounces cream cheese
⅓ cup mayonnaise
    (No. 701)
½ cup heavy cream

3½ cups canned fruit
    cocktail
½ cup chopped nuts
Few grains salt

Mash cheese. Add mayonnaise. Whip cream. Fold into cheese mixture. Drain fruit cocktail. Fold fruit, nuts, and salt into first mixture. Pack into freezing tray of mechanical refrigerator. Freeze firm. Serve on lettuce. Serves 8.

(850) SALAD MOLD

2 1/2 cups grapefruit sections
1 cup sliced dates
1 cup canned apricots
1/2 cup diced celery

2/3 cup mayonnaise
  (No. 701)
1 cup heavy cream

Drain grapefruit sections from juice. Drain apricots. Cut fruits into small pieces and combine with celery. Whip cream and add to mayonnaise. Blend with fruits and celery. Pack in trays of automatic refrigerator or pack in mold in ice and salt until frozen. Unmold and serve on lettuce and garnish with fruit salad mayonnaise (No. 702). Serves 6.

(851) FROZEN PINEAPPLE SALAD

1/2 cup cream cheese
1/4 cup mayonnaise
  (No. 701)
1/2 pound marshmallows, cut
  fine

1 small can crushed pine-
  apple
1/2 pint cream, whipped
1 cup ginger ale
Maraschino cherries for
  garnish

Cream the cheese. Add salad dressing, marshmallows, pine-apple and ginger ale. Blend well. Fold in the whipped cream. Freeze in tray of automatic refrigerator until solid. Cut into squares and serve on crisp lettuce with cherries as garnish. Serves 6.

(852) FROZEN WALDORF SALAD

2 eggs
1/2 cup sugar
1/8 teaspoon salt
1/2 cup pineapple juice
1/4 cup lemon juice

1/2 cup finely chopped
  celery
1/2 cup shredded pineapple
1 cup whipping cream
2 apples, chopped very
  fine

Beat eggs slightly. Add the sugar, salt, and fruit juices. Cook over hot water until thick. Cool. Fold in fruit and whipped cream. Pour into refrigerator tray and freeze. Cut in squares and serve on bed of lettuce. Serves 6.

(853) FROZEN FRUIT SUPREME

½ cup pears	¼ cup shredded almonds
½ cup peaches	1 cup mayonnaise
½ cup preserved figs	(No. 701)
½ cup shredded pineapple	1 cup whipping cream

Drain fruit and cut in small pieces. Whip cream and blend with mayonnaise. Combine all ingredients and freeze in refrigerator tray. Cut in squares and serve on bed of lettuce with mayonnaise. Other appropriate dressings are fruit salad mayonnaise (No. 702), banana nut mayonnaise (No. 711), marmalade mayonnaise (No. 713), honey French dressing (No. 735), or pineapple dressing (No. 748).

(854) FISH FLAKE SALADS

2 cups cold boiled fish flakes	3 tablespoons spiced vine-
1 cup minced celery	gar from sweet pickles
3 red radishes unpeeled, sliced	½ teaspoon salt
1 cup crisp cucumber, diced	Mayonnaise (No. 701)

Keep all ingredients cold. Combine fish flakes and vinegar. Combine well the fish flakes, cucumber, radishes, celery, seasonings, and mix with mayonnaise. Fill nests of lettuce leaves with the mixture and sprinkle with a dash of paprika. Serves 6.

(855) CRAB MEAT SALAD

1 pound boiled crab meat (No. 1227)	Juice of 1 lemon
	Salt—Pepper
1 head lettuce	Mayonnaise (No. 701)

Clean the lettuce and arrange into 6 nests about 4 inches across. Mix crab meat, lemon juice, seasoning as desired and enough mayonnaise to hold the crab meat together when pressed into a small cup. Invert the contents of the cup into a lettuce nest and repeat. Put a spoonful of mayonnaise over each. Not over 1 cup (total) of chopped celery, apple, hard-cooked egg (No. 202), olives, etc., may be mixed with the crab meat if desired. Serves 6.

(856) SHRIMP SALAD

1 pound boiled shrimp (No. 1272)	Juice of 1 lemon
1 head lettuce	Salt, paprika, and mayonnaise (No. 701)
2 cups finely minced celery	

Dice the shrimp and mix with celery, mayonnaise, lemon juice, and seasoning. Clean the lettuce and arrange into 6 nests about 4 inches across. Use a small cup as a mold, fill with the shrimp mixture and press firm; invert the molded contents into each lettuce nest. Add a teaspoonful of mayonnaise and paprika or crossed strips of pimiento. Serves 6.

(857) LOBSTER SALAD

This may be prepared as for shrimp salad (No. 856), using lobster meat (No. 1236) instead of shrimp. If desired, the celery may be omitted or replaced by capers, olives, etc. Serves 6.

(858) SALMON SALAD

2½ cups canned salmon	1 lemon
6 olives	½ cup mayonnaise
1 cup celery, chopped	(No. 701)

Flake the salmon. Mix with finely chopped celery and mayonnaise. Arrange on lettuce leaves and garnish with sliced olives. Serve with sliced lemon, placing a spoonful of mayonnaise on each serving. Serves 6.

(859) COLD SALMON AND STUFFED EGGS

1 pound can salmon	2 teaspoons oil, salt,
1 tablespoon lemon juice	pepper, paprika
6 hard-cooked eggs (No. 202)	1 teaspoon vinegar, cabbage or lettuce leaves
1 teaspoon mustard	

Flake the salmon, add lemon juice and let stand in a cold place. Boil the eggs hard and when cold, cut them in two lengthwise. Remove the yolks. Rub them through a sieve, blending them thoroughly with the mustard, oil, vinegar, and seasonings. Serve a mound of salmon and two pieces of stuffed egg on a cabbage or lettuce leaf. Serves 6.

(860)   SHRIMP AND GREEN PEA SALAD
IN GREEN PEPPER CUPS

1 cup boiled shrimp (No. 1272)	1 package lime gelatin
1 cup boiled green peas (No. 1823)	Salt—Pepper
	6 green peppers
½ cup mayonnaise (No. 701)	Lettuce

Remove veins from shrimp. Mix shrimp and peas. Moisten with mayonnaise. Season to taste with salt and pepper. Dissolve gelatin in 1 cup boiling water. Add 1 cup ice water. Add shrimp and peas. Wash green peppers. Slice off top. Remove seeds. Fill with shrimp-pea mixture. Chill. Serve on lettuce, garnished with mayonnaise forced through a pastry tube. Serves 6.

(861)   KIPPERED HERRING SALAD

14-ounce can kippered herring	¼ cup lemon French dressing (No. 717)
2½ cups diced, boiled beets (No. 1726)	1 head lettuce
1 sliced onion	6 deviled eggs (No. 216)

Skin and bone herring. Mix with beets. Separate onions into rings and add to mixture. Sprinkle with dressing. Chill 1 hour. Shred lettuce and make a bed. Put mound of salad on top. Arrange deviled eggs around. Serves 6. Mackerel or large sardines may be substituted for herring.

(862)   OYSTER SALAD

Scald oysters in their liquor. Drain. Cool. Serve on lettuce leaves, seasoned to taste with salt and pepper. An excellent dressing for this salad is made by adding 1 tablespoon lemon juice, ¼ cup grated horseradish, and 1 teaspoon vinegar to 2 cups whipped cream. Allow 3 oysters per serving.

(863)   SCALLOP SALAD

Follow recipe for shrimp salad (No. 856), using fried scallops (No. 1269) instead of shrimp.

(864)   SHRIMPS IN ASPIC

Cover bottom of mold with layer of aspic (No. 877) ¼ inch thick. When solid garnish with pimiento and whites of hard-cooked eggs (No. 202) cut into shapes of fish, flowers, or animals. Fill mold with shrimp (No. 1272), a few capers, and chopped nuts. Pour aspic over shrimp (just dissolved, not warm). Place in refrigerator until firm. Serve on lettuce leaves, garnished with radishes cut into rose shapes (No. 769), sliced hard-cooked eggs and tomatoes. Serves 6.

(865) JELLIED FISH SALAD WITH LEMON

1 tablespoon gelatin	¾ cup cooked salad dressing
½ cup celery	(No. 737)
1 cup flaked or canned fish, or crab meat, lobster or shrimp, cut in pieces	¼ cup chopped green pepper, or pimientos, or stuffed olives
	Salt—Paprika

Soak gelatin in ¼ cup cold water 5 minutes. Dissolve over hot water and add the dressing. Fold in the fish and celery. Add the peppers, pimientos, or olives, or some of each. Add salt and paprika to taste. Mold and chill. Serve on platter surrounded by lemons cut in quarters or into fancy shapes. Garnish with mayonnaise (No. 701), radish roses (No. 769), hard-cooked egg (No. 202) slices, and tomato slices. Serves 6.

(866)   JELLIED TUNA FISH

1 tablespoon lemon juice	½ teaspoon salt
1 tablespoon chopped parsley	⅛ teaspoon pepper
1 cup chopped celery	2 cups flaked tuna fish
1 cup cooked salad dressing (No. 737)	1 tablespoon gelatin
	¼ cup water

Add lemon juice, parsley, celery, salt, and pepper to the flaked fish. Soak gelatin in cold water 5 minutes and dissolve over hot water. Add to the cooked salad dressing and mix with the other ingredients. Pour into molds which have been dipped in cold water. Chill. Unmold. Garnish with lettuce and serve with sliced cucumbers. Serves 6.

(867) CHICKEN SALAD

To 3 cups of diced cold cooked chicken add 2¼ cups chopped celery. Season with salt and pepper and marinate in French dressing (No. 716). Chill. Moisten well with mayonnaise (No. 701) and mound in salad dish. Garnish with lettuce and sprinkle 1 tablespoon capers over the chicken. Decorate with olives or radish roses (No. 769) and slices of hard-cooked egg (No. 202). Serves 6.

(868) CHICKEN SALAD SUPREME

1 cup cold chopped cooked
  chicken
1 cup cold chopped cooked
  veal
1 cup diced celery
¼ cup chopped walnuts

½ cup mayonnaise
  (No. 701)
Salt—Pepper
Lettuce
6 stuffed olives

Mix chicken, veal, celery, walnuts, and mayonnaise. Season to taste with salt and pepper. Form into mounds on beds of lettuce in 6 salad plates. Top each mound with an olive. Serves 6. Other materials which are good, individually or in combination, in chicken salads are asparagus tips (No. 1704), chopped green pepper, shredded or chopped boiled cabbage (No. 1736), diced cooked ham, chopped celery, diced cucumbers, capers, sautéed mushrooms (No. 1801), ripe olives, diced pineapple, diced crisp bacon (No. 1464), cubed tomatoes, any cooked vegetable, diced oranges, any cooked meat, chopped boiled chestnuts (No. 3844), and hard-cooked eggs (No. 202).

(869) VEAL AND EGG SALAD

2 cups cold cooked veal,
  diced
1 cup diced boiled string
  beans (No. 1712) or
  celery, or equal parts of
  each
½ teaspoon salt

6 hard-cooked eggs
  (No. 202)
4 tablespoons salad oil
1½ tablespoons vinegar
3 tomatoes
Mayonnaise (No. 701)
Parsley and lettuce

Chop the eggs rather coarsely and combine them with the veal, string beans, oil, vinegar, salt, and a few grains of pepper. Let stand 30 minutes to marinate. Then add mayonnaise to moisten. Arrange the salad in a mound on a large platter, cover with mayonnaise. Border with lettuce and sliced tomatoes. Garnish with parsley. Serves 6.

(870)   CHEF'S SALAD

1 cup boiled green beans
  (No. 1712)
1 cup boiled carrot sticks
  (No. 1745)
1 cup celery strips
½ cup French dressing
  (No. 716)

1 head lettuce
2 cups cold cooked meat,
  diced
½ cup mayonnaise
  (No. 701)
1 tablespoon horseradish

Marinate green beans, carrots, and celery in French dressing two hours. Break lettuce into salad bowl. Combine meat with marinated vegetables and arrange over lettuce. Add mayonnaise mixed with horseradish. Toss lightly. Serves 6.

(871)   ROAST MEAT SALAD

1 head lettuce
2 cups lean cold cooked
  meat, diced
1 cup boiled potato
  (No. 1834), diced
1 onion, chopped
2 hard-cooked eggs
  (No. 202)
2 tomatoes

½ cup celery, diced
2 sweet pickles, chopped
1 green pepper
⅔ cup mayonnaise
  (No. 701)
½ tablespoon catchup
⅛ teaspoon pepper
2 teaspoons prepared
  mustard

Line salad bowl with lettuce leaves. Alternate in bowl, piles of meat, potato mixed with onion and celery, hard-cooked eggs, sliced or cut in dice and mixed with pickles. Separate piles with strips of green pepper. Garnish with quartered tomatoes. Sprinkle with salt and put on top the mayonnaise mixed with the catchup, mustard, and pepper. Chill. Serves 6.

(872) HAM, CHEESE, GREEN PEPPER SALAD

1 cup ground cooked ham
1 cup finely cut celery
6 ounces cream cheese
¼ cup chopped parsley

Salt
3 medium-size green
  peppers

Mix the ham, celery, cheese, and parsley thoroughly. Add salt to taste. Pack the mixture into peppers and chill. Slice and serve on lettuce with French dressing (No. 716). Serves 6.

(873)   HAM SALAD

2 cups diced cold cooked ham
1 teaspoon chopped onion
1 tablespoon chopped parsley
1 tablespoon chopped pickle
2 chopped hard-cooked eggs (No. 202)

Mix ingredients. Marinate in French dressing (No. 716). Chill. Serve with mayonnaise (No. 701). Serves 4. If desired, 1 cup shredded cabbage may be added to this. Other appropriate dressings are Russian mayonnaise (No. 703), horseradish mayonnaise (No. 708), curry French dressing (No. 720), chili dressing (No. 727), cooked salad dressing (No. 737), or bacon salad dressing (No. 755).

(874)   SWEETBREAD SALAD

Follow recipe for chicken salad (No. 867), using chopped, broiled sweetbreads (No. 1514) instead of chicken.

(875)   DUCK SALAD

2 cups chopped cold roast duck (No. 1556)
4 oranges, seeded and sliced
½ cup French dressing (No. 716)

Arrange duck and orange slices on lettuce leaves. Pour over dressing. Serves 6.

(876) KIDNEY BEAN AND TONGUE SALAD

2 cups cold smoked tongue, cut in julienne strips
2 cups boiled kidney beans (No. 1721)
¾ cup sweet pickle, chopped
3 tablespoons green pepper, chopped
1 cup celery, chopped
2 tablespoons pimiento, chopped
Salt and pepper
3 drops Tabasco
Mayonnaise (No. 701) or other salad dressing

Rub salad bowl with garlic. Add Tabasco to small amount of dressing. Combine all ingredients in bowl and toss lightly. using just enough dressing to bind together. Serves 8.

(877)   ASPIC JELLY

1 tablespoon gelatin	1/8 teaspoon pepper
1 pint stock (No. 501 or	Juice of 1/2 lemon
502)	1 egg white
1 teaspoon salt	1 eggshell
1 teaspoon mixed spices	

Put gelatin in 1/2 cup cold water. Soak 30 minutes. Dissolve over hot water. Add stock, salt, spices, pepper, and lemon juice. Heat slowly, stirring constantly, almost to boiling point. Add egg white and eggshell. Bring to boil while beating. Boil 1 minute. Strain through cheesecloth. Pour in mold. Chill until set.

(878)   SALAD RINGS

2 teaspoons gelatin	2 tablespoons pickle relish
2 cups cottage cheese	1 teaspoon Worcestershire
1/4 cup diced American cheese	sauce
2 tablespoons mayonnaise	1/2 teaspoon salt
(No. 701)	

Soak gelatin in 1/2 cup cold water 5 minutes. Dissolve over hot water. Combine with other ingredients and pour into 6 individual ring molds. Chill until firm. Centers may be filled with mixed or plain vegetables, or with seafood, chilled and combined with mayonnaise. Serves 6.

(879)   EGG SALAD

1. Cut the whites of hard-cooked eggs (No. 202), into eighths lengthwise. Arrange on lettuce to simulate the petals of a flower. Put yolks through ricer and arrange in the center of whites. Serve with cooked salad dressing (No. 737).

2. Cut eggs lengthwise in quarters and serve on lettuce with cooked salad dressing.

3. Chop whites finely and arrange on lettuce. Put yolk through ricer and mound in the center. Serve with cooked salad dressing.

4. Diced hard-cooked eggs and sliced cucumbers may be added to potato salad (No. 780). Eggs and fish combine very well with watercress or escarole.

(880)   CHEESE AND NUT SALAD

1 cup mild cheese	1/3 cup chopped nuts
1 tablespoon melted butter	1/3 cup chopped pimiento
1/2 cup sweet cream	1/3 cup chopped olives

Mash the cheese. Moisten with cream and melted butter. Season with salt and cayenne. Add chopped nuts, pimiento, and olives. Press into a mold and let stand 2 hours. Cut in slices and serve on lettuce with mayonnaise (No. 701). Combine mild cream cheese with pimiento. Shape into small balls and serve on head lettuce with French dressing (No. 716). Serves 6.

Other Cheese Combinations.—Grate raw carrots and combine them with cottage cheese in the proportion of half carrot and half cheese. Season with mayonnaise. Form into balls and serve on lettuce with French dressing. Dates are good stuffed with cream cheese. Slices of orange may be added. Tomatoes also may be stuffed with cheese.

(881)   MACARONI AND OLIVE SALAD

1 cup sliced boiled maca-roni (No. 2302)	1 tablespoon chopped parsley
1 cup chopped celery	1/2 cup cooked dressing
3/4 cup chopped stuffed olives	(No. 737) or mayon-
1 tablespoon chopped onion	naise (No. 701)

Mix thoroughly. Chill. Serves 6.

(882)   WATER LILY SALAD

Cut a hard-cooked egg (No. 202) in halves, lengthwise. emove yolk. Mash. Moisten half of yolk with a little cooked essing (No. 737). Form into a small round in center of a uce-lined dish. Cut each half of egg white in three strips, thwise, and arrange as petals. Sprinkle with remaining yolk. s 1.

COTTAGE CHEESE SALAD

ps cottage cheese	1 tablespoon chow-chow
p piquante mayon-ise (No. 704)	1 tablespoon chopped nuts
	Lettuce
spoon chopped 'ento	1/2 cup Russian mayon-naise (No. 703)

Mix cheese, piquante mayonnaise, chow-chow, pimiento, and nuts. Pack into small cups or molds. Chill. Unmold on lettuce leaves. Garnish with Russian mayonnaise. Serves 6.

(884) COTTAGE CHEESE AND STRAWBERRY SALAD

2 cups cottage cheese
2 cups sliced strawberries
3 tablespoons honey French dressing (No. 735)

Lettuce
½ cup fruit salad mayonnaise (No. 702)

Mix cheese, strawberries, and French dressing. Put on lettuce leaves. Garnish with mayonnaise. Serves 6.

(885) BREAD SALAD

½ cup stoned chopped ripe olives
1 cup chopped celery
1 tablespoon chopped pimiento
1 teaspoon salt
½ teaspoon paprika
1 tablespoon olive oil
1 tablespoon lemon juice

2 hard-cooked eggs (No. 202)
1½ cups bread or cracker crumbs
3 tablespoons butter or fat
Lettuce
½ cup mayonnaise (No. 701)

Mix olives, celery, pimiento, salt, and paprika. Add olive oil and lemon juice. Chill for 1 hour. Chop whites of eggs. Sauté crumbs in butter until golden brown. Drain. Add olive and celery mixture and chopped egg whites. Chill. Toss together and serve on lettuce leaves. Sprinkle with egg yolks rubbed through a sieve. Serve with mayonnaise or any preferred salad dressing. Serves 6.

(886) CUCUMBER PEAR ASPIC

1 package lime-flavored gelatin
1¾ cups hot water
2 tablespoons vinegar
½ teaspoon salt

1 cup drained, diced cucumber
1 cup diced canned pears
6 halves, canned pears
6 cream cheese balls

Dissolve gelatin in hot water. Add vinegar and ¼ teaspoon salt. Chill until slightly thickened. Season cucumber with ¼ teaspoon salt. Add pears. Fold into slightly thickened gelatin.

Turn into individual molds. Chill until firm. Unmold on bed of crisp escarole or lettuce. Garnish with halved pears and cream cheese balls. Serve with mayonnaise (No. 701) if desired. Serves 6.

(887)   CARROT AND CABBAGE SALAD (JELLIED)

1 package lemon gelatin	1 cup grated carrots
1 pint hot water	1 cup finely shredded
2 tablespoons vinegar	cabbage
1 teaspoon salt	

Dissolve gelatin in hot water. Add vinegar and ½ teaspoon salt. Chill until slightly thickened. Season carrots and cabbage with ½ teaspoon salt and fold into slightly thickened gelatin. Turn into mold. Chill until firm. Unmold on crisp lettuce. Garnish with mayonnaise (No. 701). Serves 6.

(888)   WINTER VEGETABLE SALAD BOWL

1 cup boiled cauliflower (No. 1755)	6 boiled carrots (No. 1745), cut into fourths, length-wise
1 cup boiled string beans (No. 1712)	½ head lettuce
1 cup boiled beets (No. 1726)	½ cup Russian French Dressing (No. 725)

Arrange lettuce in a salad bowl. Arrange the cauliflower, string beans, and beets in separate piles. Then place long pieces of carrot between each pile of vegetables. Pour salad dressing over the vegetables and chill ½ hour in the refrigerator. Serves 6.

(889)   HOLIDAY SALAD

Red Layer:

1 package lemon-flavored gelatin	1 can condensed tomato soup
1 cup boiling water	

Dissolve the gelatin in the boiling water. Then add the soup and mix well. Pour into a ring mold and set in refrigerator until firm.

Green Layer:

1 can condensed Scotch broth
1 can water
1 tablespoon lime juice

1 package lime-flavored
    gelatin
1 drop peppermint flavor

Add the water to the broth and heat to boiling. Dissolve the gelatin in the hot soup, add lime juice and 1 drop of peppermint flavor, if desired. Pour on the red section of mold and set in refrigerator until firm. Serves 8.

(890)   TROPICAL SALAD

Place a mound of cottage cheese in the center of a salad plate. Make a slight depression in the center and fill with strawberry preserves   Surround cheese with nosegays of water-cress. Top cress with well-chilled and thoroughly drained canned pineapple gems, about 6 to a serving. Serve at once.

(891)   LIME RING WITH PINEAPPLE

1 package lime-flavored
    gelatin
1 14-ounce can pineapple
Sirup drained from pineapple
    and water to make 1 pint
        Powdered sugar

1 cup irradiated evaporated
    milk, chilled
1 tablespoon lemon juice
1 pint red raspberries
8 sprigs of mint

Dissolve gelatin in hot sirup and water. When it begins to set, whip milk until very stiff. Add lemon juice and fold into gelatin. Pour into a ring mold which has been rinsed in cold water. Put in a cold place until set. When ready to serve, unmold on a cold platter. Fill center with pineapple gems which have been thoroughly chilled and well-drained. Top with red raspberries. Garnish with sprigs of mint which have been dipped in powdered sugar to make edges frosty. Serves 8.

(892)   WREATH SALAD

1 14-ounce can unsweetened
    sliced pineapple
Small seedless white grapes
½ cup orange juice

1 3-ounce package cream
    cheese
Watercress
8 white pillow mints

Drain pineapple slices which have been well-chilled in can. Spread one side of each slice with cream cheese which has been softened with a fork. Top cream cheese with a double row of grapes which have been cut in half lengthwise, placing cut side next to cheese. Chill in refrigerator ½ hour. Serve each slice on salad plate. Garnish with watercress. Serve with orange mint dressing which has been made by blending crushed mints with orange juice. Oranges should be well-chilled before squeezing juice. Serves 4.

(893)   HAWAIIAN CHICKEN SALAD

2½ cups cooked chicken, cut into ½-inch squares
1 14-ounce can pineapple gems, drained
1 cup celery, cut in ½-inch pieces

3 tablespoons salad oil
2 tablespoons lemon juice
¼ teaspoon salt
5 tablespoons mayonnaise (No. 701)
¼ cup shredded almonds

Combine chicken, pineapple gems, and celery. Mix salad oil, lemon juice, and salt and marinate salad for 1 hour. Then add mayonnaise and mix well. Serve on a bed of greens and sprinkle shredded almonds over the top. Serves 6.

(894)   BANANA MELON BALL SALAD

1 banana
Melon balls

Salad greens

Peel and cut banana, lengthwise, into halves. Place halves, cut sides up, side by side, in center of salad plate. Place a few melon balls at each end, between the banana halves. Garnish with crisp greens. Serve with mayonnaise (No. 701). Serves 1.

(895)   FRUIT SALAD BOWL

Orange and melon slices are swirled on a fruit mixture in a bed of curly endive. Melon balls and fresh strawberries further decorate this attractive summer salad. When serving apportion some of each fruit to each guest. Serve with honey French dressing (No. 735).

(896)   BANANA FRUIT PLATE

1 sliced canned pineapple
½ ripe banana
Salad greens

Fresh berries, grapes, or cherries

Cut pineapple slice into halves and arrange them at back of salad plate, with one slice overlapping the other. Peel and slice banana. Arrange one row of 3 or 4 overlapping slices on each side of the plate. Garnish center with greens and fill in remaining space with berries. Serve with mayonnaise (No. 701) or fruit salad mayonnaise (No. 702). Serves 1.

(897)   BANANA PINEAPPLE SALAD

    2 slices canned pineapple   Salad greens
    1 ripe banana

Place a ring of pineapple around each end of a peeled banana. Garnish with crisp salad greens and berries, if desired. Serve with mayonnaise (No. 701) or fruit salad mayonnaise (No. 702). Serves 1.

(898)   PINEAPPLE BANANA CRISSCROSS

    1 ripe banana   Cherries or berries
    2 slices canned pineapple   Salad greens

Peel and cut banana lengthwise into quarters. Place two quarters on salad plate, crossing one over the other. Cut through one side of pineapple slice and twist into S-shape so that it will stand upright where the banana pieces cross. Place a cluster of cherries or a mound of berries beside the banana. Garnish with salad greens. Serve with French dressing (No. 716). Serves 2.

(899)   CAROTENE SALAD

    1½ cups orange segments   Any desired salad dressing
    1½ cups finely cut raw carrot   Lettuce or shredded cabbage
    ½ cup raisins   ½ cup chopped peanuts

Toss orange, carrot, and raisins together lightly with 2 forks. Moisten with dressing. Serve on lettuce leaves or cabbage. Sprinkle with peanuts. Serves 6.

Breads

THE basic ingredient of bread, pastry, and most cakes is flour or meal. Wheat makes the best flour for most purposes because it contains proteins which combine in the presence of moisture to form gluten, which imparts a distinctive texture and character to wheat doughs.

Flours, except whole wheat, should always be sifted once before measuring and then put lightly into the measure and leveled. Whole-wheat flours and meals should be stirred and then measured in the same manner as white flour. Shortenings should be packed hard into the measure at room temperature. Sugar can be measured without sifting. All measurements are level. Accurate measuring is essential for good results.

Average proximate composition of different types of wheat and wheat flour[1]

Type of wheat and flour	Carbohydrates (mostly starch)	Fat	Protein	Water	Mineral matter (ash)	Type of wheat and flour	Carbohydrates (mostly starch)	Fat	Protein	Water	Mineral matter (ash)
	Per cent	*Per cent*	*Per cent*	*Per cent*	*Per cent*		*Per cent*	*Per cent*	*Per cent*	*Per cent*	*Per cent*
Hard wheat:						Soft wheat:					
Grain............	70.9	1.8	12.3	13.2	1.8	Grain...........	72.2	1.9	11.0	13.2	1.7
Whole-wheat flour.........	70.9	1.8	12.3	13.2	1.8	Whole-wheat flour.........	72.2	1.9	11.0	13.2	1.7
Straight flour....	73.7	1.1	11.5	13.2	.5	Straight flour....	75.8	1.2	9.4	13.2	.4
Patent flour.....	74.6	1.0	10.8	13.2	.4	Patent flour.....	76.7	1.1	8.7	13.2	.3

[1] Calculated on 13.2 percent moisture basis for purposes of comparison.

The average proximate composition of different types of hard-wheat and soft-wheat flours is shown in the above table.

Though no indication of vitamin content is given, experiments have shown that in general the highly refined flours contain practically none of the vitamins present in the whole-grain products.

GENERAL INSTRUCTIONS FOR WHITE BREAD

Ingredients in the following proportions will make about 3 ½ pounds of bread. The liquid may be milk, water, potato water or any combination of these.

2¾ cups liquid
½ to 1 ounce (1 to 2 cakes) yeast
3 tablespoons sugar
4 teaspoons salt

2 tablespoons fat
About 2¼ pounds, or 2¼ quarts, sifted hard-wheat flour

From these ingredients bread may be made by various methods. The common standard ways, known as the straight-dough and sponge methods, are described here, and suggestions are given for varying them.

STRAIGHT-DOUGH METHOD

With the ingredients in these proportions and with the temperature about 82° F., bread can be made according to the straight-dough method with compressed yeast in about 4 hours from the time the dough is mixed until the loaves are put into the oven. If the time must be shortened, twice or even three times as much yeast may be used. The dough must then, of course, be watched very closely, as there is more danger of letting the fermentation go too far.

Mixing.—A small quantity of the liquid, about one-half cup, should be set aside for softening the yeast. If milk is used, it must be scalded first to check the growth of bacteria, and then cooled. In this case the part reserved for soaking the yeast should be cooled quickly, and the rest while still hot may be poured over the sugar, salt, and fat.

Other liquids than milk usually do not require heating, but often this is done for convenience in dissolving and melting the sugar, salt, and fat. In any case the liquid mixture should be brought to a temperature below 100° F. before being mixed with the yeast. The exact temperature depends on that of the room and of the flour, and should be so adjusted to these as to bring the temperature of the dough to about 82° F.

The flour, except about 1 cup, should be added to the liquid and mixed thoroughly with a spoon, the hands, or a mechanical bread mixer. All the flour may be added at once if experience has shown the amount necessary. It is impossible, however, to tell beforehand exactly how much flour will be required unless flour from this same lot has already been used. The experienced bread maker tells by the feel of the dough when enough flour has been added. The quantity given in the above proportions is about right for rather strong flour. If the flour is extremely strong, 2¼ pounds will be too much, but if it is of only average strength more will be needed. Usually, with a strong flour, the dough should be about as soft as can be conveniently handled.

Kneading.—When the flour and liquid are thoroughly mixed and the dough no longer sticks to the sides of the mixing bowl, it is ready to be kneaded. The main purpose of the kneading is to develop the gluten. This first kneading should be thorough, but heavy pressure is not needed. If a bread mixer is used, it kneads as well as mixes.

If the bread is kneaded by hand, it should be turned out on a clean floured board and worked quickly with the palms of the hands until it is soft, smooth, and elastic. Since the dough is sticky at first there may be a tendency to knead in the flour on the board. Therefore only a thin film of flour should be used on the board, for as the gluten develops in the dough the stickiness disappears.

Dough made from hard-wheat flour requires more kneading than that made from soft-wheat flour. Overkneading of doughs from either flour may, however, injure the baking quality of the gluten and produce a loaf of poor texture and volume.

First rising.—After kneading, the dough should be formed into a ball and put into a greased bowl to rise. The easiest way to keep the surface from drying and cracking is to turn the dough over once or twice in the bowl so that the whole surface is thinly greased. Fat should be used sparingly, however, so that no streaks of it will show later in the bread. A clean cloth over the bowl and a plate or other tight cover will help to control the temperature, to keep out the dust, and to prevent drying. The bowl may be placed in a pan of warm water to raise the temperature of the dough, if it has cooled off, and keep it between 80° and 85° F. When the dough has risen to about double its original bulk, it should be tested with the finger to determine whether it is ready to punch down for a second rising.

Punching down.—When the dough is light enough, the center

should be punched in, the sides pulled over and pressed into the center, and the ball of dough turned with the smooth side up. This can be done in less than a minute and is preferable to taking the dough out on the board. The purpose of punching down is to let out some of the gas so that fermentation can continue without injuring the gluten by causing it to stretch too far.

Second rising.—The second rising is not used with soft-wheat flour, but with hard-wheat flour will not take so long as the first if the temperature is right. It helps to give a good texture and fine, even grain. When the dough has again risen to the same volume as before, it is ready to be punched down and divided.

Dividing.—The dough should be so divided that each piece when placed in the baking pan will fill it about half full. After being divided, the dough should be rounded into balls to seal over the cut surfaces and allowed to stand a few minutes before molding.

Molding.—The loaves are molded by flattening each of them on the board into an oblong piece and then folding and sealing the edges together with the palms of the hands. This is repeated several times, each time folding a different way. The last time the sides are brought together into the center and the loaf is placed, sealed edges down, in a greased pan for the last rising. The top surface should be lightly greased to prevent drying out and to keep the surface elastic. Otherwise a compact grain will form below the crust.

Rising in the pans.—The shape of the pan makes a difference in the volume and quality of the loaf. A shallow pan (about 4 by 8½ by 3 inches) that holds a pound or a pound-and-a-half loaf is better than a deep, narrow pan. The loaf bakes more quickly, has a crust on all sides, and makes a more attractive slice if baked singly in such a pan. The material of the pan affects the temperature of baking. Glass and enamelware require lower temperatures than such metals as tin and aluminum.

The temperature (80° to 85°F.) should be just as carefully regulated during the last rising as for the two earlier periods. The pans may be set in warm water and covered with a clean cloth. When the loaves have about doubled in bulk the surface should be lightly pressed with the finger to test whether they are ready to be baked.

Baking.—The oven should be moderately hot at first (about 385°F.) for a pound loaf. It can be baked at a higher temperature and more quickly than a pound-and-a-half loaf. Unless the oven bakes very evenly, the loaves should be turned around after they have been in about 15 minutes. The temperature of the oven should then be lowered to 350° F. If a coal or wood range is used, the temperature at the start should be 400° F. or lower.

Baking will require from 45 minutes to 1 hour, depending on the temperature of the oven and the size of the loaf. When the loaves shrink from the sides of the pan and give a hollow sound when tapped, the bread is done. Brushing the loaves with milk or butter just before they are taken from the oven oftentimes improves the color of the crusts and makes them glossy and more tender, but less crisp. As soon as the loaves are taken from the oven they should be turned out of the pans and placed on a rack to cool. They should not be covered while they are warm.

SPONGE METHOD

With dried yeast, which takes longer to become active than compressed yeast, it is generally more satisfactory to make a sponge early in the morning or the night before the bread is to be baked. With the following exceptions, the dough is mixed and handled in the same way as in the straight-dough method with compressed yeast.

The dried yeast cake should be broken up and soaked in luke-warm water until it is soft, or for about one-half hour before mixing.

If the sponge is to stand overnight, only about half as much yeast is needed.

The liquid, the yeast, and half of the flour should be mixed and left until they form a light, frothy sponge. For a quick sponge the sugar also may be mixed with these other ingredients.

When the sponge is to rise overnight, ordinary room temperature (65° to 75° F.) is warm enough; but for a shorter sponge process the temperature should be the same as for dough (80° to 85° F). When the sponge is light, it should be stirred up well. The salt, sugar, melted fat, and the rest of the flour are then added to make a dough.

After the dough is mixed it is handled in the same way as in the straight-dough method.

BREAD FROM SOFT-WHEAT FLOURS

Soft-wheat flours, because of the smaller quantity or poorer quality of the gluten, require less moisture than hard-wheat flours to make a dough of the right consistency. Therefore proportionately less liquid or more flour is used, since the dough is made a little stiffer. It will not "tighten up" during the first rising, as does hard-wheat flour dough. Instead it may become softer or slacken a little. The proportions for bread made with hard-wheat flour are based on 2¾ cups of liquid and 2¼ pounds, or 2¼ quarts, of flour. For the same quantity of liquid about 2½ pounds, or 2¾ quarts, of sifted soft-wheat flour will be required.

SPOILAGE IN BREAD

There are three principal kinds of spoilage in bread—sourness, ropiness, and mold.

Sourness or high acidity in bread results from abnormal fermentation due to the growth of lactic acid bacteria in the dough for too long a period before baking. To prevent this the rising of the dough must be stopped at the right point.

Ropiness or sliminess in bread shows itself in the center of the loaf, some time after the bread is baked. It results from the growth of certain highly resistant spore-forming bacteria. In summer, when bread is stored at relatively high temperatures, this type of fermentation may cause considerable waste. The organisms causing ropiness seem to be present in some cases in the flour, but they also may be in potatoes, or in liquid yeast that is saved from one baking to another, or on utensils.

To prevent ropiness, be sure that the utensils are not carrying the infection. Cracks or seams harbor bacteria and make them difficult to destroy. Boil the utensils in water and vinegar combined in the proportion of 1 part of vinegar to 3 parts of water. If the bread continues to be ropy and potatoes are being used, omit them from the next baking. If liquid yeast is being saved from one baking to another, discard it and make fresh yeast. If these precautions are not successful, add about 2 teaspoons of 90-grain white vinegar to the liquid ingredients for an average baking of 3½ pounds of dough.

QUICK BREADS AND PASTRY

Quick breads are so called because they are made with leavening that acts more quickly than yeast. The other essential ingredients are the same as for yeast breads—flour, fat, and liquid. Salt is added for seasoning, often sugar also, and many quick breads contain eggs.

With a few exceptions, such as popovers, which are raised by steam, quick breads require baking powder or other chemical leavening agent. Pastry, such as piecrust, has no leavening added. Air may be beaten into a batter, but generally is added by means of beaten eggs.

Ingredients and proportions for quick breads and pastry

Class	Flour, all-purpose	Baking powder	Salt	Sugar	Eggs	Milk	Fat
	Cups	*Teaspoons*	*Teaspoon*	*Table-spoons*	*Number*	*Cup*	*Table-spoon*
Popovers....................	1	....	1/8	....	2	1	1
							Teaspoon
Timbale cases..............	1	....	1/2	....	1	3/4	1
Cover batter no. 1...........	1	1 1/2	1/2	....	1	3/4	1
Cover batter no. 2...........	1 3/4	2 1/2	1/2	2	1	1	1
							Table-spoons
Fritters...................	2	3	1	2	2	1	1
Griddlecakes...............	1 1/2–1 3/4	2–2 1/2	3/4	0–1	1	1	2
Waffles...................	1 1/2	2	1/2	1	1–2	1	2
Muffins...................	2	3	1/2	0–2	1	1	2–4
Biscuits...................	3	4	1	....	....		4–6
Pastry, plain...............	1 1/2	....	1	....	....	(1)	5–6

¹ About 2 1/2 tablespoons of water.

(901)   BREAD

1 cup milk	2 1/2 teaspoons salt
3 tablespoons shortening	1 yeast cake
2 tablespoons sugar	6 1/2 cups flour

Add 1 cup water to milk. Heat. Add shortening, sugar, and salt. Dissolve yeast cake in 1/4 cup lukewarm water and add to mixture. Stir in 3 or 4 cups flour and beat thoroughly. Cover and set in a warm place to rise over night. In the morning add enough flour to make a firm dough. Knead on a floured board until smooth and elastic to touch. Cover and set in a warm place to rise until treble in bulk. Knead again. Shape into loaves and put in greased bread pans. Cover and let rise again until double in bulk. Bake in moderate oven (350° F.) 50 to 60 minutes.

(902)   BREAD

1 cup milk	1 1/2 teaspoons salt
2 tablespoons shortening	1 yeast cake
1 1/2 tablespoons sugar	2 1/2 cups flour

Heat milk. Add shortening, sugar, and salt. Dissolve yeast
cake in 2 tablespoons lukewarm water. Add to mixture. Add
1 cup flour and beat thoroughly. Cover and set in a warm place
to rise until light, about 1 hour. Add enough flour to make a
firm dough. Knead on a floured board until smooth and elastic
to touch. Cover and set in a warm place to rise until treble in
bulk. Knead again. Shape into a loaf and put in greased bread
pan. Cover and set in a warm place to rise until double in bulk.
Bake in moderate oven (350° F.) 50 to 60 minutes.

(903)   FIG BREAD

Follow recipe for bread (No. 901 or 902), adding 1 cup
chopped figs to dough.

(904)   PRUNE BREAD

Follow recipe for bread (No. 901 or 902), adding ½ cup
chopped, stewed prunes (No. 71) to dough.

(905)   FRIED BREAD BALLS

Break pieces the size of walnuts from well-raised bread dough
(No. 901 or 902). Fry 4 to 5 minutes in deep, hot fat (375° F.).
Serve as bread or with maple sirup.

(906)   FRENCH BREAD

2 teaspoons sugar	3 quarts sifted flour
1 yeast cake	½ teaspoon cornstarch
2 teaspoons salt	

Blend sugar and yeast with a knife or back of a spoon. Add
1 quart lukewarm water. Put flour in a mixing bowl. Hollow out
center and add liquid mixture. Mix and knead on a flowered
board until smooth and elastic. Cover and set in a warm place
to rise until double in bulk, about 4 hours. Knead again and
cover and set in a warm place to rise again until double in bulk.
Mold into long loaves. Put on baking sheets. Cover and again
set in a warm place to rise until double in bulk. Bake in moderate oven (350° F.) 1¼ to 1½ hours. Fifteen minutes before
cooking is finished brush with a mixture made by blending cornstarch in 2 teaspoons cold water and boiling paste 5 minutes in
⅓ cup boiling water.

(907)   RYE BREAD

6⅓ cups sifted rye flour	3 cups lukewarm water
4½ cups sifted hard-wheat flour	2 cakes yeast
	3 tablespoons sugar
5½ cups sifted all-purpose flour	5 teaspoons salt
	2 tablespoons melted fat

Sift the rye flour with the white flour and proceed as for bread (No. 901) until ready to form the loaves. Mold into long, sharply pointed loaves, place on a greased shallow pan or one on which flour or corn meal has been sprinkled. Rub fat lightly on the tops of the loaves. Cover and let rise until the bulk has increased 1¾ times. Make about three slashes with a sharp knife at an angle across the top of each loaf. Bake pound loaves for 30 to 35 minutes in a hot oven (400° F.). A pan of hot water should be placed in the oven during baking. Remove loaves from pan and glaze with a mixture of egg white and water or cooked starch paste.

(908)   CARAWAY LOAF

Add ½ cup sliced, seedless raisins and 1 tablespoon caraway seeds to French bread (No. 906) or rye bread (No. 907).

(909)   WHOLE WHEAT BREAD

1 cup milk	2 tablespoons lukewarm water
2 tablespoons shortening	
4 tablespoons sugar	2 cups flour
1 teaspoon salt	1½ to 2 cups whole wheat flour
1 yeast cake	

Heat milk and add shortening, sugar, and salt. When lukewarm add the yeast cake dissolved in the warm water. Add the flour and beat until smooth. Cover and set in a warm place to rise for about 1 hour. Add the whole wheat flour and knead until it is elastic to touch and does not stick to an unfloured board. Cover and set in a warm place to rise until double in bulk. Knead again until free from air bubbles. Put in a greased loaf pan. Cover and set in a warm place to rise until double in bulk. Bake in a moderate oven (350° F.) 50 to 60 minutes.

(910)   GRAHAM BREAD

1 cake yeast
1½ tablespoons salt
2 tablespoons sugar

2 tablespoons melted
  shortening
5 cups whole wheat flour

6 cups white flour

Dissolve yeast in 2 tablespoons lukewarm water. Add 4 cups lukewarm water, salt, sugar, and shortening. Sift flour together and add to mixture, making a firm dough. Knead on floured board until smooth and elastic to the touch. Cover and set in warm place to rise until double in bulk. Then proceed as for whole wheat bread (No. 909).

(911)   RAISIN BREAD

1 cup milk
3 tablespoons shortening
4 tablespoons sugar
1 teaspoon salt

1 yeast cake
4½ cups flour
1 cup raisins

Heat milk. Add shortening, sugar, and salt. Dissolve yeast cake in 2 tablespoons lukewarm water. Add to mixture. Add 2 cups flour and beat until smooth. Cover and set in a warm place to rise for 1 hour. Add raisins and enough flour to make a firm dough. Knead until smooth and elastic to touch. Cover and set in a warm place to rise until double in bulk. Knead again. Form into loaf and put in greased baking pan. Cover and set in warm place to rise until double in bulk. Bake in moderate oven (350°F.) 50 to 60 minutes.

(912)   CHEESE BREAD

Add ⅔ cup grated cheese to recipe for whole-wheat bread (No. 909).

(913)   PEANUT-BUTTER BREAD

Add ½ cup peanut butter to recipe for whole-wheat bread (No. 909).

(914)   COCONUT BREAD

Add ½ cup shredded coconut to recipe for whole-wheat bread (No. 909).

(915)   NUT BREAD

Add ⅔ cup chopped nuts to recipe for whole-wheat bread (No. 909).

(916)   RAISED CORN BREAD

3 cups corn meal	1½ tablespoons salt
1 yeast cake	¼ cup sugar
9 cups whole-wheat flour	¼ cup melted shortening

Pour 3 cups boiling water gradually into corn meal, mixing thoroughly. Add 1 cup cold water. Cool to lukewarm. Dissolve yeast in 2 tablespoons lukewarm water and add to mixture. Add 2 cups whole-wheat flour. Mix well. Cover and set in warm place until light, about 2 hours. Add enough whole-wheat flour to make a firm dough. Knead on a floured board until smooth and elastic to the touch. Cover and set in a warm place to rise until double in bulk. Then proceed as for whole-wheat bread (No. 909).

(917)   OATMEAL BREAD

3 cups finely ground rolled oats	2 cakes compressed yeast
9 cups sifted all-purpose flour	4 tablespoons sugar
	4 teaspoons salt
3½ cups milk	2 tablespoons fat

Mix the rolled oats with the white flour and proceed as for bread (No. 901). These ingredients make 4 pounds of bread.

(918)   SOYBEAN BREAD

4½ cups sifted soybean flour	2 cakes compressed yeast
8½ cups sifted all-purpose flour	4 tablespoons sugar
	4 teaspoons salt
2¾ cups milk	2 tablespoons fat

Sift the soybean flour with the wheat flour and proceed as for bread (No. 901). These ingredients make 4⅓ pounds of bread.

(919) LIMA BEAN BREAD

2 cups sifted lima-bean flour	3 cups milk
8½ cups sifted all-purpose flour	2 tablespoons sugar
	4 teaspoons salt
1 to 2 cakes yeast	2 tablespoons fat

Sift the lima-bean flour with the white flour and proceed as for bread (No. 901). Yield: 4½ pounds bread.

(920) GLUTEN BREAD

1 yeast cake	1 tablespoon melted shortening
3 cups lukewarm water or milk	5½ cups gluten flour
1 teaspoon salt	

Dissolve yeast in 1 cup liquid. Add balance of liquid and shortening. Sift flour and salt together and beat into liquid. Knead until smooth. Put in greased baking pans. Cover and let rise until double in bulk, about 2 hours. Bake in moderate oven (350° F.) 50 minutes.

(921) CINNAMON YEAST LOAF

4 cups well-raised bread dough (No. 901)	4 tablespoons sugar
	1 tablespoon cinnamon
2 tablespoons melted butter	1 egg yolk
1 well-beaten egg	

Knead butter, egg, and sugar into well-raised bread dough. Roll on floured board ¾-inch thick. Place in greased baking pan. Set in warm place to rise until very light. Gash top. Brush with beaten egg yolk. Sprinkle with mixture of 2 tablespoons sugar and 1 tablespoon cinnamon. Bake in moderate oven (350° F.) 45 minutes.

(922) REFRIGERATOR ROLLS

2 cakes yeast	1 teaspoon salt
¼ cup sugar	3 beaten eggs
1 cup milk	5 cups flour
½ cup shortening	

Crumble yeast and mix with sugar. Let stand 20 minutes. Scald milk. Add shortening and salt. Cool to lukewarm. Add yeast-sugar mixture and eggs. Add flour, mixing thoroughly. Turn out on floured board and knead until satiny. Place in greased bowl. Cover and set in warm place to rise until double in bulk, about 2 hours. Knead again. Form into smooth ball. Grease surface. Cover and keep in refrigerator. Take out amount required each time, and keep remainder covered in refrigerator. This may be used in the following varieties:

Cloverleaf rolls: Form dough into small balls. Dip each into melted butter and place 3 balls in each section of an oiled muffin pan. Cover, let double, and bake in hot oven (425° F.) 15 to 20 minutes.

Crescents: Roll part of dough into circular shape about ¼ inch thick. Cut in wedges. Brush with melted butter and roll up beginning at the wide end. Fasten point on top and curve into crescents. Place on greased baking sheet. Cover, let double in bulk and bake in hot oven (425 ° F.) 15 to 20 minutes.

Parker House rolls: Roll dough about ¼ inch thick. Cut with biscuit cutter. Brush with melted butter. Mark across center with dull side of knife. Fold and press edges together. Place on oiled baking sheet, cover and let double. Bake in hot oven (425° F.) 15 to 20 minutes.

Bowknots: Roll out dough about ¼ inch thick. Cut in strips ½ inch wide and about 6 inches long. Tie in knots. Place on oiled baking sheet, cover and let double. Bake in hot oven (425° F.) 15 to 20 minutes.

Rosettes: Follow directions for *bowknots.* After tieing, bring 1 end through center and the other over the side.

Fan Tan Rolls: Roll out rectangular sheet very thin. Brush with melted butter. Cut in strips about 1 inch wide. Pile 6 or 7 strips together. Cut 1½-inch pieces and place on end in oiled muffin pans. Let rise until light. Bake in hot oven (425° F.) 15 to 20 minutes.

Braids: Roll dough out ¼ inch thick and cut in strips 6 inches long and ½ inch wide. Cross 3 strips in the middle and braid from center to each end. Press ends together and fold under. Place on oiled baking sheet, let double and bake in hot oven (425° F.) 15 to 20 minutes.

(923)   HOMEMADE BISCUIT MIX

8 cups flour	4 teaspoons salt
8 teaspoons baking powder	1½ cups shortening

Sift flour and measure. Sift again with the baking powder and salt. Cut in the shortening until the mixture has a fine even crumb. Place in a closed container and keep in refrigerator, using as desired. This mixture will keep at least a month in the refrigerator. It will yield five batches with two cups of the mixture to the batch. It may be used for biscuits, dumplings, shortcake, waffles, muffins, quick coffee cake, and dozens of other things.

(924)   SWEET YEAST DOUGH

2 cakes yeast	½ cup sugar
¼ cup lukewarm water	1 teaspoon salt
1 cup milk	2 eggs, beaten
¼ cup shortening	5 cups flour

Soften yeast in lukewarm water. Scald milk. Add butter, sugar, and salt. Cool to lukewarm. Add flour to make a thick batter. Add yeast and eggs. Beat well. Add enough flour to make a soft dough. Turn out on lightly floured board and knead until satiny. Place in greased bowl, cover and let rise until double in bulk, about two hours. When light, punch down, shape into tea ring, rolls or coffee cakes. Let rise until double in bulk about ½ to ¾ hour. Bake in moderate oven (375° F.) 25 to 30 minutes for coffee cakes, 20 to 25 minutes for rolls. Yield: 2 12-inch tea rings.

(925) EGG BREAD

Prepare sweet yeast dough (No. 924). When light, cut half the dough in 6 pieces. Roll each piece in 8-inch long strip. Cross 3 of the rolls in center and braid to each end. Fasten. Place on greased baking sheet. Braid remaining 3 rolls. Place on top. Cover and set in a warm place to rise until double in bulk. Brush with beaten egg yolk and sprinkle with sugar. Bake in hot oven (400° F.) 30 minutes.

(926) HEALTH BREAD

1 cup sifted white flour	1 teaspoon soda
2 cups whole wheat flour	1½ cups milk
1 teaspoon salt	½ cup molasses
½ cup sugar	

Mix together the flour, salt, and sugar. Dissolve the soda in the milk and add the molasses. Add liquids to dry ingredients and mix thoroughly. Pour into greased pans and bake slowly 1½ hours at 325° F. Dates or raisins may be added.

(927) SPOON BREAD

1 cup corn meal	½ teaspoon soda
1 teaspoon salt	1 cup buttermilk
1 tablespoon sugar	1½ tablespoons shortening
1 beaten egg	

Put corn meal into a bowl. Pour ¾ cup boiling water over meal. Cover and let cool. Add salt, sugar, and egg. Dissolve soda in buttermilk and add to first mixture. Mix thoroughly. Add shortening. Pour into a deep, greased baking dish. Bake in hot oven (375° F.) 30 to 35 minutes.

(928) CORN BREAD

1¼ cups flour	¼ cup sugar
¾ cup corn meal	1 egg, well beaten
3 teaspoons baking powder	¾ cup milk
1 teaspoon salt	¼ cup shortening, melted

Sift together flour, corn meal, baking powder, salt and sugar; combine and add egg, milk and shortening. Stir just to moisten dry ingredients; put in greased shallow pan. Bake in moderate oven (400° F.) about 20 minutes. Makes 9 servings.

(929) DATE AND NUT BREAD

1 egg	2 cups flour
¼ cup sugar	4 teaspoons baking powder
½ cup dates	½ teaspoon salt
½ cup nut meats	1 cup milk

Beat egg and add sugar. Add nut meats broken and dates cut in pieces. Sift dry ingredients together and add alternately with milk to first mixture. Turn into greased pan. Bake at 350° F. for 45 minutes. Either all dates or all nuts may be used.

(930) BATTER BREAD

1 pint milk	4 eggs
2 tablespoons corn meal	

Heat milk. Add corn meal. Mix well. Separate eggs. Beat yolks and add to mixture, mixing thoroughly. Beat egg whites stiff. Fold into mixture. Pour in shallow, hot, greased baking pan. Bake in hot oven (400° F.) until brown, about 10 minutes.

(931) NUT BREAD

3 cups flour	1½ cups milk
3 teaspoons baking powder	1 cup chopped nuts
1 cup sugar	1 cup raisins
1 teaspoon cinnamon	2 tablespoons melted
1 teaspoon salt	shortening
1 beaten egg	

Sift flour, baking powder, sugar, cinnamon, and salt together. Combine egg and milk, mixing well. Add to first mixture, mixing thoroughly. Add nuts, raisins, and shortening. Pour into bread pan. Let stand 30 minutes. Bake in moderate oven (325° F.) 50 to 60 minutes.

(932) RAISIN BREAD

3 ½ cups flour	1 egg, beaten
4 ½ teaspoons baking powder	1 tablespoon fat
1 teaspoon salt	1 ½ cups milk
½ cup sugar (or less)	1 cup chopped raisins

Sift the dry ingredients, reserving a little flour. Add milk, egg, and melted fat, beating mixture thoroughly. Sift flour over chopped raisins and stir into mixture. Place in greased bread pan and let stand for 20 minutes. Bake in moderate oven 350° F. 45 minutes to 1 hour. Chopped dates or figs may be substituted for raisins.

(933) MOLASSES BRAN BREAD

1 teaspoon soda	1 ½ cups whole-wheat flour
½ cup molasses	1 ½ cups bran
1 ½ cups sour milk	½ cup seeded raisins

Dissolve soda in molasses. Add milk, flour, bran, and raisins. Bake 45 minutes in a moderate oven (350° F.) in a loaf pan. This may be baked in smaller molds.

(934) BANANA TEA BREAD

1 ¾ cups sifted flour	⅓ cup shortening
¾ teaspoon soda	⅔ cup sugar
1 ¼ teaspoons cream of tartar	2 eggs, well beaten
½ teaspoon salt	1 cup mashed bananas

Sift flour, soda, cream of tartar, and salt together three times. Rub shortening to a creamy consistency with the back of a spoon. Stir in the sugar, a few tablespoons at a time, and continue beating until light and fluffy. Add eggs and beat well. Add flour mixture alternately with banana, a small amount at a time. Beat after each addition until smooth. Pour into a well-greased loaf pan and bake in a moderate oven (350° F.) about 1 hour. Makes one loaf about 3 ½ x 4 ½ x 3.

(935)   ORANGE NUT BREAD

2½ cups sifted flour
1 tablespoon baking powder
1¼ teaspoons salt
1 cup chopped nuts
1 cup milk

2 beaten eggs
½ cup orange marmalade
2 tablespoons melted
shortening

Mix and sift flour, baking powder, and salt. Add nuts. Add milk and eggs and stir lightly so as to moisten. Stir in marmalade and shortening. Pour in well-greased baking pan. Bake in moderate oven (350° F.) about 1 hour.

(936)   STEAMED BROWN BREAD

1 cup white flour
1 cup whole-wheat flour
1 cup corn meal
1½ teaspoons salt
½ cup sugar

1 teaspoon soda
½ cup molasses
1½ cups buttermilk
2 tablespoons melted
shortening

Sift flour, whole-wheat flour, corn meal, salt, and sugar together. Mix soda and molasses. Add buttermilk and molasses to the dry mixture. Add shortening. Mix well. Fill a greased pudding mold ¾ full and steam 3 hours.

(937)   RAISIN BROWN BREAD

Follow recipe for steamed brown bread (No. 936), adding ½ cup flour-dredged raisins and reducing sugar to ¼ cup.

(938)   WAFFLES

2 cups flour
4 teaspoons baking powder
1 teaspoon salt
1 tablespoon sugar

1¼ cups milk
2 eggs
2 tablespoons melted
shortening

Sift flour, baking powder, salt, and sugar together. Add milk. Separate eggs. Beat yolks and add to mixture. Mix thoroughly. Beat egg whites stiff and fold into mixture. Add shortening. Heat waffle iron on both sides. Grease well. Put a little of batter in center. Close iron. Brown on 1 side. Turn. Brown on other side. Serve with honey, maple sirup, or marmalade.

(939)   WHOLE WHEAT WAFFLES

Follow recipe for waffles (No. 938), using whole-wheat flour for white flour.

(940)   PECAN SOUR CREAM WAFFLES

Follow recipe for waffles (No. 938), using 2 cups sour cream in place of milk, adding 1 teaspoon soda and ½ cup chopped pecans, and eliminating baking powder.

(941)   PINEAPPLE WAFFLES

Follow recipe for waffles (No. 938), adding ½ cup drained, crushed pineapple to batter.

(942)   BANANA WAFFLES

Follow recipe for waffles (No. 938), adding ¾ cup mashed banana pulp to batter.

(943)   BERRY WAFFLES

Follow recipe for waffles (No. 938), adding ¾ cup washed blueberries or blackberries to batter.

(944)   APPLE CINNAMON WAFFLES

Follow recipe for waffles (No. 938), adding 2 cups diced apple, 1½ teaspoons cinnamon, and 2 tablespoons sugar.

(945)   DATE WAFFLES

Follow recipe for waffles (No. 938), adding 1 cup finely chopped dates to batter.

(946)   COCONUT WAFFLES

Follow recipe for waffles (No. 938), sprinkling batter with 1 teaspoon shredded coconut before cooking.

(947)   CORN PONE WAFFLES

Follow recipe for waffles (No. 938), substituting 1 cup corn meal for 1 of the cups of flour.

(948)   NUT WAFFLES

Follow recipe for waffles (No. 938), sprinkling 1 teaspoon chopped nuts on each waffle before cooking.

(949)   CHEESE WAFFLES

Follow recipe for waffles (No. 938), adding ½ cup grated cheese to batter.

(950)   CHOCOLATE WALNUT WAFFLES

Follow recipe for waffles (No. 938), adding ¾ cup chopped walnuts, 4 tablespoons melted shortening, 6 tablespoons cocoa, ½ teaspoon cinnamon, 1 teaspoon vanilla, and ¾ cup sugar.

(951)   POPOVERS

1 cup flour	2 eggs
¼ teaspoon salt	1 tablespoon melted
1 cup milk	shortening

Mix and sift flour and salt. Add milk gradually. Add beaten egg and shortening. Beat batter five minutes with a Dover egg beater. Pour batter into greased hot iron popover pans or hot greased earthen cups. Bake in a hot oven (400° F.) 30 minutes. Reduce heat to a moderate oven (325° F.) and bake 15 minutes. Do not open oven door for the first 15 minutes of baking. This recipe makes 8 to 10 popovers.

(952)   WHOLE WHEAT POPOVERS

Follow recipe for popovers (No. 951), using whole-wheat flour instead of white flour.

(953)   FRUIT POPOVERS

After popovers (No. 951) or whole-wheat popovers (No. 952) are cooked, open at the side and fill with any desired well-sugared berries or fruit.

(954) DUMPLINGS

2 cups flour
1 teaspoon salt
4 teaspoons baking powder
3 tablespoons shortening
¾ cup milk

Sift flour, salt, and baking powder together. Rub in shortening with knife or finger tips. Add milk to make a soft dough. These are dropped, a tablespoon at a time, on chicken or meat stews the last 15 to 20 minutes of cooking. The kettle must be covered closely and cover must not be removed during cooking.

(955) WHOLE WHEAT DUMPLINGS

Follow recipe for dumplings (No. 954), using whole-wheat flour instead of white flour.

(956) SUET DUMPLINGS

1 cup flour
1 teaspoon baking powder
⅓ teaspoon salt
⅓ cup chopped suet

Mix and sift flour, baking powder, and salt. Add suet and enough cold water to just bind. Mix well. Divide into 12 dumplings and cook last 15 to 20 minutes with a meat stew.

(957) POTATO DUMPLINGS

6 finely minced boiled potatoes (No. 1834)
1 teaspoon salt
½ teaspoon pepper
2 tablespoons melted shortening
1 teaspoon nutmeg
4 beaten eggs
2 tablespoons flour
2 tablespoons bread crumbs

Beat all ingredients together thoroughly. Drop from tablespoon into boiling, slightly-salted water. Cover closely and boil until light, about 12 minutes. Yield: 20 dumplings.

(958) APPLE DUMPLINGS

Roll out plain pastry (No. 2701) to ⅛-inch thickness. Cut in large circles. Cut tart apples in thin slices. Put a small amount in center of each circle of pastry. Sprinkle with sugar and a little nutmeg and dot with butter. Moisten edge of pastry with water. Bring opposite edges to center and press tightly together. Prick top to allow steam to escape. Bake in quick oven (425° F.) 10 minutes. Reduce heat to moderate (350° F.) and bake 15 to 20 minutes longer.

(959)   PEACH DUMPLINGS

Follow recipe for apple dumplings (No. 958), using peaches instead of apples and lemon juice instead of nutmeg.

(960)   TOMATO DUMPLINGS

Follow recipe for dumplings (No. 954), using tomato juice instead of milk and eliminating shortening.

(961)   BERRY DUMPLINGS

Follow recipe for apple dumplings (No. 958), using berries instead of apples and omitting nutmeg. Dredge berries in flour to thicken juices.

(962)   CHERRY DUMPLINGS

Follow recipe for apple dumplings (No. 958), using cherries instead of apples.

(963)   ORANGE DATE DUMPLINGS

2 cups homemade biscuit mix (No. 923)	½ cup chopped dates
½ cup milk	1 cup sugar
2 tablespoons butter	¼ cup orange juice
1 teaspoon grated lemon rind	2 teaspoons lemon juice
	1 teaspoon grated orange rind

Blend milk with biscuit dough. Roll to ¼-inch thickness. Brush with melted butter. Cover with dates and lemon rind. Roll like a jelly roll. Cut in 8 slices. Place pieces in greased baking dish, cut side down. Boil remaining ingredients with 1 cup water 5 minutes. Pour sirup over biscuits. Bake in quick oven (450° F.) 30 minutes. Serves 8.

(964)   SHORTCAKES

2 cups flour	2 tablespoons sugar
5 teaspoons baking powder	¼ cup shortening
1 teaspoon salt	⅔ cup milk

Mix and sift flour, baking powder, salt and sugar. Cut in shortening with a knife or rub in with the finger tips. Add milk gradually and mix to a soft dough. Roll out on a slightly floured board to ½-inch thickness. Cut with a large cookie cutter. Bake in a quick oven (425° F.) 15 minutes. Break apart and put sliced and sweetened fruit or crushed berries between and on top of cakes. Serve with whipped cream. This recipe makes 8 short-cakes.

(965)   MEAT SHORTCAKE

2 cups homemade biscuit mix (No. 923)	2 cups diced cooked meat
Milk	2 cups medium white sauce (No. 2004)
2 tablespoons butter	

Add enough milk to biscuit mix to make a soft dough. Divide dough in 2 parts and roll on floured board about ¼-inch thick. Place one layer in greased baking pan. Brush with butter. Top with other half. Bake in hot oven (400° F.) 25 minutes. Split in 2 parts. Heat meat with sauce and serve between layers and on top of shortcake. Serves 6.

(966)   DOUGHNUTS

⅓ cup sugar	2 teaspoons baking powder
1½ tablespoons shortening	⅛ teaspoon cinnamon
1 well-beaten egg	⅛ teaspoon clove
½ cup milk	1⁄16 teaspoon mace
2 cups flour	½ teaspoon salt

Cream sugar and shortening together. Add egg and milk. Mix well. Mix and sift remaining ingredients. Add them to liquid mixture and mix thoroughly. Turn out on slightly floured board and roll to ½-inch thickness. Cut with a doughnut cutter. Fry in deep, hot fat (375° F.) until dark brown. Drain on unglazed paper. Sprinkle with confectioners' sugar. This makes 1 to 1½ dozen doughnuts.

(967)   CRULLERS

Roll out any doughnut mixture ½-inch thick. Cut in strips 3 inches by ½ inch. Twist and roll each strip. Fry same as doughnuts (No. 966).

(968)   RAISED DOUGHNUTS

⅔ cup sugar	1 yeast cake
3 tablespoons shortening	5 cups flour
1 teaspoon salt	2 well-beaten eggs
1 cup scalded milk	1 teaspoon nutmeg

Add sugar, shortening, and salt to milk. When lukewarm, add yeast cake, mixed with 2 tablespoons warm water. Add enough flour (about 2 cups) to make a sponge. Set in a warm place to rise. When light, add eggs, nutmeg, and enough flour to make a light dough. Cover and let rise until double in bulk. Knead until free from large air bubbles. Roll out on slightly floured board to ½-inch thickness. Cut with a doughnut cutter. Cover and set in a warm place to rise again until double in bulk. Put them, top side down, in deep hot fat (375° F.). Fry to delicate brown on 1 side. Turn and fry other side. Drain on unglazed paper. Sprinkle with confectioners' sugar at time of serving. This makes 30 doughnuts.

(969)   JELLY DOUGHNUTS

Follow recipe for raised doughnuts (No. 968). After the second rising, roll out on a slightly floured board to ⅛-inch thickness. Cut with a cookie cutter. Put 1 teaspoon currant jelly in the center of one round, moisten edges with water, and place another round on top. Press edges lightly together. Cover and set in a warm place to rise until double in bulk. Fry in the same way as raised doughnuts. This makes 24 doughnuts.

(970)   FRENCH CRULLERS

4 tablespoons sugar	4 tablespoons shortening
1 teaspoon salt	1 cup flour
1 teaspoon grated orange rind	3 eggs

Put sugar, salt, shortening, and orange rind in saucepan with 1 cup hot water. Bring to a boil. Add flour. Blend thoroughly. Cook until thick, stirring constantly. Cool slightly. Add one egg at a time, beating each one in thoroughly before adding another. Press dough through a pastry tube, using a rose tube, onto a well-greased square of heavy paper, in desired shape. Turn paper upside down and let crullers drop into deep, hot fat (375° F.). Fry until well puffed up and a golden brown in color, about 6 or 7 minutes. Drain on unglazed paper. Ice with confectioners' frosting (No. 3173). This makes 18 crullers.

(971) PRUNE DOUGHNUTS

Follow recipe for raised doughnuts (No. 968). After the second rising, roll out on a slightly floured board to ⅛-inch thickness. Cut with a cookie cutter. Put a teaspoon of chopped, stewed prunes (No. 71), mixed with a little lemon juice, in the center of one round. Moisten edge, cover with another round and press edges together. Cover and set in a warm place to rise until double in bulk. Fry in the same way as raised doughnuts.

(972) CHOCOLATE DOUGHNUTS

Follow recipe for doughnuts (No. 966), adding 1 square melted chocolate, ½ teaspoon vanilla, and 2 tablespoons sugar.

(973) PINEAPPLE DOUGHNUTS

Follow recipe for prune doughnuts (No. 971), using crushed pineapple instead of stewed prunes.

(974) MOLASSES DOUGHNUTS

Follow recipe for doughnuts (No. 966), adding ¼ cup sugar, 1 cup molasses, 1 teaspoon ginger, and 1 cup flour.

(975) FROSTED DOUGHNUTS

Follow recipe for doughnuts (No. 966) and, when cool, ice with caramel (No. 3183) or chocolate icing (No. 3187).

(976)   SWEET MILK GRIDDLE CAKES

2 cups flour
1 teaspoon salt
1½ teaspoons baking powder
2 tablespoons sugar

2 cups milk
1 egg
1 tablespoon melted
    shortening

Mix and sift flour, salt, baking powder, and sugar. Add milk, well-beaten egg, and shortening and mix well. Drop by tablespoons on a hot griddle, greased well, and brown on both sides. Serve hot with marmalade or honey.

(977)   SOUR MILK GRIDDLE CAKES

2 cups flour
1 teaspoon salt
1 teaspoon soda
2 cups sour milk

1 egg
1 tablespoon melted
    shortening

Mix and sift flour and salt. Dissolve soda in the sour milk and add to the flour mixture. Add beaten egg and shortening and mix well. Drop by tablespoons on a hot griddle, greased well, and brown on both sides. Serve hot with maple sirup or jam.

(978)   WHOLE WHEAT GRIDDLE CAKES

⅔ cup whole-wheat flour
1¼ cups flour
3 teaspoons baking powder
1 teaspoon salt
2 tablespoons sugar

1½ cups milk
1 egg
1 tablespoon melted
    shortening

Mix whole-wheat flour, flour, baking powder, salt, and sugar together. Add milk, beaten egg, and shortening and mix well. Drop by tablespoons on a hot griddle, greased well, and brown on both sides. Serve hot with powdered sugar or maple sirup.

(979)   BREAD CRUMB GRIDDLE CAKES

1 cup dry bread crumbs
½ teaspoon salt
1½ cups hot milk

½ cup cold milk
2 eggs, well-beaten

Mix crumbs and salt in bowl. Add hot milk. Add cold milk. Fold eggs into crumb mixture. Drop from tablespoon onto hot griddle and brown both sides. Serves 4.

(980)   BLUEBERRY GRIDDLE CAKES

1 egg
1 cup milk
2 teaspoons baking powder

1 cup flour
1/4 teaspoon salt
1/2 cup blueberries

Beat egg until light. Add salt and milk. Sift baking powder with flour and stir it into first mixture. Beat until smooth. Add blueberries. Drop from spoon onto hot griddle and brown both sides. Serves 4.

(981)   RAISIN GRIDDLE CAKES

3 cups flour
2 tablespoons sugar
1 1/2 tablespoons baking
    powder
1 teaspoon salt

1 beaten egg
1 cup milk
1 tablespoon melted
    shortening
1/2 cup sliced raisins

Mix and sift flour, sugar, baking powder, and salt together. Combine egg, milk, and shortening. Combine mixtures and beat smooth. Add raisins. Drop on well-greased hot griddle and brown both sides. Serves 6.

(982)   CORN MEAL GRIDDLE CAKES

1 cup flour
1/2 cup corn meal
3 1/2 teaspoons baking powder
3/4 teaspoon salt
1 tablespoon sugar

1 egg, beaten
1 cup milk
3 tablespoons melted
    shortening

Sift together flour, corn meal, baking powder, salt and sugar; combine and add egg, milk and shortening. Stir just to moisten dry ingredients; bake on a hot, greased griddle until browned on both sides. Serve hot with honey, maple syrup, or marmalade. Makes 14.

(983) CORN GRIDDLE CAKES

2½ cups flour
4 teaspoons baking powder
½ teaspoon salt
1 tablespoon sugar
2 cups milk

1 beaten egg
1 tablespoon melted shortening
2½ cups stewed (No. 1769) or canned corn

Mix and sift the dry ingredients. Add milk slowly and then beat in egg. Beat until smooth, about 1 minute. Add melted shortening and blend well. Add well drained corn. Drop by tablespoonfuls on a hot griddle and bake until bubbles form on top, then turn and bake on the other side. These cakes are very tender and should be handled carefully in turning or they will break. This makes about 36 griddle cakes. They should be served at once and may be used in a meal in the place of potato, or as the main dish of luncheon or supper. Serves 4-6.

(984) PANCAKES AU GRATIN

Make griddle cakes (No. 976) 5 inches in diameter. Spread with hot, creamed chicken (No. 1545). Sprinkle with grated cheese. Roll like a jelly roll. Fasten with skewers. Put in baking pan. Sprinkle with more cheese. Bake in moderate oven (350° F.) until cheese is melted.

(985) BANANA GRIDDLE CAKES

Follow recipe for sweet milk griddle cakes (No. 976), substituting 2 mashed bananas for ½ cup flour and reducing milk content to 1 cup.

(986) CEREAL GRIDDLE CAKES

Follow recipe for sweet milk griddle cakes (No. 976), substituting 1 cup any cooked cereal for 1 cup flour, adding 1 well-beaten egg, and reducing milk to 1 cup.

(987) HAM GRIDDLE CAKES

Follow recipe for sweet milk griddle cakes (No. 976), adding ½ cup finely chopped cooked ham to batter.

(988)   BUTTERED TOAST

Cut day-old bread into ¼-inch slices. Put slices in toaster or on a grate and brown some distance from heat, so that they may dry gradually. Cover one side with butter. Serve as soon as possible after toasting.

(989)   MELBA TOAST

Cut stale bread in very thin slices or ½-inch strips. Cut off crusts. Put in slow oven (250° F.) and dry thoroughly until a delicate brown.

(990)   MILK TOAST

2 slices buttered toast   ¼ teaspoon salt
   (No. 988)   1 cup scalded milk

Cut toast in small squares. Add salt to milk and pour, hot, over toast in cereal bowl.

(991)   FRENCH TOAST

1 egg, slightly beaten   1 cup sweet milk
¼ teaspoon salt   2 tablespoons sugar
5 slices of bread   Fat to grease the griddle

Add the salt, sugar, and milk to the slightly beaten egg. Dip the pieces of bread into the egg mixture. Cook the soaked slices of bread on a well-oiled griddle. Brown on one side. Turn and brown on the other. Serve with maple sirup or jelly. Served with stewed fruit, this makes a good dessert.

(992)   CREAM TOAST

Dip slices of toast into medium white sauce (No. 2004). Pour remaining sauce on the pieces of toast and serve hot.

(993)   CINNAMON TOAST

Spread buttered toast (No. 988) with a mixture of 3 parts sugar and 1 part cinnamon. Place on platter and put in moderate oven (350° F.) until sugar melts.

(994)   BAKED BREAD AND CHEESE

6 slices bread
½ pound American cheese
½ teaspoon salt
1½ cups milk

½ teaspoon paprika
Butter
2 eggs

Spread butter on slices of bread. Pile one slice above another and cut in cubes. Cut the cheese in thin slices. Put cubes of bread and slices of cheese in a baking dish, in alternate layers, sprinkling each layer with salt and paprika. Beat the eggs, add the milk, mix and pour over the bread and cheese. Bake at 350° F. until firm in the center. Serve hot. Serves 6.

(995)   GOLDEN TOAST STICKS

Cut bread in ½-inch slices. Then cut in sticks ½-inch wide. Arrange sticks on a baking sheet and bake in a 300° F. oven 20 minutes or until they are crisp throughout and evenly browned. Turn sticks once during baking. Serve with soup, allowing three sticks for each person.

(996)   CROUSTADES

Cut stale bread in 2½-inch slices, and the slices in squares, oblongs, or circles. Scoop out the centers with a fork leaving cases ¼-inch thick. Fry in deep hot fat (375° F.) until a delicate brown. Drain on unglazed paper. Fill with creamed vegetables, meat or fish.

(997)   CHEESE TOASTED CRACKERS

Sprinkle soda crackers with grated cheese and lightly with paprika. Crisp in hot oven (400° F.) until cheese melts.

(998)   TOASTED PAPRIKA CRACKERS

Spread soda or salted crackers with butter. Sprinkle with paprika. Crisp in hot oven (400° F.).

(999) CORN CAKE

1 cup corn meal	½ teaspoon salt
¾ cup flour	1 well-beaten egg
2 tablespoons sugar	1 cup milk
4 teaspoons baking powder	2 tablespoons melted fat

Mix and sift dry ingredients. Add egg, milk, and fat. Bake in shallow, greased pan in hot oven (425° F.) 20 minutes. One cup sour milk may be used instead of sweet milk, in which case add ½ teaspoon soda and use only 2 teaspoons baking powder.

(1000) JOHNNYCAKE

1 cup corn meal	1½ tablespoons melted
2 tablespoons whole-wheat	shortening
flour	1 cup boiling milk
½ teaspoon salt	1 egg
1 tablespoon sugar	

Sift corn meal and flour together. Spread thin on baking sheet and brown lightly in slow oven (275° F.). Mix flour, corn meal, salt, and sugar. Add shortening and pour milk in quickly. Separate egg. Beat the white stiff. Beat the yolk and fold into the white. Add corn meal mixture and stir in with a folding motion. Drop batter from a spoon, in rectangular shape, into a greased baking pan, leaving ½ inch between each biscuit. Bake in hot oven (400° F.) 30 minutes. Yield: 12 Johnnycakes. Or, bake in greased pan about 45 to 50 minutes.

(1001) COFFEE CAKE

3 cups flour	½ cup shortening
2 cups brown sugar	2 teaspoons baking powder
1 teaspoon salt	2 eggs
1 teaspoon cinnamon	¾ cup milk

Mix and sift flour, salt, sugar, and cinnamon. Cut in shortening with a knife or rub in with the finger tips. Reserve 1 cup of this mixture to sprinkle on top of cake. To the remainder add the baking powder and mix well. Add the beaten eggs and milk and beat thoroughly. Pour into two greased layer cake pans and sprinkle top with crumbs reserved for this purpose. Bake in a hot oven (400° F.) 20 to 25 minutes.

(1002)   APPLE COFFEE CAKE

2 cups homemade biscuit mix (No. 923)	2 tablespoons butter
2 tablespoons sugar	
1/4 cup sugar	1 teaspoon cinnamon
1 egg	1 sliced apple
3/4 cup milk	

Combine mix and 1/4 cup sugar. Beat egg slightly and add milk. Combine with first mixture. Place in oiled coffee cake pan. Brush liberally with melted butter. Sprinkle evenly with a mixture of cinnamon and 2 tablespoons sugar. Arrange thin uniform slices of apple over the top. Bake in moderate oven (375° F.) 40 to 45 minutes.

(1003)   MINCEMEAT COFFEE CAKE

5 tablespoons butter	2 teaspoons baking powder
3 tablespoons brown sugar	1/2 teaspoon salt
1 cup mincemeat	1 egg
1 1/2 cups flour	2/3 cup milk
1/2 cup sugar	

In a deep cake pan melt two tablespoons butter. Sprinkle two tablespoons brown sugar over butter and cover evenly with one cup mincemeat. Over this pour the batter made of the remaining ingredients and bake in a moderately hot oven (425° F.) 25 minutes. To make the batter, sift flour, sugar, baking powder and salt together. Beat egg, add milk, and 3 tablespoons melted butter. Add to dry ingredients and mix well. Serves 6.

(1004)   COFFEE RING

3 cups flour	1 egg
1/3 cup sugar	3/4 cup milk
5 teaspoons baking powder	3/4 cup raisins
1 teaspoon salt	1/2 cup nuts, chopped
1/4 cup shortening	

Mix and sift flour, sugar, baking powder, and salt. Cut in shortening with a knife or rub in with the finger tips. Add beaten egg and enough milk to make a soft dough. Roll out to 1/4-inch thickness into a rectangular-shaped piece. Spread lightly with melted butter, sprinkle with raisins and nuts, and 1 tablespoon sugar. Roll like a jelly roll lengthwise. Bring ends together to make a circle and press together. Put on a large greased pan and cut gashes around outside edge with scissors, 2 inches apart.

Bake in a moderate oven (350° F.) 25 to 30 minutes. Spread top with confectioners' frosting (No. 3173).

(1005) ENGLISH TEA CAKE

½ cup scalded milk	1 egg or 2 egg yolks
1 cake yeast	½ teaspoon salt
¼ cup shortening	½ cup raisins
¼ cup sugar	1½ cups flour

Soften yeast in milk which has been cooled to lukewarm. Add shortening, sugar, eggs, salt, raisins, and enough flour to make a rather stiff drop batter. Beat until smooth. Let rise until double in bulk. Stir down and fill oiled, 2-inch deep pan about ½ to ¾ full. Let rise until puffy. Bake in moderately hot oven (400° F.) 25 to 30 minutes. Make a topping of 2 tablespoons sugar, ½ teaspoon cinnamon, and ½ cup chopped nuts. Combine and sprinkle over tea cake before last rising.

(1006) CHERRY RINGS

6 ½-inch slices bread	¼ cup macaroon crumbs
2 beaten eggs	¼ cup bread crumbs
¼ cup sugar	2 tablespoons chopped
1 cup milk	almonds
⅓ teaspoon salt	½ cup cherry sauce
1 teaspoon grated orange peel	(No. 3116)

Cut bread in rings with cookie cutter. Combine eggs, sugar, milk, salt, and orange peel. Dip bread rings in mixture, then in macaroon crumbs, again in egg mixture, and finally in bread crumbs. Fry in deep, hot fat (360° F.) until golden brown. Sprinkle with sugar and almonds. Serve with hot cherry sauce. Serves 6.

(1007) SWEDISH LUNCHEON RING

2 cups homemade biscuit mix (No. 923)	1 tablespoon onion
Milk	1 pimiento, chopped
2 cups diced cooked meat	Salt and pepper
1 small green pepper, chopped	Milk or broth
	Bacon

Add enough milk to biscuit mix to make a soft dough. Roll on a floured surface to ¼-inch thickness. Spread with a mixture

of the meat, seasonings, and enough broth or milk to moisten.
Roll like a jelly roll. Form in ring. Place on cookie sheet. Cut
diagonal slashes to center and place ½ slice bacon in each slash.
Bake in moderately hot oven (375° F.) for thirty minutes.
Serve with pimiento sauce (No. 2014). Serves 6.

(1008)   GREEK FEAST CAKE

Prepare sweet yeast dough (No. 924). When light, shape into
3 round loaves. Place them close together on greased baking
sheet as a 3-leaved clover. Cover and set in a warm place to rise
until double in bulk. Brush with milk. Bake in hot oven
(400° F.) 45 minutes. When cool, glaze with confectioners'
icing (No. 3173) and garnish with nuts and candied fruits.

(1009)   BOHEMIAN BRAID

Prepare sweet yeast dough (No. 924). Divide into 9 parts.
Roll each part into long strip. Braid 4 strips and place on greased
baking sheet. Braid 3 parts and place on top. Twist remaining
2 parts and place on top, tucking ends under. Cover and set in
a warm place to rise until double in bulk. Bake in hot oven
(400° F.) 45 minutes. When cool, brush with confectioners'
icing (No. 3173) and sprinkle with chopped nuts.

(1010)   ALMOND COFFEE PUFFS

1 cake compressed yeast	½ teaspoon salt
¼ cup lukewarm water	2—2½ cups flour
½ cup milk	2 eggs
¼ cup shortening	1 cup almonds, blanched
5 tablespoons sugar	and chopped
	(No. 3632)

Soften yeast in lukewarm water. Scald milk. Add shortening,
tablespoon sugar, and salt. Cool to lukewarm. Add flour, beating
thoroughly. Add softened yeast, and then unbeaten eggs, one
at a time. Beat until mixture is smooth. Cover and let rise until
double in bulk, about 1 hour. Stir down and add ½ cup chopped
almonds. Fill oiled muffin pans ½ full. Sprinkle with remaining
almonds which have been mixed with 4 tablespoons of sugar.
Cover and let rise until doubled, about 30 minutes. Bake in

moderate oven (375° F.) 15 to 20 minutes. Yield: 2 dozen 2-inch puffs.

(1011)   BRIOCHE

3 cups sifted flour	3 tablespoons sugar
1 cup scalded milk	4 well-beaten eggs
1 yeast cake	½ teaspoon salt
1 cup melted shortening	

Put 2 cups flour in bowl. Cool milk to lukewarm. Add yeast cake and dissolve. Add mixture to flour. Beat until smooth. Cover and set in a warm place to rise until light, about 1 hour. Add shortening, sugar, eggs, remaining flour, and salt. Mix well and knead on floured board until smooth. Cover and set in a warm place to rise until very light, about 4 hours. Knead again and form into any desired shape. Cover and let rise again in warm place until light. Bake in moderately hot oven (375° F.) 20 minutes. Serves 6.

(1012)   BAKING POWDER BISCUITS

2 cups flour	4 tablespoons shortening
4 teaspoons baking powder	¾ cup milk
½ teaspoon salt	

Sift flour, baking powder, and salt together. Rub shortening in with finger tips. Add milk slowly and mix to a soft dough. Roll out on a slightly floured board to ½-inch thickness. Cut with a biscuit cutter. Bake in quick oven (450° F.) 10 to 15 minutes. Yield: 12 biscuits.

(1013)   CREAM OF TARTAR BISCUITS

3 cups flour	1½ tablespoons shortening
1 teaspoon salt	1 teaspoon soda
2 teaspoons cream of tartar	1 cup milk

Mix and sift flour, salt, and cream of tartar together. Work in shortening with the finger tips. Mix soda and milk and add to flour mixture. Mix thoroughly and knead on a floured board until satiny. Roll ¾-inch thick. Cut with biscuit cutter. Bake on greased pan, with space between, in hot oven (425° F.) 15 minutes. Yield: 12 biscuits.

(1014)   SOUR MILK BISCUITS

2 cups flour	2 tablespoons shortening
3 teaspoons baking powder	½ teaspoon soda
1 teaspoon salt	¾ cup sour milk

Sift flour, baking powder, and salt together. Rub in shortening with finger tips. Mix soda and sour milk. Add slowly to first mixture and mix to a soft dough. Roll out on slightly floured board to ½-inch thickness. Cut with a biscuit cutter. Bake in quick oven (450° F.) 10 to 15 minutes. Yield: 12 biscuits.

(1015)   BRAN BISCUITS

1 cup shredded bran	2 cups homemade biscuit
Milk	mix (No. 923)

Combine bran and biscuit mix. Add enough milk to make a soft dough. Roll to desired thickness. Cut with cookie cutter. Place on greased baking pan. Bake in hot oven (425° F.) 15 minutes. Yield: 12 biscuits.

(1016)   WHOLE WHEAT BISCUITS

Follow recipe for whole-wheat rolls (No. 1033), cutting ½ inch thick dough with round cookie cutter.

(1017)   RYE BISCUITS

1 cup rye flour	2 tablespoons sugar
1 cup flour	2½ tablespoons shortening
1 teaspoon salt	

Mix and sift flour, salt, and sugar. Work in shortening with finger tips. Add water and mix to a stiff dough. Knead for a few minutes on floured board. Cut with a cookie cutter. Prick with a fork. Bake to golden brown in moderate oven (350° F.). Yield: 10 biscuits.

(1018)   SWEET POTATO BISCUITS

1 cup sweet potatoes, mashed (No. 1882)	½ teaspoon baking soda
	1 cup buttermilk
1 tablespoon shortening	2 cups flour
1 tablespoon sugar	1 teaspoon salt

Beat potatoes, shortening, and sugar together until well blended. Dissolve baking soda in buttermilk and add to potato mixture. Mix and sift flour and salt and add to first mixture. Mix well. Roll out to ½-inch thickness on floured board. Cut with small cookie cutter. Put on greased baking pan. Bake in hot oven (400° F.) 15 to 20 minutes. Yield: 24 biscuits.

(1019) OATMEAL BISCUITS

1½ cups flour	1½ cups raw rolled oats
1 tablespoon sugar	4 tablespoons shortening
4 teaspoons baking powder	¾ cup milk
1½ teaspoons salt	

Sift flour, sugar, baking powder, and salt together. Add rolled oats and mix. Rub shortening in with finger tips. Add milk slowly and mix to a soft dough. Roll out on floured board to ¾-inch thickness. Cut with biscuit cutter. Brush tops with milk and bake in quick oven (450° F.) 15 to 20 minutes. Yield: 15 biscuits.

(1020) ORANGE BISCUITS

Follow recipe for baking powder biscuits (No. 1012), adding ½ tablespoon grated orange rind with milk. Bake with a piece of loaf sugar, dipped in orange juice, on each biscuit.

(1021) CHEESE BISCUITS

Follow recipe for baking powder biscuits (No. 1012), adding ½ cup grated cheese before adding milk.

(1022) EMERGENCY BISCUITS

Follow recipe for baking powder biscuits (No. 1012), using 1 cup milk. Drop by tablespoons into a greased pan.

(1023) BUCKWHEAT BISCUITS

Follow recipe for rye biscuits (No. 1017), using buckwheat flour instead of rve flour.

(1024)   HAM RELISH BISCUITS

2 cups homemade biscuit
    mix (No. 923)
⅔ cup chopped ham
¼ cup chopped celery
½ teaspoon chopped onions

½ teaspoon chopped
    parsley
3 tablespoons mayonnaise
    (No. 701)

Pat out dough until it is ⅓ inch thick. Spread with other ingredients and roll up. Cut off half-inch slices and bake 8 minutes in a moderate oven (350° F.). Serve warm. Yield: 12 biscuits.

(1025)   SAUSAGE BISCUITS

2 cups flour
5 teaspoons baking powder
¾ teaspoon salt

2 tablespoons shortening
¾ cup milk
8 sausages

Cut shortening into mixed and sifted dry ingredients. Add milk gradually, stirring mixture with a knife. Toss on floured pastry cloth and cut in 3-inch round biscuits. Place a pan fried sausage (No. 1469) in the center of each biscuit and roll up. Place on oiled pastry sheet and bake in 450° F. oven 15 minutes. Yield: 8 biscuits.

(1026)   COCONUT BISCUITS

2 cups homemade biscuit
    mix (No. 923)
Milk
½ cup browned coconut

2 tablespoons soft butter
¼ cup soaked seedless
    raisins
2 tablespoons brown sugar

Brown coconut by heating on cookie sheet in 350° F. oven. Mix with biscuit mix. Add milk to make a soft dough. Roll dough in a rectangle ¼ inch thick. Spread with butter and sprinkle with brown sugar and raisins. Roll up like a jelly roll and cut in slices ¾ inch thick. Place in greased muffin pans. Bake at 425° F. for 15 to 20 minutes. Yield: 8 to 12 biscuits.

(1027)   HONEY DATE BISCUITS

2 cups baking powder bis-
    cuit dough (No. 1012)
¼ cup butter

2 tablespoons honey
¼ cup chopped nuts
½ cup chopped dates

Roll dough in rectangle to ¼-inch thickness. Cream the butter. Add honey gradually. Add nuts and dates. Mix well. Spread mixture on dough. Roll as a jelly roll. Cut into 1-inch slices. Place, cut side down, on greased baking sheet. Bake in hot oven (425° F.) 25 minutes. Yield: 8 to 12 biscuits. Whole nut meats may be pressed into each biscuit before baking.

(1028) BRAN BUTTERSCOTCH BISCUITS

½ cup all-bran	½ teaspoon soda
¾ cup buttermilk	½ cup shortening
1½ cups flour	1 tablespoon softened
1 teaspoon baking powder	butter
1 teaspoon salt	½ cup brown sugar

Soak the all-bran in buttermilk. Sift flour, baking powder, salt, and soda together. Cut in shortening until mixture is like coarse corn meal. Add soaked all-bran. Stir until dough follows fork around bowl. Turn out onto floured board and knead lightly a few seconds. Roll into an oblong about ¼ inch thick. Spread with a tablespoon softened butter and sprinkle with the brown sugar. Roll up like a jelly roll and cut into 1-inch slices. Place slices, cut side down, close together in greased baking pan. Bake in hot oven (450° F.) about 12 minutes. Yield: 12 biscuits.

(1029) SCOTCH SCONES

2 cups flour	2 tablespoons sugar
1 teaspoon salt	4 tablespoons shortening
5 teaspoons baking powder	2 eggs
⅓ cup milk	

Mix and sift flour, salt, baking powder and 1 tablespoon sugar. Cut in shortening with a knife or rub in with the finger tips. Add the beaten eggs (reserving 1 egg white for the tops). Add milk and mix to a soft dough. Roll out on a slightly floured board to ½-inch thickness into a round piece and cut into quarters. Brush with white of egg and sprinkle with the remaining tablespoon of sugar. Bake in a quick oven (425° F.) 10 to 15 minutes. This recipe makes 10 to 12 scones. Cinnamon may be sprinkled on scones before baking.

(1030)   PARKER HOUSE ROLLS (YEAST)

2 cups milk	2 yeast cakes
5 tablespoons shortening	6½ cups flour
3 tablespoons sugar	¼ cup butter
3 teaspoons salt	

Heat milk. Add shortening, sugar, and salt. Dissolve yeast cakes in 4 tablespoons lukewarm water. Add to mixture. Add 2 cups flour and beat thoroughly. Cover and set in a warm place to rise until light, about 1½ hours. Add enough flour to make a firm dough. Knead on a floured board until smooth and elastic to touch. Cover and set in a warm place to rise until double in bulk. Knead again. Roll the dough to ¼-inch thickness and cut with a large, round cutter. Brush each piece with melted butter. Mark through the center with the back of a knife and fold over. Place rolls in a greased, shallow pan 1 inch apart. Cover and set in a warm place to rise until double in bulk. Bake in hot oven (400° F.) 15 to 20 minutes. Yield: 30 rolls.

(1031)   PARKER HOUSE ROLLS

Follow recipe for baking powder biscuits (No. 1012), with following changes: Roll out to ¼-inch thickness. Cut with large cookie cutter. Spread with melted butter. Fold over double and press edges together lightly.

(1032)   PLAIN YEAST ROLLS

½ cup milk	1 cake yeast
2 tablespoons shortening	½ cup lukewarm water
2 tablespoons sugar	1 egg or 2 egg yolks
2 teaspoons salt	3½ cups flour

Scald milk and add fat, sugar and salt. Soften yeast in lukewarm water. Cool milk to lukewarm and add yeast and beaten egg. Add flour to make a soft dough. Turn out on lightly floured board and knead until smooth and satiny. Place in lightly greased bowl and allow to double in bulk. Punch down and mold into rolls. Cover and set in warm place to rise until double in bulk. Bake in hot oven (400° F.) 15 to 20 minutes. Yield: 20 rolls.

(1033)   WHOLE WHEAT ROLLS

2 cups whole-wheat flour	½ teaspoon salt
1 tablespoon sugar	¼ cup shortening

Mix and sift flour, sugar, and salt. Work in shortening with finger tips. Add ⅔ cup cold water gradually, stirring constantly. Mix well and knead for a few minutes on a floured board. Then follow recipe for wheat sticks (No. 1074).

(1034)   SOUR CREAM ROLLS

2 cups thick sour cream	¼ cup sugar
1 cake yeast	4 cups flour
¼ teaspoon soda	Melted butter
2 teaspoons salt	

Scald cream and cool to lukewarm. Crumble the yeast cake and stir into ⅓ cup of the lukewarm cream. Add soda, salt, and sugar to the remaining cream and mix well. Combine the two mixtures and add flour gradually, stirring constantly until smooth. Brush with melted butter. Cover and put in a warm place and let rise to about 2½ to 3 times the original volume. Knead lightly for about one minute and cut dough in two parts. Roll out one part at a time in rectangular shape about ⅛ inch thick. Brush with butter and cut in lengthwise strips about 2 inches wide. Place strips on top of each other and cut off pieces about 1½ inches wide. Place pieces in small buttered muffin tins with the cut edges up. Let rise in a warm place until double in size. Bake in a hot oven (425° F.) 10 to 15 minutes, or until a golden brown. Brush with butter if desired. Yield: 24 rolls.

(1035)   SWEDISH RYE ROLLS

½ cake yeast	2 teaspoons salt
¼ cup lukewarm milk	2 teaspoons caraway seed
1 teaspoon sugar	5 cups rye flour
1 pint lukewarm water	

Dissolve yeast and sugar in milk. Pour in mixing bowl. Add lukewarm water, salt, caraway seed, and 2 cups rye flour. Stir well with a wooden spoon and set to rise in a warm place. In

two hours it should be well risen and full of bubbles. Stir in
more flour, enough to make a very stiff dough. Beat this and
set to rise for another two hours. Turn onto floured board,
knead well, and place in greased muffin rings or form into round
rolls. Let rise until dough starts to crack. Then, with your hand
dipped in cold water, wet the rolls and put them in the oven.
Bake at 375° to 400° F. about 15 to 18 minutes, depending on
size of rolls. This batter may be placed in a loaf pan and baked
as bread if desired, in which case bake at 350° F. 45 to 50 minutes. Yield: 24 small rolls.

(1036)   CINNAMON ROLL

Roll baking powder biscuit (No. 1012) batter ½ inch thick.
Spread with a mixture of 2 tablespoons sugar and ½ teaspoon
cinnamon. Roll like a jelly roll. Cut slices ¾ inch thick. Bake in
quick oven (450° F.) 10 to 15 minutes. Yield: 12 rolls. Chopped
nut meats may be added to the sugar-cinnamon mixture.

(1037)   PECAN ROLLS

½ cake yeast	4 cups sifted flour
¼ cup sugar	¼ cup butter
¼ cup shortening	1 cup brown sugar
1 beaten egg	1 cup chopped pecans
1 cup milk	48 whole pecans
¾ teaspoon salt	

Soften yeast in 2 tablespoons lukewarm water. Add ½ teaspoon sugar. Cream fat. Add sugar, egg, and lukewarm milk.
Add yeast. Mix and sift salt and flour. Stir into first mixture
until dough is firm. Knead 10 to 15 minutes on a floured board,
until smooth and elastic to the touch. Put dough in a greased
bowl. Set in a warm place to rise until doubled in bulk. Knead
again. Roll out in rectangular shape ¼ inch thick. Spread with
softened butter. Dredge with brown sugar. Sprinkle with
chopped pecans. Roll like a jelly roll. Cut in 1-inch thick slices.
Place 4 whole pecans, 2 teaspoons brown sugar, and ½ teaspoon
butter in each muffin pan. Press 1 roll into each hard enough
to make nuts stick. Cover and set in warm place to rise until
doubled in bulk. Bake in moderate oven (350° F.) about 20
minutes, or until lightly browned. Turn out, bottom side up,
so pecans will be on top. Yield: 12 rolls.

(1038)   RAISIN ROLLS

2 cups flour	⅔ cup milk
5 teaspoons baking powder	1 teaspoon melted butter
1 teaspoon salt	½ cup raisins
2 tablespoons sugar	¼ cup chopped nuts
3 tablespoons shortening	½ teaspoon cinnamon

Mix and sift flour, baking powder, salt, and 1 tablespoon of
sugar. Cut in shortening with a knife or rub in with the finger
tips. Add milk gradually and mix to a soft dough. Roll out on a
slightly floured board. Brush over with the melted butter.
Sprinkle with raisins, nuts, 1 tablespoon sugar, and the cinnamon. Roll like a jelly roll and cut in ¾-inch slices. Put in a
greased baking pan, cut side down, and bake in a quick oven
(425° F.) 15 minutes. Serve hot. This recipe makes 8 rolls.

(1039)   BUTTERSCOTCH ROLLS

Follow recipe for raisin rolls (No. 1038). Line a deep greased
pan with 1 cup brown sugar creamed with 2 tablespoons butter
and 1 tablespoon cold water. Lay the rolls on this mixture. Bake
in a hot oven (375° F.) 20 to 25 minutes. Turn biscuits out on
a plate and serve hot.

(1040)   PEANUT BUTTER ROLLS

2 cups homemade biscuit mix (No. 923)	½ cup peanut butter
	2 tablespoons cream

Roll dough in rectangle ¼ inch thick. Cream peanut butter
and cream. Spread on dough. Roll as a jelly roll. Slice ¾ inch
thick. Put on greased baking sheet. Bake in moderate oven
(350° F.) 15 to 20 minutes. Yield: 12 rolls.

(1041)   DAINTY ROLLS

2 cups flour	½ cup milk
4 teaspoons baking powder	Butter
1 teaspoon salt	Seedless raisins
2 tablespoons sugar	Chopped nuts
½ cup shortening	Sugar
1 egg	

Mix and sift flour, baking powder, salt, and sugar. Cut in
shortening with a knife or rub in with the finger tips. Add
beaten egg and enough milk to make a soft dough. Roll out
on slightly floured board to ¼-inch thickness and cut in 3-inch

squares. Spread each lightly with melted butter. Sprinkle with raisins, nuts, and a little sugar. Roll like a jelly roll and press ends together. Brush tops with yoke of egg diluted with 1 teaspoon water. Bake in a hot oven (400° F.) 20 minutes. Yield: 12 rolls.

(1042)   BRAN REFRIGERATOR ROLLS

1 cup boiling water	2 eggs
1 cup shortening	2 cakes yeast
¾ cup sugar	1 cup lukewarm water
1½ cups bran	7 to 8 cups flour
1½ teaspoons salt	

Pour boiling water over the shortening and stir until melted. Add sugar, bran, and salt and mix well. When cool, add beaten eggs and yeast cakes, dissolved in the lukewarm water. Add flour and knead until smooth. Put dough into a bowl and spread with a little melted shortening and cover with wax paper. Set in the refrigerator until ready to use. Pull off a small amount of the dough and shape in ball and place in greased muffin pan. Cover and let rise in a warm place until double in bulk, about 1 hour. Bake in a pre-heated oven (400° F.) for about 20 minutes. Makes 3½ dozen rolls.

(1043)   COFFEE ROLLS

1 cup milk	2 tablespoons lukewarm
¼ cup shortening	water
¼ cup sugar	4 to 5 cups flour
1 teaspoon salt	2 eggs
1 yeast cake	

Heat milk and add shortening, sugar, and salt. When lukewarm, add the yeast cake, dissolved in warm water. Add 1½ cups flour and beat well. Cover and set in a warm place to rise. When double in bulk, add the beaten eggs and mix well. Add enough flour to make a firm dough. Knead on a slightly floured board until smooth and elastic to touch. Cover and set in a warm place to rise until double in bulk. Knead again. Break off small pieces of dough, shape into balls, and flatten like biscuits. Fit into a greased loaf pan. Cover and set in a warm place to rise until treble in bulk. Brush tops with melted butter. Sprinkle with sugar, cinnamon, mace, and chopped raisins. Bake in hot oven (400° F.) 25 to 30 minutes. Yield: 30 rolls.

(1044) CLOVER LEAF ROLLS

Follow recipe for Parker House rolls (yeast) (No. 1030) with following changes: Pull off small bits of dough after the third rising. Shape in small balls. Place 3 balls in each greased muffin pan. Yield: 36 rolls.

(1045) DINNER ROLLS

Follow recipe for Parker House rolls (yeast) (No. 1030) with following changes: Roll dough to ½-inch thickness. Cut with small, round cookie cutter. Yield: 36 rolls.

(1046) CRUSTY WATER ROLLS

1 cup lukewarm water	2 egg whites
1 cake compressed yeast	3–4 cups flour
1 tablespoon sugar	¼ cup farina or white
1 teaspoon salt	corn meal
2 tablespoons melted shortening	1 egg yolk

Soften yeast in part of the water. To remainder add sugar, salt, and shortening. Add 1 cup flour, beating well. Add yeast and beaten egg whites. Mix thoroughly. Add enough more flour to make a soft dough. Knead until satiny. Oil surface lightly. Cover and let rise until doubled in bulk. Punch down. When again doubled, knead down, divide into small portions for rolls. Cover and let "rest" ten minutes. Shape into buns or Vienna rolls. Place 2½ inches apart on oiled baking sheet which has been sprinkled with farina or white corn meal. Cover and let rise until doubled. Brush with egg yolk diluted with cold water. Bake in hot oven (450° F.) 20 minutes. Place large flat pan filled with boiling water on floor of oven to give crustiness. Yield: 24 rolls.

(1047) BUTTERMILK ROLLS

1 cake yeast	¼ teaspoon soda
¼ cup lukewarm water	4 tablespoons melted
2 cups buttermilk	shortening
4 tablespoons sugar	5 cups flour
2 teaspoons salt	

Soften yeast in lukewarm water. Scald buttermilk in top of double boiler. Add sugar, salt, soda, and melted shortening.

Cool to lukewarm. Add softened yeast and half the flour, beating well. Add enough flour to make a soft dough. Turn out on lightly floured board and knead until satiny. Shape into small round biscuits and place in greased pan or roll out ½ inch thick and cut with biscuit cutter. Brush each round with melted butter, fold over like Parker House rolls (No. 1030), and place on greased baking sheet or in shallow pan. Brush lightly with melted butter. Cover and let rise until double in bulk about 1½ hours. Bake in hot oven (400° F.) 15 to 20 minutes. Yield: 6 dozen small rolls.

### (1048)			CARAMEL ROLLS

Prepare sweet yeast dough (No. 924). When light, roll ½ inch thick. Brush with melted butter. Sprinkle with ½ cup brown sugar. Roll as a jelly roll. Cut in 1-inch slices. Brush muffin cups with melted butter, allowing ½ teaspoon per cup. Add 1 teaspoon brown sugar. Put roll slices, cut side down, in cups. Set in warm place to rise until light. Bake in moderate oven (375° F.) 20 to 25 minutes.

### (1049)			ORANGE-DATE ROLLS

2 cups flour	½ cup chopped dates
1 teaspoon salt	1 cup sugar
3 teaspoons baking powder	1 cup water
⅓ cup shortening	¼ cup orange juice
½ to ⅔ cup milk	2 teaspoons lemon juice
Melted butter	1 teaspoon grated orange
1 teaspoon grated lemon	rind
rind	

Sift flour, measure, then sift with baking powder and salt. Cut in the shortening until the mixture has a fine even crumb. Add enough milk to make a soft dough for rolling. Roll out to ¼-inch thickness. Brush with melted butter. Cover with dates and lemon rind. Roll up like jelly roll. Cut in 8 pieces. Place cut side down in a greased baking dish. Pour over the boiling sirup made by boiling all the other ingredients together 5 minutes. Bake in a hot oven (450° F.) for about 30 minutes or until well browned. Yield: 8 rolls.

(1050)   POTATO ROLLS

1 cup mashed potatoes (No. 1835)	½ teaspoon salt
7 cups flour	2 well-beaten eggs
¾ cup shortening	1 cup scalded milk
½ cup sugar	1 yeast cake

Mix potatoes, 1 cup flour, shortening, sugar, and salt. Add eggs and milk, cooled to lukewarm. Dissolve yeast in ½ cup lukewarm water and add to first mixture. Cover and set in a warm place to rise 2 hours. Add 6 cups flour. Knead until smooth and elastic to the touch. Cover and set in a warm place to rise again 1½ hours. Knead. Roll out ¼ inch thick. Cut with biscuit cutter. Fold like Parker House rolls (No. 1030). Lay, with space between, on greased baking pan. Set in warm place and let rise 1½ hours. Bake in hot oven (450° F.) 20 minutes. Yield: 30 rolls.

(1051)   **FLUFFY MUFFINS**

1 cup milk	3 teaspoons baking powder
1 beaten egg	3 tablespoons sugar
¼ cup melted shortening	½ teaspoon salt
2 cups flour	

Mix milk, egg, and shortening. Sift other ingredients together and mix with first mixture lightly. Do not beat. Pour batter into greased muffin pans, ⅔ full, and bake in hot oven (425° F.) 20 to 25 minutes. Yield: 12 muffins.

(1052)   **WHOLE WHEAT MUFFINS**

1 yeast cake	1 well-beaten egg
2 cups scalded milk	2½ cups whole-wheat flour
¼ cup brown sugar	½ teaspoon salt
¼ cup melted shortening	

Cool milk to lukewarm. Add yeast cake and dissolve. Add sugar, shortening, egg, and flour, sifted with the salt. Beat until smooth. Cover and set in a warm place to rise until light. Pour into greased muffin cups, ⅔ full. Cover and set in a warm place to rise until cups are full. Bake in moderate oven (350° F.) 20 to 25 minutes. Yield: 12 muffins.

(1053)   ENGLISH MUFFINS

¼ cup boiled diced potatoes (No. 1834)	1 teaspoon salt
	1 cake yeast
1 cup boiling water	2 cups sifted flour

Measure potatoes by packing down well. Place in mixing bowl and stir in hot water. When lukewarm, add salt, crumbled yeast cake, and two cups flour and beat thoroughly for about two minutes. Cover and let rise in warm place until doubled in bulk. Turn dough out on floured board, dust lightly with flour to facilitate handling, and shape small mound of dough in three-inch rounds, ¼ inch thick. Place in muffin rings, cover and again let rise until doubled in bulk. Carefully slip spatula under muffin ring and place on slightly greased hot griddle. Care must be taken as dough is very soft and falls easily. Bake in moderate oven (350° F.) 15 minutes. Then turn and bake other side 15 minutes. Yield: 9 muffins.

(1054)   BRAN MUFFINS

1 cup sifted flour	1 egg, well beaten
1 cup bran	⅔ cup milk
3½ teaspoons baking powder	3 tablespoons melted shortening
½ teaspoon salt	
3 tablespoons brown or granulated sugar	¼ cup raisins
	¼ cup prunes, chopped

Mix and sift dry ingredients and add bran. Combine egg, milk, and shortening and add to flour mixture. Then add fruit, stirring only until mixed. Use tablespoon to dip batter into greased muffin pans and fill them ⅔ full. Bake in hot oven (425° F.) for 20 to 30 minutes, according to size of muffin. Yield: 12 muffins.

(1055)   CORN MEAL MUFFINS

½ cup corn meal	½ teaspoon salt
1 cup flour	1 tablespoon melted fat
3 teaspoons baking powder	¾ cup milk
1 tablespoon sugar	1 egg

Mix and sift dry ingredients. Add gradually milk, egg, well beaten, and melted fat. Bake in greased muffin pans in hot oven (400° F.) about 25 minutes. Yield: 8 muffins.

(1056) GRAHAM MUFFINS

1½ cups sour milk
¼ cup molasses
1½ teaspoon soda

½ teaspoon salt
2 cups graham flour

Add sour milk to molasses. Put in soda and stir until it foams. Add flour and salt. Bake in a moderate oven (350° F.) 20 to 30 minutes. Makes 12 to 16 muffins.

(1057) BLUEBERRY TEA MUFFINS

¼ cup shortening
⅓ cup sugar
2 beaten eggs
2 cups flour

5 teaspoons baking powder
1 teaspoon salt
⅔ cup milk
½ cup blueberries

Cream shortening and sugar together. Add eggs and mix well. Sift 1½ cups flour, baking powder, and salt together. Add this mixture to first mixture alternately with milk. Sprinkle blueberries with remaining flour and stir in lightly. Bake in greased muffin pans in hot oven (400° F.) 25 to 30 minutes. Yield: 12 muffins.

(1058) QUICK FRUIT MUFFINS

2 cups homemade biscuit
mix (No. 923)
¼ cup sugar
1 beaten egg
1 cup milk

½ cup dates, nut meats, blueberries, sliced cranberries, or chopped fruits

Combine biscuit mix and sugar. Put egg in cup and fill cup with milk. Add this to dough, combining thoroughly without beating. Add dates, nut meats, etc., singly or in combination, as desired. Pour into greased muffin pans. Bake in hot oven (400° F.) 20 minutes. Yield: 8 muffins.

(1059) CEREAL MUFFINS

Follow recipe for fluffy muffins (No. 1051), adding 1 cup cold, cooked or flaked cereal. Increase milk slightly if dry cereal is used and decrease milk if cooked cereal is employed. Add cereal with sifted dry ingredients.

(1060)   BREAD MUFFINS

4 cups crumbled stale bread	1 cup flour
2 cups milk	¼ teaspoon salt
3 egg yolks	2 teaspoons baking powder
1 teaspoon melted shortening	3 egg whites

Soak bread in milk 15 minutes. Beat to a smooth paste. Add yolks and shortening. Mix well. Mix and sift flour, salt, and baking powder. Add to first mixture. Mix thoroughly. Add egg whites. Fill greased muffin cups ⅔ full. Bake in hot oven (425° F.) 20 minutes. Yield: 18 muffins.

(1061)   CHERRY MUFFINS

Follow recipe for blueberry tea muffins (No. 1057), using seeded and quartered cherries instead of blueberries.

(1062)   BACONIZED CORN MUFFINS

1 cup flour	1 egg
1 cup corn meal	1 cup sour milk
¼ cup sugar	2 tablespoons melted
1 teaspoon baking powder	shortening
1 teaspoon salt	Bacon
½ teaspoon soda	

Sift flour once before measuring. Sift flour, corn meal, sugar, baking powder, soda, and salt together. Beat the egg and add milk. Combine with flour mixture. Add melted shortening and beat well. Fill oiled muffin pans ⅔ full. Sprinkle tops of muffins with uncooked diced bacon. Bake fifteen minutes in hot oven (400° F.), then set muffins under broiler so that bacon may become crisp. Yield: 8 muffins.

(1063)   BANANA BRAN MUFFINS

1 cup flour	1 egg, well beaten
½ teaspoon salt	1 cup shredded bran
½ teaspoon soda	2 tablespoons milk
1 teaspoon baking powder	2 cups bananas, thinly
2 tablespoons shortening	sliced
¼ cup sugar	

Sift flour, measure, and sift with salt, soda, and baking powder. Cream shortening, add sugar gradually, and cream well. Add egg, bran, and milk. Mix and allow to stand while slicing bananas. Add bananas and mix well. Add sifted dry ingredients, stirring as little as possible. Bake in greased muffin tins at 375° F. for 20 to 30 minutes. Yield: 12 muffins.

(1064)   GLUTEN MUFFINS

1 beaten egg	2 cups gluten flour
2 cups milk	2 teaspoons baking powder
1 teaspoon salt	

Mix egg and milk. Add salt and flour. Beat well. Add baking powder. Pour into greased muffin cups, ⅔ full. Bake in quick oven (450° F.) 15 minutes. Yield: 12 muffins.

(1065)   GRAHAM CRACKER MUFFINS

18 graham crackers	½ cup seeded raisins
2 tablespoons sugar	3 tablespoons melted
¼ teaspoon salt	butter
1 tablespoon flour	1 egg, beaten
3 teaspoons baking powder	½ cup lukewarm milk

Crumble crackers fine. Add sugar, salt, flour, and baking powder. Blend thoroughly. Cut raisins in halves and stir into dry ingredients. Add melted butter. Pour heated milk over cracker mixture. Add beaten egg. Mix lightly and fill hot, greased muffin pans ⅔ full of mixture. Bake in hot oven (400° F.) 20 minutes. Yield: 12 small muffins.

(1066)   DOUGHNUT MUFFINS

1½ tablespoons shortening	½ teaspoon nutmeg
½ cup sugar	½ teaspoon salt
1 egg	2 teaspoons baking powder
2 cups flour	½ cup milk

Cream shortening and sugar. Add egg. Beat well. Mix and sift dry ingredients. Add alternately with milk to first mixture. Bake in small greased muffin pans in hot oven (400° F.) 20 to 25 minutes. Dip in melted butter or margarine. Roll in confectioner's sugar or mixed sugar and cinnamon. Serve hot. Yield: 24 muffins.

(1067)   SALLY LUNN MUFFINS

Follow recipe for blueberry tea muffins (No. 1057), omitting blueberries and using only 4 teaspoons baking powder.

(1068)   GRAHAM GEMS

2 cups flour	1 teaspoon salt
1½ cups graham flour	2 eggs, beaten
½ cup sugar	1½ cups buttermilk
2 teaspoons soda	⅓ cup melted shortening

Mix ingredients just enough to hold them together. Half-fill greased muffin pans and bake 15 minutes in a moderate oven (350° F.). Serve warm. Yield: 8 muffins.

(1069)   APPLE GEMS

1¼ cups scalded milk	1 cup flour
4 tablespoons shortening	2 teaspoons baking powder
2 tablespoons sugar	1 teaspoon salt
⅔ cup yellow corn meal	1½ cups chopped apples
1 beaten egg	

Add shortening, sugar, and corn meal to milk and mix well. Add egg, flour, baking powder, and salt. Add apples to batter and beat thoroughly. Drop into greased muffin pans and bake in moderate oven (350° F.) 25 to 30 minutes. Yield: 12 to 14 muffins.

(1070)   GRAHAM BUNS

1 cake yeast	⅓ cup sugar
2 cups scalded milk	¼ cup melted shortening
2 cups white flour	4 cups whole-wheat flour
1 teaspoon salt	

Dissolve yeast in 2 tablespoons lukewarm water. Add milk, cooled to lukewarm, and beat in white flour, making a smooth batter. Cover and set in a warm place to rise until light, about 2 hours. Add salt, sugar, and shortening. Mix thoroughly. Add whole-wheat flour and make a firm dough. Knead on a floured board until smooth and elastic to the touch. Cover and set in warm place to rise until double in bulk. Knead again. Cover and let rise again to double bulk. Knead. Roll out ½ inch thick. Cut with cookie cutter. Form into desired shape. Put 1 inch apart on greased baking pan. Set in warm place to rise until double in bulk. Bake in moderate oven (350° F.) 20 to 25 minutes. Yield: 12 to 16 buns.

(1071) RAISIN BUNS

2 cakes yeast	1 teaspoon salt
¼ cup lukewarm water	2 eggs, beaten
1 cup milk	5 cups sifted flour
¼ cup butter	1 cup seedless raisins
½ cup sugar	

Soften yeast in lukewarm water. Scald milk. Add butter, sugar, and salt. Cool to lukewarm. Add flour to make a thick batter. Add yeast and eggs. Beat well. Add raisins and enough more flour to make a soft dough. Turn out on lightly floured board and knead until satiny. Place in greased bowl, cover and let rise until double in bulk. When light, punch down and shape into rolls. Let rise until double in bulk. Bake in moderate oven (375° F.) 20 to 25 minutes. Frost with confectioners' icing (No. 3173). Yield: 4 dozen rolls.

(1072) CINNAMON BUNS

Add ½ to ¾ cup milk to 2 cups homemade biscuit mix (No. 923). Roll out ⅓ inch thick and 8 inches wide. Brush with melted butter and sprinkle with mixture of 3 parts sugar and 1 part cinnamon. Fold over twice, making 3 layers of dough. Slice into 1-inch strips. Bake on greased baking pan in moderate oven (350° F.) 25 to 30 minutes. Allow 2 cups biscuit mix for 8 buns.

(1073) HOT CROSS BUNS

1 cup scalded milk	¼ cup shortening
1 yeast cake	½ cup raisins
6½ tablespoons sugar	1 teaspoon salt
3½ cups flour	¼ cup confectioners' icing
2 well-beaten eggs	(No. 3173)

Cool milk to lukewarm. Add yeast and 1½ tablespoons sugar. Dissolve. Add 1½ cups flour. Beat thoroughly. Cover and set aside in a warm place to rise until light. Cream shortening and

balance of sugar. Add 1 egg and raisins. Add to first mixture.
Add remaining flour, sifted with the salt. Knead until satiny.
Cover and set in a warm place to rise again until double in bulk.
Mold into round buns. Put on greased baking pan. Cover and
set in a warm place to rise until very light. Brush tops with
remaining egg. Form the design of a cross on tops with back of
a knife. Bake in moderate oven (350° F.) 15 to 20 minutes.
Top with icing. Yield: 12 buns.

(1074)   **WHEAT STICKS**

1 cup flour	1 tablespoon sugar
½ cup whole-wheat flour	1½ tablespoons shortening
1 teaspoon salt	

Mix and sift flour, salt, and sugar. Work shortening in with
the finger tips. Add ⅓ cup water gradually, stirring constantly.
Mix well and knead for a few moments on a floured board.
Roll to ½-inch thickness. Cut into strips 3 inches by ¼ inch.
Put on greased baking pan with space between and bake in moderate oven (350° F.) until golden brown, turning once. Yield:
12 sticks.

(1075)   **CORN STICKS**

1 cup sifted flour	1 cup sour milk or
1 cup corn meal	buttermilk
½ teaspoon baking soda	1 tablespoon melted
1 teaspoon salt	shortening
1 egg, beaten	

Mix and sift flour, corn meal, soda and salt. Combine egg and
milk. Add to flour mixture, stirring until well mixed. Stir in
shortening. Turn into greased bread-stick pans and bake in hot
oven (425° F.) 15 to 20 minutes. To use sweet instead of sour
milk, substitute 3 teaspoons baking powder for soda. For corn
bread, bake in greased, shallow pan in hot oven (400° F.) about
30 minutes. Yield: 12 corn sticks.

(1076)   **RYE STICKS**

Follow recipe for rye biscuits (No. 1017), but roll out ½
inch thick and cut into 3 inches by ½ inch sticks.

(1077)   **BUCKWHEAT STICKS**

Follow recipe for rye sticks (No. 1076), using buckwheat
flour instead of rye flour.

(1078)   **CREAM STICKS**

Follow recipe for wheat sticks (No. 1074), adding ⅓ cup
cream and ½ cup flour and eliminating shortening.

(1079)   **WALNUT STICKS OR BISCUITS**

Add ⅓ cup chopped walnuts to recipe for wheat sticks (No.
1074) or whole-wheat biscuits (No. 1016).

(1080)   **PINEAPPLE TEA GEMS**

1 14-ounce can pineapple	1 cup milk
gems	2 cups sifted all-purpose
¼ cup butter	flour
¼ cup sugar	5 teaspoons baking powder
½ teaspoon salt	Cinnamon
1 egg	

Cream butter. Add sugar gradually and then the well-beaten
egg. Sift baking powder, flour, and salt and add alternately
with milk to first mixture. Fill small greased muffin pans about
⅔ full. Put a well-drained gem on top of each muffin and
sprinkle with a mixture of cinnamon and sugar. Bake in a moderately hot oven (400° F.) about 20 minutes. Serve hot. Yield:
24 muffins.

(1081)   **CHEESE ROULETTES**

2 cups sifted cake flour	Melted butter
2 teaspoons baking powder	1 cup grated American
½ teaspoon salt	cheese
4 tablespoons butter or other	Salt
shortening	Paprika
⅔ cup milk	

Sift flour once, measure, add baking powder and salt, and
sift again. Cut in shortening. Add milk all at once and stir carefully until all flour is dampened. Then stir vigorously until

mixture forms a soft dough and follows spoon around bowl. Turn out immediately on slightly floured board and knead 30 seconds. Roll into oblong sheet, ⅛ inch thick. Brush with melted butter. Spread cheese evenly over dough. Sprinkle with salt and paprika. Cut in strips, 6 x ½ inches, roll each strip, and place in greased muffin pans. Or roll sheet as for jelly roll, cut in ¾-inch slices, and place slices on greased baking sheet. Bake in hot oven (425° F.) 15 to 20 minutes. Yield: 2 dozen roulettes.

(1082)   JELLY PANCAKES

1 cup sifted flour	1 cup milk
1 teaspoon baking powder	2 tablespoons melted butter
½ teaspoon salt	or other shortening
1 teaspoon sugar	2 egg whites, stiffly beaten
2 egg yolks, slightly beaten	

Sift flour once, measure, add baking powder, salt, and sugar, and sift again. Combine egg yolks and milk. Add gradually to flour mixture, beating only until smooth. Add shortening. Fold in egg whites. Bake on hot, greased griddle. Spread with jelly and roll, or roll and serve around fried sausages (No. 1469) or bacon (No. 1464). Makes six 7-inch pancakes.

(1083)   CREAM SCONES

2 cups flour	Grated rind of 1 orange
½ teaspoon baking soda	¾ cup light cream
¾ teaspoon salt	4 teaspoons vinegar
2 tablespoons sugar	1 egg, slightly beaten
4 tablespoons shortening	

Sift and measure flour. Sift again with baking soda, salt, and sugar. Cut in shortening until as fine as coarse corn meal. Add orange rind. Combine cream and vinegar. Add to flour mixture, stirring quickly to form a stiff dough. Knead slightly on slightly floured board. Roll out ⅜ inch thick. Cut in diamond shapes. Brush with egg. Place on ungreased baking sheet. Bake 10 to 12 minutes at 475° F. Yield: 12 scones.

Fish

~~~~~~

EVERY homemaker should replace meat courses with fish at least twice a week. In general, it is less costly than meat, it is rich in proteins and vitamins, and, because it is low in fats and carbohydrates, it is an excellent food for persons who get little exercise, either at work or play.

The average housewife often refrains from serving fish to her family because one or more members of the family circle express dislike for it. In this section a large number of new ways to prepare fish are given and many of them, in most cases, will overcome that obstacle.

One should be extremely careful in purchasing fish. Fresh fish must be *fresh* for it decomposes quickly. It is much better to buy preserved or frozen fish than doubtful fresh fish. Frozen fish should always be bought completely enclosed in ice. It should be thawed out slowly in the refrigerator and should be used as soon as possible after thawing.

(1101)   BROILED FISH

Only small fish, or fish that may be opened out, can be broiled. Put well-dried seasoned fish on hissing hot broiler and cook over or under heat unit until flesh leaves the bone when pierced with a fork. The inside of the fish should always be broiled first and the fish then turned and broiled on the skin side. When the fish is done, it should be carefully loosened from the broiler and slipped onto a hot platter. Allow ⅓ to ½ pound fish per serving.

(1102)   BOILED FISH

The simplest way is to wrap the fish in a piece of cheese cloth and put into a kettle of boiling water. Carrot and celery may be added if desired. Cook until the fish leaves the bone. If the fish is placed in a strainer above the water, it will be steamed, instead of boiled. Allow ⅓ to ½ pound fish per serving.

(1103)   FRIED FISH

Wipe thoroughly with cold, damp cloth. Cut off tail and head. If fish is large enough, split down middle. Clean and remove as many bones as possible. Sprinkle with salt and pepper. Sprinkle with corn meal. Dip in beaten egg, diluted with a little cold water. Roll in bread crumbs. Fry in little fat until a delicate brown. Never use butter in frying fish as it takes out flavor and gives a poor color. Allow ⅓ to ½ pound fish per person. To fry fish in batter, mix ½ cup flour, ½ teaspoon salt, ¼ teaspoon pepper, ¼ cup milk, 1 tablespoon lemon juice, 1 tablespoon olive oil, and 1 beaten egg. Dip small pieces of fish in this batter and cook in deep hot fat (375° F.) 3 to 5 minutes. Or, dip the fish in batter and sauté in little fat until well browned on both sides.

(1104)   FISH BOILED IN PARCHMENT PAPER

2 pounds boneless filets or steaks	2 tablespoons grated onion
2 tablespoons melted butter or cooking oil	1 tablespoon parsley, chopped fine
¼ teaspoon pepper	1 tablespoon lemon juice
2 tablespoons grated carrot	2 sheets parchment paper about 2 feet square

Prepare a salt solution in the proportion of 2 tablespoons salt to 1 cup cold water. Fish that is ⅝ inch thick should be kept in the salt solution for about 5 minutes, but this time may be varied from 5 to 10 minutes, depending upon thickness of flesh and variety of fish. Fill a kettle ⅔ full of water and start heating. Oil or wet both sides of parchment paper and lay flat. Cut fish to serving size pieces and divide between the two papers, arranging the pieces one layer deep on each paper. Mix the pepper with the butter and put one teaspoon each of butter, onion, and carrot over each serving of fish. Sprinkle with lemon juice

and chopped parsley. Bring edges of paper together and tie.
Immerse in boiling water. After water boils, continue cooking
until tender. This will take from 8 to 15 minutes, depending
upon thickness of flesh and variety of fish. Remove to a hot
platter, and pour juices over the fish or thicken them for a
gravy. A tightly covered steamer, lined with oiled or wet parchment paper, may be used in this method of cooking. The fish
must be laid in a single layer. Steaming will require more time
to cook than will boiling. Allow 1/3 to 1/2 pound fish per serving.

(1105)   STEAMED FISH

Cut fish into pieces for serving. Cover fish with a solution
of 1 part salt to 8 parts water. Let stand 5 minutes. Remove
fish. Drain. Place in oiled steamer and cook until tender, from
5 to 12 minutes, depending on size. Serve with cream sauce
(No. 2005) or drawn butter (No. 2025). Allow 1/3 to 1/2 pound
fish per person.

(1106)   BAKED FISH

Either stuffed whole fish or filets may be baked in the oven.
Rub the prepared fish with flour and if not a fat fish dot over
with butter. Put into a 375° F. oven until it begins to color
and then lower the temperature to 350° F. until the meat leaves
the bone easily. It should be seasoned when about half cooked.
Allow 1/3 to 1/2 pound fish per serving.

(1107)   BAKING FISH IN THE GROUND

Four pounds or more of large fish should be cleared of gills
and viscera, but head, tail, fins, and scales may be left intact.
Lean fish should have three cuts across the skin on both sides.
About 2 teaspoons salt and 3/8 teaspoon pepper should be well
spread on the inside of the body cavity. A few thin strips of
bacon or salt pork may replace the salt and a few thin slices of
onion added if desired. Dig a trench about 10 inches deep and
of equal width and long enough to hold the fish. In this hole
build a fire, adding wood until about 2 inches of coals are
formed. Remove all flaming wood and about half the hot coals.
Smooth out the remaining coals and cover 1 inch with green
grass. On this place the fish and cover with another inch layer of

grass, then cover with the rest of the live coals. Cover with warm earth from around the edges of the hole. At the end of one hour, the fish should be carefully removed. The flesh may then be separated easily from the inedible portions. Allow ⅓ to ½ pound fish per person.

(1108)   **PLANKED FISH**

Follow recipe for planked halibut (No. 1171), using any fish with white flesh.

(1109)   **FISH AND APPLES**

2 pounds filets or steaks, about ⅝ inch thick	½ teaspoon salt
	1 teaspoon sugar
2¼ pounds apples	¼ teaspoon black pepper
3 tablespoons fat	4 tablespoons melted
2 tablespoons water	butter

Cover fish with a salt solution made in the proportion of 2 tablespoons salt to 1 cup cold water and allow to stand for 3 minutes and drain. Heat slowly fat in a deep frying pan. Wash, quarter, and core apples and slice to ¼ inch thick. Place the apples into the hot fat, adding the water, salt, and sugar. Cover tightly and cook slowly with one turning, until apples are almost tender. Lay the fish, flesh side down, on the apples, cover and allow to steam 3 to 5 minutes. Remove cover, turn fish, baste it with a mixture of the pepper and butter, and place for 5 to 10 minutes under the broiler until well browned. Remove the fish to a hot platter and surround with the apples. Serves 6.

(1110)   **FISH AND CABBAGE**

3 pounds cabbage	¼ teaspoon pepper
2 pounds filets of fish	4 tablespoons garlic vine-
4 tablespoons melted	gar, green pepper vine-
butter	gar, or onion vinegar

Quarter the cabbage and soak in salted water long enough to cleanse thoroughly. Cut the cabbage into coarse shreds and boil in plenty of salted water in an uncovered kettle. For each quart of water allow 1 teaspoon salt. While the cabbage is cooking, place the fish for 3 minutes in a salt solution made in the proportion of 2 tablespoons salt to 1 cup cold water. Drain the fish and brush cooking oil on all sides. When the cabbage is almost tender, place fish, flesh side down, in a well-oiled basket or steamer and suspend over the cabbage for 5 minutes with the kettle covered. Remove fish and as soon as the cabbage is tender, spread it out on an oiled plank or heat-proof platter. Lay the fish, flesh side up, on the cabbage and baste with a mixture of butter, pepper, and vinegar. Broil the fish for 5 to 10 minutes until well browned. Allow 1/3 to 1/2 pound fish per serving.

(1111)   **FISH À LA KING**

Follow recipe for tuna fish à la king (No. 1213), using any cooked, flaked fish instead of tuna.

(1112)   **FISH PATTIES**

2 cups diced cold cooked fish   Salt—Cayenne
1 cup thin white sauce   6 patty shells (No. 2709)
   (No. 2004)

Mix fish and sauce. Heat through. Season to taste with salt and cayenne. Serve in patty shells. Serves 6.

(1113)   **HASH SUPREME**

2 cups cold cooked flaked   2 1/2 cups diced boiled potatoes
   fish   (No. 1834)
3/4 cup salt pork, diced   1/4 teaspoon pepper
3/4 cup onion, diced   1/2 teaspoon salt
1 cup diced cooked beets   1/4 cup water
   (No. 1726)   4 tablespoons garlic vine-
                                      gar

Mix the vinegar and fish flakes. Fry the pork to a golden brown, add the onion, and cook to a golden yellow. Add all of the ingredients and lastly pour over the 1/4 cup of water. Cover and let cook slowly. Stir occasionally until thoroughly heated through and the flavors are blended. Serves 6.

(1114)   **FISH PIE**

2 tablespoons butter or fat
2 tablespoons flour
¼ teaspoon salt
1 cup milk
2 cups cooked fish flakes
¾ cup boiled peas
    (No. 1823)

1 tablespoon chopped
    onion
1 tablespoon chopped
    green pepper
1 cup mashed potatoes
    (No. 1835)

Melt butter in frying pan. Add flour and brown. Add salt and milk. Heat and stir until creamy. Add fish flakes, peas, onion, and green pepper. Heat through. Turn into greased baking dish. Top with potatoes. Bake in hot oven (400° F.) 12 minutes. Serves 6.

(1115)   **FISH IMPERIAL**

2 cups cooked fish flakes
3 tablespoons vinegar
3 eggs
2 cups milk
¼ teaspoon black pepper

2 tablespoons parsley,
    chopped fine
2 tablespoons grated onion
1 teaspoon salt

Start the oven at a slow heat. Combine fish flakes and vinegar. Whip the egg whites until stiff and set aside. Beat the egg yolks, add milk, salt, pepper, onion, parsley, fish flakes, and mix well. Lastly fold in the stiffly beaten whites. Pour into greased baking dish. Garnish with strips of pimiento. Set in a pan of warm water in a moderate oven and bake slowly about 45 minutes, until a silver knife when inserted will come out clean. Serves 6.

(1116)   **FISH FLAKE OMELET**

2 cups cold cooked flaked
    fish
½ cup milk
¼ teaspoon black pepper
2 tablespoons chopped
    parsley

2 tablespoons grated onion
3 tablespoons vinegar or
    lemon juice
1 teaspoon salt
4 tablespoons melted butter
4 eggs

Light the oven for slow heat. Add the vinegar or lemon juice to the fish flakes. Heat slowly the butter in the frying pan. Beat the egg whites stiff and set aside. Then beat the egg yolks and add milk, salt, pepper, parsley, onion, and stir. Add the cold flakes and mix well. Last fold in the stiff egg whites and pour into the hot fat in the frying pan. Let cook slowly over a low heat. When cooked through, place in the oven to dry on top. When dry enough to touch without wetting fingers, remove and cut opposite edges of omelet loose from the pan. Fold over and remove to a hot platter. Serves 6.

(1117) FISH FLAKES AND CRUMBS

2 pounds cold cooked flaked salmon, bluefish, mackerel, or other fat fish of distinctive flavor	2 cups coarsely crushed crackers
2 cups milk	½ teaspoon salt
	⅓ teaspoon pepper
	2 tablespoons butter

Heat milk with seasoning and butter, stir in crackers until all are wet, and add fish, mixing it with the cracker, stirring as little as possible. If desired, 2 eggs, beaten, may be added to the wet cracker mixture and the whole heated until the egg is cooked. Then the fish flakes may be added. Serves 6.

(1118) PLAIN CREAMED FLAKES

2½ cups cold flaked cooked fish	4 tablespoons flour
6 tablespoons melted butter	2 cups milk
	Salt and pepper

Put melted butter in saucepan, stir in flour until smooth, add milk, and continue stirring until the sauce thickens. Add flakes, stir while they warm, and season as desired. Serves 6.

(1119) FISH FLAKES IN CREAM

2½ cups cold flaked cooked fish	3 tablespoons chopped parsley
¼ teaspoon pepper	2 tablespoons onion, grated
½ teaspoon salt	4 tablespoons butter
1 cup cream	

Put butter to heat in a frying pan over a slow fire. In a bowl combine other ingredients with cream, adding fish flakes last. Put into the fat and simmer slowly until thoroughly heated and seasonings are well blended. Serve on toast or with baked potatoes (No. 1837). Serves 6.

(1120) BOILED FISH AND VEGETABLE DINNER

2 pounds filets, steaks, or
    pan-dressed fish
½ pound each turnips, pota-
    toes, onions, carrots
¾ cup diced salt pork

1 pound cooked cabbage
    (No. 1736)
1 teaspoon salt
¼ teaspoon pepper

In a heavy kettle or Dutch oven, fry the pork to a golden brown, add 1 cup water and all the vegetables except the cabbage, which is cooked separately. Allow the vegetables to cook for 20 to 25 minutes, add the salt, pepper, and second cup of water. Lay the fish, flesh side down, across the vegetables, cover with the cooked cabbage, and cook the whole about 5 minutes more. Place the fish in the center of a hot platter, surrounded by the cooked vegetables. The liquid remaining in the kettle may be served in a side bowl. Allow ⅓ to ½ pound fish per serving.

(1121) FISH SOUFFLÉ

2 cups cold cooked fish flakes
2 tablespoons grated carrot
2 tablespoons grated onion
½ teaspoon pepper
½ teaspoon salt

4 eggs
2 cups well-seasoned
    mashed potatoes
    (No. 1835)

Pre-heat the oven to 360° F. Mix well with the fish flakes, the salt, pepper, onion, and carrots. Separate the egg yolks and whites. Beat the whites until stiff and set aside. Then beat the yolks until a light yellow and combine with fish flakes, then the potatoes, and lastly fold in the egg whites. Put in a greased baking dish. Set in a pan of warm water and place on the center rack of the oven. Bake slowly 30 minutes. Serves 6.

(1122) CORNING FISH FOR TEMPORARY PRESERVATION

This is the simplest method of preserving surplus fish for a day or two. Scale, clean, and trim the fish: small fish may be split through the back, larger ones split into halves or fileted. The sides of flesh should not be over one inch thick. Wash the fish, drain, and cover all surfaces with as much fine salt as will cling with careful handling, using about 1 pound of salt to 5 pounds of fish. Pack the fish in a deep vessel and store in as cool a place as possible for 4 to 6 hours. The brine formed and any excess salt should then be rinsed from the fish which should be wiped dry and again kept as cool as possible until used, preferably within two days.

(1123)　　BOILED CORNED FISH

This breakfast dish, popular with many commercial fishermen, is easily prepared by placing the corned fish (No. 1122) in cold water and heating to the simmering point. Drain off the water and repeat, cooking the fish until tender. Season with pepper and butter. It is generally eaten with potatoes which are not salted.

(1124)　　CREAMED CORNED FISH

Boil corned fish (No. 1123) and flake, separating the meat from the skin and all bones. Prepare a medium white sauce (No. 2004), omitting salt. Add the fish flakes and heat. Allow 2 cups fish and 1 cup sauce for 6 servings.

(1125)　　CORNED FISH CAKES

3 cups flaked boiled corned fish (No. 1123) of a white meated variety	3 eggs, beaten 1 tablespoon butter or cooking oil
3 cups finely diced boiled potatoes (No. 1834)	¼ teaspoon pepper 1 cup flour

Break the flakes to small pieces and mix with the potatoes and eggs. Heat the butter, add pepper, and mix thoroughly with solids. Form into flat cakes not over 1 inch thick, cover these with flour and fry in cooking oil. If desired, the eggs may be omitted and ½ cup finely chopped onions added. Serves 8.

(1126)　　BAKED FILETS OF BASS

Wipe fish with cold, damp cloth. Cut into small filets. Put in baking pan. Season to taste with salt and pepper. Cover with greased baking paper. Bake in hot oven (400° F.) 8 to 12 minutes, depending on thickness. Serve with hollandaise sauce (No. 2022). Allow ⅓ to ½ pound fish per person.

(1127)   BAKED BLUEFISH

3 pounds bluefish, split and boned	1 small onion
Salt—Pepper	½ green pepper
Juice 1 lemon	1 teaspoon chopped parsley
½-inch slice eggplant	4 ripe olives
2 heads of mushrooms	2 tablespoons butter
12 anchovy filets	1 tablespoon angostura

Put fish in greased baking dish. Sprinkle with salt, pepper, and lemon juice. Chop eggplant, mushrooms, anchovy filets, onion, green pepper, parsley, and olives separately. Combine and spread on fish. Cover with buttered brown paper and bake in moderate oven (350° F.) 20 minutes. Remove to hot platter. Add butter and angostura to dish juice and pour over fish. Serves 6.

(1128)   BROILED BLUEFISH

Follow recipe for broiled fish (No. 1101).

(1129)   PLANKED BLUEFISH

Grease well a hard-wood fish plank, about 16 by 12 inches. Heat very hot. Wipe fish with cold, damp cloth. Cut off head and tail. Split down middle. Clean and remove as many bones as possible. Place, skin side down, on plank. Brush with melted butter and sprinkle with salt and pepper. Place under broiler and cook 12 to 20 minutes, depending on size. Rim plank with duchess potatoes (No. 1846), put on with pastry tube. Put in oven and bake at moderate heat (350° F.) until potatoes are browned. Arrange hot boiled carrots (No. 1745), creamed Brussels sprouts (No. 1735), and fancy-cut pickled beets
around fish. See planked steak (No. 1305) for other possible combinations of vegetables. Allow ⅓ to ½ pound of fish per person.

(1130)   SAUTÉED BUTTERFISH

Wipe fish with cold, damp cloth. Sprinkle with salt and pepper. Dredge with flour. Fry in small amount of fat in frying pan until brown on both sides, about 10 minutes. Sprinkle with chopped parsley and lemon juice. Serve, garnished with watercress and lemon slices. Allow ⅓ to ½ pound of fish per person.

(1131) CARP

Live carp, if it has not already been dressed by the retailer, may be dressed in the home by the following method: First, cut half through the body from the back of the head and just in rear of the gills to allow free bleeding; the back fin is then cut out and the scales and outer skin removed by a process known as flensing. A very sharp, thin, pointed knife is required. The fish is grasped by the tail and the scales and outer skin shaved off in strips by working the knife toward the head without cutting into the flesh. The body cavity is then split from back to front, care being used to avoid cutting into the viscera which may then be removed as a whole. The head is then cut off back of the front fins, and the tail and other fins cut away. The fish is then thoroughly cleansed in cold water. A simpler operation which removes the entire skin is to plunge the fish (or its filets) into boiling water, allowing it to remain for about 25 seconds after boiling starts again. The skin may then be easily rubbed off while the fish is hot, and the flesh rinsed in cold water. If the boiling is continued too long, the flesh may break up. After dressing, the carp should be treated as outlined below. The treatment consists of covering the dressed fish or filet with a mixture made in the following proportions:

1 cup salt	1 teaspoon black pepper
1 cup onion, finely crushed	⅛ teaspoon mace
2 tablespoons vinegar	

Chop and crush the onion by passing through the finest plate of a food chopper, saving all the juice. Mix the ingredients thoroughly. Place the fish in a deep plate and cover all surfaces with the mixture and allow it to stand for 1 hour. The fish is then thoroughly rinsed and the mixture discarded. The fish then should be washed in a pan of cold water for about 1 minute to remove any last traces of salt on its surface. The prepared fish may be boiled, fried, broiled, or baked.

(1132) BROILED CARP

Clean and season as per recipe for carp (No. 1131). Split into filets ⅝ inch thick. Broil, according to recipe for broiled salmon steak (No. 1180), eliminating seasonings.

(1133)   FRIED CARP

Clean and season as per recipe for carp (No. 1131). Cut in filets ⅝ inch thick. Fry according to recipe for fried fish (No. 1103), eliminating seasonings.

(1134)   BOILED CARP

The fish prepared as per recipe for carp (No. 1131), is boiled for 8 minutes in salted water, allowing 1½ tablespoons salt to each quart of water. Any desired sauce may be served with the fish. Extra portions may be used for flaked fish dishes. Allow ⅓ to ½ pound of fish per serving.

(1135)   BAKED CARP

Prepare fish as per recipe for carp (No. 1131). Grease a baking pan. Lay 2 strips bacon in pan. Put in fish. Lay 2 strips bacon on top. Bake for 10 minutes in very hot oven (500° F.). Reduce oven heat to 400° F. and bake 8 to 10 minutes longer. It may be cooked with sliced onions, stewed tomatoes (No. 1893), or other suitable vegetables, if desired, or served with creole sauce (No. 2047), white sauce (No. 2004), or other sauces. An excellent dish is obtained by dipping the slices of fish into milk (without salt), rolling in sifted bread crumbs, and putting a teaspoonful of cooking oil over each service portion of fish. Allow ⅓ to ½ pound fish per serving.

(1136)   BROILED COD

Split down back. Remove backbone and as many bones as possible. Follow recipe for broiled fish (No. 1101).

(1137)   SAUTÉED CODFISH

Skin fish and remove backbone. Cut in square pieces. Season to taste with salt and pepper. Roll in corn meal or cracker crumbs. Fry in little fat until brown on both sides, about 10 minutes. Drain on unglazed paper. Serve with tartar sauce (No. 2044). Allow ⅓ to ½ pound of fish per person.

(1138)   BOILED CODFISH

1 tablespoon butter	½ bay leaf
2 tablespoons chopped celery	1 tablespoon vinegar
1 chopped onion	1 teaspoon salt
1 chopped carrot	⅛ teaspoon pepper
1 tablespoon chopped parsley	2½ pounds cod

Melt butter in pan. Add celery, onion, carrot, and parsley. Sauté 2 minutes, stirring constantly. Add 2 quarts water, bay leaf, vinegar, salt, and pepper. Bring to boil. Wipe fish with cold, damp cloth. Wrap in cheesecloth. Drop in boiling water. Cover. Reduce heat and let simmer 30 minutes. Remove fish from cloth and serve hot with egg sauce (No. 2009), garnished with parsley. Serves 6.

(1139)   CODFISH BALLS, LOAF, OR PATTIES

6 medium-sized boiled pota-	2 eggs
toes (No. 1834)	¼ teaspoon pepper
2 cups shredded salt cod	½ cup milk

Pare potatoes and mash. Add codfish and eggs. Mix thoroughly. Add pepper and milk. Beat until fluffy. Drop from spoon into deep, hot fat (375° F.) and fry until brown, about 10 minutes. Drain on unglazed paper. Serves 6. This mixture may also be baked as a loaf in a greased baking dish, browning in moderate oven (350° F.). Or, it may be molded into patties and sautéed in little fat in frying pan.

(1140)   COD AU GRATIN

Follow recipe for filet of sole au gratin (No. 1152), using cod instead of filet of sole.

(1141)   SCALLOPED FLAKED COD

Follow recipe for scalloped salmon (No. 1188), using cold, cooked, flaked cod instead of salmon.

(1142)   CREAMED CODFISH

3 cups flaked cooked cod	2 tablespoons chopped
2 cups medium white sauce	celery
(No. 2004)	1 tablespoon chopped
2 tablespoons chopped	pimiento
parsley	

Mix all ingredients and warm through. Serve on hot, buttered toast (No. 988). Serves 6.

(1143)   BOILED CUSK

Follow recipe for boiled fish (No. 1102).

(1144)   FRIED EELS

Skin eels. Split down middle and clean. Cut in 3-inch lengths and wipe dry. Roll in crumbs, dip in slightly beaten egg, diluted with 2 tablespoons water, and roll again in crumbs. Fry in deep hot fat (375° F.) 3 to 5 minutes. Garnish with parsley and slices of lemon. Serves 6.

(1145)   BROILED FINNAN HADDIE

Wash fish well. Soak 30 minutes in cold water. Drain. Cover with simmering water. Let stand 15 minutes. Drain and wipe dry. Brush with melted fat and broil over hot heat 15 minutes. Put on hot platter. Dot with butter. Sprinkle with juice of ½ lemon. Allow ⅓ to ½ pound of fish per person.

(1146)   STEAMED FINNAN HADDIE

2 pounds finnan haddie	4 tablespoons butter
filets	

Place a single layer of fish in a steamer over boiling water and cook until tender, which should take 12 minutes, more or less. Remove fish to hot platter and dress with butter and lemon juice, if desired. Serves 6.

(1147)   CREAMED FINNAN HADDIE

Cover finnan haddie with boiling water and simmer ½ hour. Discard all bones and skin. Put on hot platter. Pour over hot medium white sauce (No. 2004). Sprinkle with bread crumbs. Dot with butter. Bake in moderate oven (350° F.) 5 minutes. Allow ⅓ to ½ pound fish per serving.

(1148)   FILET OF SOLE (FLOUNDER)

1½ pounds filets of flounder	¾ cup fine bread crumbs
Salt—Pepper	1 egg

Wipe filets with a cold, damp cloth. Sprinkle with salt and pepper. Dip in crumbs, then in slightly beaten egg, diluted with water, and again in crumbs. Cook in a small amount of fat in a frying pan 8 to 10 minutes, or until brown on both sides. Garnish with lemon and parsley and serve with tartar sauce (No. 2044). Serves 4.

(1149)   STUFFED FILET OF SOLE

2 pounds boiled spinach (No. 1870)	2 tablespoons finely chopped parsley
1 teaspoon salt	2 tablespoons butter
⅛ teaspoon pepper	1 cup sliced mushrooms
½ cup cooking wine	2 medium tomatoes, peeled and quartered
¼ cup bread crumbs	
2 pounds filets of flounder	2 tablespoons flour
½ cup finely chopped onion	¼ cup whipped cream
	1 tablespoon lemon juice

Drain spinach, then chop. Add salt, pepper, ⅓ cup cooking wine, and bread crumbs. Place a mound of this dressing on one end of each filet and fold the other end over it. Place in a well-greased baking pan with onion, parsley, and remaining cooking wine. Arrange mushrooms and quartered tomatoes over the top. Cover with cooking parchment paper and bake in very hot oven (500° F.) 15 minutes. Remove stuffed filets to a heat-proof platter. Thicken gravy remaining in pan with 2 tablespoons flour, blended with a little cold water. Simmer 2 or 3 minutes, stirring constantly. Remove from heat. Add whipped cream and lemon juice. Pour over filets. Brown in broiler. Serve immediately. Serves 6.

(1150) FILETS EN CASSEROLE

1 cup bread crumbs	1 teaspoon salt
2 pounds filet of sole	½ cup melted butter
1 tablespoon vinegar	1 teaspoon prepared mus-
1 tablespoon Worcestershire	tard
sauce	⅛ teaspoon pepper
1 tablespoon lemon juice	

Cover bottom of shallow baking dish with bread crumbs and place filets on the crumbs. Make sauce of other ingredients and pour over fish. Bake in a hot oven (400° F.) 20 minutes, basting occasionally with sauce. Serves 6.

(1151) BROILED FILET OF FLOUNDER

Follow recipe for broiled fish (No. 1101).

(1152) FILET OF SOLE AU GRATIN

1½ pounds filet of sole	2 tablespoons butter
2 tablespoons chopped onion	2 tablespoons flour
2 tablespoons chopped celery	1 cup milk
Salt—Pepper	½ cup grated American
2 tablespoons lemon juice	cheese

Place filets in a shallow baking pan. Sprinkle with onion, celery, salt, and pepper. Add 2 tablespoons water and lemon juice. Bake in a very hot oven (450° F.) for 10 minutes. Melt butter. Stir in flour and add milk gradually. Cook, stirring until thickened. Add salt, pepper and cheese, reserving about 2 tablespoons for top. Heat until cheese is melted. Pour over fish, sprinkle remaining grated cheese over top, and continue baking for 10 to 15 more minutes. Serves 6.

(1153) BROILED FILET OF HADDOCK

Follow recipe for broiled fish (No. 1101).

(1154) BOILED HADDOCK

Follow recipe for boiled fish (No. 1102). Serve with egg sauce (No. 2009), garnished with hard-cooked egg (No. 202) slices and parsley.

(1155)   PLANKED HADDOCK

Substitute haddock for halibut in recipe for planked halibut (No. 1171).

(1156)   BAKED HADDOCK

Split, bone, and skin a 4-pound haddock. Put in greased baking dish. Sprinkle heavily with grated American cheese. Season to taste with salt and pepper. Dot with butter. Add enough milk to just cover. Bake in moderate oven (350° F.) 45 to 50 minutes, until nicely browned. Allow ⅓ to ½ pound dressed fish per serving.

(1157)   BAKED STUFFED HADDOCK

1 4-pound haddock	Salt—Pepper
2 cups bread stuffing	2 tablespoons melted
(No. 2063)	butter or fat

Wipe fish with cold, damp cloth. Cut off and clean head and tail. Split down middle. Clean. Remove backbone and all other bones if possible. Season to taste with salt and pepper. Put stuffing between 2 halves of fish, making a sandwich. Put in baking pan. Add ½ cup water. Brush top with butter. Bake in moderate oven (350° F.) 50 minutes to 1 hour, basting occasionally with melted butter or fat. Allow ⅓ pound fish per person. Any other suitable stuffing may be used.

(1158)   CRAB STUFFED HADDOCK

Follow recipe for baked stuffed haddock (No. 1157), adding ½ cup cooked crab meat to bread stuffing.

(1159)   CREAMED HADDOCK AND MUSHROOMS

⅔ cup canned sliced mush-	2 cups milk
rooms	2 cups flaked, cooked had-
2 tablespoons butter	dock
4 tablespoons flour	1 tablespoon chopped
½ teaspoon salt	parsley
Few grains pepper	

Sauté the mushrooms in butter until golden brown. Add flour, salt, pepper, and milk. Cook until thick, stirring constantly. Add haddock and parsley. Heat through. Serves 6.

(1160) HADDOCK AU GRATIN

Follow recipe for filet of sole au gratin (No. 1152), using haddock instead of filet of sole.

(1161) BROILED HALIBUT

Prepare same as broiled cod (No. 1136).

(1162) BOILED HALIBUT

Follow recipe for boiled fish (No. 1102).

(1163) HALIBUT STEAK

Wipe slices of halibut with a cold, damp cloth. Sprinkle with salt and pepper and dust with fine cracker crumbs. Cook in a small amount of fat in a frying pan 8 to 10 minutes or until brown on both sides. Drain on unglazed paper. Garnish with parsley and slices of lemon and serve with hollandaise sauce (No. 2022). Allow ⅓ to ½ pound of fish per person.

(1164) STUFFED HALIBUT STEAK

1 dozen oysters	1 cup bread or cracker
2 tablespoons melted butter	crumbs
or fat	⅛ teaspoon pepper
1 tablespoon chopped	2 slices halibut, cut from
parsley	the middle of fish
½ teaspoon salt	1 tablespoon lemon juice

Drain oysters. Add butter, parsley, crumbs, salt, and pepper and mix well. Wipe the fish with cold, damp cloth. Place one slice on a greased piece of muslin. Sprinkle with salt, pepper, and lemon juice and spread with the oyster stuffing. Place second slice on top and brush with melted butter. Put in a baking pan with a little water. Bake in moderate oven (350° F.) 40 to 50 minutes. Baste frequently with melted butter. Remove to hot platter, garnish with potato balls (No. 1836), parsley and slices of lemon. Serve with hollandaise sauce (No. 2022) or béarnaise sauce (No. 2032). Allow ⅓ to ½ pound of fish per person.

(1165)   BAKED HALIBUT IN TOMATOES

2 pounds halibut steak	1 slice onion
2 cups canned or stewed tomatoes (No. 1893)	1 teaspoon sugar
	¼ teaspoon rosemary
3 tablespoons butter	½ teaspoon salt
3 tablespoons flour	Few grains pepper

Wipe the fish. Place in a baking dish with half the sauce made with tomatoes, butter, flour, and seasonings. Bake in moderate oven (350° F.) 40 to 50 minutes, basting occasionally with sauce in the pan. Serve surrounded with remaining sauce. Garnish with parsley and stuffed olives. Serves 6.

(1166)   BAKED HALIBUT IN MILK

Substitute milk for tomatoes in recipe for baked halibut in tomatoes (No. 1165).

(1167)   FRIED HALIBUT FILETS

Prepare same as filet of sole (No. 1148).

(1168)   BAKED HALIBUT FILETS

Follow recipe for baked bass filets (No. 1126).

(1169)   HALIBUT AU GRATIN

Follow recipe for filet of sole au gratin (No. 1152), using halibut instead of filet of sole.

(1170)   SCALLOPED HALIBUT

Substitute cooked flaked halibut for salmon in recipe for scalloped salmon (No. 1188).

(1171)   PLANKED HALIBUT

Put a cold fish plank into a cold oven and gradually pre-heat oven and plank to 450° to 500° F. Make a salt solution in the proportions of 2 tablespoons salt to 1 cup cold water. Soak the steak in this solution for 3 minutes, drain, and thoroughly brush with cooking oil. Remove plank from oven, oil it thoroughly and place fish on plank, sprinkle it with grated onion and return plank to top rack of oven. Cook for 15 to 20 minutes, basting once or twice with dressing made of 4 tablespoons melted butter and ¼ teaspoon pepper. Remove from the oven, make an ornamental border around the steaks, of mashed potato (No. 1835). Return to the oven and cook until this is brown, garnish to suit taste with cooked vegetables. Thin slices of lemon and parsley are suggested for this purpose. Suggested combinations of cooked vegetables will be found under planked steak (No. 1305). Allow ⅓ to ½ pound fish per person.

(1172)   KIPPERED HERRING

3 pounds kippers or bloaters	Pepper
Juice of one lemon	Cooking oil or fat
4 tablespoons butter, melted	

Split fish without breaking back skin. Lay, skin down, in a single layer on an oiled pan, brush with butter and lemon juice, season with pepper as desired, and bake in moderate oven (350° F.) for not over 10 minutes. An improved dish is obtained if the fish, after seasoning is applied, is closed to its original form, wrapped in oiled or wet parchment paper, and baked for not over 10 minutes. Serves 6.

(1173)   KIPPERED HERRINGS WITH EGGS

Remove skin and bones from fish. Flake. Put in greased individual baking cup. Sprinkle with pepper. Top with raw egg. Bake in slow oven (300° F.) until egg is set. Serves 1.

(1174)   BROILED FRESH MACKEREL

Follow recipe for broiled fish (No. 1101).

(1175)   BROILED SALT MACKEREL

Let fish soak in cold water 12 hours, skin side up. Drain and wipe dry. Brush with melted fat. Broil on greased broiler, skin side down, 15 minutes, basting occasionally with melted fat. Remove to hot platter. Pour over hot medium white sauce (No. 2004). Sprinkle with chopped parsley. Or, this may be served with melted butter instead of white sauce. Allow ⅓ to ½ pound of fish per person.

(1176) BAKED MACKEREL

Follow recipe for baked haddock (No. 1156), using mackerel instead of haddock.

(1177) BAKED STUFFED MACKEREL

Follow recipe for baked, stuffed haddock (No. 1157), using mackerel instead of haddock.

(1178) FRIED PICKEREL

Wipe fish with cold, damp cloth. Leave whole or cut in pieces as desired. Sprinkle with salt, pepper, and flour. Fry in little fat 20 to 30 minutes, depending on size. Serve hot, garnished with parsley and lemon slices. Allow ⅓ to ½ pound fish per person.

(1179) BAKED RED SNAPPER

1 5-pound cleaned and boned red snapper
1 teaspoon salt
1 pound boiled shrimp (No. 1272)
1 egg

1 cup cream
½ tablespoon anchovy paste
Pepper—Paprika
1 cup sherry

Wash, drain, and rub fish with salt. Put shrimp through grinder. Beat egg and one-half cream together. Mix shrimp and anchovy paste, seasoning with pepper, salt, and paprika, then stir into the beaten egg and cream, adding sherry and mixing to a smooth paste. Place stuffing inside fish and sew together with twine. Place in baking dish, pouring over it the remaining half cup of cream. Bake in a moderate oven (350° F.) until done, about 4 hours. Serve garnished with sliced cucumbers in French dressing (No. 716). Serves 10.

(1180) BROILED SALMON STEAK

Brush slices of salmon with French dressing (No. 716) and let stand 1 hour. Put in a broiler. Brush with melted fat. Broil 12 to 15 minutes, cooking on both sides. Put on hot platter. Season to taste with salt, pepper, and lemon juice. Sprinkle with chopped parsley. Serve with béarnaise sauce (No. 2032). Allow ⅓ to ½ pound fish per person.

(1181) BOILED SALMON

Follow recipe for boiled codfish (No. 1138), using salmon instead of codfish. Serve with parsley sauce (No. 2013).

(1182) SALMON FRICASSEE

2 pounds fresh salmon, cubed	1 clove
1 chopped onion	1 blade mace
1 tablespoon sugar	1 teaspoon vinegar
1 teaspoon salt	6 small tomatoes, quartered
¼ teaspoon pepper	2 tablespoons parsley, chopped
1 teaspoon dry mustard	

Combine salmon, onion, sugar, salt, pepper, mustard, clove, mace, and vinegar in saucepan. Add 1½ cups water. Bring to a boil. Add tomatoes and parsley. Reduce heat. Cover and simmer 45 minutes. Serves 6.

(1183) CREAMED SALMON

1 cup canned salmon	2 cups medium white sauce (No. 2004)
1 tablespoon lemon juice	

Flake salmon. Add lemon juice and let stand 20 minutes. Add hot white sauce. Mix well. Heat through. Serve on buttered toast (No. 988). Serves 6.

(1184) CREAMED SALMON AND PEAS

Add 1 cup boiled peas (No. 1823) to recipe for creamed salmon (No. 1183).

(1185) SALMON BAKED IN POTATO SHELLS

1 pound canned salmon	1 chopped onion
8 medium-sized baked potatoes (No. 1837)	Salt—Pepper
½ cup milk	1 cup bread crumbs
	2 tablespoons fat

Flake salmon, removing all skin and bones. Slice off tops of potatoes and scoop out contents. Mash thoroughly, adding milk, onion, and seasonings to taste. Add salmon. Mix lightly. Stuff mixture in potato shells. Cover with crumbs. Dot with fat. Bake in hot oven (400° F.) 25 minutes. Serves 6 to 8.

(1186)   SALMON AU GRATIN

2 cups canned salmon
1 cup medium white sauce
   (No. 2004)
1 tablespoon lemon juice

¼ cup bread crumbs
1 tablespoon cooking fat
⅛ teaspoon paprika

Flake salmon. Remove all skin and bones. Combine with sauce. Stir in lemon juice. Put in greased baking dish. Cover with bread crumbs. Dot with fat. Bake in hot oven (400° F.) 20 minutes. Sprinkle with paprika. Serves 6.

(1187)   SALMON FONDUE

5 slices bread
1 cup milk
2 tablespoons butter
1 cup canned salmon

3 eggs
Salt
¼ cup grated American
   cheese

Trim crusts from the bread and cut in ½-inch cubes. Heat the milk in the upper part of a double boiler. Add bread cubes, butter, liquid from salmon, and well-beaten egg yolks. Season with salt to suit taste and cook until thickened, stirring constantly. Remove from heat and stir in the cheese. Cool for 10 or 15 minutes. Add flaked salmon. Beat egg whites until stiff and fold into the fondue mixture. Pour into a well greased baking dish. Set dish in a shallow pan of hot water and bake in a moderate oven (375° F.) about an hour or until an inserted knife blade comes out clean. Serves 6. Boiled shrimp (No. 1272), tuna, or cooked, minced clams may be substituted for the salmon.

(1188)   SCALLOPED SALMON

1½ cups cold cooked flaked
   salmon
1 cup thick white sauce
   (No. 2004)

1 tablespoon chopped
   green pepper
¼ teaspoon paprika
1 cup bread crumbs

Mix salmon, hot white sauce, green pepper, and paprika. Put in greased baking dish or individual dishes. Sprinkle with bread crumbs. Bake in hot oven (400° F.) until crumbs are brown, about 20 minutes. Serves 6.

(1189)   ESCALLOPED SALMON AND TOMATO

1 pound canned salmon	1 teaspoon sugar
1 chopped onion	¼ teaspoon pepper
2½ cups canned or stewed	3 cups bread crumbs
tomatoes (No. 1893)	2 tablespoons fat
1 teaspoon salt	

Flake salmon. Simmer onion, tomatoes, salt, sugar, and pepper until onion is tender. Add 2 cups crumbs and salmon to mixture. Turn into a greased baking dish. Top with remaining crumbs. Dot with fat. Bake in moderate oven (350° F.) 10 to 15 minutes. Serves 6.

(1190)   SALMON CROQUETTES

2 cups canned salmon	¼ teaspoon salt
3 tablespoons chopped	Few grains pepper
parsley	1 cup thick white sauce
1 tablespoon lemon juice	(No. 2004)
1 teaspoon Worcestershire	1 cup bread crumbs
sauce	1 egg

Drain salmon. Remove skin and bones. Flake. Add parsley, lemon juice, Worcestershire sauce, salt, pepper, and white sauce. Blend well. Chill. Shape into croquettes, roll in bread crumbs, dip in slightly beaten egg to which a little water has been added, and roll again in crumbs. Fry in deep hot fat (390° F.) 3 to 5 minutes. Drain on absorbent paper. Serves 4.

(1191)   SALMON LOAF

Prepare mixture for salmon croquettes (No. 1190). Put in greased baking dish. Bake in moderate oven (350° F.) 20 to 25 minutes.

(1192)   SALMON PUFF

1 cup bread crumbs	2 cups milk
1 teaspoon salt	1½ cups canned salmon
2 teaspoons prepared	4 eggs, separated
mustard	

Combine crumbs, salt, mustard, and milk in a saucepan. Cook over low heat until thick. Flake salmon and add. Beat egg yolks and add to fish mixture. Beat egg whites until stiff and fold in. Pour into buttered baking dish or individual dishes. Place in pan of warm water. Bake in a moderately hot oven (425° F.) 30 minutes. Serves 6.

(1193) DEVILED SALMON

2 tablespoons minced onion
2 tablespoons green pepper
3 tablespoons butter
1 cup canned tomato soup
1 teaspoon prepared mustard
½ teaspoon salt

1 teaspoon lemon juice
2 cups canned salmon
½ cup buttered bread crumbs
6 slices lemon
Paprika

Lightly brown onion and pepper in butter. Add soup and seasonings. Simmer for a few minutes. Add flaked salmon and pile in baking dishes. Top with crumbs. Place thin slices of lemon, sprinkled with paprika on top. Bake in hot oven (400° F.) until crumbs are browned, about 15 minutes. Serves 6.

(1194) JEWISH KEDAGREE

1 pound canned salmon or tuna fish
1 tablespoon lemon juice
2½ cups boiled rice (No. 107)

2 hard-cooked eggs (No. 202)
1 tablespoon butter
Paprika—Pepper—Salt

Flake the fish. Add lemon juice and let stand 30 minutes. Drain rice. Chop eggs. Combine all ingredients. Steam in double boiler until heated through. Press into a mold. Serve hot. Serves 4 to 6.

(1195) PAN-BROILED SARDINES

2 cans sardines

1 tablespoon lemon juice

Drain sardine oil into frying pan. When hot, lay in sardines in a single layer. Brown on both sides. Serve on toast with lemon juice and hot sardine oil. Serves 4 to 6.

(1196)   BROILED DEVILED SARDINES

2 cans large boneless sardines
4 tablespoons butter
2 teaspoons dry mustard
       1 lemon
1 teaspoon Worcestershire
    sauce
½ cup fine cracker crumbs

Drain oil from the sardines. Cream butter and work the mustard and Worcestershire into it. Spread both sides of the sardines with the deviled butter. Roll sardines in crumbs until well coated. Place in a shallow pan and broil 5 minutes or until golden brown. Serve hot with quarters of lemon. Serves 4 to 6.

(1197)   SARDINES AND MASHED POTATOES

2 cups mashed potatoes
   (No. 1835)
2 cans sardines
½ tablespoon lemon juice

Line bottom of baking dish with half of potatoes. Arrange sardines on top. Sprinkle with lemon juice. Cover with remaining potatoes. Bake in moderately hot oven (375° F.) until potatoes are brown. Serves 4 to 6.

(1198)   SARDINES AND FRIED ONIONS

6 sliced onions
¼ cup cooking fat
½ teaspoon salt
2 cans sardines

Fry onions in fat. Sprinkle with salt. Place in mound on hot platter, surrounded by sardines. Serves 4 to 6.

(1199)   SARDINES AND SPINACH

1 cup medium white sauce
   (No. 2004)
2½ cups cooked spinach
   (No. 1870)
1 teaspoon salt
¼ teaspoon pepper
2 cans sardines

Combine sauce, spinach, salt, and pepper. Heat thoroughly. Put sardines in broiler and brown both sides. Put in center of hot platter. Surround with spinach. Serves 4 to 6.

(1200) SARDINES AND EGGS ON TOAST

3 tablespoons butter	4 sliced hard-cooked eggs
3 tablespoons flour	(No. 202)
½ teaspoon salt	2 cans sardines
½ teaspoon dry mustard	6 slices toast
1½ cups milk	½ teaspoon paprika

Blend butter and flour. Add salt, mustard, and milk. Cook, stirring constantly, until thickened. Add eggs and heat. Arrange sardines on toast. Heat in broiler. Remove to hot platter. Pour over egg sauce. Sprinkle with paprika. Serves 6. If desired, 2 teaspoons chopped onion may be added to the sauce. Flaked salmon, tuna fish, or mackerel may be used instead of sardines.

(1201) SCROD

Wipe fish with cold, damp cloth. Split down back and remove backbone. Follow recipe for broiled fish (No. 1101). Allow ⅓ to ½ pound fish per serving.

(1202) BROILED SHAD

Wash, remove head and tail from shad, clean and split down the back. Remove backbone with as many other bones as possible. Place, skin side down, on a greased broiler, spread with melted fat and sprinkle with salt and pepper. Broil 20 to 25 minutes, depending on size of fish. Remove to hot platter and garnish with watercress and slices of lemon. Allow ⅓ to ½ pound fish per person.

(1203) BAKED SHAD

Split the fish down the back to remove the backbone, also the viscera and roe. Then pull out the rib bones with pair of pliers. Wash and cover with a salt solution made in the proportion of 1 tablespoon salt to 1 cup ice cold water. Let stand ½ hour or more. Drain and dry. Pre-heat the oven to 500° F. Stuff the fish with desired savory stuffing, then wrap with string to keep in the stuffing. Place on a greased baking pan and sprinkle top of fish with good cooking oil. Bake at the high temperature (500° F.) 10 minutes. Then lower the heat to 400° F. and cook 15 to 20 minutes longer. Serve at once. Allow ⅓ to ½ pound fish per serving.

(1204)   PLANKED SHAD

Follow recipe for planked halibut (No. 1171), using shad instead of halibut.

(1205)   SHAD ROE

Wash and dry the roe, using care not to break the skin. Sprinkle with salt, pepper, and flour. Melt 2 tablespoons fat in a frying pan. When hot, put in the roe and cook slowly until brown on one side. Turn and brown on the other side. Cook from 20 to 30 minutes. Garnish with lemon and parsley and serve very hot with crisp bacon (No. 1464). Allow ¼ pound roe per serving.

(1206)   FRIED SMELTS

| 1½ pounds smelts | ¾ cup fine bread crumbs |
| Salt—Pepper | 1 egg |

Wash the smelts and make a slight opening at the gills with a sharp knife or scissors. Draw them between the thumb and finger from tail to head to press the intestines out at the gill opening, keeping the fish whole. Wash and dry and sprinkle with salt and pepper. Dip in crumbs, then in slightly beaten egg, diluted with a little cold water, and again in crumbs. Fry in deep hot fat (375° F.) 3 to 5 minutes. Drain on unglazed paper and serve with tartar sauce (No. 2044). Serves 6.

(1207)   PICKLED SMELTS

Wipe fish with cold, damp cloth. Remove heads and tails. Cook in a steamer or in a colander over hot water until flesh is white, about 3 to 4 minutes. Pack in a deep dish, sprinkling each layer with salt. Pour over a sauce made by boiling 4 cups vinegar, 1 chopped onion, 3 bay leaves, and 1 tablespoon mixed spices 5 minutes. Completely cover fish with sauce, making more, using same proportions, if necessary. Cover dish. Let stand 3 days before using.

(1208)   BROILED SWORDFISH

Follow recipe for broiled salmon steak (No. 1180), using swordfish instead of salmon.

(1209)   PLANKED SWORDFISH

Take a piece of well-seasoned oak, 24 inches long, 18 inches wide, and 3 inches thick, grooved around the edge, and with several grooves cut down the surface, to hold in juices. Put this in a cold oven, gradually pre-heating plank and oven to 450° or 500° F. Make a salt solution in the proportion of 2 tablespoons salt to 1 cup water. Take a slice of swordfish about ¾-inch thickness, scrape the surface of the flesh with a knife blade, soak the fish in the salt solution for three minutes, drain and brush with cooking oil. Remove plank from oven, oil it thoroughly, and place swordfish on plank. Then place it in oven and bake for 30 minutes, basting once or twice with a sauce of 4 tablespoons melted butter, containing ¼ teaspoon pepper. About five minutes before end of the cooking period remove and garnish with mashed potato (No. 1835) piped into attractive designs around the border of the plank and any appropriate combination of cooked vegetables desired. A substitute garnish often favored is simply thin lemon slices with parsley. For other possible combinations of cooked vegetables see recipe for planked steak (No. 1305). Allow ⅓ to ½ pound of dressed fish per serving.

(1210)   BROILED LAKE TROUT

Split the trout into two filets, removing the backbone. Wash thoroughly, removing all traces of blood or membrane. Place the filets in a salt solution made in the proportion of 2 tablespoons salt to 1 cup water and allow them to remain there 8 to 10 minutes. The broiling oven should be pre-heated about 10 minutes before using. Oil the heated broiler pan, then brush the fish with oil in which pepper has been stirred. The amount of oil required will be about ¼ cup with ¼ teaspoon pepper. Place the trout on the broiler pan, skin side up, about 2 inches below the heat unit. At the end of 5 minutes the skin should be turning brown. Baste. Continue cooking until the skin is well browned, then turn the fish with flesh side up and baste again. Cook until the flesh side is well browned. Remove to hot platter, butter the top of the fish, and garnish to taste. Crisp lettuce leaves, lemon slices, and parsley are suggested. Allow ⅓ to ½ pound fish per person. Or the fish may be sautéed in little fat after rolling in flour.

(1211)   TUNA FISH CROQUETTES

Follow recipe for salmon croquettes (No. 1190), using tuna
fish instead of salmon.

(1212)   TUNA FISH SOUFFLÉ

7 ounces canned tuna fish	1 cup bread crumbs
½ teaspoon salt	¾ cup milk
½ teaspoon paprika	3 beaten egg yolks
1 teaspoon lemon juice	3 stiffly beaten egg whites

Combine flaked fish with salt, paprika, and lemon juice. Simmer bread crumbs in milk 5 minutes. Add seasoned fish and egg
yolks. Mix well. Fold in egg whites. Turn into greased baking
dish or individual dishes. Place in pan of hot water and bake in
moderate oven (350° F.) 45 to 50 minutes. Serves 6.

(1213)   TUNA FISH À LA KING

1¼ cups canned tuna fish	2 canned pimientos
1 tablespoon butter	1 cup milk
½ teaspoon salt	2 tablespoons flour

Flake the tuna and add the pimientos cut fine. Add the butter
and salt and allow them to heat thoroughly, then add the milk
into which the flour has been dissolved and cooked until smooth
and creamy. Pour into a buttered baking dish, dot over with
butter and crumbs and brown quickly in a hot oven (400° F.).
Serves 4.

(1214)   BAKED WEAKFISH

Wash fish; wipe with cold, damp cloth, and sprinkle inside
with salt and pepper. Cut gashes across the skin. Spread fish with
butter or fat and sprinkle with salt, pepper, and ½ teaspoon
Worcestershire sauce. Place fish in a baking pan on a strip of
muslin greased with butter or fat. Bake in a moderate oven
(350° F.), allowing about 15 minutes to the pound. Remove
from the muslin to a hot platter. Garnish with lemon and
parsley. The fish may be filled with a bread stuffing (No. 2063)
if desired. Allow ⅓ to ½ pound fish per person.

(1215)   FRIED WHITEBAIT

Season to taste with salt and pepper. Dredge with flour. Fry 2 to 3 minutes in deep hot fat (375° F.) or sauté until browned on both sides in little fat. Serve with lemon slices or tartar sauce (No. 2044).

(1216)   SCALLOPED WHITEFISH

Substitute cooked flaked whitefish for salmon in recipe for scalloped salmon (No. 1188).

(1217)   WHITEFISH AU GRATIN

Follow recipe for filet of sole au gratin (No. 1152), using whitefish instead of filet of sole.

(1218)   PLANKED WHITEFISH

Follow recipe for planked halibut (No. 1171), using whitefish instead of halibut.

(1219)   STEAMED CLAMS

Wash thoroughly in several waters. Put in a kettle or steamer. Add ¾ cup water for each 50 clams. Cover and steam until shells open, from 10 to 15 minutes, no longer. Overcooking makes clams tough. Serve in shells with individual cups of melted butter. The clam liquor may be served as a beverage. Allow 25 clams per serving.

(1220)   FRIED CLAMS

1 pint clams	1 slightly beaten egg
Salt—Pepper	½ cup cracker or bread
Flour for dredging	crumbs

Pick over clams, removing shell fragments. Dry between towels. Sprinkle with salt, pepper, and flour. Dip in egg, diluted with a little cold water. Roll in crumbs. Fry in deep, hot fat (375° F.) 4 to 6 minutes. Drain on unglazed paper. Serves 4.

(1221)   FRIED CLAMS IN BATTER

1 pint clams	1 teaspoon salt
¼ cup clam liquor	¼ teaspoon pepper
¼ cup milk	1 cup flour
2 beaten eggs	½ teaspoon baking powder

Pick over clams and remove shell fragments. Dry between towels. Mix clam liquor, milk, eggs, salt, and pepper. Mix and sift flour and baking powder and add to first mixture. Beat thoroughly. Dip clams in batter. Fry in deep, hot fat (375° F.) 4 to 6 minutes. Drain on unglazed paper. Serves 4.

(1222)   ROAST CLAMS

Cover with water. Sprinkle with corn meal and let stand 1 hour. Wash shells. Put in baking pan, deep side down. Bake in moderate oven (350° F.) until shells open. Remove upper shell. Season to taste with salt and pepper. Dot generously with butter. Allow 6 clams per serving.

(1223)   CLAM FRITTERS

1 cup flour	¼ cup milk
¼ teaspoon salt	2 beaten eggs
⅛ teaspoon pepper	12 chopped raw clams
¼ cup clam liquor	1 teaspoon melted butter

Mix and sift flour, salt, and pepper. Add clam liquor, milk, and eggs. Stir until well blended. Add clams and butter. Mix thoroughly. Drop from spoon into deep, hot fat (375° F.) and fry 4 to 6 minutes until well browned. Drain on unglazed paper. Serve with tartar sauce (No. 2044). Serves 4.

(1224)   CLAMS NEWBURG

1 tablespoon butter	½ teaspoon salt
1 tablespoon flour	1/16 teaspoon cayenne
1 cup cream	2 tablespoons Madeira
24 drained clams	wine
2 beaten egg yolks	

Melt butter in saucepan. Stir in flour and blend. Add cream and clams. Heat, but do not boil. When heated, add egg yolks. Heat clams through. Add salt, cayenne, and wine. Stir. Serve very hot. Serves 6.

(1225) CREAMED CLAMS

2 cups cooked clams, diced   2 cups thick white sauce
(No. 2004)

Combine clams and hot white sauce. Heat through. Serve on buttered toast (No. 988). Serves 6.

(1226) CLAM CAKES OR CROQUETTES

1 quart clams, shelled   ½ cup clam liquor
1 cup fine cracker crumbs   2 eggs, well beaten

Drain clams and save ½ cup liquor. Remove the black from soft part. Put the necks through a food chopper. Put clams in a dish and add clam liquor and enough cracker crumbs to absorb all the moisture. Let stand 10 minutes. Add eggs. Shape into flat cakes or croquettes. Drop into hot deep fat (375° F.) and cook to a golden brown. Drain on unglazed paper. Serves 6.

(1227) BOILED HARD SHELL CRABS

Prepare a boiling solution made up in the proportion of 1 quart water, ⅛ cup vinegar, 1 tablespoon salt, ½ tablespoon red pepper. While this is heating, scrub and rinse the crabs. Boil the crabs for 5 minutes and simmer 10 minutes longer. Pull off the legs and claws. Split these and remove the meat. Break off the segment that folds under the body from the rear. Holding the body of a crab in the left hand, back toward you, pull off the top shell. Discard the digestive tract and rinse in water. Split the crab and remove the hard membrane that covers the body meat with a nut pick or something similar. Allow 1 or 2 crabs per person.

(1228) SOFT SHELL CRABS

Remove the eyes and the stomach (the soft portion under the eyes) if this has not already been done. Wash and dry the crabs. Dip in flour seasoned with salt and pepper. To one egg add 2 tablespoons water and beat slightly. Dip crabs in egg, then in fine, sifted bread crumbs and fry in deep hot fat (390° F.) 3 to 5 minutes. Drain on unglazed paper. Serve with parsley and slices of lemon. Allow 1 or 2 crabs per person. To broil soft shell crabs, place on greased broiler and broil 4 to 5 minutes on each side. To bake soft shell crabs, put on greased baking pan and bake in hot oven (400° F.) 8 minutes.

(1229)   DEVILED CRABS

2½ cups cooked crab meat	3 tablespoons bread crumbs
1 tablespoon melted butter	½ teaspoon salt
1 chopped hard-cooked egg	⅛ teaspoon pepper
(No. 202)	⅛ teaspoon paprika
1 cup milk	½ tablespoon Worcester-
1 tablespoon lemon juice	shire sauce

Flake crab meat. Combine all ingredients. Put in greased individual baking dishes. Sprinkle with bread crumbs. Dot with butter. Bake in moderate oven (350° F.) until well browned. Serves 6.

(1230)   BAKED CRABS IN SHELLS

Follow recipe for deviled crabs (No. 1229), putting mixture in crab shells instead of baking dishes before cooking.

(1231)   CRAB MEAT SOUFFLÉ

4 tablespoons butter	Few grains pepper
⅓ cup flour	4 eggs
1⅓ cups milk	1½ cups cooked crab meat
1 teaspoon salt	

Melt butter in a double boiler. Add flour and mix well. Add milk gradually and cook, stirring constantly, until thickened. Add salt and pepper. Add hot mixture slowly to the well-beaten egg yolks, stirring constantly. Add flaked crab meat and cool slightly. Fold in the stiffly beaten egg whites and pour into a buttered baking dish. Bake in a moderate oven (350° F.) 50 minutes. Serves 6.

(1232)   CRABS AU GRATIN

Follow recipe for filet of sole au gratin (No. 1152), substituting cooked crab meat for filet of sole and baking not more than 15 minutes.

(1233)   **CRAB CAKES**

1 pound cooked crab meat	⅛ teaspoon black pepper
2 eggs	Pinch of cayenne pepper
4 tablespoons melted butter	Cooking fat or oil
½ teaspoon salt	Fine bread crumbs

Mix crab meat, butter, seasoning, and enough of the egg to mold into small flat cakes. Beat a little water into the remaining egg and wet the cakes with this mixture, then roll them in the crumbs. Sauté until rich brown in a heavy frying pan or deep fry at about 380°-400° F. in a well oiled frying basket. Serves 6.

(1234)   **CRAB IN WHITE WINE**

½ cup white wine	1 pound fresh cooked crab
⅛ teaspoon nutmeg	meat
⅛ teaspoon cayenne	¼ cup milk
½ teaspoon salt	¼ cup cream
2 beaten egg yolks	

Season wine with nutmeg, cayenne, and salt. Warm. Add crab meat. Simmer slowly 10 minutes, stirring frequently. Add milk and cream. Cook and stir 5 minutes longer. Remove from heat. Add yolks, diluted with a little of the sauce. Heat through. Serves 6.

(1235)   **BOILED CRAWFISH**

This small crustacean is widely distributed in streams and ponds throughout the country. The edible meat is in the tail with some in the claws. Remove the sand vein by breaking off the extreme end of the tail and drawing out the vein. Make a salt solution allowing ¼ pound salt for each quart water and in this boil the crawfish until they are red. This should take about 5 minutes. Remove edible meat from tail and claws. This may be eaten hot with melted butter, vinegar, or other desired seasonings, or cold in salads, etc.

(1236)   **BOILED LOBSTER**

Take the live lobster by the back and plunge it in boiling salted water, head first. Have water deep enough to cover. Reduce heat and simmer 35 to 40 minutes. Remove from the water and cool. Turn lobster on back and make a cut with a sharp knife from point under head to tail, through the shell. Take out the large intestine which runs the length of the tail. Crack the claws so that the meat may be easily removed. Serve ice cold in the shell with cold hollandaise sauce (No. 2022) or mayonnaise (No. 701). Allow 1 lobster per person.

(1237)   BROILED LIVE LOBSTER

Select small (chicken) lobsters. Place the lobster on its back on a cutting board and kill by cutting down between the body shell and tail segment. Then split from head to tail, remove the "lady" (or stomach) at the back of its head, and the vein that passes through the center of the tail segment. Rinse, brush the flesh with melted butter, season with salt and pepper if desired, and spread out flat on the broiler, flesh side up. Cook slowly for 10 minutes, turn and cook 10 minutes longer. Remove to a hot platter and dress with melted butter to which a little lemon juice has been added. Allow 1 lobster per serving.

(1238)   BAKED LOBSTER

Prepare live lobster as in recipe for broiled live lobster (No. 1237) and cook by baking in hot oven (400° F.) 20 to 30 minutes, depending on size. To bake a boiled lobster (No. 1236), cook in 400° F. oven 12 to 18 minutes.

(1239)   STEAMED LOBSTER

Steam live lobsters ½ hour in steamer with rapidly boiling water. Dress according to recipe for boiled lobster (No. 1236).

(1240)   LOBSTER THERMIDOR

2 1½-pound lobsters, boiled (No. 1236)	¼ teaspoon salt Pinch of cayenne
2 tablespoons butter	½ cup sautéed mush-
2 tablespoons flour	rooms (No. 1801)
1 cup cream	Parmesan cheese, grated
1 teaspoon dry mustard	

Split cold boiled lobsters by crossing claws, holding firmly and drawing a pointed knife through shell, lengthwise, from head to tail with a rapid stroke. Remove meat and discard intestinal vein. Dice meat and wash lobster shells. Make sauce by melting

butter and adding flour. When well blended, add the cream.
Keep stirring until mixture reaches boiling point, then add
mustard, salt and cayenne. Add lobster meat, finely chopped
mushrooms, and fill lobster shells with mixture, piling it high.
Sprinkle grated Parmesan cheese over top, dot it with butter
and brown under broiler. Serve one lobster to each person,
garnished with some small lobster claws and parsley.

(1241)   PLANKED LOBSTER

Prepare lobster according to recipe for broiled lobster (No.
1237). Place on greased plank. Blend 1 teaspoon Worcestershire
sauce with ¼ cup melted butter. Brush lobster meat with mixture. Season to taste with salt and cayenne. Bake in hot oven
(425° F.) 15 to 20 minutes. Put border of duchess potatoes
(No. 1846) around plank and surround lobster with a combination of cooked vegetables as given in recipe for planked
steak (No. 1305). Allow 1 lobster for 2 servings.

(1242)   LOBSTER STEW

1 pound boiled diced lobster meat (No. 1236)	1½ tablespoons butter
1 pint milk	1½ teaspoon salt

Heat the milk to the scalding point and add lobster meat.
Heat thoroughly, add butter, salt and stir well. Serves 6.

(1243)   LOBSTER NEWBURG

2 cups boiled diced lobster meat (No. 1236)	¼ teaspoon salt
1 cup cream	4 tablespoons melted butter
2 egg yolks, beaten	1 teaspoon lemon juice
1 tablespoon flour	Paprika

Heat the lobster in 3 tablespoons melted butter, using care
that the butter does not brown. In another saucepan, stir the
flour well into the other tablespoon of butter, then add the
cream, heat, and stir until it is smooth. When boiling starts,
remove from the fire, add the beaten egg yolks, and stir until
the mixture thickens. Add the diced lobster and seasoning but
do not heat again or the whole may curdle. Serve with toasted
crackers or thin, dry toast. Serves 6.

(1244)   **CREAMED LOBSTER**

Substitute diced, cooked lobster meat for clams in recipe for creamed clams (No. 1225).

(1245)   **LOBSTER CROQUETTES**

2 cups cold cooked lobster (No. 1236)	1 cup thick white sauce (No. 2004)
2 tablespoons chopped celery	1 slightly beaten egg
1 tablespoon chopped parsley	¾ cup bread crumbs
Salt—Pepper	

Chop lobster. Add parsley, celery, and hot white sauce. Mix well. Season with salt and pepper to taste. Chill. Mold into croquettes or cutlets. Roll in crumbs. Dip in egg, diluted with a little cold water. Roll again in crumbs. Fry in deep, hot fat (390° F.) 3 to 5 minutes. Drain on absorbent paper. Serves 6.

(1246)   **LOBSTER PATTIES**

Follow recipe for boiled lobster (No. 1236). Crack claws and remove meat. Discard the stomach which lies under the head, also the woolly gills. Save the fatty green substance and coral (if any) to mix with the meat. Pick out all the meat and cut in uniform pieces. To 2 cups of lobster add 2 cups medium white sauce (No. 2004) using 1 cup thin cream in place of 1 cup of the milk and heat thoroughly. Add 1 tablespoon chopped parsley and 1 well-beaten egg yolk before taking from the fire. Serve in patty shells (No. 2709). Garnish with watercress. Serves 6.

(1247)   **LOBSTER CASSEROLE**

3 ounces broad noodles	1 cup boiled lobster (No. 1236), flaked
2 tablespoons butter, melted	and boned
1 cup cream or medium white sauce (No. 2004)	Salt and white pepper

Cook noodles in boiling salted water about 10 minutes. Do not let them become too soft. Drain and mix with remaining ingredients. Turn into greased casserole and bake in a moderately hot oven (375° F.) 20 minutes, or until thoroughly heated. Serves 6.

(1248) SCALLOPED LOBSTER

Put alternate layers of seasoned cracker crumbs and boiled
lobster meat (No. 1236), diced, in a baking dish with plenty of
butter cut in small pieces. Have layer of crumbs on top. Pour
over the liquor from the lobster and enough milk to moisten.
Bake in moderate oven (350° F.) about 20 minutes or until the
crumbs are brown. Serve at once. Allow ⅓ cup of lobster and
½ cup crumbs per serving.

(1249) CHINESE-EGG-LOBSTER

1 cup canned bean sprouts	2 cups cubed boiled lobster
½ cup thinly sliced canned	(No. 1236)
bamboo shoots	4 tablespoons vegetable oil
½ cup thinly sliced canned	6 eggs
water chestnuts	1 teaspoon salt

Sauté bean sprouts, bamboo shoots, water chestnuts, and
lobster in hot oil 3 minutes. Remove mixture from frying pan
and drain water off top of oil. Reheat fat and drop eggs whole
into it. Immediately spread first mixture over the top of eggs
and stir constantly, but gently until the eggs are cooked.
Serves 6.

(1250) BAKED MUSSELS

Scrub mussels. Open shells with a knife like clams. Remove
beard. Lay mussels in baking pan. Sprinkle with salt, pepper,
and chopped onion. Lay strips of bacon on top. Sprinkle with
grated cheese. Bake in slow oven (300° F.) until bacon is crisp.
Allow 8 mussels per serving.

(1251) SCRAMBLED MUSSELS

Scrub mussels clean. Open shells with a knife. Discard beard
and take from shells. Chop. Cook with scrambled eggs (No.
209), allowing 4 mussels for each egg.

(1252) FRIED OYSTERS

Follow recipe for fried clams (No. 1220), using oysters instead of clams.

(1253)   FRIED OYSTERS IN BATTER

Follow recipe for fried clams in batter (No. 1221), using oysters instead of clams.

(1254)   BROILED OYSTERS

Dry 24 oysters between towels. Heat broiler and grease well. Dip oysters in melted butter, then in dried bread crumbs, and arrange on broiler. Broil about 3 minutes. Have ready 6 slices of toast, cut in uniform pieces. Moisten toast with hot oyster juice. Place 4 broiled oysters on each slice of toast and season with salt, pepper, and a few drops of lemon juice. Serves 6.

(1255)   SAUTÉED OYSTERS

Prepare as for fried oysters (No. 1252). Fry in little fat until brown on both sides.

(1256)   ROAST OYSTERS

Substitute oysters for clams, but do not let stand in water and corn meal, in recipe for roast clams (No. 1222).

(1257)   BARBECUED OYSTERS

3 dozen large oysters in the shell
½ pound bacon, sliced thin

Bread crumbs
Paprika

Wash oyster shells thoroughly. Open oysters, discarding the flatter shell. Separate oysters from the curved shell, but allow each to remain loosely in the shell. Cover oysters with bread crumbs and season with paprika, cover each oyster with bacon, place oysters (in their shells) in one layer under a broiler flame until the bacon is cooked through. Serve oysters in the shells. Serves 6.

(1258)   OYSTERS CASINO

1 pint oysters
½ cup minced green pepper
½ cup minced bacon

1 tablespoon lemon juice
Pepper

Drain oysters. Pick out shell fragments and arrange on a greased, oven-proof platter. Sprinkle with green pepper, bacon, lemon juice, and pepper. Bake in a hot oven (450° F.) about 10 minutes. Serves 6.

(1259) OYSTERS IN PARCHMENT

12 oysters	$\frac{1}{8}$ teaspoon pepper
1 teaspoon lemon juice	4 tablespoons oyster liquid
2 teaspoons grated onion	1 tablespoon grated celery
$\frac{1}{2}$ teaspoon salt	2 teaspoons butter

Oil or wet the parchment paper, put in the oysters, liquid, and seasonings, bring all edges of the paper together and tie. Immerse in boiling water and let cook 5 to 8 minutes or just until the edges curl. The oysters may be served on toast and the liquid poured over them, or the liquid may be thickened and served as a sauce. Serves 2. To serve more use additional parchment paper, never cooking more than 12 oysters in one unit.

(1260) OYSTER FRITTERS

Follow recipe for clam fritters (No. 1223), using oysters instead of clams.

(1261) OYSTERS BENEDICT

6 thin slices smoked ham	24 oysters

Sauté ham in frying pan until well browned. Pour drippings into another pan. Pan-fry oysters in drippings 5 minutes. Put ham on hot platter. Top with oysters. Pour over hollandaise (No. 2022) or thick, cream sauce (No. 2005). Garnish with lemon slices. Serves 6.

(1262) OYSTER OMELET

Heat oysters in frying pan with a little butter until edges begin to curl. Spread them on omelet (No. 208) just before folding.

(1263)   CREAMED OYSTERS

1 quart oysters
3 cups milk
1 cup cream
⅔ cup butter

3 tablespoons flour
Salt, pepper, and lemon
    juice to taste

Heat the milk but do not boil. Heat the oysters in their juice until the edges curl, separate and skim liquor. Sift flour into the melted butter in a saucepan, heat, and stir well. Add the hot milk and oyster juice together and beat the mixture until thick and smooth. Add cream, oysters, and seasoning. Serve on buttered toast (No. 988). Serves 6.

(1264)   OYSTERS IN SHERRY CREAM

2 dozen large oysters
Salt and pepper
¾ cup cracker crumbs

2 tablespoons sherry
    flavoring
1 cup cream

Drain oysters and remove any pieces of shell. Place in a buttered, shallow pan and sprinkle with salt and pepper. Cover with the cracker crumbs, then pour on sherry flavoring and cream. Cook under the broiler 2 minutes. Turn the oysters and cook until the edges are curled and crumbs browned. Serves 6.

(1265)   CREOLE ESCALLOPED OYSTERS

1 pint small oysters
2 cups cracker crumbs
⅓ cup melted butter
½ teaspoon salt
¼ teaspoon paprika

¼ teaspoon celery seed
¼ cup chopped pimientos
¼ cup chopped green
    peppers
1½ cups milk

Pick shell fragments out of oysters. Mix the crumbs, butter, and seasonings. Sprinkle a layer of the crumb mixture ⅓-inch thick in the bottom of a buttered baking dish. Cover with oysters. Add a little milk, then a layer of crumb mixture. Repeat until all the ingredients have been used. Be sure a layer of crumbs is on top. Bake 35 minutes in a moderate oven (350° F.). Serves 6.

(1266)   SCALLOPED OYSTERS

1½ cups bread crumbs   1 tablespoon butter
24 oysters   ½ cup oyster liquor
1 teaspoon salt   ½ cup milk
¼ teaspoon pepper

Spread bottom of greased baking dish with layer of crumbs.
Put in 8 oysters. Sprinkle with salt and pepper. Dot with butter.
Repeat, alternating layers of crumbs and oysters until all are
used, having crumbs on top. Pour over oyster liquor and milk.
Bake in moderate oven (350° F.) ½ hour. Serve with crisp
bacon (No. 1464). Serves 6. Boiled macaroni (No. 2302) may
also be used as a layer in this dish.

(1267)   OYSTER SOUFFLÉ

Follow recipe for crab meat soufflé (No. 1231), using oysters,
parboiled in their own liquor until edges begin to curl, instead
of crab meat.

(1268)   OYSTER RAREBIT

1 cup oysters   ½ teaspoon salt
2 tablespoons butter   ⅛ teaspoon cayenne
½ pound diced American   2 well-beaten eggs
    cheese

Boil oysters in their own liquor until edges begin to curl.
Drain, reserving liquor, and remove tough muscle. Melt butter
in saucepan. Add cheese, salt, and cayenne. Cook slowly. When
cheese starts to melt, add oyster liquor gradually and beat in the
eggs. Serve hot on buttered toast (No. 988). Serves 4.

(1269)   FRIED SCALLOPS

1 quart scallops   1 egg
Salt—Pepper   ¾ cup fine bread or cracker
Flour for dredging   crumbs

Wash scallops and dry between towels. Sprinkle with salt,
pepper, and flour. Dip in slightly beaten egg diluted with a little
cold water and roll in crumbs. Fry in deep hot fat (375° F.) 4
to 6 minutes. Drain on unglazed paper and garnish with slices
of crisp bacon (No. 1464) and watercress. Serves 6.

(1270)   SCALLOPS WITH BACON

1 quart scallops   ½ pound thinly sliced bacon

Boil scallops, splitting large ones, in their own liquor or water until they begin to shrink. In a baking pan, place a layer of bacon, then a layer of scallops, and cover with a second layer of bacon. Cook in moderate oven (350° F.) until bacon is crisp. Serves 6.

(1271)   SCRAMBLED SCALLOPS

Boil 1 cup scallops until they begin to shrink. Drain. Break into small pieces. Put in greased frying pan. Add 2 well-beaten eggs, 2 tablespoons milk, and salt and pepper to taste. Cook, stirring constantly, until egg is set. Serve on buttered toast (No. 988). Serves 4.

(1272)   BOILED SHRIMP

The edible meat is in the tail. Break off this segment, discarding the remainder of the animal head section as waste. Peel the cover from the meat by breaking the under shell and opening from front to back. Remove the dark sand vein from the center back of each shrimp and wash the meats in cold water. Boil a salt solution, allowing 1 tablespoon salt to each quart of water, and add the shrimp to the boiling water. Cook for 6 to 10 minutes or until shrimp are tender. Shrimp may be eaten hot or cold with desired seasonings or may be creamed, used in salads, etc.

(1273)   FRENCH-FRIED SHRIMP

1½ pounds raw shrimp   Salt—Pepper
2 beaten eggs   Sifted cracker crumbs
Juice of 2 lemons   Cooking oil or fat

Peel shrimp, wash, and remove sand vein. Place them in a bowl with lemon juice, salt and pepper, and allow to stand for 15 minutes. Dip shrimp into the beaten egg and then roll in crumbs. Fry in deep, hot fat (390° F.) 3 minutes. Serves 6.

(1274)   SHRIMP NEWBURG

2 tablespoons butter	2 cups cooked shrimps
1½ tablespoons flour	(No. 1272)
¾ teaspoon salt	2 egg yolks
Few grains cayenne	1 tablespoon sherry
½ cup cream	flavoring
¼ cup milk	

Melt butter, add flour, salt, and cayenne and mix well. Add cream and milk gradually and bring to the boiling point, stirring constantly. Add shrimps. Just before serving add the beaten egg yolks and flavoring. Serve on rounds of puff paste (No. 2703). Garnish with parsley and thin strips of pimiento. Serves 6.

(1275)   SHRIMP WIGGLE

1 pound cooked shrimp	1 can tomato soup
(No. 1272)	Cornstarch or flour
2 tablespoons butter	Baking soda
2 medium-sized onions,	Soda crackers
sliced	

Dice the shrimp. Heat butter in frying pan and fry onions until golden brown. Add tomato soup and an equal quantity of water. Heat and thicken with cornstarch or flour. When the mixture is at simmering heat, add the shrimp. Just before serving, stir in a good pinch of baking soda, and serve on toasted crackers. Serves 6.

(1276)   SHRIMP CREOLE

1 pound raw shrimp	⅛ teaspoon paprika
2 tablespoons melted butter	1 pint stewed tomato
1 cup chopped onions	(No. 1893)
1 cup chopped green pepper	Salt—Pepper
½ chopped clove garlic	

Peel shrimp, wash, and remove sand vein. Mix and stir in the butter, onion, green pepper, and garlic. Let this simmer until pepper is tender, then add tomato and seasoning and boil 5 minutes. Add shrimp to this and boil 10 minutes longer. Serves 6.

(1277)   SHRIMP ORLEANS

2 chopped onions	2 tablespoons flour
2 tablespoons butter	1 cup sour cream
1 cup boiled shrimp	¼ cup liquid from shrimp
(No. 1272)	Salt—Pepper

Sauté onions in butter to a light brown. Drain fish, reserving ¼ cup liquid. Dredge shrimp with flour and add to onions. Cook slowly 5 minutes without browning. Add sour cream and simmer slowly 20 minutes. Add shrimp liquid and season to taste with salt and pepper. Heat thoroughly. Serve on buttered toast (No. 988) with pan liquor for sauce. Serves 6.

(1278)   SHRIMP AND EGGS

1½ cups fresh cooked	1¼ teaspoons paprika
(No. 1272) or canned	9 well-beaten eggs
shrimps	½ cup cream
4 tablespoons fat	¾ cup grated cheese
1 teaspoon salt	

Sauté the shrimps in fat, directly over high heat until golden brown. Remove shrimps and place pan in which they were cooked over pan containing boiling water. Add the salt and paprika, and blend. Add eggs beaten with cream. Stir constantly from the bottom, lifting the cooked eggs so that the uncooked portion runs to the bottom of the pan. Cook until the egg is set. Add cheese, stirring well, and when melted, add the shrimps, and serve at once on hot buttered toast (No. 988). Serves 6.

(1279)   SHRIMP AND RICE, BAKED

2 cups cooked shrimp	2 tablespoons chopped
(No. 1272) cut in	parsley
pieces	Few grains cayenne
2 cups steamed rice	2 cups medium white
(No. 106)	sauce (No. 2004)
⅛ teaspoon pepper	½ cup dried bread crumbs

Mix shrimps, rice, parsley, pepper, cayenne, and white sauce. Pour in a greased baking dish and sprinkle with crumbs. Bake in a hot oven (400° F.) 20 to 25 minutes or until crumbs are brown. Serves 6.

(1280)   SHRIMP SOUFFLÉ

Follow recipe for crab meat soufflé (No. 1231), using cooked shrimp (No. 1272) instead of crab meat.

(1280A)   CASSEROLE OF SHRIMP

1 package thin noodles	5 tablespoons flour
1 12-ounce can whole kernel corn	2 cups milk
2 5¾ ounce cans shrimp	½ pound strong American cheese
1 8-oz. can sliced mushrooms	Salt—Pepper
6 tablespoons butter	

Cook noodles until tender in boiling salted water. Drain and place in a casserole. Arrange whole kernel corn, shrimp and sliced mushrooms over the noodles. Melt butter in frying pan. Add flour and stir until smooth. Add the liquid from shrimp and mushrooms, the milk and cook until sauce is thick and smooth. Stir constantly. Add cheese. Season with salt and pepper and pour sauce over other ingredients. Mix gently. Sprinkle cheese over the top. Bake in a moderately hot oven (400° F.) 30 minutes. Peas may be used in place of corn. Serves 10.

(1281)   CASSEROLE OF FISH, ITALIAN STYLE

¼ pound (1 cup) mushrooms, sliced	4 tablespoons butter
⅓ cup diced celery	1¼ teaspoon salt
1 medium onion, finely chopped	¼ teaspoon pepper
3 tablespoons quick-cooking tapioca	2 teaspoons sugar
	2 cups flaked cooked haddock or cod
	3 cups canned tomatoes

Sauté mushrooms, celery, and onion in butter until tender. Combine with tapioca and remaining ingredients in order given. Turn into greased casserole and bake in hot oven (425° F.) 25 minutes, stirring twice during first 10 minutes of baking. Place unbaked biscuits on top of fish mixture after it has baked 10 minutes; return to oven, and bake 12 to 15 minutes longer, or until biscuits are browned. Serves 8.

Meats

~~~~~~

AMERICAN homemakers, as a rule, are extravagant in the management of their meat budgets. It is estimated that almost one-third of all money spent in the United States for food is used for the purchase of meat. This far exceeds in proportion the meat expenditures of housewives in other parts of the world.

In foreign lands, where incomes are usually smaller and where the choicest and most expensive cuts of meat are not always so readily available, the woman who provides the meals for her family has been forced to turn to cuts of meat her American sisters look upon with disdain. But, though she starts with the handicap of poorer materials to work with, the foreign cook does not serve less appetizing or less health-giving meals than the American housewife. Indeed, the reverse is true in many cases.

To those who are forced to feed their families on limited budgets, a careful study of the recipes on the following pages will point out the way to economy in meats. Not economy that will make your meals less delightful or less nourishing, but *real economy* that will enable you to serve the less expensive cuts of meats in a manner that will rival the products of the world's greatest artists in the field of cooking. Efficient managers of more prosperous homes will also find a wide variety of the more expensive dishes with which to delight family and mealtime guests.

THE PURCHASE OF MEATS

Just as a good doctor or a good lawyer should be chosen to guard a family's health and its legal affairs, so should a housewife look for expert guidance in the selection and purchase of meats. In every city, town, and hamlet such an expert is usually available. Select a butcher carefully. The choice of meats is such a big subject that the housewife with her thousand and one important, daily duties can scarcely expect to become expert in the field of choosing meats. Her best guide should be her butcher, and he should be carefully chosen on the basis of his experience, reliability, ability, and honesty.

There are five principal kinds of fresh meat on the market. All of it, if shipped in interstate commerce, has been inspected by the United States government. Brief guides for the shopper who likes to see her meat before buying follow:

BEEF—Beef should be bright red and solid. The fat should be clear white and very firm.

VEAL—Veal, the flesh of very young calves, is light pink and finely grained. It has little fat but what there is should be clear white. Veal does not have as pronounced a flavor as meat from more mature animals.

LAMB—Lamb flesh is pinkish and the fat is firm and white.

MUTTON—Mutton, the flesh of more mature sheep is a darker red than lamb but the fat is very similar in appearance.

PORK—Pork meat is slightly pink with an overtone of gray. The fat is white but much softer than that of other meats. The flesh is usually streaked with fat.

PREPARATION OF MEAT FOR COOKING

Remove meat from the paper as soon as it is in the home. Put it in the refrigerator on an enamel or china plate. When ready to cook, do not wash meat or valuable juices will be lost. Merely wipe it with a cold, damp cloth.

RULES, AND METHODS OF COOKING MEATS

Never pierce the meat while it is cooking or valuable juices will be lost. As a general rule, the best results are obtained if the surface of meats are seared as soon as possible when cooking starts. This locks in the juices. After searing, cooking should be slower to develop the finest flavor and for tenderness. In particular, the tougher cuts should be cooked very slowly for a long time.

ROASTING—To roast is to cook by dry heat. It has been found that the temperature of the oven is an important factor in getting the best results. A moderately low temperature (300°-350° F.) for the greater part of the cooking period should be used, because: (1) The roast is uniformly done throughout; (2) The cooking losses are decreased; (3) The meat is more palatable; (4) The roast is plump and full; and (5) The bones and fat are not charred.

The following rules apply to all kinds of meat, beef, veal, pork, and lamb.

1. A moderately low oven temperature should be used.
2. The roast should be placed in the pan fat side up, thus eliminating basting.
3. A roast may be salted before or after cooking.
4. A roast should never be covered.
5. Water should not be added.
6. A meat thermometer is the only accurate means of telling when a roast is done.

TIME-TABLE FOR ROASTING

Roast	Weight	Oven Temperature Constant	Interior Temperature When Removed From Oven	Approximate Time Per Pound
	Pounds	Degrees F.	Degrees F.	Minutes
BEEF				
Standing Ribs...........	6–8	300	140	18–20
			160	22–25
			170	27–30
Standing Ribs (1 rib).....	1.8	350	140	33
			160	45
			170	50
Rolled ribs..............	6–8	300	140	32
			160	38
			170	48
PORK—Fresh				
Loin—Center...........	3–4	350	185	35–40
Whole.............	12–15		185	15–20
Ends.............	3–4		185	45–50
Shoulder—Whole........	12–14	350	185	30–35
Boned and rolled	4–6	350	185	40–45
Cushion.......	4–6	350	185	35–40
PORK—Smoked				
Ham—Whole...........	10–12	300	170	25
Tendered.........	10–12	300	160	15
Half.............	6	300	170	30
Tendered.........	6	300	160	20
LAMB				
Leg..................	6½–7½	300	175–180	30–35
Shoulder—Rolled........	3–4	300	175–180	40–45
Shoulder..............	4½–5½	300	175–180	30–35
VEAL				
Leg Roast..............	7–8	300	170	25
Loin.................	4½–5	300	170	30–35
Shoulder..............	7	300	170	25
Shoulder—rolled........	5	300	170	40–45

	MINUTES PER POUND
Beef—rare	22 minutes
Beef—medium	26 minutes
Beef—well done	33 minutes
Veal—well done	35 minutes
Lamb—medium	40 minutes
Lamb—well done	45 minutes
Mutton—medium	30 minutes
Mutton—well done	35 minutes
*Pork—well done	40 minutes
Cured ham—well done	20 minutes

BROILING—Broiling is the type of cooking done by exposing the food to glowing coals or flames or by exposure to the broiler unit of an electric range. The broiler or rack for holding the meat should be lightly greased and very hot before the meat is put in. The meat is placed on the rack so that its top surface is 2 to 3 inches from the source of heat. (2 inches if meat is 1 inch thick, 3 inches if meat is 2 inches thick). The meat is broiled about 10 minutes on one side, or until nicely browned. It is then turned and browned on the other side. When finished, it is seasoned, dotted with butter, removed to a hot platter, and served immediately.

TIME TABLE FOR BROILING MEATS

Beef steaks, 1 inch thick, rare	8 minutes
Beef steaks, 1 inch thick, medium	10 minutes
Beef steaks, 1 inch thick, well done	15 minutes
Beef steaks, 1½ inches thick, rare	12 minutes
Beaf steaks, 1½ inches thick, medium	15 minutes
Beef steaks, 1½ inches thick, well done	22 minutes
Beef steaks, 2 inches thick, rare	18 minutes
Beef steaks, 2 inches thick, medium	22 minutes
Beef steaks, 2 inches thick, well done	30 minutes
Minute steaks, rare	4 minutes
Minute steaks, medium	5 minutes
Minute steaks, well done	6 minutes
Hamburg patties	Same as beef steaks
Veal chops, 1 inch thick, well done	18 minutes
Lamb chops, 1 inch thick, medium	25 minutes
Lamb chops, 1 inch thick, well done	30 minutes
Mutton chops, 1 inch thick, medium	25 minutes
Mutton chops, 1 inch thick, well done	30 minutes
Pork chops, 1 inch thick, well done	22 minutes
Cured ham, ¼ inch thick, well done	10 minutes
Cured ham, ½ inch thick, well done	20 minutes
Bacon, well done	4 minutes
Frankfurters, well done	10 minutes

PAN-BROILING—Cooking steaks under 1 inch thick, in a heavy pan, and keep uncovered. No water or fat is added. Sear meat on both sides in very hot pan; reduce heat and cook 10 min. one side and brown on other side. Season, dot with butter and serve immediately on hot platter. When fat meats are pan-broiled, fat is poured off as it accumulates, to avoid frying.

SAUTEING—Sautéing is frying in a greased pan or with very little fat. It is usually used to brown meats in preparation for some other form of cooking. (See frying.)

FRYING—Frying is of two types, pan-frying, and deep fat frying. In pan-frying the meat is put in a pan with a 1- or 2-inch layer of melted fat. In deep fat frying the fat is in a kettle and the meat is plunged into the hot fat. The deep-fat method is usually used for such meat dishes as croquettes, breaded cutlets or filets, or small cuts which are dipped in batter or bread crumbs before cooking. For pre-cooked meat mixtures, such as croquettes, the temperature of the fat should be 375° F. to 400° F. If no frying thermometer is available a small cube of bread will turn a light brown in 40 to 50 seconds at 375° F. to 400° F. For raw meats the temperature of the fat should be 340° F. to 375° F., when a cube of bread will brown in 50 to 60 seconds. Never cook too much food in deep fat at one time, as it may reduce the temperature. Always test the temperature just before each new batch is cooked. Do not put wet foods in deep fat. Place all deep-fried foods on unglazed paper as soon as they are removed from the fat.

PLANKING—The planking of meats usually denotes an unusually fine or party dinner. The best planks are about 1 inch thick and of oak or some other hard wood. In a family where many planked meals are served, there should be at least two planks, one for fish and one for meats. The same plank should never be used for both. The plank should be brushed with oil or butter the first few times it is used. After 4 or 5 times this practice will be unnecessary. Planks should never be washed or scrubbed. They should be cleaned by rubbing with a dry cloth or by sandpapering. Planked meats are always pre-cooked, then placed on the plank, surrounded by cooked vegetables, and baked for a few minutes to brown the surrounding foods.

POT ROASTING (*Braising*)—The moist heat method of cooking meats of less tender cut. The meat is seasoned, and dredged with flour, if desired, then placed in a hot kettle with a small amount of fat and browned on all sides. A small amount of liquid is added and the kettle covered tightly. The meat is then cooked at simmering temperature slowly and long, until tender. Usually vegetables are cooked with the meat, adding them at the proper time so that they will be done when the meat is finished.

STEWING—Stewing is the cooking of meat in a small amount of liquid which will later be thickened for gravy. Never let a stew boil, as it will toughen and shrivel the meat. Stew in either a covered or uncovered pot, saucepan, or kettle.

FRICASSEEING—Fricasseeing is stewing in a thicker liquid. The rules for good stewing apply. If meat is well browned before fricasseeing, a brown sauce will result.

BOILING—The boiling of meats is done in thin liquid, water, or stock, sufficient to half cover the meat. The water should be boiling when meat is put into it. The kettle should be tightly covered. The water should be kept just under the boiling point. Seasonings should be added when cooking is half done. The liquid in which meats are boiled should be saved for soup stock.

BRAISING—All meat to be braised must first be sautéed until brown. It is then put in a tightly covered saucepan and cooked with vegetables and seasonings. A pot roast or other braised meat dish may be cooked in the oven. This may be convenient when the oven is to be used for cooking other foods at the same time, but if the meat only is to be cooked, it is more economical of fuel to cook on a surface burner. The method is the same in either case.

(1301)   BROILED STEAK

Steak should be tender and about 1½ inches thick. Wipe with cold, damp cloth. Place on slightly greased broiler. Cook at very high heat on 1 side 10 to 12 seconds. Turn and repeat. This sears both sides and holds in juices. Then reduce heat or move broiler farther away from heat and cook more slowly, turning occasionally. A 1½-inch steak will require from 12 to 30 minutes, depending on preference; a 1-inch steak, 8 to 20 minutes. When done, sprinkle with salt and pepper and brush top with melted butter. Serve hot. If steak is tough it can be improved by pounding. A tough steak can also be made tender by brushing both sides with a mixture of 1 tablespoon vinegar and 2 tablespoons butter, fat, or olive oil, letting stand several hours before cooking. Allow ½ to ¾ pound of steak per serving. Appropriate steak sauces are mushroom (No. 2039), béarnaise (No. 2032), and maître d'hôtel (No. 2027).

(1302)   PAN-BROILED STEAK

Steak, 1 to 1½ inches thick   Salt—Pepper
Butter

Trim excess fat from steak. Wipe with cold, damp cloth. Heat frying pan until it is sizzling hot. Grease pan with removed fat. Put steak in pan, searing it quickly on both sides, turning every few seconds. When evenly seared, reduce heat and cook more slowly. Pour any fat off as it accumulates. A 1-inch steak will be done rare in about 8 minutes. Well done will require about 12 minutes more. Remove steak to hot platter. Smear with butter. Season with salt and pepper. Garnish as desired. Allow ½ to ¾ pound per serving.

(1303)   MINUTE STEAK

As its name implies, this is a very thin steak which can be cooked very quickly, figuratively in a "minute." It is prepared and served in the same manner as pan-broiled steak (No. 1302 above), but is cooked from 4 to 6 minutes.

(1304)   FILET MIGNON

Filets are cut from the tenderloin of beef and are usually from one to two inches thick. Broil to the desired degree of doneness; spread with softened butter, sprinkle with salt and pepper and serve with broiled mushroom caps (No. 1802) or sautéed chopped mushrooms (No. 1801), French fried (No. 1812) or sautéed onions (No. 1811), or broiled tomatoes (No. 1895). Allow ½ to ¾ pound of meat per serving.

(1305)   PLANKED STEAK

Tender steak, 1½ inches   Baked stuffed tomatoes
   thick   (No. 1898)
Duchess (No. 1846) or   1 tablespoon milk
   mashed potatoes   Desired vegetables
   (No. 1835)   1 tablespoon butter
Stuffed onions (No. 1815)   Salt—Pepper
1 egg yolk   Mushroom sauce (No. 2039)

Wipe meat with cold, damp cloth. Broil on greased broiler over quick heat 12 to 15 minutes, turning frequently. Heat plank, grease with butter or fat, and put steak on it. Arrange potatoes around edge of plank with pastry tube. Place stuffed onions and tomatoes around steak. Dilute beaten egg yolk in milk and brush tops of potatoes and onions. Place in hot oven (400° F.) and bake until potatoes are browned, about 8 minutes. Remove from oven and arrange vegetables artistically inside border of potatoes. Spread butter on steak. Season with salt and pepper. Almost any combination of cooked vegetables may be used but should be chosen for blend of flavors and contrasting colors. Carrots, string beans, and peas are a combination often used. Serve with mushroom sauce. Allow ½ to ¾ pound of meat per serving.

APPROPRIATE VEGETABLES FOR PLANKED STEAK

Cauliflower (No. 1755), cauliflower flowerets (No. 1755), buttered peas (No. 1823), stuffed tomatoes (No. 1898), broiled tomatoes (No. 1895), sliced tomatoes with French dressing (No. 716), carrot strips, diced carrots (No. 1745), buttered small whole carrots (No. 1745), baked sliced egg plant (No. 1789), fried egg plant (No. 1786), broiled mushroom caps (No. 1802), sautéed mushroom caps (No. 1801), boiled onions (No. 1810), stuffed onions (No. 1815), French fried onion rings (No. 1812), buttered string beans (No. 1712), stuffed green peppers (No. 1832), diced turnips (No. 1906), fried strips of green peppers (No. 1831), nest of mashed potatoes (No. 1835) filled with peas (No. 1823), spinach (No. 1870), cucumber slices, diced beets (No. 1726), anchovies, kidney beans (No. 1721), stuffed olives, fresh corn (No. 1771), buttered asparagus (No. 1705), buttered Brussels sprouts (No. 1735), lima beans (No. 1717).

APPROPRIATE BORDER MATERIALS

Duchess potatoes (No. 1846), mashed potatoes (No. 1835), mashed sweet potatoes (No. 1882), candied sweet potato quarters (No. 1883), mashed squash (No. 1876), mashed turnip (No. 1908), baked (No. 44 or 45) or sautéed banana halves (No. 46), baked apple quarters (No. 36).

(1306) FRIED STEAK AND ONIONS

3 pounds steak, 1½ inches thick
1 teaspoon salt
⅛ teaspoon pepper

1 teaspoon flour
2 medium-sized onions, sliced
¼ cup butter or fat

Wipe meat with cold, damp cloth. Sprinkle with salt, pepper, and flour. Bring fat to a boil in frying pan. Put in steak. Put onions on steak. When well browned on bottom, turn over and brown other side. Serves 6.

(1307)   ECONOMY STEAK

2 pounds beef from shin, 1   1 diced turnip
    inch thick   1 teaspoon salt
2 diced onions   ¼ teaspoon pepper
2 sliced carrots   1 tablespoon flour

Wipe meat with cold, damp cloth. Put in pan. Cover with boiling water. Simmer at low heat 3 hours. Add onion, carrot, turnip, salt, and pepper. Increase heat slightly and simmer another hour. Remove meat and vegetables to hot platter. Thicken liquor with flour, mixed to a smooth paste with cold water, stirring and cooking to desired consistency. Serves 6.

(1308)   FRENCH FRIED STEAK

Wipe meat with cold, damp cloth. Cut into 2-inch squares. Gash each piece on both sides. Fry in hot, deep fat (380 to 390° F.) 5 to 7 minutes. Drain on brown paper. Season as desired and serve hot. Allow ½ pound of meat per serving.

(1309)   BRAISED STEAK

2 pounds round steak   1 teaspoon lemon juice
3 tablespoons butter or fat   2 cloves
3 tablespoons flour   1 teaspoon salt
3 tablespoons chopped onion   ⅛ teaspoon pepper

Wipe meat with cold, damp cloth. Cut in 4-inch squares. Melt butter in saucepan. Add meat and brown well on both sides. Remove meat. Stir in flour, blending well. Add all other ingredients and meat. Cover with boiling water. Let simmer 2½ hours. Serves 6.

(1310)   ROAST BEEF

Beef for roasting   ¼ teaspoon pepper
Salt, ½ teaspoon per pound   Flour for dredging

Wipe beef with cold, damp cloth. Sprinkle with salt, pepper, and flour. Place in roasting pan with fat side up or with pieces of fat on top. Place in oven, keeping temperature at 500° F. for 18 to 20 minutes; then reduce temperature to 300° F. and cook, basting occasionally, allowing 16 to 18 minutes per pound for rare meat, 22 to 25 minutes for medium, and 30 minutes for well-done. A meat thermometer will show 140° F. for rare, 160° F. for medium, and 175° F. for well-done. Allow ½ pound per serving. Skim excess fat off pan drippings. Add 2 table-spoons flour, mixed to a smooth paste with an equal quantity of cold water, for each cup of liquid remaining. Blend well and bring to a boil for gravy.

(1311)   BRAISED BEEF (POT ROAST)

Select a firm piece of beef, either solid or rolled. Almost any inexpensive cut will do. Wipe meat with cold, damp cloth. Brown on all sides in heavy kettle in own fat or hot lard. Add a small amount of liquid, cover kettle and cook slowly at simmering temperature until tender. Turn often to prevent burning. If preferred, strained tomatoes may be used in place of water, using ½ cup for each 2 pounds of meat. A low rack may be placed under meat after browning. Serve on hot platter with gravy made by adding two tablespoons of flour paste, mixed in cold water, to pot liquor, stirring well. Allow ½ to ¾ pound of meat per serving.

(1312)   BRAISED BEEF À LA MODE (POT ROAST)

4 pounds beef	½ cup diced turnip
1 teaspoon salt	½ cup diced onion
⅛ teaspoon pepper	1 tablespoon chopped
2 tablespoons flour	parsley
Fat for sautéing	½ bay leaf
½ cup diced celery	2 cups boiling water
½ cup diced carrot	

Wipe meat with cold, damp cloth. Sprinkle with salt, pepper, flour, and brown on all sides in heavy kettle. Surround with vegetables. Add water to half cover meat. Cover tightly and let simmer below boiling point for 4 hours. Place meat on hot platter. Drain vegetables and place them around meat. Thicken liquor with flour paste for gravy. Serves 8.

(1313)   BEEF STEW WITH DUMPLINGS

5 pounds inexpensive cut of beef with bone	1 diced small onion
1½ teaspoons salt	¾ cup diced turnip
¼ teaspoon pepper	¾ cup diced carrot
3 tablespoons flour	Dumplings (No. 954)
4 cups cubed potatoes	Boiling water

Wipe meat with cold, damp cloth; remove bone; cut in 1½-inch cubes; sprinkle with salt, pepper, and flour. Melt some of meat fat in frying pan and brown surface of beef cubes thoroughly. Put meat in kettle; add bones, drippings from frying pan, and enough boiling water to cover; boil 5 minutes. Reduce heat and let simmer 2 hours. Add carrot, turnip, and onion and let simmer ½ hour longer. Add potatoes and cook ½ hour more. Remove bones, excess pieces of fat, and skim fat from surface of stew. Serve in deep plates, surrounded with dumplings. Strained stewed tomatoes (No. 1893) may be substituted for boiling water. Stew can be thickened by adding ¼ cup of flour, mixed with ¼ cup cold water, 5 minutes before removing from heat. German beef stew is prepared by adding 1 cup of vinegar and 12 cloves to water in which meat is simmered. Dutch beef stew contains ½ pound pork and ½ pound beef liver for each 1 pound of beef. Serves 8.

(1314)   BEEFSTEAK PIE

2 pounds rump, flank, or chuck steak or roasting beef	1 cup cubed, boiled carrots (No. 1745)
1 teaspoon salt	2 cups cubed, boiled potatoes (No. 1834)
⅛ teaspoon pepper	1 medium-sized onion, in ¼-inch slices
2 tablespoons flour	
3 tablespoons cold water	2 tablespoons butter or fat
½ cup celery, chopped fine	Plain pie paste (No. 2701)

Wipe meat with cold, damp cloth; cut in 1½-inch cubes; sprinkle with salt and pepper. Place meat and onion in pan; cover with boiling water and let simmer slowly 1 hour. Line sides of a buttered baking dish with pastry. Put in layer of meat and onion. Thicken liquor in pan with paste of flour and cold water; pour over meat and onion in baking dish. Add carrots and potatoes, dotted with butter or fat. Add celery. Add another layer of meat and onion. Cover with pie paste.

Bake in hot oven (about 450° F.) until brown, about ½ hour. Canadian meat pie is made by adding sautéed lamb kidneys (No. 1494) cut in small pieces, to baking dish before cooking. Serves 6.

(1315) **BEEF POT PIE**

Follow recipe for chicken pot pie (No. 1541), using beef cut in cubes in place of chicken.

(1316) **BEEFSTEAK AND KIDNEY PIE**

1½ pounds beefsteak	¼ teaspoon pepper
½ pound beef kidney	⅛ teaspoon nutmeg
1 tablespoon flour	Plain pie paste (No. 2701)
1 teaspoon salt	1 cup stock or water

Split kidney; remove core, tough skin, and hard matter. Cut into 2-inch pieces. Cover with cold, salt water 1 hour. Drain. Wipe beef with cold, damp cloth. Cut into 2-inch pieces. Sprinkle beef and kidney with flour, salt, pepper, and nutmeg. Line the sides of a greased baking dish with pie paste. Mix beef and kidney. Place in dish. Add stock. Cover with pie paste. Bake in moderate oven (350° F.) 1¼ hours. Serves 4 to 6.

(1317) **BEEF AND KIDNEY PIE WITH SPAGHETTI**

1 pound steak	1 tablespoon butter
6 lamb kidneys	1 cup boiled spaghetti
1 large, chopped onion	(No. 2302) in small
1 teaspoon salt	pieces
¼ teaspoon pepper	Plain pie paste (No. 2701)
2 tablespoons flour	

Wash kidneys. Split in halves. Remove white cores and tubes. Soak ½ hour in cold water. Drain and dry. Cut into small pieces. Wipe steak with cold, damp cloth. Cut in small pieces. Put steak and kidney in saucepan. Cover with cold water. Bring to a boil quickly. Add onion, salt, and pepper. Reduce heat and let simmer until kidneys are tender, about 45 minutes. Add flour, well blended with melted butter, stirring well. Add hot, boiled spaghetti. Mix well. Line a baking dish with plain pie paste. Pour in cooked mixture. Cover with pie paste. Bake in hot oven (450° F.) until brown. Serves 6.

(1318)   SWISS STEAK

1½ pounds beef   ¼ cup chopped green
⅓ cup flour   pepper
½ teaspoon salt   1 cup stewed (No. 1893)
⅛ teaspoon pepper   or canned tomatoes
1 small onion, chopped   1 cup boiling water
2 tablespoons fat

Wipe meat with cold, damp cloth. Mix thoroughly flour, salt, and pepper; pound into steak with a potato masher. Cut meat in 2-inch squares. Brown steak and onions in fat in heavy pan. Add green pepper, tomatoes, and water. Cover and simmer until meat is tender, about 2 hours. Add more water if needed during cooking. The liquor can be thickened with flour paste for gravy. Serves 4.

(1319)   HAMBURG PATTIES

1 pound inexpensive steak,   ⅛ teaspoon pepper
   ground   ⅓ cup milk
2 eggs   2 tablespoons chopped onion
½ cup soft bread crumbs   2 tablespoons flour
1 teaspoon salt

Beat eggs and mix with meat, bread crumbs, milk, salt, and pepper. Brown onions in fat in frying pan; add to meat mixture. Mold into small patties and sprinkle with flour. Fry in small amount of fat, turning over until well browned on both sides. Place on hot platter. Thicken liquor in pan with flour paste made with cold water for gravy. A tablespoon of poultry dressing (No. 2064) added to meat will impart a pleasing flavor. Hamburg patties may also be fried in deep, hot fat (380° to 390° F.) for 6 to 8 minutes. Serves 4. A savory sandwich hamburg can be made by sautéing additional chopped onion and placing it between very thin patties, which can then be broiled over glowing coals or in a broiler. Hamburg patties are also delicious if a bacon strip is securely skewered around them before broiling. Italian style hamburg steak is made by adding ½ pound of grated American or Parmesan cheese and 1 chopped green pepper to each 1 pound of meat in meat mixture. Hamburg beef stew is prepared by using well-browned hamburg patties instead of beef cubes in beef stew (No. 1313).

(1320)   BROILED HAMBURG STEAK

Prepare meat mixture as for hamburg patties (No. 1319). Mold into one flat piece about 1¼ to 1½ inches thick. Broil at high heat until both sides are seared. Place on plank and garnish and bake same as planked steak (No. 1305).

(1321)   HAMBURG LOAF

Prepare meat mixture as for hamburg patties (No. 1319) and form into a loaf. Place in baking pan with slices of bacon laid on top. Bake for 45 minutes at 400° F. or for 2 hours at 300° F. Serve with gravy made by adding flour paste, mixed in cold water, to fat in pan, cooking until brown, adding boiling water if necessary. Serves 4.

(1322)   HAMBURG CASSEROLE

2 tablespoons butter	1½ cups canned corn
2 sliced onions	1 cup mashed potatoes
1 pound ground beef	(No. 1835)
1 cup canned tomato soup	1 beaten egg yolk

Melt butter in pan. Sauté meat and onions until brown. Add soup and corn. Mix thoroughly. Put into a greased baking dish. Cover with potatoes. Brush top with egg yolk. Bake in hot oven (450° F.) until brown. One cup boiled macaroni (No. 2302), mixed with ½ cup grated American or Parmesan cheese, may be substituted for corn. Serves 4.

(1323)   HAMBURG AND RICE EN CASSEROLE

1½ pounds ground beef	¼ teaspoon pepper
1 onion, finely chopped	3 cups boiled rice
1 teaspoon salt	(No. 107)
½ teaspoon powdered sage	

Mix meat, onion, salt, sage, and pepper. Put in saucepan with 1 cup water. Cook at low heat 15 minutes. Line a greased baking dish with rice. Add meat. Cover with rice. Bake in moderate oven (350° F.) 15 minutes. Serve on hot platter with tomato sauce (No. 2035), garnished as desired. Serves 6.

(1324)   BEEF, SAUSAGE, AND APPLE PATTIES

1 pound ground beef	8 slices cored but unpeeled
1 pound sausage meat	apples

Mix beef and sausage. Mold into 16 thin patties. Place slice of apple between each 2 patties. Broil at high heat until seared on both sides. Reduce heat or move further from heat and cook until apple is tender. Serves 6.

(1325)   MEAT BALLS AND DUMPLINGS

1½ pounds ground beef	1 sliced onion
1 teaspoon salt	6 dumplings (No. 954)
¼ teaspoon pepper	2 tablespoons flour
2 tablespoons butter or fat	

Season meat with salt and pepper and form into 6 patties. Melt butter in saucepan. Add onion and meat cakes and brown on both sides. Cover with boiling water. Let simmer slowly 1 hour. Remove meat. Add dumplings. Cover tightly and cook 10 minutes. Remove dumplings to hot platter with meat. Mix flour to a smooth paste with cold water and stir in liquor for gravy. If desired, vegetables, potatoes, carrots, turnips, all or any of them may be cooked with this. They should be added at times so that they will be finished with the meat and dumplings. Serves 6.

(1326)   COLLOPS

2 pounds inexpensive beef	⅛ teaspoon pepper
1 chopped onion	3 tablespoons flour
1 teaspoon salt	3 tablespoons milk

Wipe meat with cold, damp cloth. Grind. Put in saucepan with 2 quarts cold water, removing all lumps from meat. Add onion. Cover. Bring to a boil. Boil 5 minutes. Reduce heat and let simmer 1½ hours. Add salt and pepper. Mix flour to a smooth paste with milk and add slowly to pan, stirring well. Serve hot on warm platter with mashed potatoes (No. 1835), garnished as desired. Serves 4.

(1327)   STUFFED ROLL OF BEEF

1 pound top sirloin or round
  of beef, cut thin
1½ cups boiled spaghetti
  (No. 2302)
1 chopped onion
1 stalk celery, chopped
1 teaspoon salt
1 teaspoon mixed spices
¼ teaspoon pepper

1 tablespoon chopped
  parsley
2 tablespoons flour
2 tablespoons butter or fat
2 cups water, stock, or
  canned or strained
  stewed tomatoes
  (No. 1893)

Wipe meat with cold damp cloth. Mix spaghetti, onion, celery, salt, spices, pepper, and parsley. Spread on meat. Roll as a jelly roll and tie or skewer securely. Sprinkle with 1 tablespoon flour. Melt butter in frying pan and brown all over. Transfer to greased baking dish. Add liquid. Cover and bake in moderate oven (350° F.) 2 hours. Put rolls on hot platter. Thicken liquor with remaining flour, mixed to a smooth paste with cold water. Pour over meat. Boiled rice (No. 107), poultry stuffing (No. 2064), stale bread crumbs, or mashed potatoes (No. 1835) can be used instead of spaghetti. Serves 4 to 6.

(1328)   BEEF HASH

2 cups cooked roast beef
  (No. 1310) or corned
  beef, chopped fine
3 cups cold boiled potatoes
  (No. 1834), chopped
  fine
½ cup milk
¼ teaspoon salt

⅛ teaspoon pepper
Dash of Worcestershire
  sauce
1 tablespoon onion juice
  or ½ cup chopped
  onion
1 tablespoon butter or fat

Mix thoroughly all ingredients but fat. Spread evenly in a greased frying pan and fry slowly over low heat until it is well-browned underneath, about 30 to 40 minutes. Turn and fold as an omelet on a hot platter. Garnish with parsley. If desired, chopped parsley, chopped green or red peppers, or diced pimiento may be added to mixture; or 1½ cups of chopped, cold, boiled beets (No. 1726) may be added. Any other chopped cooked meats, either individually or in combination, can be used for beef. Serves 6.

(1329)   SCALLOPED BEEF

3 cups chopped, cold, roast   1½ cups medium white
  beef (No. 1310)   sauce (No. 2004)
1 tablespoon chopped   1½ cups bread crumbs
  parsley   1 teaspoon onion juice

Mix all ingredients but bread crumbs. Place layer of crumbs
in a greased baking dish; put layer of meat mixture on crumbs;
keep alternating layers, with bread crumbs on top. Bake at
425° F. until crumbs are brown, about 15 minutes. Serves 6.

(1330)   BEEF HAMBURGER PIE

1½ lb. ground beef   12 small white onions, cooked
Salt and pepper   5 or 6 potatoes
3 tablespoons fat   6 carrots
3 tablespoons flour   2 stalks celery
2 No. 2 cans tomatoes   Pastry
½ teaspoon sugar   Evaporated milk

Season meat and shape into small patties; brown in hot fat in
skillet; remove to casserole dish; add flour to fat in skillet and
blend; add tomatoes and sugar and cook to a boil; add cooked
whole onions, diced potatoes, carrots and celery. Pour over meat.
Roll pie pastry to ¼ in. thick and cut to fit top of casserole.
Glaze with evaporated milk. Place pastry on top of dish; bake
in hot oven (450° F.) about 20 minutes. Serves 6.

(1331)   BEEF CUTLETS

2 cups ground cold beef   1 tablespoon chopped
½ teaspoon onion juice   parsley
1 cup thick white sauce   1 egg
  (No. 2004)   2 tablespoons water
            ¾ cup fine bread crumbs

Add onion juice, hot white sauce, and parsley to meat; mix
well; chill. Mold into cutlets. Roll in bread crumbs and dip in
gently beaten egg and water. Roll again in crumbs. Fry in deep
hot fat (380° F.) 5 minutes. Drain on brown paper. Serves 6.

(1332)   STUFFED FLANK STEAK

1½ pounds flank steak   1 tablespoon flour
½ teaspoon salt   1½ cups poultry stuffing
⅛ teaspoon pepper   (No. 2064)

Have steak scored to cut long fibers. Sprinkle with salt, pepper, and flour. Spread stuffing on meat; form into a roll and fasten with skewers. Place in baking pan with a little fat, and brown. Add 1 cup of boiling water. Cover and bake in slow oven (325° F.) about 1½ hrs. or until tender. Place on hot platter. Thicken liquor with flour paste mixed with cold water for gravy. Serves 4.

(1333) FLANK STEAK WITH TOMATO SAUCE

1½ pounds flank steak	1 cup thick tomato soup
1 onion, chopped	(No. 571)
2 tablespoons butter	¼ teaspoon pepper
1 teaspoon salt	2 tablespoons flour

Wipe meat with cold, damp cloth. Melt butter in roasting pan. Add onion and brown lightly. Add meat and brown evenly on both sides. Sprinkle with salt and pepper. Cover with water Add ½ soup. Bake in modern oven (350° F.) 1½ hours, basting frequently. Add balance of soup last 15 minutes of cooking. Thicken liquor with flour, mixed to a smooth paste with cold water, stirring until thick. Serve meat on hot platter with this gravy. Serves 4.

(1334) KOL DOLMER

1 pound ground beef	1 teaspoon salt
½ pound ground pork	¼ teaspoon pepper
tenderloin	1 cabbage
1 cup raw rice	1 tablespoon butter
1 teaspoon sugar	1 cup milk or cream
1 chopped onion	

Mix thoroughly steak, pork, onion, salt, sugar, pepper. Boil rice (No. 107) and add to mixture. Wilt cabbage leaves by scalding with boiling water. Put some of meat and rice mixture in wilted cabbage leaf and roll into balls securely. Repeat until all material is used. Put balls in greased baking pan. Dot cabbage with butter. Add 1 cup hot water. Bake in moderate oven (350° F.) 40 minutes. Turn over and bake another 20 minutes. Heat milk or cream and pour over balls. Boiled macaroni (No. 2302) can be substituted for rice. Serves 6.

(1335)   SHORT RIBS EN CASSEROLE

2 pounds short ribs of beef	2 sliced onions
3 tablespoons French	2 cups stock or water
dressing (No. 716)	6 small potatoes

Wipe meat with cold, damp cloth. Brush with French dressing and let stand 1 hour. Put in greased baking dish. Put onion on top of meat. Add stock. Cover and bake in moderate oven (350° F.) 1 hour. Pare potatoes. Add to dish. Re-cover and bake 1 hour longer. Uncover and bake 30 minutes more. Serves 6.

(1336)   CHOPPED BEEF SWEET POTATO ROLL

4 cups mashed sweet	2 pounds chopped beef
potatoes (No. 1882)	1 egg
2 tablespoons butter	½ teaspoon grated onion
¾ to 1 cup milk	6 strips bacon
3 teaspoons salt	12 fried apple slices
¼ teaspoon pepper	(No. 39)

Combine sweet potatoes, melted butter, and milk and beat until light. Season with salt and pepper. Form into a roll about 8 inches long and chill. Mix together lightly the beef, slightly beaten egg, two teaspoons salt, one-eighth teaspoon pepper and grated onion. Pat out to about half an inch thickness on a piece of waxed paper. Place sweet potato roll in center and wrap the beef around it, lifting it up with the waxed paper. Remove paper, press edges firmly together and bake in a moderate oven (350° F.) for about 45 minutes. Garnish with bacon cooked until crisp (No. 1464) and glazed apple slices. Serves 6.

(1337)   BEEF CROQUETTES

Follow instructions for chicken croquettes (No. 1553), using beef instead of chicken.

(1338)   DUTCH CROQUETTES

1 pound pork	¼ teaspoon pepper
1 pound beef	1 tablespoon chopped
1 tablespoon chopped celery	parsley
1 tablespoon chopped onion	1 cup flour
1 teaspoon powdered sage	¼ cup butter or fat
1 teaspoon salt	

Wipe meat with cold, damp cloth. Grind both together. Mix thoroughly with celery, onion, sage, salt, pepper, and parsley. Mold into patties, balls, or cones. Roll in flour. Melt fat. When it is sizzling, put in croquettes. When bottom is well browned, turn and brown evenly all over. Serve hot with white sauce (No. 2004). Serves 6.

(1339) **RAGOUT OF BEEF**

2 pounds beef	1 tablespoon flour
½ cup flour	1 diced carrot
1½ teaspoon salt	1 diced onion
¼ teaspoon pepper	1 tablespoon Worcester-
2 tablespoons butter or fat	shire sauce

Wipe meat with cold, damp cloth and cut into small cubes. Sprinkle with half the salt and pepper and roll in flour. Melt butter in saucepan. Add meat and brown it well. Stir in 1 tablespoon flour. Add 1 cup boiling water. Bring to boiling point, stirring constantly. Add balance of salt and pepper, carrot, and onion. Cover tightly and let simmer 1 hour. Add Worcestershire sauce and serve hot. Serves 6.

(1340) **BAKED RAGOUT OF BEEF**

1 pound beef, cut in 1-inch cubes	2 cups boiled lima beans (No. 1717)
¼ cup flour	1 cup canned or strained
1 teaspoon salt	stewed tomatoes
¼ teaspoon pepper	(No. 1893)
2 tablespoons butter or fat	1 tablespoon Worcester-
2 sliced onions	shire sauce
1 sliced carrot	

Mix flour, salt, and pepper. Roll meat in mixture. Melt butter in pan. Sauté meat a light brown. Add onions. Sauté until well browned. Put alternate layers of meat and vegetables in greased baking dish. Add tomatoes, mixed with Worcestershire sauce. Cover and bake in moderate oven (350° F.) 2 to 3 hours. Serves 6. Boiled peas (No. 1823) or diced boiled potatoes (No. 1834) can be substituted for lima beans.

(1341)   MEAT AND PASTRY ROLL

2 chopped onions	¼ teaspoon pepper
2 tablespoons butter or fat	Baking powder biscuit
2 pounds ground beef	dough (No. 1012)
1 teaspoon salt	

Melt butter in frying pan. Add onions and brown slightly. Add meat and brown thoroughly, mixing well. Season with salt and pepper. Roll dough thin into a square. Spread with meat mixture. Roll as a jelly roll. Put roll in greased baking dish and bake in hot oven (375° F.) 45 minutes, turning occasionally. Serves 6.

(1342)   AMERICAN CHILI CON CARNE

2 pounds beef	2 cups canned red kidney
4 tablespoons butter	beans
4 medium-size onions, sliced	4 celery stalks, chopped
2 cups canned or strained	1 teaspoon salt
stewed tomatoes	1 teaspoon red pepper
(No. 1893)	1 teaspoon chili powder

Wipe beef with cold, damp cloth. Cut into small cubes. Melt butter in pan. Sauté meat and onions in butter until nicely browned. Put in kettle. Add tomatoes, beans, celery, salt, and pepper. Simmer 1½ hours. Add chili powder and simmer 30 minutes more. Serve hot. Serves 6 to 8.

(1343)   BAKED BEEF CAKE

1 pound round steak	1 beaten egg
1 cup sifted flour	1 teaspoon salt
2 cups milk	¼ teaspoon pepper

Wipe meat with cold, damp cloth. Dice. Make a batter with flour, milk, egg, and ½ of salt and pepper. Grease a baking dish. Put meat in. Sprinkle with balance of salt and pepper. Pour batter over meat. Bake in moderate oven (350° F.) 1 hour. Serve hot. Lamb or mutton may be substituted for beef. Serves 4.

(1344)   BEEF AND TOMATOES

2 pounds steak
3 cups canned or strained
  stewed tomatoes
  (No. 1893)

3 large onions, sliced
1 teaspoon salt
1/4 teaspoon pepper

Wipe meat with cold, damp cloth. Cut into 6 pieces. Melt a little beef fat in frying pan. Put meat in pan. Arrange onion on top of meat. Add tomatoes, salt, and pepper. Simmer at low heat until meat is tender, about 1 hour. Serve on hot platter, using liquor for sauce. Serves 6.

(1345)   FILET OF BEEF

2 pounds filet of beef
1/4 cup butter or fat
1 teaspoon salt

1/4 teaspoon pepper
3 tablespoons flour

Wipe meat with cold, damp cloth. Remove all ligaments and sinews. Brush meat with butter or fat. Sprinkle with salt, pepper, and 2 tablespoons flour. Put in pan. Bake in hot oven (450° F.) 30 minutes. Remove to hot platter. For gravy, thicken liquor with remaining flour, mixed to a smooth paste with cold water, adding boiling water if necessary. Cook until thick, stirring constantly. Mushroom (No. 2039) or tomato sauce (No. 2035) also go well with this dish. Serves 4.

(1346)   BOILED BEEF

4 pounds beef, plate, neck
  or shank

2 teaspoons salt

Wipe meat with cold, damp cloth. Place in kettle. Add cold water to half cover meat. Bring quickly to a boil. Reduce heat and let simmer until meat is tender, 3 to 4 hours. Add salt and more water, if necessary, when meat is half cooked. If desired vegetables may be cooked with the meat. To obtain brown stock meat should be seared on all sides before simmering, in which case put boiling water in kettle with beef. For gravy, skim fat off stock and thicken with a little flour, mixed to a smooth paste in cold water. Other sauces recommended are tomato (No. 2035) or horseradish (No. 2038). Allow 1/2 pound per serving.

(1347)   SOUTHERN GOULASH

2 tablespoons fat	1½ cups spaghetti
1 pound ground steak	1 teaspoon salt
1 finely chopped onion	¼ teaspoon pepper
1 cup beef broth	1 teaspoon Worcester-
(No. 529)	shire sauce

Melt fat in deep pan. Sear steak and onion in it quickly. Add other ingredients. Cover pan and cook in moderate oven (325° F.) 25 to 30 minutes. Canned or strained, stewed tomatoes (No. 1893) can be substituted for beef broth. Serves 4.

(1348)   AMERICAN BEEF CHOP SUEY

Follow instructions for making American chicken chop suey (No. 1554), using beef instead of chicken.

(1349)   BEEF SAUSAGE MEAT

2 pounds chopped beef	2 tablespoons chopped
2 teaspoons salt	parsley
1 teaspoon powdered sage	3 cups stale bread crumbs
½ teaspoon black pepper	1 well-beaten egg
¼ teaspoon paprika	

Mix all ingredients thoroughly. Tie in clean cloth. Drop in kettle of boiling water and boil 1 hour. Remove cloth when cold and use sausage in thin slices. Serves 6 to 8.

(1350)   JELLIED BEEF

Follow recipe for jellied chicken (No. 1555) using beef and beef bones, instead of chicken.

(1351)   CORNED BEEF

Wipe meat with cold, damp cloth. Put in kettle. Cover with cold water. Bring to a boil. Boil 3 to 5 minutes. Skim water. Reduce heat. Let simmer until tender, allowing about 30 minutes per pound. Let cool slightly in liquor. Put on platter. Cover with another dish. Place weight on top to press meat together. To glaze corned beef, finish cooking as above. Transfer to baking pan. Stick in 12 cloves and cover with ½ cup brown sugar.

Add a little water to pan. Bake in moderate oven (350° F.), basting frequently with sirup, until glazed, about 30 to 45 minutes. Allow ½ pound of meat per serving.

(1352) JEWISH CORNED BEEF

5 pounds brisket	6 buttons garlic
1 ounce whole black pepper	¼ teaspoon saltpeter
1 ounce whole allspice	3 bay leaves

Let meat stand in brine 24 hours. Throw this brine away and add fresh water, saltpeter and spices. Let stand two weeks in a cool place. Add salt enough to your water to hold up an egg.

(1353) PRESSED CORNED BEEF

Prepare and cook according to recipe for corned beef (No. 1351). While hot, cover with a plate and weight to hold it in shape.

(1354) SPICED BEEF

Prepare, cook, and compress same as pressed corned beef (No. 1353), hanging a small bag of mixed pickling spices in water while meat is simmering.

(1355) NEW ENGLAND BOILED DINNER

Prepare and cook corned beef (No. 1351). Add to kettle, 40 minutes before meat is done, 1 sliced cabbage, 2 turnips, 6 carrots, 8 pared potatoes, and 6 pared parsnips, cut in half. To produce corned beef and cabbage, eliminate other vegetables and put cabbage in kettle 30 minutes before meat is done.

(1356) FRIED CORNED BEEF AND CABBAGE

3 tablespoons butter or fat	4 cups cold boiled cabbage
6 thin slices corned beef	(No. 1736)
Salt—Pepper	

Melt butter in frying pan. Sauté meat quickly to golden brown on both sides. Remove to hot platter. Add cabbage to pan and sauté until heated through. Sprinkle with salt and pepper while cooking. Serves 6.

(1357)   CORNED BEEF HASH

Follow directions for meat hash (No. 1602), using corned beef for meat. Chopped vegetables, which are tasty mixed into corned beef hash are pimiento, green pepper, or onion, singly or in any combination.

(1358)   CREAMED CORNED BEEF

1½ cups chopped corned beef   2 cups medium white
                                                                   sauce (No. 2004)

Stir meat in hot sauce until heated through. Serves 6.

(1359)   CREAMED CHIPPED BEEF

1 pound dried beef   1 cup milk
2 tablespoons butter   1 tablespoon flour
1 cup cream

Soak beef in cold water 15 minutes. Drain. Pick into thin pieces. Melt 1 tablespoon butter in pan. Put in beef and brown. Add milk and cream. Bring to boil. Thicken with flour, mixed to a smooth paste with balance of butter. Stir until it boils. Serve hot over buttered toast (No. 988). Serves 6.

(1360)   CREAMED BEEF ON TOAST

1½ cups unsalted medium   ½ pound dried beef
    white sauce (No. 2004)   8 toast triangles

Separate meat and let stand covered with hot water 10 minutes to remove salt. Add to hot sauce and heat thoroughly in double boiler about 10 minutes. Serve on hot platter, garnished with toast.

(1361)   SAUTÉED CHIPPED BEEF

Soak meat in cold water 15 minutes. Drain. Sauté until crisp in little butter or fat. Allow ¼ pound meat per serving.

(1362)   CHIPPED BEEF RAREBIT

1 cup grated cheese	2 teaspoons butter
1 cup shredded, dried beef	¼ teaspoon pepper
3 cups canned or strained	2 beaten eggs
stewed tomatoes	1 teaspoon Worcester-
(No. 1893)	shire sauce

Put cheese, beef, and tomatoes in saucepan. Simmer until cheese is melted, stirring constantly. Stir in butter and pepper. Add eggs and Worcestershire sauce. Heat quickly almost to a boil and serve immediately on buttered toast (No. 988). Serves 4.

(1363)   ROAST STUFFED VEAL

Leg or shoulder of veal,	2 tablespoons flour
boned	Fat, salt pork, or bacon
½ teaspoon of salt per pound	2 cups poultry stuffing
of meat	(No. 2064)
¼ teaspoon pepper	

Wipe meat with cold, damp cloth. Sprinkle with salt, pepper, and flour. Stuff. Place in roasting pan with a little fat or surrounded by strips of salt pork or bacon. Sear for 15 minutes in hot oven (500° F.). Reduce heat to 325° F. and cook 30 minutes per pound, basting every 15 minutes, adding water if necessary. A meat thermometer will read 172° F. when meat is done. A desirable addition to the stuffing is ½ cup seedless raisins or stewed pitted prunes (No. 71). Allow ½ pound of meat per serving. Roast veal may be delightfully flavored by inserting small slices of anchovies and garlic in incisions cut in surface before roasting.

(1364)   VEAL CHOPS

Have chops 1 inch thick. Wipe with cold, damp cloth. Rub all over with butter, oil, or fat. Broil in moderate heat (350° F.) about 15 minutes, turning when brown on one side. Sprinkle with salt and pepper. Serve hot. If sautéed veal chops are desired, roll in flour, season with salt and pepper, sauté in little fat until brown, cover and cook slowly 20 minutes, turning occasionally. For breaded veal chops dip in flour, then in well-beaten egg, diluted with water, then in bread crumbs, and follow directions for sautéed veal chops. Chops should be served hot with lemon butter (No. 2029), tomato (No. 2035), or white sauce (No. 2004). Allow 1 chop per serving.

(1365)   VEAL CHOPS EN CASSEROLE

6 veal chops	1 cup sliced boiled carrots
3 tablespoons butter or fat	(No. 1745)
6 medium-size onions	1 teaspoon salt
2 cups tomato (No. 2035)	⅛ teaspoon pepper
or brown sauce	2 slices bacon
(No. 2020)	

Wipe meat with cold, damp cloth. Melt butter in frying pan. Add chops and brown quickly on both sides. Remove to a greased baking dish. Quarter onions and fry in fat 4 minutes. Put onions, carrots, salt, pepper, and bacon in dish. Add sauce. Cover and bake in moderate oven (350° F.) 1½ to 2 hours. Serves 6.

(1366)   BROILED VEAL CUTLETS

Wipe meat with cold, damp cloth. Brush with butter or pork fat. Broil in high heat 7 to 9 minutes, turning often. Season to taste. Or, pan-broil in little fat same length of time. To prepare planked veal cutlets, follow recipe for planked steak (No. 1305), choosing vegetables and garnishes appropriate for veal. Allow ½ pound of meat per serving.

(1367)   BREADED VEAL CUTLETS

2 pounds veal for cutlets,	1 egg
cut ½ inch thick	2 tablespoons cold water
1 teaspoon salt	2 tablespoons butter or fat
⅛ teaspoon pepper	2 tablespoons flour
¾ cup dry bread crumbs	

Wipe meat with cold, damp cloth. Cut into 6 pieces. Sprinkle with salt and pepper. Roll in bread crumbs. Dip in egg, well beaten in two tablespoons cold water. Roll again in crumbs. Heat fat in frying pan and cook cutlets until thoroughly browned on both sides. Remove to hot platter. Thicken liquor with flour, mixed to a paste in cold water, for sauce. Grated Parmesan cheese may be added to the bread crumbs. Alternate sauces which may be used are tomato (No. 2035) or mushroom (No. 2039). The seasoned and crumbed cutlets may be fried in deep, hot fat (380° to 390° F.) about 6 to 8 minutes, in which case drain on unglazed paper. Serves 6.

(1368) GLAZED VEAL

1 pound veal steak, in 1-inch
    cubes
¼ cup flour
½ teaspoon salt

⅛ teaspoon pepper
2 tablespoons butter or fat
⅓ cup currant jelly

Roll meat in a mixture of flour, salt, and pepper. Melt fat in pan. Add veal and cook until brown. Cover and cook slowly, turning often, until tender, 30 to 45 minutes. Heat jelly. Add ½ cup boiling water to jelly. Pour liquid over meat and cook, stirring constantly, until glazed. Serves 4.

(1369) VEAL BIRDS

1½ pounds veal steak
1½ cups poultry stuffing
    (No. 2064)

¼ cup flour
2 tablespoons butter or fat

Wipe meat with cold, damp cloth. Trim off fat and cut into 6 pieces of uniform size. Spread each piece with stuffing. Form into a roll and fasten with skewers. Brown the rolls uniformly in melted fat. Place rolls in baking dish. Thicken liquor with paste of flour and cold water and pour over rolls. Bake 1 hour at 375° F. Serves 4 to 6.

(1370) VEAL POT ROAST

Follow recipe for pot roast à la mode (No. 1312), using veal instead of beef, cooking 35 minutes per pound.

(1371) VEAL LOAF

3 pounds lean veal, chopped
    fine
¾ cup cracker crumbs
1 egg
1 tablespoon chopped onion
1 tablespoon chopped
    parsley

4 tablespoons cream
1 tablespoon salt
¼ teaspoon pepper
⅛ teaspoon nutmeg
3 tablespoons fat salt
    pork, ground
¼ cup melted butter or fat

Mix all ingredients except the last thoroughly. Press as a loaf into a pan. Cook in slow oven (325° F.) for 2¾ hours, basting occasionally with melted butter or fat. Prick top occasionally to allow fat to penetrate. May be served hot with tomato sauce (No. 2035) or cold with catchup and pickles. If desired add 1 pound chopped pork. Allow ½ pound of meat per serving.

(1372)   FRICASSEE OF VEAL

Follow recipe for chicken fricassee (No. 1540), using a breast or knuckle of veal instead of chicken.

(1373)   VEAL EN CASSEROLE

Follow recipe for hamburg casserole (No. 1322), using veal instead of beef.

(1374)   VEAL BURGERS

Follow recipe for hamburg patties (No. 1319), using veal instead of beef, cooking about 10 minutes.

(1375)   VEAL LOAF AND POTATO DRESSING

Follow directions for veal loaf (No. 1371). Soak 5 slices bread in little milk. Add 5 potatoes, boiled and mashed (No. 1835). Also add 1 chopped onion, 4 tablespoons butter, 1 teaspoon salt, and ½ teaspoon pepper. Mix thoroughly. Form into small cakes. Put in pan with veal loaf last hour of cooking. Serves 6.

(1376)   RAGOUT OF VEAL

1 tablespoon butter or fat	1 tablespoon sugar
3 onions, finely chopped	1 teaspoon salt
3 tomatoes, sliced	¼ teaspoon pepper
2 pounds veal	1 cup canned or strained
2 carrots, diced	stewed tomatoes
2 tablespoons chopped	(No. 1893)
parsley	

Melt butter in pan. Add onions and brown. Add sliced tomatoes. Wash veal and put it in pan wet. Add all other ingredients. Cover and stew slowly 2 hours. Serves 6.

(1377)   BOILED VEAL

Wipe meat with cold, damp cloth. Put in pan. Cover with water. Bring to a boil. Cover. Reduce heat and let simmer until meat is tender, about 1½ hours. Season with salt and pepper when half cooked. Remove from pan when done. Sprinkle with flour. Sauté in little fat in frying pan. Allow ½ pound per serving.

(1378)   **STEWED VEAL**

1½ pounds veal	1 blade of mace
3 cups milk or equal	¼ teaspoon pepper
amounts of water and	1 tablespoon flour
milk	1 teaspoon salt

Wipe meat with cold, damp cloth. Dice. Put in saucepan. Add milk or milk-water mixture, mace, and pepper. Cover and simmer slowly until meat is tender, 1 to 1½ hours. Thicken with flour, mixed to a smooth paste with cold water. Add salt. Stir and cook to desired consistency. Serve hot. Serves 6.

(1379)   **FRICANDEAU OF VEAL**

3 pounds veal	¼ teaspoon pepper
Salt pork	2 tablespoons chopped
2 tablespoons butter or fat	parsley
2 onions, diced	2 cups canned or stewed
2 carrots, sliced	strained tomatoes
1 cup diced celery	(No. 1893)
1 teaspoon salt	1 tablespoon flour

Wipe meat with cold, damp cloth. Rub the top with salt pork. Melt butter in pan. Add veal and brown uniformly. Add onions, carrots, celery, salt, pepper, and parsley. Cover and bake in moderate oven (350° F.) 30 minutes. Add tomatoes and cook until tender, about 30 minutes more, basting frequently. Remove meat and vegetables to hot platter. Thicken liquor with flour, mixed to a smooth paste with cold water, cooking and stirring until thick. Use for sauce. Serves 6.

(1380)   **VEAL À LA MARYLAND**

2 pounds veal for roasting	1 teaspoon salt
½ cup flour	¼ teaspoon pepper
1 egg	2 tablespoons butter
1 cup bread crumbs	

Wipe meat with cold, damp cloth. Cut in pieces, 3 inches long. Roll in flour. Dip in beaten egg, diluted with water. Roll in crumbs. Sprinkle with salt and pepper. Place in baking pan. Dot with butter or lay bacon slices on top of meat. Bake in hot oven (450° F.) 25 minutes. Serve with white sauce (No. 2004). Serves 6.

(1381)   VEAL POT PIE

Follow recipe for chicken pot pie (No. 1541), using veal cut in squares, in place of chicken.

(1382)   VEAL STEW WITH NOODLES

2 pounds breast or neck of veal	6 medium-size onions
¼ cup flour	1 cup wide noodles
2 tablespoons butter or fat	1 cup sliced celery
1 teaspoon salt	1 tablespoon paprika
⅛ teaspoon pepper	1 tablespoon chopped parsley

Wipe meat with cold, damp cloth. Cut into 6 pieces. Roll in flour and brown in melted butter in kettle. Sprinkle with salt and pepper. Cover with cold water. Bring to boiling point. Reduce heat and let simmer 1½ hours. Add onions, noodles, and celery. Cook 45 minutes longer. Serve on hot platter, garnished with paprika and parsley. Serves 6.

(1383)   VEAL PIE

2½ pounds knuckle of veal	½ cup sliced carrots
1½ teaspoons salt	2 tablespoons chopped parsley
⅛ teaspoon pepper	2 tablespoons flour
2 slices onion	Plain pie paste (No. 2701)
1 cup diced celery	

Wipe meat with cold, damp cloth; cut from bone in small pieces; sprinkle with salt and pepper. Cover bones with cold water. Add vegetables and heat slowly to boiling point. Add meat. Boil five minutes; then simmer until meat is tender. Line a baking dish with pie paste. Put meat and vegetables in dish. Thicken liquor with flour mixed to a paste with cold water: pour over mixture in baking dish. Cover with pie paste. Bake in oven at 450° F. until brown. Serves 6.

(1384)   VEAL AND RICE PIE

1 pound chopped cooked cold veal	½ cup mild cheese, grated
2 cups boiled rice (No. 107)	1 teaspoon salt
2 cups medium white sauce (No. 2004)	½ teaspoon pepper
	Plain pie paste (No. 2701)

Mix well all ingredients but pie paste. Line a greased baking dish with pie paste. Put in mixture. Cover with pie paste. Punch small hole in center of top crust to permit steam to escape. Bake in moderate oven (350° F.) until well browned, about 45 minutes. Serves 6.

(1385) VEAL SOUFFLÉ

4 egg yolks	2 cups cold roast veal
1½ cups thick white sauce	(No. 1363), diced
(No. 2004)	4 egg whites
½ teaspoon salt	

Beat egg yolks and stir into hot white sauce; mix well. Add veal and salt. Chill. Fold in the egg whites, stiffly beaten. Put in greased baking dish. Set in pan of hot water and bake in moderate oven (325° F.) about 50 minutes. Serves 6.

(1386) VEAL CURRY AND RICE

Prepare same as lamb curry and rice (No. 1408), using veal instead of lamb.

(1387) VEAL CROQUETTES

Substitute veal for lamb in recipe for lamb croquettes (No. 1414).

(1388) VEAL EN BROCHETTE

1 pound veal steak, ½-inch	½ cup flour
thick	1 teaspoon salt
½ pound fresh pork, sliced	¼ teaspoon pepper
very thin	2 tablespoons butter or fat

Wipe meat with cold, damp cloth. Cut veal in 24 squares. Cut pork in 18 squares. Roll in mixture of flour, salt, and pepper. Put alternate slices of meat on 6 small skewers. Melt butter in heavy pan. Sauté skewered meat until well browned. Cover and cook slowly, turning often, until tender, 30 to 45 minutes. Serve with brown sauce (No. 2020). Serves 6.

(1389)   JELLIED VEAL

1 knuckle of veal, well broken	1 blade of mace
1 tablespoon chopped celery	2 cloves
1 tablespoon chopped onion	1 teaspoon salt
1 tablespoon chopped parsley	¼ teaspoon pepper
1 tablespoon chopped carrot	1 tablespoon lemon juice
1 tablespoon chopped turnip	2 hard-cooked eggs, sliced
	(No. 202)

Wipe knuckle with cold, damp cloth. Put celery, onion, parsley, carrot, turnip, cloves, and mace in cheese cloth bag. Put knuckles and bag in pot. Cover with cold water. Bring quickly to a boil. Reduce heat. Cover pot and let simmer until meat and bone separate. Remove knuckle and bag. Strain liquor back into the pot and boil, uncovered, down to 1 quart. Season with salt, pepper, and lemon juice. Place some of the egg slices on bottom of a greased mold. Pour over sufficient liquor to just cover egg. Let stand until slightly jellied. Add a ¼-inch layer of liquor. Let set. Add alternate layers of meat and egg. Garnish sides with egg. Fill mold with balance of liquor. Let harden. Serve chilled. Serves 6.

(1390)   ROAST LEG OF LAMB

1 6-pound leg of lamb	1 tablespoon salt
¼ teaspoon pepper	2 tablespoons flour

Wipe meat with cold, damp cloth. Sprinkle with salt and pepper; rub with flour. Place on rack in open roasting pan, fat side up. Roast for 15 minutes at 460° F.; reduce heat to 325° F. and cook 30 minutes per pound. If meat thermometer is used it will read 180° F. when done. If layer of fat is very thin, place several bacon strips on top and basting will probably be unnecessary. According to taste lamb may be flavored by (1) rubbing meat with garlic or by inserting small pieces of garlic in the meat; (2) basting with mixture of Worcestershire sauce and tomato juice; (3) covering with buttered pineapple slices for last 45 minutes of cooking; (4) rubbing with chopped mint leaves; (5) basting with mint jelly, dissolved in hot water. For gravy leave two tablespoons of fat in pan; stir in 4 tablespoons flour and cook until brown; add 2 cups hot water; bring to boiling point, constantly stirring; cook five minutes more. The roast may be glazed by basting with ½ cup grape jelly, dissolved in ½ cup hot water, the last 40 minutes of roasting. Serves 8.

(1391)   ROAST CROWN OF LAMB

Crown of lamb with 12 to
    15 ribs
1½ teaspoons salt
¼ teaspoon pepper
1 chopped onion

Meat trimmings from
    crown
1 strip of salt pork for
    each rib

Have butcher prepare crown, reserving meat trimmings. Wipe with cold, damp cloth and sprinkle with 1 teaspoon salt and ⅛ teaspoon pepper. Tie strip of salt pork around each rib-end to prevent burning. Mix meat trimmings, onion, and balance of salt and pepper. Place in crown. Cook same as roast leg of lamb (No. 1390). Replace salt pork with paper frills. In serving, center of crown may be filled with vegetables. Serves 6 to 8.

(1392)   ROAST STUFFED SHOULDER OF LAMB

1 3-pound shoulder of lamb
¼ teaspoon pepper
1 tablespoon salt
2 tablespoons flour
2 tablespoons chopped onion
3 tablespoons fat

2 cups bread crumbs
1 teaspoon chopped mint
    leaves
1 tablespoon chopped
    celery leaves

Have shoulder blade removed, leaving pocket for stuffing. Prepare meat as for roast leg of lamb (No. 1390). Brown onion in fat. Add bread crumbs, mint leaves, celery leaves, ⅛ teaspoon pepper, and ½ tablespoon salt, mixing thoroughly. Put stuffing in pocket; sew edges. Cook same as roast leg of lamb (No. 1390). Alternate stuffings which may be used are bread (No. 2063), onion (No. 2065), celery (No. 2081), mushroom (No. 2079), sausage (No. 2073), nut (No. 2095), rice (No. 2080), etc. Serves 8.

(1393)   ROAST SADDLE OF LAMB

Select a loin weighing about 6 pounds. Prepare and cook same as roast leg of lamb (No. 1390). For roast stuffed saddle of lamb, carve the saddle in thin strips parallel to the backbone. Or, have the cut boned so that it can be carved in slices across the grain of the meat. Fill the boned saddle with mint or watercress (No. 2083) stuffing. Roll the flank underneath, sew securely, and roast as above. Allow ¾ pound per serving.

(1394) ROAST STUFFED BREAST OF LAMB

Select a breast of lamb including the foreshank. Have the butcher crack the bones of the breast so that it can be carved between the ribs. Wipe the meat with a damp cloth, remove the foreshank, cut off the meat, and grind it for the forcemeat stuffing (No. 2077). Make a pocket in the breast by cutting through the flesh close to the ribs. Sprinkle the inside of the pocket with salt and pepper, pile in the hot forcemeat stuffing lightly, and sew the edges together. Rub the outside with salt, pepper, and flour. Lay the stuffed breast, ribs down, on a rack in an open roasting pan. Do not add water. Place the roast in a hot oven (480° F.), and sear for 30 minutes. If there is not sufficient fat to keep the meat from drying out, baste with melted fat, or lay a strip or two of bacon on top. After searing, reduce the oven temperature rapidly to 300° F., and continue the cooking in the open pan until the meat is tender. The total time required will probably be 1½ to 1¾ hours. If there is more stuffing than the breast will hold, bake it in a separate dish, or use it as stuffing for onions to serve with the meat. For the baked onions, choose a large, mild-flavored variety. Cut the onions in half, crosswise, and simmer in lightly salted water until about half done. Lift the onions out and arrange in a baking dish. Remove the centers without disturbing the outer layers. Chop the onion centers and add to the forcemeat stuffing. Fill the onion shells with this mixture, cover, and bake in a moderate oven (350° F.) for about one-half hour, or until the onions are tender. Remove the cover from the baking dish during the last of the cooking so that the onions will brown well on top.

(1395) BRAISED LAMB (POT ROAST)

Follow recipe for braised beef à la mode (No. 1312), using lamb instead of beef, cooking 35 minutes per pound.

(1396) BROILED LAMB CHOPS

Whether single or double, from loin, ribs, or shoulder, have lamb chops cut in uniform thickness and the fell removed. Double loin chops may be boned, rolled, and wrapped in sliced bacon. Rib chops are often "Frenched" by trimming the rib ends bare. All lamb chops are best broiled either by direct heat or in a heavy uncovered skillet. To broil by direct heat, lay the chops on a cold greased rack and place over live coals or under an electric grill or the flame of a gas oven. If a gas oven is used, have the chops 2 or 3 inches below a moderate flame. Sear them on both sides. Place double rib chops fat side up at first so that they will also sear along that edge. After searing, lower the flame and finish the cooking at reduced temperature. Turn the chops occasionally, but do not prick the brown crust. If more convenient, after searing double chops (1½ to 2 inches thick) under the flame, transfer the broiler to a moderately hot oven (375° to 400° F.) to finish the cooking. To pan-broil, lay the chops in a heavy, sizzling-hot skillet, sear quickly on both sides, and also turn thick chops on edge so as to brown the fat. Then reduce the heat, turn the chops frequently, and finish the cooking at low temperature. Do not add water or cover the skillet. From time to time pour off excess fat so that the chops broil, not fry. If preferred, with very thick chops, after searing, slip a rack under them in the skillet, and finish the cooking in a moderately hot oven (375° to 400° F.). Allow 2 thin or 1 thick chop per serving. A slice of orange laid on each chop when half cooked imparts a delightful flavor.

(1397) PLANKED LAMB CHOPS

Prepare and cook according to instruction for broiled lamb chops (No. 1396). Serve on plank in same manner as planked steak (No. 1305). Serve with mint sauce (No. 2046) or currant jelly. Allow 1 chop per serving.

(1398) BREADED LAMB CHOPS

8 lamb chops, ¾ to 1 inch thick	2 cups cracker crumbs
1 cup flour	1 teaspoon salt
2 beaten eggs	¼ teaspoon pepper
	2 tablespoons butter or fat

Wipe chops with cold, damp cloth. Roll in flour. Dip in eggs. Roll in crumbs. Sprinkle with salt and pepper. Melt butter in pan. Put chops in pan and sauté, turning often, 10 to 12 minutes. Serve plain or with medium white sauce (No. 2004). If desired, the crumbed and seasoned chops may be fried in deep, hot fat (380° to 390° F.) about 8 minutes. Drain on unglazed paper. Allow 2 chops per serving.

(1399)   STUFFED LAMB SHOULDER CHOPS

Have lamb shoulder chops cut one to two inches thick. Wipe meat with cold, damp cloth. Remove the bone and from the cavity made, cut slits so that pockets are formed. Fill these and the cavity made by removing the bone with a savory bread dressing (No. 2063). Lay bacon slices over the top and bake chops in a moderate oven (350° F.) until done, about one hour.

(1400)   SMOTHERED LAMB CHOPS

Follow recipe for smothered pork chops (No. 1434), using lamb instead of pork.

(1401)   LAMB CHOPS EN CASSEROLE

8 thin lamb chops	4 small onions
2 tablespoons butter	4 potatoes, cubed
1 teaspoon salt	1 cup canned or strained
¼ teaspoon pepper	stewed tomatoes
4 sliced tomatoes	(No. 1893)
4 cored and peeled apples	

Wipe meat with cold, damp cloth. Melt butter in frying pan and lightly brown chops on both sides. Sprinkle with salt and pepper. Put tomato slices, apples, onions, and potatoes in baking dish. Lay chops on top. Pour in tomatoes. Cover and bake in moderate oven (350° F.) until tender, about 45 minutes. Serves 4.

(1402)   FILETS OF LAMB

Select leg meat in 1-inch slices. Pound with wooden potato masher or side of cleaver to ¾-inch thickness. Let stand several hours in French dressing (No. 716), into which a little chopped onion and parsley has been mixed. Wipe off bits of onion and parsley. Pan-fry or broil, using as little fat as possible, until well browned and tender. Allow ½ to ¾ pound per serving.

(1403)   FRICASSEE OF LAMB

Follow instructions for chicken fricassee (No. 1540), using lamb instead of chicken.

(1404) LAMB EN CASSEROLE

3 cups cold roast lamb, cut in 1-inch squares (No. 1390)
1 tablespoon butter or fat
1 cup boiled carrots diced (No. 1745)
1 cup cold boiled potato balls (No. 1834)
2 cups brown sauce (No. 2020)

8 small boiled onions (No. 1810)
½ cup boiled string beans (No. 1712)
½ cup boiled peas (No. 1823)
1 teaspoon salt
⅛ teaspoon pepper
1 teaspoon Worcestershire sauce

Brown lamb in hot butter or fat in frying pan. Put in baking dish. Add carrots, potato balls, brown sauce, onions, string beans, peas, salt, pepper, and Worcestershire sauce. Cover and bake in hot oven (400° F.) 20 minutes. Serves 6. Boiled rice (No. 107), boiled macaroni (No. 2302), or boiled spaghetti (No. 2302) can be added to baking dish before cooking. White sauce (No. 2004) can be substituted for brown sauce. The quantities of cooked vegetables can be varied to suit personal preference and the supply on hand.

(1405) LAMB STEW

2 pounds lean lamb
2 tablespoons butter or fat
½ cup sliced onion
3 cups diced turnip

1 chopped green pepper
½ cup flour
1 teaspoon salt
¼ teaspoon pepper

Wipe meat with cold, damp cloth. Cut into small pieces and roll in flour. Melt butter or fat in frying pan. Add onion. Cook until yellow. Add meat. When well browned, remove meat and onions and put in kettle. Pour 1 quart water into frying pan and then into kettle with browned fat. Cover and let simmer 1 hour. Add turnip, green pepper, salt, and pepper. Cover and cook 20 minutes longer. If desired, thicken stew by adding 1 tablespoon flour, mixed to a smooth paste with 2 tablespoons cold water, cooking 5 minutes longer, stirring constantly. Serve piping hot with roast potatoes (No. 1838). Garnish with parsley. Dry pea-beans, which have been soaked 12 hours and parboiled 1 hour, can be used in place of turnip. Serves 6.

(1406)   IRISH STEW WITH DUMPLINGS

3 pounds lamb or mutton	¼ cup flour
1 onion, sliced	1 teaspoon salt
1 cup diced carrot	⅛ teaspoon pepper
1 cup diced turnip	Boiling water
3 cups potatoes, in cubes	Dumplings (No. 954)

Wipe meat with cold, damp cloth; cut into 2-inch squares. Put in kettle, cover with boiling water, and let simmer 1½ hours. Add onion, carrot, and turnip and cook 30 minutes more. Add potatoes and cook another 20 minutes. Thicken with flour mixed to a paste in cold water. Season with salt and pepper. Serve with dumplings. Serves 8.

(1407)   RAGOUT OF LAMB OR MUTTON

2 pounds neck of lamb or	2 cups stock or hot water
mutton	1 teaspoon salt
1 tablespoon butter	¼ teaspoon pepper
1 tablespoon flour	1 bay leaf
1 diced onion	1 cup peas, fresh or
1 diced carrot	canned

Wipe meat with cold, damp cloth. Cut in 1-inch pieces. Melt butter in saucepan. Stir in flour. Add meat, carrot, and onion. Cook 20 minutes, stirring often. Add stock or hot water, salt, pepper, and bay leaf. Bring to boiling point. Cover tightly. Reduce heat and let simmer 2 hours. Remove bay leaf. Add peas. Simmer 20 minutes longer. Serve hot. Serves 4 to 6.

(1408)   LAMB CURRY AND RICE

2½ pounds lamb shoulder	1 teaspoon curry powder
3 sliced onions	½ teaspoon salt
½ teaspoon peppercorns	⅛ teaspoon pepper
1 teaspoon chopped thyme	3 cups boiled rice
1 teaspoon chopped parsley	(No. 107)
3 tablespoons butter	Boiling water
4 tablespoons flour	

Wipe meat with cold, damp cloth; cut into 1-inch pieces, removing fat; heat fat in frying pan, add lamb, and brown. Cover meat with boiling water. Add onion, peppercorns, thyme, and parsley. Simmer until meat is tender, about 2½ hours. Remove meat. Strain liquor. Melt butter and blend with flour, previously mixed with curry powder, salt, and pepper. Add this mixture to strained meat liquor; bring to boiling point. Make mound of rice on hot platter and place meat and liquor around it. Serves 6.

(1409) **POTTED LAMB**

3 pounds lamb	1 tablespoon flour
6 potatoes, sliced	2 teaspoons salt
4 sliced onions	¼ teaspoon pepper

Wipe meat with cold, damp cloth. Cut in 1-inch squares. Roll in mixture of flour, salt, and pepper. Place alternate layers of meat, onions, and potatoes in a bean pot or deep dish, having a layer of potatoes on top. Fill pot with hot water. Cover. Bake in moderate oven (350° F.) 3 hours, adding water is required. Canned or strained, stewed tomatoes (No. 1893) can be used in place of water. Serves 6.

(1410) **SCALLOPED LAMB**

2 cups cold roast lamb (No. 1390), cut in pieces	1 cup bread crumbs
2 cups medium white sauce (No. 2004)	1 tablespoon chopped parsley

Mix lamb and sauce thoroughly. Put layer of mixture in greased baking dish; cover with layer of bread crumbs, sprinkled with parsley; repeat, alternating layers with bread crumbs on top. Bake in a hot oven (400° F.) until crumbs are brown, about 20 minutes.

(1411) **LAMB PIN WHEELS**

Have a lamb breast boned, then spread with bulk sausage and roll, after the fashion of a jelly roll. Fasten the roll with wooden skewers and cut into thick slices between skewers. Lay in a baking dish and place uncovered in a moderate oven (350° F.) and cook for 30 to 40 minutes. Then pour 1 cup tomato juice over all, cover and cook slowly for half an hour longer, or until the pin wheels are tender. Serve with the tomato sauce. Allow ½ pound of meat per serving.

(1412)   LAMB PATTIES WITH BACON

1½ pounds ground cooked   ⅛ teaspoon pepper
    lamb   12 slices bacon
1½ teaspoons salt

Season lamb with salt and pepper. Shape into 12 rounded flat cakes. Wrap a strip of bacon around each and fasten with a toothpick. Arrange on greased broiler rack and broil 10 minutes. Turn patties and broil 8 minutes longer. A fine dish results if a slice of tomato is browned on each patty. Serves 6.

(1413)   LAMBURGERS

Follow recipe for hamburg patties (No. 1319), using lamb instead of beef, cooking about 10 minutes.

(1414)   LAMB CROQUETTES

2 cups chopped ground cold   2 tablespoons chopped
    roast lamb (No. 1390)   parsley
1 cup thick white sauce   1 egg
    (No. 2004)   2 tablespoons water
¾ cup fine bread crumbs

Thoroughly mix lamb, hot sauce, and parsley. Chill. Mold into croquettes or cutlets. Roll in crumbs; dip in gently beaten egg and water; roll again in crumbs. Fry in deep, hot fat (380° F.) 2 to 5 minutes. Drain on brown paper. Veal may be substituted for lamb. Serves 6.

(1415)   MINCED LAMB ON TOAST

1½ cups cold roast lamb   1 cup medium white sauce
    (No. 1390), diced   (No. 2004)
1 teaspoon chopped parsley   12 toast triangles

Add meat and parsley to very hot white sauce and serve at once on hot toast. Serves 6.

(1416)   LAMB EN BROCHETTE

1½ pounds lamb, ½ inch   ¼ teaspoon pepper
    thick   ¼ cup butter
6 slices canned pineapple   ¾ cup cracker crumbs
1 teaspoon salt

Wipe meat with cold, damp cloth. Cut meat and pineapple in 1-inch squares. Alternate pieces on 6 skewers. Sprinkle with salt and pepper. Dip in melted butter. Roll in crumbs. Broil under moderate heat (350° F.) until meat is tender. Serve on toast. Serves 6.

(1417) JELLIED LAMB

Follow recipe for jellied chicken (No. 1555), using lamb and lamb bones instead of chicken.

(1418) ROAST LEG OF MUTTON

Follow directions for roast leg of lamb (No. 1390).

(1419) BOILED MUTTON CHOPS

Choose shoulder chops. Wipe with cold, damp cloth. Sprinkle with salt and pepper. Put in pan. Cover with boiling water. Cover and simmer 30 minutes, bringing to a boil at finish. Serve hot with white sauce (No. 2004). Allow 1 or 2 chops per serving.

(1420) BRAISED LEG OF MUTTON

Leg of mutton, boned	½ bay leaf
Potato stuffing (No. 2071)	Sprig of thyme
½ cup butter	Sprig of parsley
1 slice onion	1½ teaspoons salt
1 slice carrot	12 peppercorns
1 slice turnip	4 tablespoons flour

Wipe meat with cold, damp cloth. Stuff and sew securely. Place in deep pan with ¼ cup butter. Dice the onion, carrot, and turnip and add to pan with bay leaf, thyme, and parsley. Cook 5 minutes. Add 3 cups hot water, salt, and peppercorns, pouring over mutton. Cover tightly and cook 3 hours at 300° F., uncovering for the last ½ hour. Remove to hot platter. Brown the balance of butter. Slowly stir in flour. Pour in the strained liquor. Use this for sauce. Allow ¾ pound per serving.

(1421)   BOILED LEG OF LAMB OR MUTTON

Leg of mutton
1 tablespoon salt

2 cups caper sauce
(No. 2040)

Wipe meat with cold, damp cloth. Place in kettle; cover with boiling water. Cover kettle and boil for 10 minutes; skim. Simmer slowly until meat is tender. Add salt when half done. Serve with caper sauce. Allow ¾ pound per serving.

(1422)   BROILED ENGLISH MUTTON CHOPS

6 mutton chops, 2 inches
      thick
6 lamb or mutton kidneys

1 teaspoon salt
¼ teaspoon pepper
1 tablespoon butter

Wipe chops with cold, damp cloth. Soak kidneys in cold water 1 hour. Drain. Curl thin end of each chop around a kidney and skewer securely. Put in broiler. Sear both sides quickly. Then reduce heat or move further from heat and cook more slowly 10 to 15 minutes, turning frequently. Season with salt and pepper. Dot with butter. They should be served hot with Worcestershire sauce and baked potatoes (No. 1837). Serves 6.

(1423)   BREAST OF MUTTON

3 pounds breast of mutton
2 diced onions
1 teaspoon salt
¼ teaspoon pepper
¼ teaspoon chopped thyme

1 tablespoon butter
1 tablespoon flour
2 tablespoons chopped
      parsley

This is a very economical dish. Put mutton in pan over low heat to melt out fat. Pour off fat as it gathers in pan and do not let meat brown. When most of fat is out, put mutton in kettle. Cover with boiling water. Add onion, salt, pepper, and thyme. Simmer slowly until tender, about 2½ hours. Remove from kettle. Blend flour and melted butter. Reduce kettle liquor to 1 cup. Stir in flour paste. Add parsley, or chopped capers if preferred. Stir and cook to proper consistency. Use for gravy.

This dish can be served at once or warmed over the next day. Serves 6.

(1424)   MUTTON PIE

2 pounds mutton	1 teaspoon powdered
1 teaspoon salt	cloves
12 small, tart apples	1 teaspoon cinnamon
1 cup sugar	⅛ teaspoon nutmeg

Plain pie paste (No. 2701)

Wipe meat with cold, damp cloth. Sprinkle with salt. Put in pan. Cover with boiling water. Cover and simmer until tender, about 2½ hours. Wash apples. Peel, core and slice. Mix sugar, clove, cinnamon, and nutmeg. Line a greased baking dish with plain pie paste. Cut mutton in small pieces. Put layer of mutton in dish. Sprinkle with mixture of seasonings. Add layer of apples. Alternate layers, seasoning each, until all ingredients are used. Add pan liquor. Cover with pie paste. Bake in moderate oven (350° F.) 1 hour. Serves 6.

PORK AND PORK PRODUCTS

Man may become infected with a very serious disease called trichinosis through the eating of raw pork. This disease is caused by parasites called trichinae, which are too small to be seen by the naked eye but may be present in the lean meat of hogs. The danger of trichinosis may be entirely avoided by cooking pork thoroughly.

Trichinosis may be contracted from tasting sausage during its preparation to determine when seasoning is satisfactory, from hastily cooked hamburgers that contain some pork, from imperfectly cooked fresh pork, and sausage, smoked hams, bacon, and shoulders, and from improperly prepared ready-to-eat products such as Bologna-style sausage, boneless loins, capocollo, coppa, dry or summer sausage, and Italian-style ham. When these latter products are eaten without further cooking in the home, one must be sure that they have been made in a plant where competent official inspection has insured a treatment of the pork muscle that will destroy possible live trichinae.

(1425)   ROAST CROWN OF PORK

Crown of pork   ¼ teaspoon pepper
1 teaspoon salt per pound   2 tablespoons flour

Wipe meat with cold damp cloth. Cut off excess fat. Sprinkle with salt, pepper, and flour. Put in roasting pan, fat side up. Arrange pieces of excess fat around meat. Bake in very hot oven (475° F.) 15 minutes; baste; reduce heat to 325° F. and cook until well done, allowing 40 minutes to the pound. Baste every 15 minutes. A meat thermometer will read 185° F. when well done. Serve on platter, surrounded by mashed potatoes (No. 1835) and garnished with baked apples (No. 36). Paper frills on the ends of the bones and sprigs of parsley will add to the appearance of the dish. Thicken fat in roasting pan with flour paste, mixed in cold water, for gravy. If desired, the center may be filled with cranberry (No. 2093) or other suitable stuffing. Allow ½ pound of meat per serving.

(1426)   ROAST PORK

Prepare and cook same as roast crown of pork (No. 1425), allowing 30 minutes per pound for large roasts and 45 minutes per pound for small or rolled roasts. When done a meat thermometer will read 185° F.

(1427)   ROAST SUCKLING PIG

1 suckling pig, 8 to 10   ¼ cup butter
   pounds   1 small potato
5 cups onion stuffing   1 lemon or apple
   (No. 2065)   2 cranberries
2 teaspoons salt   2 tablespoons flour
1 teaspoon pepper

Select pig from 3 to 6 weeks old. Have it cleaned by butcher. Wash well in warm water, especially the head and throat passages. Wrap cloth around a skewer for this purpose. Wash with cold water and dry. Stuff loosely. Sew securely. Tie legs in toward center. Put pig in kneeling position in roasting pan. Sprinkle with salt and pepper. Add 1 cup water to pan. Prop mouth open with a small potato. Bake in moderate oven (350° F.) about 3 hours, basting often with melted butter. Serve on platter in a bed of parsley or watercress. Replace potato in mouth with lemon or apple. Put cranberries in eye sockets.

Thicken drippings with flour, mixed to a smooth paste in cold water, adding boiling water, if necessary, for gravy. Other proper stuffings are sage and onion (No. 2069), bread (No. 2063), or mashed potatoes (No. 1835). Serves 10 to 12.

(1428)   CROWN ROAST OF SPARERIBS

2 pounds spareribs	¼ cup raisins
2 cups boiled rice (No. 107)	3 tablespoons butter or fat
2 cups bread crumbs	½ teaspoon powdered sage
1 minced carrot	2 teaspoons salt
1 large minced onion	¼ teaspoon pepper

Have butcher tie spareribs in crown roast shape. Wipe meat with cold, damp cloth. Set upright in baking dish. Mix all other ingredients thoroughly and pack in cavity. Bake in moderate oven (325° F.) 2 hours. Serve in baking dish. Serves 6.

(1429)   STUFFED FRESH HAM

6- to 8-pound ham, boned	3 cups bread stuffing
1 teaspoon salt	(No. 2063)
¼ teaspoon pepper	3 cups cider

Wipe meat with cold, damp cloth. Sprinkle with salt and pepper. Stuff. Tie securely. Put in roasting pan. Bake in hot oven (475° to 500° F.) 20 minutes. Pour cider over ham. Continue cooking in moderate oven (350° F.), allowing 30 minutes per pound or until meat thermometer reads 185° F., basting frequently with drippings. Allow ½ to ¾ pound of meat per serving.

(1430) PORK CHOPS, BROILED OR FRIED

6 pork chops, ¾ to 1 inch thick	¼ teaspoon pepper
1 teaspoon salt	1 tablespoon butter

Wipe chops with cold, damp cloth. Broil at high heat until both sides are seared. Reduce heat or move further from flame and broil 15 to 20 minutes, turning often. Sprinkle with salt and pepper. Dot with butter. To fry pork chops, have pan sizzling and sear chops rapidly on both sides. Reduce heat and cook slowly 20 to 25 minutes, turning often. Season as above. A slice of orange placed on top of each chop when almost done imparts a delightful flavor. Serves 6.

(1431)   PORK CHOPS WITH DRESSING

6 pork chops	⅛ teaspoon pepper
⅛ onion, finely chopped	¾ teaspoon salt
1½ cups bread crumbs	2 tablespoons pork fat,
1 egg	chopped

Mix onion, bread crumbs, fat, pepper, salt, and well-beaten egg with ¼ cup hot water. Spread on pork chops. Put chops close together in a pan. Add enough water to cover bottom of pan. Bake in moderate oven (350° F.) 1 hour, basting every 10 minutes. Serves 4 to 6.

(1432)   PORK CHOPS WITH CANDIED SWEETS

6 pork chops	1 teaspoon salt
6 boiled sweet potatoes	⅛ teaspoon pepper
(No. 1881)	1 tablespoon flour
¼ cup brown sugar	

Wipe chops with cold, damp cloth. Broil or fry at high heat until well browned on both sides. Lay in greased baking pan. Peel potatoes and cut in halves, lengthwise. Put in pan with chops. Sprinkle with sugar, salt, and pepper. Cover bottom of pan with a little water. Bake in moderate oven (350° F.) 45 minutes to 1 hour, basting frequently. Thicken pan liquor with flour, mixed to a smooth paste with cold water, for gravy. Serves 6.

(1433)   PORK CHOPS EN CASSEROLE

8 small potatoes	2 tablespoons butter or fat
1 teaspoon salt	3 cups milk
⅛ teaspoon pepper	8 pork chops, ¾ inch
2 tablespoons flour	thick

Wash and peel potatoes; slice thin. Place layer of potatoes in greased baking dish. Sprinkle with flour, salt, and pepper and dot with butter or fat. Repeat, until all potatoes are used. Pour in milk. Lay pork chops on top. Bake in oven at 325° F. until potatoes are tender, about 1¼ hours. A slice of orange may be placed on each chop the last 15 minutes of cooking. Serves 4.

(1434)   SMOTHERED PORK CHOPS

2 pounds pork chops, cut thick	1 green pepper, cut in rings
2 unpeeled lemons, sliced	1 teaspoon salt
1 large sweet onion, cut in rings	2 cups tomato juice
	1 tablespoon butter

Wipe meat with cold, damp cloth. Put the chops in a large covered skillet and cover the top of the meat with lemon, onion and pepper. Sprinkle with salt. Pour the tomato juice over all and dot with butter. Cover and cook on the top of the stove for 1½ hours or until done. Lift on to a hot platter, being careful to keep the rings in place and serve. Serves 6 to 8.

(1435)   STUFFED PORK CHOPS

½ cup mushrooms	1 cup canned tomato
2 tablespoons minced onion	1 teaspoon salt
½ cup boiled rice (No. 107)	¼ teaspoon pepper
2 tablespoons butter or fat	6 thick pork chops with pockets
1 cup bread crumbs	

Brush mushrooms. If skin on caps is tough, peel. If stems are tender, they may be used. Brown mushrooms, onion, and rice in frying pan with melted butter. Add bread crumbs, tomato, salt, and pepper. Let simmer 10 minutes. Let stand until cool. Stuff chops with this mixture and fasten securely with skewers. Brown chops on both sides in frying pan on top of stove, cooking until meat is heated through. Add ½ cup water. Cover tightly. Bake in moderate oven (350° F.) 1 to 1¼ hours. Serves 6.

(1436)   PORK TENDERLOIN

Wipe meat with cold, damp cloth. Beat hard to flatten. Fry in little butter or bake in greased baking pan in hot oven (400° F.), basting often with pan liquor. Allow 25 to 30 minutes for cooking, depending on thickness of meat. To devil pork tenderloin baste, while cooking, in a sauce made by mixing 3 tablespoons butter, 2 tablespoons chili sauce, ¼ cup boiling water, 2 tablespoons catchup, 1 teaspoon salt, ¼ teaspoon paprika, 1 teaspoon mustard, and 1 tablespoon Worcestershire sauce. Allow ½ pound per serving.

(1437)   STUFFED PORK TENDERLOIN

2 pork tenderloins	½ teaspoon salt
2 cups poultry stuffing	⅛ teaspoon pepper
(No. 2064)	2 tablespoons butter or fat

Have each loin split not quite through. Open both flat. Cover one with stuffing and sprinkle the other with salt and pepper. Place together with stuffing, salt, and pepper in center. Sew together. Spread with butter or fat. Bake in moderate oven (350° F.) about 50 minutes, basting every 15 minutes. Serve on hot platter garnished with fried apple rings (No. 39). Serves 6.

(1438)   BOILED PORK TENDERLOIN

Soak tenderloin 6 hours in cold water. Drain. Put in pan. Cover with boiling water. Let simmer until tender, about 2 hours. Season with salt and pepper when half cooked. Allow ½ pound per serving.

(1439)   SPARERIBS AND SAUERKRAUT

2 pounds spareribs	4 cups sauerkraut
1 teaspoon salt	

Have spareribs divided. Wipe with cold, damp cloth. Sprinkle with salt. Put in kettle. Cover with cold water. Bring to boil. Cover. Reduce heat and simmer 30 minutes. Add sauerkraut. Bring to boil. Reduce heat and simmer, uncovered, 30 minutes. Serve hot. Serves 4.

(1440)   PORK PIE

2 pounds pork	1 tablespoon chopped
1 teaspoon salt	parsley
½ teaspoon pepper	2 tablespoons chopped
Plain pie paste (No. 2701)	onion
1 pound sausage meat	1 cup stock or water
2 tablespoons catchup	

Wipe pork with cold, damp cloth. Sprinkle with salt and pepper. Line a baking dish with plain pie paste. Put in layer of sausage meat. Sprinkle with parsley and onion. Put in layer of pork, chopped in small pieces. Alternate layers until all meat is used, sprinkling between each layer with parsley and onion. A layer of sausage should be on top. Pour in stock or water and catchup. Cover with pie paste. Cut a 1-inch opening in center. Bake the pie in hot oven (450° F.) until crust begins to brown. Reduce heat and bake at (350° F.) for 2 hours. It will add to the flavor if pork is soaked for 2 hours in ½ cup of sherry or in diluted vinegar before cooking. Serves 6.

(1441)   AMERICAN PORK CHOP SUEY

Prepare same as American chicken chop suey (No. 1554), using cooked pork in place of chicken. Veal may be substituted for pork in any proportion.

(1442)   BALINESE RICE-PORK

½ cup butter	6 cups boiled rice
⅓ cup lard	(No. 107)
1 medium-sized onion	1 egg
2 cups roast pork, diced	2 tablespoons milk
½ teaspoon chili powder	½ cup diced boiled ham
1 teaspoon salt	Tomato slices
⅛ teaspoon white pepper	Cucumber slices

Melt fat, add onion, and sauté until lightly browned. Add pork and seasonings and sauté until browned. Add rice and mix well. Combine egg and milk, season to taste, and fry over low heat to make a thin omelet. Cut omelet in narrow strips. Arrange rice and meat mixture on platter, sprinkle with diced ham; garnish with egg strips, and tomato and cucumber slices. Serves 6 to 8.

(1443)   PORK EN CASSEROLE

Follow recipe for hamburg casserole (No. 1322), using pork instead of beef, adding 1 teaspoon sage to seasonings.

(1444)   PORK PATTIES

2 pounds fresh pork	¼ teaspoon pepper
1 cup stale bread crumbs	2 well-beaten eggs
1 teaspoon salt	1 tablespoon pork fat
2 tablespoons chopped onion	

Wipe meat with cold, damp cloth. Chop into very fine pieces. Mix thoroughly with bread crumbs, salt, onion, pepper, and eggs. Form into patties. Melt fat. Fry patties on both sides over hot fire until well done, about 15 minutes. Serve with fried (No. 1839) or creamed (No. 1844) potatoes. Serves 6.

(1445)   CABBAGE, STUFFED WITH PORK

Follow recipe for kol dolmer (No. 1334), using pork instead of mixture of pork and beef.

(1446)   FRIED SALT PORK

Cut in ¼-inch slices. Remove rind or gash it in several places. Put in warm pan and fry slowly until dry and browned, turning frequently. If it is too salt, place in cold water and bring to boil before frying. It can be served with medium white sauce (No. 2004) or creamed potatoes (No. 1844). Apples, cored and sliced, but unpeeled, fried in the pork fat, make a delicious garnish. Allow ¼ pound per serving.

(1447)   BAKED STUFFED HAM

12-pound ham	24 cloves
4 cups bread stuffing	1 well-beaten egg
(No. 2063)	1 cup bread crumbs
1 cup brown sugar	

Scrub ham and soak 12 hours in cold water. Remove bone. Stuff. Sew opening securely. Wrap entire ham in cheesecloth. Put in kettle. Cover with cold water. Bring to boil. Reduce heat. Cover. Let simmer 3 hours. Cool in stock. Remove cloth, rind, and fat. Rub with brown sugar. Insert cloves. Brush with egg. Sprinkle with bread crumbs. Put in roasting pan and bake in slow oven (300° F.) 1¼ hours. Chestnut stuffing (No. 2075) may be used in place of bread stuffing. Serves 16 to 20.

(1448)   BAKED VIRGINIA HAM

1 ham	1 teaspoon mustard
½ cup brown sugar	1 tablespoon whole cloves
2 tablespoons bread crumbs	

Wash ham thoroughly. Put in deep pot, cover with cold water, and bring to a boil quickly. Reduce heat and let simmer 2½ hours. Remove from pot and take off skin. Mix sugar, crumbs, and mustard and spread over ham. Stick cloves in ham. Put in roasting pan with 1 cup water and bake at 350° F. until brown, about 30 minutes. Excellent results are obtained by using grape juice in roasting pan instead of water, basting frequently. A delicious garnish is prepared by coring unpeeled apples, filling openings in each with white sugar, and baking with ham. Allow ½ pound of meat per serving.

(1449)   BAKED HAM AND SWEET POTATOES HAWAII

½ ham, 5 to 6 pounds	24 cloves
1 cup brown sugar	6 sweet potatoes
1 tablespoon bread crumbs	1 cup crushed pineapple

Wash ham thoroughly. Rub fat side with brown sugar and bread crumbs. Dot with cloves. Pare sweet potatoes. Arrange them around ham. Pour crushed pineapple over ham. Bake at 325° F. 3 hours. Serves 6.

(1450)   BOILED HAM

Scrub ham thoroughly and soak 12 hours in cold water. Skim. Bring to a boil and simmer until tender, allowing 20 to 30 minutes per pound. A meat thermometer will register 160° F. when done. To serve cold, keep in stock in cool place for 12 hours; then peel off rind. To serve hot, let cool slightly in stock before removing rind. It may also be served hot by removing rind, brushing top with well-beaten egg, sprinkling with plain or sugared bread crumbs, and browning in moderate oven (350° F.). A ham boiled in cider is delicious. Allow ½ pound of ham per serving.

(1451)   PLAIN FRIED HAM

Cut a thin slice from the center of a ham and gash the fat on the edge in several places. Place in hot frying pan and brown quickly on 1 side. Turn and brown lightly on other. Cook slowly until tender, about 10 minutes if ¼ inch thick, 15 minutes if ½ inch thick, 30 minutes if 1 inch thick. If desired, apples, cored and sliced with the skin on, may be fried in the ham fat and served. Allow ½ pound of meat per serving.

(1452)   FRIED HAM AND EGGS

Cook meat, according to recipe for plain fried ham (No. 1451) and fry eggs in ham fat. Allow ¼ pound ham and 2 eggs per serving.

(1453)   BROILED HAM

Broil thin slices of ham, either raw or boiled (No. 1450), in very hot oven (550° F.) for about 10 minutes, turning frequently. Serve with fried bananas (No. 47) or pineapple slices, sautéed in little fat until brown on both sides. Allow ½ pound per serving.

(1454)   COUNTRY STYLE HAM

Slice of ham, 1 to 1½ inches thick
1 chopped onion
4 sliced carrots

3 tablespoons seeded raisins
1 tablespoon flour
1 orange

Wipe meat with cold, damp cloth. Brown on both sides quickly in saucepan. Add onion, carrots, raisins, and 1 cup water. Cover and let simmer 1½ to 2 hours. Mix flour and orange juice, blending well. Add this mixture to pan. Bring to a boil, stirring constantly. Allow ½ pound of ham per serving.

(1455)   BAKED SLICE OF HAM

2 pounds ham, 1½ inches thick
2 tablespoons brown sugar

1 cup milk
2 tablespoons flour

Melt brown sugar in frying pan. Wipe meat with cold, damp cloth. Put in pan and brown on both sides. Add milk and bake in moderate oven (350° F.) about 30 minutes. Remove ham to hot platter. Thicken liquor with flour, mixed to a smooth paste with cold water, for gravy. One-quarter cup chopped preserved ginger, cooked with the ham, adds a delightful flavor. Pears, cored and halved lengthwise, cooked with the ham are an attractive garnish. Serves 4 to 6.

(1456) CREAMED HAM

1 slice ham, ½ to ¾ inch thick	¼ teaspoon pepper
	½ teaspoon dry mustard
2 cups thin white sauce (No. 2004)	1 teaspoon sugar

Wipe meat with cold, damp cloth. Brown in frying pan on both sides. Drain on brown paper. Put in saucepan. Add sauce, seasoned with pepper, mustard, and sugar. Cover and simmer 1¼ to 1½ hours, turning occasionally and adding sufficient milk to keep ham covered. Allow ½ pound of meat per serving.

(1457) VEAL AND HAM PIE

1½ pounds cold roast veal (No. 1363)	1 teaspoon chopped lemon rind
½ pound ham	2 hard-cooked eggs
1 tablespoon flour	(No. 202), sliced
1 teaspoon powdered herbs, salt, pepper, red pepper, and mace, mixed to taste	Plain pie paste (No. 2701)
	1 tablespoon chopped parsley

Cut veal and ham in thin slices. Mix flour, lemon rind, herbs, salt, pepper, red pepper, and mace. Roll each piece of veal in this mixture. Line a baking dish with plain pie paste. Place alternating layers of veal, ham, and eggs in dish. Add 1 cup water. Sprinkle with parsley. Cover with plain pie paste. Bake in hot oven (450° F.) for 1¼ hours.

(1458) HAM SOUFFLÉ

Prepare same as veal soufflé (No. 1385), using ground, boiled ham (No. 1450) instead of veal and omitting salt.

(1459)   HAM LOAF

3 tablespoons butter	1 cup bread crumbs
¼ cup brown sugar	¼ teaspoon pepper
2 pounds smoked ham, ground	2 eggs
	½ cup milk

Melt butter in pan. Add sugar and dissolve thoroughly. Mix ham and other ingredients and form into a loaf. Put in pan. Bake in moderate oven (350° F.) 1½ hours. Pineapple slices, slightly browned in butter and sugar, and baked under meat make a fine garnish. Serves 6.

(1460)   CREAMED HAM AND EGGS

2 cups chopped cold cooked ham	½ cup cream
	¼ teaspoon pepper
2 eggs	1 tablespoon mustard

Put ham in pan. Beat eggs and add to ham. Add other ingredients. Heat through. Serve hot on buttered toast (No. 988). Serves 4.

(1461)   FRIED HAM AND RICE

2 tablespoons butter or fat	2 cups boiled rice
2 tablespoons chopped onion	(No. 107)
1 tablespoon chopped parsley	1 teaspoon salt
1 cup chopped cold cooked ham	¼ teaspoon pepper
	1 egg

Melt fat in pan. Add onion, parsley, and ham. Sauté a light brown. Add rice, salt, and pepper. Mix well. Beat egg and mix into mixture. When heated through, serve on hot platter. Serves 6.

(1462)   HAMLETS

1 cup minced cold cooked ham	¼ teaspoon Worcestershire sauce
2 tablespoons milk	1 egg
4 slices bread	4 slices bacon
1 cup yellow cheese	

Moisten ham with milk. Spread evenly on bread. Cream cheese and add Worcestershire sauce. Beat egg and blend with cheese. Spread this mixture over ham. Put 1 slice bacon on each prepared bread slice. Put in greased baking dish and bake in hot oven (450° F.) until brown, about 10 minutes. Serves 4.

(1463)   HAM CROQUETTES

For this ham and veal can be used in any proportions. To prepare and cook, follow directions for chicken croquettes (No. 1553).

(1464)   BACON, BROILED OR FRIED

Cut in thin slices. To broil, place over dripping pan and sear at high heat, turning to brown both sides. To fry, place in sizzling pan and rapidly sear both sides. If wanted crisp, either broil or fry until all fat is out. Personal preference determines how long to cook. If fried, drain on brown paper. Allow 2 to 4 slices per serving.

(1465)   BACON ROLLS

12 bacon slices	1 small onion, finely diced
2 cups bread crumbs	1 teaspoon salt
½ cup celery, chopped	⅛ teaspoon pepper
2 teaspoons diced green pepper	1 egg
	½ cup milk

Combine bread crumbs, celery, green pepper and onion, and season with salt and pepper. Moisten with slightly beaten egg and milk. Place a tablespoon of this dressing on a slice of bacon. Roll the bacon slice around the dressing and fasten the ends with a toothpick. Cook these in the oven until the bacon is crisp and the roll is heated through. Serve while hot. Serves 4 to 6.

(1466)   FRIED BACON AND APPLES

12 slices bacon	3 tablespoons sugar
3 firm apples	

Fry bacon crisp. Remove to hot platter and keep warm. Wash and quarter apples, removing all core and seeds. Put them in hot bacon fat. Cover tightly. Fry until they are partly soft, turning once. Sprinkle on sugar. Continue frying, uncovered, until well browned. Serve hot, garnished with bacon. Pineapple rings, dipped in flour and browned in bacon fat, are also delicious with bacon. Serves 6.

(1467)   SAUSAGE MEAT

2 pounds lean pork   1 teaspoon black pepper
1 pound pork fat   1 teaspoon powdered sage
2 tablespoons salt

Grind pork and fat together and mix thoroughly. Add seasonings, mixing well. Keep in cold place at least 24 hours before
using. A teaspoon ginger can be used in mixture if desired.

(1468)   SAUSAGE PATTIES

Pan-broil in hot pan 12 to 15 minutes, pouring off liquid fat.
Drain on brown paper. Or bake in moderate oven (350° F.) 30
to 35 minutes. Allow ¼ pound sausage meat per serving.

(1469)   FRIED SAUSAGES

Puncture the skin of each sausage in several places. Put in
frying pan until crisp. Drain on unglazed paper. If desired,
when sausages are almost cooked, chop one green pepper and fry
in fat until tender. Make a sauce with 2 tablespoons pan drippings, 1 tablespoon flour, and 1 cup strained, stewed tomatoes
(No. 1893), seasoned to taste. Allow ½ pound of uncooked
sausage per serving.

(1470)   BAKED SAUSAGES

Puncture the skin of each sausage in several places. Roll in
flour. Put in baking pan. Add enough water to just cover bottom of pan. Bake in moderate oven (350° F.) until crisp, about
30 minutes, turning occasionally. Serve hot with pan liquor,
blended with a little flour, for gravy. Allow ½ pound of uncooked sausage per serving.

(1471)   SAUSAGE TURNOVERS

1 cup sausage meat   1 cup boiled rice (No. 107)
1 cup chopped ham   1 egg
1 teaspoon Worcestershire   Plain pie paste
    sauce   (No. 2701)

Fry sausage meat slowly for 10 minutes, stirring constantly.
Drain off fat. Add ham, rice, and sauce, mixing well. Beat egg
thoroughly and add to mixture. Roll pie paste thin and cut in
4-inch squares. Place 2 tablespoons of meat mixture in center of

each. Moisten edges with water and fold into triangles. Close edges with a fork. Prick the tops and bake 15 to 20 minutes at 400° F. Serves 6.

(1472) SAUSAGE AND CABBAGE

1½ pounds sausage	1 teaspoon salt
4 cups chopped cabbage	⅛ teaspoon pepper

Fry sausage in pan about 12 minutes, turning to brown evenly. Drain on brown paper. Reduce fat in pan to 3 tablespoons. Put in cabbage. Sprinkle with salt and pepper. Fry 6 minutes, turning often. Serve hot. Serves 6.

(1473) SAUSAGES AND SWEET POTATOES

2 pounds sweet potatoes	2 tablespoons butter
½ cup sugar	1 teaspoon salt
½ cup brown sugar	1 pound sausage
¼ cup water	

Parboil sweet potatoes 15 minutes. Peel and cut into strips. Put in greased baking dish. Mix sugar, brown sugar, butter, salt, water thoroughly and boil in saucepan 3 minutes. Pour sirup over sweet potatoes. Bake 40 minutes at 350° F. Put sausages on top and continue baking another 30 minutes. Serves 6.

(1474) CHINESE SWEET BONES

2 pounds sausage	1 medium-sized cucumber
4 tablespoons flour	1 teaspoon salt
1 egg	½ teaspoon pepper
4 tablespoons butter	1 tablespoon lemon juice
½ cup thinly sliced onion	2 pimientos
1½ cups thinly sliced celery	½ cup toasted almonds
2 cups water	

Cut sausage into strips four inches long and one-quarter inch thick. Roll in flour, dip in slightly beaten egg and then in flour. Place butter in frying pan and, when hot, but not smoking, brown sausage all over. Add onion and celery and cover with one cup water and simmer gently 20 minutes. Remove sausage and vegetables. Add peeled and finely diced cucumber, seasonings, lemon juice with remaining cup of water to frying pan. Cover and cook 15 minutes. Add meat and vegetables to the cucumber, reheat, turn on to serving platter and garnish with pimientos and toasted almonds. Serves 6.

(1475)   SAUSAGE LOAF

Follow recipe for ham loaf (No. 1459), using sausage meat in place of ham, and baking about 1 hour.

(1476)   FRANKFURTERS—HOT DOGS

To boil, drop in boiling water and boil 6 to 8 minutes. To broil, split and broil in moderate heat 8 to 10 minutes. To pan-broil, brown all over in little fat without splitting. Or split and brown in little fat on both sides.

(1477)   FRANKFURTERS EN CASSEROLE

¼ cup butter	2 cups diced carrots
1 chopped onion	1 tablespoon catchup
¼ cup flour	1 teaspoon salt
3 cups canned or strained	¼ teaspoon pepper
stewed tomatoes	8 frankfurters
(No. 1893)	

Melt butter in saucepan. Add onion and fry until golden brown. Stir in flour, blending well. Add tomatoes and cook until thick. Add carrots, catchup, salt, and pepper. Split frankfurters and put, meat side down, in greased baking dish. Pour in mixture. Bake in moderate oven (350° F.) 25 to 35 minutes. Serves 4.

(1478)   DEVILED FRANKFURTERS

12 frankfurters	½ pound mild cheese
3 tablespoons mustard	12 slices bacon

Split frankfurters lengthwise almost, but not quite through. Spread cut surfaces with mustard. Place slice of cheese in each slit. Wrap slice of bacon around each frankfurter and fasten with toothpicks. Sauté in a little bacon grease until bacon is crisp, turning often, about 8 to 10 minutes. If desired frankfurters may be broiled under medium heat. Bread stuffing (No. 2063) may be used for filling in place of cheese. Serves 6.

(1479)   BOLOGNA CUPS WITH HOT POTATO SALAD

6 slices large bologna, about
    ¼ inch thick
4 slices bacon
1 onion, chopped
2 tablespoons vinegar

½ teaspoon salt
⅛ teaspoon pepper
6 hot boiled potatoes
    (No. 1834)

Do not remove casing from bologna slices. Dice bacon, brown lightly in hot skillet, remove bacon. Cook bologna in bacon fat on both sides, until edges curl up to form cups. Remove to hot platter. Cook onion in bacon fat until lightly browned. Return diced bacon to skillet, add vinegar and seasonings, heat thoroughly and pour over hot sliced or cubed potatoes. Pile potato salad lightly on top of bologna, garnish with green pepper rings and parsley if desired. Serves 6.

(1480)   TRIPE

2 pounds honeycomb tripe
2 tablespoons butter or fat
2 tablespoons flour
2 cups hot milk

1 teaspoon salt
½ teaspoon pepper
1 teaspoon onion juice

Soak tripe in cold water 4 hours. Scrub it clean. Cover with cold, salted water. Bring to a boil. Cover. Reduce heat and let simmer 3½ hours, or until tripe is jellied. Drain and keep tripe in cool place until ready to use. Melt butter in saucepan. Slowly add flour and stir until smooth, being careful not to brown. Add milk slowly. Bring to a boil, stirring constantly. Add salt, pepper, onion juice, and tripe. Keep stirring until mixture is hot. Serve on hot platter. Serves 6.

(1481)   FRIED TRIPE

2 pounds honeycomb tripe
¼ cup flour

2 beaten eggs
1 cup fine bread crumbs

Follow recipe for tripe (No. 1480) through simmering. Cut tripe in cubes. Roll in flour. Dip in eggs. Roll in crumbs. Dip in deep, hot fat until golden brown. Serves 6.

(1482)   TRIPE IN BATTER

2 pounds honeycomb tripe	1 egg
1½ cups flour	½ teaspoon vinegar
¼ teaspoon salt	2½ tablespoons butter or fat

Follow recipe for tripe (No. 1480) through simmering. Cut tripe in 6 pieces. Sift 1 cup flour and salt and stir in slowly ½ cup cold water. Add egg, well-beaten, vinegar, and 1 teaspoon melted butter, mixing well. Roll tripe in balance of flour, dip in batter, and sauté until golden brown in remaining butter. Serves 6.

(1483)   LYONNAISE TRIPE

2 pounds honeycomb tripe	1 teaspoon salt
2 tablespoons butter	¼ teaspoon pepper
2 tablespoons chopped onion	1 teaspoon vinegar

Follow recipe for tripe (No. 1480) through simmering. Cut tripe in small cubes. Melt butter in pan. Add onion and brown well. Add tripe and sauté 5 minutes longer. Sprinkle with salt, pepper, and vinegar. Serve hot on buttered toast (No. 988). Serves 6.

(1484)   CALVES' BRAINS

Soak brains in cold water 1 hour. Bring to a boil. Add 1 tablespoon vinegar. Reduce heat. Let simmer 15 minutes. Plunge into cold water. Remove membrane, all blood, and any dark pieces. Season with salt and pepper. Put in pan. Cover with water. Bring almost to a boil. Remove to hot platter. Serve with a white sauce (No. 2004). Sautéed brains can be cooked by frying until well browned in little fat after cleaning and seasoning as above. Breaded brains are prepared by cleaning as above, rolling in flour, dipping in well-beaten egg, diluted in a little water, rolling in bread crumbs, and frying 6 to 8 minutes in deep fat. For brain croquettes, clean as above, then follow direction for chicken croquettes (No. 1553). Two pairs of calves' brains will serve 6.

(1485)   MARINATED BRAINS

Clean brains as in recipe for calves' brains (No. 1484). Cut in 1-inch cubes. Let them stand 1 hour in French dressing

(No. 716). Dip in fritter batter (No. 2706). Fry 6 to 8 minutes in deep fat. Serve hot with tomato sauce (No. 2035). One pair of brains will yield 3 servings.

(1486) BRAINS À LA KING

Follow recipe for chicken à la king (No. 1547), using chopped, boiled brains (No. 1484) in place of chicken.

(1487) BOILED HEARTS

Beef, calf, pork, or lamb hearts can be boiled. Remove all tubes and wash thoroughly. Cover with cold water. Bring to a boil. Cover and simmer until tender, 2 to 3 hours, depending on size. Remove fat and hard matter. Slice crosswise or cut into small pieces and serve on buttered toast (No. 988). Gravy can be made by adding flour, mixed to a smooth paste with cold water, to liquor. Allow ½ to ¾ pound of heart per serving.

(1488) SAUTÉED CALVES' HEARTS

Remove all tubes from hearts and wash thoroughly. Slice in halves. Sprinkle with salt, pepper, and flour. Sauté in butter or fat 12 to 15 minutes, turning several times. Allow 2 to 3 servings for each heart.

(1489) MOCK SQUABS

2 calves' hearts	1 sliced onion
Poultry stuffing (No. 2064)	4 slices bacon
½ cup flour	1 tablespoon chopped
3 tablespoons butter or fat	parsley
1 sliced seeded green	1 teaspoon salt
pepper	½ teaspoon pepper

Remove all tubes from hearts and wash thoroughly. Stuff with stuffing and securely close openings with small skewers. Roll hearts in flour. Melt 2 tablespoons butter and, when sizzling hot, put in hearts and brown well. Remove hearts. Add balance of butter to pan. Put in onion and pepper and brown slightly. Transfer onion and pepper to baking dish. Add hearts, bacon, and parsley. Cover with boiling water. Add salt and pepper. Cover and cook slowly until tender, about 1½ hours. Serve hot. Serves 6.

(1490)   STEWED CALVES' HEARTS

2 calves' hearts	¼ teaspoon pepper
1 finely chopped onion	1 tablespoon butter
1 stalk diced celery	1 tablespoon flour
1 teaspoon salt	

Remove all tubes from hearts and wash thoroughly. Cut in
½-inch cubes. Put in saucepan and cover with cold water.
Bring quickly to a boil. Cover. Reduce heat and let simmer until
tender, about 2 hours. Add onion, celery, salt, and pepper. Cook
another 30 minutes. Add butter and flour, mixed to a smooth
paste. Bring to a boil, stirring constantly. Serve on buttered
toast (No. 988) with mashed potatoes (No. 1835), using thickened liquor for gravy. Serves 6.

(1491)   STUFFED HEART EN CASSEROLE

1 beef heart	1 teaspoon sugar
1 cup dry bread crumbs	½ teaspoon salt
1 tablespoon butter	⅛ teaspoon pepper
2 tablespoons chopped onion	1 cup tomato sauce
2 tablespoons stewed	(No. 2035)
(No. 1893) or canned	2 tablespoons flour
tomatoes	

Soak heart in cold water 2 hours. Drain. Remove veins,
arteries, muscles, and all blood. Parboil 20 minutes. Mix all other
ingredients except flour. Fill heart with mixture and tie securely.
Put in baking dish or casserole. Pour tomato sauce over heart.
Cover and cook in oven at 325° F. for 3 hours, adding hot
water as needed. Remove heart and serve with gravy, made from
liquor, thickened with flour paste mixed in cold water. Serves 6.

(1492)   CALF'S HEAD

1 calf's head	2 tablespoons chopped celery
1 half lemon	1 bay leaf
1 tablespoon vinegar	1 egg
1 chopped onion	1 cup bread crumbs
1 chopped carrot	1 tablespoon butter
1 chopped seeded green	1 teaspoon salt
pepper	⅛ teaspoon pepper

Have butcher split head and remove fat and gristle. Remove tongue and brains and reserve for other dishes. Soak head for 3 hours in warm water, changing every hour. Wash thoroughly. Dry. Rub all over with cut side of lemon. Put in saucepan. Cover with cold water. Add vinegar, onion, carrot, celery, pepper, and bay leaf. Bring quickly to a boil. Cover. Reduce heat. Let simmer until tender, about 2 hours. Pick meat from bones. Put in baking dish. Brush top with beaten egg. Cover with buttered bread crumbs. Sprinkle with salt and pepper. Bake in hot oven (450° F.) until brown. Serve with hot white sauce (No. 2004). If desired the head meat can be served hot with parsley sauce (No. 2013) without baking. Serves 8.

(1493)   BROILED KIDNEYS

3 beef, 6 veal or pork, or 9 lamb or mutton kidneys	½ cup flour
¼ cup butter	1 teaspoon salt
	¼ teaspoon pepper

Split kidneys lengthwise. Remove fat, core, hard membrane, and tubes. Soak in cold, salt water 1 hour. Drain and dry thoroughly. Dip in melted butter. Roll in flour. Put in well greased broiler and broil in moderate heat about 12 minutes, turning to brown both sides. Sprinkle with salt and pepper and serve hot. Broiled breaded kidneys can be had by rolling them in bread crumbs instead of flour, in which case maître d'hôtel sauce (No. 2027) is delightful. Excellent results are also obtained by substituting French dressing (No. 716) for melted butter, in which case do not roll in flour or crumbs. If kidneys are very old or large, before broiling cover them with cold water, bring slowly to a boil, drain, and dry. Serves 6.

(1494)   SAUTÉED KIDNEYS

9 lamb or 6 veal kidneys	1 tablespoon butter or fat
1 teaspoon salt	12 toast triangles
⅛ teaspoon pepper	12 slices crisp bacon
2 tablespoons flour	(No. 1464)

Soak kidneys in cold water 1 hour. Drain. Pour boiling water over them. Drain. Remove veins and skin. Slice ¼ to ½ inch thick. Sprinkle with salt, pepper, and flour. Fry in butter or fat over hot fire not more than 5 minutes, turning constantly. Serve on toast garnished with bacon. Serves 6.

(1495)   STEWED KIDNEYS

3 beef, 6 veal, or 9 lamb kidneys	¼ teaspoon pepper
	1 tablespoon flour
1 finely chopped onion	1 tablespoon butter
1 teaspoon salt	

Split kidneys. Remove fat, core, hard membrane, and tubes. Cut in small pieces. Soak 1 hour in cold, salt water. Drain. Put in saucepan. Add 1 quart boiling water, onion, salt, and pepper. Cover and simmer 2 hours. Thicken with flour, mixed to a smooth paste with melted butter. Season with 1 tablespoon lemon juice or Worcestershire sauce if desired. Serve hot on buttered toast (No. 988). Serves 6.

(1496)   KIDNEY STEW

3 cups veal or beef kidneys	1 cup stewed (No. 1893) or canned tomatoes
1 small onion, sliced	
2 cups sliced carrots	⅛ teaspoon pepper
3 medium-sized potatoes, sliced	½ teaspoon paprika
	1 teaspoon Worcestershire sauce
2 teaspoons salt	

Soak kidneys in cold water 2 hours, changing water whenever it becomes cloudy. Drain. Pour boiling water over them. Remove tubes and skin. Cut in small pieces. Sprinkle with salt and pepper. Place in pot with onion and carrots. Cover with water. Cover and let simmer 30 minutes. Add potatoes, tomatoes, salt, paprika, and Worcestershire sauce. Cook until potatoes are tender, about 20 minutes more. Serves 8.

(1497)   KIDNEYS EN BROCHETTE

9 mutton kidneys	3 large tomatoes, quartered
1½ teaspoons salt	3 tablespoons butter, melted
¼ teaspoon pepper	
⅓ cup olive oil	Bacon, broiled (No. 1464)

Trim kidneys, split in halves, lengthwise, and soak in cold salted water ½ hour; drain and dry thoroughly. Season with salt and pepper and dip in oil; arrange kidney halves alternately with tomato quarters on skewers. Broil about 15 minutes, turning to brown all sides; place on hot platter, pour melted butter over each and serve with crisp bacon.

(1498) KIDNEYS À LA CREOLE

2 beef kidneys
½ teaspoon baking soda
2 tablespoons butter or fat
2 tablespoons chopped green pepper
2 tablespoons chopped onion

4 tablespoons flour
1 cup canned or strained stewed tomatoes (No. 1893)
1 teaspoon salt
¼ teaspoon pepper

Split kidneys. Remove fat, core, hard skin, and tubes. Cover with cold water. Add baking soda. Let stand 12 hours. Drain and dry. Melt butter in pan. Sauté kidneys in butter with green pepper and onion 3 minutes. Add flour, mixed to a smooth paste in cold water, and cook 3 minutes longer. Add tomatoes, 1 cup of boiling water, salt, and pepper. Let simmer until kidneys are tender, about 15 minutes. Serve on buttered toast (No. 988). Serves 4.

(1499) BROILED LIVER

1½ pounds liver
2 tablespoons butter
1 teaspoon salt

¼ teaspoon pepper
1 lemon

Soak liver in boiling water 5 minutes. Brush with butter. Broil at high heat from 6 to 8 minutes, turning often. Brush again with butter, sprinkle with salt and pepper. Squeeze on a few drops of lemon juice. Serves 6.

(1500) LIVER AND BACON

12 slices bacon
Flour for dredging

1½ pounds calf liver, ½ inch thick

Broil or fry bacon slowly. Remove and drain on brown paper. Keep warm. Wipe liver with cold, damp cloth. Dredge with flour. Fry in bacon fat, turning frequently, until well browned on both sides, about 5 to 8 minutes. Serves 6.

(1501)   FRIED LIVER

Wipe with cold, damp cloth. Dry. Dip in milk. Roll in flour, seasoned with salt and pepper. Fry in little fat until well browned on both sides, about 6 to 8 minutes. Allow ¼ to ½ pound per serving.

(1502)   FRENCH FRIED LIVER

1 pound calf liver	2 cups salt water
2 tablespoons French dressing (No. 716)	8 slices bacon

Soak liver in salt water 30 minutes. Scald in boiling water; remove outside skin and veins. Sprinkle with French dressing; let stand 1 hour. Drain and slice into 3 inch strips. Fry in deep hot fat (380° F.) 3 to 5 minutes. Drain on brown paper. Fry bacon crisp (No. 1464) and use as garnish. Serves 4.

(1503)   LIVER BAKED IN SOUR CREAM

1½ pounds liver	¼ teaspoon pepper
½ cup flour	2 tablespoons butter
1 teaspoon salt	1½ cups thick sour cream

Wipe liver with cold, damp cloth. Soak in boiling water 5 minutes. Roll in flour, seasoned with salt and pepper. Melt butter in frying pan. Brown liver on both sides. Put in greased baking dish. Blend 2 tablespoons flour with sour cream. Pour over liver. Cover. Bake in moderate oven (350° F.) 15 minutes. Uncover. Bake 25 minutes more. Canned or strained, stewed tomatoes (No. 1893) can be substituted for sour cream. Serves 4.

(1504)   LIVER WITH APPLES

8 slices bacon	2 large sour apples, chopped
1 pound beef liver, thinly sliced	1 teaspoon salt
1 medium-sized onion, chopped	¼ teaspoon pepper

Cut each bacon slice in three or four pieces. Combine in a greased casserole with liver, onion, apples (peeled and cored) and seasonings. Bake in a moderate oven (350° F.) about 1½ hours. Serves 6.

(1505)   BRAISED LIVER

2 cups diced celery	8 small carrots
1½ pounds liver	8 small onions
1 teaspoon salt	2 tablespoons flour
⅛ teaspoon pepper	12 slices crisp bacon
2 tablespoons butter or fat	(No. 1464)

Put celery in bottom of greased baking dish. Wipe liver with cold, damp cloth. Remove skin and veins. Sprinkle with salt and pepper and rub with butter or fat. Put on top of celery. Add ¼ cup of water. Cover dish and bake in moderate oven (350° F.) 45 minutes or until liver is tender. Stew carrots and onion in small amount of salted water until tender. Add to casserole. Thicken vegetable liquor with flour, mixed to a smooth paste with cold water, and pour over liver. Cover and cook 15 minutes more. Serve hot, garnished with crisp bacon. Serves 6.

(1506)   LIVER LOAF

1 pound calf liver	¼ teaspoon red pepper
1 teaspoon salt	¼ teaspoon allspice
1 teaspoon butter	¼ teaspoon nutmeg
¼ teaspoon black pepper	2 eggs

Wipe liver with cold, damp cloth. Pound it to pulp in mortar. Force through a sieve. Blend butter and seasonings with pulp. Add eggs, well beaten. Force again through sieve. Put mixture in greased mold. Set mold in pan of hot water. Cook in hot oven (400° F.) 45 minutes. Serve hot with brown sauce (No. 2020) or cold as mock pâté de fois gras. Serves 6.

(1507)   LIVER AND ONION STEW

2 pounds calf liver	2 tablespoons flour
6 slices bacon, diced	½ teaspoon salt
8 onions, sliced thin	¼ teaspoon pepper

Wipe liver with cold, damp cloth. Soak in boiling water 5 minutes. Remove and dice. Put bacon in frying pan and cook half crisp. Add liver and onions. Cook until well browned. Remove liver, bacon, and onions. Add flour, mixed to a smooth paste with cold water, salt, and pepper. Bring to a boil stirring constantly. Serve liver, bacon, and onions on buttered toast (No. 988) with pan liquor for sauce. Serves 6.

(1508)   CHICKEN LIVERS

Wash and thoroughly dry livers. Cut in small cubes. Sauté in hot butter or fat until well browned, turning often. Dredge with flour. Add 1 cup stock or water. Season with salt and pepper. Let simmer 10 minutes. Remove livers to hot buttered toast (No. 988). Thicken liquor with flour, mixed to a smooth paste with cold water, for sauce. Allow ½ pound of livers per serving.

(1509)   CHICKEN LIVERS EN BROCHETTE

Slice livers ¼ inch thick. Alternate slices of liver and thin slices of bacon, cut about same size, on skewers. Use 5 pieces of bacon and 4 of liver on each skewer. Bake in hot oven (400° F.) until bacon is crisp.

(1510)   BRAISED OXTAILS

3 tablespoons butter or fat	2 tablespoons flour
2 sliced carrots	2 oxtails
1 chopped onion	1 teaspoon salt
1 small diced turnip	⅛ teaspoon pepper
1 chopped stalk of celery	2 cloves

Melt butter in saucepan. Add onion, carrot, turnip, and celery. When very lightly browned, stir in flour, blending well. Cut oxtails into 2- to 3-inch pieces. Add them to pan. Add salt, pepper, cloves, and two cups of water. Bring to a boil, stirring constantly. Reduce heat and let simmer 2 to 3 hours. Serve hot with liquor for gravy. Serves 6 to 8.

(1511)   PICKLED PIGS' FEET

Scrub pigs' feet. Rinse. Put in pan. Cover with cold water. Bring to a boil. Pour off water. Add salted, boiling water. Cover and simmer until tender, about 5 hours. Drain and plunge into cold water. Put them in a jar. Cover with hot vinegar, spiced if desired. They can also be pickled by soaking in a bath of water in which 2 sliced green peppers, 2 sliced onions, 6 peppercorns, and 1 teaspoon salt have been boiled for 10 minutes, and to which the juice of 3 lemons has been added. Let feet remain in desired bath for 2 days before eating.

(1512) BROILED OR FRIED PIGS' FEET

To broil—Wash and rinse. Sprinkle with salt and pepper. Broil over hot heat 10 minutes, turning frequently. Serve with sauce piquante (No. 2031), tomato (No. 2035), onion sauce (No. 2037), or melted butter and lemon juice. To fry—Wash pigs' feet. Put in kettle. Cover with cold water. Bring quickly to a boil. Reduce heat and let simmer until tender, 4 to 6 hours. Add 2 teaspoons salt last hour of cooking. Let pigs' feet cool in stock. Split them. Season with salt and pepper. Roll in flour. Dip in beaten egg, diluted with water. Roll in cracker crumbs. Fry until brown in hot deep fat (370° F.). To sauté—After simmering, season with salt and pepper, roll in flour, and fry in little fat until brown on all sides. Serve fried feet with tomato sauce (No. 2035). Allow 1 pig's foot per serving.

(1513) PIGS' FEET À LA RUSSE

8 pickled pigs' feet (No. 1511)	1 tablespoon sugar
	1 teaspoon salt
2 cups canned or stewed strained tomatoes (No. 1893)	¼ teaspoon black pepper
	¼ teaspoon red pepper
1 cup vinegar	2 tablespoons mixed spices

Wash and examine feet carefully. Cut in small pieces. Put all other ingredients in a pot and bring to a boil. Add feet. Simmer 1 hour. Serve hot. Serves 6.

(1514) BROILED SWEETBREADS

2 pairs sweetbreads	1 tablespoon butter or
1 teaspoon salt	lemon butter
⅛ teaspoon pepper	(No. 2029)

Soak sweetbreads in salt water 1 hour. Drain. Put in saucepan and cover with water. Bring to a boil. Reduce heat and let simmer 30 minutes. Remove and discard fat and connective tissues from sweetbreads. Split lengthwise. Sprinkle with salt and pepper. Broil 10 minutes in hot broiler (450° F.), turning to brown both sides. Brush with butter and serve hot. Serves 4.

(1515)   BRAISED SWEETBREADS

2 pairs sweetbreads	1 bay leaf
¼ pound diced salt pork	1 sprig parsley
2 sliced carrots	1 tablespoon butter
2 sliced onions	1 tablespoon flour

Prepare and clean sweetbreads as per instruction for broiled sweetbreads (No. 1514). Put vegetables in greased baking dish. Spread pork over them. Put sweetbreads on top. Add sufficient water to cover vegetables. Cover and cook in moderate oven (350° F.) 1 hour, basting every 15 minutes. Uncover last 15 minutes to brown sweetbreads. Remove sweetbreads and vegetables to a warm platter. Thicken liquor with flour, blended to a smooth paste with melted butter. Boil liquor and constantly stir to desired consistency. Serve sweetbreads on buttered toast (No. 988) with this sauce. Serves 4.

(1516)   BREADED SWEETBREADS

2 pairs sweetbreads	1 cup fine bread crumbs
1 sprig parsley	1 egg
1 stalk celery	2 tablespoons butter or fat
½ teaspoon salt	

Soak sweetbreads in cold water 1 hour. Drain. Put in saucepan with parsley, celery, salt, and water to cover. Bring to boiling point. Reduce heat and let simmer 30 minutes. Cool in the liquor. Take out sweetbreads. Remove fat and connective tissue. Cut into small uniform cutlets. Dip in bread crumbs, then in slightly beaten egg, diluted with 2 tablespoons water, and again in crumbs. Fry quickly in butter or fat until brown, turning frequently. Serve with tomato sauce (No. 2035) or with creamed asparagus tips (No. 1705). Serves 4.

(1517)   BAKED SWEETBREADS

After cleaning according to instructions for broiled sweetbreads (No. 1514), put them in pan on top of thin slices of salt pork. Bake in hot oven (400° F.) 20 minutes, basting frequently with water or soup stock. Serve hot with brown (No. 2020) or mushroom sauce (No. 2039). One pair sweetbreads serves 2.

(1518)   SWEETBREAD CROQUETTES

2 cups cooked chopped sweetbreads	1 tablespoon chopped parsley
4 tablespoons chopped mushrooms	1 cup hot thick white sauce (No. 2004)
1 teaspoon salt	2 eggs
¼ teaspoon pepper	½ cup flour
1 tablespoon lemon juice	1 cup bread crumbs

Mix thoroughly sweetbreads, mushrooms, salt, pepper, parsley, lemon juice, 1 well-beaten egg, and hot white sauce. Set aside to cool. When cold, form into patties, little balls, or cones. Roll in flour. Dip in well-beaten egg, diluted with a little water. Roll in bread crumbs. Fry until well browned in deep fat (350° to 390° F.). Serve hot with medium white sauce (No. 2004).

(1519)   SWEETBREADS EN BROCHETTE

Clean and parboil sweetbreads as for broiled sweetbreads (No. 1514). Cut in 1-inch squares. Cut sliced bacon in 1-inch squares. On a skewer put 5 squares of bacon and 4 squares of sweetbreads alternately. Sprinkle with salt and pepper. Broil until bacon is crisp. To French fry, roll each square of sweetbreads in flour, dip in well-beaten egg, diluted with a little water, and roll in crumbs before putting on skewers. Fry in deep, hot fat (350° to 390° F.) until browned.

(1520)   SWEETBREADS BÉCHAMEL

2 pairs sweetbreads	4 tablespoons flour
½ teaspoon salt	1 cup rich milk
1 sprig parsley	1 tablespoon chopped parsley
1 stalk celery	
2 tablespoons butter	1 egg yolk

Soak sweetbreads in salt water 1 hour. Drain. Put in saucepan and cover with water. Add salt, parsley, and celery. Bring to a boil. Reduce heat and let simmer 30 minutes. Remove sweetbreads. Strain liquor, reserving 1 cup. Remove fat and connective tissues from sweetbreads. Cut into small pieces. Melt butter. Stir in flour. Add milk and reserved stock and stir until thick. Add sweetbreads and keep hot. Add parsley and well-beaten egg yolk just before serving. Serve in croustades (No. 996) or on toast. Oysters or veal may be substituted for half the sweetbreads. Serves 4.

(1521)   BOILED LAMBS' TONGUES

4 lambs' tongues	¼ teaspoon paprika
3 tablespoons butter	1 tablespoon vinegar
3 tablespoons flour	1 tablespoon capers
2 tablespoons chopped onion	2 tablespoons chopped
1 teaspoon salt	olives
½ teaspoon pepper	

Wash tongue thoroughly. Place in kettle. Cover with salted water. Bring to a boil. Skim. Cover. Reduce heat and let simmer until tender, about 1 to 1½ hours. Remove. Pour cold water over them. Remove skin and hard parts. Return to kettle. Melt butter in another pan. Stir in flour until well blended and cook until browned. Add 2 cups of liquor from kettle and all other ingredients. Bring to a boil, stirring constantly. Add tongues. Remove all to a hot platter and serve with boiled rice (No. 107). Serves 6.

(1522)   BOILED BEEF TONGUE

1 beef tongue	½ bay leaf
1 sliced carrot	½ teaspoon peppercorns
1 sliced onion	2 cloves
2 stalks diced celery	2 teaspoons salt
2 sprigs parsley	

Wash tongue thoroughly. Cover with water in kettle. Add other ingredients. Bring quickly to a boil. Reduce heat and simmer for about 3 hours or until tongue is tender. Remove tongue from kettle. Remove skin and throat part from tongue. Serve hot with almond and raisin sauce (No. 2056). The tongue may also be served cold. The throat meat may be used for hash and the liquor is rich soup stock. If smoked tongue is used, soak over night and simmer until tender, about 4 hours. Hot tongue may be served with a white sauce (No. 2004). Serves 6.

(1523)   BOILED OX TONGUE

Follow recipe for boiled beef tongue (No. 1522).

(1524)   BREADED TONGUE

Boil tongue according to instructions for boiled tongue (No. 1522). Spread a mixture of bread crumbs and well-beaten eggs on tongue and bake in moderate oven (350° F.) about ½ hour, basting frequently with canned or strained, stewed tomatoes (No. 1893) or any available wine. Serve with sautéed chopped onions and celery.

POULTRY

The flesh of poultry should be firm and plump. The tip of the breast bone should be tender. If possible, have the butcher dress and clean the bird for cooking.

A chicken should be killed by chopping off the head or by slashing the big artery in the neck. The feathers must be pulled out by hand. This task will be easier if the dead bird is plunged into boiling water but dry-picked birds are superior in flavor. After removing the feathers, singe the bird over a direct flame to remove any remaining pin feathers or hairs. Cut off the head and the legs at the lower joint. Remove the crop from the neck. Make a cut at the vent, keeping the opening as small as possible. Insert hand and loosen and remove internal organs, being sure to get the lungs and the windpipe. Do not break the gall bladder, a sac attached to the liver, as the bitter taste of its contents affects any part it touches. To clean the gizzard, cut through the muscle to a tender skin, which must be removed, together with any pebbles and stones found in the sac. Cut out the oil sac near the tail. Of the entrails reserve the liver, gizzard, and heart. Wipe the inside of the bird with a cold damp cloth.

TIMETABLE FOR ROASTING YOUNG BIRDS

	Weight[1] of bird	Oven temperature	Time
	Pounds	*°F.*	*Hours*
Chicken	4– 5	350	1½–2
Duck	5– 6	350	2–2½
Goose	10–12	325	3–4
Guinea	2– 2½	350	About 1½
Turkey	6– 9	325	2½–3
	10–13	300	3–4
	14–17	275	4½–5½
	18–25	250–275	6–8

[1] Dressed weight, that is, picked but not drawn, and including head and feet. Drawn weight is about a fifth less than the dressed weight.

(1525)   ROAST CHICKEN

4-pound chicken	1 teaspoon salt
Poultry stuffing (No. 2064)	⅛ teaspoon pepper
½ cup butter	Flour for dredging

Dress chicken (Page 375) and wipe with cold, damp cloth. Put in stuffing. Fasten wings and legs close to body with skewers or by tying. Spread 3 tablespoons butter over breast and legs. Sprinkle with salt, pepper, and flour. Also sprinkle bottom of roasting pan with flour. Place chicken on back in pan. Put in hot oven (450° F.) for 15 minutes. Baste with balance of butter, melted in ⅔ cup boiling water. Reduce oven heat to 350° F. and cook until breast is tender, about 2 hours. Baste every 10 minutes, adding water if necessary. Turn bird occasionally to brown evenly. Sprinkling with flour 2 or three times during cooking will cause a thick crust. If glazed surface is wanted, omit flour on bird. Birds up to 4 pounds require about 30 minutes of cooking per pound; larger birds about 22 to 25 minutes per pound. Many different stuffings can be used, such as chestnut (No. 2075), bread (No. 2063), celery (No. 2081), mushroom (No. 2079), corn bread (No. 2070), egg and mushroom (No. 2076), or onion (No. 2065). Serve chicken with giblet gravy (No. 2002). Serves 4 to 6.

(1526)   ROAST CAPON

Prepare and cook same as roast chicken (No. 1525). Oyster stuffing (No. 2074) is suggested.

(1527)   FRUIT GLAZED ROAST CHICKEN

1 roasting chicken, 2½ to 3 pounds dressed	½ cup sliced onion
	⅓ cup minced parsley
2 teaspoons salt	¾ cup chopped or sliced ripe olives
¼ teaspoon pepper	
8½ cups white bread cubes	½ teaspoon sage
½ cup melted butter	1½ cups canned peach-nectarine nectar
1 cup finely cut celery	

Prepare chicken for roasting. Sprinkle inside and out with salt and pepper. Heat butter in large kettle. Add bread cubes and cook and stir about five minutes. Add vegetables, olives and seasonings and cook and stir until bread cubes are slightly brown and vegetables are wilted. Remove from fire, add ½ cup nectar and stir to blend. Use to stuff chicken. Sew up opening. Bake, uncovered, in a moderate oven (350° to 375° F.) about 15 minutes. Baste with remaining nectar and continue baking, basting frequently for 2½ to 3 hours, or until tender. If evaporation is rapid, add water as and if needed. Cover pan when chicken is sufficiently brown. Any other nectar of the whole-fruit variety—apricot, plum, pear or peach—makes an equally delightful glaze and stuffing for roast chicken. Serves 6.

(1528) BROILED CHICKEN

Choose broilers from 1½ to 2 pounds. Have them split down the back. Wash. Dry thoroughly. Rub all over with butter, fat, or oil. Season with salt and pepper. Put in greased broiler and sear one side quickly at high heat (450° F.). Turn and sear other side. Reduce heat or move broiler further from heat and broil at (350° F.) until tender, about 15 minutes more. To cook broiled breaded chicken, prepare and clean chicken as above. Brush it with butter. Season with salt and pepper. Sprinkle with chopped parsley and onion. Put in baking pan. Bake in hot oven (450° F.) 10 minutes, turning once. Reduce heat. Cover and bake in moderate oven (325° F.) 25 to 30 minutes more, turning frequently. Brush over with well-beaten egg. Sprinkle with fine bread crumbs and broil at high heat until nicely browned all over. Serve with brown (No. 2020) or tartar sauce (No. 2044). Allow ¾ pounds of chicken per serving.

(1529) PLANKED CHICKEN

Broil 3 medium-sized broilers according to instructions for broiled chicken (No. 1528). Put on greased plank, skin side up, garnish, and bake in accordance with recipe for planked steak (No. 1305).

(1530) CHICKEN À LA MARYLAND

Prepare chicken as for southern style fried chicken (No. 1531). Season with salt and pepper. Roll in flour. Dip in well-beaten egg, diluted with a little water. Roll in cracker or bread crumbs. Put in greased baking pan. Dot heavily with butter or cover with slices of bacon. Bake in hot oven (450° F.) 30 minutes, basting often. If bacon is used, remove last 10 minutes of cooking. Serve hot with white sauce (No. 2004). Allow ¾ pound of chicken per serving.

(1531) SOUTHERN STYLE FRIED CHICKEN

2 small chickens, about 2½	⅛ teaspoon pepper
to 3 pounds each	1 cup flour
1 teaspoon salt	¼ cup butter or fat

Dress chicken (Page 375) and wipe with cold, damp cloth. Disjoint each bird into 4 or 6 pieces. Dip each piece in cold water, sprinkle with salt and pepper, and roll in flour. Melt fat in pan and fry chicken until well and uniformly browned, turning occasionally. Serve on hot platter with giblet gravy (No. 2002), white sauce (No. 2004), or brown sauce (No. 2020). Serves 6.

(1532)   DEEP-FRIED CHICKEN

Prepare chicken as for southern style fried chicken (No. 1531). Dip in fritter batter (No. 2706) and fry in deep fat, about 380° to 400° F., until brown. Remove to baking dish and bake in moderate oven (300° F.) until tender, about 45 minutes.

(1533)   FRIED CHICKEN

Prepare and cook same as southern style fried chicken (No. 1531), omitting flour.

(1534)   COVERED FRIED CHICKEN

Prepare chicken as for southern style fried chicken (No. 1531). Melt 2 tablespoons fat or butter in shallow pan. Put chicken in pan and cover tightly. Cook in hot oven (450° F.) until well browned on bottom, about 12 minutes. Turn and repeat cooking. Add more grease if necessary. Serves 6.

(1535)　　　　BAKED CHICKEN

Select a 3-pound chicken. Have butcher split it down back. Wash and dry thoroughly. Sprinkle with salt, pepper, and flour. Put in pan, skin side up. Dot with butter. Add 2 cups hot water. Bake in hot oven (450° F.) 15 minutes, turning once, and again 'sprinkling with salt, pepper, and flour. Baste. Reduce heat to (350° F.) and bake until tender, about 1½ to 2 hours, basting every 15 minutes and turning when bottom side is well browned. Serve with giblet gravy (No. 2002). Allow ¾ pound of chicken per serving.

(1536)　　　　CHICKEN SUPRÊME

• Fricassee chicken (No. 1540), adding a slice of onion, salt, and pepper for flavoring, and a cup of diced celery. When chicken is tender, remove from pan and strain broth. Discard onion but reserve celery for casserole. Place slices of broiled ham (No. 1453) in the bottom of a large casserole, adding 2 well-drained pineapple gems and 2 canned artichoke hearts for each serving, the celery, and chicken (which has been removed from the bone). Skim fat from broth and use broth in making fricassee sauce. Melt 2 tablespoons of butter and stir in 2 tablespoons of flour for each cup and a half of broth. Stir until smooth and slightly thickened. Pour over chicken in casserole. Prepare dumplings (No. 954). Add ground cooked chicken livers or calf liver. Drop on top of casserole mixture. Cover and place in a moderately hot oven (400° F.) for 15 minutes or until dumplings are done. Before serving sprinkle with freshly grated coconut which has been toasted. Serve with boiled rice (No. 106). Yield: A stewing chicken weighing 4¼ pounds (dressed weight) will serve six.

(1537)　　BOILED FOWL, CHICKEN, OR CAPON

Dress bird (Page 375) and wipe with cold, damp cloth. Tie securely in cheesecloth. Put on low stand in kettle of boiling water. Cover and simmer until tender, allowing 20 to 30 minutes per pound. Season water with salt and pepper when half cooked. Save liquor for stock. Allow ½ to ¾ pound of chicken per serving.

(1538) STEAMED FOWL

Dress fowl (Page 375), stuff if desired, and tie up as for roasting. Cook in a steamer for 2½ to 3½ hours, depending on size of bird. Sprinkle with salt and pepper. Rub with butter. Put drippings in baking pan. Add chicken and bake in moderate oven (350° F.) until brown, 30 to 45 minutes, basting every 5 minutes. Allow ½ to ¾ pound per serving.

(1539) CHICKEN PIE

1 4-pound fowl	⅛ teaspoon pepper
1 sliced carrot	Plain pie paste (No. 2701)
1 stalk celery	4 tablespoons flour
1 sprig parsley	½ pound sliced sautéed
1 slice onion	mushrooms (No. 1801)
1 teaspoon salt	

Dress fowl (Page 375) and wipe with cold, damp cloth. Put in saucepan and cover with water. Add carrot, celery, parsley, and onion. Bring to boiling point. Reduce heat, cover, and let simmer until fowl is tender, allowing about 30 minutes per pound. Season with salt and pepper when half done. Remove fowl from pan. Remove skin and bones, keeping meat in large pieces. Line the sides of a baking dish with plain pie paste. Put in chicken. Reduce chicken stock to 3 cups by boiling. Skim off fat and strain. Mix flour to a smooth paste in cold water. Add to stock. Bring stock to boiling point, stirring constantly. Add stock and mushrooms to chicken. Cover with pie paste. Bake at 450° F. for 15 minutes or until well browned. Serves 6.

(1540) CHICKEN FRICASSEE

1 4-pound fowl	½ small onion, sliced
1 teaspoon salt	3 peppercorns
⅛ teaspoon pepper	½ bay leaf
1 cup flour	1 teaspoon chopped parsley
4 tablespoons butter or fat	12 toast triangles

Dress fowl (Page 375) and wipe with a cold, damp cloth. Disjoint. Sprinkle with salt and pepper and roll in flour. Melt butter in frying pan and fry chicken to a delicate brown. Re-

move to saucepan, cover with water, and add onion, pepper-
corn, and bay leaf. Cover and cook slowly until bird is tender,
about 1¼ hours. Remove to hot platter. Sprinkle with parsley.
Thicken liquor with a smooth flour paste mixed with cold water
for sauce. Pour sauce around bird and garnish platter with
toast. Other good sauces to use are white (No. 2004), mushroom (No. 2039), tomato (No. 2035), or caper (No. 2040).
Serves 6.

(1541) CHICKEN POT PIE

4-pound roasting chicken	Dumplings (No. 954)
6 medium-sized potatoes	2 tablespoons butter or fat
1 teaspoon salt	2 tablespoons flour
⅛ teaspoon pepper	

Dress chicken (Page 375) and wipe with a cold, damp cloth.
Put in saucepan, cover with hot water, and bring to the boiling
point. Cover and let simmer until chicken is almost tender,
allowing about 25 minutes per pound. Add potatoes, salt, and
pepper and cook 20 minutes longer, or until potatoes are soft.
Place dumplings on top. Cover tightly and cook until dumplings
are light, about 10 minutes. Remove chicken, potatoes, and
dumplings to a hot platter. Melt butter and mix to a smooth
paste with flour. Add to liquor and bring to a boil. Serve as
sauce. Serves 6.

(1542) CHICKEN AND OYSTER PIE

2 cups diced cooked chicken	¼ teaspoon pepper
1 cup chicken gravy	1 tablespoon chopped
1 cup milk	parsley
1 cup small oysters	1 tablespoon chopped
1 tablespoon flour	celery
1 tablespoon butter	Plain pie paste (No. 2701)
1 teaspoon salt	

Put chicken in saucepan. Add gravy, milk, and oysters. Simmer 30 minutes. Melt butter and mix to a smooth paste with
flour. Stir paste into mixture in pan. Bring to boil. Add salt,
pepper, parsley, celery. Line a greased baking dish with plain
pie paste. Pour in mixture. Cover with pie paste. Bake in moderate oven (350° F.) until well browned, about 20 to 25 minutes.
Serve hot. Serves 6.

(1543)   CHICKEN DIXIE STYLE

1 three-pound fowl	¼ teaspoon black pepper
1 quart water	1 cup thin cream
2 teaspoons salt	2 cups green corn

Dress chicken (Page 375). Wipe with cold, damp cloth. Disjoint and stew until tender in water. Season with salt and pepper. Remove chicken from broth and place alternately with corn in casserole. Pour over cream and chicken broth, thickened with a little flour, mixed to a smooth paste with cold water. Bake in moderate oven (350° F.) 40 minutes. Serves 6.

(1544)   CHICKEN COUNTRY STYLE

3-pound chicken	2 large green peppers
½ cup flour	1 tablespoon sugar
2 teaspoons salt	¼ teaspoon pepper
6 tablespoons butter or fat	2½ cups canned or strained
6 medium-size potatoes	stewed tomatoes
6 small onions	(No. 1893)
6 large carrots	

Dress chicken (Page 375) and wipe with cold, damp cloth. Mix ½ teaspoon of salt with flour and roll chicken in mixture. Melt fat in frying pan and brown the chicken on all sides at high heat for about 10 minutes. Peel skins from potatoes and onions. Scrape and quarter carrots lengthwise. Seed green peppers and slice them in ½-inch strips. Mix balance of salt, sugar, and pepper with tomatoes. Place ⅔ of vegetables in bottom of kettle. Place chicken on top and add remaining vegetables. Pour tomatoes and 3 cups boiling water over all. Cover tightly and bring to a boil. Reduce heat and let simmer until tender, about 1½ hours. Serves 6.

(1545)   CREAMED CHICKEN I

Combine 2 cups cold, cooked chicken, cut in little cubes with 1 cup medium white sauce (No. 2004) and heat thoroughly. Serve on toast. Serves 6.

(1546)   CREAMED CHICKEN II

Use 2 cups cold, cooked chicken, cut in small cubes and 1 cup medium white sauce (No. 2004). Put alternating layers of chicken and sauce in greased baking dish. Cover top with buttered bread crumbs and bake in hot oven (450° F.) until brown. Serve on toast. Serves 6.

(1547) CHICKEN À LA KING

2 tablespoons butter	2 cups cooked chicken,
1 cup sliced mushrooms	diced
2 tablespoons flour	1 pimiento, in thin strips
1 teaspoon salt	¼ teaspoon pepper
2 cups milk	

Melt butter. Add mushrooms. Cover and cook about 5 minutes. Sprinkle with flour. Add all other ingredients. Let cook until sauce thickens. Serve on toast or in patty shells (No. 2709). One cup of cream or 1 cup of milk and 1 cup of chicken stock (No. 502) may be substituted for the 2 cups milk. Serves 8.

(1548) CHICKEN PILAU

3-pound fowl	1 chopped onion
2 cups rice	½ cup chopped celery
2 teaspoons salt	3 sliced tomatoes
½ teaspoon pepper	3 tablespoons butter

Dress chicken (Page 375) and wash. Dry thoroughly. Boil 2 quarts water in saucepan. Add rice and chicken. Cover and simmer until chicken is about tender, about 1½ hours, adding salt and pepper last 30 minutes of cooking. Melt butter in frying pan and brown vegetables. Add to chicken. Cover and simmer 30 minutes more. Serves 6.

(1549) CHICKEN STEW WITH DUMPLINGS

4-pound fowl	¼ cup flour
1 tablespoon salt	Dumplings (No. 954)
¼ tablespoon pepper	

Dress fowl. Wipe with cold, damp cloth. Disjoint. Put in kettle. Cover with cold water. Bring to a boil. Let simmer until tender, about 1 hour. Add salt and pepper after 30 minutes of cooking. Thicken stock with flour, mixed to a smooth, thin paste with cold water. If desired flour can be mixed to a paste with an equal amount of melted butter. Serve with dumplings. Serves 6.

(1550) CHICKEN AND SWEETBREAD CASSEROLE

¼ pound mushrooms, sliced
1 tablespoon chopped onion
3 tablespoons butter
¼ cup flour
1 cup chicken stock (No. 502)
½ cup milk
½ cup light cream

1 cup diced cooked chicken
½ cup chopped cooked sweetbreads (No. 1514)
⅜ cup blanched almonds
1 teaspoon salt
⅛ teaspoon pepper
¼ cup bread crumbs, buttered

Sauté mushrooms and onion in butter until lightly browned; stir in flour, add stock and milk gradually, and cook, stirring until thickened. Add cream, chicken, sweetbreads, almonds, salt and pepper, and bring to boiling point. Turn into greased individual casseroles and cover with crumbs. Bake in moderate oven (350° F.) until well browned. Hard-cooked eggs (No. 202) can be substituted for sweetbreads. Serves 6.

(1551) SMOTHERED CHICKEN

Select and prepare chicken as for southern style fried chicken (No. 1531). Sauté until well browned in a little butter or fat. Cover with cream or with milk and cream in equal proportions. Bring to boil. Put chicken and liquid in greased baking dish. Cover tightly and bake in moderate oven (350° F.) until tender, about ½ to ¾ hour. Allow ¾ pound of chicken per serving.

(1552) CHICKEN SAUTÉ AU CURRY

1 3-pound chicken
¼ cup flour
1 teaspoon salt
⅛ teaspoon pepper
3 tablespoons butter
2 large chopped onions
1 minced sweet apple
1 tablespoon curry powder
1 tablespoon shredded coconut

1 chopped bay leaf
⅛ teaspoon thyme
2 tablespoons chopped parsley
¼ cup chopped celery
½ clove of garlic
2 chopped peeled tomatoes
2 tablespoons chicken stock (No. 502)

Dress chicken (Page 375) and wipe with cold, damp cloth. Disjoint. Roll in flour. Sprinkle with salt and pepper. Melt butter in frying pan. Brown chicken quickly on all sides. Add onions and simmer slowly 10 minutes, turning occasionally. Add apple. Cover and cook 5 minutes more. Add other ingredients. Cover and simmer 25 minutes. Shake pan gently during cooking frequently but do not stir. Use more chicken stock if more sauce is desired. Amount of curry powder can be altered to suit taste. If creamier sauce is desired, add a little heavy cream at end of cooking. Serves 6.

(1553)   CHICKEN CROQUETTES

2 cups chopped cold roast chicken (No. 1525)
2 tablespoons chopped celery
1 cup thick white sauce (No. 2004)

Few grains nutmeg
1 egg
2 tablespoons water
¾ cup fine bread crumbs

Grind chicken very fine. Add celery, hot sauce, and nutmeg, mixing well. Chill. Mold into cutlets or croquettes. Roll in crumbs; dip into gently beaten egg and water; roll again in crumbs. Fry in deep hot fat (380° F.) 2 to 5 minutes. Drain on brown paper. A desirable addition is ½ cup chopped mushrooms, cooked any style. Serves 6.

(1554) AMERICAN CHICKEN CHOP SUEY

2 cups cold cooked chicken
1 cup boiled celery (No. 1761)
1½ cups boiled rice (No. 107)
1 teaspoon salt

⅛ teaspoon pepper
1 tablespoon butter or fat
2 tablespoons flour
1½ cups chicken stock (No. 502)

Cut chicken and celery in thin strips. Mix them with rice, salt, and pepper. Melt butter and make into a smooth paste with flour. Add stock slowly, stirring constantly. Bring to a boil, continuing stirring. Add the chicken and rice mixture and heat thoroughly. A cup of sautéed mushrooms (No. 1801) will add to this dish. Thin noodles (No. 2301), sautéed until crisp in a little fat, make an appropriate addition to this dish. Arrange them on top of mixture. Serves 6.

(1555)   JELLIED CHICKEN

3-pound chicken	3 hard-cooked eggs
2½ teaspoons salt	(No. 202)
2 tablespoons gelatin	6 sliced stoned olives
1 diced onion	½ cup sliced canned mush-
2 bay leaves	rooms
1 blade of mace	1 tablespoon chopped
3 cloves	parsley
1 teaspoon whole peppers	1 tablespoon chopped
⅛ teaspoon nutmeg	celery

Dress chicken (Page 375) and wipe with cold, damp cloth. Put in kettle. Half cover with boiling water. Cover kettle and let simmer until tender, 2 to 3 hours. Add 1½ teaspoons salt when half cooked. Remove chicken from pot, reserving liquor. Drain chicken and let cool. Remove all meat and cut in 1-inch squares. Put skin and bones in saucepan. Add 1 quart liquor from kettle. Add onion, bay leaves, mace, 1 teaspoon salt, cloves, peppers, and nutmeg. Simmer until reduced to 1 pint. Add gelatin. Strain. Put layer of chicken meat in greased mold. Cover with layer of sliced eggs, mushrooms, and olives. Alternate layers until all ingredients are used, sprinkling each layer with parsley and celery. Pour stock into mold. Unmold when well set. Serve with mayonnaise (No. 701). Serves 6.

(1556)   ROAST DUCK

1 roasting duck	1½ to 2 cups celery and
2 teaspoons salt	olive stuffing
¼ teaspoon pepper	(No. 2085)

Dress duck (Page 375) and wipe with cold, damp cloth. Sprinkle with salt and pepper. Stuff. Tie and sew securely with wings and legs close to body. Put in roasting pan, breast side up. Sear in quick oven (450° F.) for 15 minutes. Add 1 cup water and baste. Reduce heat to 350° F. and cook 20 minutes per pound, basting every five minutes. Serve with applesauce (No. 34). Other proper stuffings for duck are apple (No. 2082), peanut (No. 2096), onion (No. 2065). Cranberry orange sauce (No. 2060) or olive sauce (No. 2048) or currant jelly make desirable accompaniments for duck. Allow 1 pound per serving.

(1557)   **BROILED DUCKLING**

Follow recipe for broiled chicken (No. 1528), using duck-ling in place of chicken and cooking 25 to 30 minutes.

(1558)   **BRAISED DUCK**

4-pound duck	1 cup chopped carrot
1 teaspoon salt	2 cloves
¼ teaspoon pepper	1 bay leaf
3 tablespoons butter or fat	2 tablespoons chopped
1 cup chopped onion	parsley
1 cup chopped celery	1 tablespoon flour

Wash a dry duck thoroughly. Sprinkle with salt and pepper. Melt 2 tablespoons butter in pan. Put in duck and brown all over at high heat. Add 1 quart boiling water, onion, celery, carrot, cloves, bay leaf, and parsley. Cover and let simmer until tender, about 1½ hours. Remove duck. Blend flour and 1 tablespoon melted butter and add to pan liquor. Bring to boil, stirring constantly. Serve duck on hot platter with this gravy or mushroom sauce (No. 2039). Garnish with hominy cro-quettes (No. 129). Allow ¾ pound of duck per serving.

(1559)   **ROAST GOOSE**

8- to 10-pound goose	2 cups celery stuffing
1½ teaspoons salt	(No. 2081)
¼ teaspoon pepper	6 thin strips fat salt pork

Dress goose (Page 375), wash thoroughly and dry. Stuff and sprinkle with salt and pepper. Tie and sew securely with wings and legs close to body. Put, breast up, in roasting pan with strips of pork on top. Bake in quick oven (450° F.) for 15 minutes. Add 1 cup water and baste. Reduce heat to 350° F. and cook 20 minutes per pound, basting every 15 minutes. Remove pork strips during last 30 minutes of cooking. If de-sired, goose may be rubbed with cut side of an onion or clove of garlic before cooking. Serve with giblet gravy (No. 2002) and baked apples (No. 36) or fried apple rings (No. 39). Goose may also be stuffed with mashed potatoes (No. 1835), any fruit stuffing, or may be left unstuffed. Allow 1 pound per serving.

(1560)   ROAST TURKEY

Prepare and cook same as roast chicken (No. 1525), using about 10 cups of desired stuffing, and cooking 15 to 20 minutes per pound. Baste every half hour. Allow ¾ pound per serving.

(1561)   BROILED TURKEY

Only very small turkeys can be broiled. Prepare according to instructions for broiled chicken (No. 1528). Sear quickly at high heat (450° to 500° F.), then finish cooking at 300° to 350° F. until tender. Baste every few minutes with stock made by boiling giblets, a small onion, and 1 bay leaf together until tender. Allow ¾ pound of turkey per serving.

(1562)   BOILED TURKEY

Follow recipe for boiled fowl (No. 1537), using turkey instead of fowl.

(1563)   TURKEY CROQUETTES

Follow recipe for chicken croquettes (No. 1553).

(1564)   CREAMED TURKEY

Follow directions for creamed chicken I and II (No. 1545 and 1546).

(1565)   TURKEY HASH

Follow recipe for meat hash (No. 1602) using turkey and stuffing, if any, in place of other meat.

(1566)   OTHER TURKEY DISHES

Turkey can be substituted for chicken in almost any chicken dish. See chicken section for suggested recipes.

(1567)   ROAST GUINEA HEN

Singe, dress, draw, and wash bird thoroughly. Sprinkle with salt and pepper and rub inside of cavity with butter. Stuff with highly flavored poultry stuffing or cook with a halved onion and quartered pepper in cavity. Tie wings and legs close to body. Place strips of bacon or salt pork on top of bird. Sear in hot oven (500° F.) first 15 minutes of roasting. Reduce heat to moderate (350° F.) and cook 30 minutes more. Baste every 5 minutes with drippings. Chop giblets, sauté them with butter and add to roasting pan after bird is removed. Add a little flour, mixed to a smooth paste with cold water, for gravy. Serve with currant jelly. Roast potatoes (No. 1838) may be cooked with bird. Allow ¾ to 1 pound of bird per serving.

(1568)   ROAST SQUAB

Dress squab. Wash thoroughly. Dry. Stuff with bread stuffing (No. 2063). Sew opening securely. Tie legs and wings close to body and tie strips of bacon over breast. Roast in moderate oven (350° F.) 30 minutes, basting frequently with butter and drippings. Thicken pan drippings with a little flour, mixed to a smooth paste with cold water, adding boiling water if necessary for gravy. Season with salt and pepper. Allow 1 small or ½ large squab per serving.

(1569)   BROILED SQUAB

Dress squab. Wash and dry. Brush with butter or bacon fat. Broil at moderate heat (350° F.) 15 minutes, turning frequently. Season with salt and pepper. Serve hot on buttered toast (No. 988). For planked broiled squab, refer to recipe for planked steak (No. 1305) for garnishing and baking methods. Allow 1 small or ½ large squab per serving.

(1570)   ROAST PIGEON

Follow recipe for roast squab (No. 1568), cooking 45 minutes to 1 hour. Allow one small pigeon or one-half large pigeon per serving.

(1571)   PIGEON PIE

6 small pigeons	2 tablespoons chopped
1 teaspoon salt	parsley
¼ teaspoon pepper	2 tablespoons chopped
4 tablespoons butter or fat	celery
2 tablespoons chopped onion	2 tablespoons flour
8 cloves	Plain pie paste (No. 2701)
1 carrot, sliced	

Dress, wash, and dry pigeons. Tie legs and wings tight against body. Sprinkle with salt and pepper. Melt 2 tablespoons butter or fat in pan and sauté pigeons, searing thoroughly on all sides. Cover with water. Add onion, cloves, carrot, parsley, and celery. Cover and simmer until tender, about 3 hours. Remove pigeons and separate meat from bones. Mix flour to a smooth paste with balance of butter, melted, and stir into pan liquor, bringing to a boil. Line a greased baking dish with pie paste. Put in pigeon meat. Pour in liquor. Cover with pie paste. Bake in hot oven (450° F.) until brown. Serve hot. Serves 6.

(1572)   ROAST VENISON

For roasting, choose leg or saddle. Follow recipes for roasting lamb (No. 1390), cooking venison about 12 minutes per pound. Allow ½ pound of meat per serving.

(1573)   VENISON STEAKS

Cut steaks about ¾ inch thick. Prepare and cook same as beefsteak (No. 1301 and 1302). If flavor is too strong, venison will be improved by standing for 1 hour in a mixture of olive oil and lemon juice or French dressing (No. 716). Allow ½ pound per serving.

(1574)   FILETS OF VENISON

Follow instructions for filets of lamb (No. 1402), using venison in place of lamb. If desired, cutlets may be rolled in flour, dipped in slightly beaten egg, diluted with a little water, and rolled in bread crumbs before frying.

To Microwave

Arrange 1 lb. fish fillets in a large microwave-safe baking dish. Place thicker areas toward outer edge of dish overlapping thinner parts if necessary. Cover with waxed paper; microcook on High 5 min., rotating dish once. Let stand 1 min.

Nutritional Information (per 4 oz.) —

130 Calories, .2g Carbohydrate, 21g Protein, 4g Fat, 271mg Sodium

Did You Know?

Spices, herbs and seasonings retain their freshness longer if stored away from heat and moisture. Keep tightly closed when not in use.

McCormick®/Schilling®

For More Tips Call 1-800-MEAL TIP

Tip #82

TIP #82

Lemon Fish Fillets

MICROWAVE DIRECTIONS ON BACK

This simple tip turns any kind of fish into mouth watering Lemon Fish Fillets. Just before broiling, dot each fillet with margarine and lightly sprinkle with Lemon & Pepper Seasoning Salt.

McCormick/Schilling®

(1575) ROAST RABBIT OR HARE

Use young rabbits and hares, weighing 2 to 3 pounds. Do
not eat those with unpleasant odors. They should be drawn and
cleaned as soon as possible after killing but need not be skinned
until time to cook. If purchased they are skinned by butcher.
To skin, hang up by hind legs. Slit skin around first joint of
hind legs. Insert knife in slit and loosen skin around legs and
rump. With fingers pull tail and skin down over body until free.
Cut off head and feet. Slit down front and remove entrails,
reserving heart and liver. When ready to cook, wash thoroughly
and dry. Boil heart and liver until tender. Chop fine and mix
with poultry stuffing (No. 2064), dampened with water in
which giblets were cooked. Stuff rabbit. Sew opening. Tie or
fasten legs close to body with skewers. Place on side in roaster.
Roast in hot oven (450° F.) 15 minutes, turning once and basting frequently with melted butter or drippings. Reduce heat
and continue cooking in moderate oven (350° F.) 1¼ to 1½
hours, basting every 15 minutes. Make gravy by adding a little
flour, mixed to a smooth paste with cold water, to drippings,
blending well. Allow ¾ pound of rabbit per serving.

(1576) BROILED RABBIT OR HARE

To skin, dress, and draw follow directions for roast rabbit
or hare (No. 1575). Split in halves. Cook same as broiled chick-
en (No. 1528). Allow ¾ pound of rabbit per serving. Fried
rabbit is prepared by disjointing animal; dipping in batter
made with 2 beaten egg yolks, 3 cups milk, and 1¼ cups flour;
frying in butter in heavy pan 15 minutes; and cooking more
slowly 30 to 45 minutes, turning often. After rabbit has been
taken from pan, add ¼ cup flour, mixed to a smooth paste with
cold water, and 1½ cups milk to pan drippings. Season to taste
with salt and pepper. Bring to a boil, stirring constantly, and
serve as gravy. Garnish with currant jelly and sprigs of parsley.

(1577) RABBIT STEW

Follow recipe for Brunswick stew (No. 1580), using rabbits
instead of squirrels.

(1578)   **HASSENPFEFFER**

1 2½- to 3-pound hare	1 teaspoon salt
2 tablespoons butter	¼ teaspoon pepper
2 tablespoons chopped bacon	1 tablespoon mustard seed
2 chopped carrots	1 chopped onion
1 bay leaf	¼ cup canned mushrooms
8 cloves	1 cup cream
1 clove of garlic	

Skin, dress, draw, and clean hare according to instructions for roast rabbit or hare (No. 1575). Cut meat from bones. Melt butter in saucepan. Add bacon, carrots, bay leaf, cloves, garlic, salt, pepper, mustard seed, onion, mushrooms, and hare meat. Brown well. Add 1 cup water or vinegar. Cover and simmer until tender, about 1 hour. Add cream. Mix well and serve hot. Serves 6.

(1579)   **ROAST SQUIRREL**

Follow instructions for roast rabbit (No. 1575), using squirrels instead of rabbits and rubbing animals with butter, oil, or fat before cooking. One squirrel provides two servings.

(1580)   **BRUNSWICK STEW**

2 grey squirrels	2 cups canned or strained
1 tablespoon salt	stewed tomatoes
4 potatoes, pared and cubed	(No. 1893)
1 cup canned corn	¼ pound diced salt pork
2 diced onions	1 tablespoon butter
1 cup lima beans	1 tablespoon flour
½ teaspoon pepper	

Skin, dress, draw, and clean squirrels according to instructions for roast rabbit or hare (No. 1575). Disjoint. Put 8 cups water and salt in kettle. Bring to boil. Add squirrels, potatoes, corn, onion, beans, tomatoes, and salt pork. Cover and simmer 2½ hours, stirring every 30 minutes. Add flour, mixed to a smooth paste with butter. Mix well. Cover and cook 15 minutes more. Season with pepper and stir until slightly thickened. Serves 6 to 8.

(1581)   SQUIRREL POT PIE

3 grey or fox squirrels	1 teaspoon salt
½ cup flour	¼ teaspoon pepper
3 tablespoons butter	Rounds of biscuit crust
1 chopped onion	

Skin, dress, draw, and clean squirrels according to instructions for roast rabbit or hare (No. 1575). Disjoint. Roll in flour. Melt 2 tablespoons butter in saucepan. Sauté squirrel until brown. Add 1 quart boiling water, onion, salt, and pepper. Cover closely and simmer 1 hour. Lay rounds of crust on squirrel. Cover. Boil 15 minutes. Remove crusts and squirrel to hot platter. Blend 1 tablespoon flour and 1 tablespoon melted butter and add to liquor, mixing well. Pour over squirrel and crusts. If desired lemon juice, sherry, or Worcestershire sauce may be added to gravy before serving. Serves 6 to 8.

(1582)   POSSUM

Plunge animal into very hot but not boiling water 2 minutes. Pull out or scrape off hair without damaging skin. Slit belly from throat to hind legs. Remove entrails, feet, eyes, and brains. Do not remove head or tail. Wash thoroughly. If possible, freeze for 3 or 4 days. When ready to cook, wipe with a cold, damp cloth. Sprinkle with salt and pepper. Put in roasting pan. Add 1 cup water and juice of 1 lemon. Bake in hot oven (400° F.) 15 minutes, turning once. Cover. Reduce heat and bake in moderate oven (350° F.) 1¼ to 1½ hours.

(1583)   ROAST GROUSE

Pick, singe, dress and clean grouse, inside and out. Sprinkle with salt and pepper. Brush with oil or fat. Tie wings and legs close to body. Put in roasting pan. Add 1 cup boiling water. If desired lay strip of bacon over bird. Bake in hot oven (450° F.) 15 minutes, basting frequently with melted butter or pan drippings. Reduce heat and bake 25 minutes more in moderate oven (350° F.). Remove birds. Add a little flour, mixed to a smooth paste with cold water, to pan liquor. Cook until well blended. While grouse is cooking, boil the livers. Pound into a thick paste with butter, pepper, salt, and some juice from pan.

Spread this mixture on toast and serve grouse on top. Garnish as desired. Prairie chickens, partridges, and pheasants may all be prepared and cooked in the same manner. If desired birds may be stuffed with poultry stuffing (No. 2064) before cooking. Allow 1 grouse per serving.

(1584)   BROILED GROUSE

Pick, singe, dress, and clean grouse. Split down back. Brush with butter or oil. Sprinkle with salt and pepper. Broil birds in moderate heat about 18 minutes, turning to insure even browning. Allow 1 grouse per serving.

(1585)   SMOTHERED GROUSE

Pick, singe, dress, and clean grouse. Split down back. Rub with oil or butter. Sprinkle with salt and pepper. Brown lightly in little fat. Cover closely and steam at low heat (300° F.) 45 minutes. Add a little flour, mixed to a smooth paste with cold water, to pan liquor and use for gravy. Allow 1 grouse per serving.

(1586)   PHEASANT

To roast pheasant select hens from 2½ to 3½ pounds. Prepare and cook according to instructions for roast chicken (No. 1525), allowing about 1 hour for cooking. Baste frequently. Baked pheasant is prepared by disjointing the dressed and cleaned bird, covering with light cream, and baking, covered, ½ to ¾ hour in a moderate oven (350° F.). To smother pheasant, disjoint and cover with cream as above; then cover and let simmer ½ to ¾ hours. Braised pheasant is prepared by browning disjointed bird in melted butter after seasoning and rolling in flour and then simmering bird for 30 minutes in covered pan with chopped bacon, carrots, sliced celery, chopped onion, chopped parsley, water or stock, and desired spices and seasonings. One pheasant will provide 4 servings.

(1587)   ROAST WILD TURKEY

Prepare and cook according to instructions for roast turkey (No. 1560), allowing 20 to 25 minutes per pound for roasting.

(1588)   ROAST WILD DUCK OR GOOSE

Carefully pick, singe, draw, and clean, inside and out. Sprinkle inside and out with salt and pepper. Stuff with bread stuffing (No. 2063) or place an onion or apple in cavity. Sew opening and tie legs and wings close to body. Rub body with butter or oil or cook with slices of bacon on breast. Bake in moderate oven (350° F.) about 18 minutes per pound, basting often. Serve with currant jelly and gravy made from pan drippings and giblets. Mallards, widgeons, teals, redheads, and canvasbacks are all prepared in the same manner. The latter is the best eating. Some persons prefer wild duck very rare, in which case bake at high heat (475° F.) for 15 minutes. Allow 1 pound of duck per serving.

(1589)   BROILED WILD DUCK

Carefully pick, singe, draw, and clean, inside and out. Split them down back. Brush with butter or oil. Sprinkle with salt and pepper. Broil at moderate heat (350° F.) until tender, about 18 minutes, turning often. Serve on buttered toast (No. 988) with maître d'hôtel sauce (No. 2027) or lemon butter (No. 2029). Garnish with chopped parsley. Allow 1 pound duck per serving.

(1590)   SALMI OF WILD DUCK

See recipe for salmi of game (No. 1594).

(1591)   WOODCOCK AND SNIPE

Pick, singe, dress, and clean birds. Discard feet. Dip lower legs in boiling water and remove skin. Skin head, remove eyes, and twist head around so as to use bill as skewer to hold bird in shape. Wrap birds in slices of bacon or salt pork. Broil at medium heat for 12 minutes, turning often. Or, bake in hot oven (450° F.) for 15 minutes. Serve on buttered toast (No. 988). Some bird-flesh lovers prefer to have the birds cooked without drawing entrails which shrivel and are easily removed after cooking. Allow 1 bird per serving.

(1592)   QUAIL

Follow recipes for preparing and cooking grouse (No. 1583, 1584, and 1585), cooking quail at same temperatures about 2/3 as long. Allow 1 quail per serving.

(1593)   PARTRIDGE

Follow recipes for preparing and cooking grouse (No. 1583, 1584, 1585), cooking about 10 minutes longer to roast or steam and 5 minutes longer to broil. Allow 1 partridge per serving.

(1594)   SALMI OF GAME

2 cups diced cooked game, any kind	1/4 teaspoon pepper
	1 teaspoon powdered sage
1 tablespoon butter	1 tablespoon flour
1/2 pound bacon, chopped	2 cups hot stock or water
1 diced onion	3 tablespoons Worcester-
1 sliced carrot	shire sauce
1 teaspoon salt	

Melt butter in saucepan. Add bacon, onion, carrot, salt, pepper, and sage. Cook for five minutes, stirring constantly. Stir in flour, blending well. Add stock and let simmer slowly 30 minutes. Add Worcestershire sauce and strain. Add game and simmer 10 minutes more. Serve on buttered toast (No. 988). If raw game is used, sauté in little fat until well browned, add to gravy at same point as cooked game, but then simmer 30 to 45 minutes. Serves 6.

(1595)   STUFFED SNAILS

24 canned snails	1 tablespoon chopped
24 snail shells	celery
2 tablespoons butter	1 teaspoon chopped onion
2 tablespoons chopped parsley	1/8 teaspoon pepper

Force snails into shells. Pack opening with a mixture of the other ingredients. Bake in a moderate oven (350° F.) 30 minutes. Serve hot. To prepare fresh snails, soak live snails in salt water 5 hours. Wash and rinse several times. Boil 30 minutes. Pick snails from shells and boil in fish stock (No. 504) 3 to 4 hours. Then treat as canned snails. Serves 6.

(1596)   FRIED FROGS' LEGS

Only the hind legs of frogs can be eaten. Cut off the feet. Peel off skin, turning inside out. Wipe with cold, damp cloth. Season with salt and pepper. Roll in flour. Dip in well-beaten egg, diluted with a little water. Roll in cracker crumbs. They may be dipped in fritter batter (No. 2706) instead, in which case omit flour and egg. Fry in deep, hot fat until golden brown, about 3 minutes. Serve with tartar sauce (No. 2044). They may also be sautéed in a little butter without egging or crumbing, in which case serve plain, seasoned with salt and pepper, or with white sauce (No. 2004). If desired legs may be seasoned by soaking in a mixture of lemon juice, salt, and pepper 1 hour before rolling in flour. Allow 2 legs per serving.

(1597) FROGS' LEGS WITH MUSHROOMS

12 frogs' legs	⅛ teaspoon pepper
½ cup mushrooms, canned or fresh	1 cup milk
	½ cup meat (No. 501) or chicken stock (No. 502)
3 tablespoons butter	
1 tablespoon flour	2 egg yolks
½ teaspoon salt	1 tablespoon cream

Prepare frogs' legs for cooking according to recipe for fried frogs' legs (No. 1596). If fresh mushrooms are used, peel caps and cut off stems. Melt butter in pan. Put in legs and mushrooms and sauté to a light brown. Sprinkle with flour, salt, and pepper. Add milk and stock. Bring to boil. Cover. Reduce heat and let simmer 10 minutes. Beat egg yolks with cream and add to pan. Stir well but do not boil. Serve hot with buttered toast (No. 988), garnished as desired. Serves 6.

(1598)   FROGS' LEGS FRICASSEE

12 frogs' legs	3 tablespoons butter
¼ cup flour	½ cup heavy cream
1 teaspoon salt	1 tablespoon chopped parsley
⅛ teaspoon pepper	

Skin frogs' legs as for fried frogs' legs (No. 1596). Sprinkle with flour, salt, and pepper. Melt butter. Brown legs in butter for

3 minutes, turning frequently. Remove legs. Blend 1 tablespoon flour into pan butter. Add cream slowly. Cook over low heat for 5 minutes, stirring constantly. Add legs and parsley. Serve on hot platter. Serves 6.

(1599)   BOILED TERRAPIN AND TURTLE

Diamond back Chesapeake and Long Island terrapin are preferred. They should always be purchased alive. Plunge into boiling, salted water. Boil until skin on head and feet can be rubbed off. Drain. Wash in cold water. Repeat draining and washing three times. Drain finally. Rub skin from legs and pull out nails. Cover with cold, salted water. Bring to a boil. Reduce heat. Cover and let simmer until legs can be dented, about ½ to ¾ hour. Separate from shells. Remove and discard intestines and gall bladder, a sac near the neck. Place turtle in pot, with the liver, heart, and eggs, if any. Season with salt and pepper. Cover and simmer until meat is ready to drop from bones. Remove meat and serve hot with medium white sauce (No. 2004).

(1600)   TURTLE À LA KING

Prepare according to instructions for chicken à la king (No. 1547), using chopped, cooked turtle meat instead of chicken.

(1601)   WARMED-OVER MEATS

1 tablespoon butter	1 teaspoon catchup
1 tablespoon flour	½ teaspoon salt
1 cup stock	⅛ teaspoon pepper
½ teaspoon Worcestershire sauce	2 cups cold cooked meat, in slices

Melt butter in pan. Stir in flour. Blend well. Add stock and seasonings. Bring to boil. Add meat and cook slowly until heated through. Serve hot. Serves 6.

(1602)   MEAT HASH

2 cups chopped cooked meat	1 teaspoon chopped onion
2 cups chopped potato	1 teaspoon chopped celery
1 teaspoon salt	2 tablespoons butter
¼ teaspoon pepper	¼ cup milk or meat stock

Meat should be chopped first. Add potato and chop together. Melt fat in frying pan. Spread hash evenly in pan, moisten with liquid to which seasonings have been added, and cook slowly 20 minutes, shaking occasionally to prevent sticking. If desired, hash may be put in greased pan and baked in moderate oven (350° F.). Serves 6.

(1603) MEAT LOAF

3 pounds chopped cold cooked meats in any proportions
2 eggs
1 teaspoon salt
1 teaspoon pepper
1 onion
2 cups bread crumbs
1 cup milk
⅓ cup tomato catchup
1 teaspoon Worcestershire sauce

Mix all the ingredients together thoroughly and shape into a loaf. Place in pan and bake 30 minutes in moderate oven (350° F.). Serves 6. Pan gravy (No. 2001) or tomato sauce (No. 2035) goes well with this.

(1604) MEAT BALLS

2 cups chopped cold cooked meat in any proportion
1 teaspoon chopped chives
1 teaspoon thyme
1 teaspoon chopped marjoram
1 teaspoon chopped parsley
2 tablespoons flour
¼ teaspoon salt
⅛ teaspoon pepper
2 tablespoons butter

Mix thoroughly chopped meat and herbs. Form into balls or patties. Roll in flour, mixed with salt and pepper. Brown well in hot butter. Serves 6. Pan gravy (No. 2001) or tomato sauce (No. 2035) goes well with this.

(1605) MEAT TURNOVERS

Follow instructions for sausage turnovers (No. 1471), substituting any chopped, cold, cooked meat for sausage and ham. Any combinations of meat, in any proportions, can be used. If quantity of meat is too small, add boiled rice (No. 107) or chopped, boiled potatoes (No. 1834).

(1606)   MEAT PIE

2 onions, thinly sliced   ¼ teaspoon pepper
2 cups sliced cold cooked   2 cups canned or fresh
   meat   sliced tomatoes
2 tablespoons flour   2 cups bread crumbs
1 teaspoon salt   1 tablespoon butter

Put alternate layers of onion and meat in greased baking dish
until all is used. Sprinkle each layer with flour, salt, and
pepper. Pour in canned tomatoes or lay fresh tomato slices,
peeled, as top layer. Put bread crumbs on top. Dot with butter.
Bake in moderate oven (350° F.) until brown or until tomatoes are soft. Serve hot. Serves 6.

(1607)   MEAT SOUFFLÉ

2 cups milk   1 egg yolk
1 tablespoon flour   1 tablespoon chopped
1 tablespoon butter   parsley
1 teaspoon salt   2 tablespoons chopped
¼ teaspoon pepper   onion
½ cup bread crumbs   1 tablespoon chopped
2 cups chopped cold   celery
   cooked meat

Melt butter in pan. Stir in flour, blending well. Add milk,
salt, and pepper. Cook five minutes, stirring constantly. Add
crumbs, parsley, onion, and celery. Cook 3 minutes more. Add
meat and well-beaten egg yolk, mixing well. Pour mixture
into greased baking dish. Bake in moderate oven (350° F.) 35
minutes. Serve hot. Serves 6.

(1608)   BAKED RICE AND MEAT

2 cups cold cooked meat, cut   2 onions, chopped
   in cubes   1 tablespoon Worcester-
2 cups meat stock   shire sauce
1 cup canned tomato   2 tablespoons butter
1 teaspoon salt   ½ cup uncooked rice
¼ teaspoon pepper

Put meat, stock, tomato, salt, pepper, 1 onion, and Worcestershire sauce in pan. Heat 10 minutes. Melt butter in frying pan.
Add remaining onion and rice. Brown slightly. Add to other
mixture. Turn all into a greased baking dish and bake 40 minutes in moderate oven (350° F.). Serves 6.

(1609)   SHEPHERD'S PIE

2 cups cold cooked meat, cut
   in pieces
1½ cups hot mashed potatoes
   (No. 1835)
½ teaspoon salt
⅛ teaspoon pepper

Few drops onion juice
3 tablespoons leftover
   gravy
1 egg yolk
2 teaspoons cold water

Grease a baking dish and line bottom with mashed potato. Season meat with salt, pepper, and onion juice; moisten with gravy; place in dish. Cover evenly with mashed potatoes. Spread top with egg yolk, beaten in cold water. Bake in hot oven (425° F.) until brown and heated through, about 20 minutes. Individual pies may be made in small dishes or custard cups, cooking about 15 minutes. Serves 6.

(1610)   SCALLOPED MEAT

2 cups chopped cold cooked
   meat
¼ cup bread crumbs
1 tablespoon butter
1 tablespoon flour
1 cup stock, milk, or water
1 teaspoon salt

¼ teaspoon pepper
2 tablespoons chopped
   parsley
2 tablespoons chopped
   celery
2 tablespoons chopped
   onion

Put layer of bread crumbs in greased baking dish. Add meat. Melt butter in frying pan. Stir in flour, blending well. Add liquid slowly. Cook 5 minutes, stirring constantly. Add other ingredients. Pour over meat. Bake in moderate oven (350° F.) 30 minutes. Serves 6.

(1611)   MEAT STEW

2 cups cold cooked meat, in
   2-inch cubes
2 onions, sliced
2 tablespoons fat
1 cup diced carrot

6 medium-size potatoes,
   quartered
3 tablespoons flour
Dumplings (No. 954)

Brown meat and onions in melted fat in deep pan. Add carrot and potatoes. Cover with hot water or meat stock. Cover and let simmer until vegetables are almost soft. Thicken by adding flour, mixed to a smooth paste in cold water. Drop dumplings on top. Cover and cook until dumplings are light, about 15 minutes longer. Serves 6.

(1612)   MEAT CROQUETTES

Prepare and cook same as chicken croquettes (No. 1553). Any cooked meat or any combination of meats can be used.

(1613)   MINCED MEAT ON TOAST

Mix two cups of any finely ground or chopped, cooked meat in gravy, white sauce (No. 2004), or tomato sauce (No. 2035). Heat thoroughly, add a little butter, and season to taste. Serve on toast. Serves 6.

(1614)   CREAMED MEAT

2 cups medium white sauce (No. 2004)
2 cups chopped cold cooked meat

¼ cup boiled peas (No. 1823)
¼ cup sliced broiled mushrooms (No. 1802)

Into hot sauce mix other ingredients and keep on heat until heated thoroughly. Serves 6.

(1615)   AMERICAN CHOP SUEY

Follow recipe for American chicken chop suey (No. 1554), using any other cold, cooked meat instead of chicken.

(1616)   MEAT FRITTERS

1 cup sifted flour
1 teaspoon baking powder
½ teaspoon salt
2 teaspoons sugar
1 beaten egg
¾ cup chopped cooked meat

1 cup milk
1 tablespoon chopped celery
1 tablespoon chopped onion
1 slice chopped broiled bacon (No. 1464)

Sift flour, baking powder, salt, and sugar together. Combine egg and milk and add, blending smooth. Stir in other ingredients. Let fall from tablespoon into deep, hot fat (340° to 375° F.) and fry until golden brown, 2 or 3 minutes. This provides 10 fritters.

(1617)   BAKED TAMALES

1½ cups corn meal
1 tablespoon salt
2 cups chopped cold cooked
   meat

1 teaspoon chili powder
1 cup beef stock (No. 501)
   or water

Boil 2 cups water and salt. Stir in corn meal until mixture resembles mush. Season meat with chili powder. Put layer of corn meal in baking dish. Add meat. Cover with balance of corn meal. Pour in beef stock. Bake in moderate oven (350° F.) until nicely browned. Serves 6.

(1618)   HUNGARIAN SAUSAGE LOAF

2 pounds bulk pork sausage
4 cups bread crumbs
1 egg

1 cup sour cream
Paprika

Combine sausage, bread crumbs, slightly beaten egg, and sour cream. Season with paprika. Pack firmly into a loaf pan. Bake in a moderate oven (350° F.) until done, about 1½ hours. Serves 6.

(1619)   STUFFED SAUSAGE ROLL

2 pounds bulk sausage
2 cups diced raw apples

2 cups bread crumbs
2 small onions, diced

Pat the sausage on waxed paper into a flat rectangular shape about ½ inch thick. Mix the apples, onions and bread crumbs and spread this over the meat. Roll like a jelly roll, tucking the edges in. Place in a baking dish and bake in a moderate oven (350° F.) until done, about 45 minutes. Serves 6.

Vegetables

~~~~~~~~~~~~~~~~~~~~~~~~~~~~

THE past decade has seen the American homemaker turn more and more to vegetables as a source of appetizing, health-giving meals. The sales of many popular vegetables have doubled, tripled, and quadrupled in that period.

There are several reasons for this increase. In general, vegetables in season are economical in comparison with meats and fish. They can be prepared in many tempting ways which will delight the entire family. They provide, if chosen in the proper proportions, practically all necessary vitamins and chemicals for body health.

Unless wisely purchased, there can be much waste in vegetables. Following are given the best-known methods for selecting the best and avoiding the poor.

ARTICHOKES

A compact, heavy, globular, plump globe or French artichoke, which yields slightly to pressure, and which has large, tightly clinging, fleshy leaf scales of a good green color, is the most desirable. Freshness is indicated by the green color, which with age or injury becomes brownish.

ASPARAGUS

Asparagus to be its best must be fresh, tender, and firm, with close, compact tips. A tender stalk is brittle and is easily punctured. A wilted appearance or a spreading tip is often an indication that considerable time has elapsed since cutting. Stalks of this type may or may not be freshened by placing in water.

LIMA BEANS, FRESH

The pods of the best unshelled lima beans should be well filled, clean, bright, fresh, and of dark-green color. The shelled lima bean should be plump, with tender skin, and the skin should be of good green or greenish-white color. Dried, shriveled, spotted, yellowed, or flabby pods of unshelled lima beans may be old or may be affected by disease.

FABA or FAVA BEANS

The same factors that constitute quality in the lima, and the same factors of condition, should be looked for when buying these beans.

SNAP BEANS

The best snap beans should be clean, fresh in appearance, firm, crisp, tender, free from blemish, and all in a lot should be of the same stage of maturity so that they will cook uniformly. Firm, crisp, tender beans will snap readily when broken. Pods in which the seeds are very immature are the most desirable. Generally, length is unimportant. If the seeds are half grown or larger, the pods are likely to be tough, woody, and stringy.

BEETS

Good beets should be smooth and free from blemish. Beets that are rough or ridged or that have deep growth cracks are wasteful and may be tough or woody. It is expected that beets will have some soil on them, but those that are caked with it are difficult to clean. Soft, flabby, or shriveled beets are wasty and usually poor in flavor.

BEET TOPS

Beet tops of good quality are young, fresh, tender, and clean. Old, coarse, heavy-veined, heavy midribbed leaves are usually tough and generally undesirable. Flabbiness and wilting are the factors of condition that most frequently affect beet tops, but freshness can be restored if the tops are not old and the condition is not too far advanced. Occasionally beet tops may be found to be in a slimy condition. Such stock should be avoided.

BROCCOLI

Italian sprouting broccoli to be of good quality should be fresh, clean, and not overmature. The stalks should be tender and firm, and the buds in the clusters or heads should be compact and should not have reached the stage of development at which the color of the flower is evident. The general color should be either darkish green or purplish green depending on the variety. Overmature sprouting broccoli is usually woody, tough, or stringy. Overmaturity is indicated by the bud clusters or heads which will be open to the extent that the full yellow or purple color of the blossom is distinct.

BRUSSELS SPROUTS

Brussels sprouts of good quality are hard or firm, compact, fresh, of bright appearance, and of a good green color. Puffy brussels sprouts, although edible, are usually of poor quality and flavor. Those that are wilted or have yellowed leaves are usually aged or stale and because of their wastiness should be avoided.

CABBAGE

Prime heads of cabbage should be reasonably solid, hard, or firm and heavy or fairly heavy for their size; they should be closely trimmed, that is, the stems should be cut close to the head, and all except three or four of the outer or wrapper leaves should be removed. Early or new cabbage usually is not so solid or firm as cabbage of the late or winter crop. The defects of cabbage are readily detected. Worm injury, decay, yellowing of the leaves, and burst heads are the most common. Heads containing them should be avoided.

CARROTS

Good quality carrots are firm, clean, fresh in appearance, smooth, well-shaped and of good color. Usually, although not always true, poor color of carrots is associated with poor quality. The tops of bunched carrots should be fresh and green.

CAULIFLOWER

Fine quality in cauliflower is indicated by white or creamy-white, clean, heavy, firm, compact curd, with the jacket or outer leaves, fresh, turgid, and green. "Riciness" (a term used to describe the curd when the flower clusters have begun to grow, giving the curd a ricelike or granular appearance) is not objectionable unless it is associated with an advanced stage of spreading of the flower clusters. Age is indicated by the yellowing of the leaves, particularly if the leaves drop from the stalk when handled, but other factors may cause yellowing of the leaves.

CELERY

The most desirable celery is that of medium length, thickness, and solidity, with stalks or "branches" that are brittle enough to snap easily. Pithy or stringy celery is undesirable. Pithiness can be detected by pressing or twisting the stalks and stringiness can be detected by breaking. Freezing injury may cause a browning and drying of the tops, which may later decay. Celery is subject to a trouble called blackheart that is usually followed by rots which attack the heart of the stalk. The rot, if present, can be seen by separating the branches and examining the heart.

CHARD

The leaves of chard should be crisp, tender, fresh, and free from insect injury. The stalks should be fleshy and crisp. Stalks that are wilted or rubbery may be tough, coarse, and stringy.

CHICORY, ENDIVE, ESCAROLE

Crispness, freshness, and tenderness are the essential factors of quality. Wilted plants can be freshened by being placed in water, but they may be wasty and should be examined carefully for decay, which may appear as a browning of the leaves or as a slimy rot. Tough, coarse-leaved plants are undesirable since the usually delicate bitter flavor is likely to be so intensified as to be objectionable.

COLLARDS

Collards of good quality are fresh, crisp, clean, and free from insect injury. Wilting and yellowing of the leaves indicate age or other form of damage. Sometimes worm injury will be found in the form of perforated leaves.

CORN, GREEN

A good ear of corn is one that has a fresh green husk and a cob that is well filled with bright, plump, milky kernels that are just firm enough to offer slight resistance to pressure. Dry, yellowed, or straw-colored husks are an indication of age or damage. Corn that is too immature is unsatisfactory. The kernels on cobs of immature corn are very small and very soft, and when cooked they lack flavor.

CUCUMBERS

Cucumbers for slicing purposes should be firm, fresh, bright, well-shaped, and of good color. The flesh should be firm and the seeds immature. Withered or shriveled cucumbers should be avoided. Their flesh is generally tough or rubbery and somewhat bitter. Overmaturity is indicated by a generally overgrown puffy appearance. The color of overmature cucumbers is generally dull and not infrequently yellowed, the flesh is rubbery and tough, the seeds are hard, and the flesh in the seed cavity is almost jelly-like.

DANDELIONS

Large, tender-leaved, fresh green plants are the best. Age or damage is indicated by wilted, flabby, yellow, or tough leaves.

EGGPLANTS

Heavy, firm eggplants free from blemish and of a uniform dark color are the most desirable. Age, poor handling, keeping too long, or picking too soon, will cause eggplants to be wilted, shriveled, soft, or flabby.

GARLIC

Sound, plump cloves of garlic with the outer skin or sheath unbroken are the most desirable. Such cloves are usually found in garlic bulbs that are clean, compact, and well cured—that is, dry but not soft or spongy and with the outer skin intact. Soft or spongy garlic is undesirable.

GREENS

Greens to be of good quality must be fresh, young, green, and tender. Plants or leaves of any of the leafy vegetables to be used as greens which are poorly developed, injured by insects or show excessive dirt, coarse stems, dry or yellowish leaves, are usually lacking in quality and are wasty.

KALE

Kale of good quality is usually of a dark- or bluish-green color, clean, and has a fresh appearance. Some kale has a bronzed or brownish appearance. Such kale is not attractive but the flavor is usually not harmed, as the condition is probably brought about by cold weather during the growing period. Plants with wilted and yellow leaves should be avoided unless they can be trimmed without too much waste.

LETTUCE

Head lettuce to be of good quality should be fresh, crisp, tender, and fairly firm to hard. It should be free from decay, and should not have an excess of outer or wrapper leaves. Occasionally lettuce that has well-developed seed stems is found on the markets. Usually such lettuce has a bitter flavor and is wasty. A seed stem that is objectionable although it has not burst through the head can usually be detected by wide spaces between the outer leaves at their base and a knoblike swelling protruding beyond the normal contour of the head.

MUSTARD GREENS

Mustard greens should be fresh, tender, crisp, and of a good green color. Wilted, dirty, discolored, or spotted leaves are indications of poor condition and quality. Mustard with such leaves is usually old and wasty. A common indication of age and toughness is the presence of seed stems.

OKRA

Young, tender, fresh, clean pods of small-to-medium size ranging from 2 to 4 inches in length usually are of good quality. Pods that are in good condition, fresh, and tender, will snap easily when broken, they are easily punctured. Pods that have passed their prime will present a somewhat dull, dry appearance.

ONIONS

Bright, clean, hard, well-shaped, mature onions with dry skins are usually of good quality. Onions in which the seed stem has developed are undesirable. Usually the neck of such stock is thick and a tough woody condition of the stem or neck is noticeable. The tough stem extends from the very base of the bulb, causing much waste. Decay generally appears as a rot attacking either the outer scales or the scales in the center of the bulb.

ONIONS, LEEKS, and SHALLOTS

Green onions, leeks, and shallots of good quality have green fresh tops, and medium-sized necks which are well-blanched for at least 2 or 3 inches from the root and which are young, crisp, and tender. Bruised, yellowed, wilted, or otherwise damaged tops are not attractive and may indicate poor quality or damaged necks.

PARSLEY

General appearance is the factor of quality for parsley. It should be bright, green, fresh, and free from dirt and yellowed leaves. Slightly wilted stock can be revived by placing it in water. Badly wilted stock is unattractive and practically worthless.

PARSNIPS

Smooth, firm, well-shaped parsnips of small to medium size are generally of the best quality. Soft, flabby, or shriveled roots are usually pithy or fibrous.

PEAS

Peas of the best quality are young, fresh, tender, and sweet. Quality is indicated by the color and condition of the pod, which should be bright green, somewhat velvety to the touch, and fresh in appearance. The pods should be well to fairly well filled, and the peas contained therein well developed. Pods of immature peas are usually flat, are dark green in color, and may have a wilted appearance. Pods that are swollen, of poor color, or more or less flecked with grayish specks, may be in an advanced stage of maturity.

PEPPERS

Peppers to be of good quality, must be mature, firm, well-shaped, thick-fleshed, and of good color and fresh appearance. Immature peppers are usually soft, pliable, thin-fleshed, and pale in color. Peppers in which the seeds are undeveloped are immature. In mature peppers the seeds are hard. A firm pepper may yield to slight pressure, but it should not be shriveled, limp, or pliable.

POTATOES

Potatoes that are sound, smooth, shallow-eyed, and reasonably clean are usually of good quality. Medium-sized potatoes are usually the most desirable for general use, but selection on the basis of size should be governed by the use for which they are intended. Dirty potatoes are unattractive, but the presence of dirt does not injure the eating quality. Wilted, leathery, discolored potatoes should be avoided. They may have been dug too early or injured by some other means. Occasionally both new and old potatoes show a green color on some part of the surface. This condition is known as sunburn. Sunburned potatoes should be avoided as they usually have a bitter taste that makes them largely inedible. Potatoes may sometimes have a hollow center known as hollow heart. The size of the cavity may be very small and cause no appreciable waste; or it may be very large, causing considerable waste. Another serious defect known as blackheart is sometimes found—a black, often slimy center in the potato.

Potatoes injured by freezing are sometimes found on the market during the winter. Bad cases are indicated by the potato being wet and leaky; or when cut across, it may show a black ring just within the outer surface. In such potatoes the flavor is usually affected, and the flesh turns dark in cooking.

RADISHES

A good radish is well-formed, smooth, firm, tender, crisp, and mild in flavor. The condition of the leaves is not always an indication of quality. While they may be fresh, bright and green the radishes may be spongy and pungent.

SALSIFY (OYSTER PLANT)

Smooth, firm, well-shaped roots of medium size are generally of the best quality. Soft, flabby, or shriveled roots are usually in poor condition.

SPINACH

Well-developed stocky plants with fresh, crisp, clean leaves of good green color are best. Small, straggly, or overgrown stalky plants are often tough. Bruising and crushing may occur in handling; such spinach is very wasty. Plants with yellow leaves, seed stems, or very coarse leaf stems may be tough and woody. Wilted spinach or that which shows yellowing should be critically examined. Decay may be present in the form of a soft, slimy rot.

SQUASH

Summer squash should be fresh, fairly heavy for the size, free from blemish, and the rind so tender that it can be very easily punctured. Winter squash should be heavy for its size and free from blemish, and the rind should be hard.

SWEET POTATOES

Good sweet potatoes are smooth, well-shaped, firm, and of bright appearance. The most common defects of sweet potatoes found upon the markets are decay, misshape, and growth cracks. Badly misshapen potatoes and those with growth cracks are undesirable only from the viewpoint of waste in preparation.

TOMATOES

Good-quality tomatoes are mature, firm but not overripe, fairly well formed, plump, smooth, of good color, and free from blemish. There are many defects in tomatoes which are serious only from the standpoint of waste in preparing for table. Catfaces or scars around the blossom end are typical of the defects within this class.

TURNIPS

Turnips that are smooth, firm, with few leaf scars around the crown, and with very few fibrous roots at the base are usually of good quality. The condition of the tops of bunched turnips is an indication of quality. The tops should be fresh, green, young, and turgid. Yellowed or wilted tops of bunched turnips may indicate damage of some kind, possibly caused by long keeping.

TIME CHART FOR STEAMING VEGETABLES

The times in this chart are for young, tender vegetables, cooked covered, in from one-half to a cup and a third of water. Increase time for old vegetables, for high altitudes, or for greater "doneness."

Vegetable	Method of Preparation	Cooking Time	Your Time
Asparagus	Tied in serving-sized bundles	18-20 min.	
Beans, Green or Wax	Cut in thin slivers, lengthwise	18-20 min.	
Beans, Green or Wax	Cut crosswise	25-30 min.	
Beans, Lima	Shelled	20-25 min.	
Beets	Shredded	15-18 min.	
Beets	Diced or sliced thin	20-25 min.	
Beets	Whole, with 1" stems	35-45 min.	
Broccoli	Stalks split	25-30 min.	
Brussels Sprouts	Whole	20-25 min.	
Cabbage	Shredded	10-12 min.	
Carrots	Shredded	10-12 min.	
Carrots	Quartered or sliced crosswise	20-25 min.	
Cauliflower	Separated into flowerets	15-18 min.	
Cauliflower	Whole	25-30 min.	
Chard, Swiss	No water added	18-20 min.	
Corn on Cob	Whole	8-12 min.	
Kohlrabi	Sliced or quartered	25-35 min.	
Onions	Small, whole	20-25 min.	
Onions	Medium, whole	30-35 min.	
Parsnips	Quartered lengthwise	25-35 min.	
Peas, Green	Shelled	18-22 min.	
Potatoes, White	Medium, whole	25-30 min.	
Potatoes, Sweet	Medium, whole	25-30 min.	
Spinach	No water added	10-15 min.	
Squash, Hubbard	Cut in 2" pieces	25-30 min.	
Squash, Summer	Cut in thin slices	10-15 min.	
Tomatoes	Sliced or quartered, no water	10-15 min.	
Turnips, White	Sliced or cut in 1" cubes	20-25 min.	
Turnips, Yellow	Sliced or cut in 1" cubes	25-30 min.	

(1701) ARTICHOKES

Cut stem and tough outside leaves from French artichokes. Remove the thistle-like center or "choke." Soak in salted water ½ hour. Boil about 25 minutes in salted water to which 1 tablespoon vinegar has been added. Drain. Serve with hollandaise sauce (No. 2022) or with vinaigrette dressing (No. 746). Allow 1 artichoke per serving.

(1702) JERUSALEM ARTICHOKES

Cube or slice and cook in boiling salted water 20 minutes. Serve with white sauce (No. 2004). After boiling this may be put in greased baking dish, covered with white sauce, sprinkled with grated cheese, and be baked in moderate oven (350° F.) until brown. Or, the boiled cubes may be sautéed in a little butter with chopped onion.

(1703) STUFFED ARTICHOKES

Wash thoroughly. Remove thistle-like center. Remove hearts with potato scoop. Chop hearts. Mix with an equal amount of bread crumbs and add enough melted butter to moisten. Add a little chopped ham and season with pepper. Stuff into artichokes. Tie securely. Put in greased baking pan. Add a little stock (No. 501) or water. Bake in moderate oven (350° F.) 1 hour. Allow 1 artichoke per serving.

(1704) BOILED ASPARAGUS

Tough lower ends should be cut off. Cook in deep saucepan standing upright. The steam will cook the tender tips while the hard stalks will be cooked in the boiling water. Or break into 1 inch pieces, cooking tough parts first and adding the tender tips the last 15 minutes. Allow 6 stalks per serving.

(1705) ASPARAGUS ON TOAST

Boil tied bunch of asparagus 25 minutes in boiling salted water. Drain. Arrange on buttered toast (No. 988). Spread generously with butter. Season with salt and pepper to taste.

Allow 6 stalks per serving. Appropriate sauces to be used instead of butter are vinaigrette dressing (No. 746), medium white sauce (No. 2004), hollandaise sauce (No. 2022), or béarnaise sauce (No. 2032).

(1706)   GRILLED ASPARAGUS

2½ cups boiled asparagus (No. 1704), cut in pieces	1½ cups bread crumbs
½ cup grated cheese	1 tablespoon melted butter
	Salt—Pepper—Paprika

Drain asparagus. Mix cheese, crumbs, and butter. Add seasonings to taste. Roll asparagus in crumbs. Place on broiler pan and heat through, turning frequently to brown evenly. Serve on hot platter, garnished with parsley and pimiento. Serves 6.

(1707)   HUNGARIAN ASPARAGUS

2½ cups boiled asparagus (No. 1704), cut in pieces	1 cup buttered bread crumbs
¼ cup sour cream	

Drain asparagus. Lay in single layer in greased baking dish. Cover with crumbs. Add cream. Bake in moderate oven (350° F.) until crumbs are golden brown. Serves 6. If desired, the asparagus may be rolled in crumbs before being placed in dish.

(1708)   BAKED BEANS

2 cups dried beans, pea, lima, or kidney	¼ teaspoon mustard
½ cup cubed salt pork	⅛ teaspoon pepper
¼ cup molasses	2 tablespoons butter

Rinse beans in colander with cold water. Cover with cold water and soak 12 hours. Drain. Cover with salted boiling water. Simmer slowly 1½ hours. Drain. Put in greased baking dish or bean pot with salt pork scattered in. Mix molasses, mustard, pepper, and 2 cups hot water. Add to beans. Dot with butter. Cover and bake in moderate oven (350° F.) until beans are soft, about 3 hours. Uncover last 30 minutes of cooking to brown beans. Serves 6.

(1709)   PICNIC BEANS

1 1-pound 14-ounce can baked beans with molasses and pork	¼ teaspoon dry mustard
2 tablespoons dark brown sugar	1 14-ounce can pineapple gems
Dash of salt	2 tablespoons sirup, drained from gems
	4 slices bacon, if desired

Pour beans into an oven casserole or 4 individual casseroles. Add brown sugar, salt, mustard, pineapple gems which have been drained and 2 tablespoons of the pineapple sirup. Mix well, cover and bake in a moderately hot oven (375° F.) 25 to 30 minutes or until beans are very hot. Beans may be topped with bacon slices before placing in the oven, if desired. Serves 4.

(1710)   BEAN LOAF

½ pound baked beans (No. 1708)	½ onion, chopped
½ cup tomato juice	Salt—Pepper

Mix ingredients, seasoning to taste with salt and pepper. Mold into a loaf. Put in greased baking pan. Bake 30 minutes in moderate oven (350° F.) Serve with tomato catchup or slices of onion. If desired, 1 cup grated cheese or chopped nuts may be added to loaf. Serves 6.

(1711) BEAN AND PEANUT CROQUETTES

2 cups baked beans (No. 1708)	1 cup stewed tomatoes (No. 1893)
2 tablespoons butter or fat	1 cup roasted peanuts, chopped
2 tablespoons chopped onion	1½ teaspoons salt
1 tablespoon chopped green pepper	⅛ teaspoon pepper
3 tablespoons flour	1 cup bread crumbs
1 beaten egg	

Rub beans through a coarse sieve. Melt butter or fat. Add onion and green pepper. Sauté until slightly browned. Add flour and tomatoes. Cook, stirring constantly, until thickened. Add bean pulp, peanuts, salt, pepper, and ¼ cup crumbs. Mix thoroughly. Mold into croquettes. Roll in beaten egg, diluted with a little cold water. Roll in crumbs. Let stand 10 minutes. Fry in deep hot fat (375° F.) until brown. Drain on unglazed paper. Serves 6.

(1712)   STRING OR WAX BEANS

Remove strings from green or wax beans. Cut through, lengthwise, and then in halves, crosswise. Cook in a small amount of boiling water until tender, adding a little salt during the last few minutes of cooking. Drain and serve at once. They may be covered generously with butter. Allow ¼ pound raw beans per serving.

(1713)   BEANS WITH BROWN BUTTER

2½ cups cooked green or wax beans (No. 1712)
2 tablespoons butter

⅛ teaspoon nutmeg
Dash pepper

Drain the liquid from the beans and reduce, by boiling, to about one-half cup. Brown the butter in a saucepan by heating and stirring it constantly until lightly browned. Add the beans, liquid, nutmeg, and pepper, and simmer together for a few minutes. Serves 4 to 6.

(1714)   STRING BEANS WITH CELERY

Cook a pound sliced string beans (No. 1712) with a dash each of salt and sugar in small amount of water, until tender. Without draining, add one cup boiled diced celery (No. 1761) and dress with cream. Season to taste with salt, pepper, and nutmeg. Serves 6.

(1715) STRING BEANS WITH ROSEMARY

2 pounds string beans
Salt—Pepper
4 tablespoons olive oil

1 clove garlic
½ teaspoon rosemary

String the beans and cut them in half. Put a layer into a saucepan. Salt them, then add another layer and more salt and so on until all are used. Add ½ cup water, cover tightly, and steam ½ hour over slow heat. Cook down the little water that remains. Heat the oil in a frying pan, add garlic, split lengthwise and speared with toothpicks, and let it brown on all sides. Add beans. Add rosemary. Stir well and add a dash of pepper and more salt if needed. Cover closely and cook for 10 minutes. Discard garlic and serve either hot or cold. Serves 6.

(1716)   JEWISH SWEET, SOUR BEANS

2 tablespoons cooking oil	1½ tablespoons vinegar
2 tablespoons flour	⅛ teaspoon cinnamon
1 tablespoon brown sugar	2½ cups cooked green beans
¼ teaspoon salt	(No. 1712)

Heat oil. Add flour and stir until smooth. Add other ingredients. Cover and simmer until liquid is reduced about ⅔. Serves 6. The amounts of sugar and vinegar may be changed to suit individual taste. The juice of pickled peaches or pears is good in this dish.

(1717)   BOILED LIMA BEANS

Soak dried lima beans in water 12 hours. Drain. Cook in boiling salted water until tender. Drain. Add salt and butter. For creamed lima beans serve these in thin white sauce (No. 2004). Allow ¼ pound raw, shelled beans per serving.

(1718)   LIMA BEAN AND PEANUT ROAST

2½ cups boiled lima beans (No. 1717)	½ cup milk
1 cup roasted shelled peanuts	1 teaspoon salt
2 cups mashed potatoes (No. 1835)	¼ teaspoon paprika
1 beaten egg	⅛ teaspoon white pepper
	1 teaspoon chopped onion

Drain beans. Chop peanuts fine. Put layer of potatoes in greased baking dish. Add layer of beans, then a layer of peanuts. Repeat until all ingredients are used. Mix other ingredients and pour over mixture in dish. Bake in moderately hot oven (375° F.) 30 minutes. Serve with tomato (No. 2035) or cheese sauce (No. 2008). Serves 6.

(1719)   LIMA BEANS EN CASSEROLE

¼ pound salt pork
2½ cups boiled lima beans
  (No. 1717)
1 small onion, sliced

½ cup diced carrots
1 tablespoon butter
½ teaspoon salt
⅛ teaspoon pepper

Fry fat out of salt pork. Put in greased baking dish. Add other ingredients. Half fill dish with water. Cover and bake in slow oven (300° F.) until carrots are tender. Serves 6.

(1720)   LIMA BEAN TOMATO RAREBIT

4 tablespoons butter
3 tablespoons flour
½ teaspoon salt
Dash cayenne
½ teaspoon Worcestershire
  sauce

2½ cups boiled lima beans
  (No. 1717)
2½ cups stewed tomatoes
  (No. 1893)
1 cup diced American
  cheese

Melt butter over hot water. Add flour, salt, cayenne, and Worcestershire sauce. Drain liquid from beans and tomatoes and add to butter-flour mixture. Cook, stirring constantly, until thick. Add beans, tomatoes, and cheese. Heat thoroughly in double boiler. Serve on buttered toast (No. 988). Serves 8.

(1721)   BOILED DRIED BEANS

Pick over beans. Soak in water 10 hours. Drain. Cover generously with fresh water. Add slight amount of salt to water. Boil, covered, until tender, 2 to 3 hours. Some of the bean varieties which may be cooked this way are the black, kidney, lima, pea, soy, and yellow-eye. One cup dried beans yields about 2½ cups boiled beans.

(1722)   KIDNEY BEAN RAREBIT

4 tablespoons butter
½ green pepper, finely
  chopped
¾ pound American cheese

2 cups boiled kidney beans
  (No. 1721)
¼ cup milk
Salt—Pepper

Toast or crackers

Melt butter. Add green pepper and cook over low heat 5 minutes. Slice cheese and add to mixture. Stir constantly over low heat until cheese is melted. Add kidney beans and the milk. Stir until well blended and heat through. Season with salt and pepper. Serve on toast or crackers. Serves 6.

(1723) BAKED KIDNEY BEANS

2 tablespoons diced onion
2 tablespoons diced pimiento
1/3 cup catchup

2 1/2 cups boiled kidney beans
(No. 1721)
2 strips bacon

Mix together the onion, pimiento, catchup, and beans. Pour into a shallow baking dish. Cut the bacon in two-inch pieces and arrange on top of beans. Bake in a moderate oven (375° F.) for 1 hour, or until bacon is crisp. Serves 5. Plain baked beans (No. 1708) or baked beans with tomato sauce (No. 2035) may be used instead of kidney beans.

(1724) SPANISH KIDNEY BEANS

2 1/2 cups boiled kidney beans
(No. 1721)
1/4 pound bacon, chopped

1 cup stewed tomatoes
(No. 1893)
1 onion chopped

Place layer of beans in greased baking dish. Sprinkle with some of bacon, tomatoes, and onion. Repeat until all ingredients are used. Bake in slow oven (300° F.) until bacon is crisp. Serves 4 to 6.

(1725) SHELL BEANS

Cook same as string beans (No. 1712), using very little water which should all be absorbed in cooking.

(1726) BOILED BEETS

Wash beets. Cut off most of stalks and roots. Cook in boiling salted water until tender. Peel. Slice into warm dish. Season to taste with salt and pepper. Serve hot with vinegar or spread generously with butter. Allow 2 small beets per serving.

(1727)   **BEET GREENS**

Select young beet tops. Wash carefully in several waters to remove all grit. Put entire plants, including roots, in pan. Cover with boiling water and boil rapidly until tender, about ½ hour. Season with salt during cooking. Chop coarsely. Add butter and serve hot.

(1728)   **BEETS PIQUANTE**

6 small beets	1 tablespoon sugar
1 tablespoon butter	1 teaspoon salt
¼ cup water	⅛ teaspoon pepper
¼ cup vinegar	

Cook beets in boiling salted water until tender. Melt butter and add water, vinegar, sugar, salt, and pepper and bring to the boiling point. Remove skins of beets. Slice and reheat in sauce. Serve very hot. Serves 6.

(1729)   **SAUTÉED BEETS**

2 cups boiled beets, cubed	1 teaspoon sugar
(No. 1726)	Salt—Pepper
3 tablespoons butter	Lemon juice

Sauté beets in butter until almost dry. Add sugar, salt, and pepper during cooking. Put on hot dish. Sprinkle with lemon juice. Serves 4.

(1730)   **STUFFED BEETS**

6 medium-sized boiled beets	1 tablespoon butter
(No. 1726)	Salt—Pepper
1 cup boiled peas (No. 1823)	

Cut beets in halves, crosswise. Hollow out some of pulp. Mix insides with peas and butter. Season to taste with salt and pepper. Heat through. Pile into beet cups and serve hot, garnished with a sprig of parsley. Serves 6.

(1731) BEET HASH

2½ cups boiled beets, diced   6 boiled potatoes
    (No. 1726)   (No. 1834), chopped
       2 tablespoons fat

Drain beets. Mix with potatoes. Melt fat in frying pan. Add vegetable mixture. Cook, stirring occasionally, until well browned. Serves 6.

(1732) DICED BEETS AND BACON

2½ cups diced boiled beets   4 slices bacon, chopped
    (No. 1726)   Salt—Pepper

Fry bacon crisp (No. 1464). Add beets and heat through. Season to taste with salt and pepper. Serves 4 to 6. A teaspoon of vinegar may be added if desired.

(1733) BEET AND TOMATO EN CASSEROLE

2½ cups diced boiled beets   ½ cup grated cheese
    (No. 1726)   2 cups bread crumbs
2½ cups stewed tomatoes   2 tablespoons fat
    (No. 1893)   Salt—Pepper

Put ½ beets into bottom of greased baking dish. Add half the tomatoes then half the cheese in layers. Season to taste with salt and pepper. Add ½ bread crumbs. Dot with 1 tablespoon fat. Repeat. Brown in moderate oven (350° F.) 20 minutes. Serves 6.

(1734) BROCCOLI WITH ONION SAUCE

1 bunch broccoli   Salt—Pepper
2 tablespoons minced onion   2 teaspoons lemon juice
3 tablespoons butter

Cut off woody portions of broccoli and the large outer leaves. Wash and soak in salted water a few minutes. Then cook, uncovered, in boiling salted water 15 to 20 minutes, or until tender. Sauté onion in butter until lightly browned. Add salt, pepper, and lemon juice. Add broccoli and heat 1 minute. Serves 4.

(1735)   BRUSSELS SPROUTS

Wash and clean 1 quart of Brussels sprouts and remove any withered leaves. Soak in cold salt water for 1 hour. Drain. Cover with boiling salted water and cook 20 to 25 minutes in uncovered saucepan. Drain and heat in 1½ cups medium white sauce (No. 2004). Serves 6.

(1736)   CABBAGE

Cut a head of cabbage in quarters and let stand in cold water 1 hour. Shred and discard the hard core. Cook in a small amount of boiling salted water 20 minutes. Drain and season with salt and pepper. Serves 4.

(1737)   SAUTÉED CABBAGE

5 tablespoons butter or fat	¼ cup water
6 cups finely shredded cabbage	1 tablespoon sugar
	¼ teaspoon mustard
¼ cup milk or cream	½ teaspoon salt

Melt butter and fry cabbage in it slowly 10 to 15 minutes. Mix other ingredients with ¼ cup water and add to the cabbage. Mix well and heat thoroughly. Serves 6.

(1738)   SCALLOPED CABBAGE

3 cups cooked shredded cabbage (No. 1736)	2 cups medium white sauce (No. 2004)
1 cup soft bread crumbs	½ cup grated cheese

Mix cabbage and white sauce together. Put a layer of cabbage in a greased baking dish, add a layer of crumbs, and repeat process until all the ingredients are used. Sprinkle with cheese. Bake in a hot oven (375° F.) about 20 minutes or until brown. Serves 6.

(1739)   STUFFED CABBAGE

1 medium-sized cabbage	½ cup milk
1 pound beef	1 beaten egg
1 slice bacon or salt pork	Salt—Pepper
1 onion	1 green pepper
½ cup bread crumbs	

Select solid cabbage, not too large. Remove outside leaves. Cut out stalk end, leaving a hollow shell. Chop uncooked beef with bacon and onion. Add crumbs soaked in milk, beaten egg, salt, and pepper. Shape mixture into balls or cakes, arrange in cabbage. Arrange strips of sweet pepper on top of cabbage, tie in cheesecloth, then steam or boil until tender. Serve with to-mato sauce (No. 2035). Serves 6.

(1740)   FRIED SAUERKRAUT

2½ cups sauerkraut   3 tablespoons butter

Drain sauerkraut. Fry a light brown in melted butter. Serves 4.

(1741)   SAUERKRAUT AND POTATOES

¼ pound diced bacon   6 boiled potatoes
3½ cups sauerkraut   (No. 1834)
Salt—Pepper   ½ tablespoon melted fat

Fry bacon until crisp (No. 1464). Add sauerkraut and season to taste with salt and pepper. Cook slowly 10 minutes. Turn onto hot platter. Arrange potatoes on top. Brush potatoes with fat. Serves 6.

(1742)   SCALLOPED SAUERKRAUT AND
TOMATOES

2½ cups stewed tomatoes   2 cups bread crumbs
(No. 1893)   2½ cups sauerkraut
Salt—Pepper
2 tablespoons butter

Drain tomatoes, reserving liquid. Put solid parts in greased baking dish. Sprinkle with salt and pepper. Dot with butter. Cover with layer of crumbs. Add layer of sauerkraut. Alter-nate layers, seasoning and dotting each with butter, until all ingredients are used. Have layer of buttered crumbs on top. Add tomato liquid. Bake in hot oven (400° F.) 20 minutes. Serves 6.

(1743)   SAUERKRAUT AND APPLE

¼ cup butter or fat
2 tablespoons flour
2½ cups sauerkraut

¼ cup vinegar
3 whole cloves
2 tablespoons brown sugar
1 large apple, chopped fine

Melt butter or fat in pan. Add flour and stir until smooth. Add sauerkraut, vinegar, cloves, brown sugar, and ¾ cup water. Cover and let simmer 20 minutes. Add apple just before serving. Serves 6.

(1744)   SAUERKRAUT COTTAGE PIE

1 cup cooked meat, minced
1 cup sauerkraut, chopped
¼ cup stock (No. 501)
   or gravy

¼ teaspoon pepper
2 cups mashed potatoes
   (No. 1835)
1 tablespoon fat

Mix meat, sauerkraut, stock, and pepper. Add salt if necessary. Turn into greased baking dish. Top with mashed potatoes. Dot with fat. Bake in moderate oven (350° F.) until potato is brown, about 30 minutes. Serves 6.

(1745)   BOILED CARROTS

Wash and scrape hard skin from carrot. Put in boiling water and boil until tender, adding salt during cooking.

(1746)   CREAMED CARROTS

Use sliced boiled carrots (No. 1745) instead of mixed vegetables in recipe for creamed vegetables (No. 1914).

(1747)   STEAMED CARROTS

2 tablespoons butter
2 cups scraped and sliced
   carrots

2 tablespoons chopped
   onion
Salt—Pepper

Melt butter and put with other ingredients in a double boiler. Steam until tender. Serves 6.

(1748) FRIED CARROTS

Cut off small tips of boiled carrots (No. 1745). Cut in halves or quarters, according to the size of the carrot. Dip pieces in milk, and roll in flour or bread crumbs until thoroughly covered. Fry in deep hot fat (375° F.) until a delicate brown. Drain on unglazed paper. Sprinkle with salt and serve hot. Allow 1 carrot per serving.

(1749) DICED CARROTS AND BACON

2½ cups diced boiled carrots (No. 1745)	¼ pound bacon
	1 onion, chopped

Chop bacon and sauté until almost crisp. Drain off part of fat. Add carrots and onion to bacon and sauté until brown. Serves 6.

(1750) BAKED DICED CARROTS

2½ cups diced boiled carrots (No. 1745)	1½ cups medium white sauce (No. 2004)
1 cup bread crumbs	2 tablespoons fat

Put layer of carrots in bottom of greased baking dish. Cover with some of sauce and a layer of crumbs. Dot with fat. Continue to alternate layers until all ingredients are used with layer of crumbs on top. Bake in moderate oven (350° F.) 30 minutes. Serves 6.

(1751) BELGIAN CARROTS

2½ cups diced boiled carrots (No. 1745)	1 onion, chopped
2 tablespoons butter	Salt—Pepper
2 teaspoons powdered sugar	1 tablespoon chopped parsley

Mix all ingredients. Put in greased baking dish. Bake in moderate oven (350° F.) 15 to 20 minutes. Serves 6.

(1752)   CALIFORNIA CARROTS

8 medium-sized carrots	1 tablespoon flour
1 teaspoon salt	½ cup consommé
1 onion, minced	(No. 507)
½ clove garlic	½ cup sauterne win
1 tablespoon butter	Salt—Pepper

Parsley

Scrape and slice or dice carrots. Parboil 10 minutes in boiling salted water. Drain. Fry minced onion and half a small clove of garlic in butter. When yellow, remove and discard garlic. To onion and butter add flour. Blend well. Stir in consommé and sauterne wine. Season to taste. Put in partially cooked carrots and let simmer until tender, adding a little more consommé if sauce gets too thick. Garnish with parsley. Serves 6.

(1753)   PEANUT AND CARROT LOAF

2 tablespoons butter or fat	2 cups carrots, chopped
3 tablespoons flour	1 cup dry bread crumbs
1½ cups stewed tomatoes	¼ cup chopped parsley
(No. 1893)	1½ teaspoons salt
2 cups roasted peanuts,	⅛ teaspoon pepper
chopped	

Melt butter. Add flour and tomatoes. Cook, stirring constantly, until thickened. Add other ingredients. Mix thoroughly. Mold into a loaf. Line a greased loaf pan with paper. Pack in the mixture. Bake in hot oven (400° F.) 1 hour. Serves 6.

(1754)   CARROT AND SPINACH MOLD

1½ cups boiled carrots	1½ teaspoons salt
(No. 1745), cubed	1½ cups boiled spinach
3 tablespoons butter, melted	(No. 1870), chopped
1 egg, well beaten	Sprigs of parsley

Mash carrots with a fork and mix with beaten egg and 1 tablespoon melted butter and ½ teaspoon salt. Fill small greased molds half-full of the carrot mixture. Season the chopped spinach with remaining salt and butter and fill molds to top with spinach, packing them tightly. Place molds in pan of hot water and bake in a moderate oven (350° F.) 20 minutes. Turn out on hot platter and serve garnished with parsley. Serves 6.

(1755)   BOILED CAULIFLOWER

Prepare and cook same as boiled cabbage (No. 1736), breaking cauliflower into small pieces. One cauliflower serves 6.

(1756)   CREAMED CAULIFLOWER

Mix 1 boiled cauliflower (No. 1755) with 2 cups medium white sauce (No. 2004). Heat through. Serves 6.

(1757)   FRENCH FRIED CAULIFLOWER

1 medium-sized head cauliflower	1 egg
1 cup bread crumbs	2 tablespoons cold water
	Salt—Pepper

Break the cauliflower into flowerets and cook gently 10 minutes. Drain. Roll in bread crumbs, then in the mixture of egg and water and again in crumbs. Fry in deep hot fat (375° F.) until browned. Drain on absorbent paper. Sprinkle with salt and pepper and serve very hot. Serves 6.

(1758)   CAULIFLOWER AU GRATIN

1 boiled cauliflower (No. 1755), broken in pieces	2 cups medium white sauce (No. 2004)
	½ cup grated cheese

Drain cauliflower. Put in greased baking dish. Pour over sauce. Sprinkle with cheese. Bake in hot oven (400° F.) 20 to 25 minutes. Serves 6.

(1759)   BOILED CELERIAC

Prepare same as boiled celery (No. 1761).

(1760)   CELERY

Celery should be carefully washed and broken apart. The tender heart should be used on table or in salads. The tough outer stalks can be used for cooking or soup. It can be kept crisp in ice water or in a cold covered container.

(1761)   BOILED CELERY

Scrub stalks clean. Remove all tough strings. Slice thin in saucepan. Cover with water. Boil gently until tender. Season with salt during cooking.

(1762)   CREAMED CELERY

1½ tablespoons butter or fat	¾ cup liquid in which
3 tablespoons flour	celery was boiled
1 teaspoon salt	1 large bunch celery, cut
⅛ teaspoon pepper	in ½-inch lengths
¾ cup milk	and boiled (No. 1761)

Melt butter in pan. Add flour, salt, and pepper. Blend well. Add celery liquid and milk. Bring to a boil, stirring constantly. Add celery. Heat through. Serves 6. This can be turned into a greased baking dish, sprinkled with bread crumbs and grated cheese, and baked in moderate oven (350° F.) 20 minutes.

(1763)   CELERY, CREOLE STYLE

1 cup diced celery	2 teaspoons finely chopped
2 tablespoons finely chopped	green pepper
onion	⅓ cup canned or stewed
1 tablespoon butter	tomatoes (No. 1893)

⅓ teaspoon salt

Put celery in saucepan with ½ cup boiling water and boil 10 minutes or until tender. Melt butter, add onion, salt and pepper, and cook slowly 5 minutes and stir in the tomatoes, add celery and cook the entire mixture 10 to 15 minutes longer. Serves 4.

(1764) CHAYOTE

Pare either before or after boiling. Slice 1 inch thick. Boil, covered, in little salted water 20 to 25 minutes, until tender. Drain. Serve with melted butter or any desired sauce. Allow 1 chayote for 5 servings. Pan-fried chayote is prepared by dipping slices of boiled chayote in bread crumbs and sautéing in little butter until brown on both sides. Or the boiled slices may be dipped in fritter batter (No. 2706) and cooked in deep, hot fat (375° F.) until golden brown. To bake chayote put boiled slices in greased baking dish, add medium white sauce (No. 2004) to cover, sprinkle with crumbs and grated cheese, and bake in moderate oven (350° F.) 15 minutes.

(1765) CHICORY OR ENDIVE

Wash carefully in several waters. Tie each head securely. Put in generous amount of boiling, salted water and cook until tender, about ½ hour. Drain. Sauté in small amount of butter 8 to 10 minutes, turning occasionally to cook evenly. Season to taste with salt and pepper. Serve hot. Allow 1 pound chicory for 4 servings.

(1766) CORN ON THE COB

Remove outer husks from corn. Peel back inner husks. Remove silk. Replace inner husks. Tie with strips of husk. Drop into a generous amount of boiling water and boil 7 to 10 minutes.* Serve in husks or stripped. Plenty of butter, salt, pepper. Or, the husks may be removed before boiling. (*Cooking time varies with freshness and state of maturity of corn, from 3 to 15 min. Over-boiling makes corn tough.)

(1767) OVEN ROASTED CORN

Place ears of corn (with husks) in a moderate oven (350° F.) and bake 30 minutes. Remove husks and silk and serve with butter. Allow 1 or 2 ears per serving.

(1768) PAN ROAST CORN-ON-THE-COB

Remove husks and silks from corn. Soak in cold water for ½ hour. Arrange ears of corn in a large heavy skillet or a heavy

Dutch oven. Add ½ cup water, cover tightly, and steam over medium heat 5 to 8 minutes. Remove cover and allow water to evaporate. Add 1 tablespoon butter and ⅛ teaspoon salt for each ear of corn. Continue cooking for 5 minutes, rolling corn to prevent browning. Allow 1 or 2 ears per serving.

(1769)   STEWED CORN

Shave kernels off ears of corn without cutting too close to cob. Put in saucepan. Add a little butter and enough water to cover bottom of pan. Cook gently about 15 minutes, seasoning with salt and pepper during cooking.

(1770)   CREAMED CORN

2½ cups stewed corn   1 cup white sauce
   (No. 1769)   (No. 2004)
              Salt—Pepper—Paprika

Heat corn in double boiler 10 minutes. Mix with hot white sauce. Season to taste with salt, pepper, and paprika.

(1771)   BUTTERED CORN

Cut kernels from boiled corn on the cob (No. 1766). Mix with butter. Sprinkle with salt. Allow 1 ear per serving.

(1772)   FRIED CORN

Sauté 2½ cups stewed corn (No. 1769) in a little butter in frying pan until slightly browned. Season to taste with salt and pepper. Serve hot.

(1773)   CHILI CORN À LA CRÈME

2½ cups stewed corn   ¼ teaspon chili powder
   (No. 1769)   ¼ teaspoon salt
½ cup light cream

Drain the corn and add remaining ingredients. Heat. Serves 4.

(1774) SAUTÉED CORN CAKES

2½ cups stewed corn
   (No. 1769)
1 slightly beaten egg
1 teaspoon salt

½ teaspoon paprika
⅛ teaspoon white pepper
2 tablespoons flour
½ cup corn meal

Drain corn. Chop fine. Add egg, salt, paprika, pepper, and flour. Mold into small cakes. Roll in corn meal. Sauté in little fat until brown on both sides. Serve hot with cheese (No. 2008) or tomato sauce (No. 2035). Serves 6.

(1775) CORN LOAF

2½ cups stewed corn
   (No. 1769)
1 cup thick white sauce
   (No. 2004)
1½ cups bread crumbs

¾ teaspoon salt
½ teaspoon paprika
2 tablespoons fat
1 onion, chopped

Drain corn and use liquor for white sauce, adding milk if necessary. Mix corn, sauce, and 1 cup crumbs. Add salt and paprika. Melt fat and brown onion in it. Add to mixture. Put in greased baking dish. Cover with remaining crumbs. Dot with butter. Bake in moderate oven (350° F.) 30 to 40 minutes. Serve hot with cheese sauce (No. 2008) or tomato sauce (No. 2035). Serves 6.

(1776) CORN PUDDING

2 cups stewed corn
   (No. 1769)
2 cups milk
3 eggs
1 tablespoon butter
1 tablespoon minced onion

2 tablespoons sugar
¼ cup minced green
   pepper
1 minced pimiento
1 teaspoon salt

Beat eggs slightly, add the milk, sugar, and salt. Combine corn with other ingredients and add to the milk mixture. Mix well. Turn into a buttered casserole and bake in moderate oven (325° F.) 1 hour. Serve hot with cheese (No. 2008) or tomato sauce (No. 2035). Serves 6.

(1777)   CORN FRITTERS

2 cups raw corn	1/8 teaspoon pepper
1 well-beaten egg	1 tablespoon melted butter
1 1/2 teaspoons sugar	1/4 cup flour
1/3 teaspoon salt	1/2 teaspoon baking powder

Combine corn, egg, sugar, salt, pepper, and butter. Mix and sift flour and baking powder. Add to first mixture. Mix thoroughly. Drop batter from spoon into little fat in hot frying pan and brown both sides. Serves 6.

(1778)   BAKED CORN

2 tablespoons butter or fat	2 cups canned or stewed
2 tablespoons flour	corn (No. 1769)
1 1/4 cups milk	Salt—Pepper
1 tablespoon sugar	2 well-beaten eggs

Melt fat in pan. Add flour. Blend well. Add milk slowly. Bring to a boil, stirring constantly. Add corn and sugar. Season to taste with salt and pepper. Add eggs. Mix thoroughly. Turn into greased baking dish. Bake in moderate oven (350° F.) 25 to 30 minutes. Serves 6.

(1779)   CORN AND TOMATOES

1 1/4 cups stewed tomatoes	1 teaspoon sugar
(No. 1893)	Salt—Pepper
2 1/2 cups stewed corn	Pinch of soda
(No. 1769)	1 tablespoon butter

Mix tomatoes and corn. Simmer, covered, 15 minutes. Add other ingredients. Heat through. Serves 6.

(1780)   BAKED CORN AND CARROTS

12 medium-sized carrots	1 1/2 cups stewed (No. 1769)
1 small onion, sliced	or canned whole grain
2 tablespoons butter	corn
2 1/2 tablespoons flour	6 slices broiled bacon
1 1/4 cups milk	(No. 1464)
Salt—Pepper	

Cook the carrots and onion in boiling salted water until tender. Drain and place in a buttered baking dish. Boil down liquid to ¼ cup. Melt the butter in a double boiler and add the flour and mix well. Add the milk and carrot liquid gradually and cook, stirring constantly, until thickened. Season with salt and pepper. Add corn and pour over the carrots. Bake in a hot oven (375° F.) until heated through. Top with the bacon. Serves 6.

(1781)   BOILED CUCUMBERS

Pare cucumbers. Cut, crosswise, into ½-inch slices. Boil in salted water until tender, about 10 minutes. Drain. Serve hot on buttered toast (No. 988) with white sauce (No. 2004). Allow 1 cucumber for 2 servings.

(1782)   CREAMED CUCUMBERS

Pare cucumbers. Slice thin into hot medium white sauce (No. 2004). Simmer until tender. If desired, sliced hard-cooked eggs (No. 202) may be added to sauce.

(1783)   FRIED CUCUMBERS

2 tablespoons butter or fat	2 tablespoons sugar
2 tablespoons chopped onion	3 tablespoons vinegar
4 large cucumbers, sliced	1½ teaspoons salt
¼ cup water	⅛ teaspoon pepper
½ cup sour cream	⅛ teaspoon paprika
1 egg yolk	

Melt butter, add onion and fry until a delicate brown. Add sliced cucumbers and water. Cook until water is absorbed and cucumbers browned. Mix sour cream, beaten egg yolk, sugar, vinegar, salt, pepper, and paprika. Add to cucumbers and cook slowly until mixture begins to boil. Serves 6.

(1784)   DANDELION GREENS

Wash in several waters. Boil in salted water 15 minutes. Drain. Blanch by pouring cold water over them. Drain. Chop. Season to taste with salt and pepper. Add a little butter and a piece of bacon, if desired. Heat in frying pan until almost dry.

(1785)   **DASHEEN**

Prepare same as potatoes (any style).

(1786)   **FRIED EGGPLANT**

Pare eggplant and cut in thin slices. Sprinkle with salt and let
stand under a weight until some of the juices run out. Drain off
liquid and sprinkle with flour. Dip in slightly beaten egg, diluted
with 2 tablespoons water and seasoned with ½ teaspoon salt
and ⅛ teaspoon pepper. Cover with fine dry bread crumbs. Fry
in little fat 8 to 10 minutes, turning once to brown both sides.
Serves 6.

(1787)   **BAKED EGGPLANT**

2 cups eggplant pulp	Salt—Pepper
2 eggs	1 cup corn flakes
½ cup milk	1 tablespoon butter

Parboil the eggplant about 20 minutes. Cool. Remove the
skin. Press the pulp through a colander. Beat the eggs and milk
together. Add the pulp and seasonings. Put the mixture in a
buttered baking dish. Sprinkle the corn flakes over the top. Dot
with butter and bake in moderate oven (350° F.) until lightly
browned. Serves 6.

(1788)   **EGGPLANT AU GRATIN**

1 large eggplant	⅛ teaspoon pepper
1 cup grated cheese	Few grains cayenne
1 teaspoon salt	2 tablespoons butter or fat

Pare eggplant and cut in slices. Cook in boiling salted water
until tender. Drain well and mash. Put in a layer in a greased
baking dish, sprinkle with cheese, salt, pepper, and cayenne and
dot with butter or fat. Repeat this process until all the ingredients are used, having a layer of cheese on top. Bake in a hot
oven (400° F.) 20 minutes. Serves 6.

(1789) BAKED SLICED EGGPLANT

1 eggplant   ¼ teaspoon pepper
⅓ cup melted butter   ½ cup bread crumbs
1 teaspoon salt

Cut eggplant, crosswise, into 8 ½-inch slices and peel. Brush each slice with melted butter. Add remaining melted butter, salt, and pepper to crumbs. Dip slices into buttered crumbs. Bake, uncovered, on baking sheet in a 450° F. oven 18 minutes. Serves 4.

(1790) SCALLOPED EGGPLANT AND ONIONS

1 medium-sized eggplant   Buttered crumbs
4 medium-sized onions   Salt and ground pepper-
2 tablespoons butter   corns

Peel eggplant. Cut into ¾-inch cubes. Boil until tender and drain. Peel onions, cut in ¼-inch slices. Parboil 5 minutes. Drain well and sauté in butter until tender, but not browned. Put eggplant and onions in alternate layers in a buttered baking dish, seasoning each layer with salt and pepper and covering last one with buttered crumbs. Brown in moderately hot oven (375° F.). Serves 6.

(1791) STUFFED EGGPLANT

1 large eggplant   ½ onion, chopped
½ cup minced ham   Salt—Pepper
2 tablespoons butter

Cut eggplant in halves. Scrape out insides and mix with ham. Put in saucepan. Cover with boiling water and boil until tender. Drain. Add butter and onion. Season with salt and pepper to taste. Fill each half of hull with mixture. Dot with butter. Bake in moderate oven (350° F.) 15 minutes. Serves 6. Bread crumbs, seasoned with chopped onion, also make a delicious stuffing.

(1792) CURLY ENDIVE

Follow recipe for chicory (No. 1765) through boiling, cooking about 20 minutes.

(1793)   ESCAROLE

Follow recipe for chicory (No. 1765) through boiling, cooking about 20 minutes.

(1794)   BOILED FENNEL

Wash in several waters. Tie bunches securely. Put in saucepan. Just cover with boiling, salted water and boil until tender, about 12 minutes. Season to taste with salt and pepper. Serve with melted butter. One pound fennel serves 4.

(1795)   KALE

Select tender leaves. Wash in several waters. Cook, uncovered, in boiling salted water until tender. Drain and chop. Season to taste with salt and pepper. Add a little butter or cream. Reheat for 5 minutes.

(1796)   KOHLRABI

Wash and pare kohlrabi and cut in thin slices. Cover with boiling salted water and cook, uncovered, until tender, about 40 minutes. Drain and heat in medium white sauce (No. 2004). Serves 6.

(1797)   BOILED LEEKS

Wash. Cut off stalks within 2 inches of white. Boil in salted water, uncovered, until tender, about 20 minutes. Serve with melted butter. Allow 1 bunch per serving.

(1798)   STEWED LENTILS

Wash lentils carefully in several waters. Drain. Put in saucepan. Cover with water. Boil slowly until tender. Salt and butter should be added during cooking. If desired, an onion can be added during cooking and removed when done. One pound lentils serves 6.

(1799)   **LETTUCE**

Wash carefully and thoroughly. Keep in covered container in refrigerator. Native lettuce must be separated leaf by leaf before washing. Iceberg or California lettuce may be cut in halves or quarters. Discard hard center. Shred large, mature, outer leaves for salads.

(1800)   **STEWED LETTUCE**

Wash and remove all wilted leaves from lettuce. Put heads in pan. Nearly cover with stock (No. 501). Cook, covered, in moderate oven (350° F.) 30 minutes. Remove lettuce to hot platter. Thicken liquid with a little flour, blended with an equal amount of melted butter. Season to taste with salt and pepper. Pour over lettuce.

(1801)   **SAUTÉED MUSHROOMS**

Peel and stem mushrooms. Rinse in water. Sauté 8 to 10 minutes in little butter, turn frequently to brown evenly. Serve on buttered toast (No. 988) with medium white sauce (No. 2004). One pound mushrooms serves 6.

(1802)   **BROILED MUSHROOMS**

Peel and stem mushrooms. Rinse in water. Put mushrooms carefully in pre-heated broiler. Brush with butter. Broil over hot heat 5 to 7 minutes, turning to cook both sides. Season with salt and pepper. Serve on buttered toast (No. 988) with thick or medium white sauce (No. 2004). Allow 1 pound mushrooms for 6 servings.

(1803)   **STEWED MUSHROOMS**

Trim off damaged or tough parts of stalks. Peel caps if skin is tough. Put in saucepan. Add a little water. Cover and cook about 7 minutes. Season to taste with salt, pepper, and butter. Serve on buttered toast (No. 988) with white sauce (No. 2004). Allow 1 pound for 6 servings.

(1804)   CREAMED MUSHROOMS

18 large mushrooms   Salt—Pepper
1/4 cup butter   1 cup cream
Flour for dredging

Wash and remove stems from mushrooms. Peel caps if skin
is tough. Melt butter in saucepan. Add mushrooms. Cover
closely and cook slowly 10 minutes. Dredge with flour. Season
to taste with salt and pepper. Cover with cream. Cover and
cook slowly 5 minutes longer. Serve on buttered toast (No. 988).
Serves 6.

(1805)   SCALLOPED MUSHROOMS

2 1/2 tablespoons butter   Salt—Pepper
1 tablespoon flour   1 tablespoon chopped
2 cups stock (No. 501)   parsley
2 cups mushrooms   1/4 cup crumbs

Melt 1 tablespoon butter. Stir in flour, blending well. Add
hot stock. Peel and stem mushrooms. Chop stalks and add to
mixture. Simmer, stirring occasionally, until liquid is reduced
one half. Season to taste with salt and pepper. Add parsley. Put
mushroom caps in greased baking dish. Add sauce. Sprinkle with
crumbs. Dot with remaining butter. Bake in hot oven (400° F.)
8 to 10 minutes. Serves 6.

(1806)   MUSHROOM OMELET

Add cooked mushrooms (No. 1800, 1801, or 1802) to omelet
(No. 208) before cooking.

(1807)   SHERRIED MUSHROOMS

12 mushrooms   2 tablespoons sherry
1/2 teaspoon butter   1 cup beef juice, pressed
12 bits of butter, size of   from rump steak
  marbles

Peel and stem mushrooms. Melt butter in saucepan. Remove
from heat and set in mushrooms upside down. Place one bit of
butter in center of each. Return to heat. Cook 2 or 3 minutes,

depending on size of mushrooms. Add beef juice and sherry. Simmer until mushrooms are tender. Season. Serves 4.

(1808) MUSTARD GREENS

Follow recipe for chicory (No. 1765) through boiling, cooking about 18 minutes.

(1809) STEWED OKRA

50 okra pods	Salt—Pepper
¼ pound lean ham, chopped	1 tablespoon butter
1 cup stock (No. 501)	1 tablespoon flour
1 cup stewed tomatoes (No. 1893)	2 tablespoons chopped parsley

Wash pods and cut off both ends. Put in saucepan. Add ham, stock, and tomatoes. Season to taste with salt and pepper. Simmer, covered, 30 to 40 minutes. Blend butter and flour and add to mixture. Cook slowly, stirring constantly, until thickened. Put in heated dish. Sprinkle with parsley. Serves 6.

(1810) BOILED ONIONS

Remove outer skins. Cook in boiling salted water until soft. Season to taste with salt and pepper. Add butter generously. Allow 1 or 2 onions per serving.

(1811) SAUTÉED ONIONS

2 tablespoons butter or fat	¼ teaspoon pepper
2 cups onions, sliced	⅛ teaspoon paprika
1 teaspoon salt	

Melt butter in frying pan. Add onions and sprinkle with seasonings. Mix thoroughly. Cover and cook slowly 30 minutes, stirring frequently. Serves 6.

(1812) FRENCH FRIED ONIONS

Slice 5 Bermuda onions thin. Fry in deep hot fat (375° F.) until brown. Drain on unglazed paper. Sprinkle with salt. Serves 6.

(1813)   CREAMED ONIONS

Boil 6 medium-sized onions (No. 1810). Mix with 1½ cups hot medium white sauce (No. 2004). Heat thoroughly. Serves 6.

(1814)   BAKED ONIONS

3 tablespoons butter	Salt—Pepper
¾ cup chopped nuts	24 small white onions
1 tablespoon sugar	

Heat butter, nut meats, sugar, salt, and pepper in baking dish. Add peeled onions and stir until completely covered with nut meats. Cover dish tightly and bake at 350° F. 1 hour. Serves 4.

(1815)   STUFFED ONIONS

6 large boiled onions (No. 1810)	2 tablespoons tomato catchup
¾ cup chopped cooked meat	Salt—Pepper
2 tablespoons melted butter or fat	¼ cup bread crumbs

Slice off top and remove centers from onions. Combine meat, butter, and catchup and season to taste with salt and pepper. Stuff mixture in onions. Put in greased baking dish, cover, and bake in moderate oven (350° F.) 1 hour. Remove cover. Sprinkle with crumbs. Dot with butter. Bake, uncovered, until crumbs are brown. Serves 6. Diced boiled beets (No. 1726) may be substituted for meat.

(1816)   STUFFED BERMUDA ONIONS

6 Bermuda onions	1 tablespoon parsley, chopped
2 tablespoons butter	2 tablespoons green pepper, chopped
2 tablespoons flour	
1 cup milk	
½ teaspoon salt	1 pound canned salmon
3 hard-cooked egg yolks (No. 202), crumbled	½ cup bread crumbs

Peel onions and cut off tops. Cook in boiling salted water 20 minutes. Drain and remove center sections, leaving onion cups.

Melt butter in skillet and add flour blending to smooth paste. Add milk and salt and cook, stirring constantly, until smooth and thickened. Add egg yolks, chopped parsley, green pepper, and flaked salmon. Fill mixture into onion cups. Sprinkle with bread crumbs, dot with butter, and bake in a 350° F. oven for 30 minutes. Serves 6.

(1817)   BOILED PARSNIPS

Scrape skins from parsnips. Slice into saucepan. Cover with water. Boil slowly until tender, about 1 hour. Add salt during cooking. Serve with egg sauce (No. 2009).

(1818)   FRIED PARSNIPS

Scrape the skins off boiled parsnips (No. 1817). Cool. Slice lengthwise. Season to taste with salt and pepper. Dip in melted butter. Dip in flour. Fry in deep hot fat (375° F.) until brown on both sides.

(1819)   SAUTÉED PARSNIPS

Scrape the skins off boiled parsnips (No. 1817). Slice. Season to taste with salt and pepper. Dredge with flour. Sauté in little fat until lightly browned.

(1820)   BAKED PARSNIPS

Put boiled parsnips (No. 1817) in greased baking dish. Season with salt and pepper. Brush with butter or fat. Bake in moderate oven (350° F.) until brown.

(1821)   PARSNIP FRITTERS

4 boiled parsnips (No. 1817)	1 teaspoon flour
Salt—Pepper	1 beaten egg

Scrape skins from parsnips. Mash. Season to taste with salt and pepper. Mix with flour and egg. Form into little cakes. Fry in little fat until well browned on both sides.

(1822)   PARSNIP PUFFS

5 parsnips	Few grains pepper
3 tablespoons milk	2 eggs
2 tablespoons melted fat	2 tablespoons water
1 teaspoon salt	½ cup dried bread crumbs

Cook parsnips in boiling salted water until tender. Drain and mash and add milk, fat, salt, and pepper. Add one beaten egg. Set aside to cool. Shape into small balls. Roll in crumbs, then in beaten egg, diluted with water, and again in crumbs. Fry in deep hot fat (350° F.) until brown. Drain on unglazed paper. Serves 6.

(1823)   BOILED PEAS

Remove peas from pods. Let stand in cold water ½ hour. Drain. Cook in little boiling water until tender. Sprinkle with salt. Spread generously with butter.

(1824)   PEAS IN THE POD

Leave peas in pod. Wash thoroughly. Cook them in boiling, salted water 20 to 25 minutes, or until tender. Serve in pods with mayonnaise (No. 701) or melted butter.

(1825)   BOILED CHICK PEAS

Substitute chick peas for beans in recipe for boiled dried beans (No. 1721).

(1826)   CREAMED PEAS

2 tablespoons butter	2 cups milk
2 tablespoons flour	2½ cups boiled peas
Salt—Pepper	(No. 1823)

Melt butter. Add flour and stir until smooth. Season with salt and pepper. Add milk. Heat, stirring constantly, until it bubbles. Add peas. Heat thoroughly. Serves 6. A French-style sauce can be made by substituting ½ cup cream for milk and reducing butter to 1 tablespoon and flour to ½ tablespoon.

(1827) PEAS AND CHEESE

2½ cups boiled peas   1 cup grated cheese
  (No. 1823)   ¾ teaspoon salt
  3 tablespoons fat   ⅛ teaspoon pepper

Mix ingredients and cook slowly until cheese melts. Serve on buttered toast (No. 988). Serves 6.

(1828) PEAS ANGLAISE

¼ cup chopped scallions   2½ cups boiled peas
2 tablespoons butter   (No. 1823)
½ teaspoon flour   Salt—Pepper
¼ teaspoon sugar

Sauté scallions in butter three minutes. Mix flour and sugar and add to scallions. Add peas and liquor. Season to taste with salt and pepper. Cook five minutes. Serves 4.

(1829) PEAS WITH LETTUCE

1 quart peas   1 small onion
2 tablespoons butter   1 teaspoon sugar
1 head lettuce, the heart   ¼ cup water

Put all ingredients into a stewpan. Cover and place over the fire. Cook for 5 minutes, tossing the vegetables several times. Draw the pan back where the contents will simmer slowly for ½ hour. Serves 6.

(1830) PEAS AND PEANUT ROAST

1 clove garlic   1 teaspoon salt
1 cup mashed boiled peas   ⅛ teaspoon pepper
  (No. 1823)   ⅙ teaspoon paprika
1 cup chopped roasted   3 tablespoons melted fat
  peanuts   1 egg
1 cup bread crumbs   1½ cups milk
1 cup cottage cheese

Rub a baking dish with cut clove of garlic. Mix peas, peanuts, bread crumbs, and cheese. Add seasonings and fat. Separate egg. Add yolk to mixture. Add milk. Mix well. Beat egg white stiff and fold into mixture. Grease the garlic-rubbed baking dish. Put mixture in dish. Bake in moderate oven (350° F.) 35 minutes. Serves 6.

(1831)   FRIED PEPPER RINGS

Wash peppers. Slice thin, crosswise. Remove seeds and hard tissue. Dip slices in beaten egg, diluted with a little cold water. Dip in bread crumbs. Sauté in little fat until brown on both sides. Or fry in deep, hot fat (375° F.) until browned. Drain on unglazed paper. One pepper will serve 2 .

(1832)   STUFFED PEPPERS

6 green peppers	2 tablespoons butter or fat
1 cup minced cold cooked	1 teaspoon chopped onion
meat	1 teaspoon salt
1 cup chopped tomatoes	¼ teaspoon pepper
1 cup boiled rice (No. 107)	

Wash peppers. Cut a slice from stem end and remove all insides. Mix other ingredients and stuff in peppers. Put in baking dish. Add 1 cup hot water. Bake in hot oven (400° F.) 35 minutes. Serves 6. Bread crumbs may be substituted for rice. Almost any combination of cooked meats or vegetables may be used. Chopped nuts are good, added to stuffing.

(1833)   GREEN PEPPERS IN OLIVE OIL

Wash and remove seeds from 10 sweet green peppers. Parboil in salted water. Drain and dry on a cloth. Put 1 clove garlic in a frying pan with ½ cup olive oil. When hot, remove the garlic, and add the peppers, quartered. Cook until the peppers begin to brown. Add salt and pepper to taste. Serves 8.

(1834)   BOILED POTATOES

Wash potatoes and let stand 1 hour in cold water. Pare and boil in salted water until soft. Drain and keep hot until ready to serve. Do not cover them.

(1835)   MASHED POTATOES

Select uniform- and medium-sized potatoes. Wash, pare, and let stand in cold water 1 hour. Boil in salted water until tender. Drain. Mash or force through a ricer. To each 6 potatoes add 2 tablespoons butter or fat, 1 teaspoon salt, ⅛ teaspoon pepper, and 4 tablespoons hot milk. Beat with a fork until creamy. Serve hot. Allow 1 potato per serving. If desired, buttermilk may be substituted for sweet milk.

(1836)   FRENCH FRIED POTATOES

Peel potatoes. Slice in strips 2 inches long, ¾ inch wide, and ½ inch thick. Put in ice water. Let stand 1 hour. Drain and dry between towels. Fry in deep fat (325° F.) until a golden brown. Drain on unglazed paper. Allow 1 potato per serving. For Parisienne potatoes scoop out little balls with potato scoop and fry as above.

(1837)   BAKED POTATOES

Select medium-sized potatoes. Wash with a vegetable brush to remove all particles of dirt. Soak in cold water 1 hour. Bake in a hot oven (400° F.) 40 to 50 minutes or until soft. Rub skins with butter or fat to soften them. Serve at once as they become soggy if allowed to stand.

(1838)   ROAST POTATOES

Wash potatoes and let stand in cold water 1 hour. Pare and parboil 10 minutes. Drain and put in pan with roast ¾ of an hour before roast is done. Sprinkle with salt and pepper. Baste them when meat is basted and bake until soft and well browned. Or, these may be roasted alone in a greased baking pan if brushed generously with butter or fat.

(1839) SAUTÉED OR BROILED POTATOES

5 medium-sized potatoes   Salt—Pepper
¼ cup fat

Wash potatoes but do not peel. Cook in boiling salted water until just tender. Drain. Pare and cut into ¼-inch slices and sauté in hot fat until nicely browned on both sides or broil over moderate heat, turning to brown both sides. Sprinkle with salt and pepper and serve at once. Serves 6.

(1840)   JULIENNE OR SHOESTRING POTATOES

Peel potatoes. Cut in strips ¼ inch by ¼ inch by 2 inches. Soak 45 minutes in ice water. Drain and dry between towels. Fry in deep fat (325° F.) until golden brown. Drain on unglazed paper. Allow 1 potato per serving.

(1841)   GERMAN FRIED POTATOES

Wash and pare potatoes and slice very thin. Soak them in cold water 1 hour. Drain and dry thoroughly. Put a small amount of butter or fat in a frying pan. Add the potatoes, sprinkle with salt, and cover with a tight fitting lid. Fry slowly until tender and brown, turning occasionally to prevent burning. Allow 1 medium-sized potato per serving.

(1842)   HASHED BROWNED POTATOES

Melt 2 tablespoons fat in a frying pan. Add 2 cups finely chopped cold boiled potatoes (No. 1834), 1 tablespoon chopped parsley, ½ teaspoon salt, and few grains pepper. Mix thoroughly, then allow the potatoes to brown on the under side. Fold over like an omelet. Serves 6.

(1843)   LYONNAISE POTATOES

Slice 1 small onion thin and fry in 1 tablespoon fat until a delicate brown. Add 2 cups cold boiled potatoes (No. 1834), cut in ¼-inch slices. Sprinkle with ½ teaspoon salt and few grains cayenne. Let potatoes brown on the under side, fold over and turn out on hot platter. Sprinkle with 1 teaspoon chopped parsley. Serves 6.

(1844)   CREAMED POTATOES

1 cup milk
1½ tablespoons flour
1 tablespoon butter

2 cups sliced cold boiled
    potatoes (No. 1834)
1 teaspoon chopped parsley

Heat milk. Stir in flour and butter. Heat and stir until smooth and thick. Add potatoes and parsley. Heat, shaking occasionally, until potatoes are heated through. Serves 6. If desired, this can be turned into a greased baking dish, sprinkled with bread crumbs and grated cheese, and baked in moderate oven (350° F.) 20 to 25 minutes.

(1845)   POTATOES AU GRATIN

Grease a baking dish. Arrange slices of cold boiled potatoes (No. 1834) on bottom. Sprinkle with grated cheese, salt, and pepper. Dot with butter. Repeat process until all materials needed are used. Add enough milk to almost cover top layer. Bake in hot oven (400° F.) 20 to 25 minutes. Allow 1 medium-sized potato per serving.

(1846)   DUCHESS POTATOES

Select potatoes of uniform size, wash, pare and let stand in cold water 1 hour. Boil in salted water until tender. Drain off all the water and force through a potato ricer. To 3 cups hot riced potatoes add 2 tablespoons butter or fat, 1 teaspoon salt, few grains paprika, and the beaten yolks of 3 eggs. Force through a pastry bag into different shapes such as pyramids, roses, circles. Brush over with a beaten egg yolk diluted with 1 tablespoon water. Bake in a moderate oven (350° F.) 15 minutes or until a delicate brown. This is an excellent garnish for planked steak or fish.

(1847)   SCALLOPED POTATOES

Follow recipe for potatoes au gratin (No. 1845), eliminating cheese and sprinkling a little flour on each layer. Or, use thin slices of raw potatoes, soaked 1 hour in cold water, and bake in moderate oven (325° F.) 1¼ hours.

(1848)   DUTCH POTATOES

1 small onion, chopped	2 tablespoons chopped
1 tablespoon fat	parsley
3 medium-sized potatoes, cubed	Salt—Pepper

Brown onion in fat. Add potato, parsley, and seasonings. Barely cover with water. Cook until potatoes are tender. Serves 6.

(1849) POTATOES HASHED IN CREAM

3 cups diced boiled potatoes (No. 1834)	2 cups light cream (about)
3 tablespoons butter	Salt—Pepper

Dice potatoes in small, even-sized cubes. Melt butter in heavy frying pan. Add potatoes and stir over medium heat until butter is absorbed. Add cream and cook over low heat about 20 minutes, until mixture is thick. Season to taste with salt and pepper. Serves 6.

(1850) WHOLE POTATOES IN SPANISH SAUCE

¼ cup butter	2 tablespoons chopped pimiento
¼ cup chopped onion	
2 tablespoons chopped green pepper	4 cups tiny white boiled potatoes (No. 1834)

Melt the butter and add the chopped onion, green pepper, and pimiento. Simmer for five minutes. Add the drained potatoes and cook until golden brown. Season to taste. Serves 6.

(1851) GREEN ONION POTATOES

4 large potatoes	1 teaspoon salt
4 tablespoons butter	¼ teaspoon pepper
¼ to ⅓ cup milk	¼ cup green onions

Wash, peel and quarter potatoes. Cook in boiling salted water to cover about 20 minutes or until tender. Drain. Mash. Add butter and heated milk gradually, beating continuously until light and fluffy. Season with salt and pepper. Chop onions fine, including about 3 inches of green stem and fold into potatoes, just before serving. Serves 6.

(1852) STUFFED BAKED POTATOES

6 medium-sized baked potatoes (No. 1837)	1 teaspoon salt
	¼ teaspoon pepper
¼ cup hot milk	⅛ teaspoon paprika
2 tablespoons butter or fat	

Cut a cross in the side of each potato. Turn back corners. Scoop out insides without breaking skin. Combine with other ingredients. Mash and beat until light. Fill potato skins with mixture. Dot with butter. Brown in moderate oven (350° F.). Serves 6. Grated cheese may be sprinkled on potatoes before cooking. Chopped onion and chopped cooked ham may be added to stuffing, if desired.

(1853)   BELGIAN POTATOES

1 quart thinly sliced potatoes	1 teaspoon salt
1/4 cup butter, melted	1/8 teaspoon paprika
	1 tablespoon lemon juice

Put the potatoes into a baking dish. Pour over them half the melted butter to which the seasonings have been added. Bake in a hot oven until potatoes are half cooked. Stir lightly, add remainder of butter mixture, and continue to bake until potatoes are tender and the edges are brown and crisp. Serves 6.

(1854) BAKED POTATOES WITH SAUSAGE

Wash, pare potatoes, and remove centers with an apple corer. Put in each potato a part of a sausage. Place in baking pan in a moderate oven (350° F.) and bake until potatoes are brown, about 40 minutes. Baste with fat while baking. Sprinkle with salt and pepper. Allow 1 potato per serving.

(1855)   POTATO CROQUETTES

2 cups mashed potatoes (No. 1835)	2 tablespoons butter
1/8 teaspoon white pepper	1/4 teaspoon celery salt
1/2 teaspoon salt	1/4 cup flour
2 eggs	1 cup bread crumbs

Beat 1 egg, mix with potatoes, and add other ingredients. A little milk is sometimes needed if potatoes are dry. Heat mixture in a saucepan, stirring. When it leaves the side of the pan, turn it on to flat dish. Cool. Mold into croquettes. Roll in flour. Dip in other well-beaten egg, diluted with a little cold water. Roll in bread crumbs. Fry in deep, hot fat (375° F.) until well browned. Serves 6.

(1856)   POTATO CAKES

Mold cold mashed potatoes (No. 1835) into patties. Dredge with flour. Fry in little fat, turning once to brown both sides.

(1857)   POTATO PANCAKES

3 medium-sized raw potatoes	1 egg
1 tablespoon flour	1 teaspoon salt
1 tablespoon cream	

Grate potatoes. Add other ingredients. Stir well. Cook by spoonfuls in heavy frying pan in hot fat. Serves 6.

(1858)   POTATO FRITTERS

3 cups hot mashed potato (No. 1835)	Few grains pepper
	2 tablespoons flour
2 tablespoons fat	1 tablespoon chopped parsley
1 teaspoon salt	
1 teaspoon sugar	2 eggs

To the potatoes add fat, salt, sugar, pepper, flour, and parsley. Add beaten egg yolks and mix well. Fold in stiffly beaten egg whites. Drop by tablespoons in deep hot fat (375° F.) and fry 5 to 8 minutes or until a delicate brown. Drain on unglazed paper. Serve hot. Serves 6.

(1859)   POTATO PUFFS

½ cup fat	½ teaspoon salt
½ cup flour	¼ teaspoon pepper
2 eggs	3 boiled potatoes, pared and riced (No. 1834)
⅛ teaspoon nutmeg	

Mix fat with ½ cup boiling water. Bring to a boil. Stir in flour and cook until well blended. Cool. Beat in eggs, one at a time. Add other ingredients. Drop from spoon in deep hot fat (350° F.) and fry 10 minutes. Yield: 10 puffs.

(1860)   STUFFED MASHED POTATO

2 cups mashed potato (No. 1835)	½ cup thick white sauce (No. 2004)
1 cup boiled peas (No. 1823)	1 cup bread crumbs
	1 beaten egg

Mold potatoes into small balls. Combine peas and sauce. Push finger into center of balls and fill hole with pea mixture. Mold to completely cover peas with potato. Roll balls in crumbs. Dip in egg, diluted with a little cold water. Roll again in crumbs. Fry in deep hot fat (375° F.) until well browned. Drain on unglazed paper. Serves 6.

(1861) POTATO SOUFFLÉ

3 cups hot mashed potatoes (No. 1835)	2 teaspoons chopped parsley
2 tablespoons butter or fat	1/8 teaspoon cayenne
2 tablespoons chopped onion	3 eggs
1 teaspoon salt	

Combine potatoes, butter, onion, parsley, cayenne, and salt. Separate eggs. Beat yolks and add to mixture, mixing thoroughly. Beat egg whites stiff and fold into mixture. Put in greased baking dish. Set in pan of water. Bake in moderate oven (350° F.) 50 to 60 minutes. Serves 6.

(1862) POTATO CHIPS

Peel potatoes. Cut, crosswise, in very thin slices. Let stand, covered with ice water, 45 minutes. Drain and dry between towels. Fry in deep fat (325° F.) until golden brown. Drain on unglazed paper. Sprinkle liberally with salt.

(1863) CHEESED POTATO CHIPS

Spread out potato chips (No. 1862) in shallow pans. Sprinkle generously with grated American cheese. Bake in hot oven (400° F.) 10 minutes. Serve hot.

(1864) MASHED PUMPKIN

Follow recipe for mashed squash (No. 1876).

(1865) BAKED PUMPKIN

Follow recipe for baked squash (No. 1878).

(1866)   CREAMED RADISHES

2 cups sliced radishes   2 cups medium white sauce
(No. 2004)

Simmer radishes in water until tender, about 20 minutes. Drain. Add to hot white sauce. Serves 6.

(1867)   SALSIFY

Prepare according to directions for parsnips, either boiled (No. 1817), fried (No. 1818 or 1819), or as fritters (No. 1821).

(1868)   CREAMED SCALLIONS

3 bunches scallions
4 tablespoons butter
4 tablespoons flour
1 teaspoon salt
1/4 teaspoon pepper
1 cup milk

1 cup beef broth
(No. 529)
2 tablespoons minced parsley
1 teaspoon onion juice or Worcestershire sauce

Wash scallions. Remove root ends and any wilted green shoots. Cut in inch pieces and cook in large amount of boiling salted water about 10 minutes, until tender. Melt the butter and stir in flour and seasonings. When well blended, add milk and broth slowly, stirring constantly over low heat until mixture thickens and boils. Add the parsley and onion juice or Worcestershire sauce. Drain scallions and add to sauce. Serves 6.

(1869)   SCAROLA

Same as escarole (No. 1793).

(1870)   BOILED SPINACH

Cut leaves from roots. Wash in several waters, making certain that all sand is removed. Put in saucepan. Heat gradually in own juice and boil until tender. Season to taste with salt, pepper, and butter. Allow 1 pound uncooked spinach for 3 servings.

(1871) CREAMED SPINACH

Heat 4 cups chopped, boiled spinach (No. 1870) in 2 cups medium white sauce (No. 2004). Serves 6.

(1872) SPINACH AND EGG

2 pounds spinach	1 teaspoon salt
2 tablespoons butter or fat	2 chopped hard-cooked
1 teaspoon chopped onion	eggs (No. 202)
¼ teaspoon mustard	½ cup spinach water
⅛ teaspoon pepper	6 slices bacon

Pick over spinach and wash thoroughly. Cook in saucepan using only the water which clings to the leaves. Add ½ teaspoon salt. When tender, drain and chop. Melt butter. Add onion, mustard, pepper and salt. Sauté until onion is slightly browned. Add spinach, eggs, and spinach water. Heat thoroughly. Garnish with crisp bacon. (No. 1464). Serves 6.

(1873) SPINACH WITH WILTED LETTUCE AND BACON

1 head lettuce, shredded	½ teaspoon salt
1 cup boiled spinach	⅓ pound of sliced bacon
(No. 1870), chopped	½ cup vinegar
1 chopped onion	

Mix lettuce, spinach, and onion in hot serving dish. Sprinkle with salt. Sauté bacon until crisp. Strain and sprinkle bacon on greens. Heat vinegar with 1 tablespoon of bacon fat. Pour over mixture. Mix with fork. Serves 6.

(1874) SPINACH TIMBALES

2 cups boiled spinach	⅛ teaspoon paprika
(No. 1870)	Dash cayenne
2 tablespoons butter	Few drops onion juice
2 slightly beaten eggs	2 teaspoons lemon juice
1 cup milk	1 cup tomato sauce
¾ teaspoon salt	(No. 2035)
⅛ teaspoon pepper	

Combine all ingredients except sauce. Pack in greased timbale molds. Bake at low heat (300° F.) in pan of hot water until firm. Unmold and serve with hot sauce. Serves 6.

(1875)   SPINACH SOUFFLÉ

2½ cups boiled spinach (No. 1870)
Salt—Pepper—Nutmeg
1 tablespoon butter
½ cup milk
1 tablespoon flour
1 beaten egg

Chop spinach fine. Heat. Rub through a coarse sieve. Reheat and add butter, blended to a smooth paste with flour. Season to taste with salt, pepper, and nutmeg. Add milk and egg. Beat until light. Pour into individual greased baking dishes. Bake in moderate oven (350 ° F.) 15 minutes. Serves 6.

(1876)   SUMMER SQUASH

Wash and quarter. Cook 30 minutes, or until tender, in a steamer or colander over boiling water. Mash, adding salt to taste and a little cream or butter.

(1877)   SQUASH IN CREAM

Butter a deep baking dish. Peel 4 summer squashes and remove the seeds. Slice the squash into the dish, sprinkle with salt and pepper, and dot with 3 tablespoons butter. When dish is full, place in a hot oven (400° F.) and cover. When tender, add 1 cup cream and cook, uncovered, until done. When slightly browned, sprinkle with parsley, and serve in the cooking dish. Serves 6.

(1878)   BAKED SQUASH

Small Hubbard squash
1 teaspoon salt
3 tablespoons butter or fat
⅛ teaspoon pepper
3 tablespoons chopped onion
⅛ teaspoon paprika
2 tablespoons chopped green pepper
¼ cup fine bread crumbs

Cut squash in pieces, pare and boil in salted water 30 minutes or until tender. Drain and mash. Melt butter. Add onion and pepper and sauté slowly 5 minutes. Add onion, green pepper, salt, pepper, and paprika to the squash. Mix well and turn into a greased baking dish. Sprinkle with crumbs, salt, and pepper and bake in a hot oven (400° F.) 25 minutes. Serves 6.

(1879)   SAUTÉED SQUASH

Pare summer squash and cut in uniform pieces. Sprinkle with salt, pepper, and flour. Dip in slightly beaten egg, diluted with 2 tablespoons water, then in fine dry bread crumbs. Fry in small quantity of fat 6 to 8 minutes. Brown on both sides. Serves 6.

(1880)   BAKED SQUASH WITH BACON

3 pound Hubbard squash	½ to ⅔ cup milk
Melted butter	1 cup diced bacon
Salt—Pepper	

Cut squash in pieces and remove seeds and stringy portions. Brush with butter, sprinkle with salt and pepper, and bake in a moderate oven (350° F.) until tender. Scoop out the inside. Mash and add the hot milk and additional salt to taste. Pour into a buttered baking dish. Fry bacon until crisp (No. 1464). Drain and sprinkle over squash. Bake in a moderate oven (350° F.) 25 to 30 minutes. Serves 6.

(1881)   BOILED SWEET POTATOES

Boil sweet potatoes with jackets on, following recipe for boiled potatoes (No. 1834).

(1882)   MASHED SWEET POTATOES

Mash boiled sweet potatoes (No. 1881) and add salt to taste, a little butter, and cream. Beat until light.

(1883)   CANDIED SWEET POTATOES

Select medium-sized potatoes. Scrub with a vegetable brush to remove all particles of dirt. Boil in water until tender. Drain off water and remove the skins. Cut in halves, lengthwise, and put them in a greased shallow pan. Make a sirup by boiling ⅔ cup sugar, ⅓ cup water, and 1½ tablespoons butter or fat 5 minutes. Pour this over the sweet potatoes. Bake in a hot oven (400° F.) 20 minutes or until a delicate brown, basting occasionally with the sirup. Allow 1 potato for 2 servings.

(1884) FRENCH FRIED SWEET POTATOES

Parboil large sweet potatoes 10 minutes. Peel and cut in strips, 3 inches long. Fry in deep hot fat (325° F.) until a delicate brown. Drain on unglazed paper. Sprinkle with salt. Allow ½ potato per serving.

(1885)   ROAST SWEET POTATOES

Prepare and cook same as roast potatoes (No. 1838).

(1886) BAKED STUFFED SWEET POTATOES

6 sweet potatoes	¼ teaspoon grated orange
2 tablespoons butter	rind
1 egg yolk	¼ teaspoon salt
⅛ teaspoon white pepper	

Wash potatoes. Bake in moderate oven (350° F.) until soft when pressed, about 45 minutes. Cut off the tops and carefully remove and mash the pulp. Reserve the potato cases. Add other ingredients to the pulp. Beat well and roughly refill the cases. Bake 20 minutes in a slow oven (300° F.). Serves 6.

(1887)   SWEET POTATOES AND APPLES

Grease casserole with butter. Pare, core and cut 6 apples into thick slices. Place a layer in the dish. Cover with slices of 3 boiled sweet potatoes (No. 1881) and top with apples. Sprinkle with ½ cup sugar and dot with butter. Repeat until all ingredients are used. Place casserole in a pan of boiling water and bake in slow oven (325° F.) 1 hour. Serves 6.

(1888)   SPICED SWEET POTATO BALLS

3 large sweet potatoes	⅛ teaspoon nutmeg
1 cup chopped nuts	⅛ teaspoon allspice
2 tablespoons butter	⅛ teaspoon cinnamon
½ teaspoon salt	½ cup flour

Scrub potatoes to remove all dirt. Boil with skins on until tender. Peel and mash. Mix with other ingredients. Shape into balls. Roll in flour. Fry in deep hot fat (375° F.) until well browned. Serves 6.

(1889) ORANGE SWEET POTATOES

2½ cups sliced boiled sweet
   potatoes (No. 1881)
3 tablespoons butter
3 tablespoons brown sugar

1 tablespoon grated orange
   rind
2 tablespoons orange juice

Sauté the sweet potatoes in butter until browned on one side. Turn and sprinkle with sugar, orange rind, and orange juice. Cover and brown slowly on other side. Serves 5.

(1890) SWEET POTATO CROQUETTES

2 cups hot mashed sweet
   potato (No. 1882)
2 tablespoons fat
1 teaspoon salt
⅛ teaspoon pepper

1 teaspoon sugar
2 eggs
½ cup fine bread crumbs
2 tablespoons water

Mix sweet potato with fat, salt, pepper, sugar, and one well-beaten egg. Beat well. If mixture is too stiff, add a little hot milk. Shape into croquettes. Roll in crumbs, dip in beaten egg, diluted with water, and roll again in crumbs. Fry in deep hot fat (375° F.) until golden brown and drain on unglazed paper. Serves 6.

(1891) SWEET POTATO PUFFS

2 cups mashed sweet
   potatoes (No. 1882)
2 beaten egg yolks

1 cup cream
½ teaspoon salt
2 well-beaten egg whites

Mix potatoes, yolks, cream, and salt. Heat in saucepan. When very hot, remove from heat and add egg whites. Beat until light. Pile loosely on buttered platter. Brush with egg white. Heat in moderate oven (350° F.) until brown. Serves 6.

(1892) SWISS CHARD

Cook leaves the same as spinach (No. 1870) and the midribs like celery (No. 1761).

(1893) STEWED TOMATOES

Pour boiling water over tomatoes. Plunge into cold water. Drain. Remove skins and hard parts. Quarter. Put in saucepan. Season to taste with salt and pepper. Bring slowly to a boil. Serve hot.

(1894) FRIED TOMATOES, CREAM GRAVY

3 tablespoons fat	⅛ teaspoon pepper
4 tablespoons flour	4 large tomatoes
2 tablespoons sugar	2 cups milk
1½ teaspoons salt	

Melt fat in frying pan. Mix flour, sugar, salt, and pepper. Cut tomatoes in ½-inch slices. Dip in flour mixture and fry in fat until brown. Remove to a hot platter. Put the milk in the pan and bring to boiling point, stirring constantly until it thickens. Add a little salt, if necessary. Pour over the tomatoes and serve hot. Serves 6.

(1895) BROILED TOMATOES

1 cup chopped cooked chicken	6 tomatoes
Flour for dredging	2 tablespoons grated cheese
¼ cup milk	Salt—Pepper

Dredge chicken with flour. Put in saucepan. Moisten with milk. Heat until thickened. Wash tomatoes. Cut in halves, crosswise. Spread them with chicken mixture. Sprinkle with cheese. Season to taste with salt and pepper. Put into broiler. Broil at moderate heat until delicately browned on top. Serves 6.

(1896) BROILED TOMATOES WITH CHEESE

6 slices stale bread	12 slices bacon
12 slices tomato	Salt—Pepper
6 slices American cheese	

Place the sliced cheese on bread. On this place two slices tomato and two slices bacon. Place on rack in broiler until bacon is crisp and cheese well melted. Serve very hot and garnish with sprigs of parsley, if desired. Serves 6.

(1897) CREOLE TOMATOES

Cut in halves 6 ripe tomatoes. Place in a baking pan and cover each tomato with a thick layer of equal parts of chopped green pepper and onions. Season with salt, pepper, and butter. Bake in a hot oven (450° F.) 15 minutes. Pour cream sauce (No. 2005) over tomatoes after placing each on a square of fresh buttered toast (No. 988). Serves 6.

(1898) BAKED STUFFED TOMATOES

2 cups soft bread crumbs	2 tablespoons sugar
1 teaspoon salt	3 tablespoons fat
⅛ teaspoon pepper	6 tomatoes

Mix bread crumbs with salt, pepper, 1 tablespoon sugar, and 2 tablespoons melted fat. Cut thin slice from stem end of tomatoes and remove a little of the center. Sprinkle with salt, pepper, and sugar. Fill with the stuffing. Dot with small bits of fat and bake in a moderate oven (350° F.) 1 hour. Serves 6. Two cups of shredded cabbage, seasoned with 1 chopped onion, salt, and pepper is another good stuffing. Or, tomatoes may be filled with balls of sausage meat. Buttered corn flakes may be sprinkled on tomatoes before cooking. One cup cooked, quartered shrimps (No. 1272) may be substituted for 1 cup crumbs.

(1899) BLUSHING BUNNY

2½ cups stewed tomatoes (No. 1893)	1 cup chopped mild cheese
Salt—Pepper	3 well-beaten eggs

Heat tomatoes. Season with salt and pepper. Stir in cheese. When cheese has melted, add eggs and stir until thick. Serve on buttered toast (No. 988). Serves 6.

(1900) BAKED TOMATO EN CASSEROLE

2 onions	1 teaspoon salt
3 tablespoons fat	⅛ teaspoon paprika
2 cups stewed (No. 1893) or canned tomatoes	⅛ teaspoon pepper

Cut onions in slices and fry in fat until a delicate brown. Add other ingredients. Mix well. Put in a baking dish and cook in a quick oven (425° F.) 50 minutes, stirring occasionally. Serve on slices of toast. Serves 6.

(1901) TOMATOES BAKED WITH CREAM SAUCE

2½ cups stewed tomatoes   Salt—Pepper
    (No. 1893)   1 cup medium white sauce
2 tablespoons sugar   (No. 2004)

Chop tomatoes. Add sugar. Season to taste with salt and pepper. Put in greased baking dish. Bake in moderate oven (350° F.) 30 minutes. Pour over sauce. Bake 10 minutes more. Serves 6.

(1902) TOMATOES OR CORN WITH BEANS

2½ cups boiled green beans   1 cup milk
    (No. 1712)   2 tablespoons chopped
2½ cups stewed tomatoes   onion
    (No. 1893) or stewed   2 teaspoons sugar
    corn (No. 1769)   Salt—Pepper
4 strips bacon   ½ cup buttered bread
4 tablespoons flour   crumbs
1 tablespoon butter

Drain beans and tomatoes. Reduce drained liquid, by boiling, to one cup. Cut bacon into ½-inch lengths. Fry until crisp. Strain, leaving bacon fat in pan. Stir in flour and butter until smooth. Add milk and liquid from vegetables. Cook until thick and smooth, stirring constantly. Add onion and sugar. Season to taste with salt and pepper. Add beans, tomatoes, and bacon. Mix well. Turn into shallow, greased baking dish. Top with crumbs. Bake in moderate oven (375° F.) 30 minutes. Serves 10. Baked beans (No. 1708) can be substituted for green beans or corn.

(1903)   TOMATOES AND ROLLED OATS

1 cup soup stock (No. 501)   ½ cup rolled oats
    or water   1 teaspoon salt
1 cup stewed tomatoes   3 tablespoons melted fat
    (No. 1893)

Bring stock or water to boil. Stir in tomatoes. Add oats slowly, stirring constantly. Add salt. Cook slowly, uncovered, until dry. Add fat. Serve hot. Serves 4.

(1904)   SCALLOPED TOMATOES

2 cups bread crumbs	Salt—Pepper
2½ cups stewed tomatoes	2 tablespoons butter
(No. 1893)	

Cover bottom of greased baking dish with 1 cup bread crumbs. Add tomatoes. Season to taste with salt and pepper. Stir remaining crumbs in melted butter and cover tomatoes. Bake in moderate oven (350° F.) until well browned. Serves 6.

(1905)   TOMATO SCRAPPLE

2½ cups stewed tomatoes	1 teaspoon sugar
(No. 1893)	Salt—Pepper
1 onion, chopped	1 cup chopped roasted
1 carrot, chopped	peanuts
1 cup corn meal	

Mix tomatoes, onion, carrot, corn meal, sugar and season to taste with salt and pepper. Cook slowly until thick, about 1 hour. Beat in peanuts. Pack into an oiled pan or baking powder tin. Cool. Slice and fry in little fat. Serves 8.

(1906)   BOILED TURNIPS

Peel and slice. Boil in slightly salted water until tender about 1 to 1¼ hours. Season to taste with butter, salt, and pepper.

(1907)   TURNIP GREENS

Follow recipe for chicory (No. 1765) through boiling, cooking about 25 minutes.

(1908)   MASHED TURNIPS

Mash boiled turnips (No. 1906) adding butter, salt, pepper, and milk to get desired consistency and taste.

(1909)   HASHED TURNIPS

Chop 3 cups boiled and drained turnips (No. 1906) into rather large pieces. Return to the stewpan and add 1 teaspoon of salt, ¼ teaspoon of pepper, 1 tablespoon of butter and 4 tablespoons of water. Cook over a very hot fire until the turnips have absorbed all the seasonings. Serve at once. Serves 6.

(1910)   CREAMED TURNIPS

Follow recipe for creamed vegetables (No. 1914), using boiled turnips (No. 1906) instead of mixed vegetables.

(1911)   FLUFFY YELLOW TURNIP

2 tablespoons fat	1 tablespoon sugar
1 tablespoon chopped onion	1/8 teaspoon pepper
3 cups yellow turnips, mashed (No. 1908)	Few grains cayenne
	2 egg yolks
1 teaspoon salt	2 egg whites

Melt fat, add onion, and fry until a delicate brown. Add turnips, salt, sugar, pepper, cayenne and mix well. Add beaten egg yolks. Fold in the stiffly beaten egg whites. Put in a greased baking dish and bake in a hot oven (400° F.) 20 to 25 minutes. Serves 6.

(1912)   VEGETABLE MARROW

Prepare according to recipe for summer squash (No. 1876).

(1913)   BUTTERED VEGETABLES

Most vegetables may be served buttered. After they are boiled and drained, they should be returned to the stove and the butter and seasoning added. The pan should be well shaken so the butter will coat the vegetables.

(1914)   CREAMED VEGETABLES

2½ cups mixed cooked vegetables	1 tablespoon flour
	¼ teaspoon dry mustard
½ cup light cream	Salt—Pepper
2 tablespoons butter	

Drain vegetables and add ½ cup of the liquid to cream. Melt butter. Add flour and mustard. Season to taste with salt and pepper. Add liquid. Cook until thick, stirring constantly. Add vegetables. Heat thoroughly. Serves 6. If desired, ½ cup grated cheese or sliced hard-cooked eggs (No. 202) may be added with vegetables. Serves 6.

(1915) SCALLOPED VEGETABLES

Fill bottom of caserole or baking dish with diced (cooked or canned) vegetables. Pour over with layer of medium white sauce (No. 2004). Continue to alternate with vegetable and white sauce to the top of the dish, making the top layer one of white sauce. Add a small chip of butter occasionally as the dish is being filled. Scatter soft crumbs over the top and bake until browned in a moderate oven (350° F.).

(1916) PURÉED VEGETABLE

Rub well cooked vegetable through a sieve. Season to taste, add small amount of butter. Reheat and serve. Suitable vegetables for puréeing are peas, carrots, beets, winter squash, string beans, spinach, asparagus, cauliflower.

(1917) SUCCOTASH

2 cups stewed corn
  (No. 1769)
¼ cup butter

2 cups boiled lima beans
  (No. 1717)
Salt—Pepper

Mix corn, beans, and butter. Season to taste with salt and pepper. Heat thoroughly. Serves 6. If desired, this may be served with warm milk poured over.

(1918) SUCCOTASH SOUFFLÉ

3 tablespoons butter
4 tablespoons flour
1 cup milk
¾ teaspoon salt
Dash cayenne
½ teaspoon dry mustard

2½ cups succotash
  (No. 1917)
½ cup grated American
  cheese
4 eggs

Blend butter and flour together and add milk and seasonings. Cook until thickened, stirring constantly. Add succotash and remove from heat. Stir in the cheese and well-beaten egg yolks and fold in the stiffly beaten egg whites. Pour into a medium-size casserole. Set in a shallow pan of hot water and bake in a moderate oven (350° F.) about 1 hour, or until firm and well browned. Serves 8. Stewed corn (No. 1769) or drained and chopped mixed vegetables may be used instead of succotash.

(1919)   MIXED VEGETABLE HASH

3 cups cooked vegetables   Salt—Pepper

Sauté vegetables on hot greased frying pan. Season with salt and pepper. This goes well with poached eggs (No. 207). Serves 6.

(1920)   VEGETABLES AU GRATIN

Put creamed vegetables (No. 1914) in greased baking dish. Sprinkle with bread crumbs and grated cheese, if desired. Dot with butter. Bake in moderate oven (350° F.) 15 minutes or until crumbs are browned. Serves 6.

(1921)   VEGETABLES LYONNAISE

2 medium-sized onions
3 tablespoons butter
2½ cups cooked peas
    (No. 1823)
Salt—Pepper

2½ cups stewed corn
    (No. 1769)
2 tablespoons chopped
    parsley

Slice onions thin. Separate into rings. Sauté until golden brown in butter. Drain vegetables and add liquid to onions. Simmer until reduced to ½ cup. Add peas and corn. Season to taste with salt and pepper. Heat thoroughly. Sprinkle with parsley just before serving. Serves 6.

(1922)   BAKED MACÉDOINE

3 tablespoons butter or fat
1 tablespoon chopped onion
2 tablespoons chopped
    pimiento
2 cups canned or stewed
    tomatoes (No. 1893)
1 cup stewed corn
    (No. 1769)
1½ cups boiled rice
    (No. 107)

2 tablespoons flour
1 hard-cooked egg,
    chopped (No. 202)
1 tablespoon chopped
    parsley
2 teaspoons salt
⅛ teaspoon pepper
1 teaspoon Worcestershire
    sauce
½ cup grated cheese

Melt butter, add onion and pimiento, and cook 3 minutes. Add flour and mix well. Add tomatoes and stir until mixture thickens slightly. Add corn, rice, egg, and seasonings. Put in a baking dish, sprinkle cheese over the top and bake in a hot oven (400° F.) 20 minutes. Any combination of cooked vegetables is good in this dish. Peas, lima beans or carrots may be substituted for the corn. Serves 6.

(1923) VEGETABLE FRITTERS

1¾ cups flour
1 teaspoon salt
Few grains pepper
3½ teaspoons baking powder
2 eggs
½ cup milk
½ cup cooked carrots (No. 1745), chopped
¼ cup cooked peas (No. 1823)
¼ cup cooked lima beans (No. 1717)
1 tablespoon chopped parsley
2 tablespoons melted fat

Mix and sift flour, salt, pepper, and baking powder. Beat eggs and add milk. Add to the flour mixture and beat thoroughly. Add carrots, peas, lima beans, parsley, and fat and mix well. Drop by tablespoons into deep hot fat (375° F.) and fry until a delicate brown. Drain on unglazed paper. Serve hot with cheese sauce (No. 2008). Serves 6.

(1924) VEGETABLE PIE

1 small onion, sliced
3 tablespoons butter
1 tablespoon flour
1½ teaspoons salt
⅛ teaspoon pepper
2 cups cooked mixed vegetables
1 cup mashed potatoes (No. 1835)
1 egg, slightly beaten

Sauté onion in butter until soft. Add flour, salt, and pepper. Mix well. Add vegetables without draining. Simmer slowly, stirring constantly, until mixture thickens. Turn into greased baking pan. Combine egg and potatoes and beat until fluffy. Spread potatoes over vegetable mixture. Bake in moderately hot oven (400° F.) until brown. Serves 6.

Sauces · Stuffings

SAUCES, STUFFINGS, ACCOMPANIMENTS

S AUCES add greatly to the savor and appearance of meals. They also provide the clever homemaker with an opportunity to get into the diet food values found wanting in the principal items on the menu.

(2001)   PAN GRAVY

To each cup of pan liquid add, gradually, 2 tablespoons flour mixed till smooth, with an equal quantity of cold water. Cook as white sauce (No. 2004). Strain.

(2002)   GIBLET GRAVY

Pour off the fat from the pan in which poultry has been roasted, saving 4 tablespoons. Add 3 tablespoons flour and stir until it browns. Measure water in which the giblets were cooked and add enough water to make 3 cups. Add to the browned flour and stir until smooth and thickened. Add liver, gizzard, and heart, chopped fine. Season with salt and pepper. Reheat and serve in hot gravy boat with the poultry.

(2003)   FISH SAUCE OR GRAVY

2 tablespoons butter	½ cup liquid from boiled
2 tablespoons flour	fish
1½ cups milk, scalded	2 tablespoons lemon juice

1 egg yolk

Melt **butter.** Add flour and heated milk gradually. Add liquid from fish and lemon juice just before removing from fire. Just before serving, beat sauce into yolk of egg. Serve hot. One table-spoon catchup may be added, if desired.

(2004) WHITE SAUCE

Proportions for ingredients of white sauce

Consistency	Milk	Flour	Butter or other fat	Use of sauce
	Cup	*Table-spoon*	*Table-spoon*	
Thin	1	1	1	Heavy milk soups.
Thin-medium.	1	1½	1½	Creamed dishes of starchy vegetables or of cereals; also gravy.
Medium	1	2	2	Creamed dishes of succulent vegetables, hard-cooked eggs, diced meat, and fish; also gravy.
Thick	1	3	2-3	Binder for croquettes, meat loaf, and soufflés

The ingredients for white sauce may be combined in any of several ways. Choice of method depends upon the quantity of sauce to be made and upon the proportion of fat to flour. When equal quantities of fat and flour are used and not more than a pint of sauce is being made, the following method is economical of time and utensils and yields a smooth sauce: Soften the fat or melt it at a very low temperature, blend thoroughly with the flour, add the milk, and heat slowly, stirring constantly until the mixture thickens, and boil until the starch is cooked. In making more than a pint of sauce, use the same method of blending fat and flour, but add hot milk and finish the cooking in a double boiler to save time and the energy required for stirring. For a very large quantity of sauce mix the flour into a thin paste with cold milk, combine this paste with the rest of the milk which has been heated, stir while cooking, and beat in the fat at the last.

(2005) CREAM SAUCE

Substitute cream for milk in white sauces (No. 2004).

(2006)   **ANCHOVY SAUCE**

Add ½ teaspoon anchovy paste to 1 cup thin white sauce (No. 2004) or cream sauce (No. 2005).

(2007)   **CELERY SAUCE**

Add ½ cup chopped, boiled celery (No. 1761) to 1 cup thin white sauce (No. 2004) or cream sauce (No. 2005).

(2008)   **CHEESE SAUCE**

Add 1 cup grated cheese to medium white sauce (No. 2004) or cream sauce (No. 2005) after it has thickened and stir until cheese has melted.

(2009)   **EGG SAUCE**

Add 1 chopped hard-cooked egg (No. 202) and 2 teaspoons chopped parsley to hot medium white sauce (No. 2004) or cream sauce (No. 2005).

(2010)   **GOLDEN SAUCE**

Mix 2 beaten egg yolks into medium white sauce (No. 2004) or cream sauce (No. 2005). Reheat. Add 1 teaspoon lemon juice or vinegar just before serving.

(2011)   **LOBSTER SAUCE**

Add chopped, boiled lobster meat (No. 1236) to medium white sauce (No. 2004) or cream sauce (No. 2005).

(2012)   **OYSTER SAUCE**

Scald 12 oysters in their own juice until edges curl. Add to medium white sauce (No. 2004) or cream sauce (No. 2005) just before serving.

(2013)   **PARSLEY SAUCE**

Follow recipe for thin white sauce (No. 2004) or cream sauce (No. 2005) and add 3 tablespoons chopped parsley.

(2014)   PIMIENTO SAUCE

Put 3 pimientos through a sieve and add to hot medium white sauce (No. 2004) or cream sauce (No. 2005).

(2015)   RAVIGOTE SAUCE

To 1 cup thin white sauce (No. 2004) add 1 tablespoon each minced chives, chervil, tarragon, and shallot, ¼ cup lemon juice, 1 tablespoon tarragon vinegar, and 1 tablespoon butter.

(2016)   SHRIMP SAUCE

Add 1 cup chopped, boiled shrimps (No. 1272) to 1 cup medium white sauce (No. 2004) or cream sauce (No. 2005).

(2017)   VELOUTÉ SAUCE

Substitute chicken broth (No. 511) for milk in recipe for white sauce (No. 2004), reducing quantity of liquid 25%.

(2018)   SAUCE ALLEMANDE

Add the beaten yolk of 1 egg and 1 tablespoon lemon juice to each cup of velouté sauce (No. 2012). If preferred, the lemon juice may be replaced by cream and a little grated Parmesan cheese added, cooking a little longer to melt cheese.

(2019)   CHAUDFROID SAUCE

Soak 1 tablespoon gelatin in cold water 5 minutes. Stir into 1 cup hot velouté sauce (No. 2017). Let cool until slightly firm and spread on cold meats. For brown sauce make velouté sauce with stock (No. 501). For yellow sauce add 2 beaten egg yolks to chaudfroid sauce before taking from heat.

(2020)   BROWN SAUCE

2 tablespoons melted butter	2 cups stock (No. 501)
1 slice onion	Salt—Pepper
2 tablespoons flour	

Melt butter. Add onion and brown. Remove onion and stir in flour, blending well. When brown, add stock. Season to taste with salt and pepper. Cook until it boils and is smooth. One bouillon cube, dissolved in 2 cups hot water, may be substituted for stock.

(2021)   BORDELAISE SAUCE

Replace 1 cup stock in brown sauce (No. 2020) with 1 cup Bordeaux wine.

(2022)   HOLLANDAISE SAUCE

½ cup butter	Speck cayenne pepper
2 egg yolks	1 tablespoon lemon juice
½ teaspoon salt	

Melt the butter in a saucepan. Beat the egg yolks in a bowl with beater at high speed until thick and lemon-colored. Add the salt, cayenne pepper, and 3 tablespoons melted butter, a drop at a time, beating meanwhile. Then add the remaining butter, alternately with the lemon juice, until all has been added. Store in the refrigerator until ready to use. This sauce melts readily when served on hot vegetables. Serves 6.

(2023)   MOCK HOLLANDAISE SAUCE

2 egg yolks	3 tablespoons lemon juice
1 cup thick white sauce	Few grains cayenne
(No. 2004)	

Add beaten egg yolks to the hot white sauce and mix well. Bring slowly to the boiling point, stirring constantly. Remove from fire, add lemon juice and cayenne.

(2024)   SAUCE TRIANON

Add 3 tablespoons sherry wine to recipe for hollandaise sauce (No. 2022).

(2025)   DRAWN BUTTER

6 tablespoons butter	Salt—Pepper
3 tablespoons flour	

Melt 3 tablespoons butter. Add flour and cook, stirring constantly, until smooth. Add 2 cups hot water. Season to taste with salt and pepper. Bring to boiling point and boil 5 minutes. Add remaining butter.

(2026) BROWN BUTTER SAUCE

¼ pound butter
3 tablespoons vinegar
1 tablespoon chopped parsley
Salt—Pepper

Heat butter slowly in a frying pan until it browns. Add vinegar, parsley, and season to taste with salt and pepper. Chopped onion may be added if desired.

(2027) MAÎTRE D'HÔTEL BUTTER OR SAUCE

½ cup butter
1½ teaspoons lemon juice
1 teaspoon minced parsley
⅛ teaspoon pepper
⅛ teaspoon salt

Cream the butter, gradually working in the lemon juice, salt, and pepper. When well blended, work in the parsley, and with butter paddles roll into balls about ¾ inches in diameter. Chill and place one butter ball at the side of each serving of fish. The butter will melt when put on hot food.

(2028) ANCHOVY BUTTER

Add ½ teaspoon anchovy paste and a dash of cayenne pepper to recipe for maître d'hôtel butter (No. 2027). The butter will melt when put on hot food.

(2029) LEMON BUTTER

4 tablespoons butter, melted
1 teaspoon lemon juice
⅛ teaspoon pepper

Blend all together. Serve hot.

(2030) MINT BUTTER

Add 1 tablespoon chopped mint and omit parsley in recipe for maître d'hôtel butter (No. 2027). The butter will melt when put on hot food.

(2031)   HOT TARTAR SAUCE

1 tablespoon vinegar
¼ shallot, chopped fine
1 teaspoon capers, chopped fine
1 teaspoon pickles, chopped fine
1 teaspoon olives, chopped fine

1 teaspoon parsley, chopped fine
¼ teaspoon powdered tarragon
1 cup medium white sauce (No. 2004)

Mix vinegar, shallot, capers, pickles, olives, parsley, and powdered tarragon. Have white sauce very hot. Add mixture and mix well. Serve very hot.

(2032)   BÉARNAISE SAUCE

¼ cup fat
4 egg yolks
½ teaspoon salt
Few grains cayenne

1 tablespoon tarragon vinegar
½ teaspoon onion juice
1 tablespoon chopped parsley

Mix fat and beaten egg yolks together. Add salt and cayenne and cook over hot (not boiling) water until thick, stirring constantly. Add vinegar and onion juice and cook 20 minutes, still stirring. Remove from fire and add chopped parsley. Serve immediately.

(2033)   BÉCHAMEL SAUCE

1½ cups chicken stock (No. 502) or broth (No. 511)
1 slice onion
1 slice carrot
Bit of bay leaf
Sprig of parsley

6 peppercorns
¼ cup butter
¼ cup flour
1 cup scalded milk
½ teaspoon salt
⅛ teaspoon pepper

Cook stock 20 minutes with onion, carrot, bay leaf, parsley, and peppercorns. Strain. Melt butter. Add flour and gradually hot stock and milk. Season with salt and pepper. Equal parts of stock and milk may be used.

(2034) NEWBURG SAUCE

2 tablespoons butter	2 tablespoons sherry
1 teaspoon onion	flavoring
Red pepper	1 cup cream
Salt	3 egg yolks

Gently cook the butter, onion, salt, and pepper 5 minutes. Add the flavoring and cook 3 minutes. Add cream to egg yolks and beat well. Combine with the butter mixture and heat gently until the sauce bubbles but does not boil.

(2035) TOMATO SAUCE

½ tablespoon onion, chopped	Salt—Pepper
1 tablespoon parsley, finely	4 tablespoons flour
chopped	4 tablespoons fat
2 cups tomatoes	

Simmer the onion and parsley in the tomatoes about 20 minutes. Strain. Follow directions for white sauce (No. 2004) using tomato mixture in place of milk.

(2036) COCKTAIL SAUCE

6 tablespoons tomato	4 tablespoons lemon juice
catchup	Celery salt
2 tablespoons horseradish	Tabasco sauce

Shake ingredients until well mixed, adding celery salt and Tabasco sauce to suit taste.

(2037) ONION SAUCE

1 tablespoon fat	1 tablespoon flour
2 tablespoons sugar	1 cup beef broth
2 onions, sliced fine	(No. 529)
Salt	1 tablespoon vinegar

Brown the sugar in the fat. Add onions and cook, then add flour and brown a little more. Add broth, vinegar, and salt. Cook until a smooth, creamy brown sauce results. Put through a strainer.

(2038)   HORSERADISH SAUCE

2 tablespoons shortening	⅓ cup horseradish
3 tablespoons flour	½ teaspoon Worcestershire
1½ cups meat (No. 501) or	sauce
fish stock (No. 504)	Few grains cayenne pepper
½ teaspoon salt	

Cook flour in shortening and add stock and salt. Cook till smooth and thick and add remaining ingredients. Serve at once. Tomato juice may be substituted for part of the stock.

(2039)   MUSHROOM SAUCE

4 tablespoons flour	1 cup sliced fresh or
4 tablespoons fat	canned mushrooms
2 tablespoons chopped	Salt—Pepper
onions	2 cups stock (No. 501)

Brown flour in saucepan. Melt fat in another pan. Add onions and mushrooms and brown slightly. Strain. Add flour and seasonings to taste to fat. Mix well. Add stock gradually, stirring constantly. Cook until thickened. Add onions and mushrooms. Simmer 2 minutes.

(2040)   CAPER SAUCE

1 tablespoon butter or fat	1 cup stock (No. 501)
2 tablespoons flour	or fish stock (No. 504)
½ teaspoon salt	2 tablespoons capers
⅛ teaspoon pepper	

Melt butter, add flour, salt, and pepper and mix well. Add stock and bring to the boiling point, stirring constantly. Add capers.

(2041)   SPANISH SAUCE

2 tablespoons butter or fat	3 tablespoons cooked ham,
2 tablespoons chopped onion	chopped
2 tablespoons flour	3 tablespoons boiled celery
½ teaspoon salt	(No. 1761), chopped
Dash cayenne	2 tablespoons boiled carrots
Dash pepper	(No. 1745), chopped
1 cup strained tomato juice	

Melt butter, add onion, and sauté until a delicate brown. Add flour, salt, cayenne, and pepper and mix well. Add tomato juice and bring slowly to the boiling point, stirring constantly. Add ham, celery, and carrots. Serve hot.

(2042) BARBECUE SAUCE

1 medium-sized onion
2 tablespoons butter
2 tablespoons vinegar
2 tablespoons brown sugar
4 tablespoons lemon juice
1 cup catchup
½ cup chopped parsley

½ tablespoon prepared mustard
½ cup water
3 tablespoons Worcestershire sauce
Salt
Cayenne pepper

Brown onion in butter. Add remaining ingredients. Simmer 30 minutes.

(2043) MUSTARD SAUCE

1 tablespoon butter
1½ teaspoons flour
1 teaspoon dry mustard
2 tablespoons vinegar

1 tablespoon prepared mustard
1 teaspoon sugar
1 cup hot stock (No. 501)

Salt—Pepper

Melt butter. Add flour. Cook, stirring until smooth. Add dry mustard, vinegar, prepared mustard, sugar, and stock. Simmer slowly 10 minutes, stirring occasionally. Season to taste with salt and pepper. A cold mustard sauce may be made by substituting 1 tablespoon boiling water for butter.

(2044) TARTAR SAUCE

1 cup mayonnaise
   (No. 701)
1 tablespoon minced pickles

1 tablespoon minced parsley
1 tablespoon minced capers
1 tablespoon minced onion

Mix ingredients thoroughly and serve cold.

(2045) HOT MAYONNAISE

Add one cup mayonnaise (No. 701) to one cup hot white sauce (No. 2004) for string beans, asparagus, and French artichokes.

(2046)   MINT SAUCE

8 stalks mint, or	2 tablespoons sugar
2 tablespoons dry mint	½ cup vinegar

Wash mint and pick leaves from stems. Chop fine. Add sugar to vinegar. Pour over mint leaves. Let stand 1 hour.

(2047)   CREOLE SAUCE

¾ cup minced onion	1 garlic clove, minced
1 cup minced sweet pepper	1 teaspoon salt
2 cups stewed (No. 1893)	⅜ teaspoon pepper
or canned tomato	⅛ teaspoon paprika
4 tablespoons melted butter	

Place the butter, onion, pepper, and garlic in a saucepan and simmer about 10 minutes or until tender. Then add tomato, and seasoning. Boil 5 minutes. Serve hot.

(2048)   OLIVE SAUCE

12 green olives	1 tablespoon flour
1 tablespoon butter	1 cup stock (No. 501)
1 tablespoon chopped onion	1 clove
1 tablespoon diced carrot	Salt—Pepper

Remove stones from olives. Put in saucepan. Cover with water and boil 30 minutes. Drain and chop coarsely. Melt butter in frying pan. Add onion and carrot and sauté until brown. Add flour and cook, stirring constantly, until smooth. Add stock gradually. Add clove. Season to taste with salt and pepper. Let simmer 15 minutes, stirring occasionally. Strain. Add olives. Reheat.

(2049)   SWEET PEPPER SAUCE

2 tablespoons butter	1 cup chopped sweet
1 clove garlic, minced	peppers
½ onion, diced	½ teaspoon salt
1 tablespoon flour	⅛ teaspoon pepper
1 cup boiling water	½ teaspoon minced parsley

Melt butter. Add the garlic and onion. Fry until yellow. Stir in the flour, water, and sweet peppers. Season with salt, pepper and parsley.

(2050) CUCUMBER SAUCE

Grate a cucumber. Drain. Season pulp with 2 teaspoons vinegar. Season to taste with salt and pepper.

(2051) CURRY SAUCE

1 tablespoon butter	2 cups hot milk or stock
1 teaspoon onion juice	(No. 501)
1 tablespoon curry powder	Salt—Pepper
2 tablespoons flour	

Melt butter and add onion juice. Mix curry powder and flour and add to butter. Stir until smooth. Add milk or stock. Season to taste with salt and pepper. Bring to boiling point, stirring constantly.

(2052) CURRANT JELLY SAUCE

½ cup currant jelly	2 teaspoons lemon juice
2 tablespoons hot water	Few grains salt

Break up jelly with fork. Add other ingredients. Grape or wild plum jelly can be substituted for currant jelly.

(2053) BREAD CRUMB SAUCE

6 tablespoons butter	1 teaspoon chives, minced
4 tablespoons bread crumbs	Salt—Pepper

Melt butter and add crumbs and chives. Season with salt and pepper. Sauté until brown.

(2054) GINGERSNAP SAUCE

4 gingersnaps	1 cup hot water
½ cup brown sugar	1 lemon, sliced
4 tablespoons vinegar	¼ cup seeded raisins
Few drops onion juice	¼ cup shaved almonds

Crush gingersnaps and add other ingredients. Cook until smooth. Add more vinegar, if necessary.

(2055)   RAISIN SAUCE

6 tablespoons raisins	Few grains salt
2 cups cold water	Few grains paprika
2 tablespoons flour	1½ tablespoons lemon juice
2 tablespoons fat	

Bring the raisins and cold water slowly to the boiling point and let simmer 15 minutes. Melt fat, add dry ingredients, and blend thoroughly. Add raisins and liquid. Stir constantly and boil 5 minutes. Remove from fire and add lemon juice.

(2056)   ALMOND AND RAISIN SAUCE

2 tablespoons butter or fat	½ cup almonds, cut in
4 tablespoons flour	strips
3 cups meat stock	1 tablespoon sugar
(No. 501)	¼ cup vinegar
1 cup raisins	

Melt butter, add flour, and mix well. Add stock and stir until it thickens. Stir in raisins, almonds, sugar, and vinegar. Season with salt and pepper if necessary.

(2057)   BOILED CIDER APPLE SAUCE

2 quarts sweet apples, cored	1 quart sweet cider reduced
and pared	by boiling ½
Maple or brown sugar	

Put apples in a kettle. Add cider. Simmer 3 or 4 hours. If cider is sour, add maple sugar or brown sugar to taste.

(2058)   CIDER AND RAISIN SAUCE

¼ cup sugar	¼ cup seedless raisins
1 tablespoon cornstarch	4 small pieces stick
⅛ teaspoon salt	cinnamon
1 cup cider	8 whole cloves

Mix the sugar, cornstarch, and salt, and add the cider and the raisins. Put in the spices tied up in a piece of cheesecloth. Boil the mixture for about 10 minutes and take out the spices. Serve the sauce hot with ham.

(2059)   APPLE-HORSERADISH SAUCE

2 tablespoons white vinegar	3 tablespoons grated
3 apples	horseradish
2 teaspoons sugar	

Grate the peeled apples into vinegar and blend at once so apples will remain white. Add grated horseradish and sugar.

(2060)   CRANBERRY ORANGE SAUCE

½ teaspoon dry mustard	½ tablespoon flour
⅔ cup chicken broth (No. 511)	2 tablespoons chicken broth (No. 511)
½ cup strained cranberry sauce (No. 54)	2 teaspoons butter
½ cup orange juice	Dash of cayenne
Piece of orange peel	Salt to taste

Moisten the mustard with a little chicken broth. Make a smooth paste and add the chicken broth. Start it in a saucepan. Add remaining ingredients. Simmer 15 minutes. Cook, stirring constantly, until sauce thickens slightly. Remove peel before serving.

(2061)   FRESH MINT CHUTNEY

1 bunch fresh mint	½ teaspoon salt
1 small onion	Dash cayenne pepper
½ teaspoon pepper	2 tablespoons lemon juice

Chop mint and onion together. Add seasoning and lemon juice and put through meat grinder. Beat well.

(2062)   CHAMPAGNE SAUCE

1 cup champagne	2 tablespoons mushrooms, chopped
1 teaspoon sugar	
2 cloves	1 slice onion, chopped
8 peppercorns	1 slice carrot, chopped
1 bay leaf	2 tablespoons flour
2 tablespoons butter	1 cup stock (No. 501)
Salt—Pepper	

Simmer champagne, sugar, cloves, peppercorns, and bay leaf 5 minutes. Melt butter in frying pan. Add mushrooms, onion, and carrot. Sauté until brown. Add flour and stock. Season with salt and pepper. Bring to boiling point, stirring constantly. Strain champagne and add to mixture. Simmer 8 minutes.

STUFFINGS

Stuffings need not be cooked inside bird or meat. They can be placed in pan around the roast or can be baked separately in baking pans or molds.

(2063) BREAD STUFFING

2 cups bread crumbs	¼ cup celery, cut fine
½ cup melted butter	1 small onion, chopped

Sauté the celery and onion in the fat until soft and add to the bread crumbs. Mix well.

(2064) POULTRY STUFFING

1 small onion	⅛ teaspoon pepper
3 tablespoons butter or fat	1 teaspoon poultry
3 cups soft bread crumbs	seasoning
1 teaspoon salt	

Slice onion and sauté in butter until a delicate brown. Add bread crumbs, salt, pepper, and poultry seasoning and mix well.

(2065) ONION STUFFING

6 tablespoons fat	¼ cup onion, finely
1½ to 2 cups hot water	chopped
4 cups toasted bread cubes	1 tablespoon celery,
½ teaspoon salt	chopped
1 tablespoon sage	1 tablespoon parsley,
⅛ teaspoon pepper	chopped

Melt 4 tablespoons fat in hot water. Mix with remaining ingredients. Yield: Stuffing for 4-pound chicken.

(2066) GIBLET STUFFING

Add giblets from bird, simmered in water until tender and chopped, to poultry stuffing (No. 2064).

(2067)   TRICKY STUFFING

2 eggs	2 apples
4 carrots	½ cup peanuts
2 cups bran flakes	Salt—Pepper

Beat eggs until light. Add grated carrots, bran flakes, chopped apple, and peanuts. Season to taste with salt and pepper.

(2068)   CRACKER STUFFING

8 cups cracker crumbs	3 teaspoons poultry
½ pound salt pork	seasoning
1 medium-sized onion	1 teaspoon salt

Put crackers, salt pork, and onion through food chopper. Add seasoning and salt, then stir and at the same time add enough boiling water to make it moist and fluffy.

(2069)   SAGE AND ONION STUFFING

12 medium-sized onions	2 tablespoons butter,
1½ cups stale bread crumbs	melted
1 tablespoon chopped parsley	Salt and pepper to taste
1 teaspoon powdered sage	

Peel and cook onions in boiling salted water until tender, drain and chop. Add the rest of ingredients and mix well.

(2070)   CORN BREAD STUFFING

6 tablespoons butter or fat	4 cups corn bread crumbs
⅓ cup chopped onion	¼ teaspoon thyme
⅔ cup chopped celery	½ teaspoon salt
3 tablespoons chopped	¼ teaspoon pepper
parsley	

Melt butter in frying pan. Add onion, celery, and parsley. Sauté until lightly browned. Remove from heat and mix thoroughly with other ingredients.

(2071)   MASHED POTATO STUFFING

2 cups mashed potatoes,
   highly seasoned
   (No. 1835)
½ cup chopped boiled
   onions (No. 1810)

2 egg yolks
2 tablespoons melted fat
¼ teaspoon sage

Mix ingredients in order given.

(2072)   SWEET POTATO STUFFING

2 cups hot mashed sweet
   potatoes (No. 1882)
2 tablespoons chopped
   onion

1 cup soft bread crumbs
2 tablespoons melted
   butter

Combine sweet potatoes and crumbs. Season with onion and moisten with butter. One cup of sausage meat makes a delicious addition to this stuffing.

(2073)   MINCED HAM OR SAUSAGE STUFFING

4 cups bread crumbs
½ cup minced ham or
   sausage meat
1 tablespoon minced parsley
1½ teaspoons salt
1 egg

4 tablespoons melted butter
1 teaspoon marjoram
½ teaspoon onion salt
¼ teaspoon pepper
¼ teaspoon mace

Put together in the order given and moisten with hot milk.

(2074)   OYSTER STUFFING

3 cups soft bread crumbs
1 teaspoon salt
⅛ teaspoon pepper
Few drops onion juice

1 tablespoon chopped
   parsley
25 oysters
2 tablespoons butter or fat

¼ cup oyster liquor

Mix crumbs, salt, pepper, onion juice, and parsley. Clean oysters, removing particles of shell, and add to the crumbs. Moisten with butter melted in hot oyster liquor. Mix thoroughly.

(2075)   CHESTNUT STUFFING

3 cups soft bread crumbs
1 teaspoon salt
¼ teaspoon pepper
3 tablespoons butter or fat

¼ cup hot milk
2 cups boiled chestnuts
   (No. 3844)

Mix bread crumbs, salt, and pepper. Moisten with butter, melted in the hot milk. Chop the chestnuts rather fine and add to the bread crumb mixture. Mix thoroughly.

(2076)   EGG AND MUSHROOM STUFFING

4 cups stale bread cubes
Stock (No. 501)
2-inch piece salt pork
¼ cup mushrooms, chopped
1 hard-cooked egg
   (No. 202), chopped

1 teaspoon salt
¼ teaspoon pepper
½ teaspoon poultry
   seasoning
Few drops onion juice

Cut bread in small cubes. Add hot stock to moisten and allow to stand 15 minutes. Dice pork and fry lightly. Add mushrooms and brown. Combine with bread, egg, and seasonings.

(2077)   FORCEMEAT STUFFING

2 cups ground lean meat
   from the foreshank
2 cups fine dry bread crumbs
2 tablespoons butter or other
   fat
¼ cup chopped celery
1 tablespoon chopped onion

1 sprig parsley, cut fine
⅛ teaspoon celery seed
¼ teaspoon savory
   seasoning
1 teaspoon salt
⅛ teaspoon pepper

Melt the butter in a skillet, add the celery and onion, and cook for two or three minutes. Add the ground meat, and stir until the juice evaporates and the meat browns slightly. Then add the bread crumbs and seasonings and stir until well mixed.

(2078)   SPINACH STUFFING

1½ cups drained boiled
   spinach (No. 1870)
2 tablespoons grated
   onion
4 tablespoons butter

2 tablespoons lemon juice
2 cups soft fine bread
   crumbs
Salt—Pepper

Combine ingredients and season to taste.

(2079)   MUSHROOM STUFFING

¼ pound mushrooms	1 small onion, finely
4 tablespoons butter	minced
2 cups bread crumbs	Salt—Pepper

Chop mushrooms and cook slowly in butter for about 5 minutes. Add bread crumbs and seasonings. Moisten with a little hot water.

(2080)   RICE STUFFING

1½ tablespoons onion, chopped	2 cups soup stock (No. 501)
1 tablespoon fat	½ teaspoon poultry
¾ cup uncooked rice	seasoning
1 teaspoon salt	

Cook onion in fat until tender. Add rice and simmer until the rice is a golden tint, then add soup stock, salt, and poultry seasoning. Cover and steam for twenty minutes, until rice is tender.

(2081)   CELERY STUFFING

2 cups toast crumbs	½ teaspoon salt
1 cup diced celery	⅛ teaspoon pepper
1 small onion, minced	¼ teaspoon sage
4 tablespoons melted fat	

Toast bread and crumble into small pieces. Fry celery and onion in fat for a few minutes. Add to crumbs together with seasonings. Add a little water and mix thoroughly.

(2082)   APPLE STUFFING

5 tart apples, diced	¼ cup chopped parsley
¼ cup diced salt pork	½ cup sugar
½ cup chopped celery	2 cups fine dry bread
½ cup chopped onion	crumbs

Fry the salt pork until crisp, and remove the pieces from the skillet. Cook the celery, onion, and parsley in the fat for a few minutes and remove them. Put the apples into the skillet, sprinkle

with the sugar, cover, and cook until tender, then remove the lid and continue to cook until the juice evaporates and the pieces of apples are candied. Add the other ingredients to the apples.

(2083) MINT OR WATERCRESS STUFFING

3 cups fine dry bread crumbs
½ cup fresh mint leaves, or 1½ cups finely cut watercress leaves and stems
6 tablespoons butter

3 tablespoons chopped celery
1½ tablespoons chopped onion
¾ teaspoon salt
Dash of pepper

Melt the butter in a skillet and add the onion and celery. Cook for a few minutes and add the mint leaves or the finely cut cress and the other seasonings, stir in the bread crumbs, and mix all the ingredients together. When using watercress allow the liquid which cooks out to evaporate before the bread crumbs are added.

(2084) RICE AND APRICOT STUFFING

3 cups flaky boiled rice (No. 107)
3 tablespoons butter or other fat
1 small onion, chopped
1 sprig parsley, chopped

1 cup chopped celery and tops
½ teaspoon savory seasoning
¼ pound dried apricots
Salt to taste

Fry the onion, parsley, and celery in butter a few minutes. Add rice and other seasonings. For the apricots, wash and dry them first, then cut into strips with the scissors, and mix with the rice and seasonings.

(2085) CELERY AND OLIVE STUFFING

3 cups soft bread crumbs
1 cup chopped celery
½ cup chopped olives
1 teaspoon salt
¼ teaspoon pepper

⅛ teaspoon paprika
Few drops onion juice
3 tablespoons butter or fat
½ cup hot water

Mix bread crumbs, celery, olives, salt, pepper, paprika, and onion juice. Moisten with butter, melted in hot water. Mix thoroughly.

(2086)   PRUNE AND APPLE STUFFING

3 cups bread crumbs
¼ cup melted fat
1 teaspoon salt
1 cup apples, pared, cut
in eighths, and stewed in
a little sugar (No. 41)

Few grains pepper
½ cup soaked stewed and
stoned prunes (No. 71)
½ cup nut meats, broken
into pieces, if liked

Mix all ingredients thoroughly.

(2087)   RAISIN STUFFING

2 tablespoons butter or fat
1 tablespoon chopped onion
1 cup finely cut celery and
tops
2 tablespoons chopped
parsley

2½ cups fine dry bread
crumbs
½ pound seeded chopped
raisins
Grated rind of ½ lemon
½ teaspoon salt

Cook the onion, celery, and parsley in the fat for a few minutes. Mix the raisins thoroughly with the bread crumbs, stir in
the cooked vegetables, and add the lemon rind and salt.

(2088)   LEMON STUFFING

⅓ cup melted shortening
1½ cups stale crumbs
2 teaspoons minced parsley
1 teaspoon poultry
seasoning

¾ teaspoon salt
Grated rind of 1 lemon
⅓ teaspoon pepper
2 eggs
Milk

Pour the fat over the crumbs. Add the various seasonings and
flavorings and stir all well together. Beat the eggs and add.
Moisten with milk if necessary.

(2089)   ORANGE STUFFING FOR DUCK

3 cups stale bread cubes,
toasted
½ cup hot water
2 teaspoons grated orange
rind
⅔ cup orange pulp
2 cups diced celery

¼ cup melted butter
1 beaten egg
½ teaspoon salt
Dash of pepper
¼ cup poultry
seasoning

Soften bread cubes in hot water for 15 minutes. Add remaining ingredients. Combine lightly. Stuff duck.

(2090) APRICOT STUFFING

2½ cups stewed unsweetened
    apricots (No. 42)
2 cups soft bread crumbs
2 cups cracker crumbs
¼ cup melted butter

¼ cup minced celery
½ cup shredded almonds
1½ teaspoons salt
Dash of pepper

Cut apricots into small pieces. Add the remaining ingredients and stir well.

(2091) PARSLEY STUFFING

3 cups dry bread crumbs
1 small onion, chopped
3 tablespoons chopped
    parsley

3 tablespoons melted
    shortening
1 teaspoon salt
¼ teaspoon pepper

1 cup milk

Combine in order given and toss together with a fork to keep it light.

(2092) SHREDDED WHEAT STUFFING

8 shredded wheat biscuits
2 teaspoons herb dressing
1 tablespoon minced parsley

2 teaspoons salt
½ cup butter
½ cup boiling water

Roll and sift the shredded wheat biscuits. Mix with the dressing, parsley, and salt. Melt the butter and add the boiling water to it. Mix with the dry ingredients, stirring well.

(2093) CRANBERRY STUFFING

1 cup fresh stewed cran-
    berries (No. 54), chopped
¼ cup sugar
¼ cup chopped celery
2 tablespoons chopped
    parsley

4 tablespoons butter
4 cups stale bread crumbs
½ teaspoon sweet
    marjoram
1 teaspoon salt

Combine cranberries and sugar. Cook celery and parsley in butter until celery in tender. Blend all together.

(2094) CONSOMMÉ AND RIPE OLIVE STUFFING

2 dozen ripe olives	1 teaspoon salt
4 cups dry bread cubes	¼ teaspoon pepper
1 cup consomme (No. 507)	1 tablespoon minced onion

Remove the seeds from the ripe olives. Chop the olives, then add remaining ingredients and mix well. Four cups bread cubes will use up one medium dry loaf.

(2095)   NUT STUFFING

½ to 1 cup chopped nuts	3 tablespoons melted
1 tablespoon finely chopped	butter or fat
onion	2½ cups soft bread crumbs
2 or 3 sprigs parsley,	½ teaspoon salt
chopped	⅛ teaspoon pepper
½ cup cut celery	Savory seasoning, if desired

Cook the onion, parsley, and celery in the fat for a few minutes, add the bread crumbs and seasonings, and stir until well mixed and hot. Add the nuts just before stuffing the fowl.

(2096)   PEANUT STUFFING

3 cups soft bread crumbs	1 tablespoon chopped
¾ cup chopped peanuts	parsley
½ teaspoon onion juice	2 tablespoons butter or fat
1 teaspoon salt	½ cup stock (No. 501)
⅛ teaspoon pepper	or water

Mix bread crumbs and peanuts. Add onion juice, salt, pepper, and parsley. Moisten with butter, melted in hot stock or water. Mix thoroughly.

(2097)   BRAZIL NUT STUFFING

1 cup chopped onion	8 cups bread crumbs
½ cup chopped celery	2 teaspoons poultry
⅔ cup butter or fat	seasoning
1½ cups thinly sliced	2 teaspoons salt
Brazil nuts	¼ teaspoon pepper

Cook onions and celery in butter 5 minutes. Combine Brazil nuts, bread crumbs, and seasonings and add to cooked mixture. Mix well. This makes enough to stuff about a 10-pound turkey. If a more moist stuffing is desired add a little hot water, stock, or milk.

(2098) PECAN STUFFING FOR TURKEY

2 tablespoons onion, chopped	½ cup melted butter
2 cups bread crumbs	½ teaspoon salt
1½ cups milk	⅛ teaspoon black pepper
½ cup raisins	1 teaspoon sage
½ cup chopped pecans	2 eggs

Mix ingredients, pouring hot milk over bread crumbs.

(2099)   BUTTERNUT STUFFING

4 cups sifted bread crumbs	4 cups hot mashed
1½ teaspoons poultry seasoning	potatoes (No. 1835)
1½ cups butternut meats	1 teaspoon salt
1 egg, well beaten	½ teaspoon pepper
½ cup cream	

Mix crumbs with poultry seasoning, and then with nut meats. Mix egg with cream and add to potatoes. Add seasonings and beat. Put two mixtures together.

(2100)   TOASTED ALMOND STUFFING

1 cup hot milk	1 teaspoon poultry
½ cup melted butter	seasoning
2 eggs, lightly beaten	1 teaspoon salt and pepper
4 cups cracker crumbs	mixed
4 cups bread crumbs	1½ cups chopped toasted
1 tablespoon onion juice	almonds (No. 3831)
1 cup chopped celery	

Pour the hot milk, melted butter, and the two eggs over the bread and cracker crumbs. Let stand 10 minutes. Add onion juice, chopped celery, poultry seasoning, salt and pepper, and chopped almonds.

(2101)   RICE AND HAZELNUT STUFFING
FOR WILD FOWL

½ cup hazelnuts, chopped
2 cups boiled wild rice
   (No. 108)
2 tablespoons finely chopped
   onion
1 cup cut celery

1 tablespoon chopped green
   pepper
4 tablespoons melted
   butter or fat
¼ teaspoon salt
⅛ teaspoon pepper

Cook the onion, green pepper, and celery in the fat for a few minutes. Add the rice and seasonings, and stir until well mixed and hot. Add the nuts just before stuffing the fowl. Chopped boiled chestnuts (No. 3844) can be substituted for hazelnuts.

ACCOMPANIMENTS

(2102)   ROYAL CUSTARD

1 cup bouillon (No. 505)   2 eggs

Beat bouillon and eggs until light. Pour into mold. Set in pan of boiling water and bake in moderate oven (350° F.) until firm. Cool. Cut into cubes.

(2103)   YORKSHIRE PUDDING

1 cup flour
½ teaspoon salt
1 cup milk
2 egg yolks

1 tablespoon melted butter
   or fat
2 egg whites

Mix and sift flour and salt. Add milk, beaten egg yolks, and butter. Mix well. Fold in the stiffly beaten egg whites. Cover the bottom of an earthenware baking dish with drippings from roast beef. Pour the batter into the baking dish. Bake in a hot oven (400° F.) 20 minutes. Baste with drippings from the roast after it is well risen. Cut in squares and serve on platter with the roast.

(2104)   CRANBERRY AND APPLE ICE

2 cups cranberries
1 cup sugar

2 cups tart apples, grated

Cook cranberries rapidly in 1 cup water until steaming. Reduce heat and simmer until skins burst, about 5 minutes. Rub through a medium sieve. Add enough hot water to make 2 cups pulp and liquid. Add sugar and cook 2 minutes, stirring constantly. Cool. Add apples. Mix well. Pour into refrigerator freezing tray and freeze rapidly to a mush. This makes a garnish for fruit cocktails or an accompaniment to roast meats and poultry. Serves 8 to 12.

(2105)   **CROÛTONS**

Cut stale bread in thick slices. Remove the crust and cut bread in small cubes. Drop in deep hot fat (375° F.) and fry until a delicate brown. Remove with a skimmer and drain on unglazed paper. Serve a few croûtons in each portion of soup.

(2106)   **CINNAMON ORANGE SLICES**

1½ cups sugar	2 cinnamon sticks
½ cup water	3 oranges
Juice of 1 lemon	

Make a sirup of sugar, water, juice and cinnamon. Wash oranges and cut in thick slices. Place in hot sirup and boil gently, without covering until rind is clear. Chill in sirup before serving as a meat garnish.

(2107)   **SPICED PRUNE GARNISH**

1½ cups granulated sugar	12 large prunes, soaked in
1½ cups hot water	cold water
1 piece stick cinnamon	6 lettuce cups
12 whole cloves	

Combine the sugar, water, and spices and heat to the boiling point. Add prunes, cover, and cook until tender, about 20 minutes. Remove prunes from sirup and cool slightly. Carefully remove the stones. Place two or three prunes in each lettuce cup and arrange on platter around meat loaf or other meat dish.

Cheese

CHEESE, despite what looks like high cost, is economical to use. There is no wastage. It is rich in proteins and calories. Many varieties contain an abundance of fats. It can be prepared quickly in many different ways and is often the answer to the perplexing question of what to serve unexpected guests.

(2201) COTTAGE CHEESE

Heat sour milk to about 100° F. and turn into a strainer lined with cheesecloth. Pour over 1 quart hot water. Let curd hang in cheesecloth bag until all whey has drained off. Add enough cream and melted butter to moisten. Add salt.

(2202) WELSH RAREBIT

2 tablespoons butter or fat	Few grains cayenne
2 tablespoons flour	1 cup thin cream
¼ teaspoon mustard	1½ cups grated cheese
½ teaspoon salt	1 egg

Toast

Melt butter. Add flour, mustard, salt, and cayenne and mix well. Add cream slowly and bring to the boiling point, stirring constantly. Add cheese and stir until melted. Remove from fire. Beat the egg well and pour hot sauce on it. Mix well. Serve hot on toast. Serves 4.

(2203)   RAREBIT SUPREME

2 tablespoons butter	1 teaspoon mustard
1½ tablespoons chopped onion	1 cup tomato juice
2 tablespoons chopped green	1¼ cups grated cheese
pepper	1 well-beaten egg
2 tablespoons flour	½ cup cream
1 teaspoon salt	1 cup cooked flaked
⅛ teaspoon cayenne	crab meat (No. 1227)

Melt butter in pan. Add onion and pepper and sauté until lightly browned. Mix flour, salt, and cayenne and add to mixture. Add mustard and tomato juice. Simmer slowly, stirring constantly, until smooth and thickened. Add cheese and stir thoroughly. Stir in egg. Simmer 3 minutes, stirring constantly. Remove from heat. Add hot cream and crab meat. Mix well. Heat through. Serve on buttered toast (No. 988). Serves 6.

(2204)   ALE RAREBIT

3 cups grated cheese	1 cup ale
1½ tablespoons butter	2 beaten egg yolks

Melt cheese and butter. Add ½ cup ale. Mix remaining ale with yolks and stir into cheese. Cook, stirring constantly, until smooth and thick. Pour over buttered toast (No. 988). Serves 4.

(2205)   TUNA FISH RAREBIT

Add ½ cup flaked tuna fish to Welsh rarebit, eliminating salt and substituting 1 teaspoon Worcestershire sauce for mustard.

(2206)   SARDINE RAREBIT

Place broiled sardines (No. 1195) on buttered toast (No. 988) before pouring Welsh rarebit (No. 2202) over.

(2207)   CRUMB RAREBIT

1 cup bread crumbs	1 well-beaten egg
1 cup milk	½ teaspoon salt
1 teaspoon butter	⅛ teaspoon pepper
½ cup cheese, grated	

Soak crumbs in milk 10 minutes. Melt butter and cheese in frying pan. Add crumbs, egg, salt, and pepper. Heat thoroughly, stirring constantly. Serve on buttered toast (No. 988) or crackers. Serves 4.

(2208)   BACON AND BEAN RAREBIT

1 cup baked beans
   (No. 1708)
¼ cup diced bacon
1 tablespoon finely minced
   onion
¼ cup minced American
   cheese

½ cup tomato soup
   (No. 571) or cream of
   tomato soup (No. 570)
½ teaspoon dry mustard
1 teaspoon Worcester-
   shire sauce

Put the bacon in pan, add the onion, and cook till golden brown. Add the beans, tomato soup or purée, and the seasonings. When thoroughly heated, add the cheese and stir slowly till the cheese is melted. Serve on top thin slices of toast or toasted crackers. Serves 4.

(2209)   MUSHROOM SOUP RAREBIT

2 tablespoons butter
2 tablespoons flour
1 cup milk
1 cup cream of mushroom
   soup (No. 551)
1 tablespoon tomato
   catchup

½ teaspoon salt
Dash pepper
1 teaspoon Worcester-
   shire sauce
1 cup grated sharp
   American cheese

Blend butter and flour together in a double boiler. Add milk and cook until thickened, stirring constantly. Add soup, catchup, salt, pepper, and Worcestershire sauce and heat thoroughly. Remove from heat and stir in the cheese. Serve on toast or toasted corn bread. Serves 6.

(2210)   MEXICAN CHEESE

2 tablespoons butter or fat
2 tablespoons chopped green
   pepper
2 tablespoons flour
1 teaspoon salt
¼ teaspoon mustard
Few grains cayenne

1 cup strained tomato
   juice
1 cup stewed (No. 1769)
   or canned corn
1½ cups grated cheese
1 egg

Melt butter, add green pepper, and cook until soft. Add flour, salt, mustard, and cayenne and mix well. Add tomato juice slowly and cook until thick, stirring constantly. Add corn and cheese and cook until cheese is melted. Remove from fire. Beat the egg well and pour the hot sauce on it. Mix well. Serve hot on toast. Serves 6.

(2211)   CHEESE SOUFFLÉ

1 cup grated cheese	3 egg yolks
1 cup thick white sauce	3 egg whites
(No. 2004)	

Add the cheese to the hot white sauce and stir until melted. Cool. Add the beaten egg yolks. Fold in the stiffly beaten egg whites. Pour into a greased baking dish. Stand in a pan of warm water and bake in a moderate oven (325° F.) 50 to 60 minutes. Serves 6.

(2212)   CHEESE FONDUE

1½ cups milk	⅛ teaspoon pepper
2 cups soft bread crumbs	⅛ teaspoon paprika
3 eggs	1 tablespoon melted butter
1½ cups grated cheese	or fat
1 teaspoon salt	

Pour milk over the bread crumbs. Add beaten eggs, cheese, salt, pepper, paprika, and butter. Mix well. Pour into greased individual baking dishes and bake in moderate oven (350° F.) 20 to 25 minutes. Serves 6.

(2213)   CORN-CHEESE FONDUE

1 cup milk	1 tablespoon butter
1½ cups bread crumbs	Salt—Pepper—Paprika to
1 cup stewed corn	taste
(No. 1769)	3 egg yolks, beaten until
1 cup grated American	thick
cheese	3 egg whites, beaten stiff

Mix well the milk, crumbs, corn, cheese, butter, and seasonings. Add the egg yolks and fold in the stiffly beaten egg whites. Bake in individual buttered dishes in a moderate oven (350° F.) until firm. Serves 6.

(2214)   CHEESE BALLS OR CROQUETTES

½ pound grated American cheese	⅛ teaspoon salt
2 cups soft bread crumbs	Few grains cayenne
3 eggs	1 egg
1 teaspoon Worcestershire sauce	2 tablespoons water
	½ cup dry bread crumbs

Mix cheese, soft crumbs, 3 beaten eggs, Worcestershire sauce, salt, and cayenne. Form into balls. Dip in slightly beaten egg, diluted with water, roll in dry crumbs, and fry in deep hot fat (375° F.) until a delicate brown. Drain on unglazed paper. Serve hot with tomato sauce (No. 2035). Serves 6.

(2215)   SCRAMBLED CHEESE

⅓ cup milk	⅓ teaspoon paprika
2 tablespoons butter	1 cup grated cheese
4 beaten eggs	1 tablespoon chopped parsley
1 teaspoon salt	

Heat milk and butter in pan set in hot water or double boiler. Add eggs, salt, and paprika. Cook, stirring constantly, until thickened. Add cheese and parsley and continue stirring until slightly set. Turn onto buttered toast (No. 988) and garnish with broiled bacon (No. 1464). Serves 4.

(2216)   BAKED COTTAGE CHEESE

Cream ½ pound cottage cheese with salt, pepper, and sugar to taste. Put in baking dish. Add enough cream to barely moisten. Heat thoroughly in moderate oven (350° F.). Beat. Repeat heating and beating twice more. Return to oven and brown on top. Serves 4.

(2217)   BAKED CELERY AND CHEESE

1¼ cups grated cheese	1 cup boiled celery
2 eggs	(No. 1761)
1 teaspoon Worcestershire sauce	1 cup boiled macaroni (No. 2302)
2 cups milk	Salt—Pepper

Combine cheese, eggs, Worcestershire sauce, and milk. Beat until light. Combine celery and macaroni and put in bottom of greased baking dish. Sprinkle with salt and pepper. Add cheese-egg mixture. Set in pan of hot water. Bake in moderate oven (350° F.) until set, about 35 to 45 minutes. Turn out on hot platter and serve with cheese sauce (No. 2008), garnished with sautéed mushroom caps (No. 1801). Serves 6.

(2218)   BAKED CHEESE AND OLIVE

2 cups bread, broken in pieces
3 tablespoons melted butter
1 cup grated cheese
½ cup sliced stuffed olives

3 beaten eggs
1 teaspoon mustard
¼ cup liquid from olives
2 cups hot milk

Stir bread in 2 tablespoons butter. Line bottom of greased baking dish with ⅔ cup buttered crumbs. Add layer of ½ cup cheese, then ¼ cup olives. Repeat layers of crumbs, cheese, and olives. Top with remaining crumbs. Brush with remaining butter. Mix eggs, mustard, liquid from olives, and milk, blending well. Pour over mixture in dish. Bake in moderate oven (350° F.) 35 to 45 minutes. Serves 6.

(2219)   BAKED CHEESE AND APPLES

Use 3 cored, pared, and sliced apples instead of sliced olives in baked cheese and olive (No. 2218), eliminating liquid from olives.

(2220)   CHEESE AND SPINACH LOAF

4 cups boiled spinach (No. 1870), chopped
2 cups grated cheese
1 cup boiled rice (No. 107)
1 tablespoon horseradish

2 tablespoons melted butter
1 teaspoon salt
¼ teaspoon pepper

Combine ingredients. Mold into a loaf. Put in greased baking pan. Bake in moderate oven (350° F.) 15 to 18 minutes. Serve garnished with slices of hard-cooked egg (No. 202). Tomato sauce (No. 2035) goes well with this. Serves 6.

(2221)   CHEESE AND NUT ROAST

½ cup grated cheese   1 chopped onion
½ cup chopped nuts   2 teaspoons lemon juice
½ cup bread crumbs   Salt—Pepper
1 tablespoon butter

Combine cheese, nuts, and crumbs. Melt butter. Add onion and sauté until well browned. Add ¼ cup hot water, lemon juice, and salt and pepper to taste. Add dry mixture and mix well by stirring. Turn into greased baking dish. Bake in moderate oven (350° F.) until brown. Serve with mushroom sauce (No. 2039). Serves 6. Cooked rolled oats (No. 101) or boiled rice (No. 107) may be used instead of bread crumbs.

(2222) COTTAGE CHEESE AND PEANUT LOAF

Use 1 cup cottage cheese instead of grated cheese and peanuts instead of chopped nuts in recipe for cheese and nut roast (No. 2221).

(2223)   CHEESE CUTLETS

1 cup grated cheese   1½ cups mashed potatoes
1½ cups boiled dried beans   (No. 1835)
(No. 1721)   Salt—Pepper

Combine ingredients, adding salt and pepper to taste. Shape into cutlets, ½ inch thick. Fry until brown on both sides in little fat. Serve with tomato (No. 2035) or horseradish sauce (No. 2038). Serves 6.

(2224)   CHEESE LOAF

½ pound American cheese   6 small sweet pickles,
4 hard-cooked eggs   chopped
(No. 202)   1 small onion, chopped
Dash cayenne

Allow cheese to stand at room temperature until softened. Force through coarse sieve. Mash yolks of eggs with fork. Chop whites. Add eggs, pickles, onions, and cayenne to cheese and blend thoroughly. Press in buttered mold. Chill thoroughly. Remove to small platter and slice. Serves 6.

(2225) CURRIED COTTAGE CHEESE AND EGGS IN RICE NESTS

2 tablespoons butter	1½ cups cottage cheese
2 tablespoons flour	Salt—Pepper
¾ cup milk	6 hard-cooked eggs
1 teaspoon curry powder	(No. 202)
½ teaspoon onion juice	Hot boiled rice (No. 107)

Melt butter in a double boiler. Add flour and mix well. Add milk gradually and cook, stirring constantly, until thickened. Add curry powder, onion juice, cottage cheese, and salt and pepper to taste. Fold in the diced eggs, reserving six slices for garnish. Reheat. Serve on nests of rice. Serves 6.

(2226) CHEESE PUDDING

3 eggs, well beaten	Salt—Pepper
2 cups grated cheese	½ cup milk
2 cups bread crumbs	

Combine eggs, cheese, and crumbs and season to taste with salt and pepper. Turn into greased individual baking dishes. Moisten with milk. Bake in moderate oven (350° F.) 25 to 35 minutes. Serves 6.

(2227) CHEESE APPLES

Soften 8-ounce package American cheese with a fork. Add ½ cup finely chopped nut meats and 12 small pickled onions, finely chopped. Mix well and form into small balls, apple shaped. Roll one side in paprika and stick in a whole clove for "blossom" end. Makes one dozen.

(2228) CHEESE PIN WHEELS

Baking powder biscuit dough (No. 1012)	1 cup grated American cheese
⅓ cup melted butter	

Roll dough into oblong piece ¼ inch thick. Spread with melted butter and sprinkle ½ cup grated cheese. Roll as for jelly roll and cut in 1-inch slices. Place slices in greased pan or muffin pans and sprinkle remaining grated cheese over the muffins. Bake in hot oven (400° F.) 15 to 20 minutes. Or, the rolled dough can be brushed with melted butter and all the cheese sprinkled over the dough.

(2229)   CHEESE TORTE

⅛ pound of butter	¾ pint heavy sour cream
25 graham crackers, crumbled	4 eggs, separated
	½ cup sugar
½ pound cream cheese	Pinch of salt
½ pound cottage cheese	1 teaspoon vanilla

Melt butter. Add cracker crumbs, reserving three teaspoons. Line a buttered baking dish with crumbs. Blend cheese well. Add sour cream and mix well. Add egg yolks, sugar, salt, and vanilla, and mix well. Fold in stiffly beaten egg whites. Turn into greased large or individual baking dishes. Sprinkle reserved crumbs over top. Bake in hot oven (375° F.) 35 minutes. Cool before serving.

(2230)   TRÈS BIENS

Place enough slices of tomato to cover a slice of bread. Sprinkle with salt and pepper, then a slice of cheese, next a slice of onion, then a ring of green pepper, and last, two strips of bacon laid over the top. Bake in a hot oven (400° F.) about 20 minutes or until bacon is crispy. Do not put under broiler. Serve with any desired sauce.

(2231)   COTTAGE CHEESE PIE

2½ teaspoons cornstarch	2 teaspoons lemon juice
½ cup cream	Grated rind of ¼ lemon
½ pound cottage cheese	¼ teaspoon cinnamon
1 tablespoon melted butter	Plain pie pastry
2 eggs	(No. 2701)
⅔ cup sugar	Powdered sugar

Dissolve cornstarch in cream. Drain cheese and rub in through a sieve twice. Add butter. Separate eggs. Beat yolks until light. Add sugar and beat until thoroughly blended. Add cheese, cream, lemon juice, rind, and cinnamon. Beat egg whites stiff and fold in, reserving a little. Line a greased pie tin with pastry. Brush with reserved egg white. Pour in cheese mixture. Bake in moderate oven (350° F.) 25 to 35 minutes. Sprinkle with powdered sugar and a dash of cinnamon. Serves 4.

(2232)   **CHEESE CUPS**

1 cup flour   ½ cup grated American
¼ teaspoon salt   cheese
            ⅓ cup shortening

Mix and sift flour and salt. Cut cheese and shortening into mixture. Add 3 tablespoons cold water. Roll out on floured board ⅛ inch thick. Cut in squares and line muffin tins so that corners stick out. Bake in hot oven (425° F.) until brown, about 15 minutes. Remove. Cool and serve filled with buttered (No. 1913) or creamed vegetables (No. 1914). Serves 8.

(2233)   **CHEESE CAKE**

½ cup melted butter   Rind of ½ lemon, chopped
2 cups zwieback crumbs   fine
½ cup powdered sugar   ½ teaspoon salt
1 teaspoon cinnamon   ½ teaspoon vanilla
4 eggs   1 cup cream
¾ cup granulated sugar   2 cups cream cheese
¼ cup lemon juice   ¼ cup flour

Combine butter, 1 cup crumbs, sugar, and cinnamon. Blend thoroughly. Separate eggs. Combine yolks, granulated sugar, and ½ cup water. Cook, stirring constantly, in a double boiler until mixture coats a metal spoon. Stir in lemon rind, lemon juice, salt, and vanilla. Beat egg whites slightly and stir into cream. Blend cheese and flour and add to cream. Combine liquid mixtures. Stir in crumb mixture. Turn into greased baking pan. Sprinkle remaining crumbs on top. Bake in slow oven (275° F.) 1 hour. Leave cake in oven 45 minutes after cooking is finished. Serves 6.

(2234)   **CHEESE STRAWS**

Roll out plain pastry (No. 2701) to ⅛-inch thickness. Sprinkle with salt, cayenne, and grated American cheese. Fold in 3 layers. Roll out again, spread, and roll as before. Cut in strips ½ inch wide and 4 or 5 inches long. Bake in hot oven (400° F.) 5 or 6 minutes.

(2235) CHEESE CREAM PUFFS

¼ cup shortening	½ cup grated American
½ cup flour	cheese
½ teaspoon salt	2 eggs
Few grains cayenne	

Bring shortening and 1 cup hot water to boiling point. Add flour, salt, and cayenne, stirring constantly and cook until mixture leaves sides of pan. Add cheese and mix well. Cool. Add unbeaten eggs, one at a time, beating well after each egg is added. Drop by teaspoons on a greased pan, making small balls. Bake in moderate oven (350° F.) 30 to 40 minutes. Yield: 48 puffs.

(2236) CHEESE FINGERS

1 cup flour	2 tablespoons shortening
½ teaspoon baking powder	4 tablespoons grated
⅛ teaspoon cayenne	cheese
½ teaspoon salt	

Mix and sift flour, baking powder, cayenne, and salt. Cut in shortening with a knife or rub in with finger tips. Add cheese and enough cold water to hold mixture together. Roll out on floured board to ¼-inch thickness. Cut in very thin strips with a knife or pastry jagger. Bake in a hot oven (400° F.) 20 minutes. Yield: 50 fingers.

(2237) CATCHUP CHEESE FINGERS

Mix grated American cheese to a smooth paste with tomato catchup, using about two tablespoons catchup to every ¼ pound cheese. Cut sliced sandwich bread in narrow strips, toasted on one side, then spread untoasted side heavily with cheese mixture. Toast under broiler and serve at once with cream soups or vegetable salads.

(2238) CHEESE CRACKERS

Sprinkle grated cheese on crackers or thin melba toast (No. 989). Heat in hot oven (450° F.) until cheese melts. Sprinkle with paprika.

(2239)   CORN SOUP ROQUEFORT

2 cups corn chowder
   (No. 547)
½ cup milk
Salt

¼ cup crumbled Roque-
   fort cheese
Paprika

Empty soup in a saucepan, add milk, salt to suit taste, **and** heat, stirring to blend ingredients. Just before serving, **add** cheese. Add a dash of paprika to each serving. Any cream soup may be used instead of corn chowder. Serves 6.

(2240)   CHEESE FRITTERS

1 cup steamed rice
   (No. 106)
1 egg
½ cup grated American
   cheese

1 tablespoon milk
2 teaspoons prepared **mustard**
¼ teaspoon salt
Buttered cracker crumbs
¼ teaspoon paprika

Mix the rice thoroughly with the beaten egg, milk, **grated** cheese and seasonings. Shape into balls, roll in buttered **cracker** crumbs, and fry in deep fat (375° F.) until brown. Serves 6.

(2241)   CHEESE FAVORITE

½ cup grated American
   cheese
1½ tablespoons melted butter
¼ teaspoon salt
¼ teaspoon paprika

3 eggs
2 teaspoons prepared
   mustard
Toast points

Mix grated cheese, butter, salt and paprika. Beat eggs **until** light, add mustard and pour into the cheese mixture. Cook **in** double boiler, stirring constantly until the mixture is smooth and creamy. Serve on hot toast points and garnish with paprika. Serves 6.

Macaroni · Spaghetti

THE principal uses to which macaroni, noodles, spaghetti, and vermicelli are adapted are usually in combinations with meats, eggs, and vegetables. However, there are many tasty dishes in which these dried pastes can be made into an economical main course.

Because most macaroni, etc., is bought in packages, it would always be best to carefully study the cooking directions given by the manufacturer as variations in the grade of flour cause changes in the time and methods of cooking for best results. The methods and times given in the following recipes are average and, if used, will always yield satisfactory dishes.

(2301)   **NOODLES**

¼ teaspoon salt   1 slightly beaten egg
1 cup flour

Mix and sift flour and salt. Add gradually to egg until a stiff dough is formed. Knead a few minutes on floured board. Roll out to ¹⁄₁₆-inch thickness. Let stand ½ hour. Cut in long ¼-inch wide strips. Dry thoroughly. Noodles may be cut into any size strips or any tiny fancy shapes. This makes 1½ cups raw noodles.

(2302)   **BOILED MACARONI**

Boil macaroni in salted water until tender. Drain in sieve or colander. Pour boiling water over the macaroni to prevent sticking. Keep hot over hot water. Spaghetti, vermicelli, and noodles

(No. 2301) are cooked the same way. If desired, butter may be added before serving.

(2303)   CREAMED MACARONI

Substitute boiled macaroni (No. 2302) for noodles in recipe for creamed noodles (No. 2316).

(2304) ELBOW MACARONI À LA GOLDENROD

8 ounces elbow macaroni	1 pimiento, chopped
2 tablespoons butter	2 tablespoons minced
2 tablespoons flour	parsley
2½ cups milk	3 hard-cooked eggs
Salt—Pepper	(No. 202)

Cook macaroni as directed on package and drain. Melt butter, stir in flour, and add milk gradually. Stir over low fire until smooth and thick. Season to taste with salt and pepper. Add pimiento, parsley, and chopped whites of the eggs. Combine this sauce with the macaroni. Arrange on a large platter, sprinkle center with egg yolks, pressed through a sieve, and garnish with parsley and pimiento. Serves 6.

(2305)   BAKED MACARONI

4 cups boiled macaroni	½ cup buttered bread
(No. 2302)	crumbs
2 cups medium white sauce	
(No. 2004)	

Combine macaroni and sauce. Turn into greased baking dish. Top with crumbs. Bake in hot oven (400° F.) until brown. Serves 6.

(2306)   MACARONI WITH CHEESE

1 cup macaroni	¼ cup chopped or grated
1⅓ cups white sauce	cheese
(No. 2004)	Buttered crumbs

Break macaroni into pieces 1 inch long, boil, strain, and rinse. Stir cheese into hot, well-seasoned white sauce and put macaroni and sauce in buttered baking dish in layers. Sprinkle buttered crumbs on top and brown well in hot oven (400° F.). Serves 6.

(2307)   CHEESE MACARONI WITH EGGS

Add 3 sliced hard-cooked eggs (No. 202) to white sauce in recipe for macaroni with cheese (No. 2306).

(2308)   MACARONI AND TOMATOES

Substitute boiled macaroni (No. 2302) for spaghetti in recipe for spaghetti and tomatoes (No. 2327).

(2309) MACARONI WITH OYSTERS OR CLAMS

Place 8 to 12 raw oysters or clams as one of the center layers in recipe for macaroni and tomatoes (No. 2308).

(2310) MACARONI WITH BACON-TOMATO SAUCE

Use macaroni in place of spaghetti in recipe for spaghetti with bacon-tomato sauce (No. 2329).

(2311) MACARONI WITH ITALIAN SAUCE

Use macaroni instead of spaghetti in recipe for spaghetti with Italian sauce (No. 2328).

(2312)   CREOLE MACARONI

Substitute 2 cups creole sauce (No. 2047) for white sauce and grated cheese in recipe for macaroni with cheese (No. 2306). Serves 6.

(2313) SAUSAGE AND MACARONI LOAF

2 pounds link sausages	½ pound grated American
1 cup macaroni	cheese
2 tablespoons butter	2 eggs slightly beaten
2 tablespoons flour	Salt
1 cup milk	

Cook macaroni in boiling salted water until tender, about 20 minutes. Make a white sauce by combining butter and flour, gradually adding milk and cooking until thickened. Melt cheese in white sauce, add slightly beaten eggs and macaroni. Season. Brown link sausages in frying pan and place in a border around inside of loaf pan. Pour macaroni mixture inside sausage border. Bake in moderate oven (350° F.) 40 minutes. Tomato sauce (No. 2035) may be served with this. Serves 6.

(2314)   MACARONI AND CHIPPED BEEF EN CASSEROLE

4 cups boiled macaroni (No. 2302)
1 cup chipped beef

2 cups thin white sauce (No. 2004)
¼ cup bread crumbs

Put a layer of macaroni in a greased baking dish or casserole, then a layer of chipped beef and a layer of white sauce. Repeat until all the ingredients are used. Sprinkle top with seasoned bread crumbs and bake in hot oven (400° F.) 20 to 25 minutes. Serves 6.

(2315) MACARONI AND CHEESE CROQUETTES

1 cup grated cheese
1 teaspoon onion juice
1 cup thick white sauce (No. 2004)
4 cups boiled elbow macaroni (No. 2302)

3 slices broiled bacon (No. 1464), chopped
1½ teaspoons chopped parsley
1 cup bread crumbs

Combine cheese and onion juice with hot white sauce. Add other ingredients. Mix well. Mold into croquettes. Dip in crumbs. Fry in deep hot fat (375° F.) 4 minutes or until crumbs are browned. Drain on unglazed paper. Or, mold into small patties and fry in little fat in frying pan, turning once to brown both sides. Serves 6.

(2316)   CREAMED NOODLES

Combine 4 cups boiled noodles (No. 2302) with 2 cups medium white sauce (No. 2004). Heat, stirring frequently, until they will dish without running.

(2317) NOODLES WITH BUTTERED CRUMBS

Into six quarts of actively boiling salted water drop little by little one pound of fine noodles (No. 2301). Cook until tender, then drain well through a colander. Put a large lump of butter in the bottom of a pan, add the noodles, and stir with a fork so that they are all well coated with butter. Place in a hot dish and sprinkle with buttered toasted crumbs made by toasting bits of bread in the oven until a golden brown, then rolling them into a powder with a rolling pin. Melt plenty of butter in a frying pan and heat the crumbs in this.

(2318) BAKED NOODLES, CHEESE, AND HAM

4 cups boiled noodles (No. 2302)	⅔ cup grated cheese
1 cup ham, cut fine	2 cups thin white sauce (No. 2004)

Put a layer of noodles in a greased baking dish. Sprinkle with ham and cheese, then cover with a layer of white sauce. Repeat until all the ingredients are used. Sprinkle top with cheese. Bake in hot oven (400° F.) 20 to 25 minutes. Serves 6.

(2319)   NOODLES WITH SARDINES

1 can sardines	1 cup thin white sauce (No. 2004)
2 tablespoons butter or oil	½ cup grated cheese
2½ cups boiled noodles (No. 2302)	

Sauté the sardines in the oil in frying pan. Mix the noodles, white sauce and grated cheese. Steam until hot in double boiler. Pour the sardines and oil into the noodle mixture. This may be heated for 5 minutes and served or it may be turned into a greased baking dish, sprinkled with bread crumbs, and baked in a hot oven (400° F.) for about 10 minutes. Serve hot. Serves 4 to 6.

(2320)   HAM WITH NOODLES

2 cups boiled noodles (No. 2302)	3 cups ground cooked ham
3 cups thin white sauce (No. 2004)	1 cup buttered bread crumbs

Make alternate layers of noodles and ham in a shallow baking dish. Pour on the white sauce. Sprinkle buttered crumbs over the top. Bake about 20 minutes in a moderately hot oven (375° F.). Serves 6. As a variation, tomato sauce (No. 2035) may be substituted for white sauce.

(2321)   SAUSAGE WITH NOODLES

6 sausages	1 cup stewed prunes
4 cups boiled wide noodles	(No. 71)
(No. 2302)	1 pimiento
1 cup browned bread	¾ cup water
crumbs	

Place sausages in pan with water. When water cooks out, brown nicely on all sides. Season hot noodles and place in center of platter. Sprinkle with fine bread crumbs browned in butter. Arrange sausages on noodles and place prunes around the edge of platter. Garnish with pimiento. As a variation, the noodles may be prepared with cheese sauce (No. 2008) or tomato sauce (No. 2035). Serves 6.

(2322)   VIENNESE NOODLES

8 ounces wide egg noodles	½ cup chopped almonds or
¼ cup butter	Brazil nuts
	2 teaspoons poppy seeds

Cook wide egg noodles (No. 2302) and drain. Melt 1 tablespoon butter. Add chopped nuts and stir over low heat until light brown. Add remaining butter, the egg noodles, and poppy seeds and stir lightly until heated thoroughly. Serve with any creamed meat or fish dish, or with creamed mushrooms (No. 1804). Serves 6. This may also be served as an entrée with tomato (No. 2035) or any desired sauce.

(2323)   NOODLE OMELET

Sauté boiled noodles (No. 2302) in little fat until delicately browned and add to egg mixture before cooking omelet (No. 208).

(2324)   EGG NOODLE NESTS

8 ounces fine egg noodles	1 tablespoon lemon juice
2 eggs	6 stewed apricots
⅓ cup sugar	(No. 42)
½ cup milk	Dry cake crumbs
Grated rind 1 orange	

Cook fine egg noodles, broken in short lengths (No. 2302), and drain. Beat eggs slightly. Add sugar, milk, orange rind, and lemon juice. Combine with egg noodles and place over boiling water. Cook 10 minutes. Fill individual baking cups or ramekins with this mixture, leaving a hollow in center. Place apricot in each hollow. Sprinkle with stale cake or macaroon crumbs and brown quickly in hot oven (400° F.) or under broiler. Serve with apricot juice or whipped cream. Canned peaches, pears, pineapple chunks, or any stewed fruits or berries can be substituted for apricots. Serves 6.

(2325)   CREAMED SPAGHETTI

Substitute boiled spaghetti (No. 2302) for noodles in recipe for creamed noodles (No. 2316).

(2326)   BAKED SPAGHETTI

½ pound spaghetti	2 cups canned or stewed
2 tablespoons butter or fat	tomatoes (No. 1893)
1½ tablespoons onion, chopped	1 teaspoon salt
	¼ teaspoon pepper
1½ tablespoons green pepper, chopped	⅛ teaspoon paprika
	1 tablespoon sugar
1 cup grated cheese	

Boil spaghetti in salted water until tender. Drain. Melt butter in pan and sauté onion and green pepper until soft. Add tomatoes, salt, pepper, paprika, and sugar. Simmer 10 minutes. Add spaghetti and mix well. Add ½ cup cheese. Turn into greased baking dish. Sprinkle with remaining cheese. Bake in hot oven (400° F.) until cheese is brown, 20 to 25 minutes. As a variation, this dish can also be made by adding ground sausage meat or ham. Serves 6.

(2327)   SPAGHETTI AND TOMATOES

Put a layer of boiled spaghetti (No. 2302) in the bottom of a greased baking dish. Add layer of tomato sauce (No. 2035). Dot with ¼-inch cubes of bacon and onion. Continue alternating layers to fill dish. Cover with buttered crumbs and grated cheese, if desired. Bake in hot oven (400° F.) 20 to 25 minutes. Four cups boiled spaghetti serves 6.

(2328) SPAGHETTI WITH ITALIAN SAUCE

½ pound ground veal
½ pound ground pork
½ pound ground beef
½ pound sausage
¼ pound butter
1¼ pounds onions, chopped
¼ clove garlic, cut fine
1 green pepper, chopped
2 sprigs parsley, chopped
½ pound mushrooms, sliced

2½ cups tomato purée
1 cup catchup
½ teaspoon Worcestershire
   sauce
2 teaspoons lemon juice
2 teaspoons salt
¼ teaspoon pepper
8 ounces spaghetti
Grated Parmesan cheese

Brown meats in butter in iron skillet. Add onions, garlic, pepper, and parsley. Cook until slightly brown. Add mushrooms, tomato purée, catchup, and ½ cup water, Worcestershire, lemon juice, salt, and pepper. Simmer, covered, 1½ hours. Boil spaghetti in salted water until soft, keeping it whole. Pour sauce over spaghetti and serve on platter. Sprinkle top generously with grated Parmesan cheese. Serves 8.

(2329) SPAGHETTI WITH BACON-TOMATO SAUCE

4 slices bacon, diced
1 onion, sliced
¾ cup stewed tomatoes
   (No. 1893)
½ teaspoon salt

⅛ teaspoon pepper
⅛ teaspoon allspice
Dash cayenne
4 cups boiled and drained
   spaghetti (No. 2302)

Heat bacon in frying pan. Add onion, tomatoes, salt, pepper, allspice, and cayenne. Bring to boiling point. Cover and let simmer 30 minutes. Pour over hot spaghetti. Sprinkle with grated Parmesan cheese if desired. Serves 6.

(2330) SPAGHETTI LUNCHEON CASSEROLE WITH MUSHROOMS

¼ pound stewed mushrooms (No. 1803)	Dash cayenne
¼ cup chopped onion	¼ cup grated American cheese
3 tablespoons butter	3 cups boiled spaghetti
2 tablespoons flour	(No. 2302)
1 cup milk	½ cup buttered bread
¼ cup chopped pimientos	crumbs
½ teaspoon salt	

Drain and save the liquid from the mushrooms. Brown mushrooms and onion in the butter. Add flour and blend well. Add milk and the liquid from the mushrooms and cook until thick and smooth. Add chopped pimientos and season with salt and cayenne. Remove from heat and stir in the cheese. Combine with the spaghetti and place in a buttered baking dish. Top with bread crumbs and bake in a moderately hot oven (400° F.) about 20 minutes. Serve hot with tomato (No. 2035) or any desired sauce. Serves 8.

(2331) SPAGHETTI CROWN WITH SAVORY SPINACH

3 cups boiled spaghetti (No. 2302)	15 fried cocktail pork sausages (No. 1469)
1 cup tomato sauce (No. 2035)	2½ cups boiled spinach (No. 1870)
3 eggs, beaten	¼ cup French dressing
½ teaspoon salt	(No. 716)
1 tablespoon horseradish	

Combine the spaghetti with the eggs and salt. Grease and flour a basin (6 inches in diameter) and turn the spaghetti mixture into it. Place the sausages upright around the spaghetti close to the edge of the pan. Bake in a moderate oven (375° F.) 35 minutes or until firm. Turn out on a plate and then invert onto a chop platter so that crown is right side up. Combine the spinach with the French dressing and horseradish and heat thoroughly. Place in mounds around the spaghetti crown. Serve with tomato sauce. Serves 5.

(2332)   SPAGHETTI WITH TUNA FISH

1 onion, chopped	1 cup tomato soup
½-pound can tuna fish	(No. 571)
2 cups boiled spaghetti	½ teaspoon sugar
(No. 2302)	1 teaspoon salt
½ cup tomato sauce	⅛ teaspoon pepper
(No. 2035)	¼ teaspoon paprika
1 teaspoon chopped parsley	Dash cayenne

Sauté the onion in the oil from the tuna fish. Flake the fish. Add all ingredients to the onion and oil. Let simmer 20 minutes or until thoroughly hot. Rub the serving dish with cut clove of garlic. Pour the spaghetti mixture into it and serve hot. Serves 4 to 6. Salmon may be used in place of tuna fish.

(2333)   SPAGHETTI WITH CORN

Substitute stewed (No. 1769) or buttered corn (No. 1771) for tuna fish and 1½ tablespoons butter for tuna fish oil in recipe for spaghetti with tuna fish (No. 2332).

(2334)   SPAGHETTI WITH MINCED HAM

Combine 2 cups minced cooked ham with spaghetti in recipe for spaghetti with bacon-tomato sauce (No. 2329) and do not use cheese.

(2335) SPAGHETTI WITH BUTTERED CRUMBS

Substitute spaghetti for noodles in recipe for noodles with buttered crumbs (No. 2317).

(2336) SPAGHETTI WITH OYSTERS OR CLAMS

Place 8 to 12 raw oysters or clams as one of center layers in recipe for spaghetti and tomatoes (No. 2327).

(2337)   SPAGHETTI AND KIDNEYS

Place 6 lamb kidneys, skinned, cleared of tubes and hard membranes, and halved, as top layer in recipe for spaghetti and tomatoes (No. 2327) and bake in hot oven (400° F.) about 30 minutes or until kidneys are tender. Serves 6.

(2338)   SPAGHETTI AND SAUERKRAUT

2½ cups boiled spaghetti   1 cup tomato sauce
    (No. 2302)   (No. 2035)
2½ cups sauerkraut   6 slices bacon

Put layer of spaghetti in bottom of greased baking dish. Add layer of sauerkraut. Repeat, alternating layers, until all ingredients are used. Add sauce. Top with bacon. Bake in hot oven (400° F.) 20 to 25 minutes or until bacon is crisp. Serves 6.

(2339)   GOLDEN EGG VERMICELLI

3 hard-cooked eggs   6 slices buttered toast
    (No. 202)   (No. 988)
1 cup thin white sauce   3 cups boiled vermicelli
    (No. 2004)   (No. 2302)

Remove shells from eggs and separate yolks from whites. Chop whites and mix with hot white sauce. Pour over toast. Rub egg yolks through sieve and sprinkle over sauce. Surround with vermicelli. Serves 6.

(2340) ANCHOVY OR SARDINE VERMICELLI

3 cups boiled vermicelli   2 tablespoons grated cheese
    (No. 2302)   2 tablespoons oil from fish
2 cups medium white sauce 1 tablespoon chopped
    (No. 2004)   parsley
1 tablespoon chopped onion 12 anchovies or sardines

Put vermicelli in greased baking dish. Combine sauce, onion, cheese, oil, and parsley. Pour over vermicelli. Top with anchovies or sardines. Bake in hot oven (400° F.) 20 minutes or until browned. Serves 6.

Desserts

THE dessert which closes a meal will often be remembered long after the other courses are forgotten. Whether or not the luncheon, dinner, or supper is, on the whole, good or bad, the dessert will often classify it. This fact is amply illustrated by low-priced meals served by caterers. Invariably these experts in preparing and serving meals always provide large quantities of tasty and delightful-appearing ices and cakes to close the meal. However deficient they might have been in the quality or quantity of other courses, they give everybody an opportunity to gorge himself on desserts.

The clever homemaker will select desserts that go well with meals. Where the main part of the meal consists of foods with large fatty content, such as meats or fish, fruits provide an appropriate dessert. Where the meal is largely vegetarian, heavy puddings or dishes rich in cream or eggs, are a proper close to a meal.

(2401) SOFT CUSTARD

2 cups milk	¼ teaspoon salt
3 slightly beaten eggs	1 teaspoon vanilla
⅓ cup sugar	

Put 1¾ cups milk in saucepan. Cover and bring to boiling point. Reduce heat. Combine eggs, sugar, salt, and remaining milk. Add to scalded milk, stirring constantly. Cook, stirring constantly, until a coating forms on a spoon. Remove and cool. Add vanilla. Serve in tall glasses with whipped cream and coconut or use as a pudding sauce. Yield: 2¼ cups custard.

(2402) BAKED CUSTARD

2 eggs	2 cups scalded milk
2 tablespoons sugar	½ teaspoon vanilla
Few grains salt	Few grains nutmeg

Beat eggs. Add sugar and salt. Add scalded milk, vanilla, and nutmeg. Mix well. Pour into custard cups. Set cups in pan of hot water and bake in a slow oven (300° F.) 25 minutes. Test with silver knife. When it is done, the custard will not stick to the knife. Serves 6. A good topping is a sprinkling of graham cracker crumbs, browned in a little butter and brown sugar.

(2403) APRICOT CUSTARD

Serve soft custard (No. 2401) over stewed apricots (No. 42) and top with whipped cream.

(2404) CARAMEL CUSTARD

Follow recipe for baked custard (No. 2402) but melt sugar to a golden brown over slow heat before adding.

(2405) CHOCOLATE CUSTARD

Add 1 square melted, unsweetened chocolate or ⅓ cup cocoa to recipe for baked custard (No. 2402).

(2406) COCONUT CUSTARD

Add 1½ tablespoons shredded coconut to baked custard (No. 2402) before cooking.

(2407) COFFEE CUSTARD

Substitute 1 cup strong coffee (No. 301) for equal amount of milk in recipe for baked custard (No. 2402).

(2408) CUSTARD WITH FRUIT

3 eggs	1 teaspoon vanilla
3 cups milk	¼ teaspoon lemon extract
¼ cup sugar	¼ teaspoon salt
¼ teaspoon nutmeg	

Beat the eggs slightly and combine with the remaining ingredients. Pour into a basin (6 inches wide and 2½ inches deep). Place in a shallow pan of hot water and bake in a moderate oven (350° F.) about 40 minutes or until an inserted knife blade comes out clean. Chill. Unmold on a chop plate and surround with canned fruit. Serves 6 to 8.

(2409)   MACAROON CUSTARD

Add ¼ pound crumbed macaroons to soft custard (No. 2401) just before removing from heat.

(2410)   PEACH CUSTARD

Add ⅓ cup cream to soft custard (No. 2401) when cooking is finished and 2 cups sliced peaches after cooling. Serve with whipped cream.

(2411)   PINEAPPLE CUSTARD

2½ cups crushed pineapple   5 egg yolks, stiffly
½ cup sugar   whipped

Combine ingredients. Mix lightly. Turn into 1 large mold or individual molds, which have been wet in cold water. Set in pan of warm water. Cover and bake in slow oven (300° F.) until set. Chill. Unmold and garnish with whipped cream. Serves 6.

(2412)   TUTTI-FRUTTI CUSTARD

Add ¼ cup mixed chopped candied cherries, pineapple, and orange peel to baked custard (No. 2402) just before baking. If desired, chopped nut meats may be added with cherries, pineapple, and peel.

(2413)   FLOATING ISLAND

Top soft custard (No. 2401) with one teaspoon beaten egg white flavored with powdered sugar and vanilla.

(2414)   JUNKET

    2 cups milk   ½ teaspoon vanilla
    2 tablespoons sugar   2 teaspoons lukewarm
    2 teaspoons rennet, or   water
       1 junket tablet

Heat the milk to lukewarm (99° F.) in double boiler. Add sugar and flavoring and stir until sugar is dissolved. Add junket dissolved in water and pour into dish from which custard is to be served. Let stand until cool and firm. Serve with cream, soft custard (No. 2401), fruit, or fruit sirup. Cinnamon, nutmeg, coconut, chocolate, cocoa, or other flavor may be substituted for vanilla. Serves 6.

(2415)   CARAMEL JUNKET

   Melt and brown sugar in a frying pan before adding to junket (No. 2414).

(2416)   CHOCOLATE JUNKET

   Add 1 square melted, unsweetened chocolate to recipe for junket (No. 2414).

(2417)   COFFEE JELLY

    2 tablespoons gelatin   1½ cups strong coffee
    ⅓ cup sugar   (No. 301)

Soak gelatin in ⅔ cup cold water 5 minutes. Add 1 cup boiling water and stir until gelatin is dissolved. Add coffee and sugar. Pour into mold. Chill. Serve with whipped cream. Serves 6.

(2418)   LEMON JELLY

    2½ tablespoons gelatin   ½ cup lemon juice
    1 cup sugar   Grated rind of ½ lemon

Soak gelatin in ½ cup cold water 5 minutes. Add sugar and 2 cups boiling water. Stir until dissolved. Add lemon juice and rind. Mix well. Strain through cheesecloth into mold. Chill. Serve plain or with custard (No. 2401), plain cream, or whipped cream.

(2419) ORANGE JELLY

Add ⅔ cup orange juice, reduce lemon juice to 2 tablespoons, and omit lemon rind in recipe for lemon jelly (No. 2418).

(2420) FRUIT GELATIN

| 1 tablespoon gelatin | 1 cup mixed fruit, diced |
| ⅓ cup sugar | |

Soak gelatin in 2 tablespoons cold water 5 minutes. Add 1 cup boiling water and sugar and stir until dissolved. Cool. Drain fruit and stir lightly into jelly when congealing starts. Turn into molds. Chill. Serve plain or with cream or whipped cream. Serves 6.

(2421) FRUIT DE LUXE

12-ounce can cherry juice	1 cup heavy cream
1-pound can pears	2 tablespoons sugar
1 package lemon-flavored	1 teaspoon vanilla
gelatin	1-pound can apricots

Heat cherry juice with ½ cup sirup from pears. Add gelatin and stir until dissolved. Cool until congealing starts. Pour into ring mold and chill until firm. Unmold on large plate. Whip cream, gradually adding sugar and vanilla. Pile in center of ring. Arrange pears and apricots around ring. Loganberry or cranberry juice may be substituted for cherry juice. Peach halves and pineapple chunks may be used instead of pears and apricots. Serves 6.

(2422) GRAPE FRAPPÉ

1½ tablespoons gelatin	1 tablespoon lemon juice
1½ cups grape carbonated	1 cup cream
beverage	

Soak gelatin in 3 tablespoonfuls of cold water 5 minutes. Add ⅓ cup boiling water. Cool. Add lemon juice and grape beverage. When nearly stiffened beat until light and spongy. Add cream, beating into the mixture. Serve very cold in sherbet glasses with spoonful of whipped cream on top. Serves 6.

(2423)   ORANGE CHARLOTTE

2 tablespoons gelatin
2 tablespoons lemon juice
½ cup sugar

1 cup orange carbonated
   beverage
1 egg white, beaten stiff

Soak gelatin in ⅓ cup cold water and dissolve over boiling water. Stir until dissolved. Add lemon juice and sugar. Cool. Add orange beverage. When mixture is nearly firm beat well. Add white of egg, folding into mixture. Line a mold with strips of stale cake, lady fingers, macaroons or vanilla wafers, pour in mold and chill. Serves 5.

(2424)   MARSHMALLOW PUDDING
WITH BANANAS

1 tablespoon gelatin
¾ cup sugar

3 stiffly beaten egg whites
3 bananas, shredded

Soak gelatin in ¼ cup cold water 5 minutes. Add ¼ cup boiling water and sugar. Stir until dissolved. Cool, stirring occasionally, until congealing starts. Add egg whites and beat until very light. Add bananas and stir lightly. Chill until set. Serve with whipped cream. Serves 4.

(2425)   BANQUET PUDDING

4 eggs
½ cup sugar
1 pint light cream
1 tablespoon granulated
   gelatin

½ teaspoon vanilla
Few drops almond extract
1 tablespoon sherry
   flavoring

Beat eggs. Gradually add sugar and hot cream. Cook in double boiler until mixture barely coats the spoon. Add gelatin, which has been soaked 5 minutes in ¼ cup cold water, to hot mixture, stirring it thoroughly. Add flavorings. Turn into wet mold to cool. Serve with fruit sauce. Serves 6.

(2426)   BROWN CHIFFON

1⅛ tablespoons gelatin
1 pint root beer

2 egg whites, beaten stiff
½ cup cream, whipped

Soak gelatin in ¼ cup cold water, then dissolve over boiling water. Cool. Add root beer. Set in cool place to stiffen. When nearly firm, fold in the egg whites and whipped cream and put into refrigerator until firm. Serve in sherbet glasses. Serves 6.

(2427)   MOCK NESSELRODE PUDDING

2½ tablespoons gelatin	10 macaroons, crumbed
1 cup cold milk	1 teaspoon vanilla
4 egg yolks	½ teaspoon almond extract
¾ cup sugar	2 tablespoons sherry
3 cups scalded milk	flavoring
¾ cup chopped raisins	4 egg whites

Soak gelatin in cold milk 5 minutes. Beat egg yolks and sugar together and pour the scalded milk on them. Put in a double boiler, or over hot water and cook, stirring constantly until custard coats the spoon. Add gelatin and stir until dissolved. Take from the fire and add raisins, macaroon crumbs, vanilla, almond extract and sherry flavoring. Mix well. Fold in stiffly beaten egg whites. Set in a pan of ice water and beat until thick. Pour into a mold which has been dipped in cold water and chill thoroughly. Turn out of mold onto a plate and decorate with whipped cream and maraschino cherries. Serves 6.

(2428)   BAVARIAN CREAM

1½ tablespoons gelatin	⅛ teaspoon salt
½ cup cold milk	1½ cups scalded milk
3 egg yolks	1 teaspoon vanilla
½ cup sugar	½ pint cream, whipped

Soak gelatin in cold milk 5 minutes. Beat yolks, sugar, and salt together until light. Add scalded milk and mix thoroughly. Cook in double boiler or over hot water, stirring constantly, until mixture coats a metal spoon. Add gelatin. Stir until dissolved. Set in pan of cold water and stir until it begins to thicken. Add vanilla and fold in whipped cream. Turn into a mold which has been dipped in cold water. Chill until firm. Serves 6.

(2429)   SPANISH CREAM

Substitute 3 stiffly beaten egg whites for whipped cream in recipe for Bavarian cream (No. 2428).

(2430)   CHOCOLATE BAVARIAN CREAM

Add ⅓ cup cocoa to recipe for Bavarian cream (No. 2428), adding with scalded milk.

(2431)   COFFEE BAVARIAN CREAM

Substitute 1½ cups strong coffee (No. 301) for 1½ cups scalded milk in recipe for Bavarian cream (No. 2428).

(2432)   DATE BAVARIAN CREAM

Add ⅔ cup chopped dates to recipe for Bavarian cream (No. 2428).

(2433)   FIG BAVARIAN CREAM

Add ⅔ cup chopped figs to recipe for Bavarian cream (No. 2428).

(2434)   MELBA BAVARIAN CREAM

Serve Bavarian cream (No. 2428) with berry-jelly sauce (No. 3114).

(2435)   NUT BAVARIAN CREAM

Add ⅔ cup chopped nuts to recipe for Bavarian cream (No. 2428).

(2436)   ORANGE OR PINEAPPLE BAVARIAN CREAM

Substitute 1 cup orange juice or 1 cup grated pineapple and the juice of ½ lemon for scalded milk in recipe for Bavarian cream (No. 2428).

(2437)   FRESH PEACH BAVARIAN CREAM

Add 1 cup fresh peach pulp, well mashed, to recipe for Bavarian cream (No. 2428) and omit vanilla.

(2438) PISTACHIO BAVARIAN CREAM

Add ⅓ cup chopped pistachio nuts to recipe for Bavarian cream (No. 2428).

(2439) PLUM BAVARIAN CREAM

2½ cups canned red plums	2 tablespoons sherry
1 package pineapple gelatin	2 egg whites
½ cup heavy cream	

Drain the sirup from the plums and add enough water to make 2 cups liquid. Heat to boiling point. Remove from heat and add gelatin, stirring until dissolved. Chill until mixture starts to congeal. Whip cream and fold into gelatin mixture. Add sherry and then fold in the stiffly beaten egg whites. Remove seeds from plums and cut each piece of fruit in two. Add to gelatin mixture. Chill until firm. Black cherries or red pitted cherries may be used instead of red plums. Serves 8.

(2440) PRUNE BAVARIAN CREAM

Substitute stewed prunes (No. 71) for red plums in recipe for plum Bavarian cream (No. 2439).

(2441) STRAWBERRY BAVARIAN CREAM

Substitute 1 cup juice from mashed strawberries for equal amount of milk in Bavarian cream (No. 2428).

(2442) VANILLA BLANC MANGE

½ cup sugar	2 beaten egg yolks
3 tablespoons cornstarch	1 teaspoon vanilla
3 tablespoons flour	2 egg whites, stiffly
¼ teaspoon salt	beaten
3 cups scalded milk	

Mix sugar, cornstarch, flour, and salt. Add milk and mix well, Cook over boiling water until thick, stirring constantly. Cover and cook 15 minutes longer. Remove from fire, pour on the yolks and cook 2 minutes longer over boiling water, stirring constantly. Add vanilla. Fold in stiffly beaten egg whites. Pour into a mold or individual molds. Chill. Serve with chocolate sauce (No. 3107). Serves 6.

(2443)   CHOCOLATE BLANC MANGE

Add 1½ squares melted, unsweetened chocolate to recipe for vanilla blanc mange (No. 2442). Serve with whipped cream.

(2444)   COFFEE BLANC MANGE

Substitute 1½ cups strong coffee (No. 301) for equal quantity of milk in vanilla blanc mange (No. 2442).

(2445)   STRAWBERRY BLANC MANGE

Add ⅓ cup crushed strawberries to vanilla blanc mange (No. 2442) when cold.

(2446)   FRUIT CORNSTARCH

Add 2½ cups chopped fruits, one kind or a mixture, to recipe for vanilla blanc mange (No. 2442).

(2447)   ALMOND PEACH CREAM

1 cup whipping cream	2½ cups sliced peaches
2 tablespoons sugar	½ cup shredded coconut
¼ teaspoon almond flavoring	

Whip cream and add sugar and flavoring. Fold in peaches and coconut. Chill. Serves 6.

(2448)   COEUR DE CRÈME

½ pound cream cheese	1 tablespoon confectioners'
½ pint heavy cream	sugar
Dash of paprika	Pinch of salt

Blend cheese, cream, sugar, paprika, and salt together thoroughly but lightly. Dampen a piece of cheesecloth and spread as smoothly as possible in special heart-shaped basket or mold. Pack cheese mixture in this and chill in refrigerator for several hours. Unmold the coeur on a wreath of shiny green leaves and remove cloth. Serve with rich preserves or fresh strawberries, sugar, and cream.

(2449)   GINGANA CREAM

1 cup heavy cream	3 bananas, mashed
2 tablespoons confectioners' sugar	1 tablespoon lemon juice
1/16 teaspoon salt	1 cup gingersnap crumbs

Whip cream until slightly stiff. Add sugar and salt. Combine bananas and lemon juice and fold into cream. Fold in crumbs. Cover and chill in refrigerator. Serve very cold in sherbet glasses. Serves 6.

(2450)   FRIED CREAMS

2 eggs	1 teaspoon vanilla
1/2 cup sugar	3/4 cup fine dried bread
6 tablespoons flour	crumbs
1/4 teaspoon salt	1 egg
2 cups scalded milk	2 tablespoons water
1 teaspoon butter or fat	

Beat eggs and add sugar, flour, salt, and milk. Mix well and cook over hot water until thick, stirring constantly. Remove from fire, add butter or fat, and cool slightly. Add vanilla. Pour into a small greased pan to 3/4-inch thickness. Put in ice box overnight. Cut into pieces 2 inches long and 1 inch wide. Roll each piece in crumbs, dip in beaten egg, diluted with water, and roll again in crumbs. Fry in deep hot fat (375° F.) until a delicate brown. Drain on unglazed paper. Serve with powdered sugar or maple sirup. Serves 6.

(2451)   PEACH FLUFF

6 fresh peaches	1/2 pint heavy cream
2 tablespoons powdered sugar	1/2 teaspoon almond extract
1/2 pound marshmallows	1/2 teaspoon vanilla extract

Sprinkle sugar over peaches which have been peeled and cut in small pieces. Cut marshmallows into small pieces and mix with peaches. Whip cream to which flavoring has been added and fold into peaches. Chill. Serves 6.

(2452) RHUBARB FLUFF

2 cups stewed rhubarb (No. 75)	⅔ cup sugar
Juice ½ lemon	1 cup whipped cream

Mix rhubarb, lemon juice, and sugar. Cool. Fold in whipped cream. Serve in sherbet glasses. Serves 6.

(2453) CHOCOLATE SOUFFLÉ

2 tablespoons fat	3 squares melted
3 tablespoons flour	unsweetened chocolate
1 cup milk	3 egg yolks
½ cup sugar	1 teaspoon vanilla
½ teaspoon salt	3 stiffly beaten egg whites

Melt fat and blend in flour. Add milk slowly and bring to a boil, stirring constantly. Add sugar and salt. Mix chocolate with 3 tablespoons hot water and add to mixture. Cool. Add egg yolks and beat until light. Add vanilla. Fold in egg whites. Turn into greased baking dish. Set in pan of hot water. Bake in moderate oven (350° F.) 40 to 45 minutes. Serve hot with whipped cream or custard sauce (No. 3103). Serves 6.

(2454) APPLESAUCE SOUFFLÉ

2½ cups applesauce (No. 34)	¼ teaspoon nutmeg
½ cup sugar	3 stiffly beaten egg whites
¼ teaspoon salt	2 tablespoons sliced
½ teaspoon cinnamon	almonds

Mix applesauce, sugar, salt, cinnamon, and nutmeg. Fold in egg whites. Turn into greased baking dish. Sprinkle with almonds. Place in shallow pan of hot water and bake in moderate oven (350° F.) until firm, about 40 minutes. Serve with whipped cream or custard sauce (No. 3103). Serves 8.

(2455) APRICOT SOUFFLÉ

Substitute ¼ cup apricot jam for unsweetened chocolate in recipe for chocolate soufflé (No. 2453), reduce sugar to ¼ cup, and omit vanilla.

(2456)   **BLUEBERRY SOUFFLÉ**

Substitute ⅔ cup blueberries for chocolate in recipe for chocolate soufflé (No. 2453), reduce sugar to ¼ cup, and omit vanilla.

(2457)   **CUSTARD SOUFFLÉ**

2 tablespoons butter	2 eggs
¼ cup flour	¼ cup sugar
1 cup scalded milk	¼ teaspoon salt

To melted butter add flour and, gradually, hot milk. Bring to boiling point and pour onto egg yolks, beaten until thick and lemon-colored, sugar, and salt. Cool. Cut and fold in stiffly beaten egg whites. Bake in same manner as chocolate soufflé (No. 2453).

(2458)   **DATE OR FIG SOUFFLÉ**

Substitute ⅔ cup chopped dates or figs for chocolate in chocolate soufflé (No. 2453), reduce sugar to ¼ cup, and omit vanilla.

(2459)   **LEMON OR ORANGE SOUFFLÉ**

Substitute the grated rind of 2 lemons or 1 orange for chocolate in chocolate soufflé (No. 2453) and omit vanilla.

(2460)   **MARASCHINO SOUFFLÉ**

Substitute ⅓ cup chopped maraschino cherries for chocolate in chocolate soufflé (No. 2453), reduce sugar to ¼ cup, and omit vanilla.

(2461)   **NUT SOUFFLÉ**

Substitute ⅔ cup chopped nuts for chocolate in chocolate soufflé (No. 2453).

(2462) PRUNE SOUFFLÉ

½ cup bread crumbs	¼ teaspoon cinnamon
½ cup chopped nuts	1 cup stewed prune pulp
½ cup prune juice	1 tablespoon lemon juice
2 tablespoons sugar	Grated rind 1 lemon
½ teaspoon salt	2 eggs

Combine bread crumbs, nuts, prune juice, sugar, salt, and cinnamon. Make prune pulp by rubbing stewed prunes (No. 71) through a sieve. Add pulp, lemon juice and rind to mixture. Separate eggs. Beat yolks until light and lemon-colored. Add to mixture. Beat egg whites stiff and fold in. Turn into greased baking dish. Set dish in pan of hot water. Bake in moderate oven (350° F.) until firm, 35 to 45 minutes. Serve with whipped cream. Serves 6.

(2463) STRAWBERRY SOUFFLÉ

Substitute ⅓ cup quartered strawberries for chocolate in chocolate soufflé (No. 2453) and omit vanilla.

(2464) VANILLA SOUFFLÉ

Omit chocolate from chocolate soufflé (No. 2453) and increase vanilla to 2 teaspoons.

(2465) APPLE SNOW

4 tart apples	3 egg whites, stiffly beaten
Powdered sugar	

Pare, quarter, and core apples. Place in double boiler and steam until soft. Rub through a sieve. Add powdered sugar to taste. Stir apple pulp gradually into egg whites. Pile lightly on serving dish. Serve with custard sauce (No. 3103). Serves 4.

(2466) BERRY FLUMMERY

5 cups berries, any kind	3 tablespoons cornstarch
½ cup sugar	½ teaspoon nutmeg

Bring berries to boiling point. Rub through a sieve. Dissolve sugar in ½ cup water. Add cornstarch and stir smooth. Add mixture to berry pulp. Add nutmeg. Cook over hot water, stirring constantly, until thickened. Serve hot or cold with plain cream or custard (No. 2401). Serves 6.

(2467)   FRUIT WHIP

1 cup mashed fruit pulp, any kind individually or in combination	1 egg white ¼ cup powdered sugar

Put all ingredients in a bowl and beat until stiff, 10 to 15 minutes. Pile in sherbet glasses. Chill. Serve with whipped cream. Serves 6.

(2468)   APPLESAUCE WHIP

3 cups applesauce (No. 34) 6 tablespoons sugar 1 tablespoon lemon juice ½ tablespoon vanilla	½ tablespoon almond extract 2 tablespoons gelatin 2 egg whites

Add sugar, lemon juice, vanilla, and almond extract to applesauce. Soak gelatin in 2 tablespoons cold water 5 minutes. Dissolve over hot water. Stir into applesauce mixture. Fold in stiffly beaten egg whites. Cover and chill. Serve with soft custard (No. 2401). Serves 8.

(2469)   APRICOT WHIP

Make fruit whip (No. 2467), using mashed apricot pulp.

(2470)   PRUNE WHIP

Make fruit whip (No. 2467), using the pulp of stewed prunes (No. 71).

(2470A)   RHUBARB WHIP

Substitute rhubarb sauce (No. 75) for applesauce in applesauce whip (No. 2468).

(2471)   PLUM PUDDING

¼ cup shortening
1 cup sugar
3 cups soft bread crumbs
1 teaspoon baking powder
1 teaspoon salt
¼ teaspoon nutmeg
½ teaspoon cinnamon
¼ teaspoon mace
¼ teaspoon clove
3 beaten eggs

¾ cup scalded milk
2 tablespoons chopped
    orange peel
2 tablespoons chopped
    lemon peel
1½ cups raisins
¼ cup currants
¼ cup chopped figs
½ cup nuts, cut in pieces
½ cup grape juice

Cream shortening and sugar together. Add bread crumbs, baking powder, salt and spices. Add eggs and mix thoroughly. Add milk. Add orange and lemon peel, raisins, currants, figs, nuts, and grape juice to the first mixture, and beat thoroughly. Fill greased pudding mold ¾ full. Cover tightly and steam 4 hours. Serve with orange (No. 3139) or hard sauce (No. 3105).

(2472)   RED PLUM PUFF PUDDING

8 large, fresh red plums,
    halved and seeded
½ cup water
2½ tablespoons quick-cooking
    tapicoa
⅔ cup sugar
⅛ teaspoon salt
½ cup sifted cake flour

6 tablespoons sugar
2 egg yolks, beaten until
    thick and lemon-
    colored
2 egg whites
⅛ teaspoon salt
¼ teaspoon cream of tartar

Bring to a boil plums and water. Combine tapioca, sugar, and salt. Add gradually to fruit mixture and boil briskly 1 minute. Pour into greased baking dish and keep hot. Sift flour once and measure. Add sugar gradually to egg yolks, beating until light. Beat egg whites and salt until foamy. Add cream of tartar and beat until stiff enough to hold up in peaks, but not dry. Fold egg yolk mixture into egg whites. Then fold in flour, a small amount at a time. Stir hot tapioca-fruit mixture. Turn batter over mixture. Bake in moderate oven (325° F.) 50 minutes, or until cake is baked. Serve warm. Serves 8. *For golden puff pudding* substitute 4 cups sliced fresh peaches for plums. Increase the tapioca to 3 tablespoons and the sugar to ¾ cup. Add 2 tablespoons lemon juice. *For blueberry puff pudding* substitute 2 cups blueberries and 2 cups sliced apples for plums.

Increase tapioca to 3 tablespoons and sugar to ¾ cup. Add 2 tablespoons lemon juice.

(2473) BREAD PUDDING

1½ cups bread crumbs	¼ teaspoon salt
3 cups hot milk	1 tablespoon fat
2 beaten eggs	½ teaspoon vanilla
⅔ cup sugar	½ cup chopped nuts

Combine crumbs, milk, eggs, sugar, salt, and fat. Mix well. Add vanilla and nuts. Turn into greased baking tin. Bake in moderate oven (350° F.) 35 to 40 minutes or until firm. Serve with whipped cream. Serves 6.

(2474) BREAD AND BUTTER PUDDING

⅓ cup raisins	⅔ cup sugar
5 thin slices stale bread	2 cups milk
¼ cup butter, melted	½ teaspoon vanilla
2 eggs	

Line bottom of greased pudding dish with raisins. Cut bread slices in 3 strips, crosswise. Dip each in melted butter and arrange on top of raisins. Beat remaining ingredients together and pour over bread. Set dish in pan of hot water. Bake in hot oven (375° F.) until bread is browned and a knife blade comes out clean. Serve plain or with cream. Serves 6.

(2475) SPICED BREAD PUDDING

1 cup toasted bread crumbs	½ teaspoon nutmeg
1 cup brown sugar	1 teaspoon cinnamon
1 teaspoon soda	1 cup sour milk
½ teaspoon ground cloves	1 cup raisins

Combine crumbs, sugar, soda, cloves, nutmeg, and cinnamon. Add milk and raisins. Mix well. Turn into greased pudding dish. Bake in moderate oven (325° F.) 1 hour. Serves 4 to 6.

(2476) CABINET PUDDING

Follow recipe for bread and butter pudding (No. 2474) using sweet rolls, sweet buns, sponge cake (No. 3003), or lady fingers (No. 3042) instead of bread. If desired, substitute crushed pineapple for raisins and omit vanilla. Serve with custard sauce (No. 3103).

(2477) CHERRY BREAD PUDDING

Add 1½ cups stoned and chopped cherries to recipe for **bread** pudding (No. 2473) and increase sugar to 1 cup.

(2478) CHOCOLATE BREAD PUDDING

Add 2 squares melted, unsweetened chocolate or ⅔ cup cocoa to recipe for bread pudding (No. 2473).

(2479) COFFEE BREAD PUDDING

Follow recipe for bread pudding (No. 2473), substituting 1½ cups strong coffee (No. 301) for an equal quantity of milk and omitting vanilla.

(2480) COTTAGE PUDDING

¼ cup butter or fat	3 teaspoons baking powder
¾ cup sugar	½ teaspoon salt
2 eggs	¾ cup milk
2¼ cups flour	1 teaspoon vanilla

Cream fat, sugar, and eggs together. Mix and sift flour, baking powder, salt. Add alternately with milk to first mixture. Add vanilla. Beat well. Turn into greased baking pan or muffin tins to a depth of 1 to 1½ inches. Bake in hot oven (400° F.) 20 to 25 minutes. Serve with lemon (No. 3129) or custard sauce (No. 3103). Serves 6.

(2481) CHOCOLATE COTTAGE PUDDING

Add 1½ squares melted, unsweetened chocolate or ⅓ cup cocoa, mixed to a smooth paste with hot water, to recipe for cottage pudding (No. 2480).

(2482) FRUIT COTTAGE PUDDING

Add ¾ cup berries or diced fruit, well drained and mixed with a little of the flour, to recipe for cottage pudding (No. 2480).

(2483) BLUEBERRY COTTAGE PUDDING

Use blueberries for fruit in fruit cottage pudding (No. 2482).

(2484) BAKED INDIAN PUDDING

¼ cup corn meal	⅛ teaspoon ginger
5 cups milk	¼ teaspoon cinnamon
¼ cup molasses	1 tablespoon fat
½ teaspoon salt	

Mix corn meal with 1 cup milk. Scald the remaining milk in a double boiler or over hot water. Add corn meal, molasses, salt, ginger, cinnamon and fat and mix well. Pour into a greased baking dish and cook in a slow oven (275° F.) 2 hours. Serve with cream or custard sauce (No. 3103). Serves 6.

(2485) RICE PUDDING

2 eggs	1 teaspoon vanilla
½ cup sugar	2 cups steamed rice
½ teaspoon salt	(No. 106)
2¼ cups milk	Dash nutmeg

Separate eggs. Beat yolks. Add sugar, salt, milk, vanilla, and rice. Stiffly beat egg whites and fold into mixture. Turn into baking dish. Sprinkle with nutmeg. Bake in moderate oven (350° F.) 45 minutes. Serves 6.

(2486) RICE CREAM PUDDING

1 tablespoon gelatin	¼ teaspoon salt
½ cup rice, boiled in milk	½ teaspoon vanilla
(No. 107)	½ cup heavy cream
1 tablespoon sugar	

Soak gelatin in 3 tablespoons cold water 5 minutes. Dissolve over hot water. Add rice, sugar, salt, and vanilla. Mix thoroughly. Cool. Whip cream and fold into mixture. Mold or pile on dessert dishes. Serve cold. Serves 4.

(2487) APPLE RICE PUDDING

Add 4 stewed apples (No. 41) to recipe for rice cream pudding (No. 2486).

(2488)   RICE MERINGUE PUDDING

Bake rice pudding (No. 2485). When done, top with meringue (No. 3205). Return to hot oven to brown.

(2489)   PEACH RICE PUDDING

3 eggs
¼ cup sugar
¼ teaspoon salt
1½ cups evaporated milk or cream

2½ cups canned sliced peaches
½ teaspoon nutmeg
¼ teaspoon cinnamon
Few drops almond extract

1½ cups cooked rice (No. 107)

Beat eggs. Add sugar and salt and beat well. Add milk and sirup drained from peaches. Cook in a double boiler until mixture coats a spoon, stirring frequently. Remove from heat and add spice and flavoring. Combine with peaches and rice. Chill and serve. Pears, pineapple, or apricots may be used instead of peaches. Serves 12.

(2490)   TAPIOCA CREAM

1 cup scalded milk
¼ cup minute tapioca
⅓ cup sugar

1 egg
¼ teaspoon salt
½ teaspoon vanilla

To milk add tapioca and cook in double boiler until it is transparent. Add half the sugar to milk and half to egg yolks, slightly beaten, and salt. Pour hot mixture slowly on egg mixture. Return to double boiler and cook until it thickens, stirring constantly. Add egg whites, beaten stiffly. Flavor with vanilla. Serve cold. Serves 4.

(2491)   TAPIOCA CUSTARD PUDDING

1 pint scalded milk
2 eggs, slightly beaten
⅓ cup minute tapioca

½ cup sugar
1 teaspoon salt
1 tablespoon butter

Add tapioca to milk and cook in double boiler 30 minutes. To sugar and salt add the eggs. Pour this gradually on hot mixture. Turn into buttered pudding dish. Add butter. Put in pan of hot water. Bake in slow oven (325° F.) 30 minutes. One cup of almost any chopped, canned, or stewed fruits or berries may be added. Serves 6.

(2492) APPLE TAPIOCA

½ cup minute tapioca
1 teaspoon salt
3 cups apples, pared, cored,
   and sliced

1 cup brown sugar
2 teaspoons lemon juice
⅓ teaspoon nutmeg
¾ teaspoon cinnamon

Cook the tapioca and salt in 4 cups hot water in a double boiler 15 to 20 minutes or until the tapioca is clear. Stir frequently. Put the apples in a greased baking dish. Cover with sugar, mixed with the spices, and lemon juice. Pour the tapioca mixture over this and bake in a moderate oven (350° F.) about 45 minutes. Serves 8.

(2493) CHOCOLATE TAPIOCA

1½ cups milk
2 tablespoons minute
   tapioca
1 egg
3 tablespoons sugar

⅛ teaspoon salt
1 teaspoon vanilla
2 squares unsweetened
   chocolate

Scald 1 cup milk in top of double boiler. Add tapioca and cook for 20 minutes or until tapioca is transparent. Stir frequently. Beat egg yolk. Add sugar and salt. Put tapioca mixture with egg yolk. Put over bottom of double boiler and cook until thickened. Remove from heat and fold in white, beaten stiffly, vanilla and chocolate blended with half cup scalded milk. Serves 4.

(2494) COFFEE TAPIOCA

1 egg yolk
1 cup evaporated milk
⅓ cup minute tapioca
⅔ cup sugar
¼ teaspoon salt

1 cup water
2 cups strong coffee
   (No. 301)
1 egg white
1 teaspoon vanilla

Mix egg yolk with small amount of milk in saucepan. Add remaining milk, tapioca, sugar, salt, water, and coffee. Bring mixture to boil over direct heat, stirring constantly. Remove from fire. Beat egg white until just stiff enough to hold shape. Fold hot tapioca mixture gradually into egg white. Cool. When slightly cool, stir in flavoring. Chill. Serve in parfait glasses with caramel sauce (No. 3109). Serves 8.

(2495)   TAPIOCA MERINGUE PUDDING

Top any tapioca pudding with meringue (No. 3205) when done and return to oven to brown.

(2496)   PINEAPPLE TAPIOCA

2 ½ cups crushed pineapple   ⅓ cup sugar
¼ cup minute tapioca   ⅛ teaspoon salt

Mix all ingredients and cook in a double boiler or in a pan set in hot water until tapioca is clear, about 20 minutes. Chill. Serve with cream. Serves 4 to 6.

(2497)   INDIAN TAPIOCA PUDDING

⅓ cup minute tapioca   ½ teaspoon salt
¼ cup corn meal   2 tablespoons butter
1 quart milk, scalded   1 ½ cups cold milk
1 cup molasses

Combine tapioca and corn meal and sprinkle into the scalded milk. Stir and cook until the tapioca becomes transparent. Add molasses, salt, and butter. Pour into a breased baking dish. Add cold milk without stirring. Bake in a moderate oven (350° F.) about 1 hour. Serve cold with whipped cream. Chopped dates may be added if desired. Serves 8.

(2498)   PRINCESS PUDDING

1 cup minute tapioca   ½ pint currant or other
3 ½ cups boiling water   tart jelly
½ cup sugar   ½ teaspoon salt

Cook tapioca in water with sugar and salt until clear and jellied. Add jelly and stir until dissolved. Chill and serve very cold with whipped cream or soft custard (No. 2401). Serves 8.

(2499)   ANGEL PUDDING

5 eggs   ½ cup walnut meats
½ teaspoon cream of tartar   ¾ cup dates, chopped
2 tablespoons sugar

Beat eggs until foamy. Add cream of tartar and beat stiff. Add sugar gradually, mixing well. Combine nuts and dates and fold into mixture. Put a little water in bottom of greased baking pan. Turn in pudding. Bake in moderate oven (350° F.) 20 minutes. Serve hot with whipped cream or lemon sauce (No. 3129). Serves 6.

(2500)   STEAMED CHOCOLATE PUDDING

1 tablespoon fat	1½ teaspoons baking
¾ cup sugar	powder
1 egg	½ cup milk
1½ cups flour	2 squares unsweetened
½ teaspoon salt	chocolate

Cream fat, sugar, and egg together. Mix and sift flour, baking powder, and salt and add alternately with the milk to the first mixture. Beat thoroughly. Add melted chocolate and mix well. Fill greased pudding mold ¾ full. Cover tightly and steam 1 hour. Serve with whipped cream. Serves 4.

(2501)   CARAMEL PUDDING

1 cup brown sugar	¼ cup cornstarch
4 cups milk	4 egg whites
¼ cup butter	1 cup granulated sugar
4 egg yolks	

Bring sugar and milk to boiling point, stirring constantly. Add butter. Beat yolks and cornstarch together and add to first mixture. Cook, stirring constantly, until thick. Turn into greased baking pan. Bake in moderate oven (350° F.) until brown. Beat egg whites with sugar and brush on top. Return to oven and brown top. Serves 6.

(2502)   BUTTERSCOTCH NUT PUDDING

1½ cups brown sugar	6 tablespoons flour
3 tablespoons butter	⅛ teaspoon salt
1¾ cups scalded milk	½ cup nuts, chopped
3 egg yolks	Whipped cream
½ cup cold milk	

Dissolve the brown sugar and butter in the scalded milk. Combine slightly beaten egg yolks with the cold milk. Mix with flour and salt. Add first milk mixture and nuts. Pour in a greased pan. Cover and steam in moderate oven (325° F.) 45 minutes. Serve with whipped cream. Serves 6.

(2503)   BUTTERSCOTCH PUDDING

Omit nuts from recipe for butterscotch nut pudding (No. 2502).

(2504)   BLACKBERRY PUDDING

¼ cup shortening	¼ cup milk
¾ cup sugar	1 teaspoon vanilla
1 cup sifted flour	2 egg whites, beaten
¼ teaspoon salt	3 cups blackberries
1 teaspoon baking powder	

Cream the shortening and stir in ½ cup sugar gradually. Sift the dry ingredients together and add alternately with the milk to first mixture. Fold in the stiffly beaten egg whites. Add vanilla. Mix blackberries with the remaining ¼ cup sugar. Place in bottom of greased pudding dish. Pour batter over them and cover mold tightly. Bake at moderate heat (350° F.) 1¼ hours. Serves 4 to 6.

(2505)   BLUEBERRY PUDDING

Use blueberries or huckleberries instead of blackberries in recipe for blackberry pudding (No. 2504).

(2506)   COCONUT PUDDING

Substitute 1 cup shredded coconut for blackberries in blackberry pudding (No. 2504).

(2507)   JAM PUDDING

½ cup butter	1 cup sugar
3 beaten eggs	1 teaspoon soda
1 cup jam	1 cup buttermilk
1½ cups flour	½ teaspoon cinnamon

Cream butter with eggs and jam. Add flour slowly, beating to blend. Add sugar and beat light. Dissolve soda in buttermilk and add to batter. Add cinnamon and beat light. Turn into greased baking pan. Bake in moderate oven (350° F.) about 20 minutes. Serve hot with cream sauce (No. 3101). Serves 6.

(2508) STEAMED DATE PUDDING

3 tablespoons shortening	½ teaspoon salt
2 cups flour	1 cup milk
¾ teaspoon soda	¾ cup molasses
1 teaspoon ground cloves	½ pound dates, stoned and
1 teaspoon cinnamon	cut
¼ teaspoon allspice	

Melt shortening. Sift flour, measure, add dry ingredients and sift again. Mix molasses and milk and add to dry ingredients. Add shortening. Fold in dates. Pour into a greased mold, cover, and bake in moderate oven (325° F.) 2 hours. Serve with lemon sauce (No. 3129) or foamy sauce (No. 3104). Serves 6.

(2509) STEAMED FIG PUDDING

Use chopped figs instead of dates in recipe for steamed date pudding (No. 2508).

(2510) GINGER PUDDING

Add 2 teaspoons ground ginger with dry ingredients and omit dates in recipe for steamed date pudding (No. 2508).

(2511) PRUNE PUDDING

4 stiffly beaten egg whites	15 stewed prunes (No. 71)
4 teaspoons sugar	¼ teaspoons cream of
⅛ teaspoon salt	tartar

Beat sugar and salt into egg whites. Mash prunes, adding cream of tartar. Beat into first mixture. Turn into buttered baking dish. Bake in moderate oven (350° F.) 20 minutes. Serve hot or cold with whipped cream. Serves 4.

(2512) DATE TORTE

½ cup flour	½ cup sugar
⅛ teaspoon salt	½ teaspoon vanilla
1 teaspoon baking powder	1 cup chopped nut meats
2 eggs	1 package dates, sliced

Sift dry ingredients. Beat the eggs. Beat in the sugar gradually. Add the vanilla, nuts, and dates. Stir in the dry ingredients. Bake in a shallow pan which has been lined with paper and oiled, in a moderate oven (350° F.) about 1 hour. Cut in pie-shaped pieces and serve with hard sauce (No. 3105). Serves 6.

(2513) STEAMED MOLASSES PUDDING

1 egg
¾ cup molasses
1 teaspoon soda
½ cup water

1½ cups flour
½ teaspoon salt
1 cup raisins
2 tablespoons melted fat

Beat egg and add molasses. Dissolve soda in water and stir into the egg mixture. Sift flour and salt, add, and beat thoroughly. Dredge raisins with flour and stir in lightly. Add fat. Fill greased pudding mold ¾ full. Cover closely and steam 1¼ hours. Serve hot with foamy sauce (No. 3104). Serves 6.

(2514) LEMON SPONGE PUDDING

1 cup sugar
1 tablespoon flour
Pinch of salt
2 egg yolks

1 cup milk
Rind and juice of 1 lemon
2 tablespoons butter
2 egg whites, stiffly beaten

Sift the sugar, flour, and salt and blend with the beaten egg yolks. Add the milk, lemon juice, and rind, beating thoroughly. Melt butter and add. Fold in the stiffly beaten egg whites and bake in pudding dish set in a pan of hot water ¾ hour in moderate oven (350° F.). Serve cold. Serves 6.

(2515) STEAMED CRANBERRY PUDDING

4 tablespoons fat
⅔ cup granulated sugar
¼ teaspoon salt
2½ cups flour

3 teaspoons baking powder
¼ teaspoon nutmeg
2 eggs, beaten
1½ cups chopped cranberries

Cream the fat and sugar. Add other ingredients and 1 cup cold water. Half fill a greased pudding mold. Cover tightly and steam for 2 hours. Serve hot with lemon (No. 3129) or any other fruit-flavored sauce. Serves 6.

(2515A) STEAMED CHERRY PUDDING

Substitute chopped cherries for cranberries in recipe for steamed cranberry pudding (No. 2515).

(2516) PEACH CRISP PUDDING

¼ cup butter	2 cups diced peaches and
½ cup sugar	juice
4 cups bread cubes	1 tablespoon lemon juice

Cream butter and sugar together. Add bread cubes to sugar mixture and blend well. Mix fruit and lemon juice with the bread. Pour into greased individual baking dishes and bake in a moderate oven (375° F.) 35 minutes. Garnish with peaches and whipped cream if desired. Serve hot. Apricots or crushed pineapple may be substituted for peaches. Hot lemon sauce (No. 3129) goes well with this. Serves 6.

(2517) PEACH CRUMBLE PUDDING

6 to 8 peaches, peeled and halved	½ cup sifted flour
	⅛ teaspoon nutmeg
¼ cup brown sugar	¼ cup butter

Place peaches in greased baking dish. Work remaining ingredients together to consistency of fine crumbs and sprinkle over peaches. Bake in a moderate oven (350° F.) 25 to 30 minutes. Serve warm. Serves 6.

(2518) ROLY-POLY PUDDING

2 cups flour	5 tart apples, sliced
4 teaspoons baking powder	½ teaspoon cinnamon
1 teaspoon salt	½ teaspoon nutmeg
5 tablespoons shortening	½ cup sugar
½ cup milk	

Mix and sift flour, baking powder, and salt. Rub in 3 tablespoons shortening with finger tips. Add milk and mix to a soft dough. Turn out on floured board and pat into oblong shape. Spread with remaining 2 tablespoons softened shortening. Cover with a layer of thinly sliced apples and sprinkle with cinnamon, nutmeg, and sugar. Roll like a jelly roll. Bake in moderate oven (350° F.) 30 to 40 minutes. Slice 1 inch thick and serve hot with lemon sauce (No. 3129).

(2519)   CORN FLAKE PUDDING

1 quart corn flakes	1/4 cup sugar
1 quart milk	1/4 teaspoon ginger
2 eggs	1/4 teaspoon cinnamon
1/2 teaspoon salt	Vanilla
1/4 cup molasses	1 tablespoon butter

Stir all together. Turn into greased baking dish. Dot with butter. Place the dish in a pan of water and put in oven. Bake for 3/4 to 1 hour in a moderate oven (350° F.). Serves 8.

(2520)   CHOCOLATE CORN FLAKE PUDDING

Add 1 1/2 squares melted, unsweetened chocolate to recipe for corn flake pudding (No. 2519), increasing sugar to 1/2 cup and omitting molasses.

(2521)   SAGO PUDDING

Substitute sago for corn meal in baked Indian pudding (No. 2484). When done, this may be topped with meringue (No. 3205) and returned to oven to brown.

(2522)   SEA MOSS PUDDING

1 cup sea moss	1/2 teaspoon salt
1 quart milk	1 1/2 teaspoons vanilla
1 cup sugar	

Soak moss in cold water about 15 minutes. Pick out discolored pieces. Scald milk in top of double boiler. Add sugar, salt, and moss. Cook in double boiler about 25 minutes. Strain. Let cool a little. Add vanilla. Pour into mold or molds that have been dipped in cold water. Chill. Unmold. Serve with cream, cream sauce (No. 3101), chocolate sauce (No. 3107), or any fruit sauce. Serves 8.

(2523)   SNOW PUDDING

1/2 cup lemon-flavored gelatin	2 egg whites, stiffly beaten

Dissolve gelatin in 1 cup boiling water. Cool. When congealing has started, fold in egg whites. Serve with soft custard (No. 2401). Serves 4.

(2524) SOUR MILK PUDDING

1 teaspoon soda	1 teaspoon cinnamon
1 cup sour milk	¼ teaspoon salt
2 cups bread crumbs	⅛ teaspoon nutmeg
½ cup shortening	1 cup chopped nuts
1 cup sugar	1 cup raisins
2 eggs	1 teaspoon vanilla
1 cup flour	

Combine soda and milk. Add bread crumbs. Let stand 10 minutes. Beat shortening while adding sugar slowly. Beat in eggs, one at a time. Mix and sift flour, cinnamon, salt, and nutmeg. Add to shortening alternately with the milk mixture. Add nuts, raisins, and vanilla. Turn into greased baking dish. Cover and bake in moderate oven (350° F.) 1¼ hours. Serve with any fruit sauce. Serves 8.

(2525) GRATED SWEET POTATO PUDDING

3 cups grated raw sweet potatoes	2 tablespoons butter, melted
½ cup sugar	½ cup chopped nuts
½ cup maple sirup	½ teaspoon salt
1 cup milk	2 eggs, well beaten
1 teaspoon nutmeg	

Combine sweet potatoes, sugar, maple sirup, milk, nutmeg, butter, nuts, and salt. Add eggs and pour into buttered shallow pan. Bake in a moderately hot oven (375° F.) 50 to 60 minutes. Serves 6.

(2526) DELMONICO PUDDING

5 eggs	2 tablespoons cornstarch
½ cup sugar	4 cups milk

Separate eggs. Beat yolks light. Add 5 tablespoons sugar. Beat again until very light. Mix cornstarch to a smooth paste with a little milk and add to yolks. Bring remaining milk just to boiling point and stir into mixture. Cook, stirring constantly, until thickened. Turn into greased baking dish. Bake in moderate oven (350° F.) until firm. Beat egg whites to stiff froth with remaining sugar. Spread on pudding. Return to oven and brown. Serves 6.

(2527)   KUCHEN PUDDING

1½ cups sifted flour	2½ cups canned apricot
½ teaspoon salt	halves, drained
2 teaspoons baking powder	1½ tablespoons butter
½ cup shortening	1½ tablespoons flour
⅓ cup sugar	(additional)
1 teaspoon vanilla	4 tablespoons sugar
1 well-beaten egg	(additional)
¼ cup milk	½ teaspoon cinnamon
¼ cup sirup from apricots	

Mix and sift flour, salt, and baking powder. Cream shortening, sugar, and vanilla together. Add egg. Combine milk and ¼ cup apricot sirup and add alternately with the flour to creamed mixture. Pour into a greased baking pan (8 x 8 inches). Arrange apricot halves on top, pressing into batter. Boil remaining juice from apricots 5 minutes. Add other ingredients. Mix well and pour over pudding. Bake in moderately hot oven (375° F.) 45 minutes. Sliced peaches or pineapple chunks may be used in place of apricots.

(2528)   CHARLOTTES

Line the bottom and sides of a mold with ladyfingers (No. 3042). Fill with any desired Bavarian cream. When set, unmold on plate. These may be made in large or individual molds.

(2529)   CHARLOTTE RUSSE

Line small cake molds with ladyfingers (No. 3042) or ¼-inch slices of any kind of cake. Fill center with whipped cream or any desired soft dessert. Serve thoroughly chilled.

(2530)   APPLE BROWN BETTY

½ to 1 cup sugar	3 cups sliced or chopped
¼ teaspoon cinnamon	apples
¼ teaspoon nutmeg	¼ cup water
¼ teaspoon salt	Juice and grated rind of 1
1½ cups soft bread crumbs	lemon
3 tablespoons butter	

Mix sugar, spices, and salt. If apples are very tart, use additional sugar—up to 1 cup. Grease a 1½-quart casserole. Put in a third of the crumbs, then half of the apples. Sprinkle with half of the sugar mixture. Repeat. Mix water, lemon juice and rind; pour over. Put on remaining crumbs and dot with butter. Cover and bake in moderate oven (350° F.) 1¾ hours. Serves 6. Rhubarb, peaches, pineapple, bananas, or cherries may be used instead of apples.

(2531)   APPLESAUCE BROWN BETTY

Substitute 2½ cups applesauce (No. 34) for apples in apple brown betty (No. 2530).

(2532)   PEACH BROWN BETTY

See apple brown betty (No. 2530).

(2533)   APPLE PAN DOWDY

1 quart apples, sliced	⅛ teaspoon nutmeg
1 cup light brown sugar	4 tablespoons butter
½ teaspoon cinnamon	½ cup cider
⅛ teaspoon clove	

Butter a pudding dish. Put in sliced apples and spread sugar over the apples and sprinkle the spices over the sugar. Dot top with butter. Add cider and cover with homemade biscuit dough (No. 923), ¼ inch thick. Leave holes for the steam to escape. Bake in moderate oven (350° F.) until apples are tender and crust is well browned. Serve with whipped cream. Serves 6.

(2534)   PEACH COBBLER

2½ cups canned sliced peaches	¼ teaspoon cinnamon
2 tablespoons granulated tapioca	Dash nutmeg
¼ cup sugar	1 tablespoon butter
¼ teaspoon salt	Baking powder biscuit dough (No. 1012)

Empty the peaches into a shallow baking dish. Add tapioca and let stand about 10 minutes. Add the sugar, salt, and spice. Mix well. Dot top with butter. Roll biscuit dough to a thickness of ¼ inch. Prick and arrange over the top of the peach mixture. Bake in hot oven (400° F.) about 30 minutes, or until well browned. Apricots, blackberries, blueberries, black or red raspberries may be used instead of peaches. Serves 8.

(2535)   DUTCH APPLE CAKE

After cottage pudding (No. 2480) is in pan, but before cooking, top batter with thin slices of apple. Sprinkle with cinnamon and sugar. Dot with butter or fat. Bake in moderate oven (350° F.) until apples are tender, about 45 minutes. Serve hot with whipped cream.

(2536)   APPLE DELIGHTS

2 cups flour	1 cup milk
1½ teaspoons baking powder	1 egg
½ teaspoon salt	6 soft ripe apples
¼ cup shortening	Sugar

Mix and sift flour, baking powder, and salt. Cut in shortening with a knife. Add milk and beaten egg and mix well. Drop tablespoons of batter into well greased muffin pans. Peel apples, cut in halves, and take out cores. Put on top of batter, cut side up, and fill the holes with sugar. Bake in a hot oven (400° F.) 25 minutes or until apples are tender. Serve hot with cream or sweetened whipped cream, dusted with cinnamon. Serves 6.

(2537)   APPLE CROW'S NEST

4 tart apples, cored, pared, and sliced	1 cup flour
1½ tablespoons butter	2 teaspoons baking powder
¾ cup sugar	¼ teaspoon salt
2½ teaspoons cinnamon	3 tablespoons shortening
	¼ cup milk

Arrange apples in greased pie tin and dot with butter. Sprinkle with 1 tablespoon sugar and 1½ teaspoons cinnamon. Sift flour, baking powder, salt, and ¼ cup sugar together twice. Cut in shortening with a knife or finger tips. Add enough milk gradually to make a soft dough. Spread over apples. Bake in hot oven (400° F.) until apples are tender, about 25 minutes. Turn out upside down. Mix remaining sugar and cinnamon and stir into apples. Serve hot with whipped cream, sprinkled with cinnamon and chopped nuts. Serves 6.

(2538) CRANBERRY ROLL

2 ½ cups flour
4 teaspoons baking powder
1 teaspoon salt
¼ cup sugar

2 tablespoons shortening
1 beaten egg
¾ cup milk
2 cups cranberries

Mix and sift flour, baking powder, salt, and sugar. Work in shortening with finger tips. Add egg and just enough milk, gradually, to make a soft dough. Roll out on floured board to ½-inch thickness. Spread surface generously with butter or fat. Cover with cranberries. Roll as a jelly roll. Put in greased baking pan. Brush top and sides with butter or fat. Bake in quick oven (450° F.) until it begins to brown. Reduce heat to 350° F. and bake 45 minutes longer. Slice 1 inch thick and serve hot with lemon (No. 3129) or hard sauce (No. 3105). Serves 6.

(2539) PEAR BRICKLE

½ cup heavy cream
2 tablespoons sugar
½ cup crushed peanut brittle

1 teaspoon vanilla
1-pound canned sliced pears

Whip cream. Add sugar and vanilla. Combine lightly with peanut brittle and pears. Serve over slices of plain or toasted angel food cake (No. 2902). Garnish with additional peanut brittle, maraschino cherries, or red jelly. Crushed pineapple, sliced apricots, peaches, fruit cocktail, or white cherries may be used instead of pears. Serves 8.

(2540) BLUEBERRY SLUMP

1 quart blueberries
3 cups water
2 cups sugar
1 ½ cups flour

1 ½ teaspoons baking powder
¼ teaspoon salt
Milk

Boil the berries, water, and sugar in a broad saucepan until there is plenty of juice. Mix the flour, baking powder, and salt together and add sufficient milk to make a soft dough. Pour over the berries. Cover closely. Cook for 15 minutes on top of stove. Turn out on hot platter and serve with egg sauce (No. 3126). Serves 6.

(2541)   PINEAPPLE PEACH CRISP

7 slices bread	2½ cups canned crushed
¼ cup butter	pineapple
⅔ cup brown sugar	1 cup canned sliced peaches
¼ cup shredded almonds	

Spread both sides of the bread with butter. Cut the bread in squares or strips and arrange part of them in the bottom of a shallow pan (8 x 8 inches). Sprinkle with half the sugar, pour the pineapple and peaches over the mixture, and sprinkle with the almonds and remaining sugar. Cover with remaining bread squares and bake in moderate oven (350° F.) 40 minutes. Serve with whipped cream. Serves 8 to 10.

(2542)   PEACH BASKET TURNOVER

2 egg yolks	½ teaspoon salt
1 cup sugar	1 teaspoon vanilla
⅓ cup liquid drained from	1 cup brown sugar
peaches	2 tablespoons shortening
2 stiffly beaten egg whites	1 can drained sliced
1 cup flour	peaches
1 teaspoon baking powder	

Beat yolks with ½ cup sugar until light. Add ⅓ cup peach liquid and remaining sugar. Beat 5 minutes. Fold in egg whites. Mix and sift flour, baking powder, and ¼ teaspoon salt. Add to first mixture and mix thoroughly. Add vanilla. Cream brown sugar and shortening together. Add peaches and remaining salt and place in shallow, greased baking pan. Pour over batter. Bake in hot oven (400° F.) 45 minutes. Turn out upside down. Serve hot with fruit juice and whipped cream. Serves 6.

(2543)   UNIVERSAL DESSERT

½ cup heavy cream	½ cup shredded toasted
2½ cups stewed raspberries	almonds (No. 3831)
(No. 49)	Pound cake (No. 2979)

Whip cream and combine lightly with drained berries and ¼ cup almonds. Line a shallow dish with thin slices of cake. Spread with half the fruit mixture. Add another layer of cake and remaining fruit. Sprinkle with remaining almonds. Chill

several hours. Serve with whipped cream. Strawberries, loganberries, or blackberries may be substituted for raspberries.
Serves 8.

(2544)　　　　　FIGS ANNETTE

2½ cups stewed figs (No. 55)　　¼ teaspoon nutmeg
¼ cup sugar　　　　　　　　　Dash cinnamon
1 tablespoon cornstarch　　　　3 tablespoons lemon juice
1 tablespoon butter　　　　　　1 teaspoon grated lemon
⅛ teaspoon salt　　　　　　　　　rind

Drain figs. Add ¼ cup sugar to sirup and bring to boiling
point. Blend cornstarch with ¼ cup cold water and add to
sirup. Cook, stirring constantly, until thickened. Cook 10 minutes longer over hot water. Add other ingredients. Place 2 or 3
figs on slices of sponge cake (No. 3003) or on individual shortcakes (No. 964). Pour over sauce. Serves 6.

(2545)　　GRAHAM CRACKERS AND
MARSHMALLOWS

½ pound graham crackers,　　10 maraschino cherries,
　crumbed　　　　　　　　　　chopped
½ pound marshmallows,　　　½ cup chopped walnuts
　chopped in small pieces　　½ cup orange juice
½ pound pitted dates,　　　　Juice ½ lemon
　chopped

Mix well and pack into cake tin lined with waxed paper.
Chill and serve with whipped cream. Serves 8.

(2546)　　TUTTI FRUTTI DESSERT

3 cups left-over canned or　　1 teaspoon baking powder
　stewed fruit　　　　　　　　½ teaspoon salt
¾ cup flour　　　　　　　　　1 egg
¾ cup sugar

Pour fruit (one kind or an assortment) in shallow baking
dish. Sift dry ingredients together in a bowl. Add unbeaten egg
and mix well. Then spread mixture over fruit. Bake in a moderately hot oven (375° F.) approximately 30 minutes, or until
brown. Serve warm with cream. Serves 6.

FROZEN DESSERTS

The best method for freezing desserts must be determined by the available equipment.

When freezing is to be done in an automatic refrigerator, the mixture should be thoroughly chilled before putting in the freezing compartment. No hot foods should be placed in box during freezing period and ice cubes should not be made at the same time. The refrigerator door should be opened as little as possible. In all cases it is best to study carefully the directions for freezing given by the manufacturer of the refrigerator as methods differ in various makes. All frozen desserts having gelatin or custard bases should be thoroughly stirred at 45-minute intervals until quite thick. Do not stir, during freezing, those desserts with a whipped cream base or those into which egg whites or whipped cream have been folded.

To freeze in rock salt and ice in a crank freezer, never fill container more than ⅔ full to provide room for expansion and for the lightening of the cream by the incorporation of air bubbles. Cover the container closely, placing wax paper over the top of container before putting on the lid. Pack ice receptacle with a mixture of 3 parts broken ice and 1 part rock salt. Turn crank slowly at first and faster as mixture hardens.

To freeze in a vacuum-pack freezer, fill container ⅔ full. At least once during freezing the cover must be removed, the cream scraped from the sides of the container, and the mixture thoroughly stirred or beaten.

(2547)   VANILLA ICE CREAM

1½ cups top milk	⅛ teaspoon salt
2 eggs	2 teaspoons vanilla
½ cup sugar	1 cup whipping cream
1 tablespoon cornstarch	

Scald milk. Separate eggs. Beat yolks and add sugar and cornstarch. Combine this mixture with milk. Cook over water 20 to 25 minutes, stirring occasionally. Cool. Beat egg whites until stiff. Add salt and fold into cooked mixture. Add vanilla. Pour into refrigerator freezing tray and chill to a heavy mush. Beat until fluffy. Whip cream and fold into mixture. Return to tray and freeze. Serves 6.

(2548) ## FRENCH ICE CREAM

2 cups milk	1 cup sugar
5 egg yolks	2 cups cream
Few grains salt	1 tablespoon vanilla

Scald the milk in a double boiler or over hot water. Beat egg yolks, salt, and sugar together until light. Pour the scalded milk on them and stir until well mixed. Return to boiler and cook until the mixture coats the spoon, stirring constantly. Remove from fire. Add cream and stir well. Cool. Add vanilla. Chill and freeze. Serve with chocolate sauce (No. 3107). Yield: 1 quart ice cream.

(2549) ## CHOCOLATE ICE CREAM

1 ounce unsweetened chocolate	⅔ cup water
	1 teaspoon vanilla
⅔ cup sweetened condensed milk	⅔ cup whipping cream

Melt chocolate in top of double boiler. Add condensed milk and stir until mixture thickens. Add water slowly and mix well. Chill thoroughly. Add vanilla. Whip cream slightly and fold into the chilled chocolate mixture. Pour into freezing tray and freeze. After the mixture is half frozen remove from the refrigerator, beat until smooth and replace in freezing unit until frozen. Serves 6.

(2550) ## STRAWBERRY ICE CREAM

4 egg yolks	2 cups strawberry juice
1 cup sugar	and pulp
2 cups cream	

Beat eggs with ½ cup sugar. Add remaining sugar to cream and bring to boiling point. Stir cream gradually into eggs. Strain. Cool. Stir in strawberry juice and pulp. Freeze.

(2551) ## COFFEE ICE CREAM

Add ¾ cup strong black coffee (No. 301) to recipe for French ice cream (No. 2548).

(2552)   FROZEN PUDDING

1½ cups orange juice
¼ cup lemon juice
½ cup sugar
2 cups cream
⅓ cup powdered sugar
2 teaspoons vanilla

½ cup raisins, chopped
dates, chopped mara-
schino cherries, or
chopped stewed prunes
(No. 71), all 1 kind
or in combination

½ cup chopped walnuts

Mix fruit juices. Add sugar and dissolve. Beat cream thick. Add fruit juices, powdered sugar and vanilla. Stir in raisins, dates, prunes or cherries, and walnuts. Chill. Freeze. Yield: 1½ quarts.

(2553)   APRICOT ICE CREAM

1 pound dried apricots
1 cup sugar
1 tablespoon candied ginger
Juice ½ lemon

1 cup evaporated milk
½ teaspoon unflavored
gelatin

Scald milk. Soften gelatin in 2 teaspoons cold water and dissolve in milk. Chill until icy cold and whip. Cook apricots in enough water to cover. When boiling add sugar and ginger. Simmer until fruit is thick and mushy. Add lemon juice and cool. Fold into whipped milk mixture. Turn into refrigerator freezing tray and freeze. Serves 6.

(2554)   BANANA ICE CREAM

Add 3 mashed bananas to vanilla ice cream (No. 2547) just before freezing.

(2555)   BUTTERSCOTCH ICE CREAM

Substitute brown sugar for white sugar in vanilla ice cream (No. 2547) and add ½ tablespoon butter during cooking.

(2556)   CARAMEL ICE CREAM

Make vanilla ice cream (No. 2547) but melt and brown sugar in frying pan before adding.

(2557) MARSHMALLOW ICE CREAM

Add ½ cup marshmallows, chopped into small pieces, to chocolate ice cream (No. 2549) just before freezing.

(2558) CHOCOLATE MINT ICE CREAM

1 cup hard after-dinner cream mints	1 ounce unsweetened chocolate, coarsely
¾ cup milk	grated
1 cup heavy cream	Oblong vanilla sugar wafers
Green food coloring	

Add mints to milk. Melt at low heat, stirring constantly. Cool thoroughly. Whip cream stiff and fold mint mixture into it until well blended. Tint a delicate green color. Pour into tray of electric refrigerator and freeze to a mush-like consistency. Stir and fold in grated chocolate. Place split sugar wafers in the bottom of a freezing tray and fill with partly frozen mint and chocolate mixture. Return to refrigerator and continue freezing until firm. Unmold so that sugar wafers are on top. Serves 6.

(2559) CINNAMON ICE CREAM

Place small stick of cinnamon candy in milk before scalding for vanilla ice cream (No. 2547).

(2560) FRUIT COCKTAIL ICE CREAM

Substitute crushed mixed fruits for crushed pineapple in recipe for pineapple ice cream (No. 2567).

(2561) HARLEQUIN ICE CREAM

1 quart whipping cream	1 cup macaroon crumbs
Confectioner's sugar	1 cup strawberry jam
2 ounces unsweetened chocolate, melted	½ cup shredded almonds

Divide cream in four portions and whip. To first part add 5 tablespoons confectioner's sugar and the chocolate, slowly. Spread on bottom of refrigerator tray and place in refrigerator while preparing next layer. To the second portion of cream add same amount of sugar and macaroon crumbs. Spread this carefully over first layer and return to refrigerator. The third layer is made by adding the strawberry jam to another portion of cream, and the fourth layer is composed of the remaining cream, the almonds, and five tablespoons of sugar.

(2562)   MAPLE ICE CREAM

Substitute ¼ cup maple sugar for an equal quantity of white sugar in recipe for vanilla ice cream (No. 2547) and omit vanilla.

(2563)   PEACH ICE CREAM

Follow recipe for vanilla ice cream (No. 2547), reducing vanilla content to ½ teaspoon and adding ½ teaspoon almond extract with vanilla and 1½ cups mashed and sweetened peaches when folding in whipped cream.

(2564)   PEACH MALLOW ICE CREAM

1 cup crushed fresh peaches	20 marshmallows
3 tablespoons sugar	½ pint whipping cream

Sprinkle peaches with sugar and let stand 20 minutes. Put marshmallows and ¼ cup water in top of double boiler. Cook, stirring occasionally, until liquid. Add peaches. Cool. Whip cream stiff and combine with cold mixture. Pour into refrigerator freezing tray and freeze. Serves 6.

(2565)   PEANUT BRITTLE ICE CREAM

Add ½ to ¾ cup crushed peanut brittle to vanilla ice cream (No. 2547) when folding in whipped cream.

(2566)   PEPPERMINT CANDY ICE CREAM

1 cup crushed candy mints	1½ cups cream
1½ cups hot milk	⅛ teaspoon salt

Dissolve the candy in the hot milk over heat. Add cream and salt. Chill. Freeze until quite firm. Beat with rotary beater until light and creamy. Continue freezing. Serve with hot fudge sauce (No. 3108). Serves 6.

(2567)   PINEAPPLE ICE CREAM

1 egg	1½ cups crushed pineapple
½ cup sugar	1 teaspoon vanilla
2 cups evaporated milk	1 cup whipping cream
Few grains salt	

Beat egg, add sugar, evaporated milk and salt. Cook over hot water until thick, stirring constantly. Chill. Add pineapple and vanilla. Whip cream and fold in the pineapple mixture. Pour into the freezing tray and freeze. After the mixture is half frozen remove from the refrigerator, beat until smooth and replace in freezing unit. Serves 6.

(2568)   PISTACHIO ICE CREAM

Add 1 teaspoon pistachio extract and omit vanilla in recipe for vanilla ice cream (No. 2547) or French ice cream (No. 2548). Color pale green with vegetable coloring.

(2569)   PUMPKIN ICE CREAM

4 cups light cream	½ teaspoon ground ginger
2 beaten eggs	½ teaspoon ground cloves
1¼ cups brown sugar	¼ teaspoon salt
1 teaspoon cinnamon	1¼ cups mashed (No. 1864)
½ teaspoon nutmeg	or canned pumpkin

Put cream in saucepan. Cover and bring to boiling point. Reduce heat. Add eggs, sugar, and seasonings. Cook, stirring constantly, until a coating forms on spoon. Stir in pumpkin. Heat thoroughly. Chill and freeze. Yield: 1 quart.

(2570)   TUTTI-FRUTTI ICE CREAM

3 cups milk	1 cup raisins
2 slightly beaten eggs	1 cup chopped maraschino
¾ cup sugar	cherries
2 tablespoons cornstarch	2 cups cream, whipped
24 macaroons, toasted and powdered	1 teaspoon vanilla

Put 2½ cups milk in saucepan. Cover and bring to boiling point. Reduce heat. Combine eggs, sugar, cornstarch, and remaining milk. Add gradually to scalded milk while stirring. Cook, stirring constantly, until a coating forms on spoon. Chill. Start to freeze. When freezing starts, add macaroons, raisins, cherries with their liquid, whipped cream, and vanilla. Freeze. Yield: 1½ quarts.

(2571) WALNUT ICE CREAM

Add ½ cup chopped walnuts, ¼ cup strong coffee (No. 301), and 1 tablespoon powdered sugar to vanilla ice cream (No. 2547), when mushy, and finish freezing.

(2572) ORANGE SHERBET

Add 3 well-beaten egg whites and ⅔ cup heavy cream to orange ice (No. 2594) when mixture is chilled but before freezing starts.

(2573) LEMON SHERBET

Add 3 well-beaten egg whites and ⅔ cup heavy cream to lemon ice (No. 2592) when mixture is chilled but before freezing starts.

(2574) PINEAPPLE SHERBET

1½ cups sugar	Juice of 1 lemon
2 cups shredded pineapple	1 egg white

Boil 4 cups water and sugar together 10 minutes. Drain pineapple and add with the lemon juice. Cool. Freeze. When partly frozen, fold in stiffly beaten egg white. Continue freezing. If canned pineapple is used, reduce sugar to ¾ cup. Yield: 1 quart sherbet.

(2575) BANANA SHERBET

3 cups sugar	4 bananas, cut in small
Juice of 4 lemons	pieces
1 stiffly beaten egg white	

Bring sugar to a boil in 6 cups water. Let cool slightly. Add lemon juice and bananas. Chill. Freeze. When congealing starts, add egg white and continue freezing.

(2576) BUTTERMILK SHERBET

2 cups buttermilk	1 teaspoon vanilla
1 cup crushed pineapple	1/16 teaspoon salt
⅔ cup sugar	1 egg white

Mix buttermilk, all but 2 tablespoons sugar, salt, pineapple, and vanilla. Freeze to a mush. Beat egg white until stiff and add the 2 tablespoons sugar. Transfer frozen mixture to cold mixing bowl. Beat until fluffy. Add egg white and return to freezing tray. Freeze quickly without further stirring.

(2577)   CHERRY SHERBET

2½ cups cherries   1 pound sugar

Stone and chop cherries. Add sugar and 1 quart water. Bring to boiling point, stirring frequently. Chill and freeze.

(2578)   GINGER SHERBET

Stir ½ cup chopped preserved ginger into 1 quart lemon ice (No. 2592) when at mushy stage and continue freezing.

(2579)   GRAPE SHERBET

Use 2 cups grape juice instead of crushed pineapple in recipe for pineapple sherbet (No. 2574) and reduce amount of water to 3 cups.

(2580)   LIME SHERBET

1 tablespoon gelatin   3 egg whites, whipped stiff
1 cup sugar   ½ cup almonds or pistachio
4 cups lime carbonated   nuts, chopped
     beverage

Soak gelatin in 2 tablespoonfuls of cold water 5 minutes. Add ½ cup boiling water and stir until dissolved. Cool. Add sugar and lime beverage. When partly frozen, at thick mush stage, add egg whites and nuts. Freeze. Serves 8.

(2581)   LIQUEUR SHERBET

Stir ½ cup claret or sherry into 1 quart lemon ice (No. 2592) when frozen to mushy stage.

(2582)   LOGANBERRY SHERBET

2 teaspoons gelatin	1 teaspoon grated orange
¾ cup sugar	rind
¼ teaspoon salt	1 12-ounce can logan-
¼ cup orange juice	berry juice
½ cup cream, whipped	

Soak gelatin in ¼ cup cold water 5 minutes. Bring sugar, salt, and ½ cup water to boiling point. Remove from heat. Add gelatin, orange juice, and rind. Stir until gelatin is dissolved. Add loganberry juice. Chill. Start freezing. When mushy, remove and beat with rotary beater. Fold in whipped cream. Finish freezing. Almost any fruit juice or combination of fruit juices and mashed pulp may be substituted for loganberry juice. Serves 6.

(2583)   PEACH SHERBET

½ teaspoon gelatin	Juice 1 orange
1 cup sugar	1 cup fresh peach pulp
Juice ½ lemon	1 egg white

Soak gelatin in ¼ cup cold water 5 minutes. Boil sugar and 2 cups water 10 minutes, and dissolve gelatin in hot sirup. Cool. Add orange and lemon juice and peach pulp which has been forced through very coarse sieve. Freeze to the mushy stage. Fold in stiffly beaten egg white. Continue freezing without stirring. Yield: 1 quart.

(2584)   ITALIAN SORBET

2 cups sugar	1½ cups orange carbonated
2 cups water	beverage
2 tablespoons gelatin	1½ cups grape carbonated
1 cup orange juice	beverage
½ cup lemon juice	1 cup lemon carbonated
	beverage

Boil sugar and water gently 20 minutes. Add gelatin. Cool. Add fruit juices and lastly the beverages. Freeze. Ginger ale may be substituted for part or all of above beverages. Serves 16.

(2585) TEA SHERBET

2 quarts tea (No. 306)
Juice of 3 lemons
1 cup sugar
2 beaten egg whites
¼ teaspoon salt

Mix tea, lemon juice, and sugar. Chill. Freeze to mushy stage. Add egg whites and salt. Finish freezing.

(2586) WINE SHERBET

Stir 1 cup wine into 1 quart orange ice (No. 2594) when frozen to mushy stage. Champagne or any bubbling or still wine may be used.

(2587) APRICOT ICE

2 cups stewed apricots
    (No. 42)
½ cup sugar
1 tablespoon corn sirup
Juice and grated rind 1
    lemon

Rub apricots through a sieve. Add other ingredients with 2 cups hot water. Strain. Chill. Freeze.

(2588) BERRY WATER ICE

2½ cups berries, any kind
1 pound sugar
Juice of 2 lemons

Bring berries to a boil in 2 cups water. Add sugar and lemon juice. Stir until dissolved. Let stand in warm place 1 to 2 hours. Rub through a sieve. Add 2 additional cups water. Mix well. Taste and add more sugar if necessary. Chill and freeze.

(2589) CRANBERRY ICE

½ cup sugar
2½ cups stewed cranberries
    (No. 54)
1 tablespoon gelatin
1 stiffly beaten egg white

Boil sugar in 1 cup water 3 minutes. Add cranberries and boil 5 minutes longer. Rub through a sieve. Soak gelatin in 4 tablespoons cold water 5 minutes. Add hot cranberry mixture and stir until gelatin is dissolved. Cool. Combine mixture with egg white. Chill and freeze. Yield: 1 quart.

(2590)   PINK FRUIT ICE

3 cups pineapple juice	2 cups sugar
3 cups orange juice	3 cups strawberry car-
½ cup lemon juice	bonated beverage

Mix well and freeze. Serves 15.

(2591)   GRAPE ICE

1½ cups grape carbonated	1½ teaspoons lemon juice
beverage	1½ to 2 tablespoons sugar
Few grains salt	

Chill ingredients before combining. Freeze. Orange, strawberry or cherry carbonated beverages may be substituted for the grape, depending upon flavor or color desired. Serves 5.

(2592)   LEMON ICE

2¼ cups sugar	Juice of 1 orange
Juice of 4 lemons	Grated rind of 1 lemon

Dissolve sugar in 1 quart water and boil 10 minutes. Strain juices and add to sirup. Add rind and mix thoroughly. Chill and freeze. Yield: 1 quart ice.

(2593)   MINT ICE

1½ cups sugar	½ cup chopped mint or ½
¾ cup white corn sirup	teaspoon mint essence
1¾ cups water	2 cups grapefruit sections
6 tablespoons lemon juice	and juice

Cook sugar, sirup, and 1 cup water to soft boil stage (238° F.). Add lemon juice, and remaining water. Cool. Add mint. Cut the canned grapefruit sections into pieces and add fruit and juice to cooled sirup. Freeze. Yield: 2 quarts.

(2594)   ORANGE ICE

2 cups sugar	Juice 1 lemon
Juice 6 oranges	Grated rind 1 orange

Make same as lemon ice (No. 2592).

(2595) PEACH ICE

Substitute peach compote (No. 59) for apricots in apricot ice (No. 2587).

(2596) PINEAPPLE ICE

1 cup crushed pineapple	Juice of ½ orange
Juice of 1 lemon	1½ cups powdered sugar

Rub pineapple through a sieve into 2 cups hot water. Add other ingredients. Chill. Freeze.

(2597) STRAWBERRY ICE

Follow recipe for berry water ice (No. 2588), using mashed strawberries for berries.

(2598) CHOCOLATE MOUSSE

Follow directions for making coffee mousse (No. 2599) substituting 2 ounces melted, unsweetened chocolate for coffee and 1 teaspoon vanilla for 1 tablespoon mocha essence.

(2599) COFFEE MOUSSE

2 cups cream	½ cup strong coffee
½ cup powdered sugar	(No. 301)
⅛ teaspoon salt	1 tablespoon mocha essence

Whip the cream, sugar, and salt together until stiff. Add coffee and mocha essence and mix well. Chill and freeze. Serve with whipped cream. Yield: 1½ quarts.

(2600) CRANBERRY MOUSSE

1 cup evaporated milk	1¼ cups canned cranberry
2 tablespoons lemon juice	sauce, cut in small
¼ cup sugar	cubes

Chill milk thoroughly and whip until stiff. Add lemon juice and whip until very stiff. Fold in the cold cranberry sauce and sugar. Mix lightly, but thoroughly. Freeze. Serves 6.

(2601)   DATE MOUSSE

½ package dates   4 egg yolks
1 cup orange juice   ½ teaspoon salt
1 teaspoon orange rind   1 cup cream, whipped

Cook pitted dates with ½ cup water over a low heat for 10 minutes. Rub through coarse sieve. Add orange juice and rind, beaten egg yolks, and salt. Stir over boiling water until egg yolks thicken, about 5 minutes. Cool. Fold in whipped cream and freeze. Serves 8 to 12.

(2602)   FRUIT MOUSSE

Follow directions for making coffee mousse (No. 2599), adding 2 cups chopped and drained fruit and 1 teaspoon vanilla and omitting coffee and mocha essence.

(2603)   RASPBERRY MOUSSE WITH
                    MARSHMALLOWS

1 cup sweetened raspberry   20 marshmallows, cut in
    juice   small pieces
Juice ½ lemon   1 cup heavy cream
              1 cup sugar

To obtain juice from berries, crush a pint of raspberries slightly, add 1 cup sugar, and let come to a boil slowly. Stir to keep from burning. Press through a sieve and measure. Add water to make a cup of juice if necessary. While hot, add marshmallows and dissolve. Cool and add lemon juice, then fold into the cream which has been whipped. Freeze. Serves 6.

(2604)   STRAWBERRY MOUSSE

Use strawberries, heated to the boiling point and rubbed through a sieve, for fruit in fruit mousse (No. 2602). Raspberries, loganberries, blackberries, cherries, alone or in combination, may be used in place of strawberries.

(2605)   VANILLA MOUSSE

Substitute ½ cup water for strong coffee and 1 tablespoon vanilla for mocha essence in recipe for coffee mousse (No. 2599). Serve with fudge sauce (No. 3108) or berry-jelly sauce (No. 3114). If desired, chopped nuts, chopped maraschino cherries, and raisins may be added to this.

(2606)   MACAROON BISQUE

Add ½ cup almond macaroon crumbs to vanilla ice cream (No. 2547) when folding in whipped cream.

(2607)   ANGEL PARFAIT

¾ cup sugar	1½ teaspoons vanilla
¼ cup water	2 cups whipping cream
2 egg whites	

Cook sugar and water, stirring until sugar is dissolved, then without stirring until it spins a thread. Beat egg whites until stiff. Add sirup slowly, while continuing to beat. Add flavoring and cream, which has been beaten until thick but not stiff. Freeze quickly without stirring.

(2608)   PISTACHIO PARFAIT

Add 1 teaspoon almond extract and a little green vegetable coloring to recipe for angel parfait (No. 2607).

(2609)   APRICOT FREEZE

2 eggs	3½ cups stewed apricots
½ cup sugar	(No. 42)
⅛ teaspoon salt	2 teaspoons vanilla
½ cup milk	Few drops almond extract
½ cup heavy cream, whipped	

Beat the eggs with a rotary beater until very thick, about 5 minutes. Add sugar gradually and continue to beat until thick and smooth. Add salt, milk, sirup from the apricots, and flavorings. Mix well. Chill. Freeze until mushy. Remove and beat with rotary beater. Fold in the whipped cream and the apricots that have been mashed. Continue freezing. When the sides and bottom of mixture become frozen, stir well. Finish freezing. Serves 10 to 12.

(2610)   FROZEN PRUNE WHIP

1½ cups stewed prunes
  (No. 71)
½ cup granulated sugar
¼ teaspoon ground cloves
2 cups milk
¼ teaspoon salt

⅓ cup granulated sugar
  (additional)
1 teaspoon vanilla extract
1 tablespoon plain gelatin
2 eggs
1 cup whipping cream

Remove pits from prunes and cut in small pieces. Combine with sugar, spice and heat to dissolve sugar. Chill. Combine 1½ cups milk, salt, and ⅓ cup sugar and scald. Add flavoring and gelatin moistened in remaining ½ cup milk and stir to dissolve gelatin. Pour over beaten eggs, stirring briskly. Chill until thick. Whip cream stiff and fold into chilled gelatin mixture. Add prune mixture. Freeze, stirring once or twice during process. Serves 6.

(2611)   ORANGE FLUFF

¾ cup sugar
Grated rind of 2 oranges
1 cup orange juice

½ teaspoon gelatin
2 cups whipping cream

Cook sugar in ⅔ cup cold water until a little of the mixture dropped in cold water forms a soft ball. Remove from heat. Add orange rind and ¼ cup orange juice. Sprinkle gelatin on one tablespoon cold water and add to mixture. Mix well and chill. Whip the cream until stiff and add to mixture. Put balance of orange juice in refrigerator freezing tray. Pour the mixture on top and freeze. Serves 6 to 8.

(2612) FROZEN GRAPENUT WITH WHIPPED
CREAM

½ cup grapenuts
½ cup granulated sugar

1 pint whipping cream
1 teaspoon vanilla

Whip cream, fold in the ½ cup grapenuts and allow to stand one hour or until grapenuts begin to soften. Fold in sugar and vanilla and pour into tray and freeze.

(2613) ROOT BEER CRÈME

2 cups root beer
2 cups cream

Few grains salt

Chill ingredients before combining. Freeze. Sarsaparilla may be used in place of root beer. Serves 8.

(2614) FROZEN WHIPPED CREAM

Whip ½ pint heavy cream until slightly thickened. Add 2 tablespoons confectioners' sugar and ½ teaspoon vanilla. Pour into freezing tray of an electric refrigerator and freeze until firm.

(2615) GLORIFIED RICE

½ cup steamed rice
   (No. 106)
⅓ cup sugar
Pinch of salt

½ cup milk
½ cup chopped dates
1 cup whipping cream
1 teaspoon vanilla

Combine rice and milk and cook slowly 15 minutes. Cool and add chopped dates, sugar, vanilla, salt and fold in whipped cream. Pour into tray and freeze lightly.

(2616) FROZEN CHARLOTTES

Line the bottom and sides of mold with ladyfingers (No. 3042). Fill with any desired ice cream, either one flavor or in combination. Turn out. Garnish with whipped cream.

(2617) SNOWBALLS

Roll balls of firmly frozen ice cream in shredded coconut just before serving.

(2618) BOMBES

Line a melon mold with any preferred ice cream. Fill center with any desired mousse. Freeze. Or the center may be filled with almost any pudding, whip, soufflé, custard, or cream.

(2619) SPUMONI

Line a round-bottom mold with vanilla ice cream (No. 2547). Add a layer of chocolate ice cream (No. 2549). Fill with mixture of chopped nuts and maraschino cherries, raisins, and whipped cream. Freeze solid. Unmold.

(2620) BANANA CARAMEL ICE CREAM
Automatic Refrigerator

1 cup mashed ripe bananas	⅓ cup milk
2 teaspoons lemon juice	2 egg whites
¼ cup firmly packed brown sugar	1 cup whipping cream
	2 egg yolks
¼ teaspoon salt	1 teaspoon vanilla extract

Mix together bananas and lemon juice. Add sugar, salt and milk, stirring until mixed. Beat egg whites until stiff. Whip cream until thickened but not stiff. Beat egg yolks until thick. Combine banana mixture, egg whites, egg yolks, cream and vanilla. Turn into freezing trays of an automatic refrigerator. Freeze, with indicator at coldest setting, stirring every 30 minutes until mixture begins to hold its shape. Then freeze until firm. Serves 8.

VARIATIONS

BANANA CARAMEL NUT ICE CREAM—Make Banana Caramel Ice Cream adding ½ cup coarsely chopped nut meats during final stirring. Pecans, walnuts, Brazil nuts, peanuts or almonds can be used.

BANANA DATE ICE CREAM—Make Banana Caramel Ice Cream adding ½ cup date paste during final stirring. To make date paste, simmer ½ cup cut pitted dates with ½ cup water for 10 minutes. Cool.

BANANA PRALINE ICE CREAM—Make Banana Caramel Ice Cream adding ½ cup coarsely chopped buttered pecans during final stirring. To butter pecans, heat ½ cup pecans in 1 tablespoon butter until lightly browned. Sprinkle very lightly with salt.

BANANA RAISIN ICE CREAM—Make Banana Caramel Ice Cream adding raisin paste during final stirring. To make raisin paste, simmer ½ cup cut seedless raisins with ¼ cup orange juice until liquid has evaporated. Cool.

BANANA RAISIN AU RHUM ICE CREAM—Make Banana Caramel Ice Cream adding raisin rum mixture during final stirring. To make raisin rum mixture, mix ½ cup cut seedless raisins with 2 tablespoons rum flavoring or rum and let stand 10 minutes.

Pies

~~~~~~

PIE is the great American dessert. In every corner of the land millions of persons are eating pie every day, at every meal. Despite the witticisms often aimed at them, many New England families still serve pie as a breakfast delicacy. It is in a great number of lunch boxes. In some of its varieties it forms the dessert for meals served in every place, from the humblest home to the great hotels and restaurants.

The filling for pies must be a combination of the proper ingredients prepared in the correct way. But, above all, pie-making success depends upon a tender flaky crust. The following simple rules will be a guide toward good results:

RULES FOR GOOD PIE-MAKING

1. Keep shortening in refrigerator until ready to use. Have water cold. In warm weather, it is a good plan to chill the flour and shortening mixture before and after adding the water. It will take a little longer, but success is more certain.

2. Cut shortening into flour until the mixture is coarse and granular.

3. Cold water should be added a little at a time, tossing the mixture with a fork until all particles are moistened. Press into a ball and divide into two parts.

4. Rolling out the dough calls for a delicate touch. Place ball on a lightly floured board or canvas, roll with short strokes toward the edges, keeping it round. Roll ⅛ inch thick. Never turn dough while rolling. Lift with spatula and dust board with

flour, if it sticks. The dough for the upper crust is rolled thinner than ⅛ inch.

5. The lower crust should be about 2½ inches greater in diameter than the upper crust, and the upper crust should be slightly larger than the pie it is to cover.

6. The lower crust should be placed in the pan so that it covers the surface smoothly. And be sure no air lurks beneath the surface, for the air, expanding in baking, will push the crust out of shape.

7. The short slashes cut in center of upper crust are there for the purpose of permitting the steam to escape, but they may be decorative, too.

8. After rolling out dough for pie shell, the entire surface should be pricked to allow air to escape. The pastry is put into pan and trimmed ½ inch larger than pan, then the edge rolled under and fluted.

9. The perfect fruit pie keeps the filling within bounds; the lower crust is as tender and flaky as the upper. A deep pie plate should be used to prevent the juices from escaping. With very juicy fruits, the lower crust may be brushed over with egg white. A little thickening helps, too, but men, those judges of good pie, do not like too much of any kind, so use it sparingly.

10. In making custard pies, the crust should be baked at a high temperature until set, then the filling added and the baking continued at a low temperature until the custard is done.

(2701)   **PLAIN PASTRY**

> 2 cups flour   ⅔ cup shortening
> ¾ teaspoon salt

Mix and sift flour and salt. Cut in the shortening with a knife. Add only water enough to hold the ingredients together. Do not knead. Divide dough in 2 parts and roll out thin on a slightly floured board. Line a pie pan with one-half the pastry. Pinch pastry with the fingers to make a fancy edge and prick bottom and sides with a fork. Bake in a very hot oven (460° F.) 10 to 15 minutes. For a 2 crust pie, line pie pan with pastry, put in a filling, cover with top crust and bake as directed for pies. If a less rich pastry is desired, use only ½ cup shortening. Yield: 2 pastry shells. Flaky pastry (No. 2702) may be used wherever this is called for.

(2702)   FLAKY PASTRY

2 cups flour   ⅔ cup shortening
1 teaspoon salt

Mix and sift flour and salt. Cut in 2 tablespoons of the shortening with a knife. Add enough water to make a stiff dough.
Roll out in an oblong piece on a slightly floured board and dot
with bits of shortening, using ⅓ the remaining quantity. Fold
over ends to the center and fold again to make 4 layers. Press
ends together and roll out. Dot again with shortening, fold and
roll. Repeat this process a third time. Chill thoroughly. This
pastry may be used wherever plain pastry (No. 2701) is called
for.

(2703)   PUFF PASTE

2 cups flour   1 cup shortening
1½ teaspoons salt

Mix and sift flour and salt. Cut in 2 tablespoons shortening
with a knife. Add just enough water to bind. Knead 5 minutes.
Cover. Chill. Roll on slightly floured board to ¼-inch thickness in rectangular shape with square corners. Slightly soften
remaining shortening and lay out in a flat circular shape in the
center of ½ the dough. Fold other half over it. Press edges
tightly together to hold in air. Fold right side over and left
side under enclosed shortening. Chill. Roll out again in rectangular shape. Fold ends toward center making 3 layers. Chill. Repeat this process 4 times. Chill. Paste should be made at least
24 hours before cooking and should be kept ice cold.

(2704)   HOT WATER PASTRY

½ cup shortening   ¾ teaspoon salt
1½ cups flour   ¼ teaspoon baking powder

Cream shortening with fork in ¼ cup boiling water. Mix
and sift flour, salt, and baking powder. Add dry mixture gradually to shortening, blending well. Form into a ball and store in
a refrigerator until ready to use. Yield: 1 pastry shell.

(2705) GRAHAM CRACKER PASTRY

¼ cup butter, melted   1 cup graham cracker
¼ cup sugar   crumbs

Mix all ingredients well. Knead lightly. Keep in refrigerator in mixing bowl. Before using, bring to room temperature. Yield: 1 pastry shell.

(2706) FRITTER BATTER

2 cups sifted flour   2 eggs, beaten
3 teaspoons baking powder   1 cup milk
1 teaspoon salt   1 tablespoon fat, melted
2 tablespoons sugar

Sift the dry ingredients together. Combine the beaten eggs, milk, and melted fat. Add gradually to the dry ingredients, stirring only until the batter is smooth.

(2707) COVER BATTERS

With the addition of 1½ teaspoons of baking powder, sifted with the dry ingredients, the timbale batter (No. 2710) may be used as a cover batter for frying sliced eggplant, sliced onion rings, shrimp, oysters, scallops, and fish. A somewhat thicker cover batter is used for frying more juicy vegetables or fruits.

(2708) TART SHELLS

Roll out puff paste (No. 2703) to ⅛-inch thickness. Fit over inverted pie, muffin, or patty tins. Prick with a fork. Bake in quick oven (425° F.) 15 to 20 minutes.

(2709) PATTY SHELLS

Roll out puff paste (No. 2703) to ¼-inch thickness. Cut with a floured, round biscuit cutter. From half the rounds of dough remove centers with a smaller cutter. Wet edges of whole rounds and place rings on them. Brush tops with beaten egg, diluted with 1 tablespoon cold water, being careful not to moisten the sides. Chill until stiff. Bake in hot oven (400° F.) 20 minutes. Bake the removed centers in quick oven (450° F.) 10 minutes. Use as covers for filled tarts.

(2710)   TIMBALE CASES

1 beaten egg	1 cup sifted flour
¾ cup milk	½ teaspoon salt
1 teaspoon melted fat	

Combine egg, milk, and fat. Add flour and salt and beat until smooth. Let stand 30 minutes. Heat timbale or rosette iron in deep, hot fat (375° F.). Remove iron and drain. Dip iron into batter, nearly to depth of iron. If batter slips off, iron is too hot. Immerse batter-covered iron in the hot fat and fry 30 seconds until light and crisp. Drain on unglazed paper. Yield: 30 cases.

(2711)   DANISH PASTRY

2½ cups flour	¾ cup shortening
1½ teaspoons salt	1 beaten egg

Mix and sift flour and salt. Work in shortening with finger tips. Add egg and enough ice water to bind mixture. Chill. Roll out to ⅛-inch thickness. Fit over inverted muffin tins. Trim. Prick and bake in quick oven (425° F.) 12 minutes.

(2712)   NUT PASTRY

Substitute the same amount of finely ground pecans for ½ the shortening in plain pastry (No. 2701).

(2713)   VOL-AU-VENT

Make same as patty shells (No. 2709) but larger and thicker.

(2714)   APPLE PIE

Plain pastry (No. 2701)	⅛ teaspoon salt
6 cups pared cored apples, sliced ¼-inch thick	¼ teaspoon cinnamon
⅔ cup sugar	1 teaspoon lemon juice
¼ teaspoon nutmeg	2 teaspoons butter

Lightly roll half of the pie crust to ⅛-inch thickness and about 2½ inches larger than a 9-inch pie plate. Fold it in half and fit it into the pie plate. In rolling the pie crust use only enough flour to prevent sticking, handling the dough very lightly and never turning it. Press the pie crust lightly to fit the pie pan and trim even with the edge of the pan, using a knife. Fill the pie shell with the apples. Mix sugar, nutmeg, salt, cinnamon, and lemon juice. Sprinkle over apples and dot with the butter. Moisten the edge of the crust with cold water. Roll the other half of the pie crust to $\frac{1}{8}$-inch thickness and about 1 inch larger than the diameter of the plate. Fold this in half and make 3 slits, each $\frac{1}{2}$-inch in length, in the center of the folded side. Adjust over the filling, then carefully fold the edge of the upper crust under the lower crust all the way around. Finish by pressing the edges together with a fork dipped in flour. If a glazed surface is desired, brush top of pie with top milk, cream or melted butter, or slightly beaten egg white. Bake for 40 minutes at 425° F. in a preheated oven.

(2715)   ONE-CRUST APPLE PIE, I

4 large tart apples	1 tablespoon fat
$\frac{1}{2}$ cup sugar	Plain pastry (No. 2701)
Few grains nutmeg	Whipped cream

Wash, pare, and core apples. Cut in thin slices. Put them in the bottom of pie pan and sprinkle with sugar and nutmeg. Dot with small bits of fat. Roll plain pastry thin and fit over the apples. Trim off edge of the pastry and press with fingers or fork to make a fancy edge. Prick top to allow steam to escape. Bake in a quick oven (425° F.) 10 minutes. Reduce heat to a moderate oven (325° F.) and bake 20 minutes. Cool. Turn out upside down on a serving dish. Cover with whipped cream, sweetened and flavored.

(2716)   ONE-CRUST APPLE PIE, II

4 large tart apples	1 tablespoon fat
Plain pastry (No. 2701)	$\frac{1}{4}$ teaspoon nutmeg
1 cup sugar	$\frac{1}{8}$ teaspoon cinnamon

Wash, pare, and cut apples in quarters. Remove the cores. Line a pie pan with plain pastry, pinch with fingers to make a fancy edge, and arrange apples in it. Pour the sugar over them and dot with small bits of fat. Sprinkle with nutmeg and cinnamon. Bake in quick oven (425° F.) 10 minutes. Reduce heat and bake 20 minutes more in moderate oven (325° F.).

(2717) APPLE PIE WITH MELTED CHEESE

After an apple pie (No. 2714) is baked, cover the top with American cheese cut into thin slices or grated, and put in a slow oven (300° F.) until the cheese is melted. Serve at once.

(2718) BERRY PIE

3 cups berries	Plain pastry (No. 2701)
1 cup sugar	1 tablespoon butter
2 tablespoons cornstarch	1 tablespoon lemon juice
or 4 tablespoons flour	for blueberry pie
⅛ teaspoon salt	

Mix fruit with combined sugar, cornstarch or flour, and salt, and if blueberries, lemon juice. Line pie pan with pastry. Fill with berries and dot with butter. Moisten pastry edge and put top pie crust in place. The upper crust should be cut in several places so that steam can escape. Crimp edge and bake in a hot oven (425° F.) for about 10 minutes, then reduce the oven temperature to moderate (325° F.) for about 30 minutes to finish baking.

(2719) BLUEBERRY PIE

Follow recipe for apple pie (No. 2714), using 3½ to 4 cups blueberries, 2 tablespoons flour or 1½ to 2½ tablespoons quick-cooking tapioca and the amounts of spice, sugar, salt, lemon juice, and butter given in apple pie recipe. More sugar may be added if fruit is tart. Blackberry, plum, grape, rhubarb, or peach pie may be made in the same way.

(2720) CARROT PIE

Plain pastry (No. 2701)	1 egg, well beaten
1 cup grated raw carrot	¼ teaspoon ginger
⅔ cup sugar	¼ teaspoon cinnamon
1½ cups milk	¼ teaspoon salt

Line a pie pan with plain pastry. Mix other ingredients and put in pan. Top with layer of pastry. Wet edges of pastry with water. Press together and trim. Gash top. Bake in hot oven (425° F.) 10 minutes. Reduce heat to moderate (325° F.) and bake 45 to 50 minutes longer.

(2721)   CHEESE PIE

1 cup cottage cheese	2 beaten eggs
1 cup seedless raisins, sliced	Juice 1 lemon
½ cup corn sirup	Grated rind 1 lemon
2 tablespoons butter	Plain pastry (No. 2701)
2 tablespoons cream	

Rub cheese through a coarse sieve and mix thoroughly with raisins, sirup, butter, cream, eggs, and lemon juice and rind. Line a pie pan with pastry. Turn in mixture. Bake in hot oven (425° F.) 10 minutes. Reduce heat and continue baking in moderate oven (325° F.) until firm. Shredded coconut may be substituted for raisins. Honey or granulated sugar may be used in place of corn sirup. If neither raisins or coconut are used in filling, jelly, jam, or preserves may be spread on top after baking.

(2722)   CHERRY PIE

Plain pastry (No. 2701)	2½ cups canned or stewed
Sugar to taste	cherries (No. 53)

Line pie pan with plain pastry. Drain cherries. Sprinkle with sugar to taste. Pour over sirup from cherries. Top with layer of pastry. Wet edges of pastry. Press together and trim. Gash top. Bake in quick oven (425° F.) 10 minutes. Reduce heat and bake 20 minutes longer in moderate oven (325° F.).

(2723)   LATTICE CHERRY PIE

Top cherry pie (No. 2722) with ⅜-inch wide strips of plain pastry (No. 2701), placed crisscross, instead of with a solid crust. Moisten edge of lower crust and ends of strips and place a strip of dough around edge to hold strips in place.

(2724)   CHERRY MINCE PIE

2½ cups canned or stewed	1 cup mincemeat
pitted cherries (No. 53)	
1 tablespoon tapioca	Plain pastry (No. 2701)

Combine cherries in their liquid with mincemeat and tapioca. Line pie plate with pastry. Turn mixture into pie pan. Crisscross top with long strips of pastry. Wet ends of strips with water and press to pastry lining. Bake in hot oven (425° F.) 10 minutes. Reduce heat and bake in moderate oven (325° F.) 20 minutes longer.

(2725) MOCK CHERRY PIE

2 cups cranberries, coarsely chopped
1 cup seedless raisins
3 tablespoons flour

1 cup sugar
1/8 teaspoon salt
Plain pastry (No. 2701)
1 tablespoon fat

Combine cranberries and raisins. Add flour, sugar, and salt. Line a pie pan with plain pastry and fill with mixture. Dot with fat. Moisten edge of pastry. Cover with a top crust. Press edges together and trim. Prick top to let steam escape. Bake in quick oven (425° F.) 10 minutes. Reduce heat and bake 25 minutes longer in hot oven (375° F.).

(2726) CHESS PIE

Puff paste (No. 2703)
1/3 cup butter
1/2 cup sugar

3 egg yolks, well beaten
1/2 teaspoon vanilla
Meringue (No. 3205)

Line a pie plate with puff paste. Chill. Cream butter and sugar. Add yolks and vanilla. Turn into pie plate. Bake in moderate oven (350° F.) until very light. Top with meringue. Bake again in moderate oven (350° F.) 12 minutes. Cut in pieces to serve while hot.

(2727) CHOCOLATE PIE

Plain pastry (No. 2701)
2 ounces unsweetened chocolate
3 well-beaten eggs
1 cup sugar

2 tablespoons soft bread crumbs
1 1/2 cups milk
1/2 cup chopped nuts
1 cup cream, whipped

Line a pie tin with pastry. Pinch edge with fingers to make fancy. Shave chocolate and melt over hot water. Add sugar, crumbs, and chocolate to eggs. Mix thoroughly. Stir in milk. Turn into pie tin. Bake in hot oven (375° F.) 20 minutes or until set. Chill. Sprinkle with nuts. Top with whipped cream. Garnish, if desired with half cherries and whole nuts.

(2728) CRANBERRY AND BANANA PIE

2½ cups cranberries
1¾ cups sugar

Plain pastry (No. 2701)
3 sliced bananas

Stem, pick over, and wash cranberries. Add sugar and ½ cup hot water. Cook, covered, until berries stop popping. Line a pie pan with plain pastry. Put in ⅓ of cranberry mixture. Add a layer of bananas. Continue alternating layers until all ingredients are used. Put layer of pastry on top. Wet edges of pastry with water. Press together and trim. Gash top. Bake in hot oven (425° F.) 10 minutes. Reduce heat and bake in moderate oven (325° F.) 10 minutes longer.

(2729) CRANBERRY APPLESAUCE PIE

2 teaspoons gelatin
1¾ cups cranberry sauce
   (No. 54)
2½ cups applesauce (No. 34)
2 tablespoons lemon juice
2 tablespoons sugar

⅛ teaspoon salt
1 baked plain pastry pie
   shell (No. 2701)
½ cup heavy cream
¼ teaspoon nutmeg

Soak gelatin in ¼ cup cold water 5 minutes. Dissolve over hot water. Combine cranberry and applesauce. Add lemon juice, sugar, and salt. Beat smooth with a rotary beater. Add gelatin. Mix thoroughly. Turn into pastry shell. Whip cream and spread over top. Sprinkle with nutmeg.

(2730)   DATE PIE

Substitute 1 cup stoned, chopped dates for 6 cups raw apples in recipe for apple pie (No. 2714).

(2731)   DREAM PIE

1¾ cups sugar
¾ cup water
4 cups cranberries
2 tablespoons flour
¼ teaspoon salt
3 eggs, separated

1 teaspoon vanilla
2 teaspoons butter
Baked plain pastry shell
   (No. 2701)
3 tablespoons powdered
   sugar

Cook sugar and water to a sirup. Add cranberries and cook until they stop popping. Cool slightly. Mix flour, salt, and egg yolks until smooth. Stir in 3 tablespoons of the juice of the cooked cranberries. Add to berries and simmer several minutes. Add the vanilla and butter. Cool. Pour into pie shell. Cover with meringue made by beating the stiffly beaten egg whites and the powdered sugar together. Bake in a moderate oven (350° F.) 15 minutes.

(2732)   **EGGNOG PIE**

1 tablespoon granulated gelatin	¼ teaspoon salt
¼ cup cold water	1 cup heavy cream, whipped
1 cup boiling water	2 tablespoons whisky or
2 eggs, well beaten	one teaspoon vanilla
3 tablespoons powdered sugar	1 baked plain pastry shell (No. 2701)

Soften gelatin in cold water. Dissolve in boiling water. Chill until slightly thickened. Beat with rotary beater until fluffy. Beat eggs well. Add salt. Beat in sugar. Fold into gelatin. Fold in cream. Add whisky or vanilla. Chill again until thickened. Turn into baked shell and chill until firm. Garnish with additional whipped cream if desired.

(2733)   **FIG PIE**

2 eggs, well beaten	¾ pound dried figs, stewed (No. 55)
2 tablespoons granulated sugar	1 baked plain pastry shell (No. 2701)
¼ teaspoon salt	

Meringue (No. 3205)

Combine eggs, sugar, salt, and figs. Cook slowly until egg thickens. Turn into baked shell. Top with meringue. Brown in moderate oven (350° F.) 10 to 12 minutes.

(2734)   **GOOSEBERRY PIE**

Substitute gooseberries for blueberries in recipe for blueberry pie (No. 2719).

(2735)   GRAHAM CRACKER PIE

3 cups graham cracker   3 cups applesauce
  crumbs   (No. 34)

Put layer of crumbs on bottom and sides of greased pie plate. Add layer of applesauce and a layer of crumbs. Continue alternating layers until all ingredients are used, having a layer of crumbs on top. Sprinkle applesauce layers with sugar if necessary. Chill. Remove from plate and cut as a baked pie.

(2736)   CONCORD GRAPE PIE

7 cups Concord grapes   ¾ teaspoon salt
3 tablespoons cornstarch   Grated rind of 1 orange
1½ cups sugar   Plain pastry (No. 2701)

Wash and stem grapes. Slip skins from pulp. Heat pulp to boiling and boil 5 minutes. Then rub through sieve to remove seeds. Combine cornstarch, sugar, salt, and orange rind with grape pulp. Cook until thickened, stirring constantly. Add grape skins and cool. Line a pie pan with plain pastry. Turn in mixture. Top with ⅜-inch wide strips of pastry, laid crisscross. Moisten ends of strips with water. Put another strip around pie to hold crossed strips in place. Bake in hot oven (425° F.) 10 minutes. Reduce temperature to 325° F. and bake 20 minutes more.

(2737)   CONCORD GRAPE PIE WITH CHEESE
CREAM TOPPING

1½ quarts Concord grapes   1 tablespoon lemon juice
½ cup sugar   1 baked plain pastry shell
½ cup flour   (No. 2701)
Few grains salt   1 cup whipping cream
1½ tablespoons butter   ½ cup cottage cheese

Wash the grapes and separate pulp from skins. Cook pulp slowly until soft, then press through a sieve. Mix the pulp and skins and heat in a double boiler. Mix the sugar, flour, and salt and add gradually to the grapes. Cook, stirring constantly, until thickened. Add butter and lemon juice and cool slightly. Pour into baked pie shell and cool. Top with whipped cream mixed with the cottage cheese.

(2738)   GRAPE AND TOMATO PIE

3 partly green tomatoes
1½ cups Concord grapes
Plain pastry (No. 2701)
1¼ cups sugar

3 tablespoons flour
Salt
Cream

Wash tomatoes and grapes. Line pie pan with pastry. Sprinkle ¼ cup sugar on pastry. Slice tomatoes rather thin and place a layer over the sugar. With a sharp knife cut each grape almost through. Remove seeds and lay open over the tomatoes till fairly well covered. Cover this with ½ each of the sugar and flour and a sprinkle of salt. Repeat, making two layers in all. Cover with top crust. Moisten edges of pastry with water. Press edges tightly together and trim. Brush top of crust with cream and bake in hot oven (425° F.) 10 minutes. Decrease to 350° F. and continue baking 30 minutes, or until well browned.

(2739)   HUCKLEBERRY PIE

Substitute huckleberries for blueberries in recipe for blueberry pie (No. 2719).

(2740)   JELLY PIE

3 tablespoons flour
1 cup sugar
1 tablespoon melted butter
½ cup jelly

2 beaten eggs
1 baked plain pastry shell
(No. 2701)

Mix and sift flour and sugar. Add butter. Mix jelly and 1 cup warm water and add to flour-sugar mixture. Stir mixture into eggs. Turn into baked pastry shell. Bake in moderate oven (350° F.) 15 minutes.

(2741)   TWO-CRUST LEMON PIE

1 tablespoon cornstarch
1 cup sugar
Plain pastry (No. 2701)

Juice and grated rind 1
lemon
1 egg, slightly beaten

Combine cornstarch and sugar. Add lemon juice and rind, 1 cup water, and egg. Cook few minutes and cool. Line a pie pan with plain pastry. Turn in mixture. Cover with layer of pastry. Wet edges of pastry with water. Press together and trim. Gash top. Bake in a hot oven (425° F.) 10 minutes. Reduce heat to moderate (325° F.) and bake 20 to 25 minutes longer.

(2742) LEMON FLUFF PIE

3 egg yolks
¼ cup lemon juice
1 teaspoon grated lemon
    rind

3 egg whites
½ cup sugar
⅛ teaspoon salt
Pastry shell (No. 2701)

Beat egg yolks. Add lemon juice and grated rind. Cook slowly until rather thick. Cool mixture and fold in egg whites, beaten stiff with sugar and salt. Pour into baked pastry shell (No. 2701). Bake 30 minutes at 325° F.

(2743) MINCE PIE

Follow directions for making apple pie (No. 2714), using 3 cups prepared mincemeat as the filling. For any other cooked pie filling, follow this same recipe.

(2744) MOLASSES PIE

1 cup molasses
1 tablespoon flour

1 lemon
Plain pastry (No. 2701)

Blend molasses and flour. Cut and chop lemon, and add juice, pulp, and rind to molasses. Line a pie pan with pastry. Turn in mixture. Make a top crust with layer of pastry. Wet edges of pastry with water. Press together and trim. Bake in hot oven (425° F.) 10 minutes. Reduce heat and continue baking in moderate oven (325° F.) 20 minutes.

(2745) ORANGE PIE

Substitute orange juice and orange pulp for pineapple juice and pulp in recipe for pineapple pie (No. 2751) and add 1 tablespoon lemon juice before combining with yolks.

(2746) PEACH PIE

Pare 8 peaches and slice thin. Simmer in ⅓ cup water 10 minutes. Add sugar to taste. Line a pie pan with plain pastry (No.

2701) and pour the filling into it. Dot with small bits of fat. Moisten edge of pastry, cover with a top crust, and press edges together. Prick top with a fork to allow steam to escape. Bake in a quick oven (425° F.) 10 minutes. Reduce heat to moderate oven (350° F.) and bake 15 to 20 minutes.

(2747) PEACH PIE SUPREME

1 package orange-flavored gelatin
1½ cups hot peach juice and water

2½ cups canned sliced peaches, drained
1 baked 9-inch pie shell (No. 2701)

Dissolve gelatin in hot peach juice and water. Add peaches. Chill. When slightly thickened, turn into cold baked pie shell (No. 2701). Chill until firm. Serve with whipped cream, if desired.

(2748) PEACH-BLACKBERRY PIE

Substitute 1¼ cups sliced peaches and 1¼ cups clean blackberries for cherries in lattice cherry pie (No. 2723), adding 1 tablespoon lemon juice, a dash of nutmeg, and a dash of cinnamon.

(2749) PEAR PIE

Substitute pears for peaches in recipe for peach pie (No. 2746).

(2750) PECAN PIE

3 eggs
½ cup sugar
1 cup corn sirup
⅛ teaspoon salt

1 teaspoon vanilla
¼ cup butter or fat, melted
Plain pastry (No. 2701)
1 cup pecans

Beat eggs. Add sugar, sirup, salt, vanilla, and butter or fat. Line pie pan with plain pastry. Put in pecans in a layer. Add mixture. Bake in moderate oven (350° F.) 50 to 60 minutes. The nuts will rise to top and form a crusted layer.

(2751) PINEAPPLE PIE

½ cup flour	2 cups canned pineapple,
1 cup sugar	cut in small pieces
¼ teaspoon salt	Baked plain pastry shell
⅔ cup pineapple juice	(No. 2701)
1 cup hot water	3 tablespoons confec-
1 tablespoon fat	tioners' sugar
3 egg yolks, beaten	3 egg whites

Mix flour, sugar, and salt together. Add the pineapple juice and water and bring slowly to the boiling point, stirring constantly. Cook 15 minutes over hot water. Remove from fire, add fat and well-drained pineapple. Pour this mixture on the yolks and mix well. Pour the filling into pie shell. Cover with a meringue made by beating the confectioners sugar into the stiffly beaten egg whites. Bake in a moderate oven (325° F.) 15 minutes or until a delicate brown. This filling may be used for pineapple tarts (No. 2829).

(2752) PRUNE PIE

Substitute stoned stewed prunes (No. 71) for apples in recipe for apple pie (No. 2714).

(2753) PUMPKIN PIE

Plain pastry (No. 2701)	1¼ teaspoons cinnamon
2 cups mashed pumpkin	¼ teaspoon cloves
(No. 1864)	¼ teaspoon ginger
1 cup milk	¼ teaspoon nutmeg
3 egg yolks, beaten	1 teaspoon salt
½ cup sugar	3 egg whites, stiffly beaten

Line a pie pan with plain pastry and pinch with fingers to make a fancy edge. Mix the pumpkin and milk together. Add the yolks. Add the sugar mixed with the cinnamon, clove, ginger, nutmeg, and salt. Mix well. Fold in the egg whites. Turn into pie pan. Bake in a quick oven (450° F.) 10 minutes, reduce heat to hot oven (375° F.), and bake 20 minutes longer or until the filling is firm.

(2754) NUT PUMPKIN PIE

Add ¼ cup chopped nuts to filling in recipe for pumpkin pie (No. 2753).

(2755) SHERRY PUMPKIN PIE

Substitute ¼ cup sherry for an equal quantity of milk in recipe for pumpkin pie (No. 2753).

(2756) RAISIN PIE

1½ cups seedless raisins	1 tablespoon lemon juice
1 tablespoon flour	1 cup chopped walnuts
½ cup sugar	Plain pastry (No. 2701)
Grated rind 1 lemon	

Wash raisins. Cook in 1½ cups boiling water until tender. Mix and sift flour and sugar and add slowly to raisins, stirring until thickened. Add lemon rind and juice and nuts. Cool. Line a pie pan with plain pastry. Turn in mixture. Top with a layer of pastry. Wet edges of pastry. Press together and trim. Gash top to let steam escape. Bake in quick oven (425° F.) 10 minutes. Reduce heat and bake 20 minutes longer in moderate oven (325° F.).

(2757) SOUR CREAM RAISIN PIE

Plain pastry (No. 2701)	½ teaspoon cinnamon
1 cup seedless raisins	¼ teaspoon salt
2 tablespoons flour	1 cup sour cream
1 cup sugar	1 beaten egg
½ teaspoon nutmeg	

Line a pie pan with pastry. Grind raisins and combine with all other ingredients. Turn into pan. Top with a layer of pastry. Wet edges of pastry. Press together and trim. Gash top to let steam escape. Bake in quick oven (425° F.) 10 minutes. Reduce heat and bake 20 minutes longer in moderate oven (325° F.).

(2758)   RHUBARB PIE

3 cups rhubarb	2 tablespoons flour
Plain pastry (No. 2701)	⅛ teaspoon salt
1 cup sugar	2 eggs, beaten

Peel rhubarb and cut in one-half inch pieces before measuring. Line a pie pan with plain pastry. Mix sugar, flour, salt, and eggs. Add to the rhubarb and turn into pie pan. Moisten edge of pastry with water. Cover with top crust. Press edges together and trim. Gash top to let steam escape. Bake in quick oven (425° F.) 10 minutes. Reduce heat and continue baking in moderate oven (325° F.) 30 minutes.

(2759)   RHUBARB AND PINEAPPLE PIE

Substitute 1 cup crushed pineapple for an equal quantity of rhubarb in recipe for rhubarb pie (No. 2758). Arrange rhubarb and pineapple in alternating layers.

(2760)   EGGLESS RHUBARB LEMON PIE

½ cup stewed rhubarb	1½ tablespoons butter
(No. 75)	½ teaspoon lemon extract
¾ cup sugar	Baked plain pastry shell
¼ cup cornstarch	(No. 2701)

Combine rhubarb, 1 cup boiling water, and sugar. Mix cornstarch to a smooth paste with ¼ cup cold water and add. Cook over boiling water 10 minutes, stirring constantly. Add butter and lemon extract. Turn into baked shell. Cool.

(2761)   SQUASH PIE

Substitute mashed squash (No. 1876) in recipe for pumpkin pie (No. 2753).

(2762)   STRAWBERRY PIE

Wash and stem ripe strawberries. Roll them in powdered sugar and fill a baked plain pastry shell (No. 2701). Top with whipped cream. Chill.

(2763)   SWEET POTATO PECAN PIE

¼ cup butter	⅓ cup milk
½ cup brown sugar	½ teaspoon salt
1 cup mashed sweet potatoes	1 teaspoon vanilla
(No. 1882)	1 cup broken pecans
3 eggs	Plain pastry (No. 2701)
⅓ cup corn sirup	

Cream together the butter and sugar. Add mashed potatoes and slightly beaten eggs. Mix well. Combine with sirup, milk, salt, vanilla, and pecans. Line pie pan with plain pastry. Turn mixture into pan. Bake in hot oven (425° F.) 10 minutes. Reduce heat and continue baking in moderate oven (325° F.) 35 to 45 minutes longer. The pecans may be omitted.

(2764)   SWEET POTATO PIE

Omit pecans from sweet potato pecan pie (No. 2763) and increase amount of mashed sweet potato to 1½ cups.

(2765)   TURNIP PIE

Substitute mashed turnip (No. 1908) for pumpkin and ¾ cup brown sugar for ½ cup granulated sugar in recipe for pumpkin pie (No. 2753).

(2766)   WASHINGTON PIE

⅓ cup shortening	½ teaspoon salt
1 cup sugar	½ teaspoon vanilla
2 eggs, well beaten	2 teaspoons baking powder
½ cup milk	Raspberry jam
1¾ cups flour	Confectioners' sugar

Cream shortening. Add half the sugar gradually. Beat until light. Add remaining sugar to eggs. Combine mixtures. Mix and sift flour, baking powder, and salt and add alternately with milk to first mixture. Beat thoroughly and add vanilla. Bake in buttered layer cake tins 20 to 30 minutes in moderately hot oven (375° F.). Use raspberry jam between layers and sprinkle top with confectioners' sugar.

(2767) APPLE MERINGUE PIE

When baking is finished, top one-crust apple pie II (No. 2716) with meringue (No. 3205) and return to oven to brown slightly.

(2768) APPLESAUCE MERINGUE PIE

3½ tablespoons cornstarch	2 egg yolks
¼ cup cold milk	2 cups applesauce
4 cups hot milk	(No. 34)
½ cup sugar	Baked plain pastry shell
1 tablespoon butter	(No. 2701)
1 teaspoon vanilla	Meringue (No. 3205)

Mix cornstarch to a smooth paste with cold milk. Stir into hot milk. Cook, stirring constantly, until thick. Remove from heat. Add sugar, butter, vanilla, and yolks. Mix thoroughly. Put applesauce in baked pie shell. Add cooked custard. Top with meringue (No. 3205). Bake in moderate oven (350° F.). 15 minutes.

(2769) APRICOT MERINGUE PIE

1 pound dried apricots	3 slightly beaten egg yolks
2 cups milk	1 teaspoon vanilla
1 tablespoon butter	Baked plain pastry shell
¼ teaspoon salt	(No. 2701)
4 tablespoons cornstarch	Apricot meringue
1 cup sugar	(No. 3208)

Simmer apricots in 3 cups water until tender. Rub through a fine sieve. Scald milk, butter, and salt in top of double boiler. Mix cornstarch and sugar, and add to milk, stirring until thick. Stir egg yolks into mixture. Cook 2 minutes. Add vanilla and 1½ cups of apricot pulp and liquid mixture. Cool. Turn into pastry shell. Top with apricot meringue. Bake in moderate oven (350° F.) 15 minutes.

(2770) BLACKBERRY MERINGUE PIE

⅓ cup sugar	2 tablespoons lemon juice
2 tablespoons cornstarch	1 tablespoon butter
¼ teaspoon salt	1 8-inch baked pastry
¼ teaspoon cinnamon	shell (No. 2701)
2½ cups canned or stewed blackberries (No. 49)	2 egg whites
	4 tablespoons sugar

Combine the ⅓ cup sugar, cornstarch, salt, and cinnamon with the sirup drained from the blackberries. Cook in a double boiler until smooth and thick, stirring constantly. Continue cooking for 10 minutes. Remove from heat and add the lemon juice, butter, and berries. Pour into the pastry shell. Beat the egg whites until stiff. Add the sugar gradually and beat until it will stand in peaks. Spread over pie and bake in a moderate oven (350° F.) about 15 minutes or until well browned. Blueberries, raspberries, strawberries, gooseberries, or loganberries may be substituted for blackberries.

(2771)   BUTTERSCOTCH MERINGUE PIE

Plain pastry (No. 2701)   Butterscotch filling
Meringue (No. 3205)   (No. 3156)

Roll pastry and line pie plate. Make edge as desired. Prick several times with a fork. Bake in a hot oven (450° F.) 12 to 15 minutes, until crust is done. Let crust cool and fill with butterscotch filling. Top with meringue.

(2772)   LEMON MERINGUE PIE

1½ tablespoons fat   Grated rind of ½ lemon
8 tablespoons flour   Baked plain pastry shell
1 cup sugar   (No. 2701)
¼ teaspoon salt   2 tablespoons confec-
2 cups water   tioners' sugar
2 egg yolks, beaten   2 egg whites, stiffly beaten
Juice of 1 lemon

Melt fat. Add flour, sugar, salt, water, and yolks. Mix well. Cook over hot water until thick, stirring constantly. Remove from fire, add lemon juice and rind and mix well. Pour into the baked pie shell. Cover top with meringue (No. 3205) made by beating the confectioners' sugar into egg whites. Bake in moderate oven (325° F.) until a delicate brown, about 15 minutes. This filling may also be used for lemon tarts (No. 2825).

(2773)   ORANGE MERINGUE PIE

Substitute orange juice and rind for lemon juice and rind in recipe for lemon meringue pie (No. 2772).

(2774)   PEACH MERINGUE PIE

Baked plain pastry shell   2 cups custard filling
    (No. 2701)   (No. 3152)
2 cups canned peach   Meringue (No. 3205)
    halves, drained

Fill pastry shell ½ full with custard filling. Add layer of peach halves. Top with meringue. Bake in moderate oven (350° F.) 12 to 15 minutes.

(2775)   PEAR MERINGUE PIE

Substitute canned pears for peaches in peach meringue pie (No. 2774).

(2776)   PINEAPPLE AND RAISIN MERINGUE PIE

2 cups raisins   2 cups crushed pineapple
1 cup brown sugar   6 tablespoons granulated
1 teaspoon salt   sugar
4 tablespoons flour   Baked plain pastry shell
3 eggs, separated   (No. 2701)

Cover raisins with water and cook until they are tender. Mix the sugar, salt, and flour together and add. Let boil several minutes until thick, then add to the beaten egg yolks. Add the crushed pineapple. Cool and pour into a baked pie shell. Beat the egg whites, add 6 tablespoons granulated sugar, and beat until all the sugar is dissolved. Cover filling and bake meringue in a moderate oven (350° F.) about 15 minutes.

(2777)   BANANA FRUIT CHIFFON PIE

1 cup mashed bananas   ½ cup granulated sugar
2 tablespoons lemon juice   3 egg yolks
½ cup orange juice   1 tablespoon gelatin
¼ teaspoon grated lemon   ⅓ cup cold water
    rind   3 beaten egg whites
¼ teaspoon grated orange   1 baked plain pastry shell
    rind   (No. 2701)
⅓ teaspoon salt

Mix together the bananas, juices, rinds, salt, sugar, and yolks of eggs. Cook in a double boiler until thick. Stir in the gelatin which has been soaked for 5 minutes in cold water and stir until dissolved. Cool. Add the whites and pour into pie shell. Chill until firm.

(2778)   CHERRY CHIFFON PIE

1 cup cherry juice	2 egg whites, beaten frothy
½ package cherry gelatin	1 baked plain pastry shell
½ cup chopped cherries	(No. 2701)
¼ cup sugar	

Bring juice to a boil. Add gelatin and dissolve. Chill. When congealing starts, add cherries. Mix thoroughly and chill again. Beat sugar and egg whites together until stiff. Fold into first mixture. Turn into pastry shell. Chill.

(2779)   CHOCOLATE CHIFFON PIE

¾ cup sugar	1 teaspoon vanilla
4 egg yolks, well beaten	¼ teaspoon salt
⅓ cup milk	4 egg whites, beaten frothy
2 ounces unsweetened	1 baked plain pastry shell
chocolate	(No. 2701)
½ tablespoon gelatin	

Beat 6 tablespoons sugar into yolks. Cook in double boiler, stirring constantly, until creamy. Bring milk to boiling point and shave in chocolate. Blend thoroughly. Soak gelatin in 1 tablespoon cold water 5 minutes. Dissolve in milk-chocolate mixture. Add vanilla and salt and pour milk mixture into egg mixture. Mix well and chill. Beat egg whites with remaining sugar until stiff. Fold into chilled chocolate mixture. Turn into pastry shell. Chill. Yield: 1 9-inch pie.

(2780)   GRAPEFRUIT CHIFFON PIE

Substitute an equal amount of grapefruit juice and rind for lemon juice and rind in lemon chiffon pie (No. 2781).

(2781)   LEMON CHIFFON PIE

½ tablespoon gelatin
4 egg yolks
½ teaspoon salt
1 cup sugar
Grated rind 1 lemon

Juice 1 lemon
4 egg whites, stiffly beaten
Baked plain pastry shell
    (No. 2701)
1 cup cream, whipped

Soak gelatin in 2 tablespoons cold water 5 minutes. Dissolve over hot water. Mix yolks, salt, ½ cup sugar, lemon juice, and rind in top of double boiler. Cook, stirring constantly, until thick. Add gelatin and cook 1 minute longer. Beat egg whites to peaks with remaining sugar. Fold liquid mixture into egg whites. Turn into baked pastry shell. Top with whipped cream. Cool.

(2782)   LIME CHIFFON PIE

Substitute lime juice and rind for lemon juice and rind in recipe for lemon chiffon pie (No. 2781).

(2783)   LOGANBERRY CHIFFON PIE

1 cup graham cracker
    crumbs
3 tablespoons melted butter
1 tablespoon gelatin
12-ounce can loganberry juice
1 cup sugar

¼ teaspoon salt
2 tablespoons lemon juice
1 teaspoon grated lemon
    rind
1 cup heavy cream
1 stiffly beaten egg white

Mix crumbs and butter and line a 9-inch pie pan. Soak gelatin in ½ cup cold water 5 minutes. Dissolve over hot water. Add to the fruit juice and sugar. Stir until sugar is dissolved. Add salt, lemon juice, and rind. Whip the cream. Fold ½ cream and egg white into mixture. Turn into crumb-lined pan. Chill until firm. Top with remaining cream. Sprinkle a few graham cracker crumbs on top. Almost any fruit juice can be substituted for loganberry juice.

(2784)   ORANGE CHIFFON PIE

Add the juice of 1 orange and 1 tablespoon grated orange rind to recipe for lemon chiffon pie (No. 2781), omitting lemon rind and reducing lemon juice to 1 tablespoon.

(2785) STRAWBERRY CHIFFON PIE

1½ tablespoons gelatin
1 cup crushed strawberries
½ cup sugar
⅛ teaspoon salt

1 egg white, stiffly beaten
1 cup cream, whipped
1 baked plain pastry shell
 (No. 2701)

Soak gelatin in ¼ cup cold water 5 minutes. Dissolve over hot water. Sprinkle sugar on berries and let stand until sugar dissolves. Add gelatin and salt, mixing well. Chill. When congealing starts, beat until light with a rotary beater. Fold in egg white and whipped cream. Pile into baked shell. Chill.

(2786) PUMPKIN CHIFFON PIE

1 tablespoon gelatin
¼ cup water
½ cup milk
1 cup sugar
1¼ cups mashed pumpkin
 (No. 1864)
3 egg yolks, slightly beaten

½ teaspoon each salt, nutmeg, cinnamon and
 ginger
3 egg whites
Baked plain pastry shell
 (No. 2701)

Dissolve the gelatin in water 5 minutes. Combine milk, ½ cup sugar, pumpkin, yolks, and spices and cook over boiling water until thick. Remove from stove and add gelatin. When this begins to set up add beaten egg whites to which ½ cup sugar has been added. Pour into baked pie shell and place in refrigerator.

(2787) CREAM PIE

1 tablespoon fat
8 tablespoons flour
⅔ cup sugar
¼ teaspoon salt
2 egg yolks, beaten
2 cups milk

1 teaspoon vanilla
Baked plain pastry shell
 (No. 2701)
2 tablespoons confec-
 tioners' sugar
2 egg whites

Melt fat. Add flour, sugar, salt, milk, and yolks and cook over hot water until thick, stirring constantly. Add vanilla. Pour into a pie shell. Cover top with a meringue made by beating the confectioners' sugar into the stiffly beaten egg whites. Bake in a moderate oven (325° F.) 15 minutes, or until a delicate brown.

(2788)   ALMOND CREAM PIE

Add ½ cup chopped almonds and ½ cup chopped walnuts to recipe for cream pie (No. 2787).

(2789)   APPLE CREAM PIE

Add 1½ cups applesauce (No. 34) to recipe for cream pie (No. 2787) and reduce milk content to 1¼ cups.

(2790)   BANANA CREAM PIE

Make cream pie (No. 2787), filling shell with alternate layers of sliced bananas and filling.

(2791)   BOSTON CREAM PIE

3 tablespoons sugar	1 tablespoon vanilla
2 cups milk	2 Washington pie layer
2 tablespoons cornstarch	cakes (No. 2766)
1 beaten egg	

Dissolve sugar in 1½ cups milk. Combine cornstarch with remaining milk. Combine mixtures. Add egg. Cook slowly, stirring constantly, until thick. Add vanilla. Spread filling between layers of cake. Sprinkle powdered sugar on top.

(2792)   BUTTERSCOTCH CREAM PIE

Substitute 1 cup brown sugar for ⅔ cup granulated sugar in recipe for cream pie (No. 2787).

(2793)   CHOCOLATE CREAM PIE

2 tablespoons fat	2 egg yolks, beaten
6 tablespoons flour	1 teaspoon vanilla
1½ cups milk	Baked plain pastry shell
2 ounces unsweetened	(No. 2701)
chocolate, shaved	2 tablespoons confec-
¾ cup sugar	tioners' sugar
¼ teaspoon salt	2 egg whites, stiffly beaten

Melt fat and add flour, milk, chocolate, sugar, and salt. Heat slowly to boiling point, stirring constantly, until thick and smooth. Remove from heat. Add yolks and vanilla. Turn into pastry shell. Beat confectioners' sugar into egg whites until a stiff meringue is formed. Top pie with meringue. Bake in moderate oven (325° F.) until a delicate brown, about 15 minutes. Whipped cream may be substituted for meringue. One-half cup chopped pecans may be added to filling just before turning into pastry shell.

(2794)   COCONUT CREAM PIE

⅓ cup sugar	1½ cups scalded milk
2 tablespoons cornstarch	1 tablespoon butter
¼ teaspoon salt	½ cup shredded coconut
3 egg yolks	½ teaspoon vanilla

Add sugar, cornstarch, and salt to egg yolks. Pour scalded milk into this, return to double boiler, stir and cook until thickened. Add the butter, coconut, and vanilla. Pour into a pie tin, lined with plain pastry (No. 2701). Bake in a hot oven (450° F.) until the crust is set, then reduce the temperature to 325° F. The pie may be covered with meringue (No. 3205).

(2795)   COFFEE CREAM PIE

Omit unsweetened chocolate in recipe for chocolate cream pie (No. 2793) and substitute ¾ cup strong coffee (No. 301) for an equal amount of milk.

(2796)   DATE CREAM PIE

Add ⅔ cup chopped dates to filling for cream pie (No. 2787).

(2797)   NUT AND RAISIN CREAM PIE

Stir ⅔ cup chopped nuts and raisins, either individually or in combination, into cream pie (No. 2787) filling and sprinkle a few on top.

(2798)   ORANGE CREAM PIE

Make cream pie (No. 2787), placing a layer of sliced oranges on bottom of crust before adding cream filling.

(2799)   VANILLA CREAM PIE

Omit chocolate from recipe for chocolate cream pie (No. 2793) and increase vanilla to 2 teaspoons.

(2800)   CUSTARD PIE

Plain pastry (No. 2701)	½ teaspoon salt
3 eggs, slightly beaten	3 cups bottled milk
¾ cup granulated sugar	1 teaspoon vanilla

Roll the pie crust to ⅛-inch thickness and 2 inches larger than the diameter of the plate. Line a 9-inch pie plate with this pie crust, fitting it loosely. Fold back the edge of the pie crust all the way around and bring this double fold to an upright position. Flute the double fold of pie crust in the following manner: Place the floured tip or knuckle of the index finger of the right hand against the fold on the inside of the pie crust rim, so that it is between the tips of the thumb and index finger of the left hand, which are on the outside of the pie crust rim. Pinch gently, then remove the fingers and continue this same fluting motion around the entire rim of the pie. Combine the eggs, sugar, and salt. Add the milk and vanilla, and pour into the pastry shell. Bake at 450° F. in a preheated oven for 30 to 40 minutes or until a silver knife inserted in the center comes out clean.

(2801)   APPLE CUSTARD PIE

Add 1½ cups applesauce (No. 34) to recipe for custard pie (No. 2800) and reduce quantity of milk to 2 cups.

(2802)   CARAMEL CUSTARD PIE

Melt and brown sugar in frying pan before adding in recipe for custard pie (No. 2800).

(2803)   COCONUT CUSTARD PIE

Add ¼ cup shredded coconut to custard mixture in recipe for custard pie (No. 2800).

(2804)   **COFFEE CUSTARD PIE**

Substitute 1½ cups strong coffee (No. 301) for an equal quantity of milk in recipe for custard pie (No. 2800).

(2805)   **DATE CUSTARD PIE**

Simmer ¼ cup dates 20 minutes in the milk to be used in recipe for custard pie (No. 2800). Rub dates through a sieve and add pulp with the milk to custard.

(2806)   **LEMON CUSTARD PIE**

Add the grated rind of 2 lemons to recipe for custard pie (No. 2800) and omit vanilla.

(2807)   **MACAROON CUSTARD PIE**

Substitute ½ teaspoon almond extract for 1 teaspoon vanilla in recipe for custard pie (No. 2800) and sprinkle pie with ½ cup macaroon crumbs before baking.

(2808)   **ORANGE CUSTARD PIE**

Add grated rind of 2 oranges to recipe for custard pie (No. 2800) and omit vanilla.

(2809)   **SQUASH CUSTARD PIE**

Add 2 cups mashed squash (No. 1876), 1 tablespoon melted butter, ½ teaspoon nutmeg, 1 teaspoon cinnamon, ¼ teaspoon powdered cloves, and ¼ teaspoon ginger to recipe for custard pie (No. 2800), substitute 1¼ cups brown sugar for ¾ cup granulated sugar, and reduce milk to 2 cups.

(2810)   **VANILLA CUSTARD PIE**

Increase amount of vanilla to 2 teaspoons in recipe for custard pie (No. 2800).

(2811) FRIED PIES

Follow recipe for plain pastry (No. 2701), using only ½ cup shortening. Roll out pastry to ⅛-inch thickness. Cut in large circles. Put a tablespoon of seasoned applesauce in center of pastry. Moisten edges with cold water. Fold over so as to make a semi-circle. Press edges together with tines of a fork. Fry in deep hot fat (375° F.) until a delicate brown. Drain on unglazed paper.

(2812) ALMOND MERINGUE TARTS

½ cup jam or preserves	¾ cup chopped almonds
6 baked tart shells	½ cup meringue
(No. 2708)	(No. 3205)

Divide jam and put on bottom of tart shells. Fold nuts into meringue and put on jam. Bake in moderate oven (350° F.) 10 minutes. Serves 6.

(2813) APPLE AND CHEESE TARTS

Plain pastry (No. 2701)	½ pound American cheese,
6 to 8 tart juicy apples	finely sliced
1½ cups granulated sugar	1 teaspoon cinnamon
½ teaspoon nutmeg	

Line eight small muffin pans with plain pastry. Fill each with thinly sliced apples, sugar, and cheese. Sprinkle with cinnamon and nutmeg. Cover each with strips of pastry and bake 30 to 40 minutes in a moderate oven (350° F.) or until pastry is browned and apples are tender.

(2814) APPLE TARTS

Fill baked tart shells (No. 2708) with applesauce (No. 34). Top with whipped cream and sprinkle lightly with cinnamon, nutmeg, chopped nuts, or candied ginger.

(2815) APRICOT TARTS

1 can apricots	Danish pastry shells
½ can sugar	(No. 2711)

Stew contents of can of apricots with sugar slowly until apricots are becoming transparent, about 20 minutes. Strain and continue to cook sirup until thick. Place 1 apricot in each shell. Pour over a little sirup and garnish with whipped cream. Marshmallows may be used for topping instead of whipped cream.

(2816)   BANBURY TARTS

1 cup mixture of chopped	1 beaten egg
dates, figs, raisins, and	Juice of 1 lemon
nuts	Grated rind of 1 lemon
1 cup brown sugar	Plain pastry (No. 2701)
1 tablespoon flour	

Mix all ingredients but pastry. Roll pastry to ⅛-inch thickness and cut in squares, 3x3 inches. Put some of mixture in center of each square. Moisten edges with cold water. Fold over diagonally and press edges together with fork. Bake in hot oven (400° F.) until pastry is brown, 15 to 20 minutes. Yield: 8 tarts.

(2817)   FRIED BANBURY TARTS

Form Banbury tarts (No. 2816), using a plain pastry (No. 2701) made with ½ cup shortening. Fry in deep, hot fat until brown, about 10 minutes. Drain on unglazed paper. Sprinkle with powdered sugar. Yield: 8 tarts.

(2818)   BUTTERSCOTCH TARTS

Plain pastry (No. 2701)	1½ cups milk
2 eggs, separated	4 tablespoons butter
1 cup brown sugar	1 teaspoon vanilla
⅛ teaspoon salt	4 teaspoons granulated sugar
4 tablespoons flour	

Lightly roll the pie crust to ⅛-inch thickness. Cut into rounds with a 4-inch or 5-inch floured cookie cutter. Then fit these rounds over the back of muffin pans, and trim. Prick the entire surface of each and bake at 450° F. 12-15 minutes in a preheated oven. Then remove from oven, cool, and carefully lift from muffin pans. Invert on a cake rack. Meanwhile combine beaten egg yolks, brown sugar, salt, flour, milk, and butter in saucepan and cook, stirring constantly until it thickens. Cover, reduce heat, and cook slowly 15 minutes, stirring occasionally. Cool, add vanilla and fill the tart shells. Cover with a meringue made from the egg whites and 4 tablespoons granulated sugar. Yield: 12 tarts.

(2819)   CHERRY TARTS

2½ cups canned red cherries   1 tablespoon cornstarch
½ cup sugar   6 tart shells (No. 2708)

Drain the juice from the cherries. Combine the cherry juice, 1 cup boiling water, and sugar. Bring to the boiling point and strain. Make a smooth paste of the cornstarch and a little cold water. Add this to the hot sirup, stirring constantly. Cook, still stirring, until the mixture thickens. While hot pour this over the cherries. Let the filling cool before filling the tart shells. Serve with whipped cream, hard sauce (No. 3105), or custard sauce (No. 3103). Sliced or chopped canned peaches, pineapple, apricots, strawberries, loganberries, raspberries, Royal Anne cherries, blackberries, blueberries, or cranberries may be substituted for the red sour pitted cherries in the recipe.

(2820)   CRANBERRY TARTS

¼ cup cornstarch   1 cup cranberry sauce
1 cup sugar   (No. 54)
½ cup molasses   8 baked tart shells
½ teaspoon salt   (No. 2708)
1 tablespoon butter

Mix cornstarch and sugar. Add 1 cup boiling water. Cook, stirring constantly, until boiling rapidly. Add molasses and salt. Cook 8 minutes. Stir in cranberry sauce and butter. Turn into tart shells. Serves 8.

(2821)   CRANBERRY BANANA TARTS

1 cup cranberry sauce   3 bananas, sliced
(No. 54)   6 baked tart shells
½ cup sugar   (No. 2708,

Crush cranberry sauce. Add sugar and 1 cup water. Bring to a boil and boil 5 minutes. Cool. Put bananas in tart shells. Add cooked sauce. Serves 6.

(2822)   GOOSEBERRY TARTS

Wash 4 cups of gooseberries and drain. Cook slowly with 1½ cups sugar and ¼ cup water until berries are tender, stirring constantly until sugar is melted. Add 1 tablespoon fat and 1 teaspoon grated lemon rind. Cool. Pour into baked tart shells (No. 2708). Yield: 12 tarts. Garnish with whipped cream, flavored and sweetened.

(2823)   GRAPE TARTS

½ cup grape juice	6 baked tart shells
1 cup sugar	(No. 2708)
1 teaspoon cornstarch	1 cup whipped cream
1 cup grapes	

Bring grape juice and sugar to boiling point with ½ cup water. Blend cornstarch to a smooth paste with a little cold water and stir in. Cut grapes in halves and remove seeds. Put in sirup. Simmer until grapes are soft. Turn into tart shells. Top with whipped cream and 1 raw grape in each tart. Serves 6.

(2824)   HICKORY NUT TARTS

1 cup chopped hickory nut meats	2 tablespoons cream
½ cup seedless raisins	¼ teaspoon salt
1 cup sugar	12 baked tart shells
2 egg yolks, beaten	(No. 2708)
	Whipped cream

Mix nuts, raisins, sugar, yolks, cream, and salt thoroughly. Pile in tart shells. Bake in moderate oven (350° F.) 12 minutes. Top with whipped cream. Serves 12.

(2825)   LEMON TARTS

1½ cups sugar	2 tablespoons grated lemon
½ cup flour	rind
2 tablespoons cornstarch	12 baked tart shells
½ teaspoon salt	(No. 2708)
3 eggs	6 tablespoons sugar
6 tablespoons lemon juice	(additional)

Combine 1½ cups sugar, flour, cornstarch, and salt. Add 2¼ cups boiling water gradually, stirring constantly. Separate eggs. Beat yolks and pour hot mixture over them, stirring constantly. Cook slowly 5 minutes. Add lemon juice and rind. Mix well. Cool. Pour into tart shells. Cover with meringue (No. 3205) made from egg whites and 6 tablespoons sugar. Yield: 12 tarts.

(2826)   MACAROON TARTS

Add ½ cup macaroon crumbs to filling for lemon tarts (No. 2825).

(2827)   ORANGE RHUBARB TARTS

2 pounds rhubarb, broken in small pieces	1 tablespoon gelatin
2 oranges, peeled and seeded	12 baked tart shells (No. 2708)
1½ cups sugar	Whipped cream

Combine rhubarb with orange segments, cut in small pieces, and sugar. Put in greased baking dish. Bake in moderate oven (350° F.) 50 to 60 minutes. Soak gelatin in 2 tablespoons cold water and dissolve over hot water. Stir into cooked fruit. Cool. Fill tart shells with chilled mixture and top with whipped cream.

(2828)   PEACH TARTS

Remove skins and slice peaches thin. Cook in a small amount of water until tender. Drain liquid from peaches. To 1 cup liquid add ½ cup sugar and cook until thick. Cool. Just before serving put peaches in a baked plain pastry shell (No. 2701) and pour the sirup over the peaches. Cover with whipped cream, flavored and sweetened.

(2829)   PINEAPPLE TARTS

¾ cup sugar	2 egg yolks, slightly beaten
2 tablespoons flour	
½ cup water	Baked tart shells
1 cup crushed pineapple	(No. 2708)
¼ teaspoon salt	

Mix sugar and flour. Pour on water gradually, while stirring constantly. Boil five minutes. Add pineapple, egg yolks, and salt. Fill tart shells. Cover with meringue (No. 3205) and bake in slow oven (300° F.) until delicately brown.

(2830)   PUMPKIN TARTS

Plain pastry (No. 2701)	2 tablespoons melted butter
2½ cups mashed pumpkin	1 tablespoon molasses
(No. 1864)	1 teaspoon cinnamon
2 cups brown sugar	¾ teaspoon ground ginger
4 beaten eggs	½ teaspoon nutmeg
1 cup milk	½ teaspoon salt

Line 6 tart tins with plain pastry. Mix other ingredients well. Pile in tart shells. Bake in moderately hot oven (375° F.) 40 minutes. Serve hot or cold. If cold, top with layer of cottage cheese. Serves 6.

(2831)   STRAWBERRY TARTLETS

½ cup sugar	½ cup heavy cream
¼ teaspoon salt	Plain pastry (No. 2701)
2 tablespoons flour	3 cups washed hulled
2 well-beaten eggs	strawberries
1 cup scalded milk	¾ cup currant jelly
½ teaspoon vanilla	

Combine sugar, salt, flour, and eggs. Add milk slowly. Cook slowly, stirring constantly, until thick. Add vanilla. Fold in cream. Roll pie crust to ⅛-inch thickness. Cut into rounds with 4- or 5-inch cookie cutter. Fit these rounds over the back of muffin pans and trim. Prick the entire surface of each. Bake at 450° F. 12 to 15 minutes. Remove from oven. Cool. Lift from pans. Invert on cake rack. Fill shells half full of milk-egg mixture. Put layer of strawberries in tarts. Heat jelly until it melts and put 1 tablespoon over each tart. Yield: 12 tarts.

(2832)   APPLE TURNOVERS

Roll out plain pastry dough (No. 2701) into rounds about the size of a large saucer. On ½ round arrange thin slices of apple. Sprinkle with a mixture of sugar, cinnamon, and a little salt. Dot with butter. Moisten the rim of pastry with water. Fold over uncovered half of pastry and press edges together with a fork. Prick top. Bake in hot oven (400° F.) until apples are tender, about 20 minutes.

(2833)   CHERRY TURNOVERS

Substitute stoned and sliced cherries for apples in recipe for apple turnovers (No. 2832) and omit cinnamon. Serve with cherry sauce (No. 3116).

(2834)   MINCEMEAT TURNOVERS

2½ cups sifted flour	Cold water
¾ teaspoon salt	1 cup mincemeat
⅔ cup shortening	

Sift flour and salt together. Cut in shortening. Add cold water to make a stiff dough. Roll out ⅛ inch thick and cut into 3-inch squares. Place a tablespoon of mincemeat on each square. Fold into triangular shapes and press edges with tines of fork. Bake in hot oven (450° F.), 12 to 15 minutes or until delicately golden in color. Serve hot or cold. Yield: 12 turnovers.

(2835)   BANANA BUNDLES

6 bananas	1 teaspoon cinnamon
½ cup sugar	Plain pastry (No. 2701)

Peel and cut the bananas in half, crosswise. Roll in sugar and cinnamon which have been thoroughly mixed. Place on a square of pastry about ⅛ inch thick and roll completely around the banana. Bake in a hot oven (425° F.) 35 to 40 minutes or until brown. Serve hot with whipped cream or hard sauce (No. 3105).

(2836)   BUTTERSCOTCH STACKS

Plain pastry (No. 2701)	3 egg yolks
3 tablespoons butter	1½ cups milk
1½ cups brown sugar	6 tablespoons flour
¾ cup boiling water	⅜ teaspoon salt

Roll pastry to about ⅛-inch thickness and cut into rounds with a cookie cutter. Place on a cookie sheet and bake in a hot oven (400° F.) about 10 minutes. Cool. Melt butter, add sugar, allow to brown, then gradually add water. Beat egg yolks, add small amount of measured milk and the flour, and smooth. Add remainder of milk and salt. Pour this slowly into sugar mixture and cook until thick, stirring constantly. Cool and place a spoonful on top of each pastry round. Stack these in threes and top with whipped cream.

(2837) FRUIT PASTRIES

Roll out plain pastry (No. 2701) to ¼-inch thickness. Cut in circles. Put a tablespoon of fruit filling in center of 1 piece of pastry, moisten the edge, and cover with another circle. Press edges firmly together with fork. Bake in a quick oven (425° F.) 15 to 20 minutes.

(2838) JELLY PASTRIES

Substitute jelly or jam for fruit filling in recipe for fruit pastries (No. 2837).

(2839) PEANUT CREAM PASTRIES

2 tablespoons flour	1 cup milk
¼ cup sugar	½ teaspoon vanilla
⅛ teaspoon salt	Plain pastry (No. 2701)
1 egg	Chopped peanuts

Mix flour, sugar, and salt. Add beaten egg and milk. Cook over hot water until thick, stirring constantly. Cool. Add vanilla. Roll out plain pastry to ¼-inch thickness. Cut in square, round, or rectangular shaped pieces. Prick with a fork and bake in a quick oven (450° F.) 12 to 15 minutes. Cool. Serve 2 as a portion, with the custard filling between and on top of pastries. Sprinkle thickly with chopped peanuts.

(2840) ALLEGRETTI SQUARES

1½ cups plain pastry (No. 2701)	Chocolate pudding (No. 2500)
Meringue (No. 3205)	

Roll out pastry dough ⅛ inch thick into 12 squares of equal size. Tube pudding, in fancy designs, on each square. Dot with meringue. Brown lightly in hot oven (450° F.).

(2841) COCONUT DATE STRIPS

Plain pastry (No. 2701)
2 tablespoons fat
⅛ teaspoon salt
3 tablespoons brown sugar

3 tablespoons coconut, shredded
¼ cup chopped dates

Roll out pastry on slightly floured board in rectangular sheet about ¼ inch thick. Spread with softened fat and sprinkle with salt. Mix sugar, coconut, and dates and sprinkle over ½ the pastry. Fold over the other half and cut into strips 1 inch wide, making them uniform in length. Bake in a hot oven (400° F.) 10 to 15 minutes.

(2842) LEMON FANCHONETTES

Substitute two-crust lemon pie filling (No. 2741) for pumpkin pie filling in recipe for pumpkin fanchonettes (No. 2843).

(2843) PUMPKIN FANCHONETTES

Cut large circles from plain pastry (No. 2701) rolled to ⅛-inch thickness. Fit into small fluted pans. Pinch with fingers to make a fancy edge. Fill with pumpkin pie filling (No. 2753). Bake in quick oven (425° F.) 15 to 20 minutes. Garnish before serving with a spoonful of whipped cream.

(2844) FRUIT PIE ALASKAN

1 tablespoon cornstarch
¼ teaspoon salt
¼ cup sugar
2 cups shredded pineapple
1 9-inch baked pie shell (No. 2701)

1 pint vanilla ice cream (No. 2547)
3 egg whites
6 tablespoons sugar, additional

Mix together the cornstarch, salt, and ¼ cup sugar. Add the pineapple and cook until clear and slightly thickened, stirring constantly, about 5 minutes. Cool and spread over the bottom and sides of the pie shell. Pack the ice cream over the fruit mixture. To make meringue, beat the egg whites until stiff. Add the sugar gradually and beat until it stands in peaks. Spread meringue over the top making sure there are no air holes. Bake in a very hot oven (500° F.) about 3 or 4 minutes until browned. Serves 8.

(2845) ICE CREAM PIES

Follow recipe for fruit pie Alaskan (No. 2844), using any desired fruit and ice cream combination. If desired, fruit may be omitted. Individual pies can be made in tart shells.

(2846) LEMON ANGEL PIE

4 egg yolks	2 egg whites, stiffly beaten
¾ cup sugar	1 baked pie shell (No. 2701)
¼ cup lemon juice	Lemon meringue (No. 3209)
1 tablespoon butter	

Cream egg yolks and sugar together. Add lemon juice. Cook in double boiler or in pan set in hot water, stirring frequently, until stiffened, about 10 minutes. Add butter. Remove from heat. Fold in egg whites. Pour into pie shell. Top with meringue. Brown in moderate oven (325° F.) 15 minutes.

(2847) ORANGE ANGEL PIE

Substitute orange juice for lemon juice in recipe for lemon angel pie (No. 2846).

(2848) LIME ANGEL PIE

Substitute lime juice for lemon juice in recipe for lemon angel pie (No. 2846)

(2849) MERINGUE SHELLS

2 cups granulated sugar	¼ teaspoon salt
6 egg whites	½ tablespoon vinegar
1 teaspoon vanilla	

Sift sugar: Beat salted egg whites until frothy. Add half of sugar, 2 tablespoons at a time, beating after each addition until sugar is dissolved. When half the sugar has been added, gradually beat in vinegar. Continue adding sugar, 2 tablespoons at a time. Add vanilla. Spoon or force mixture through pastry tube onto wet paper spread on cookie sheet. Bake in very slow oven (250° to 275° F.), for 45 to 60 minutes. Place meringues on a damp table top to steam for a minute or two before removing from paper. Makes 12 to 16 meringues.

Cakes

ALL cakes contain flour and sugar. Most of them contain liquid and leavening. Some of them contain fat; others do not. In a general way they are classified as cakes containing fat and cakes without fat. But cookies and doughnuts, both of which contain fat, have other characteristics that distinguish them.

Fine soft-wheat flour is best for cakes, especially the richer cakes. The liquid is preferably milk. Granulated sugar is preferred to powdered, and a solid fat which can be creamed is better than an oil. Baking powder or soda, and sour milk or soda and molasses are the usual leavening in cakes containing fat. Pound cake, however, has no leavening and no liquid, and the true sponge cakes, which contain no fat, are leavened by air beaten into the eggs.

As the quantity of sugar, fat, and eggs increases in a cake batter, the proper proportioning of the ingredients becomes more important, careful measuring is essential, and the method of combining has more effect on the baked product.

The object is to build up a stable mixture which will not separate. This is formed best when all the ingredients are at room temperature (70° F.). Then the fat creams more readily, and the egg whites beat more quickly and to a larger volume.

The ingredients for foundation cake and rich cake are combined in the following way: Cream the fat until it is soft, add the flavoring and the finely granulated sugar, gradually stirring until the mass increases in volume and becomes light and fluffy, due to the enclosed air. Continue the creaming and slowly add the well-beaten egg yolks. If the egg yolks are added too rapidly the mixture may curdle.

Sift the dry ingredients together and add them alternately with the liquid. The first and last additions should be the dry ingredients. The addition of too much liquid at one time may cause the mixture to separate. Beat in the dry ingredients and stir in the liquid. Then fold in the beaten egg whites. The resulting mixture should be a smooth, fairly thick batter.

When the pans containing cakes in loaves or layers are taken from the oven they should not be removed from the pan until the cake cools partially and becomes firmer. Cake is too soft and hot for handling when it first comes from the oven. It should be removed from the pan, however, before it reaches room temperature or has a chance to sweat.

Because of their delicate texture, sponge cakes require more careful mixing and baking than other types of cake. The eggs should be brought to room temperature before they are beaten in order to obtain a fine-grained cake of largest volume.

The recipes in the following chapter should give good results to the careful homemaker who lives at sea level or at elevations not above 3,000 feet. Above that level cakes made in accordance with the following recipes have a tendency to be coarse, dry, and crumbly. The high altitude affects the steam generated in cooking, the baking powder, soda, shortening, and sugar. As altitudes get higher, for good cake success it is often necessary to reduce the quantities of any or all of those ingredients. For the homemaker who lives up in the high places the Colorado State College, Fort Collins, Colorado, has made an exhaustive study of this condition and has pamphlets which they generously distribute to persons faced with this problem.

(2901)   **PLAIN CAKE**

3 cups sifted flour	1 beaten egg
4 teaspoons baking powder	1 cup milk
½ teaspoon salt	¼ cup melted shortening
1 cup sugar	1 teaspoon vanilla

Sift flour, baking powder, salt, and sugar together. Combine all other ingredients. Combine 2 mixtures and stir until smooth. Pour into a greased pan. Bake in moderate oven (365° F.) 25 minutes. If formed into cupcakes, bake in moderately hot oven (375° F.) 20 minutes.

(2902)   ANGEL FOOD CAKE

1 cup sifted flour	½ teaspoon salt
1 to 1¼ cups sugar	¾ teaspoon cream of tartar
8 egg whites	1 teaspoon vanilla

Sift the flour and half the sugar together several times. Beat the egg whites with the salt until frothy. Add the cream of tartar and beat until the egg foam starts to peak. Fold in the other half of the sugar to form a meringue. Then fold in the flour-sugar mixture gradually and gently, and when the whole is partly blended add the vanilla. Only a gentle folding motion should be used in mixing, for stirring tends to release the air depended on for leavening. A tube pan is best for baking angel food, and a fairly large cake will require about an hour in an oven at a temperature of 325° F. After baking, invert the cake and remove from the pan when almost cold.

(2903)   CHERRY ANGEL FOOD CAKE

⅓ cup maraschino cherries, sliced or chopped	¾ teaspoon vanilla
	1 cup egg whites
¼ teaspoon salt	1¼ cups granulated sugar
1 teaspoon cream of tartar	1 cup sifted cake flour
¼ teaspoon almond flavoring	

Drain cherries thoroughly. Add salt, cream of tartar, almond flavoring, and vanilla to egg whites. Beat until foamy but not stiff. Beat in sugar, 2 tablespoons at a time. Sift flour 3 times and fold into mixture. Pour a layer in the bottom of an ungreased cake pan. Sprinkle in ½ cherries. Add remainder of batter. Top with remaining cherries. Bake in moderate oven (325° F.) 50 minutes. Remove pan. Invert and allow to hang until cake cools and pulls away from sides of pan.

(2904)   COCOA ANGEL FOOD

Substitute ¼ cup cocoa for an equal quantity of flour in recipe for angel food cake (No. 2902). Sift cocoa with flour.

(2905)   LEMON ANGEL CAKE

Substitute the grated rind of ½ lemon for vanilla in angel food cake (No. 2902).

(2906) ORANGE ANGEL CAKE

Substitute grated rind of ¼ orange for vanilla in angel food cake (No. 2902). Spread with orange icing (No. 3200) and top with orange segments if desired.

(2907) MOCK ANGEL CAKE

1 cup milk	2 egg whites, beaten stiff
1 cup flour	1 teaspoon vanilla
1 cup sugar	Fondant (No. 3169)
3 teaspoons baking powder	

Heat milk almost to boiling point. Mix and sift flour, sugar, and baking powder 3 times. Pour milk gradually into dry mixture, blending well. Fold in egg whites. Add vanilla. Pour into ungreased pan and bake in slow oven (300° F.) 45 minutes. Cool. Cover with fondant.

(2908) APPLE UPSIDE-DOWN CAKE

¼ cup butter or other fat	¼ teaspoon salt
½ cup sugar	½ cup milk
1 egg	2 to 4 firm-fleshed apples
1 teaspoon vanilla	2 teaspoons cinnamon
1½ cups sifted flour	mixed with ¼ cup
2 teaspoons baking powder	sugar
Hard sauce or whipped cream	

Cream the fat, while adding the sugar, well-beaten egg, and vanilla. Sift the dry ingredients together and add alternately with the milk to the first mixture. Spread a thick coating of fat on the bottom and sides of a glass baking dish or a very heavy pan. Pare, quarter, and slice the apples thin. Spread in an overlapping layer on the bottom of the baking dish and sprinkle with the cinnamon and sugar. Pour the cake mixture over the apples. The batter is rather thick and may need to be smoothed on top with a knife. Bake in a very moderate oven (300° to 325° F.) 45 minutes. Loosen the sides of the cake, turn it out carefully, upside down, and the top will be covered with a neat layer of transparent apples. Serve hot with hard sauce (No. 3105) or whipped cream.

(2909)   PINEAPPLE UPSIDE-DOWN CAKE

Substitute canned pineapple slices for apple in apple upside-down cake (No. 2908) and omit cinnamon.

(2910)   APPLESAUCE CAKE

½ cup shortening	1 teaspoon salt
1½ cups brown sugar	1 teaspoon cinnamon
1 egg	½ teaspoon clove
1 cup thick applesauce	1½ to 2 cups flour
(No. 34)	1 teaspoon soda

Cream shortening, sugar, and egg together. Dissolve soda in applesauce and add. Sift salt, cinnamon, and clove with part of the flour and add to the first mixture. Add enough more flour to make a fairly stiff batter. Pour into a greased loaf pan and bake in moderate oven (350° F.) 50 to 60 minutes. 1 cup raisins may be added to the batter.

(2911)   DRIED APPLE CAKE

2 cups dried apples	2 eggs, well beaten
2 cups molasses	1½ teaspoons soda
1 cup seeded raisins	2 teaspoons cinnamon
1 cup butter	½ teaspoon cloves
1 cup sour milk	½ teaspoon grated nutmeg
1 cup brown sugar	3 cups flour

Soak dried apples 10 hours in cold water. Drain, chop fine, and cook slowly with molasses one hour. Add raisins. Stir well and let cool. Cream butter, gradually adding sugar, beaten eggs, cooled mixture, sour milk and flour mixed and sifted with soda and spices. Turn into a well-buttered loaf pan, and bake in moderate oven (350° F.).

(2912)   APRICOT CHERRY TURNOVER CAKE

2¼ cups flour	8 egg yolks
4 teaspoons baking powder	1 teaspoon vanilla
1 teaspoon salt	Butter
¾ cup shortening, butter or	Brown sugar
other fat	5 cups canned apricot
1¼ cups granulated sugar	halves
¾ cup milk	Maraschino cherries

Sift flour. Measure and sift again with baking powder and salt. Cream shortening with sugar and 2 tablespoons milk until light. Beat egg yolks light and add to creamed mixture. Add vanilla to milk and add alternately with dry mixture to creamed mixture. Spread a pan with butter. Over this pack a ¼-inch layer of brown sugar. Drain apricots and dry between towels. Press a cherry into each. Place apricots, cut side down, on sugar. Pour batter over fruit. Bake in moderate oven (350° F.) 1 hour. Turn out upside down.

(2913)   CHOCOLATE RIBBON CAKE

3 cups sifted cake flour
3 teaspoons baking powder
½ teaspoon salt
⅔ cup shortening
1½ cups sugar
2 eggs and 2 egg yolks, well beaten
1 cup milk

1 teaspoon vanilla
3 squares unsweetened chocolate, melted and cooled
2 tablespoons sugar
¼ cup hot water
½ teaspoon soda
2 tablespoons butter

Sift flour once, measure, add baking powder and salt, and sift together three times. Cream shortening thoroughly, add sugar gradually, and cream together until light and fluffy. Add eggs and beat well. Add flour, alternately with milk, beating until smooth. Add vanilla. Combine remaining ingredients. Cool slightly. Turn a generous ⅓ batter into greased 9-inch layer pan. Add chocolate mixture to remaining batter; turn into two greased 9-inch layer pans. Bake in moderate oven (375° F.) 30 minutes. Spread with seven-minute frosting (No. 3174), arranging light layer between dark ones. Top with chocolate icing (No. 3187).

(2914)   BIRTHDAY CAKE

½ cup shortening
1½ cups sugar
3 eggs
2¼ cups flour

1 teaspoon salt
3 teaspoons baking powder
⅔ cup milk
1 teaspoon almond extract

Cream shortening, sugar, and eggs together. Mix and sift flour, salt, and baking powder and add alternately with the milk to the first mixture. Add almond extract and beat thoroughly. Pour into a greased tube pan. Wrap a button, thimble, ring, and dime in separate pieces of wax paper and put into the cake batter. Bake in a moderate oven (350° F.) 50 to 60 minutes. Cover and decorate with ornamental frosting (No. 3176)

(2915) BLUEBERRY TEA CAKE

2 tablespoons butter	1½ cups flour
1 cup sugar	⅓ cup milk
2 eggs, separated	1½ cups blueberries

Cream the butter and sugar together until well blended. Beat egg yolks and add. Add the flour alternately with the milk. Fold in the stiffly beaten egg whites. Pour half of the batter into a greased oblong baking pan, cover with the floured blueberries and then with the remaining batter. Bake in a moderate oven (350° F.) 35 minutes. Sprinkle with powdered sugar while still warm and cut in 2-inch squares.

(2916) BREAD CRUMB CAKE

3 egg yolks	2 teaspoons baking powder
1 cup sugar	1 tablespoon melted
3 tablespoons cold water	shortening
¾ cup chopped walnuts	1 teaspoon vanilla
1 cup soft bread crumbs	3 egg whites

Beat egg yolks until thick and lemon-colored. Add sugar and water. Add the nuts, bread crumbs, baking powder, and shortening. Mix well. Add vanilla and fold in stiffly beaten egg whites. Bake in 2 greased layer cake pans in a hot oven (400° F.) 15 to 20 minutes. When cool, spread whipped cream, sweetened and flavored, between layers and on top of cake.

(2917) BUTTERSCOTCH CAKE WITH MARSHMALLOWS

1¾ cups flour	¼ cup water
2 teaspoons baking powder	1 teaspoon vanilla
1 teaspoon salt	2 eggs
½ cup shortening	¼ cup milk
1½ cups brown sugar	12 marshmallows

Sift the flour. Measure and sift again with the baking powder and salt. Mix the shortening, sugar, and water and cook over low heat until the sugar is dissolved. Cool and add vanilla. Add eggs one at a time, beating well after each addition. Alternately add sifted dry ingredients with the milk. Beat until smooth, being careful not to overheat. Pour into a 9-inch cake pan lined with paper. Place marshmallows at intervals on top of batter. Bake in a moderate oven (350° F.) 50 minutes.

(2918) MARASCHINO CHERRY CAKE

4½ cups cake flour	1½ teaspoons vanilla extract
4½ teaspoons baking powder	½ teaspoon almond extract
1 teaspoon salt	2 egg yolks
¾ cup shortening	5 egg whites
2¼ cups sugar	¼ cup maraschino cherries
1¾ cups milk	

Sift flour once. Measure and sift with baking powder and salt. Cream shortening. Continue creaming, gradually adding 1½ cups sugar and 3 tablespoons of milk. Add egg yolks and flavorings to milk. Add sifted dry ingredients alternately with the milk mixture to the creamed shortening and sugar. Beat egg whites until stiff, but not dry. Add remaining sugar and beat until sugar is dissolved. Fold into cake mixture. Pour batter into three oiled 9-inch layer pans. Sprinkle ¼ cup finely cut pieces of maraschino cherries over the batter. Bake in a moderately hot oven (375° F.) 25 minutes. Frost with seven-minute icing (No. 3174).

(2919) CHOCOLATE REFRIGERATOR LAYER CAKE

2 8-inch cake layers	½ cup semi-sweet
(No. 2953)	chocolate sirup
1 cup heavy cream	

Split each layer in half, making four layers in all. Whip the cream until it begins to thicken. Add the chocolate sirup all at once, and continue to beat until the mixture is smooth, thick, and well blended. Spread between the cake layers and top with the remainder. Chill in the refrigerator for 24 hours. Then cut as a cake and serve. Serves 8 to 10.

(2920)   CITRON TEA CAKE

½ cup shortening
½ teaspoon salt
1 teaspoon vanilla
¾ teaspoon nutmeg
1 cup brown sugar
2 eggs

2½ teaspoons baking powder
2 cups sifted flour
½ cup citron, finely cut
½ cup nuts, finely cut
¾ cup water

Combine shortening, salt, vanilla, and nutmeg. Add brown sugar gradually and cream until light and fluffy. Add eggs, one at a time, beating thoroughly after each addition. Add baking powder to flour and sift three times. Add 1 tablespoon to citron and nuts and mix thoroughly. Add small amounts of flour to creamed mixture, alternately with water, mixing after each addition, until smooth. Add citron and nuts, and mix well. Pour batter into deep round 7- or 8-inch pan, well greased. Bake in moderate oven (350° F.) 1 hour. Sift confectioners' sugar over the top and serve in slices.

(2921)   CRUMB CAKE

½ cup shortening
1½ cups brown sugar
2½ cups sifted flour
2½ teaspoons baking powder

1 teaspoon cinnamon
1 teaspoon salt
1 beaten egg
¾ cup milk

Mix shortening, sugar, and 2 cups flour to a fine crumb. Reserve ¾ cup of this crumb. Sift remaining flour, baking powder, cinnamon, and salt. Combine with crumb mixture. Add egg and milk and mix well. Pour into an 8-inch square pan which has been lined with oiled paper. Sprinkle reserved crumbs on top. Bake in moderately hot oven (375° F.) 35 to 40 minutes.

(2922)   DATE CAKE

4 eggs
1½ cups brown sugar
⅔ cup shortening
3¼ cups flour
5 teaspoons baking powder

1 teaspoon salt
1 teaspoon cinnamon
½ teaspoon nutmeg
¾ cup milk
1½ cups chopped dates

Separate eggs. Cream yolks, brown sugar, and shortening. Mix and sift flour, baking powder, salt, cinnamon, and nutmeg.

Add dry mixture to first mixture alternately with milk. Beat egg whites well. Stir into mixture. Add dates, mixing well. Turn into a greased loaf pan. Bake in moderate oven (350° F.) 50 to 60 minutes. Cool and frost as desired.

(2923) DEVIL'S FOOD CAKE

2 cups cake flour	1 teaspoon vanilla
1½ cups sugar	2 squares (2 oz.) unsweet-
¾ teaspoon salt	ened chocolate, melted
½ cup shortening	and cooled
2 eggs	1 teaspoon baking soda
1 cup milk	1 tablespoon hot water

Sift flour, measure and resift 3 times with sugar and salt. The last time sift directly into large mixing bowl. Add shortening (room temperature), eggs, and ½ cup of milk. Stir with a spoon to blend. Beat with an electric mixer using low speed or by hand with wooden spoon for 2 minutes by the clock. Scrape sides of bowl twice during beating. Add the combined vanilla, melted cooled chocolate, soda and water and the remaining milk. Beat for 2 more minutes. Pour into two 8-inch layer cake pans with bottoms lined with thin plain paper. Bake at 350° F. (moderate) for 20 to 25 minutes or, until cake tests done. Cool 5 minutes before removing from pan. Place on cake coolers to cool thoroughly. Frost with caramel (No. 3183) or any desired frosting.

(2924) BANANA DEVIL'S FOOD CAKE

2 cups cake flour	1½ cups brown sugar
1 teaspoon salt	2 eggs
½ teaspoon soda	⅓ cup mashed ripe banana
2 teaspoons baking powder	2 squares unsweetened
½ cup shortening	chocolate
¾ cup buttermilk or sour	1 teaspoon vanilla
milk	

Sift flour once. Measure and sift again with salt, soda, and baking powder. Cream shortening, 2 tablespoons buttermilk or sour milk, and sugar together until light and fluffy. Add eggs, one at a time, beating after each addition. Add banana pulp, then melted chocolate. Combine remaining milk and vanilla. Add dry ingredients alternately with milk to creamed mixture. Beat well. Pour into an oiled 10 by 14-inch pan and bake in a moderate oven (350° F.) 45 minutes. Frost with caramel coconut frosting (No. 3184).

(2925) FEATHERWEIGHT CAKE

1 cup sugar	2 teaspoons baking powder
½ cup shortening	⅔ cup milk
2 cups flour	3 egg whites
½ teaspoon salt	1 teaspoon vanilla

Cream shortening with sugar until the mixture is very light. Mix and sift flour, salt, and baking powder, and add alternately with the milk to the first mixture. Fold in egg whites which have been beaten until stiff but not dry. Add vanilla. Turn batter into two greased layer pans. Bake in a moderate oven (350° F.). Ice with any desired icing.

(2926) FOUNDATION CAKE

½ cup shortening	4 teaspoons baking powder
½ teaspoon vanilla	½ teaspoon salt
1½ cups sugar	1 cup milk
2 well-beaten egg yolks	2 beaten egg whites
3 cups sifted flour	

Cream shortening, vanilla, and sugar together until light and fluffy. Continue creaming while adding yolks slowly. Sift flour, baking powder, and salt together and add alternately with milk to creamed mixture. Beat in the dry ingredients. Fold in beaten egg whites. Turn into lightly greased pan. For a layer cake, bake in moderate oven (365° F.) 25 minutes. For a loaf cake bake in 325° F. oven 40 to 45 minutes.

(2927) CHOCOLATE CAKE

Add 2 ounces melted, unsweetened chocolate just before egg whites are folded into foundation cake (No. 2926), reduce shortening to ⅜ cup, and reduce flour to 2⅞ cups.

(2928) WHITE CAKE

Use 4 to 6 egg whites and omit egg yolks in recipe for foundation cake (No. 2926).

(2929) YELLOW CAKE

Use 4 to 6 egg yolks and omit egg whites in recipe for foundation cake (No. 2926).

(2930)   FOUR-EGG CAKE

4 eggs	3 teaspoons baking powder
¾ cup shortening	1 teaspoon salt
1½ cups sugar	¾ cup milk
3 cups flour	2 teaspoons vanilla

Separate eggs. Cream yolks, shortening, and sugar together. Mix and sift flour, baking powder, and salt. Add this mixture alternately with milk to egg-shortening mixture. Beat egg whites stiff. Add vanilla. Fold into dough. Turn into greased cupcake pans or into 3 greased layer cake pans. Bake cupcakes in quick oven (425° F.) 20 minutes; layer cakes in hot oven (400° F.) 25 minutes. Spread layers and top of cake with seven-minute icing (No. 3174), to which has been added ½ cup chopped nuts, ¼ cup chopped candied cherries, and ½ cup chopped raisins.

(2931)   ALMOND CAKE

Follow recipe for four-egg cake (No. 2930). Add ½ cup blanched almonds and ¼ cup candied cherries, cut in thin strips. Substitute ½ teaspoon almond flavoring for ½ teaspoon of the vanilla. Bake in a greased loaf pan in a moderate oven (350° F.) 60 to 80 minutes.

(2932)   CURRANT SPICE CAKE

Follow recipe for four-egg cake (No. 2930). Add 1 teaspoon cinnamon, ½ teaspoon clove, ¼ teaspoon nutmeg and ¾ cup currants. Mix these with the flour before adding. Bake in a greased loaf or round pan in a moderate oven (350° F.) 60 to 80 minutes. Top with seven-minute icing (No. 3174).

(2933)   NUT CAKE

Follow recipe for four-egg cake (No. 2930). Add 1 cup English walnuts or other preferred nuts, cut in pieces and mixed with a little of the flour. Bake in a greased loaf pan in a moderate oven (350° F.) 60 to 80 minutes.

(2934)   RAISIN CAKE

Follow recipe for four-egg cake (No. 2930). Add ¾ cup raisins mixed with a little of the flour. Bake in a greased loaf pan in a moderate oven (350° F.) 60 to 80 minutes.

(2935)   FRUIT CAKE

2 cups shortening	2 pounds currants
2 cups light brown sugar	1 pound nut meats
7 eggs	2 pounds raisins, seeded
4 cups flour	and finely chopped
2 teaspoons mace	½ pound date meats, finely
2 teaspoons cinnamon	chopped
2 teaspoons baking powder	½ pound citron, thinly
Few grains salt	sliced and cut into
2 tablespoons fruit juice	short strips
2 tablespoons milk	

Cream shortening. Add sugar gradually and beat for 5 minutes. Beat egg yolks until light and lemon-colored and whites until stiff and dry. Add these to the butter and sugar mixture. Add milk, fruit juice, chopped nuts, and fruit that have been rolled in flour. Lastly, add well sifted dry ingredients. Beat mixture thoroughly and place in deep, round cake pans lined with several thicknesses of oiled paper. Bake 3 to 4 hours in a slow oven (275° F.). If the oven is difficult to regulate, cover the cake with several thicknesses of oiled paper the last hour of the baking.

(2936)   COFFEE FRUIT CAKE

1 cup shortening	4 cups flour
2 cups brown sugar	1 teaspoon salt
4 eggs	1 teaspoon clove
1 cup strong coffee	1 teaspoon nutmeg
(No. 301)	2 teaspoons cinnamon
1 teaspoon soda	1 pound currants
1 cup molasses	1 pound raisins

Cream shortening and sugar together. Add eggs one at a time, blending in thoroughly. Stir in coffee. Add soda mixed with molasses. Mix and sift flour, salt, and spices. Add enough of the flour mixture to the fruit to keep it from sticking together. Add the remainder to the first mixture. Add fruit and mix thoroughly. Line bottom of a large pan with several layers of greased brown paper and grease sides of pan. Pour in the cake batter and bake in a very slow oven (250° F.) 2 to 3 hours. A small pan of water in the oven helps to keep the cake from burning during the long cooking.

(2937) FUDGE CAKE

½ cup shortening
1¼ cups brown sugar
1 teaspoon vanilla
3 ounces melted, unsweetened chocolate

2 eggs
2 cups sifted flour
1½ teaspoons baking powder
½ teaspoon soda
1 cup milk

Cream shortening and brown sugar together. Add vanilla. Add eggs, one at a time, beating thoroughly after each addition. Beat in chocolate gradually. Sift flour, baking powder, and soda together and add alternately with milk to first mixture. Beat until smooth. Turn into greased pan or pans. In loaf pan bake in moderate oven (325° F.) 1 hour. In layer cake pans bake in moderate oven (350° F.) 25 minutes.

(2938) GINGERBREAD

2 cups sifted cake flour
2 teaspoons baking powder
¼ teaspoon soda
2 teaspoons ginger
1 teaspoon cinnamon
½ teaspoon salt

⅓ cup shortening
½ cup sugar
1 egg, well beaten
⅔ cup molasses
¾ cup sour milk or buttermilk

Sift flour once, measure, add baking powder, soda, spices, and salt, and sift together three times. Cream shortening thoroughly, add sugar gradually, and cream together until light and fluffy. Add egg and molasses; then flour, alternately with milk. Beat after each addition until smooth. Pour into greased pan or a ring mold. Bake in moderate oven (350° F.) 1¼ hours. Serve with whipped cream. As a variation use gingerbread as the base for fruit shortcakes. Serves 6.

(2939)   REFRIGERATOR GINGERBREAD

2 cups flour	½ teaspoon soda
1½ teaspoons baking powder	½ teaspoon salt
1 teaspoon ginger	½ cup shortening
1 teaspoon cinnamon	½ cup sugar
¼ teaspoon allspice	½ cup buttermilk
¼ teaspoon cloves	2 eggs
¼ teaspoon nutmeg	½ cup molasses

Sift flour and measure. Sift again with baking powder, ginger, cinnamon, allspice, cloves, nutmeg, soda, and salt. Cream shortening and sugar with 2 tablespoons buttermilk. Add eggs and mix well. Add molasses. Add dry ingredients and remaining milk alternately to creamed mixture. Keep covered in refrigerator until ready to bake. Bake in 2 9-inch layer cake pans in moderate oven (350° F.) 30 minutes.

(2940)   GINGER CAKE

5 tablespoons shortening	½ cup sour milk
½ cup sugar	1¾ cups flour
1 egg	2 teaspoons ginger
½ cup molasses	1 teaspoon cinnamon
1 teaspoon soda	½ teaspoon salt

Cream shortening, sugar, and egg together. Stir in molasses. Dissolve soda in the sour milk. Mix and sift flour, ginger, cinnamon, and salt. Add alternately with the sour milk to the first mixture. Turn into a greased shallow pan. Bake in hot oven (400° F.) 25 to 30 minutes. Serve hot with whipped cream.

(2941)   GINGERBREAD SHORTCAKE

2 cups flour	⅓ cup shortening
1 teaspoon baking powder	½ cup sour milk
1 teaspoon soda	1 egg
1 teaspoon ginger	1 cup molasses
2 teaspoons cinnamon	1 cup heavy cream

Sift together the dry ingredients. Heat to boiling the molasses and shortening. Add the milk and egg to the dry ingredients and stir quickly into the hot molasses mixture. Bake in a moderate oven (375° F.) 20 to 25 minutes, in two greased 8-inch layer pans. Cool and cover with whipped cream to serve.

(2942) GOLDEN GLORY CAKE

4½ cups cake flour
4 teaspoons baking powder
1½ teaspoons salt
1 cup shortening
2⅔ cups sugar

1½ cups canned unsweet-
ened pineapple juice
4 egg yolks
1½ teaspoons vanilla
4 egg whites

Sift flour. Measure and sift again with the baking powder and salt. Cream shortening with 2 cups sugar and 2 tablespoons pineapple juice until light and fluffy. Add unbeaten egg yolks and beat well. Alternately add the sifted dry ingredients with remaining pineapple juice. Add vanilla. Mix until smooth. Fold in the egg whites beaten until stiff but not dry. Add remaining sugar and beat until it just disappears. Bake in three 8-inch layers in a moderately hot oven (375° F.) 25 to 30 minutes. Spread golden icing (No. 3192) between layers and on top and sides of cake.

(2943)   GOLD CAKE

½ cup shortening
1 cup sugar
8 egg yolks
1½ cups flour

4 teaspoons baking powder
1 teaspoon salt
½ cup milk
1 teaspoon vanilla

Cream shortening and sugar together. Add well-beaten egg yolks. Mix and sift flour, baking powder, and salt and add alternately with the milk to the first mixture. Add vanilla and beat thoroughly. Bake in 2 greased layer cake pans in a hot oven (400° F.) 20 minutes. When cool, put layers together, and ice top and sides with honey frosting (No. 3193).

(2944)   GRAHAM CRACKER CAKE

½ cup shortening
1 cup granulated sugar
3 eggs
1 cup milk
2 teaspoons baking powder

24 graham crackers, crumbed
1 cup chopped nuts
½ teaspoon salt

Cream shortening and sugar together. Beat yolks of eggs till light and add. Add milk. Roll the crackers fine. Mix baking powder with cracker crumbs. Add to other mixture together with salt and chopped nuts. Add beaten whites of eggs. Bake in 2 layers in moderately hot oven (375° F.). When cool, spread whipped cream between layers and on top of cake.

(2945) GUMDROP CAKE

½ cup butter
1 cup sugar
2 eggs, beaten
2¼ cups flour
¼ teaspoon salt
2 teaspoons baking powder

1 teaspoon vanilla
¾ cup milk
¾ cup raisins
1 pound gumdrops, black ones removed, chopped fine

Cream butter, while adding sugar and beaten eggs. Sift flour, salt, and baking powder together over chopped candy and raisins. Dredge well. Add vanilla to milk and add flour mixture and milk, to first mixture alternately. Bake in a large greased loaf tin in a slow oven (275° to 300° F.) 1½ hours.

(2946) HONEY CAKE

1 cup honey
1 cup sugar
½ cup melted shortening
2 slightly beaten eggs

2 cups flour
1 teaspoon baking powder
1 teaspoon caraway seeds

Cream honey, sugar, shortening, and eggs. Mix and sift flour, baking powder, and seeds. Combine mixtures and mix until smooth. Turn into baking pan and bake in moderately hot oven (375° F.) 30 to 40 minutes.

(2947) JELLY ROLL

2 eggs
⅞ cup sugar
Grated rind 1 lemon
1 cup flour
1½ teaspoons baking powder

¼ teaspoon salt
3 tablespoons milk
Jelly
Confectioners' sugar

Beat eggs. Add sugar and beat well. Add rind. Sift flour with baking powder and salt and add, alternately with milk, to first mixture. Pour into a shallow pan, about 14 x 10 inches, lined with wax paper. Bake in moderate oven (350° F.) 15 to 20 minutes. Turn out on damp cloth. Spread with jelly and roll up. Wrap in wax paper and cool. Sprinkle with confectioners' sugar just before serving.

(2948) CHOCOLATE ROLL

4 egg whites	1 teaspoon baking powder
½ cup sugar	½ teaspoon salt
4 egg yolks	1 cup cream
4 tablespoons cold water	½ teaspoon vanilla
4 tablespoons cocoa	2 tablespoons confec-
1 cup flour	tioners' sugar

Beat egg whites until stiff. Add sugar gradually, beating constantly. Add beaten egg yolks and water. Mix and sift cocoa, flour, baking powder, and salt and fold into the first mixture. Line a long shallow pan with greased paper. Pour the batter into the pan. Bake in a hot oven (400° F.) 15 to 20 minutes. Turn out on a damp cloth and cool slightly. Beat cream stiff with vanilla and confectioners' sugar and spread on cake. Roll like a jelly roll (No. 2947). Sprinkle with powdered sugar.

(2949) FRUIT ROLL

¾ cup cake flour	3 tablespoons cornstarch
1 teaspoon baking powder	¼ teaspoon salt
4 eggs	Dash nutmeg
¼ teaspoon salt	Dash cinnamon
¾ cup sugar	2½ cups canned or stewed
Juice of ½ lemon	raspberries (No. 49)
1 teaspoon grated lemon rind	Juice of ½ lemon
⅓ cup sugar	1 tablespoon butter

Sift the flour. Measure and sift again with baking powder. Put the eggs and salt in a bowl. Set the bowl in a larger bowl of hot water and beat until eggs are thick and lemon colored. Remove bowl from water and add the sugar, a tablespoon at a time, beating after each addition. Add lemon juice and rind and fold in the dry ingredients. Grease a shallow pan. Pour the batter into the pan and bake in a moderately hot oven (400° F.) 15 minutes. Turn from the pan onto a cloth covered with confectioners' sugar. Quickly spread with the fruit mixture and roll. Wrap in the cloth and cool on a rack. Slice and serve with whipped cream. To make the fruit filling: Mix together the sugar, cornstarch, salt, nutmeg, and cinnamon. Drain the sirup from the raspberries and heat to boiling. Stir in the dry ingredients and cook until thick and clear. Place over hot water and continue to cook 10 minutes. Remove from heat and stir in the raspberries, lemon juice, and butter.

(2950)   ORANGE CREAM ROLL

Substitute orange filling (No. 3165) for jelly in recipe for jelly roll (No. 2947).

(2951)   PISTACHIO ROLL

Cook jelly roll (No. 2947). Use cream, whipped with a little powdered sugar and almond extract, for filling. Ice with seven-minute frosting (No. 3174).

(2952)   JIFFY CAKE WITH SELF ICING

4 tablespoons shortening	1½ teaspoons baking powder
1 cup sugar	1 teaspoon vanilla
1 egg	½ cup grated sweet
½ cup milk	chocolate
⅓ teaspoon salt	½ cup chopped almonds
1½ cups sifted flour	

Combine shortening, sugar, egg, milk, salt, flour, baking powder, and vanilla. Beat with a rotary beater until light and smooth. Pour into deep cake pan. Mix chocolate and almonds and spread evenly over cake. Bake in moderate oven (350° F.) 35 to 40 minutes.

(2953)   LAYER CAKE

⅓ cup shortening	3 teaspoons baking powder
¾ cup sugar	½ teaspoon salt
2 eggs	½ cup milk
1½ cups flour	1 teaspoon vanilla

Cream shortening, sugar, and eggs together. Mix and sift flour, baking powder, and salt and add alternately with the milk to the first mixture. Add vanilla and beat thoroughly. Bake in 2 greased layer cake pans in a hot oven (400° F.) 20 to 25 minutes. Cool. Put layers together with any cream filling, chocolate (No. 3158), pineapple (No. 3167), lemon (No. 3163), orange (No. 3165), or coconut (No. 3159). Ice top with confectioners' frosting (No. 3173).

(2954)   CHOCOLATE LAYER CAKE

Use fudge icing (No. 3191) between layers and on top and sides of baked layer cake (No. 2953).

(2955)   COFFEE LAYER CAKE

Use coffee filling (No. 3160) between layers and on top and sides of baked layer cake (No. 2953).

(2956)   LEMON LAYER CAKE

Use lemon icing (No. 3194) between layers and on top and sides of baked layer cake (No. 2953).

(2957)   ORANGE LAYER CAKE

Use orange icing (No. 3200) between layers and on top and sides of baked layer cake (No. 2953).

(2958)   STRAWBERRY LAYER CAKE

Spread strawberry jam between layers of baked layer cake (No. 2953) and sprinkle top with powdered sugar.

(2959)   VANILLA LAYER CAKE

Use boiled icing (No. 3171) between layers and on top and sides of baked layer cake (No. 2953).

(2960)   CHOCOLATE CHIP LAYER CAKE

1 8-ounce package semi-sweet chocolate	1 cup sugar
2¼ cups sifted cake flour	½ cup shortening
2¼ teaspoons baking powder	3 egg whites, unbeaten
½ teaspoon salt	¾ cup milk
	1½ teaspoons vanilla

Cut each small square of chocolate in 4 to 6 pieces. Sift flour once, measure, add baking powder and salt, and sift together three times. Cream butter thoroughly, add sugar gradually, and cream together until light and fluffy. Add egg whites, one at a time, beating thoroughly after each. Add flour, alternately with milk, a small amount at a time, beating after each addition until smooth. Add vanilla. Grease two 8-inch pans, lined with waxed paper, and grease again. Pour about ⅙ of batter into each pan. Sprinkle ⅙ of chopped chocolate over each lot. Repeat, ending with chocolate. Bake in moderate oven (375° F.) 30 minutes, or until done. Frost with your favorite frosting, decorating with shredded chocolate. To make cupcakes, add chopped chocolate to cake batter with vanilla. Bake in greased cupcake pans in moderate oven (375° F.) 20 minutes, or until done.

(2961)   MARBLE CAKE

¾ cup shortening
2 cups sugar
1½ cups milk or water
4 egg whites
3¼ cups flour
½ teaspoon salt

3 teaspoons baking powder
3 teaspoons vanilla
2 ounces unsweetened
    chocolate
¼ teaspoon soda

Cream shortening, sugar, and 2 tablespoons milk or water until light and fluffy. Beat unbeaten egg whites one at a time into mixture. Sift flour and measure. Sift again with salt and baking powder. Add sifted dry ingredients alternately with remaining liquid to cream mixture. Add vanilla. Melt chocolate and combine with soda. Divide batter into 2 equal parts. Add chocolate mixture to one part. Drop batter by spoonfuls into a greased and floured cake pan, alternating the white and chocolate batter until all is used. Bake in moderate oven (350° F.) 50 minutes.

(2962)   MARBLE REFRIGERATOR CAKE

2 cups scalded milk
½ cup carmelized sugar
3 eggs
½ cup sugar
5 tablespoons flour
1 ounce unsweetened,
    melted chocolate

1 cup nut meats
1 teaspoon vanilla
Chocolate (No. 3079)
    and vanilla wafers
    (No. 3091)
Whipped cream

Pour the scalded milk and caramelized sugar on the eggs which have been beaten with the half-cup sugar and flour. Cook over water till thick. Add the melted chocolate to ½ the batter and the nutmeats and vanilla to the rest. Line a pan with chocolate and vanilla wafers. Pour the chocolate mixture in first, then the other filling, and top with whipped cream. Chill well and serve.

(2963) MARMALADE REFRIGERATOR CAKE

2 small packages gingersnaps,
    crumbled
1 tablespoon gelatin
½ cup unsalted butter

¾ cup confectioners' sugar
3 eggs
¼ cup orange marmalade
½ cup whipping cream

Line a mold with gingersnaps, crumbling bits to cover bottom completely. Soak gelatin in 2 tablespoons cold water 5 minutes. Dissolve over hot water. Cream butter with ½ cup sugar until fluffy. Separate eggs. Beat yolks well. Add to butter-sugar mixture. Fold in gelatin and then marmalade. Beat egg whites fluffy. Add remaining sugar to whites and beat to a meringue. Fold into first mixture. Turn into the mold. Chill 24 hours. Turn out, inverted, on plate. Whip cream and use to decorate cake. Ring with half circles of gingersnaps, standing them erect to hide rim.

(2964)   MARSHMALLOW CAKE

½ cup shortening	4 egg whites
1½ cups sugar	¼ teaspoon cream of tartar
½ cup milk	⅛ teaspoon salt
2 cups flour	1 teaspoon vanilla
3 teaspoons baking powder	

Cream the shortening, adding sugar gradually. Mix and sift flour, baking powder, cream of tartar, and salt. Add them alternately with milk to creamed mixture. Add stiffly beaten egg whites and the flavoring. Bake in layer cake pan about 30 minutes in a moderate oven (350° F.). Put layers together with marshmallow frosting (No. 3197) and ice with confectioners' frosting (No. 3173).

(2965)   MILE-A-MINUTE CAKE

1¾ cups flour	1⅓ cups brown sugar
2 teaspoons baking powder	2 eggs
1 teaspoon salt	½ cup milk
½ teaspoon cinnamon	½ pound dates, stoned and
½ teaspoon nutmeg	chopped
⅓ cup shortening	½ cup nuts, chopped

Sift the flour. Measure and sift again with the baking powder, salt, and spices. Combine all ingredients in the order given, adding the pitted, chopped dates and chopped nuts last. Beat all together 5 minutes. Bake in a 9-inch square pan in a moderate oven (350° F.) 50 to 60 minutes. Ice with peanut butter icing (No. 3201).

(2966)   QUICK MINCE COFFEE CAKE

2 cups flour	½ cup milk
4 teaspoons baking powder	1 cup mincemeat
½ teaspoon salt	¼ cup cream
¼ cup sugar	3 tablespoons sugar
⅓ cup shortening	1 teaspoon cinnamon
2 eggs	

Sift flour. Measure and sift again with baking powder, salt, and ¼ cup sugar. Cut in the shortening. Beat one egg. Add milk and stir into the dry ingredients, mixing only enough to moisten them. Put into a greased 8-inch pan. Spread the mincemeat over the dough. Beat the remaining egg and mix with cream. Pour over mincemeat topping. Sprinkle with the sugar and cinnamon, mixed. Bake in a moderate oven (375° F.) 1 hour. Serve hot as a dessert with whipped cream or pudding sauce.

(2967)   MOLASSES CAKE

½ cup shortening	1 teaspoon cinnamon
½ cup sugar	¼ teaspoon clove
3 eggs	¼ teaspoon mace
¾ teaspoon soda	1 teaspoon salt
⅔ cup molasses	½ cup milk
2¼ cups flour	½ cup raisins

Cream shortening, sugar, and egg yolks together. Add soda, mixed with the molasses. Mix and sift flour, cinnamon, clove, mace and salt, and add alternately with the milk to the first mixture. Stir in beaten whites. Dredge the raisins lightly with flour and stir in lightly. Pour into a greased loaf pan and bake in a moderate oven (350° F.) 50 to 60 minutes.

(2968)   MOTHER'S TEA CAKES

⅓ cup shortening	1½ cups flour
1 cup sugar	1 teaspoon baking powder
½ teaspoon salt	½ cup milk
2 eggs	½ teaspoon vanilla

Cream shortening, sugar, salt, and eggs together. Beat until light and soft. Mix and sift flour and baking powder and add to the first mixture alternately with the milk. Add vanilla. Beat thoroughly and pour into well-greased shallow baking pan. Bake in hot oven (400° F.) 30 minutes. When partly cool, dust with powdered sugar, cut in squares, and serve while warm.

(2969)　　　　　　　NUN'S CAKE

1 cup butter	3 cups sifted cake flour
1½ cups sugar	2½ teaspoons baking powder
5 egg yolks	1 teaspoon salt
2 egg whites	1 teaspoon vanilla
¾ cup milk	¼ teaspoon mace

Cream the butter, add sugar gradually and continue creaming. Add egg yolks and whites gradually, beating constantly, until light and fluffy. Sift flour, baking powder, salt, and mace together three times. Add to egg mixture, alternately with milk. Add vanilla. Bake in a greased pan in moderate oven (350° F.) 1 hour.

(2970)　　　　　　　ORANGE CAKE

3 eggs	3 teaspoons baking powder
⅔ cup shortening	1 teaspoon salt
1½ cups sugar	1 cup orange juice
3 cups flour	

Separate eggs. Cream yolks, shortening, and sugar together. Mix and sift flour, baking powder, and salt. Add to first mixture alternately with orange juice. Beat egg whites and stir into mixture. Pour into 3 greased layer cake pans. Bake in hot oven (400° F.) 20 to 25 minutes. Spread orange frosting (No. 3200) between layers and on top of cake.

(2971)　　　QUICK ORANGE CAKE

½ cup melted butter	4 teaspoons baking powder
1 cup sugar	¼ teaspoon salt
2 eggs	Rind of 2 oranges
¾ cup orange juice	3 tablespoons sugar
2 cups flour	(additional)

Add hot butter to 1 cup sugar. Add well-beaten eggs and orange juice. Add sifted dry ingredients and beat well. Pour into a greased pan. Grate orange rind and mix with 3 tablespoons sugar. Sprinkle on cake. Bake 50 minutes at 350° F.

(2972)   SUNNY ORANGE CAKE

3 cups flour	3 eggs
4 teaspoons baking powder	1 cup milk
1 teaspoon salt	1 teaspoon vanilla
1⅔ cups sugar	¼ cup orange juice
½ cup shortening	

Sift flour and measure. Sift 3 more times with baking powder, salt, and sugar. Soften shortening, but do not melt, and add to dry mixture. Combine other ingredients and add slowly to first mixture. Beat 1 minute. Bake in 2 9-inch layer cake pans in a moderately hot oven (375° F.) 25 to 30 minutes. Ice with boiled egg yolk icing (No. 3179).

(2973)   ORANGEADE CAKE

1 orange	½ teaspoon salt
1 cup raisins or dates	1 teaspoon soda
½ cup nuts	2 cups sifted cake flour
½ cup shortening	¾ cup orange juice
1 cup sugar	1 cup sugar
2 eggs	⅓ cup orange juice
1 teaspoon maple flavor	(additional)

With sharp knife remove the outer, bright colored layer of orange peel from orange. Combine with raisins or dates and nuts. Put through food chopper using finest knife. Cream shortening and sugar thoroughly. Add eggs and maple flavor, beating in well. Add chopped fruit and nut mixture. Sift salt and soda with flour and add alternately with orange juice. Turn into greased pan measuring 8 x 13 inches and bake in a moderate oven (350° F.) about 1 hour. While still very hot spread with the 1 cup sugar mixed with the ⅓ cup orange juice. This orange mixture forms a tempting sugar coating on cake. Serve warm or cool in the pan and serve.

(2974)   ORANGE REFRIGERATOR CAKE

1 cup orange juice	¼ cup orange pieces
1 tablespoon gelatin	1 cup whipping cream
⅓ cup sugar	24 ladyfingers (No. 3042)
½ cup boiling water	or sponge cake
12 marshmallows	(No. 3003)

Soften gelatin in ¼ cup orange juice 5 minutes. Add the sugar and boiling water. Stir to dissolve. Add ¾ cup orange juice. While gelatin mixture cools, combine marshmallows cut into bits, and orange pieces. When gelatin begins to stiffen, beat until fluffy. Fold in orange pieces, marshmallows, and the whipped cream. Line a spring pan with waxed paper. Arrange a layer of ladyfingers or sponge cake on bottom and sides, with ladyfingers rounded side out. Pour in filling. Chill in refrigerator 6 to 8 hours. Unmold and garnish with whipped cream and orange sections. Serves 8.

(2975) ORANGE DATE CAKE

2 cups flour	½ cup butter
¼ teaspoon salt	1 cup sugar
2 teaspoons baking powder	3 eggs
½ package pitted dates	1 teaspoon grated orange
¼ cup orange juice	rind

Sift dry ingredients. Cut the dates in eighths. Mix dates through the flour with the fingertips. Cream the butter, adding the sugar gradually, then beaten eggs and grated orange rind. Stir in the flour alternately with the orange juice. Pour the batter into a loaf pan which has been greased and lined with greased paper. Bake in a moderate oven (325-350° F.) 50 to 60 minutes. Ice with boiled egg yolk icing (No. 3179), orange icing (No. 3200), or garnish with whipped cream.

(2976) PEACH CAKE

½ cup shortening	2 teaspoons baking powder
1 cup sugar	¼ teaspoon salt
2 eggs	½ cup milk
2 cups flour	1 cup diced fresh peaches

Cream shortening and sugar. Add eggs, one at a time, beating well. Sift flour, measure, and sift again with baking powder and salt. Add alternately with milk to first mixture. Add peaches and mix. Bake in 9-inch square pan 30 to 35 minutes at 375° F. Serve warm with lemon sauce (No. 3129) or top with sweetened whipped cream.

(2977) PEPPERMINT STICK CANDY LAYER CAKE

2⅔ cup flour
3 teaspoons baking powder
1 teaspoon salt
½ cup shortening
1½ cups sugar
1¼ cups milk
1 egg yolk

1 teaspoon vanilla
3 egg whites
½ cup finely ground peppermint stick candy
½ cup coarsely ground peppermint stick candy

Sift flour and measure. Sift again with baking powder and salt. Cream shortening. Continue creaming, gradually adding ⅘ cup of sugar and 3 tablespoons milk. Add egg yolk and vanilla to remaining milk. Add sifted dry ingredients alternately with milk to creamed mixture. Beat egg whites stiff but not dry. Beat in remaining sugar. Fold into cake batter. Pour into 2 9-inch layer pans with wax paper in bottom. Sprinkle with the finely ground peppermint candy. Bake in moderately hot oven (375° F.) 25 minutes. Ice with seven-minute icing (No. 3174), colored pink. Sprinkle coarsely ground peppermint candy over top and sides of cake.

(2978) PORK CAKE

¼ pound salt pork, chopped fine
2 cups flour
½ teaspoon baking soda
1 teaspoon cinnamon
¼ teaspoon allspice
¼ teaspoon nutmeg

¼ teaspoon cloves
½ cup raisins
½ cup currants
2 ounces citron, chopped
1 well-beaten egg
½ cup molasses
½ cup sugar

Pour ½ cup boiling water over pork and let stand 10 minutes. Sift flour, baking soda, cinnamon, allspice, nutmeg, and clove together. Add raisins, currants, and citron to dry mixture. Mix well. Beat egg, sugar, and molasses together and add to soaking pork. Gradually add flour-fruit mixture. Mix well. Line a greased loaf pan with greased wax paper. Turn in mixture. Bake in slow oven (300° F.) 1½ to 1¾ hours or until thoroughly done.

(2979) POUND CAKE

1 cup shortening	1 ½ teaspoons salt
1 ½ cups sugar	⅛ teaspoon mace
5 eggs	1 teaspoon vanilla
2 cups flour	

Cream shortening and sugar together. Add eggs, one at a time, beating well after the addition of each egg. Add the flour, salt, and mace. Add vanilla and beat thoroughly. Bake in a greased loaf pan in a moderate oven (350° F.) 60 to 80 minutes.

(2980) BRIDE CAKE

Substitute 8 egg whites for 5 eggs in recipe for pound cake (No. 2979).

(2981) CHERRY-NUT POUND CAKE

Add ¼ cup chopped preserved cherries and ¼ cup chopped nut meats to recipe for pound cake (No. 2979).

(2982) COCONUT POUND CAKE

Add ⅔ cup shredded coconut to recipe for pound cake (No. 2979).

(2983) COFFEE POUND CAKE

Add 2 tablespoons powdered coffee to recipe for pound cake (No. 2979), creaming it with shortening and sugar.

(2984) FRUIT POUND CAKE

Add ½ cup seedless raisins, ⅓ cup chopped preserved cherries, ¼ cup grated orange peel, ¼ cup grated lemon peel, and ¼ cup chopped nuts to recipe for pound cake (No. 2979). Place halved almonds on top of cake before baking.

(2985) LEMON POUND CAKE

Add ¼ cup grated lemon rind to recipe for pound cake (No. 2979).

(2986) MAPLE POUND CAKE

Substitute ½ cup maple sugar and ½ cup brown sugar for equal amounts of granulated sugar in recipe for pound cake (No. 2979).

(2987) ORANGE POUND CAKE

Add ½ cup grated orange rind to recipe for pound cake (No. 2979).

(2988) RAISIN POUND CAKE

Add 1¼ cups seedless raisins to recipe for pound cake (No. 2979).

(2989) VANILLA POUND CAKE

Increase vanilla to 2 teaspoons in recipe for pound cake (No. 2979).

(2990) WALNUT POUND CAKE

Add ⅔ cup chopped walnuts to recipe for pound cake (No. 2979).

(2991) PUMPKIN CAKE

½ cup shortening
1 cup brown sugar
½ cup granulated sugar
1 egg or 2 egg yolks
¾ cups mashed pumpkin
    (No. 1864)
2 cups flour

¼ teaspoon soda
3 teaspoons baking powder
1 teaspoon salt
1 teaspoon cinnamon
⅔ cup chopped nut meats
⅓ cup sour milk

Cream shortening and sugars together. Add egg and pumpkin. Sift flour, soda, baking powder, salt, and cinnamon together. Add nut meats and add dry mixture alternately with sour milk to creamed mixture. Mix well. Turn into 2 8-inch layer pans with oiled paper in the bottom. Bake in moderate oven (350° F.) 25 minutes. Cool. Put together with spiced whipped cream (No. 3210) between layers.

(2992)   QUICK CAKE

1 cup sugar	¼ cup melted shortening
1½ cups flour	2 eggs
2 teaspoons baking powder	Milk
½ teaspoon salt	1 teaspoon vanilla

Mix sugar, flour, baking powder, and salt and sift three times. Put shortening in measuring cup, add eggs, and fill cup with milk. Add liquid to the sifted flour mixture. Add vanilla and beat thoroughly. Bake in 2 greased layer cake pans in hot oven (400° F.) 15 to 20 minutes. Cool. Put layers together and ice top with quick frosting (No. 3170). This cake may also be baked in greased muffin pans.

(2993)   SEAFOAM CAKE

1 cup flour	10 egg whites, beaten stiff
1½ cups sugar	1 teaspoon vanilla
1 teaspoon baking powder	

Mix and sift flour, sugar, and baking powder 3 times. Add gradually to egg whites, stirring after each addition. Add vanilla. Turn into greased pan, lined with wax paper. Bake in moderate oven (350° F.) 35 to 45 minutes.

(2994)   BANANA SHORTCAKE

See shortcakes (No. 964).

(2995)   CURRANT SHORTCAKE

See shortcakes (No. 964). Top with meringue (No. 3205).

(2996)   GRAPEFRUIT SHORTCAKE

See shortcakes (No. 964).

(2997)   HUCKLEBERRY SHORTCAKE

See shortcakes (No. 964).

(2998)   ORANGE SHORTCAKE

See shortcakes (No. 964).

(2999)   STRAWBERRY SHORTCAKE

See shortcakes (No. 964).

(3000)   SNOW CAKE

¼ cup shortening	½ cup milk
1 cup sugar	1 teaspoon vanilla
1⅔ cups flour	¼ teaspoon almond extract
½ teaspoon baking powder	2 beaten egg whites

Cream shortening and sugar together. Mix and sift flour and baking powder and add alternately with milk to creamed mixture. Add vanilla and almond extract. Fold in egg whites. Turn into a narrow, greased cake pan. Bake in moderate oven (350° F.) 30 to 40 minutes.

(3001)   OLD FASHIONED SPICE CAKE

2 cups flour	¼ teaspoon allspice
2 teaspoons baking powder	½ cup raisins
1 teaspoon cinnamon	1 cup sugar
1 teaspoon salt	½ cup shortening
¼ teaspoon nutmeg	1 cup milk
¼ teaspoon cloves	1 egg

Sift flour. Measure and sift together with other dry ingredients. Add raisins. Cream sugar and shortening with 2 tablespoons milk. Add egg and mix well. Add sifted dry ingredients alternately with remaining milk. Bake 30 to 40 minutes in loaf pan at 350° F. Serve with whipped cream.

(3002) BLACK WALNUT OR BUTTERNUT SPICE CAKE

1 cup black walnuts or butternuts, broken	1 tablespoon baking powder
½ cup butter or other fat	½ teaspoon cinnamon
2 cups brown sugar	½ teaspoon nutmeg
3 eggs	½ teaspoon ground clove
3 cups sifted flour	¾ cup milk
½ teaspoon salt	

Place the broken nuts in boiling water for a few minutes and drain. Cream the fat and sugar together and add the well-beaten egg yolks. Sift together the dry ingredients. Add the dry ingredients alternately with the milk to the first mixture. Add the nuts. Fold in the well-beaten egg whites. Bake either in greased muffin tins (⅔ full) or in 3 8½-inch layer-cake pans in a moderate oven (350° F.) about 20 minutes, or until lightly browned.

(3003) PLAIN SPONGE CAKE

1 cup sifted flour	1 teaspoon lemon rind,
4 or 5 eggs	grated
1 cup sugar	½ teaspoon salt
2 tablespoons lemon juice	

Sift the flour three times. Beat the egg yolks until thick and lemon-colored. Gradually add half the sugar, beating thoroughly, and then the lemon juice and rind. Beat until thick. Beat the egg whites and salt until they start to peak but will still flow. Fold in the rest of the sugar, then the yolk mixture. Fold in the flour gently. Pour the batter as soon as it is mixed into an ungreased baking pan. For a large or medium-sized loaf a tube pan is best, because the center opening allows the mixture to heat evenly. Powdered sugar sifted over the top makes a more desirable crust. The oven should be ready for the cake as soon as it is mixed and in the pan. A large or medium-sized sponge cake should be baked in a slow oven (300° F.) 50 to 60 minutes. After baking, invert the cake to cool, but remove from the pan before it is entirely cold.

(3004) COCOA SPONGE CAKE

Substitute ¼ cup cocoa for an equal amount of flour in recipe for plain sponge cake (No. 3003) and substitute 1 tablespoon water for an equal amount of lemon juice. Sift cocoa with flour.

(3005) MOCHA CAKE

Put coffee filling (No. 3160) between 2 layers of baked sponge cake (No. 3003) and on top and sides. Sprinkle macaroon crumbs on sides of cake and use pastry tube to put cream on top.

(3006) ORANGE SPONGE CAKE

5 egg yolks	2 teaspoons baking powder
1¼ cups sugar	⅛ teaspoon salt
½ cup orange juice	1 tablespoon grated orange
½ cup water	peel
2 cups sifted cake flour	5 egg whites

Beat egg yolks, sugar, and orange juice for 10 minutes with a rotary hand or electric beater. Add water and beat 2 minutes. Add flour, sifted with baking powder and salt. Beat about 1 minute, or only until dry ingredients have been quickly and thoroughly blended into mixture. Fold in grated peel and egg whites, beaten stiff but not dry. Bake in 9-inch ungreased tube pan in moderate oven (350° F.) 70 minutes. Invert pan until cake is cold. Remove. Cut crosswise in 3 equal layers. Spread gold icing (No. 3182) between layers and on top of cake. Decorate with orange sections or sprinkle with coconut just before serving.

(3007) RICH CAKE

1 cup shortening	4 teaspoons baking powder
½ teaspoon vanilla	½ teaspoon salt
2 cups sugar	1 cup milk
4 well-beaten egg yolks	4 beaten egg whites
3 cups sifted flour	

Mix and bake same as foundation cake (No. 2926).

(3008) SUNSHINE CAKE

1 cup sifted flour	¾ teaspoon cream of tartar
6 whites and 3 yolks of eggs	1 teaspoon flavoring
1 to 1¼ cups sugar	½ teaspoon salt

Mix and bake as directed for plain sponge cake (No. 3003).

(3009) SWEDISH TEA CAKES

½ cup butter	1 egg white
¼ cup brown sugar	½ cup chopped walnuts
1 egg yolk, slightly beaten	Jelly
1 cup sifted flour	

Cream butter and blend in sugar. Add egg yolk, then flour. Roll dough into small balls 1 inch in diameter. Dip in egg white, then roll in chopped nuts. Place on greased cookie sheet and press centers down with finger. Bake 5 minutes in a slow oven (300° F.). Remove and press down centers again. Bake 15 minutes longer. Cool slightly. Fill centers with jelly. Yield: 12 cakes.

(3010)   TWO-EGG CAKE

½ cup shortening	1¾ cups sifted cake flour
1 cup granulated sugar	2 teaspoons baking powder
2 eggs, separated	½ cup milk
½ teaspoon salt	½ teaspoon vanilla

Cream shortening 1 minute at high speed. Add sugar gradually, beating swiftly. Add eggs, unbeaten, one at a time, and beat well. Add sifted dry ingredients alternately with the milk to which the vanilla has been added. Beat well. Pour batter into a loaf pan 8 x 8 x 2 inches, well greased and lightly floured, or lined with waxed paper. Cut through the batter to break any large air bubbles. Or if preferred, turn into two greased 8-inch layer cake pans or into 2 dozen greased cupcake pans. For a loaf cake, bake for 50-60 minutes at 350° F. A layer cake is baked for 25-30 minutes at 375° F. and cupcakes for 20-30 minutes at 375° F. After removal from oven, loosen edges, invert on rack, removing pan and turn right side up. Cool. Frost with fudge frosting (No. 3191) or any desired frosting.

(3011)   WEDDING CAKE

½ pound shortening	½ tablespoon ginger
¾ pound brown sugar	½ tablespoon clove
6 eggs	3 pounds raisins
½ cup molasses	1 pound currants
1 cup grape juice	½ pound lemon and orange
½ pound flour	peel, chopped
1½ tablespoons cinnamon	½ pound citron, chopped
1 tablespoon mace	

Cream shortening and sugar together. Add the beaten eggs, molasses, and grape juice and mix well. Mix and sift flour, cinnamon, mace, ginger, and clove. Add enough of the sifted flour mixture to the fruit to keep it from sticking together. Add remaining flour and fruit to the first mixture and beat thoroughly. Line bottom of a large round pan with greased paper and grease sides of pan. Pour mixture into it and bake in a very slow oven (225° F.) 3 to 4 hours. A small pan of water in the oven helps to keep the cake from burning during the long cooking. Ice and decorate with ornamental frosting (No. 3176).

(3012) CUPCAKES

½ cup shortening	2 teaspoons baking powder
1 cup sugar	½ teaspoon salt
3 eggs	½ cup milk
1¾ cups flour	1 teaspoon vanilla

Cream shortening, sugar, and eggs together until light and fluffy. Sift flour, baking powder, and salt and add alternately with milk to creamed mixture. Add vanilla. Beat thoroughly. Turn into greased cupcake pans. Bake in moderately hot oven (375° F.) 15 to 20 minutes. Yield: 18 cupcakes.

(3013) SOUR CREAM CUPCAKES

1 tablespoon shortening	1½ cups flour
1 cup sugar	1½ teaspoons salt
2 eggs	½ teaspoon cream of tartar
½ teaspoon soda	⅛ teaspoon mace
½ cup sour cream	

Cream shortening, sugar, and eggs together until light and fluffy. Dissolve soda in sour cream. Sift flour, salt, cream of tartar, and mace together and add alternately with cream to first mixture. Beat thoroughly. Bake in greased cupcake pans in hot oven (400° F.) 15 to 20 minutes. Yield: 18 cupcakes.

(3014) SPICED CUPCAKES

½ cup shortening	1 tablespoon hot water
1 cup sugar	2½ cups flour
2 eggs	½ teaspoon salt
⅓ cup seeded raisins, chopped	½ teaspoon clove
	½ teaspoon mace
⅓ cup currants, chopped	1½ teaspoons cinnamon
⅓ cup nuts, chopped	¾ cup sour milk
1 teaspoon soda	

Cream shortening, sugar, and egg yolks together. Add raisins, currants and nuts. Add soda, dissolved in hot water. Mix and sift flour, salt, and spices and add alternately with the sour milk to the first mixture. Fold in one stiffly beaten egg white. Turn into well-greased muffin pans and bake in a hot oven (375° F.) 15 to 20 minutes. Yield: 18 cupcakes.

(3015) FROZEN CUPCAKES

1 cup heavy cream	$\frac{1}{16}$ teaspoon salt
$\frac{1}{4}$ cup sugar	$\frac{1}{2}$ teaspoon vanilla
$2\frac{1}{2}$ tablespoons chopped nuts	1 tablespoon maraschino
$1\frac{1}{2}$ cups crumbled sponge	cherry juice
cake (No. 3003)	3 tablespoons chopped
crumbs	maraschino cherries

Whip the cream stiff and then fold in the rest of the ingredients, lightly but thoroughly. Fill tiny cups with the mixture and place in freezing tray of refrigerator. Garnish with maraschino cherries and candied ginger. Serves 4.

(3016) FILLED CUPCAKES

Make cupcakes (No. 3012). Cool. Cut in halves, crosswise. Remove portion of cake. Fill with whipped cream. Return to original shape and ice with boiled frosting (No. 3171) or creamy chocolate frosting (No. 3188).

(3017) FILLED CHOCOLATE CAKES

Mix batter for devil's food cake (No. 2923). Bake in greased cupcake pans in moderately hot oven (375° F.) 15 to 20 minutes. While hot remove a small square from top of each cake and insert marshmallow. Ice with boiled frosting (No. 3171).

(3018) PETITS FOURS

Bake a sponge (No. 3003) or pound cake (No. 2979) in a shallow pan so that the finished cake is not more than 1 inch high. When cool, slice in 1-inch strips. Then cut into various fancy shapes, half moons, circles, triangles, etc. Cut each small cake in half, crosswise. Remove a portion of insides and fill with whipped cream, custard (No. 2401), or any desired filling. Put together again and dip in any desired icing or icings. Where a large number are prepared it adds to the beauty of the table to color the tiny cakes in various brilliant colors. Garnish tops with nuts, candied fruits, maraschino cherries, etc., with an eye to beauty as well as taste. Various designs can also be made on tops of cakes with various-colored frostings. Place each cake in a paper cup.

(3019) CREAM PUFFS

½ cup shortening   4 eggs
1 cup boiling water or milk   1 teaspoon salt
1 cup flour

Add shortening to water and bring to a boil. Add flour all at once and stir vigorously until ball forms in center of pan. Cool slightly. Add unbeaten eggs, one at a time, beating after adding each egg. Mixture should be very stiff. Shape on oiled cookie sheet by dropping from spoon or using pastry bag and tube. Bake fifteen minutes in hot oven (450° F.). Reduce temperature to moderate (350° F.) and continue baking for thirty minutes or until done. If in doubt, remove one from oven to test. Cool. Fill with cream filling (No. 3151), ice cream, or whipped cream. Makes 2 dozen small puffs.

(3020) CHOCOLATE CREAM PUFFS

Fill baked cream puffs (No. 3019) with chocolate cream filling (No. 3158) and frost with chocolate icing (No. 3187).

(3021) COFFEE CREAM PUFFS

Fill baked cream puffs (No. 3019) with coffee filling (No. 3160) and frost with caramel icing (No. 3183).

(3022) VANILLA CREAM PUFFS

Fill baked cream puffs (No. 3019) with cream filling (No. 3151) and frost with boiled icing (No. 3171).

(3023) ECLAIRS

Prepare as for cream puffs (No. 3019). Press dough through pastry bag and tube onto greased shallow pan in strips 4 inches long and 1 inch wide. Bake same as cream puffs and fill as desired. Ice with any desired frosting.

(3024) CHOCOLATE ECLAIRS

Fill baked eclairs (No. 3023) with chocolate cream filling (No. 3158) and frost with chocolate icing (No. 3187).

(3025) COFFEE ECLAIRS

Fill baked eclairs (No. 3023) with coffee filling (No. 3160) and frost with caramel icing (No. 3183).

(3026) VANILLA ECLAIRS

Fill baked eclairs (No. 3023) with cream filling (No. 3151) and frost with boiled icing (No. 3171).

(3027) CAROLINES

Make like eclairs (No. 3023) about 2 inches long.

(3028) MARGUERITES

Follow recipe for boiled frosting (No. 3171). Add 1 cup of chopped nuts and 1 tablespoon melted shortening. Beat the mixture until it will hold its shape. Drop by teaspoons on soda or salted crackers. Bake in a moderate oven (350° F.) 15 minutes or until a delicate brown.

(3029) COCONUT BARS

Stale bread   Coconut
Sweetened condensed milk

Cut bread in strips 1 inch wide, 1 inch thick, and 3 inches long. Dip in condensed milk and roll in coconut. Place on greased baking sheet and bake in a hot oven (425° F.) until delicately browned.

(3030) DATE BARS

1 cup nuts, chopped   ¼ cup flour
1 cup stoned dates, chopped   1 tablespoon melted
1 cup powdered sugar   shortening
2 beaten eggs   ½ teaspoon salt
1 tablespoon lemon juice

Combine nuts, dates, sugar, and eggs. Mix well. Add other ingredients and mix thoroughly. Turn, ¼ inch thick, into greased, shallow pan. Bake in moderate oven (350° F.) 20 to 25 minutes. While hot, cut into strips or bars and roll in powdered sugar.

(3031)   SQUASH GEMS

⅔ cup mashed squash   1 teaspoon baking soda
   (No. 1876)   2 teaspoons cream of
1 cup milk   tartar
½ cup sugar   ¼ teaspoon salt
1 well-beaten egg   2 tablespoons melted
2 cups flour   butter

Combine squash and milk. Stir in sugar and egg. Mix and sift
flour, baking soda, cream of tartar, and salt. Add to first mixture. Add butter. Beat thoroughly. Turn into hot, greased cupcake pans. Bake in hot oven (400° F.) 20 to 30 minutes or
until done.

(3032)   SCOTCH FANS

1 cup shortening   1 teaspoon salt
¾ cup brown sugar   1 egg yolk
2¼ cups flour

Cream shortening and sugar together. Add flour and salt and
knead until ingredients hold together. Roll out on slightly
floured board to ¼-inch thickness. Cut in circles with large
fluted cookie cutter, then cut each circle in 3 fan-shaped pieces.
Brush with egg yolk diluted with 1 tablespoon water. Bake in a
slow oven (300° F.) 15 to 20 minutes. Yield: 36 fans.

(3033)   MARSHMALLOW GRAHAM CRACKER
                    DATE ROLL

18 graham crackers,   1 cup walnut meats, cut
   crumbed fine   fine
1 pound dates, pitted and   ¾ cup milk
   cut into small pieces   1 teaspoon vanilla
16 marshmallows, cut into
   eighths

Mix all ingredients in the order given. Then form into rolls
about 2 inches in diameter, wrap in waxed paper, and chill in
the refrigerator. Serve cut in cold slices with a very hot lemon
sauce (No. 3129). Serves 12.

(3034)   APRICOT SQUARES

½ cup butter	9 ripe apricots
1 cup sugar	1 teaspoon grated orange
2 eggs	rind
1 cup flour	3 teaspoons butter
1 teaspoon baking powder	3 teaspoons brandy

Cream butter and half the sugar. Add eggs and beat very light. Sift flour with baking powder and stir into creamed mixture. Pour into a buttered and floured, square cake pan. Press apricot halves, pitted but not peeled, into the batter, skin side down. Place in each half ⅓ teaspoon of butter and an equal amount of brandy. Sprinkle over all the remaining sugar and orange rind mixed. Bake in a moderate oven (350° F.) 30 minutes and cut in nine squares.

(3035)   BLUEBERRY SQUARES

2 cups flour	⅔ cup milk
4 teaspoons baking powder	1½ cups berries
¼ teaspoon salt	½ cup granulated sugar
5 tablespoons shortening,	½ teaspoon cinnamon
melted	

Mix flour, baking powder, and salt. Add shortening and milk. Mix lightly and pour at once into a buttered shallow pan. Press down until soft dough is about ⅔ inch thick. Quickly spread with other ingredients mixed together. Bake 12 minutes in a moderately hot oven (375° F.). Cut in squares and serve fresh with butter.

(3036)   BUTTERSCOTCH SQUARES

¼ cup butter	½ teaspoon salt
1½ cups brown sugar	⅓ cup heavy cream
2 eggs	½ cup chopped nuts
1½ cups flour	

Cream butter. Add ¾ cup sugar and cream thoroughly. Add 1 egg and beat well. Mix the flour and salt and add to the first mixture alternately with the cream. Spread ⅛ inch thick on buttered cookie sheets. Brush with the remaining egg, well beaten, and sprinkle with the remaining sugar mixed with the nuts. Bake in a moderate oven (350° F.) 15 to 20 minutes. Cut into 2-inch squares while still hot. Yield: 70 to 75 squares.

(3037)   CHOCOLATE ROBINS

½ cup flour
½ teaspoon salt
¼ cup shortening
½ cup chopped nuts

2 squares chocolate, melted
2 eggs
1 cup sugar
1 teaspoon vanilla

Sift flour once. Measure, add salt, and sift again. Place shortening in mixing bowl and cream until soft. Add warm melted chocolate and stir until thoroughly blended. Beat the whole eggs until very light and fluffy. Add sugar, a small amount at a time, beating after each addition. Add egg mixture to chocolate mixture and fold in flour, nuts, and vanilla. Bake in shallow oiled pan 25 to 30 minutes at 350° F. Cool and cut into squares.

(3038)   DATE SQUARES

1 cup hot water
1 cup chopped pitted dates
¼ cup shortening
¾ cup sugar
2 eggs

1¾ cups sifted flour
1 tablespoon cocoa
½ teaspoon cinnamon
¼ teaspoon cloves
1 tablespoon lemon juice

1 cup chopped nut meats

Pour hot water over dates and let stand. Cream shortening, adding sugar gradually and the eggs one at a time, beating well after each addition. Sift flour with cocoa and spices and add alternately with water drained from dates and lemon juice. Blend in dates and nuts. Put in well-greased square tin and bake in a moderate oven (350° F.) 30 to 40 minutes. Sprinkle with confectioners' sugar while warm and cut in squares when cool.

(3039)   BROWNIES

1 cup sugar
1½ tablespoons cocoa
¼ cup butter, melted
1 egg

1 teaspoon vanilla
½ cup flour
½ cup chopped walnuts

Cream sugar, cocoa, and butter together and add other ingredients, mixing well. Spread dough in shallow, greased and floured pan. Bake in a moderate oven (350° F.) 30 minutes. Turn out and cut into pieces while warm.

(3040) BANGOR BROWNIES

1 cup flour	1 egg
1 teaspoon baking powder	2 squares melted,
Few grains salt	unsweetened chocolate
¼ cup melted shortening	1 cup nuts, chopped
⅓ cup molasses	

Sift flour, baking powder, and salt together. Mix other ingredients in the order given and beat thoroughly. Spread the mixture evenly on a cake pan that has been lined with oiled paper. Bake about 15 minutes in a slow oven (325° F.). Remove the paper from the cake as soon as it is taken from the oven and cut into small squares or strips with a sharp knife.

(3041) CARAMEL BROWNIES

1 cup flour	2 cups brown sugar
2 teaspoons baking powder	2 eggs
1 teaspoon salt	2 teaspoons vanilla
⅝ cup shortening	1 cup chopped nuts

Sift flour. Measure and sift again with baking powder and salt. Melt shortening. Add sugar, eggs, vanilla, and sifted dry ingredients mixed with the nuts. Spread thinly in a well oiled and floured pan 10 by 15 inches. Bake in a moderate oven (350° F.) 30 minutes. Cool and cut.

(3042) LADYFINGERS

3 eggs, separated	⅛ teaspoon salt
⅔ cup powdered sugar	½ teaspoon vanilla
½ cup sifted cake flour	

Mix flour, salt, and ⅓ cup sugar and sift together three times. Beat egg whites until stiff and gradually beat in remaining sugar. Fold in vanilla and egg yolks beaten until thick and very light colored. Carefully fold in the flour-sugar mixture, sprinkling about three tablespoons at a time over surface. Press through pastry tube on ungreased paper-lined pans, making strips 4 x ¾ inches or bake in ladyfinger pans. Dust with additional powdered sugar and bake in a moderate oven (350° F.) 10 to 12 minutes. Batter may be dropped from teaspoon to make rounds if desired. Yield: 24 ladyfingers.

(3043) NAPOLEONS

Bake three layers of puff paste (No. 2703). Cool. Put cream filling (No. 3151) between layers and frost tops with boiled icing (No. 3171). Sprinkle with finely chopped nuts and cut in 3 x 2-inch rectangles.

(3044) FIG NEWTONS

½ cup shortening	½ teaspoon salt
1½ cups sugar	3 cups flour
1 well-beaten egg	3 teaspoons baking powder
½ cup milk	1 cup figs, chopped
1 teaspoon vanilla	

Cream butter and 1 cup sugar. Add egg and beat until light. Mix milk and vanilla. Sift salt, flour, and baking powder together and add alternately with milk to creamed mixture. Blend well. Roll out to ⅛-inch thickness on slightly floured board in a rectangle. Put figs in saucepan with remaining sugar and 1 cup boiling water. Boil 5 minutes. Cool. Spread cooked mixture over ½ of the dough. Cover with uncovered half of dough. Cut in oblongs. Bake in quick oven (400° F.) 12 to 15 minutes.

(3045) HERMITS

1 cup shortening	1 teaspoon allspice
1½ cups sugar	1 teaspoon cinnamon
3 eggs	1 teaspoon clove
½ teaspoon soda	1 teaspoon nutmeg
3 cups flour	1½ cups raisins
1½ teaspoons salt	½ cup chopped nuts

Cream shortening, sugar, and eggs together until light and fluffy. Dissolve soda in 2 teaspoons water and add. Sift flour, salt, allspice, cinnamon, clove, and nutmeg together and add to creamed mixture. Add raisins and nuts and mix well. Drop by teaspoons on greased baking sheet. Bake in moderate oven (350° F.) 15 to 20 minutes. Yield: 70 cookies.

(3046) BRAN BUTTERSCOTCH COOKIES

1½ cups shortening	1 cup shredded bran
2 cups brown sugar	3 cups flour
2 eggs	2 teaspoons baking powder

Cream shortening. Add sugar, well-beaten eggs, and bran. Mix well. Sift the flour with the baking powder and add to the first mixture. Shape into a roll and store in refrigerator. When needed, slice thin and bake on cookie sheet in hot oven (425° F.) about 12 minutes.

(3047) BROWN SUGAR COOKIES

7 cups sifted flour	4 cups brown sugar
1 tablespoon soda	1 cup melted butter
1 tablespoon cream of tartar	4 eggs

Mix ingredients well and form into a roll and let stand in refrigerator. Slice and bake at 400° F. 8 to 10 minutes, or until lightly browned. Yield: 100 cookies.

(3048) BUTTERSCOTCH COOKIES

3/4 cup shortening	1 teaspoon baking powder
3/4 cup brown sugar	1/4 teaspoon soda
1 teaspoon vanilla	1/2 teaspoon salt
4 cups sifted flour	2 well-beaten eggs

Cream shortening and sugar together. Add vanilla. Sift flour, baking powder, soda, and salt together and add alternately with eggs to creamed mixture, beating well after each addition. Shape into rolls 3 inches thick and 6 inches long. Wrap each in wax paper and chill several hours. Cut in slices and bake in moderately hot oven (375° F.) 8 minutes. Yield: 36 cookies.

(3049) CHOCOLATE NUT COOKIES

2 ounces chocolate, melted	1/2 teaspoon soda
1/2 cup shortening	1 teaspoon baking powder
1 cup brown sugar	1/2 cup milk
1 egg	1 teaspoon vanilla
1 1/2 cups flour	1 cup nut meats, chopped
1/4 teaspoon salt	

Add melted chocolate to creamed shortening, sugar, and egg mixture. Add the sifted dry ingredients alternately with the milk and the vanilla and the nut meats last. Drop on cookie sheet. Bake 15 to 20 minutes at 400° F. Yield: 24 cookies.

(3050)   CHOCOLATE WALNUT DOLLARS

½ cup butter	1 teaspoon baking powder
1 cup sugar	½ teaspoon cinnamon
1 egg	½ cup chopped walnuts
2 tablespoons milk	2 ounces melted unsweet-
1 teaspoon vanilla	ened chocolate
2½ cups flour	

Cream butter, sugar, and slightly beaten egg. Add vanilla. Add dry ingredients, which have been sifted together, alternately with milk. Add chocolate and nut meats. Form into roll. Chill and slice thinly. Bake in a moderate oven (350° F.) about 10 minutes. Yield: 40 cookies.

(3051)   COCOA DATE DROP COOKIES

½ cup shortening	2 tablespoons cocoa
¾ cup sugar	½ cup milk
1 egg	1 teaspoon vanilla
2 cups sifted flour	¾ cup chopped dates

Cream shortening, adding sugar gradually. Add egg and beat well. Add flour sifted with cocoa, alternately with milk to which the flavoring has been added. Stir in dates sprinkled with flour. Drop by teaspoonfuls on greased baking sheet and bake in moderate oven (350° F.) 12 to 15 minutes. Yield: 40 cookies.

(3052)   COCONUT ORANGE JUMBLES

¾ cup shortening	¼ teaspoon salt
1¼ cups sugar	½ teaspoon baking soda
2 eggs	¾ cup orange juice
1 cup shredded coconut	3 tablespoons grated
2½ cups sifted flour	orange peel

Cream shortening and sugar together. Beat in eggs. Beat in coconut. Sift flour, salt, and baking soda together and add alternately with orange juice to creamed mixture. Beat until smooth while adding. Drop by teaspoons on ungreased baking sheet. Sprinkle with additional coconut and orange peel. Bake in hot oven (425° F.) 10 to 12 minutes. Yield: 48 cookies.

(3053)   CORN FLAKE COOKIES

1 cup shortening	1 cup raisins
1½ cups sugar	2 cups flour
2 well-beaten eggs	2 teaspoons baking soda
¼ cup milk	2 cups corn flakes

Cream shortening and sugar. Add eggs and beat until light. Add milk and raisins. Sift flour with baking soda and add, blending well. Add corn flakes. Roll to ¼-inch thickness on slightly floured board. Cut with a cookie cutter. Place on baking sheet and bake in moderate oven (350° F.) 12 to 15 minutes. **Yield: 48 cookies.**

(3054)   CRISP COOKIES

1 cup shortening	4 cups sifted flour
2 teaspoons vanilla	4 teaspoons baking powder
2 cups sugar	½ teaspoon salt
2 eggs, separated	¼ cup milk

Mix ingredients as for drop cookies (No. 3056). Form dough into a roll. Wrap in wax paper and chill. Cut off thin slices and bake in moderately hot oven (375° F.) 10 to 12 minutes. Yield: 72 cookies.

(3055)   ROLLED COOKIES

Make dough as for crisp cookies (No. 3054). Roll on lightly floured board to ¼-inch thickness. Cut into any desired shape and bake on greased baking sheet in moderately hot oven (375° F.) 10 to 12 minutes. Yield: 72 cookies.

(3056)   DROP COOKIES

¾ cup shortening	4 cups sifted flour
3 teaspoons vanilla	4 teaspoons baking powder
1½ cups sugar	½ teaspoon salt
2 eggs, separated	¾ cup milk

Cream shortening, vanilla, and sugar together until light and fluffy. Continue creaming while adding well-beaten eggs slowly. Sift flour, baking powder, and salt together and add alternately with milk to creamed mixture. Drop small portions of mixture on greased baking sheet and bake in moderately hot oven (400° F.) 12 to 15 minutes. Yield: 72 cookies.

(3057) DROP FRUITETTES

2 cups flour
2 teaspoons baking powder
½ teaspoon salt
½ cup butter
½ cup sugar
½ teaspoon vanilla

¼ teaspoon lemon extract
1 egg
⅓ cup sliced candied citron
½ cup chopped nuts
1-pound can fruit cocktail

Sift flour. Measure. Sift again with baking powder and salt. Cream butter, adding sugar gradually, then flavoring and slightly beaten egg. Add flour and ½ cup of the sirup from the fruit cocktail. Carefully mix in the citron, nuts, and fruit cocktail that has been thoroughly drained. Drop from a teaspoon on a buttered baking sheet. Bake in a moderately hot oven (400° F.) about 15 minutes, or until brown. Yield: 36 cookies.

(3058) GINGERSNAPS

1 cup sugar
1 cup molasses
1 cup butter
1 egg
1 teaspoon cinnamon

2 teaspoons ginger
2 teaspoons soda
1 tablespoon cider vinegar
1 teaspoon vanilla
Flour to make stiff dough

Combine sugar, molasses, butter, egg, cinnamon, ginger, and soda. Mix well. Add vinegar, vanilla, and enough flour to make a stiff dough. Roll very thin. Cut with cookie cutter. Bake in moderate oven (325° F.) 10 to 12 minutes. Yield: 48 gingersnaps.

(3059) GINGER COOKIES

½ cup shortening
½ cup molasses
½ cup sugar
½ teaspoon nutmeg
½ teaspoon cinnamon
½ teaspoon ginger

1 beaten egg
½ cup chopped nuts
2½ cups flour
½ teaspoon baking powder
⅔ teaspoon salt

Cream shortening, molasses, sugar, nutmeg, cinnamon, and ginger together. Mix well and bring slowly to boiling point. Cool. Add egg and nuts, combining well. Sift flour, baking powder, and salt together and add to first mixture. Mix thoroughly. Shape into a roll about 2½ inches in diameter. Roll in wax paper and store in refrigerator. Slice and bake in moderately hot oven (375° F.) 12 minutes. Yield: 48 cookies.

(3060) REFRIGERATOR GINGER COOKIES

1 cup shortening	5½ cups flour
1 cup sugar	½ teaspoon soda
1 cup molasses	2 teaspoons baking powder
1 egg	1 tablespoon ginger

Blend shortening, sugar, and molasses. Add egg and mix well. Sift flour once. Measure and sift with other dry ingredients. Add to first mixture. Chill. Form into rolls. Wrap in wax paper and allow to stand 24 hours in refrigerator. Slice ⅛ inch thick and bake 10 to 12 minutes at 400° F. Yield: 80 cookies.

(3061) HAZELNUT COOKIES

¼ pound sweet chocolate	2 egg whites
¼ pound finely chopped hazelnuts	¼ teaspoon cinnamon
	Few grains ground clove
¼ pound finely chopped almonds	2 tablespoons melted shortening
⅔ cup powdered sugar	

Melt chocolate over hot water. Add chopped nuts and sugar and mix well. Add stiffly beaten egg whites, spices, and shortening. Mix well. Chill. Roll out thin, a small quantity at a time, on slightly floured board. Cut with cookie cutter. Place on greased pans and bake in moderate oven (325° F.) 12 to 15 minutes. Yield: 4 dozen cookies.

(3062) LACE WAFERS

2 tablespoons shortening	2½ cups rolled oats
1 cup sugar	2½ teaspoons baking powder
2 eggs	1 teaspoon vanilla
½ teaspoon salt	¼ teaspoon almond extract
½ teaspoon nutmeg	

Cream shortening, sugar, and eggs together until light and fluffy. Combine salt, nutmeg, rolled oats, and baking powder and add to creamed mixture. Mix thoroughly. Add vanilla and extract. Drop by teaspoons on greased baking pan. Bake in moderate oven (350° F.) 12 to 15 minutes. Yield: 60 cookies.

(3063)   ALMOND MACAROONS

3 egg whites	10 drops almond extract
1 cup sugar	1 tablespoon melted
½ pound finely chopped	shortening
almonds	

Beat egg whites. Add sugar gradually, beating constantly. Add almonds, flavoring, and shortening. Mix well. Drop by teaspoons on wet paper which has been placed on inverted pan or bread board. Bake in slow oven (275° F.) 30 to 40 minutes. Yield: 48 macaroons.

(3064)   CANADIAN MACAROONS

2 egg whites	½ cup walnut meats,
½ cup granulated sugar	chopped
½ cup brown sugar	1 cup shredded coconut
1 tablespoon flour	1 teaspoon vanilla
2 cups corn flakes	

Beat egg whites until very stiff. Add sugar, flour, and other ingredients. Mix well and drop by teaspoonfuls on buttered cookie sheet. Bake 20 minutes in a moderate oven (350° F.). Yield: 60 macaroons.

(3065)   OATMEAL MACAROONS

1 cup sugar	¾ teaspoon salt
1 tablespoon melted	2½ cups rolled oats
shortening	2 teaspoons baking powder
2 eggs	1 teaspoon vanilla extract

Mix sugar with shortening. Add egg yolks, salt, and rolled oats. Add baking powder, beaten egg whites, and vanilla. Mix thoroughly. Drop on greased tins about ½ teaspoon to each macaroon, allowing space for spreading. Bake about 10 minutes in a moderate oven (350° F.). Yield: 60 macaroons.

(3066)   MOLASSES CRISPS

¼ cup shortening	1 cup flour
½ cup sugar	¾ teaspoon salt
¾ cup molasses	

Melt shortening. Add sugar and molasses and bring to boiling point. Cool slightly. Add flour and salt. Drop by teaspoons on greased baking sheet. Bake in moderate oven (350° F.) 12 to 15 minutes. Turn around finger to form a roll while warm. Yield: 36 cookies.

(3067) REFRIGERATOR NUT COOKIES

1 cup nuts, finely chopped	1 teaspoon vanilla
½ cup butter or other fat	2 cups sifted flour
1 cup brown sugar	2 teaspoons baking powder
1 egg, beaten	½ teaspoon salt

Cream the fat and sugar and add the egg and the vanilla. Sift the dry ingredients together, add the nuts, and combine with the first mixture. Stir until blended. Chill and then form into a roll of the desired size. Roll in wax paper and chill thoroughly. When solid, cut crosswise in thin slices with a sharp knife. Bake for about 10 to 15 minutes, or until lightly browned, in a moderate oven (350°-375° F.). Allow the cookies to become crisp on the baking sheet. If desired, add two squares of melted chocolate with the beaten egg and vanilla to the creamed fat and sugar. Replace the cup of brown sugar with a scant cup of white sugar. Yield: 48 cookies.

(3068) OATMEAL COOKIES

1½ cups flour	1 egg, well beaten
2 teaspoons baking powder	½ cup milk
½ teaspoon salt	1½ cups uncooked oatmeal
½ cup shortening	¾ cup raisins
1 cup sugar	1½ tbs. grated orange rind

Sift together flour, baking powder and salt; cream shortening and sugar until light. Combine egg and milk; add alternately with oatmeal. Stir in raisins, orange rind, and dry ingredients. Drop from teaspoon onto greased cookie sheets; bake in moderate oven (375° F.) about 12 minutes. Yield: 48 cookies.

(3069) OATMEAL JELLY COOKIES

Make a slight depression in center of oatmeal cookies (No. 3068) before baking and fill with currant jelly.

(3070) PEANUT DROP COOKIES

2 cups brown sugar
1 cup shortening
½ teaspoon salt
2 eggs
1 teaspoon vanilla
2 cups flour

½ teaspoon soda
1 teaspoon baking powder
1 cup corn flakes
2 cups rolled oats
1½ cup peanuts with skins
    left on

Cream the sugar with the shortening and salt. Add the eggs and vanilla and beat until creamy. Sift the flour, soda, and baking powder together and add to first mixture. Add other ingredients. Drop by small spoonfuls on cookie sheet and bake in a moderately hot oven (400° F.) 12 to 15 minutes. Yield: 72 cookies.

(3071) PEANUT BUTTER COOKIES

2 cups sifted flour
1½ teaspoons baking powder
½ teaspoon salt
2 tablespoons shortening
½ cup peanut butter

1 cup sugar
1 egg
1 teaspoon vanilla
⅓ cup milk
½ cup peanuts, chopped

Sift flour, baking powder, and salt together. Cream shortening and peanut butter together. Beat in other ingredients one at a time. Stir in flour mixture, blending well. Chill. Roll out to ¼-inch thickness on slightly floured board. Cut with cookie cutter. Place on ungreased baking sheet. Sprinkle with peanuts. Bake in moderate oven (350° F.) 12 to 15 minutes. Yield: 50 cookies.

(3072) PEASANT COOKIES

1 cup butter
1 cup sugar
1 tablespoon molasses

¾ cup chopped nuts
2¾ cups sifted flour
1 teaspoon baking soda

Cream butter. Blend in sugar and molasses. Add nuts, then sifted dry ingredients. Form dough into rolls and chill thoroughly. Cut into thin slices. Bake on greased cookie sheet in moderate oven (350° F.) about 12 to 15 minutes. Yield: 60 cookies.

(3073)   PECAN WAFERS

½ cup shortening	½ cup chopped pecans
1 cup brown sugar	½ teaspoon salt
2 eggs	½ teaspoon maple extract
4 tablespoons flour	

Cream shortening and sugar. Add eggs, one at a time, beating well after each is added. Stir in flour and blend well. Add nuts, salt, and extract. Drop by teaspoons, 5 inches apart, on greased baking sheet. Spread out very thin with spoon. Bake in slow oven (300° F.) 10 to 12 minutes. If desired, these may be turned around finger to form rolls while warm. Yield: 36 wafers.

(3074)   SOUR CREAM COOKIES

½ cup shortening	½ teaspoon cinnamon
1 cup sugar	¼ teaspoon salt
1 beaten egg	½ cup sour cream
2 cups flour	½ cup raisins or chopped
½ teaspoon baking soda	nuts, or a combination
½ teaspoon nutmeg	of both

Cream shortening and sugar. Add egg and continue creaming until light. Sift flour, baking soda, nutmeg, cinnamon, and salt together and add alternately with cream to creamed mixture. Stir in raisins or nuts. Drop by teaspoons on greased baking sheets. Bake in moderately hot oven (375° F.) 10 to 12 minutes. Yield: 36 cookies.

(3075)   SUGAR COOKIES

⅔ cup shortening	1½ teaspoons salt
1¼ cups sugar	2 teaspoons baking powder
2 eggs	Grated rind 1 orange
3 cups flour	1 tablespoon orange juice

Cream shortening, sugar, and eggs together until light and foamy. Sift flour, salt, and baking powder together and add to first mixture. Add orange rind and juice. Mix until smooth. Chill. Roll to ¼-inch thickness, on slightly floured board. Cut with cookie cutter. Sprinkle with sugar and bake in moderate oven (350° F.) 12 to 15 minutes. Yield: 60 cookies.

(3076)   ALMOND COOKIES

Substitute 1 teaspoon vanilla for orange rind and juice in recipe for sugar cookies (No. 3075). After cookies have been cut, brush with egg and dip in chopped almonds. Cook same as sugar cookies.

(3077)   BUTTER COOKIES

Use butter as shortening in recipe for sugar cookies (No. 3075) and substitute 1 teaspoon vanilla for orange rind and juice.

(3078)   CARAWAY SEED COOKIES

Add 2 tablespoons caraway seeds to recipe for sugar cookies (No. 3075).

(3079)   CHOCOLATE COOKIES

Add ½ cup cocoa, mixed with 3 tablespoons hot water or coffee (No. 301), to recipe for sugar cookies (No. 3075) when eggs are added and substitute 1 teaspoon vanilla for orange juice and rind.

(3080)   CINNAMON COOKIES

Add 1 teaspoon powdered cinnamon and eliminate orange rind and juice in recipe for sugar cookies (No. 3075).

(3081)   COCONUT COOKIES

Add 1 cup shredded coconut to recipe for sugar cookies (No. 3075).

(3082)   FIG COOKIES

Add ⅔ cup chopped figs to recipe for sugar cookies (No. 3075) and substitute brown sugar for granulated sugar and 1 teaspoon vanilla for orange rind and juice.

(3083)   HALLOWE'EN COOKIES

Cut sugar cookies (No. 3075) into half moons, witches, elves, pumpkins, etc. Ice cookies with orange icing (No. 3200) and decorate with tiny black candies.

(3084)   LEMON COOKIES

Substitute lemon rind and juice for orange rind and juice in recipe for sugar cookies (No. 3075).

(3085)   MAPLE SUGAR COOKIES

Substitute ¾ cup maple sugar for an equal amount of granulated sugar and eliminate orange rind and juice in recipe for sugar cookies (No. 3075).

(3086)   NUT COOKIES

Prepare recipe for sugar cookies (No. 3075). Before baking, brush cookies with egg white and sprinkle with chopped nuts and sugar.

(3087)   ORANGE COOKIES

Use the grated rind of 2 oranges in recipe for sugar cookies (No. 3075).

(3088)   RAISIN COOKIES

Add ⅔ cup raisins to recipe for sugar cookies (No. 3075).

(3089)   SAND TARTS

Substitute 1 teaspoon vanilla for orange juice and rind in recipe for sugar cookies (No. 3075). Cut into diamonds or squares, brush with white of egg, sprinkle with sugar and cinnamon, and place an almond in the center of each cookie.

(3090)   SPICE COOKIES

Sift ⅛ teaspoon clove, ¼ teaspoon nutmeg, and ½ teaspoon cinnamon with flour in recipe for sugar cookies (No. 3075) and substitute 1 teaspoon vanilla for orange juice and rind.

(3091)   VANILLA COOKIES

Substitute 1½ teaspoons vanilla for orange rind and juice in recipe for sugar cookies (No. 3075).

(3092)   FILLED COOKIES

Roll out sugar cookie dough (No. 3075) ⅛ inch thick. Cut into circles. Put 1 teaspoon jam in center of ½ the circles. Top with other circles, pressing edges firmly together. Bake same as sugar cookies. Another good filling is made by combining 1 cup chopped raisins, figs, or dates with 1 cup sugar and ¼ cup water and boiling until fruit is tender.

(3093)   YORK COOKIES

½ cup butter	½ teaspoon soda
½ cup sugar	¼ teaspoon nutmeg
1 cup flour	1 tablespoon lemon or
1 egg	orange juice
1 tablespoon milk	

Mix the butter and sugar to a cream and add flour gradually. Beat up an egg with the milk and mix all together. Add the soda, nutmeg, and lemon or orange juice. Spread very thin on a baking sheet. Sprinkle with sugar and bake in a moderately hot oven (375° F.) until a golden brown. Cut in squares.

(3094)   CHOCOLATE CHIP COOKIES

1 8-ounce package semi-sweet chocolate	1 cup flour
½ cup shortening	½ teaspoon salt
¼ cup brown sugar	½ teaspoon soda
½ cup white sugar	½ cup broken nut meats
1 well-beaten egg	1 teaspoon vanilla

Cut each square of chocolate into 4 pieces. Cream shortening. Add sugars gradually while creaming until light and fluffy. Add egg and mix well. Sift flour once. Measure. Sift again with salt and soda. Combine mixtures thoroughly. Add chocolate, nut meats, and vanilla. Drop from teaspoon on greased baking sheet. Bake in moderate oven (375° F.) 10 to 12 minutes. Yield: 50 cookies.

Frostings

SAUCES, ICINGS, FILLINGS, MERINGUES

SAUCES! Icings! Frostings! Fillings! Meringues! These are the delightful finishing touches that raise dishes above the average. They turn old familiar recipes into something brand new and their wide range of coloring, texture, and flavorings enable the clever homemaker to surprise her family and friends at every meal. *Frostings* are made of sugar and liquid heated to a desired temperature, combined with egg white and stirred to the desired consistency. *Icings* are sugar mixtures which are not cooked.

(3101)   **CREAM SAUCE**

1 cup sugar	1 cup cream
1 egg white	1 teaspoon vanilla
3 egg yolks	

Combine ingredients and beat until very light. Heat over hot water, beating until foamy. Remove from heat. Add vanilla. Stir well.

(3102)   **CREAMY SAUCE**

¼ cup butter	1 well-beaten egg
2 cups confectioners' sugar	1 teaspoon vanilla
½ cup cream	

Cream butter and sugar. Add other ingredients and beat until well blended and light.

(3103)   CUSTARD SAUCE

1 cup milk
2 beaten egg yolks
2 tablespoons sugar

1/8 teaspoon salt
1/4 teaspoon vanilla

Scald milk over hot water. Beat yolks, sugar, and salt together and pour milk over them. Cook over hot water, stirring constantly, until mixture coats the spoon. Chill. Add vanilla.

(3104)   FOAMY SAUCE

1/4 cup sugar
2 tablespoons flour
1/2 teaspoon salt
1 cup milk
1 egg yolk

2 tablespoons sherry
   flavoring
Few grains nutmeg
2 egg whites

Mix sugar, flour, and salt together. Add milk and beaten egg yolk and cook over hot water until thick. Add flavoring and nutmeg. Fold in the stiffly beaten egg whites.

(3105)   HARD SAUCE

1 cup confectioners' sugar
1/2 cup butter

1/2 teaspoon vanilla
1/8 teaspoon salt

Combine ingredients and cream well. Press into mold. When firm unmold and serve.

(3106)   WHIPPED CREAM SAUCE

1 egg white
3/4 cup powdered sugar
1 egg yolk

3/4 cup heavy cream
1 teaspoon vanilla
Few grains salt

Beat egg white until stiff and add sugar gradually, while beating constantly. Add egg yolk, beaten until thick and lemon-colored, cream, beaten until stiff, flavoring, and salt.

(3107)   CHOCOLATE SAUCE

1 1/4 cups milk
1 cup powdered sugar
1/2 tablespoon butter or other
   fat

2 ounces unsweetened
   chocolate
1 teaspoon vanilla
1/8 teaspoon salt

Cook milk, chocolate, and fat over a slow fire and stir until chocolate melts and the mixture is thick. Add sugar and cook until it thickens again, stirring constantly. Add vanilla and salt. Mix well.

(3108)   HOT FUDGE SAUCE

  1 ounce chocolate   ⅓ cup hot water or hot
  2 tablespoons butter   strong coffee
 1½ cups sugar   (No. 301)
  1/16 teaspoon salt   ⅓ cup thin cream
      1 teaspoon vanilla

Bring water in bottom of double boiler to a boil. Melt chocolate in top of double boiler. Add butter, sugar, salt, and hot water or coffee. Heat until all sugar crystals are dissolved. Cook about ten minutes. Remove from heat, add cream and vanilla. Beat well, and serve hot.

(3109)   CARAMEL SAUCE

Butter the inside of a granite saucepan. Add 2 ounces unsweetened chocolate and melt over hot water. Add 2 cups light brown sugar and mix well. Add 1 ounce butter and ½ cup rich milk. Cook until the mixture forms a soft ball in cold water, then take from fire, and flavor with vanilla.

(3110)   CARAMEL NUT SAUCE

Add ½ cup chopped nut meats to recipe for caramel sauce (No. 3109) after cooking.

(3111)   BUTTERSCOTCH AND CORN SIRUP
                       SAUCE

  ½ cup corn sirup   ¼ cup butter
 1½ cups brown sugar

Combine ingredients with 1 cup boiling water. Cook slowly to the soft ball stage (238° F.). Cool.

(3112)   CREAMY CHOCOLATE SAUCE

1 ounce unsweetened
   chocolate
1 cup sugar
Few grains salt

½ to ¾ cup light cream
Cinnamon if desired
1 teaspoon vanilla

Cut chocolate into small pieces. Add sugar, 1 cup water, and salt and let boil 5 minutes. Remove from fire, cool, and add flavoring and cream.

(3113)   APRICOT SAUCE

1 cup canned mashed
   apricots, drained
Sugar

1 cup heavy cream,
   whipped

Rub apricots through a sieve and combine with cream. Mix well, sweetening with sugar as desired.

(3114)   BERRY-JELLY SAUCE

1 cup berry juice
½ cup red currant jelly

½ cup sugar
1 teaspoon cornstarch

Combine juice, jelly, and sugar. Bring to boiling point. Add cornstarch, mixed to a smooth paste with 1 tablespoon cold water. Boil 1 minute. Serve hot or cold.

(3115)   BRAZIL CREAM SAUCE

2 egg yolks
1 cup confectioner's sugar
½ cup ground Brazil nuts

1 tablespoon cherry or
1 teaspoon vanilla
   extract

Beat egg yolks and stir in the sifted sugar, nuts, and flavoring.

(3116)   CHERRY SAUCE

1 tablespoon cornstarch
Cold water
Lemon juice

2 cups canned cherries and
   juice
A little red coloring

Mix cornstarch with a little cold water, bringing it to a pour-ing consistency. Add cherries and juice and red coloring. Cook, stirring constantly. When thickened and smooth, put pan over hot water and cook 5 to 10 minutes. Add a dash of lemon juice just before serving.

(3117) HOT CHERRY GLAZE

2 tablespoons cornstarch	1½ cups hot cherry juice
½ cup sugar	2 tablespoons lemon juice
¼ teaspoon salt	¼ teaspoon almond extract

Mix cornstarch, sugar, and salt. Pour the hot fruit juice over the dry ingredients, stirring constantly. Cook until thick and clear. Remove from fire and add the lemon juice and flavoring. A drop or two of red coloring may be added, if desired.

(3118) CIDER SAUCE

1 teaspoon cornstarch	1 tablespoon melted butter
⅔ cup sugar	2 well-beaten egg yolks
½ cup cider	

Blend cornstarch smooth in 1 tablespoon cold water. Boil it 10 minutes with 1 cup water and sugar, stirring until sugar dissolves. Remove from heat. Warm cider and add to mixture with butter and yolks. Mix well.

(3119) COCONUT SAUCE

Add 1 cup shredded coconut and 2 beaten egg whites to recipe for hard sauce (No. 3105).

(3120) CHOCOLATE MINT SAUCE

2 cups sugar	¾ cup milk
Dash of salt	1 tablespoon butter
2 ounces unsweetened chocolate	¼ cup crushed peppermint candy

Combine sugar, salt, chocolate, milk, and butter, and heat slowly, stirring until sugar is dissolved and chocolate melted. Boil, covered, 2 minutes; then boil, uncovered, until a small amount forms a very soft ball when dropped into cold water (230° F.). Remove from heat. Add crushed mints and beat slightly. Serve hot or warm. If it seems too thick, dilute with a small amount of cream. Yield: 2 cups sauce.

(3121)   COCOA SAUCE

½ cup cocoa   1 cup sugar
1 cup water   1 tablespoon butter
¼ teaspoon salt   1 teaspoon vanilla

Cook cocoa and water together until it is smooth and thick. Add sugar and salt and cook a few minutes longer. Add butter and vanilla.

(3122)   COCONUT SAUCE

Add ½ cup shredded coconut to recipe for custard sauce (No. 3103).

(3123)   COFFEE SAUCE

Substitute ½ cup strong coffee (No. 301) for lemon juice and peel in recipe for lemon sauce (No. 3129) and omit nutmeg.

(3124)   CRIMSON SAUCE

½ cup red currant jelly   4 maraschino cherries
2 teaspoons lemon juice   finely cut
Dash of salt   1 teaspoon cherry juice

Combine the jelly, 2 tablespoons hot water, lemon juice, and salt. Add the cherries and juice.

(3125)   FLUFFY CUSTARD SAUCE

Add 1 stiffly beaten egg white to recipe for custard sauce (No. 3103) just before removing from heat.

(3126)   EGG SAUCE

2 eggs, beaten light   ½ teaspoon vanilla
⅔ cup sugar

Beat the sugar thoroughly into the eggs and then add vanilla.

(3127)   GOURMET SAUCE

1 cup berry-jelly sauce   ½ cup whipped cream
   (No. 3114)   ¼ cup milk
1 egg yolk

Mix ingredients thoroughly.

(3128)   CREAMY HARD SAUCE

Add ½ cup heavy cream, whipped, to recipe for hard sauce
(No. 3105).

(3129)   LEMON SAUCE

1 tablespoon cornstarch   2 tablespoons lemon juice
½ cup sugar   1 cup boiling water
1 teaspoon grated lemon   2 tablespoons butter
   peel   Nutmeg—Salt

Combine cornstarch, sugar, lemon peel, lemon juice. Add
water slowly, stirring constantly. Boil 5 minutes. Remove from
heat. Add butter. Season to taste with nutmeg and salt. Serves 4.

(3130)   LEMON HARD SAUCE

⅓ cup butter   3 tablespoons lemon juice
2¼ cups powdered sugar   1 stiffly beaten egg white
1 egg yolk

Cream butter, sugar, egg yolk, and lemon juice together until
light and foamy. Fold in egg white.

(3131)   LEMON DATE SAUCE

Add ⅓ cup chopped dates to recipe for lemon sauce (No.
3129).

(3132)   LEMON MARSHMALLOW SAUCE

Add ⅓ cup marshmallows, cut in tiny pieces, to recipe for
lemon sauce (No. 3129).

(3133)   LEMON RAISIN SAUCE

Add ⅓ cup chopped raisins to recipe for lemon sauce (No. 3129).

(3134)   MAPLE SUGAR SAUCE

¼ pound maple sugar	½ cup heavy cream
2 well-beaten egg whites	1 teaspoon lemon juice

Boil maple sugar with ½ cup water until sirup will spin a 10-inch thread when dropped from a spoon. Pour sirup over egg whites slowly, beating vigorously. Add cream and lemon juice. Mix well.

(3135)   GOLDEN MARSHMALLOW SAUCE

1 cup brown sugar	8 marshmallows
1¼ cups boiling water	1 teaspoon vanilla extract

Combine sugar and water and simmer gently for 15 minutes. While hot, add the marshmallows and stir until creamy and smooth. Cool and add vanilla.

(3136)   HOT MARSHMALLOW SAUCE

1 cup sugar	1 tablespoon sherry
½ cup water	flavoring
¼ pound marshmallows	½ teaspoon vanilla

Put sugar and water in a saucepan. Place over the fire and stir until sugar is dissolved. Cook without stirring until the sugar will spin a thread when dropped from the tip of a spoon (238° F.). Add marshmallows which have been softened in the oven, but not browned. Beat until sauce is smooth. Add flavoring. Keep hot over water. If too thick, thin with a few drops of boiling water.

(3137)   MOCHA SAUCE

2 egg yolks	½ cup strong coffee
¼ cup sugar	(No. 301)
⅛ teaspoon salt	1 cup whipped cream

Beat yolks, sugar, and salt together. Add coffee slowly while beating. Cook over hot water, stirring constantly, until thickened. Strain. Cool. Fold in cream.

(3138)   NUTMEG SAUCE

1 cup sugar
1 tablespoon flour
Few grains salt

1 tablespoon butter
1 teaspoon nutmeg

Mix the sugar, flour, and salt. Add 2 cups boiling water and stir. Then add the butter and cook 5 minutes. Add the nutmeg.

(3139)   ORANGE SAUCE

1 tablespoon cornstarch
½ cup sugar
1 teaspoon grated orange
   peel

1 cup orange juice
1 tablespoon lemon juice
2 tablespoons butter

Mix cornstarch, sugar, peel, and orange juice. Boil 5 minutes. Remove from fire. Add lemon juice and butter. Serve hot.

(3140)   ORANGE CREAM SAUCE

2 egg yolks
½ cup sugar

1 orange (juice and grated
   rind)
1 cup whipping cream

Beat egg yolks until very thick. Add sugar and the juice and grated rind of 1 orange. Cook slowly until thick, stirring constantly. Chill, and fold in cream which has been beaten until thick. Serve cold, or partially frozen, on puddings or on any plain cake.

(3141)   ORANGE PINEAPPLE SAUCE

1 orange, juice and rind
⅔ cup sugar
½ cup pineapple juice

3 egg yolks, well beaten
1 cup cream

Bring pineapple juice, sugar, and juice and rind of orange to boiling point and add to yolks. Cook in double boiler until thick. Cool and add cream which has been whipped.

(3142) PEACH SAUCE

Substitute canned peaches for apricots in recipe for apricot sauce (No. 3113).

(3143) STEAMED PUDDING SAUCE

½ cup butter	4 tablespoons cream
1 cup brown sugar	½ cup dates, finely chopped

Cream butter well then add brown sugar and cream together. Add dates.

(3144) RASPBERRY SAUCE

½ cup sugar	2 teaspoons cornstarch
1 cup raspberry jelly	

Combine sugar and ½ cup water. Bring to a boil, stirring until sugar is dissolved. Add jelly and cornstarch, blended to a smooth paste with 2 tablespoons cold water. Bring again to a boil. Remove from heat. Strain. Serve hot or cold.

(3145) RUM SAUCE

1 egg yolk	1 egg white, stiffly beaten
2 tablespoons rum	½ cup cream, whipped
2 tablespoons confectioners' sugar	Grated rind 1 lemon

Beat the egg yolk with the rum and sugar. Add the stiffly beaten egg white and whipped cream, and lastly the grated lemon rind.

(3146) SEA FOAM SAUCE

2 tablespoons butter	1 egg yolk
½ cup sugar	1 stiffly beaten egg white
2 tablespoons flour	1 teaspoon vanilla

Cream the butter and add the sugar which has been mixed with the flour. Add the yolk and beat well. Add ½ cup boiling water and cook over hot water until thick. Cool and just before serving, fold in the stiffly beaten egg white. Flavor with vanilla.

(3147) SPICED SAUCE

⅓ cup brown sugar
1-inch stick cinnamon
1 tablespoon grated lemon
    peel

Small piece root ginger
2 whole cloves
1 tablespoon cornstarch
1 tablespoon lemon juice

Put sugar in saucepan. Add cinnamon, ginger, lemon peel, cloves, and 1½ cups water. Simmer, covered, 20 minutes, stirring occasionally. Strain. Add cornstarch, blended with 2 tablespoons cold water, and lemon juice.

(3148) STRAWBERRY SAUCE

Add 1 cup mashed strawberries or other berries and 1 well-beaten egg white to recipe for hard sauce (No. 3105).

(3149) VANILLA SAUCE

1 cup milk
½ cup sugar
2 egg yolks

2 tablespoons sugar
1 teaspoon vanilla
1 tablespoon butter

Bring milk and ½ cup sugar to a boil, stirring until sugar is dissolved. Beat yolks and 2 tablespoons sugar together until light and lemon-colored. Pour milk over eggs, stirring vigorously. Heat, without boiling, until thickened. Remove from heat. Add vanilla and butter.

(3150) WINE SAUCE

3 egg yolks
½ cup sugar

2 tablespoons rum
1 cup white wine

Combine ingredients and beat until light. Heat over hot water, beating vigorously until hot.

(3151) CREAM FILLING

⅓ cup flour
⅔ cup sugar
¼ teaspoon salt
2 cups milk

2 tablespoons butter
3 egg yolks, beaten
½ tablespoon vanilla

Mix flour, sugar, and salt. Scald milk and add to dry mixture, stirring while adding slowly. Cook over hot water, stirring until thick, about 15 minutes. Add butter. Pour mixture over egg yolks, stirring constantly. Cool. Add vanilla.

(3152)   CUSTARD FILLING

2 cups milk
3 eggs
⅓ cup sugar

⅛ teaspoon salt
⅛ teaspoon nutmeg

Scald milk. Beat eggs slightly and add sugar and salt. Stir constantly while adding the hot milk. Pour into pie crust. Sprinkle with nutmeg. Makes 1 9-inch pie.

(3153)   GINGER APPLESAUCE FILLING

½ cup applesauce (No. 34)
2 tablespoons preserved
    ginger, chopped

½ cup heavy cream,
    whipped

Rub applesauce through a sieve. Add ginger and fold into cream.

(3154)   BANANA BUTTER

4 ripe bananas
1 cup white sugar
2 eggs, well beaten

2 tablespoons butter
Grated rind and juice 1
    lemon

Mash bananas and beat to a pulp with a fork. Add butter, sugar, lemon, and eggs. Put all together in a smooth granite pan and cook until as thick as custard, stirring constantly. Seal in an airtight jar. Use as a filling for cakes and pastries.

(3155)   BANANA FILLING AND ICING

1 cup cream
½ cup confectioners' sugar
1 cup banana pulp

½ teaspoon vanilla
Few grains salt

Beat cream until stiff and add sugar. Fold in banana pulp, vanilla, and salt.

(3156)   BUTTERSCOTCH FILLING

3 tablespoons butter
1½ cups brown sugar
¾ cup boiling water
3 egg yolks

1½ cups milk
6 tablespoons flour
⅜ teaspoon salt

Melt butter. Add sugar and allow to brown. Gradually add water. Beat egg yolks. Add small amount of the measured milk and the flour. Stir until smooth. Add remainder of milk and salt. Pour this slowly into sugar mixture and cook until thick, stirring constantly. Cool and pour into baked, cooled pastry shell. Cover with meringue (No. 3205).

(3157)   CARAMEL FILLING

1 cup brown sugar   ¼ cup cream
2 tablespoons butter

Combine ingredients. Cook over hot water, stirring frequently, until smooth and of proper consistency.

(3158)   CHOCOLATE CREAM FILLING

Melt 2 ounces unsweetened chocolate in scalded milk in recipe for cream filling (No. 3151) and increase amount of sugar to 1 cup.

(3159)   COCONUT CREAM FILLING

Add 1 cup shredded coconut to recipe for cream filling (No. 3151).

(3160)   COFFEE FILLING

Add ¼ cup powdered coffee to milk before scalding in recipe for cream filling (No. 3151).

(3161)   DATE CREAM FILLING

Add ¼ pound chopped dates and 1 teaspoon grated lemon rind to milk before it is added in recipe for cream filling (No. 3151).

(3162)   FRUIT FILLING

¾ cup chopped figs   ½ cup sugar
½ cup chopped dates   ½ cup boiling water
¼ cup chopped raisins   3 tablespoons lemon juice

Mix figs, dates, and raisins. Add sugar, water, and lemon juice and cook over hot water until thick. Spread while hot between layers of cake.

(3163)   LEMON CREAM FILLING

1 beaten egg yolk	⅛ teaspoon grated lemon
½ cup sugar	peel
2 tablespoons cornstarch	½ tablespoon butter
¼ cup lemon juice	

Combine yolk, sugar, cornstarch, ½ cup water, lemon juice, and lemon peel. Cook 15 minutes over hot water, stirring frequently. Add butter. Cool.

(3164)   MARSHMALLOW CREAM FILLING

¾ cup sugar	16 marshmallows, cut in
⅓ cup corn sirup	quarters
2 egg whites, stiffly beaten	

Cook sugar, corn sirup, and ¼ cup water together in a saucepan until it spins a long thread (240° F.) when dropped from a metal spoon. Remove from heat and immediately add the marshmallows. Beat until thoroughly blended. Pour the hot sirup over the egg whites and continue beating until mixture is smooth.

(3165)   ORANGE FILLING

6 tablespoons sugar	1 tablespoon butter
3 tablespoons cornstarch	½ teaspoon grated orange
1 egg yolk	peel
1 cup orange juice	

Mix sugar and cornstarch in upper part of double boiler. Add beaten egg and orange juice. Place over boiling water and cook 10 to 15 minutes, until thickened, stirring frequently. Remove from heat and add butter and grated orange peel. Cool. Yield: filling for 3 layer cake.

(3166)   PECAN FILLING

3 eggs	2 cups corn sirup
1 tablespoon granulated	1 teaspoon vanilla
sugar	¼ teaspoon salt
2 tablespoons flour	1 cup whole pecans

Beat eggs until light. Mix sugar and flour and add to eggs. Beat well. Add sirup, vanilla, salt, and ¾ cup pecans. Pour into pie crust. Top with remaining pecans.

(3167) PINEAPPLE FILLING

½ cup sugar	1 cup pineapple, cut in
4 tablespoons flour	pieces
⅛ teaspoon salt	¾ cup pineapple juice
1 egg	1 tablespoon fat

Mix sugar, flour, and salt. Add beaten egg, pineapple, and juice. Cook in a double boiler or over boiling water until thick, stirring constantly. Add fat and mix well. Cool.

(3168) STRAWBERRY FILLING

1 cup crushed strawberries, sweetened to taste	½ cup heavy cream, whipped

Fold berries into cream.

(3169) FONDANT

2½ cups sugar	⅛ teaspoon cream of tartar
1 cup water	

Combine ingredients. Heat to the boiling point, stirring until sugar is dissolved. Continue boiling, brushing sirup from sides of pan until the temperature reaches 238° F. or until a small amount of sirup dropped into cold water will form a soft ball. Remove to shallow dish. When lukewarm, stir until white and creamy. Add any desired flavoring. Cool. When ready to use for icing, warm slightly over hot water.

(3170) QUICK FROSTING

1 cup sugar	½ teaspoon vanilla
1 egg white	

Put sugar, ¼ cup water, and egg white in saucepan and cook over boiling water. Beat constantly until frosting is the proper consistency to spread. Add vanilla.

(3171)   BOILED FROSTING

1¾ cups sugar
½ cup water

2 egg whites
1 teaspoon vanilla

Cook sugar and water together, stirring until the sugar is dissolved. Boil, without stirring, to 238° F. or until the sirup forms a soft ball when tested in cold water. Pour over the stiffly beaten egg whites and beat constantly until the mixture holds its shape. When cool, add vanilla.

(3172)   BROWN SUGAR FROSTING

Substitute brown sugar for white sugar in boiled frosting (No. 3171) and cook until 240° F. is reached.

(3173)   CONFECTIONERS' ICING

1½ tablespoons fat
1½ cups confectioners' sugar
3 tablespoons cream

⅛ teaspoon salt
1 teaspoon vanilla

Cream fat and continue creaming while slowly adding sugar. Add cream, salt, and vanilla and mix smooth.

(3174)   SEVEN-MINUTE FROSTING

2¼ cups sugar
1½ tablespoons white corn
     sirup

7½ tablespoons water
3 egg whites
1½ teaspoons vanilla

Combine all ingredients, except vanilla, in top of double boiler and mix well. Cook over boiling water 3 minutes. Remove from fire but leave over hot water and beat with rotary beater 7 minutes, or until of a consistency to spread. Add vanilla and blend well.

(3175)   REFRIGERATOR FROSTING

2 cups sugar
⅓ cup light corn sirup
⅓ cup water

2 egg whites
1 teaspoon vanilla

Cook sugar, corn sirup, and water together, stirring until sugar is dissolved. Boil, without stirring, until it forms a rather firm ball when dropped in cold water. Pour over stiffly beaten egg whites, beating constantly. Continue to beat until mixture holds its shape. Add vanilla. Store in a covered jar in the refrigerator. If it becomes too hard, add a few drops of hot water before using.

(3176)   ORNAMENTAL ICING

1 egg white	½ teaspoon lemon juice
2¾ cups confectioners' sugar	

Beat egg with 1 cup sugar until stiff. Add lemon juice and beat in. Add remaining sugar, a small amount at a time, beating after each addition. Any desired coloring may be beat into this icing.

(3177)   ALMOND ICING

Add ¼ teaspoon almond extract and reduce quantity of vanilla to ½ teaspoon in recipe for confectioners' icing (No. 3173).

(3178)   APPLE SNOW FROSTING

1 cup sugar	1 apple, grated
1 egg white	½ teaspoon vanilla

Cook sugar and ¼ cup water together, stirring until sugar is dissolved. Cook to 240° F. or until it forms a rather firm ball when tested in cold water. Pour sirup gradually over the stiffly beaten egg whites. Add apple and continue beating until the mixture will hold its shape. Add vanilla.

(3179)   BOILED EGG YOLK FROSTING

2 cups sugar	1 teaspoon orange juice
1 teaspoon vinegar	1 teaspoon lemon juice
2 tablespoons butter	1 teaspoon grated orange
2 egg yolks, well beaten	rind
1 teaspoon baking powder	

Combine sugar, vinegar, and ½ cup hot water. Bring to boiling point, stirring constantly. Cover and cook without stirring until sirup spins a thread 10 to 12 inches long. Add butter. Pour the sirup over egg yolks in a fine stream, beating vigorously. Add other ingredients. Beat with rotary beater until mixture is creamy. Cool and store in refrigerator.

(3180)   BOILED CORN SIRUP FROSTING

2½ cups sugar
½ cup corn sirup
¼ teaspoon salt

2 egg whites, well beaten
1 teaspoon vanilla

Cook sugar, sirup, salt, and ½ cup water together to the firm ball stage (240° F.). Pour over egg whites slowly, beating vigorously. Add vanilla. Continue beating until frosting stands in peaks. Cool and keep in refrigerator.

(3181)   BROWN BUTTER ICING

¼ pound butter
¼ cup light cream
Confectioner's sugar

1 teaspoon vanilla
½ cup nut meats

Brown the butter in a saucepan, being careful not to burn it. After it is melted, add the light cream and enough confectioners' sugar to make the right consistency to spread. Add the vanilla and nut meats.

(3182)   GOLD FROSTING

1 tablespoon gelatin
4 egg yolks
¾ cup sugar
1 cup orange juice

1 teaspoon grated orange
   peel
4 egg whites
¼ cup sugar

Orange sections

Soften gelatin in ¼ cup cold water 5 minutes. Cook egg yolks, sugar, and orange juice in top of double boiler until thickened, about 10 minutes. Add gelatin, stirring to dissolve. Add grated peel. Cool. Beat egg whites until stiff, gradually adding the ¼ cup sugar. Fold into cooked orange mixture. Spread between layers and on top of cake. Chill in refrigerator. Decorate with fresh orange sections just before serving or sprinkle with coconut.

(3183)   CARAMEL FROSTING

2 cups brown sugar
1 cup granulated sugar
1 cup sour cream or milk

1 tablespoon butter
1 teaspoon vanilla
Cream or top milk

Combine the sugars and sour cream in a large saucepan and cook slowly until the sugars are dissolved. Cook until a little of the mixture dropped in cold water forms a soft ball. Remove from heat, add butter and vanilla, and cool to 145° F. or until the outside of the saucepan feels warm to the touch. Beat until quite stiff, then add enough cream while beating to make of a spreading consistency. Frosts and fills a two-layer cake, 8 inches in diameter.

(3184)   CARAMEL COCONUT FROSTING

1½ cups brown sugar	½ teaspoon vanilla
¾ cup cream or milk	1 cup moist coconut
2 tablespoons butter	

Cook sugar and cream or milk until it forms soft ball when dropped in cold water (238° F.). Add butter and flavoring. Cool. Beat until consistency to spread. Frost cake. Sprinkle with coconut and place under broiler until coconut is delicately browned.

(3185)   CARAMEL PECAN FROSTING

Add ½ cup chopped pecans to caramel coconut frosting (No. 3184) when beating after cooling. Omit broiling.

(3186)   CHOCOLATE FLUFF

1 cup cream	¼ teaspoon salt
1 teaspoon vanilla	¾ cup sugar
4 tablespoons cocoa	

Mix well and whip until thick. Chill. Serve on sheet or loaf cake, layer cake, or cupcakes.

(3187)   CHOCOLATE FROSTING

Add 3 ounces melted, unsweetened chocolate to recipe for boiled corn sirup frosting (No. 3180) after all of the sirup has been added.

(3188)   CREAMY CHOCOLATE FROSTING

4 ounces unsweetened chocolate, grated
1½ cups milk
1½ cups powdered sugar

1 teaspoon vanilla
1 tablespoon fat
Salt

Cook chocolate, milk, and sugar together, stirring constantly until sugar is dissolved. Then stir only enough to prevent burning. Cook to the soft ball stage (240° F.). Add vanilla, fat, and a few grains salt. Beat to proper consistency.

(3189)   COCONUT FROSTING

Add ½ cup shredded coconut to recipe for seven-minute frosting (No. 3174) after cooking is finished and sprinkle more coconut on cake after frosting is put on.

(3190) COCONUT MARSHMALLOW FROSTING

Add 1 cup marshmallows, cut in tiny pieces, and ½ cup shredded coconut to boiled frosting (No. 3171).

(3191)   FUDGE FROSTING

2 ounces unsweetened cooking chocolate
1 cup milk
2 cups granulated sugar
⅛ teaspoon salt

2 tablespoons white corn sirup
2 tablespoons butter
1 teaspoon vanilla

Add chocolate to milk. Cook slowly until smooth and blended, while stirring. Add sugar, salt, and corn sirup. Stir until sugar is dissolved and mixture boils. Continue cooking until mixture forms a very soft ball when a little is dropped in cold water. Add butter and vanilla. Cool to lukewarm. Beat until thick enough to spread. Makes enough to frost a loaf cake about 8″ x 8″ x 2″.

(3192)   GOLDEN ICING

¼ cup butter
¼ teaspoon salt
¼ cup canned crushed pineapple

2 egg yolks
6 cups sifted confectioners' sugar
¼ cup pineapple juice

Cream butter and salt with egg yolks. Add well drained pine-apple and sugar. Add pineapple juice gradually to make proper consistency.

(3193) HONEY ICING

Beat ½ cup honey into boiled frosting (No. 3171) after it has been beaten with egg whites.

(3194) LEMON FROSTING

Substitute lemon rind and juice for orange rind and juice in recipe for orange frosting (No. 3200).

(3195) MAPLE SUGAR FROSTING

Substitute crumbled maple sugar for white sugar in boiled frosting (No. 3171).

(3196) MARBLE ICING

1½ cups sugar	2 egg whites
5 tablespoons water	¼ teaspoon peppermint
1 tablespoon white corn	extract
sirup	1 ounce bitter chocolate

Combine all ingredients except peppermint and chocolate in top of double boiler and mix well. Stir over hot water until sugar is dissolved. Beat with rotary beater over boiling water until frosting is fluffy and will hold its shape. Add flavoring and blend well. Spread frosting over top and sides of cake. Melt chocolate and pour across cake in ¼-inch strips about an inch apart. Then draw a knife across through the strips at 1 inch intervals.

(3197) MARSHMALLOW FROSTING

½ pound marshmallows	½ teaspoon vanilla
1 cup sugar	Salt
1 egg white, stiffly beaten	

Slice marshmallows into small pieces and melt over hot water. Cook sugar in ¼ cup water to soft ball stage (240° F.). Pour sirup over egg white. Beat until stiff. Add marshmallows and beat until smooth and of the right consistency to spread. Add vanilla and a few grains salt.

(3198)   MOCK MARSHMALLOW FROSTING

2 teaspoons gelatin   ½ teaspoon vanilla
2 cups sugar

Soak gelatin in 6 tablespoons cold water 5 minutes. Dissolve over hot water. Cook sugar with ½ cup water, stirring constantly, until it will spin a 10-inch thread when dropped from a spoon. Pour sirup over gelatin. Add vanilla and beat until thick and white. If desired, chopped nuts may be added to this.

(3199)   MOCHA ICING

Add 2 tablespoons cocoa and substitute strong coffee (No. 301) for cream in recipe for confectioners' icing (No. 3173).

(3200)   ORANGE FROSTING

1 teaspoon light corn sirup   1 egg white
⅞ cup sugar   3 tablespoons orange juice
¼ teaspoon grated orange   Few grains salt
   peel   ½ teaspoon lemon juice

Beat together in top part of double boiler all ingredients except lemon juice. Place over rapidly boiling water and beat constantly with rotary beater 6 to 7 minutes, until stiff enough to stand in peaks. Remove from heat. Add lemon juice. Continue beating until of consistency to spread. Yield: frosting for top and sides of cake.

(3201)   PEANUT BUTTER ICING

2 cups confectioners' sugar   1 teaspoon nutmeg
3 tablespoons peanut butter   4-6 tablespoons milk
1 teaspoon cinnamon

Combine all ingredients. Add the milk slowly until of the right consistency.

(3202) LEMON SEVEN-MINUTE FROSTING

Substitute 3 tablespoons lemon juice for an equal amount of water in seven-minute frosting (No. 3174) and add ¼ teaspoon grated lemon peel.

(3203)   SPICED ICING

1 egg white	Confectioners' sugar
2 tablespoons sweet cream	¼ teaspoon mace

Add cream to unbeaten egg white and mix well. Add sugar, a little at a time, until icing is the right consistency to spread. Add mace and mix well.

(3204)   STRAWBERRY ICING

¼ cup strawberries, crushed   3 cups confectioners' sugar

Mix ingredients thoroughly.

(3205)   MERINGUE

3 egg whites	1 teaspoon lemon juice
¼ teaspoon salt	6 tablespoons sugar
¼ teaspoon vanilla	

Beat egg whites until bubbly. Add salt, vanilla, and lemon juice. Continue beating until egg whites form a thick foam. Add sugar, a tablespoon at a time, beating after each addition. After last addition of sugar, beat until mixture piles and sugar is dissolved.

(3206)   FRENCH MERINGUE

3 egg whites	¼ teaspoon salt
1 cup sugar	½ teaspoon vanilla

Combine egg whites, sugar, and salt in saucepan. Beat steadily with a rotary beater while cooking over hot water until mixture is stiff. Remove from heat. Cool. Add vanilla and beat in thoroughly.

(3207)   ITALIAN MERINGUE

1 cup sugar	3 stiffly beaten egg whites
¼ teaspoon salt	½ teaspoon vanilla

Combine sugar, salt, and ¼ cup boiling water. Bring to a boil, stirring until sugar is dissolved. Cook to soft ball stage (240° F.). Pour sirup over egg whites in fine stream, beating vigorously during and after pouring until mixture is firm. Add vanilla and beat in thoroughly.

(3208)   APRICOT MERINGUE

¼ teaspoon salt	3 egg whites
¼ teaspoon vanilla	6 tablespoons sugar
1 teaspoon lemon juice	½ cup apricot sirup

Add salt, vanilla, and lemon juice to egg whites. Beat to a stiff foam. Add sugar, a tablespoon at a time, beating after each addition. With the last sugar beat until mixture piles well and the sugar is dissolved. Fold in sirup, made by stewing apricots and rubbing some of the cooked pulp through sieve into juice.

(3209)   LEMON MERINGUE

2 egg whites	1 teaspoon lemon juice
4 tablespoons sugar	

Beat egg whites frothy. Continue beating while adding sugar gradually until egg holds its shape in peaks. Fold in lemon juice.

(3210)   SPICED WHIPPED CREAM

1 cup heavy cream	1 teaspoon cinnamon
3 tablespoons confectioners' sugar	1 teaspoon ginger

Whip cream until stiff and add sugar and spices.

Sandwiches

~~~~~~~~~~~~~~~~~~~~~~~~~~~~~~~~

THERE is no end to the variety of sandwiches available to the clever homemaker. Practically any article of food can be adapted in some form or other for sandwiches. Almost any kind of bread, biscuits, rolls, muffins, or buns can be used for the outer covers.

For parties thin sandwiches can be cut into almost any desired shape or size to fit in with a particular occasion. An almost endless array of color combinations is also available. For box lunches, either for school, business, or outings, the sandwich provides an easy method of preparation and any dietary requirement can be met.

In making sandwiches it is always best to cream the butter before spreading in order to cover the bread evenly. The coating of butter helps to prevent moist fillings from making the bread soggy. To keep sandwiches fresh they should be closely wrapped in wax paper and kept in as cool a place as is possible.

(3301)   MISCELLANEOUS MEAT SANDWICHES

Use day-old bread, either graham, whole-wheat, rye, rolls, or white bread. Arrange slices so they will fit together. Cream butter or butter substitute so that it will spread easily. If well-spread with butter, a moist filling will not make the bread soggy. Following are some suggested fillings:

Minced ham with cream or salad dressing.
Any left-over meat, minced, with cream or salad dressing.
Dried beef, plain or frizzled (No. 1361).

Slices of cooked beef, ham, pork, veal, tongue, poultry, or lamb, sprinkled with salt or spread with a salad dressing.

Cooked beef or pork liver, put through a food grinder, mixed to a paste with melted butter, and seasoned with salt, pepper, and onion juice.

Chopped cooked liver, mixed with an equal quantity of chopped hard-cooked eggs (No. 202).

Tiny, well-browned sausages (No. 1469) with a little grated onion.

Chopped cooked chicken, diced celery, chopped pimiento, chopped ripe olives, grated onion, salt, pepper, and mayonnaise (No. 701).

Slices of corned beef, tongue, or any prepared meat, with or without lettuce and tomatoes.

Minced cooked ham with salad dressing, chopped hard-cooked eggs (No. 202), chopped parsley, and chopped celery.

Minced cooked ham with chopped pickles, and salad dressing.

Sliced ham with cream cheese and shredded lettuce, chopped watercress, or thin slices of crisp cucumber.

Slices of cold, cooked meats in combination.

Chicken salad (No. 867) and lettuce.

Chopped cooked ham, mixed with chopped cooked turkey or chicken, salt, pepper, and mayonnaise (No. 701).

Minced, cooked meat (any kind), mixed with chopped celery, salt, pepper, and mayonnaise (No. 701).

Slices of crisp bacon (No. 1464).

Cooked chicken livers, chopped very fine, mixed with chopped hard-cooked egg yolk (No. 202), chopped onion, salt, pepper, and mayonnaise (No. 701).

Mixed, cooked lamb, combined with mint sauce (No. 2046), on a lettuce leaf.

Minced, cooked poultry, mixed with chopped nut meats, chopped green pepper, salt, paprika, and mayonnaise (No. 701).

Minced cooked ham, mixed with peanut butter and mayonnaise (No. 701).

Minced corned beef, mixed with mustard and mayonnaise (No. 701).

(3302) MISCELLANEOUS FISH SANDWICHES

Prepare and butter bread as for miscellaneous cold meat sandwiches (No. 3301) and spread with any of the following:

Tuna fish or salmon, plain or mixed with salad dressing, and lettuce.

Minced sardines, sprinkled with lemon juice, and garnished with lettuce leaf.

Anchovy paste, mixed with cream cheese or sprinkled with lemon juice.

Boiled shrimp (No. 1272), chopped celery, and chili sauce.

Tuna fish or salmon, diced celery, chopped pimiento, chopped ripe olives, grated onion, salt, pepper, and mayonnaise (No. 701).

Minced sardines, mixed with minced ham, chopped pickle, mustard, catchup, and lemon juice.

Minced boiled shrimps (No. 1272), mixed with chopped cucumber, salt, paprika, and mayonnaise (No. 701).

Minced sardines, mixed with horseradish, butter, lemon juice, and paprika.

Flaked fish, mixed with any combination of chopped green peppers, onion, pimiento, tomatoes, and chives and moistened with mayonnaise (No. 701).

Tuna fish or salmon, topped with slices of crisp bacon (No. 1464).

Minced sardines, mixed with chopped cucumber.

(3303)   MISCELLANEOUS CHEESE SANDWICHES

Prepare and butter bread as for miscellaneous cold meat sandwiches (No. 3301) and spread with any of the following:

Cream cheese with chopped nuts, olives or peppers, or a combination of these.

Sliced cheese with salad dressing or mustard on rye bread.

Cottage cheese with onions and cream or salad dressing used with brown bread. Pimiento may also be added.

Add India relish to well seasoned fresh cottage cheese.

Add chopped English walnuts to cottage cheese.

Chopped parsley, cottage cheese, and salad dressing.

Grated cheese, with chopped sweet pickle and mayonnaise (No. 701).

Cream cheese, blended with tomato catchup.

Cottage cheese, mixed with almost any fruit jam or jelly.

Mixture made by combining 2 cups grated cheese, 1 tablespoon butter, 1 teaspoon salt, 1 teaspoon mustard, dash cayenne, 2 well-beaten eggs, 1/2 cup milk, and dash pepper. Cook and beat until mixture is thick and smooth and add 4 pimientos, chopped fine.

Roquefort cheese, cream, chopped ripe olives, chopped celery, and lettuce leaf.

Grated cheese, chopped dates, chopped almonds, lemon juice, mayonnaise (No. 701), and lettuce leaf.

Cream cheese, milk, chopped gingerroot, chopped almonds, salt, and paprika.

Cream cheese, mixed with chopped sweet pickles and peanut butter.

Grated cheese, mixed with chopped pimiento and mayonnaise (No. 701).

Cream cheese, mixed with butter, pepper, salt, paprika, and Worcestershire sauce.

Grated cheese, mixed with chopped green pepper, mustard, and Worcestershire sauce.

Cold Welsh rarebit.

Cream cheese, seasoned with anchovy paste.

Cream cheese, mixed with chopped celery and cooked salad dressing (No. 737).

Cream cheese, mixed with chopped dates.

Cream cheese, mixed with crushed pineapple.

Grated Parmesan cheese, seasoned with cayenne and Worcestershire sauce and moistened with melted butter.

Cream cheese, mixed with chopped maraschino cherries.

(3304) MISCELLANEOUS EGG SANDWICHES

Prepare and butter bread as for miscellaneous cold meat sandwiches (No. 3301) and spread with any of the following:

Chopped hard-cooked egg (No. 202) mixed with salad dressing.

Scrambled eggs (No. 209), plain or in milk, or with bits of diced, crisp bacon (No. 1464).

Scrambled eggs (No. 209), mixed with stewed tomatoes (No. 1893) and a little grated onion, if desired.

Chopped hard-cooked egg (No. 202), mixed with chopped dill pickle and mayonnaise (No. 701).

Chopped hard-cooked egg (No. 202), mixed with chopped watercress, salt, paprika, and mayonnaise (No. 701).

Slices of hard-cooked egg (No. 202) arranged on lettuce leaves, dipped in French dressing (No. 716).

Chopped deviled eggs (No. 216) on lettuce leaves.

Chopped hard-cooked egg (No. 202), mixed with chopped olives and French dressing (No. 716).

Chopped hard-cooked egg (No. 202), mixed with diced broiled bacon (No. 1464) or minced ham and mayonnaise (No. 701).

Chopped hard-cooked egg (No. 202), mixed with chopped celery, chopped pimiento, and mayonnaise (No. 701).

(3305) MISCELLANEOUS FRUIT SANDWICHES

Prepare and butter bread as for miscellaneous cold meat sandwiches (No. 3301) and spread with any of the following:

Chopped dates, mixed with butter and sprinkled with lemon juice.

Chopped dates, mixed with an equal amount of peanut butter or cream cheese, seasoned with salt, and sprinkled with lemon juice.

Jams, jellies, or preserves.

Mashed ripe bananas, mixed with chopped peanuts or peanut butter.

Chopped celery, apple, nuts, or olives, in any proportion, and salad dressing.

One cup chopped raisins, mixed with ¼ cup chopped nuts and mayonnaise (No. 701).

Chopped ripe olives, chopped onion, chopped celery, cream cheese, and chopped pimiento.

Sliced stuffed olives.

Sliced olives with dressing made by cooking to boiling point 2 eggs, ½ cup sugar, 1 teaspoon flour, 1 teaspoon butter, 1 teaspoon mustard, 1 cup cream, ½ cup vinegar, and 1 teaspoon salt.

Chopped raisins, mixed with grated orange rind and sprinkled with orange juice.

Chopped dates, mixed with grated orange rind and sprinkled with lemon juice.

Mashed, stewed prunes (No. 71), mixed with peanut butter, lemon juice, and cream.

Mashed, canned apricots, mixed with chopped nut meats.

Chopped dates, mixed with chopped nut meats.

A mixture of chopped dates, figs, and raisins.

Crushed pineapple and chopped pecans, with or without cream cheese.

Chopped stewed figs (No. 55).

(3306) MISCELLANEOUS VEGETABLE SANDWICHES

Prepare and butter bread as for miscellaneous cold meat sandwiches (No. 3301) and spread with any of the following:

Plain lettuce with salad dressing.

Sliced tomato or sliced tomato and lettuce with salt, pepper, and salad dressing.

Diced pickled cucumber, mixed with cottage cheese.

Chopped pickled beets, mixed with cottage cheese.

Chopped celery, apples, nuts, or olives, in any proportions, and salad dressing.

Mixed pickles, sour or sweet, with chopped hard-cooked eggs (No. 202).

Left-over beans, mashed or rubbed through a sieve, mixed with tomato sauce (No. 2035) or salad dressing and chopped sour pickle or chutney

Creamed mushrooms (No. 1804).

Mashed, cooked beans, seasoned with chopped onion, pickle relish, or horseradish, and moistened with mayonnaise (No. 701).

Slices of onion and salad dressing.

Chopped pimientos, mashed to a paste with grated cheese or ground left-over meats and mayonnaise (No. 701).

Cucumber slices, sprinkled with grated onion, lettuce leaf, mayonnaise (No. 701).

Tomato pulp, mixed with chopped ripe olives and mayonnaise (No. 701).

Chopped celery, mixed with chopped olives and mayonnaise (No. 701).

Chopped green pepper, mixed with chopped onion, chopped ripe olives, and mayonnaise (No. 701).

Chopped boiled spinach (No. 1870), mixed with chopped hard-cooked eggs (No. 202), chopped onion, and mayonnaise (No. 701).

Grated raw carrot, mixed with mashed, boiled peas (No. 1823) and mayonnaise (No. 701).

A mixture of chopped onion, chopped parsley, chopped green pepper, chopped cucumber, chopped celery, tomato pulp, and mayonnaise (No. 701) on lettuce leaf.

Mashed, left-over beans, mixed with diced, crisp bacon (No. 1464), mustard, and catchup.

Mashed, left-over beans, mixed with chopped celery and mustard.

Washed and carefully selected watercress, which has been marinated 3 minutes in French dressing (No. 716).

Grated raw carrot, sprinkled with lemon juice, on lettuce leaves, which have been dipped in French dressing (No. 716).

Chopped celery, mixed with peanut butter.

Sliced cranberry sauce (No. 54), sprinkled with chopped celery.

Grated raw carrots, mixed with shredded cabbage and raisins.

Chopped green pepper.

Sliced radishes.

Any washed and selected salad greens.

Mixture of shredded cabbage, chopped, boiled beets (No. 1726), chopped green pepper, chopped ripe olives, and Russian dressing (No. 725).

(3307) MISCELLANEOUS COLD SANDWICHES

Prepare and butter bread as for miscellaneous cold meat sandwiches (No. 3301) and spread with any of the following:

Jelly.

Peanut butter.

Chopped nut meats, either all one kind or in combination, mixed with mashed hard-cooked eggs (No. 202) and mayonnaise (No. 701).

Chopped nut meats, mixed with jelly.

Honey, mixed with lemon juice and chopped nut meats.

Chopped olives, mixed with chopped nut meats and chopped, cooked meat.

Maple sugar.

Peanut butter, mixed with jelly or jam.

Honey, mixed with peanut butter.

Peanut butter, mixed with diced, crisp bacon (No. 1464) and mayonnaise (No. 701).
Sliced pickles.

(3308)   OPEN SANDWICHES

These are sandwiches made with only the lower slice of bread. Otherwise make the same as any other sandwich and garnish with appropriately colored items such as crumbled hard-cooked egg yolks (No. 202), sliced olives, minced parsley, pimiento, lemon slices, nut meats, etc.

(3309)   HOT MEAT SANDWICHES

Butter slices of toast generously. Top with hot slices of any cooked meat or poultry and cover with gravy.

(3310)   THREE-DECKER CLUB SANDWICHES

Take 3 slices toasted bread. Butter 1 side of 1 slice and place, butter side up on dish. Cover with lettuce leaf. Brush with mayonnaise (No. 701). Add slices of any desired meat, poultry, fish, or vegetables. Spread with more mayonnaise. Butter another slice of toast on both sides. Put on sandwich. Add slices of crisp bacon (No. 1464), onion, or tomato slices. Spread with more mayonnaise. Butter third slice of toast and place, butter side down, on sandwich. Cut diagonally.

(3311)   BROWN AND WHITE BREAD
                        SANDWICHES

Use 1 slice white bread and 1 slice dark bread in making any plain sandwich. Use alternating slices of dark and white bread in tiered sandwiches.

(3312)   CHILLED CHECKERBOARDS

Cut 3 slices each of whole-wheat and white bread, ½ inch thick. Remove crusts. Spread a slice of white bread with creamed butter or softened cheese, and place a slice of whole-wheat on it. Spread this with creamed mixture. Place on it a slice of white bread, making whole-wheat bread the middle layer. Repeat this process with remaining slices, beginning with whole wheat so that a slice of white bread is the middle layer this time. Trim each pile evenly, and cut each pile in 3 1-inch slices. Spread these slices with creamed mixture, and put together in such a way that a white block will alternate with a whole wheat one, forming a checkerboard at ends. There will be two "checkered" loaves. Wrap each loaf in waxed paper, and place in refrigerator to chill. When ready to serve, slice about ¼ inch thick. Serves 4.

(3313)   CHILLED CORNUCOPIAS

Remove crusts from all sides of a fresh loaf of bread. Slice bread very thin, crosswise, with a sharp knife. Spread each slice with a soft sandwich filling. Place a sprig of parsley or watercress at one corner. Roll corners at left and right of sprig toward the center to form a cornucopia. Overlap, and spread with soft butter to seal. Place close together in shallow pan, cover with damp cloth, and place in refrigerator to chill. Serves 6.

(3314)   CHILLED PINWHEELS

Remove the crusts from top and sides of a fresh, close-textured loaf of bread. With a sharp knife, cut bread lengthwise in slices ⅛ to ¼ inch thick. Discard bottom crust. Spread the long slices of bread with creamed butter, softened cheese, or any very smooth spread. Lay alternating strips of green pepper and pimiento, crosswise, 1 inch apart, over entire strip of bread; or lay about four stuffed olives lengthwise on one end of bread. Beginning at one end, roll the bread as for jelly roll. Spread a little soft butter on the last lap of bread to make it stick, wrap the small rolls in waxed paper, and place in refrigerator to chill. When ready to serve, slice about ¼ inch thick. Serves 6.

(3315)   ROLLED SANDWICHES

Remove all crusts from any sandwich made with fresh bread. Roll up and skewer with toothpicks. Wrap in wax paper and chill in refrigerator.

(3316)   SALAD LOAF SANDWICH

Cut off crusts from 1 whole loaf of fresh bread. Slice, lengthwise, into ½-inch slices. Butter 2 slices on 1 side and 2 slices on both sides. Put 1 slice of former, butter side up, into loaf pan. Spread with chicken, meat, lobster, shrimp, or any desired salad. Cover with slice of bread, buttered on both sides. Add more salad, then other slice of bread, buttered on both sides. Spread again with more salad and top with remaining slice bread. Cover with wax paper. Put weight on top. Chill in refrigerator. Slice, crosswise, for serving and garnish with lettuce, olives, hard-cooked egg slices (No. 202), radishes, celery, and pickles. Serves 8.

(3317) SALAD LOAF SANDWICH IN CHEESE

Make salad sandwich loaf (No. 3316) with vegetable salad (No. 795). Blend chopped parsley with cream cheese and spread over entire loaf.

(3318) GINGERBREAD AND WHITE BREAD RIBBON SANDWICHES

Spread 2 slices of white bread with creamed butter on one side and one slice of gingerbread with creamed butter on both sides. Put together with gingerbread in the center. Make a second sandwich loaf, alternating gingerbread with white bread. Wrap in wax paper, cover with damp cloth and put in cool place. Cut in ½-inch slices and serve. Cream or cottage cheese with nuts or dates also may be used for filling.

(3319) CRISPY SANDWICHES

¼ cup butter   ½ bunch celery, chopped
¼ cup peanut butter   Salt

Cream the two butters, adding salt to season. Spread both top and bottom slices of bread with the butter, cover the bottom slice with celery and press slices firmly together. Cream cheese can be substituted for peanut butter.

(3320) SAUTÉED JAM SANDWICHES

Spread jam between 2 slices buttered bread. Sauté sandwich in little butter until brown on both sides. Sprinkle with cinnamon and powdered sugar. Serve hot.

(3321)   SPANISH SANDWICHES

2 tablespoons chopped pimiento	½ teaspoon salt
	Dash paprika
2 tablespoons chopped onion	1 egg, well beaten
1 tablespoon butter	6 slices buttered toast
1 cup tomato juice	(No. 988)
1 cup grated cheese	

Sauté pimiento and onion in butter 5 minutes. Add tomato juice, cheese, salt, and paprika and cook 5 minutes longer or until cheese is melted. Stir small amount into egg. Return to hot mixture and cook 2 minutes longer. Serve on hot toast. Serves 6.

(3322)   CLUB SANDWICH

Cut white bread in ¼-inch slices and toast on one side. Spread untoasted side with butter. Lay a crisp lettuce leaf on the bread and spread with mayonnaise (No. 701). On top of lettuce put layers of sliced chicken, sliced tomatoes and crisp bacon (No. 1464) or cold ham. Season well with salt and pepper and cover with top piece of toast. Cut in halves diagonally.

(3323)   TURKEY CLUB SANDWICH

Cut white bread in ¼-inch slices. Cut off and discard crusts. Spread creamed butter on bread. Place slice of turkey meat on one slice bread. Season to taste with salt and pepper. Add slice of ham. Add layer of cranberry sauce (No. 54). Dot generously with a mixture of mayonnaise (No. 701), chopped lettuce, and chopped pickles. Top with another slice bread. Cut diagonally.

(3324)   EGG CLUB SANDWICH

Substitute sliced hard-cooked egg (No. 202) for sliced chicken in recipe for club sandwich (No. 3322).

(3325)   BAKING POWDER BISCUIT
SANDWICHES

Roll out baking powder biscuit dough (No. 1012) to ½-inch thickness. Cut into rounds. Place a sausage on each round.

Moisten edges of dough. Fold over and press together with sausage in center. Bake in hot oven (475° F.) 12 to 15 minutes.

(3326) TOASTED RAW BEEF SANDWICHES

Spread scraped raw beef, seasoned to taste with salt and pepper, between 2 slices buttered bread. Brown sandwiches on both sides by broiling, grilling, or toasting. Serve hot.

(3327) BROILED BACON, CHEESE, AND TOMATO SANDWICH

Cut white bread in ¼-inch slices and trim off crusts. Spread lightly with butter. Cover bread with thin slices of American cheese. Then put slices of tomato on the cheese and sprinkle with salt and pepper. Lay 2 strips of bacon over the top. Put in broiler and broil until cheese melts and bacon is crisp.

(3328) STEAK SANDWICH

Broil a thin slice of steak rare (No. 1301). Place on slice of buttered toast (No. 988). Add 2 slices broiled bacon (No. 1464). Season to taste with salt, pepper, and any favorite meat sauce. Top with another slice of buttered toast and cut diagonally. Serve, garnished with sliced tomatoes, fried onions (No. 1811), and pickles.

(3329) CHICKEN WAFFLE SANDWICH

Place slices of cooked chicken, seasoned with chopped celery and mayonnaise (No. 701), and a lettuce leaf between 2 freshly made waffles (No. 938). Cover with gravy.

(3330) CHICKEN SALAD SANDWICH

Cut thin slices of white bread and trim off crusts. Spread lightly with butter. Make a filling of cold cooked chicken, cut in small cubes, and half the quantity of finely cut celery, seasoned with salt and pepper and moistened with mayonnaise (No. 701). Spread between two slices of bread. Cut in halves diagonally.

(3331)   OPEN CHOPPED HAM SANDWICHES

1 cup cooked ham, chopped	2 tablespoons chopped sour
1 hard-cooked egg	pickle
(No. 202), chopped	Few grains pepper
2 tablespoons chopped green	Mayonnaise (No. 701)
pepper	Plain rolls (No. 1032)

Mix together ham, egg, green pepper, pickle, and pepper. Moisten with a little mayonnaise. Split rolls. Spread both halves lightly with butter. Spread and cover with some of the ham mixture. Decorate tops with thin slices of pickle and strips of green pepper. Serve open.

(3332)   HOT HAM AND CHEESE
SANDWICH

Cut slices of white bread and trim off crusts. Spread lightly with butter. On one slice arrange a slice of ham and a thin slice of cheese and put another slice of bread on top. Mix ¾ cup milk, 1 beaten egg, and ¼ teaspoon salt together, dip sandwich in it and sauté in hot fat until brown on both sides. Drain on unglazed paper. Serve hot.

(3333)   TOASTED CHEESE SANDWICHES

Place slice of American cheese between 2 slices buttered bread with crusts trimmed off. Brown sandwiches on both sides by broiling, grilling, or toasting. Serve hot.

(3334)   BAKED CHEESE SANDWICH

1 pound American cheese	1 teaspoon Worcestershire
1 teaspoon mustard	sauce
½ teaspoon baking powder	1 egg
Speck of cayenne	2 tablespoons milk

Put cheese through chopper. Rub in other ingredients and mix to a creamy consistency. Spread on slices of bread from which the crust has been removed. Set in hot oven (500° F.) and bake to a light brown. The bread is crispy on the edges and cheese mixture is puffy. Serve at once.

(3335)   CHEESE SANDWICH PASTE

2 cups grated cheese
½ cup milk
2 well-beaten eggs
1 teaspoon ground white
   mustard

1 teaspoon salt
1 tablespoon butter
Dash cayenne
Dash pepper

Melt cheese. Add milk and eggs. Stir well. Add other ingredients. Cook until eggs are set. Remove from heat. Set pan in cold water and beat until thick and smooth. If desired, chopped sweet red peppers may be added after cooking.

(3336)   CHEESE DREAMS

Cut thin slices of bread and trim off crusts. Sprinkle thin slices of American cheese with salt, paprika, and cayenne and put between two slices of bread. Cut in halves and dip in a mixture of 1 beaten egg, ½ cup milk, and ¼ teaspoon salt. Fry in little fat until brown on both sides. Drain on unglazed paper and serve hot.

(3337)   SALMON CLUB SANDWICH

Arrange slices of tomato on toast. Spread with mayonnaise (No. 701). Cover with lettuce leaves. Sprinkle with French dressing (No. 716). Add layer of flaked, canned salmon or tuna fish and top with another slice of toast. Cut diagonally.

(3338)   SARDINE, HAM, AND BACON SANDWICH

12 sardines
1 cup chopped cooked ham
2 tablespoons chopped sweet
   pickles
1 teaspoon prepared mustard
1 teaspoon catchup
1 teaspoon lemon juice

12 slices bread or toast
2 tablespoons shredded
   lettuce
1 tablespoon mayonnaise
   (No. 701)
12 slices broiled bacon
   (No. 1464)

Remove skin and bones from sardines and chop with ham and pickles. Add mustard, catchup, and lemon juice and mix well. Spread on slices of buttered bread or toast. Sprinkle with lettuce. Dot with mayonnaise. Arrange 2 slices bacon on each sandwich and top with another slice of buttered bread or toast. Serves 6.

(3339) HOT SARDINE SANDWICHES

2 tablespoons butter	2 tablespoons catchup
2 tablespoons flour	½ cup grated sharp Ameri-
1 cup milk	can cheese
½ teaspoon salt	2 cans sardines
⅛ teaspoon paprika	6 slices toast

Blend together the butter and flour in a double boiler. Add milk and seasonings and cook until thickened, stirring constantly. Stir in the cheese. Arrange three or four sardines on each slice of toast. Place under the broiler until heated and serve with sauce over each sandwich. Yield: 6 sandwiches.

(3340) GRILLED CRAB MEAT AND EGG SANDWICHES

1 can crab meat	1 teaspoon prepared
Yolks of 4 hard-cooked eggs	mustard
(No. 202)	1 beef bouillon cube
1 tablespoon melted butter	¼ cup boiling water

Mix flaked crab meat with yolks of hard-cooked eggs which have been forced through a sieve. Moisten with melted butter, mustard, and beef bouillon cube, dissolved in water. Spread mixture between thin slices of buttered bread. Brush outside of bread with melted butter, place on heated grill, and cook until golden brown.

(3341) LOBSTER SANDWICH

Spread 2 slices bread or toast with mayonnaise (No. 701). Place thin slices boiled lobster (No. 1236) on 1 slice. Sprinkle with chopped hard-cooked eggs (No. 202). Add lettuce leaf and top with other slice of bread or toast.

(3342) SPICY SHRIMP SANDWICHES

1¼ cups boiled shrimp	1 teaspoon grated onion
(No. 1272)	2 teaspoons horseradish
¼ cup finely chopped sweet	¼ cup mayonnaise
pickle	(No. 701)
¼ cup chopped celery	Pepper
1 teaspoon lemon juice	Salt

Chop shrimp into small pieces. Add pickle, celery, lemon juice, and grated onion. Mix thoroughly. Add pepper and salt to taste. Combine horseradish and mayonnaise with shrimp mixture. Spread on buttered slices of bread or use for making canapes. **Yield: 2 cup spread.**

(3343)   FRIED EGG SANDWICH

Place a fried egg (No. 203), cooked on both sides and sprinkled with chopped onion, if desired, between 2 slices bread or buttered toast (No. 988).

(3344)   HAM AND EGG SANDWICHES

3 beaten eggs	1 tablespoon chopped onion
1 cup chopped cooked ham	Salt—Pepper

Combine ingredients, seasoning as desired. Pour as patties, the proper size for sandwiches, into hot, greased pan. Brown well on both sides. Place between slices of buttered toast (No. 988), bread, or rolls. **Yield: filling for 4 sandwiches.**

(3345) TOMATO AND CHEESE SANDWICH

Place 2 slices tomato on slice of buttered toast (No. 988). Mix 2 tablespoons cottage cheese with chopped watercress and chopped olive and spread on tomato. Top with another slice buttered toast.

(3346) GRAVY AND CRANBERRY SAUCE SANDWICH

Butter 2 slices bread. Spread 1 slice with any cold, left-over meat gravy and the other with cranberry sauce (No. 54). Press together.

(3347)   BROILED BAKED BEAN SANDWICH

1 slice toast	Grated or sliced American
1 heaping spoonful baked	cheese
beans (No. 1708)	½ slice bacon

Place a heaping spoonful of beans on slice of toast. Cover with grated or sliced American cheese. Top with half slices of bacon and broil slowly until bacon is crisp and cheese melted. Arrange on plate and garnish with fresh cucumber pickle. Serve at once.

(3348)   PIMIENTO SANDWICH FILLING

3 tablespoons flour	1 egg
½ teaspoon mustard	1 cup water
½ teaspoon salt	½ cup vinegar
2 tablespoons sugar	2 tablespoons butter
¼ teaspoon paprika	1 cup chopped pimientos

Mix the dry ingredients. Add water, vinegar, and beaten egg. Mix well and cook until thickened, stirring constantly. Add the butter and pimientos and cook gently about 3 minutes. Cool and store in the refrigerator in a jar. This may be used for sandwich filling or salad dressing. The sandwich bread may be spread with a meat or fish paste before the pimiento filling and lettuce are added.

(3349)   BAKED BEAN SANDWICH

Toast slices of bread. Butter and spread with baked beans (No. 1708). On this place a thin slice of Bermuda onion and cover the top with slices of bacon. Arrange in broiler pan and place in oven so that food is about 3 inches below broiling unit. Broil about 8 minutes, or until bacon is done.

(3350) BANANA PEANUT BUTTER SANDWICH

8 slices bread	2 bananas, sliced
Peanut butter	Butter

Spread 4 slices bread with peanut butter. Place banana slices on peanut butter. Butter remaining slices of bread and use to top sandwiches. Yield: 4 sandwiches.

(3351)   BANANA HAM SANDWICH

¾ cup cooked ham, chopped	1 teaspoon onion, chopped
¼ cup celery, diced	1 banana
1½ teaspoons prepared mustard	8 slices bread
	Butter

Mix ham, celery, onion, and mustard. Dice banana and mix lightly with ham mixture. Spread 4 slices bread with mixture. Spread remaining bread with butter and use to top sandwiches. Yield: 4 sandwiches.

(3352)   BANANA RAISIN SANDWICH

1 cup chopped raisins	8 slices bread
1 teaspoon salt	2 bananas, peeled
Mayonnaise (No. 701)	Butter

Mix raisins and salt. Add enough mayonnaise to moisten. Spread 4 slices bread with raisin mixture. Slice bananas and place on mixture. Spread butter on remaining bread and use to cover sandwiches. Yield: 4 sandwiches.

(3353)   SOUTHERN HAM SANDWICH

6 pieces corn bread, about 3 inches square	1 can condensed cream of mushroom soup
6 slices ham, boiled or baked	½ cup milk

Stir milk into soup. Heat, but do not boil. While the sauce is heating, split the pieces of corn bread and toast them. Then place the ham between the toasted slices of corn bread and pour the hot mushroom sauce over the top.

(3354)   FUDGE SANDWICH

Make fudge (No. 3801). After beating turn out in thin layer onto any desired sweet crackers or cookies. Top with other cookies. Chill.

(3355)   PENUCHI SANDWICH

Substitute penuchi (No. 3802) for fudge in recipe for fudge sandwich (No. 3354).

Church and Grange

LARGE quantity cooking for church, grange, or lodge suppers has its own problems. The menu should always be planned with due regard to available cooking and serving equipment. Foods, which may be readily kept warm for an extended period of time, should be served. The same general dietary rules, which apply to meals for the large or small family, should be observed in the preparation of meals for a large group. If the main course of the meal is rich in fats or starch, serve a fruit dessert. If a salad provides the principal course, a rich dessert may be served.

Large luncheons and suppers are usually festive occasions and the room and table should be tastefully and appropriately decorated. Throughout the warm months there is available an abundance of flowers, fall brings lovely foliage in rich, seasonable colors, and the clever use of crepe paper at other seasons will make the diners acquire the mood the occasion demands.

At such luncheons, dinners, or suppers the guests should not be gorged with food. Portions should be made dainty and as pleasing in appearance as is possible. Great care should be taken in measuring portions in order that one half of the guests are not skimped to overfeed those who were served first.

Almost any dish in this entire volume can be produced in sufficient quantity to feed large numbers. The proper amount of ingredients to purchase can be determined by simple multiplication. In some recipes, however, the method of preparing for large numbers varies from the small-family procedure to such an extent that instructions are given in this chapter. Recipes which require exact cooking times at exact temperatures

should be avoided in large-quantity cooking because it is difficult to maintain even temperatures for long periods in heavy-
duty stoves in which several dishes are being cooked at once,
with the frequent opening and shutting of the oven doors.

(3401)   CHOCOLATE

2 pounds chocolate	1/2 teaspoon salt
3 pounds sugar	16 quarts hot milk

Melt chocolate. Add sugar and 4 quarts boiling water and
stir until smooth. Boil 10 minutes. Add salt. Pour into the hot
milk. Beat well with an egg beater and keep hot over boiling
water. Serve with whipped cream. Serves 100.

(3402)   COCOA

3 cups cocoa	1/2 teaspoon salt
4 cups sugar	16 quarts hot milk

Mix cocoa, sugar, salt, and 1 quart warm water together until
smooth. Add 2 quarts boiling water and boil 10 minutes. Pour
into the hot milk. Bring to boiling point, stirring constantly.
and beat with an egg beater for a few minutes. Keep hot over
boiling water. Serve with whipped cream. Serves 100.

(3403)   COFFEE

4 cups ground coffee	9 quarts water

Tie the coffee in thick cheesecloth bags, leaving plenty of
room for coffee to swell. Let stand in the water several hours.
Bring slowly to boiling point and boil 5 minutes. Remove the
bags and keep coffee hot for serving. Serves 50.

(3404)   RECEPTION PUNCH

8 cups sugar	2 quarts iced tea
2 quarts water	(No. 307)
1/2 cup crushed mint leaves	2 gallons water
3 quarts orange juice	2 quarts ginger ale
1 quart pineapple, grape, or berry juice	Orange and lemon slices and mint sprigs
1 quart lemon juice	

Boil sugar with the 2 quarts water about 5 minutes. Add
crushed mint. Cool and strain. Add fruit juices, tea, and remaining water. Just before serving add ginger ale. Pour over
ice in punch bowls. Garnish with slices and sprigs. Serves 100.

(3405)   ORANGE JUICE PUNCH

1 quart orange juice	1 quart vanilla ice cream
1 quart orange sherbet	(No. 2547)
(No. 2572)	1 quart cold ginger ale

Beat orange juice, sherbet, and ice cream with rotary beater until well mixed. Add ginger ale. Stir well. Serves 30.

(3406)   FRUIT CUP

3 1/4 quarts canned sliced peaches	2 quarts grapefruit segments
3 quarts canned crushed pineapple	3 cups fruit juice

Drain fruit, reserving juice. Cut into proper-size pieces for serving. Add to juice. Chill. Cherries, grapes, or other fruits may be added or substituted. Serves 50.

(3407)   VEGETABLE SOUP

3 quarts stewed (No. 1893) or canned tomatoes	2 cups rice
	6 onions
1/4 cup salt	1 1/2 quarts celery
3 teaspoons pepper	3 quarts potatoes
2 bay leaves	1 quart carrots
2 cups butter or fat	1 pint turnips

Put tomatoes in a large soup kettle with 5 gallons water or any meat or vegetable stock. Add salt, pepper, bay leaves, butter or fat, and rice. Clean and pare vegetables and chop into small pieces. Add to soup. Cover and simmer slowly 2 hours. Serves 50.

(3408)   CLAM CHOWDER

1 bushel soft clams, in the shell, or 1/2 bushel razor clams, in the shell	1 pound diced salt pork
	1 teaspoon pepper
	3 tablespoons salt
3 quarts potatoes, peeled and sliced	1 1/2 gallons water
	2 gallons milk
1 quart sliced onions	

Wash clams thoroughly in fresh water to remove sand. Place clams in a pan and cover with clean, salt water. Sprinkle a handful of corn meal over them and let stand 2 to 3 hours. The clams will try to get the meal and in so doing will work out sand in shell. Put clams in kettle. Add water and boil until clams open. Drain, reserving liquid. Shell clams. Remove stomach contents, cut off dark necks, and rinse the bodies. Razor clams should be cut into 1-inch lengths. Put diced pork into kettle and fry brown. Add the sliced onions and cook to a golden yellow. Add the sliced potatoes, seasonings, and clam liquor. Cook until the potatoes are half done. Then add the clams and continue cooking until the potatoes are soft. Then add the milk which has been heated. If desired, the chowder may be slightly thickened with flour. Hard crackers may be added to the chowder immediately before serving. Serves 32.

(3409) FISH CHOWDER

15 pounds fish, cleaned, and trimmed but not split	1 pound diced salt pork
	1 teaspoon pepper
2 quarts potatoes, peeled and sliced	3 tablespoons salt
	1½ gallons water
1 quart sliced onions	2 gallons milk

In a heavy kettle, fry the diced pork to a golden brown. Add the potatoes and onions in alternate layers. Add the seasoning and water. Lay the fish in a boiling basket on top of the whole and simmer until the potatoes are cooked. Remove fish and separate the flesh from the skin and bones. Return the flesh to the chowder. Have the milk hot, but not boiled, and pour it into the chowder and mix the whole with a minimum of stirring. The milk may be slightly thickened if desired. Just before serving, add hard crackers to the chowder. Serves 32.

(3410) POTATO SALAD

8 quarts potatoes	½ cup chopped parsley
1½ quarts chopped celery	Lettuce
2 tablespoons salt	1 quart mayonnaise
1 quart French dressing (No. 716)	(No. 701)
	Stuffed olives

Wash, pare, and cube potatoes. Cook in boiling salted water until tender. Drain and cool. Add celery, salt, and parsley. Toss with a salad fork to mix. Add French dressing and let stand 3 hours. Serve on lettuce leaves, garnished with mayonnaise and stuffed olives. Serves 50.

(3411)   TUNA FISH OR SALMON SALAD

8 pounds canned tuna fish
  or salmon
1 gallon chopped celery
2 cups cooked dressing
  (No. 737)
½ cup heavy cream

2 cups mayonnaise
  (No. 701)
Lettuce
9 tomatoes
1 bunch parsley

Break fish into medium-size pieces. Add celery. Whip cream, mix with cooked dressing and mayonnaise, and add to first mixture. Mix lightly. Serve on lettuce leaves, garnished with tomato slices and parsley. Serves 50.

(3412)   CHICKEN SALAD

4 quarts cooked chicken, cut
  in small pieces
4 quarts chopped celery
1 tablespoon salt
1 teaspoon pepper
1 pint French dressing
  (No. 716)

2 quarts cooked salad dressing (No. 737) or
  mayonnaise (No. 701)
Lettuce
8 hard-cooked eggs
  (No. 202), sliced

Combine chicken, celery, salt, pepper, and French dressing. Let stand 2 hours. Add salad dressing or mayonnaise. Mix well. Serve on lettuce leaves, garnished with egg. Serves 50. Chopped ham may be substituted for any part of the chicken.

(3413)   TOMATO GELATIN SALAD

5 cups canned condensed
  tomato soup
2 cups cold water

5⅓ tablespoons gelatin
1 teaspoon salt
2 cups lemon juice

Salad dressing

Heat tomato soup to boiling. Soften gelatin in cold water 5 minutes. Mix softened gelatin with hot soup, stirring until dissolved. Add salt and lemon juice. Pour into shallow oblong pans. Chill thoroughly. When firm, cut into 50 squares. Serve on crisp lettuce with mayonnaise (No. 701) or cooked salad dressing (No. 737). Serves 50.

(3414) SOUTHERN CORN BREAD

2 quarts flour	6 eggs, beaten
½ cup sugar	1½ tablespoons soda
¾ cup baking powder	1½ quarts buttermilk
4 tablespoons salt	1 cup melted shortening
3½ cups corn meal	

Mix and sift flour, sugar, baking powder, and salt. Stir in corn meal and mix well. Add eggs. Add soda, dissolved in buttermilk, and shortening. Beat thoroughly. Bake in greased shallow pans in quick oven (425° F.) 35 minutes. Serves 50.

(3415) BAKING POWDER BISCUITS

6½ quarts flour	3 cups shortening
½ cup salt	2 quarts milk
¾ cup baking powder	

Mix and sift flour, salt, and baking powder. Cut in shortening with a knife or rub in with the finger tips. Add milk slowly to make a soft dough. Roll out on slightly floured board to ¾-inch thickness and cut with a biscuit cutter. Put on a greased baking sheet and bake in a quick oven (425° F.) 10 to 15 minutes. Yield: 100 biscuits.

(3416) FRIED FISH, CRUMBLED IN CORN MEAL

16 pounds fish filets or 24 pounds small fish, heads removed, either split or whole	1 quart flour
	1 quart medium fine yellow corn meal
	⅝ cup salt
Fat for frying	

Sift together the flour, corn meal, and salt. Dip fish in water and roll in the above crumbing mixture. Heat fat in frying pan and, when smoking begins, place a single layer of fish in the pan and cook 3 minutes. Then turn fish and cook on the other side. Or, put fish in a single layer in deep, hot fat (385° F.) and brown evenly about 4 to 8 minutes. Garnish with lemon slices. Serves 32.

(3417)   BROILED FISH

16 pounds fish filets or 24 pounds small fish, heads removed, either split or whole	1 pint cooking oil 2 tablespoons salt 1/3 teaspoon pepper

Wash the fish and wipe dry. Mix the cooking oil, salt, and pepper, and brush this over the fish. If a broiler is available and there is a good bed of live coals, the fish is placed skin side down on the well-oiled broiler and cooked 5 minutes or until the skin is covered with brown bubbles. The fish is then turned and the flesh side similarly cooked. Baste while cooking. Garnish with lemon slices. Serves 32.

(3418)   BOILED FISH AND EGGS IN WHITE SAUCE

20 pounds dressed fish 5 tablespoons salt	2 1/3 cups vinegar 12 quarts water

Put the washed fish into a boiling basket or wrap in cheese-cloth. Boil in the mixture of salt, vinegar, and water 8 to 12 minutes, depending upon the variety of fish. Separate the fish flesh from skin and bones. Serve hot with a white sauce (No. 2004) made from 4 1/2 quarts milk, 1/2 pound butter, 1/2 pound flour, and 1 dozen chopped hard-cooked eggs (No. 202). Serves 32.

(3419)   BOILED FISH WITH SPANISH SAUCE

24 pounds dressed fish 5 tablespoons salt 2 1/2 cups vinegar 12 quarts water	6 1/2 quarts stewed tomatoes (No. 1893) 3 quarts sliced onions 2 tablespoons sugar
1 1/2 cups butter	

Put the washed fish into a boiling basket or wrap in cheese-cloth. Boil gently in the mixture of salt, vinegar, and water only long enough to be able to separate fish flesh from bones and skin. The fish flesh should be kept in as large pieces as possible. Simmer the tomatoes and sliced onions until the latter are tender. Add the fish flesh which has been separated from skin and bones. Add butter and sugar. Simmer the whole, with minimum stirring, until flavors are blended. Garnish with hard-cooked egg (No. 202) slices. Serves 32.

(3420) CLAM BAKE WITH POTATOES AND SWEET CORN

2 bushels clams in the shell	6 dozen ears sweet corn, all
3 pecks sweet potatoes or	but inside layer of husk
small white potatoes	removed
Melted butter	

Prepare a rock platform about 20 feet long, 4 feet wide, and 8 to 10 inches deep. Provide plenty of firewood and about 20 bushels of fresh wet rock weed, avoid dead or dry weed. Keep a brisk fire well spread over the rock platform for 1 to 2 hours or until it is well heated. Remove smoking wood. The food should be ready for cooking. Cover the hot stones and live embers at once with about 4 inches of wet rock weed. Spread the food over this, then cover it with another 4-inch layer of wet rock weed. Over the whole, spread a heavy canvas or similar cover to hold in the steam. Allow the food to cook for about 40 minutes or until the potatoes are soft. By eating near the cooking place, food may be kept covered and hot until used. The clams will open during the cooking. The loose cover around the neck of the clam should be removed and the dark neck may be cut or bitten off. The clams are dipped into hot melted butter as eaten. Small lobsters, filets of fish in wax paper, and other foods may be added. Serves 32.

(3421) OYSTER ROAST

3 bushels medium or large	5 pounds melted butter
oysters in the shell	Salt—Pepper

Wash and rinse oysters in fresh water. Place, deep side down, on a sheet iron plate. Roast 10 to 15 minutes over a clear fire or at high heat. Serve with butter, salt, and pepper on the side. Serves 32.

(3422)   FISH CAKES

8 pounds fish flakes	Salt
1 gallon boiled potatoes	Pepper
(No. 1834)	Crumbing mixture or flour
1 dozen eggs, beaten	Cooking oil, salt pork, or
⅓ cup butter, melted	other frying medium

Boiled or left-over fish may be used for flakes. The flesh separated from skin and bones should be coarsely chopped. The potatoes should be chopped, and then mixed with the chopped fish, beaten eggs, butter, and seasoning. The amount of the latter will depend upon the original cooking of the fish, and the cooking fat. Mold the mixture into cakes about ¾ inch thick and 2½ inches in diameter and chill if possible. Roll the cakes in crumbs or flour and sauté until brown on both sides in frying medium. The cakes may also be deep fried. For this method of cooking, the cakes should be crumbed and placed in a single layer in a well oiled frying basket. Cook to a golden brown in fat heated to 385° F. Serves 32.

(3423)   CREAMED FISH

16 pounds fish flakes	2½ quarts medium white sauce
Salt—Pepper	(No. 2004)

The fish flakes should be prepared from boiled fish after separation from skin and bones. The amount of seasoning will depend upon the original cooking of the fish. To the white sauce may be added chopped hard-cooked eggs (No. 202), minced onions, grated cheese, minced green peppers, chopped mushrooms, or other similar material. Serves 32.

(3424)   PINEBARK STEW

1 pound bacon	1 pound butter
15 pounds white-meated fish,	5 cups catchup
dressed and split	2 teaspoons black pepper
5 pounds diced potatoes	1 teaspoon red pepper
1½ pounds sliced onions	1 bottle Worcestershire
2 tablespoons curry powder	sauce
2 tablespoons salt	

A large Dutch oven or heavy kettle and a large frying pan are desirable for cooking the stew. Mince the bacon and fry it dry in the kettle. Add the onion and cook to a golden yellow. Add the potatoes, salt, and 1 tablespoon curry powder. Add just enough water to cover the potatoes and simmer about 20 minutes. Then add the split fish, mixing it with the potatoes and onions. Cook the whole about 10 minutes or until the potatoes are soft. While the fish is cooking, melt the butter in the frying pan and mix the other ingredients into the hot butter. Dip the liquor from the kettle into the frying pan with constant stirring, the result being a rich bark-colored gravy or sauce. Serve large pieces of fish with the potatoes, on toast with rice (No. 107), the gravy being poured over the portions of stew as served. Serves 32.

(3425) ESCALLOPED SALMON

10 one-pound cans salmon	2¾ cups flour
3 quarts broken bread	½ teaspoon paprika
4 quarts milk	2 tablespoons salt
4 bay leaves	1 cup buttered crumbs
1½ cups fat	

Mix salmon with broken bread. Add bay leaves to milk and scald. Remove bay leaves. Melt fat, blend with flour, and add to scalded milk, stirring rapidly. Add salt and paprika and cook 15 minutes. Combine the two mixtures and pour into greased pans. Sprinkle buttered crumbs on top. Bake in a moderate oven (350° F.) 30 minutes. Tuna fish may be substituted for salmon if desired. Serves 50.

(3426) CREAMED CHICKEN

½ pound butter	6¾ quarts milk
½ pound chicken fat	½ gallon rich chicken stock
1 pound 2 ounces flour	(No. 502)
1 ounce salt	4 pounds chicken meat,
Few grains pepper	cooked and cubed

Make white sauce (No. 2004) of first seven ingredients. Add chicken just before serving and heat thoroughly. Serve on biscuits or in patty shells (No. 2709). The amount of chicken may be increased when the price permits. Serves 50.

(3427) CHICKEN Á LA KING

6 quarts cold, cooked chicken, cut in cubes	¼ cup chopped parsley
	1 pound mushrooms
1 can pimiento, chopped	2 tablespoons fat
2 tablespoons salt	3 quarts white sauce
1 tablespoon pepper	(No. 2004)

Combine chicken, pimiento, salt, pepper, and parsley. Mix well. Peel mushrooms and slice. Sauté 10 minutes in fat. Add white sauce, mix thoroughly, and turn into chicken mixture. Heat over boiling water, stirring frequently. Serve on buttered toast (No. 988) or in patty shells (No. 2709). Serves 50.

(3428) CORNED BEEF LOAF

12 pounds cooked corned beef hash (No. 1357)	8 ounces chopped onions
	1 quart milk
1 dozen eggs	

Beat eggs and combine with hash. Add onions and milk. Shape into 6 equal-size loaves. Place in greased loaf pans. Bake in moderately hot oven (375° F.) 15 minutes. Serve with creole sauce (No. 2047). Serves 50.

(3429) BARBECUED CORNED BEEF

5 pounds cooked corned beef (No. 1351)	1 cup chili sauce
	1 cup prepared mustard
1 cup butter	½ cup Worcestershire sauce
1 cup catchup	¼ teaspoon cayenne

Slice corned beef. Cream butter, while gradually adding other ingredients. Brush meat slices generously with mixture. Put in baking pan and bake in moderately hot oven (375° F.) 15 minutes. Serves 50.

(3430) MASHED POTATOES

15 pounds potatoes	¼ cup salt
1½ quarts scalded milk	¼ cup butter or fat, melted

Pare potatoes. Wash and boil (No. 1834) until tender. Mash until smooth. Add other ingredients. Beat until light and fluffy. Serves 50.

(3431) BAKED BEANS

4 quarts pea beans	½ cup sugar
6 tablespoons salt	2 teaspoons mustard
¼ cup soda	2 teaspoons paprika
1 cup molasses	1 pound chopped salt pork

Soak beans in cold water to cover 10 hours. Drain. Cover with water. Add salt. Simmer until almost tender. Drain. Add other ingredients and 3 quarts hot water. Bake in shallow, greased pans in moderate oven (350° F.) 1¼ to 1½ hours. Serve with tomato catchup. Serves 70.

(3432) BAKED BEAN LOAF

6½ quarts baked beans (No. 3431)	About 5 cups milk
10 cups bread crumbs	1 tablespoon salt
1 cup finely chopped onion	Pepper
8 eggs	Paprika

Mix the beans and onion. Beat the eggs. Combine the ingredients, form into loaves, put into buttered baking pans, and bake in a moderately hot oven (400° F.) until brown, about 25 minutes. Serve with chili sauce. Serves 50.

(3433) STUFFED GREEN PEPPERS

8 pounds cooked corned beef hash (No. 1357)	2 cups chili sauce
6 tablespoons chopped onion	16 large green peppers

Mix hash, onion, and chili sauce. Cut peppers into thirds, remove seeds and hard membrane, and wash. Fill each section with hash mixture. Place in a single layer in shallow pan with ¼ inch water in bottom. Bake in moderate oven (350° F.) 30 minutes. Serves 48.

(3434)   ESCALLOPED CORN

6 quarts stewed corn (No. 1769)	2 teaspoons salt
4 quarts milk	1 teaspoon pepper
1 cup fat	2 quarts cracker or bread crumbs
½ cup finely chopped onion	

Heat milk, fat, and onion. Add salt and pepper and pour over crumbs. Alternate with a layer of corn, crumbs, and corn in a greased pan. Sprinkle with buttered crumbs on top. Bake in a moderate oven (350° F.) until brown, about 45 minutes. Serves 50.

(3435)   ESCALLOPED CARROTS AND CHEESE

6 quarts boiled carrots (No. 1745), diced	2¼ pounds grated cheese
3 quarts medium white sauce (No. 2004)	2 quarts buttered crumbs
	Salt—Pepper

Sprinkle salt and pepper over carrots. Place all ingredients in alternate layers in greased baking pan with a layer of crumbs on top. Bake in moderate oven (350° F.) 40 minutes or until cheese is melted and crumbs are golden brown. Boiled onions (No. 1810) or boiled (No. 1721) or baked red kidney beans (No. 1708) may be substituted for carrots. Serves 50.

(3436)   RAISIN SAUCE FOR BAKED HAM

6 cups vinegar	¾ cup mustard
6½ quarts water	¾ cup flour
12 cups brown sugar	6 cups raisins

Mix dry ingredients. Add raisins, vinegar, and water. Cook to a sirup and serve hot over ham. Serves 100.

(3437)   MACARONI AND CHEESE

5 pounds macaroni	2 pounds cheese, cut in small pieces
¼ cup salt	
6 quarts thin white sauce (No. 2004)	1 quart soft bread crumbs
	½ cup fat

Break macaroni in pieces. Cook in 2 gallons boiling salted water until tender. Drain. Add white sauce and cheese to the macaroni. Put in greased shallow baking pans. Cover with crumbs and dot with small bits of fat. Bake in moderate oven (350° F.) 50 to 60 minutes. Serves 50.

(3438) COTTAGE PUDDING

1 cup shortening	1 teaspoon ground cloves
3 cups sugar	1 teaspoon nutmeg
1 tablespoon vanilla	1 teaspoon salt
4 eggs	5 cups flour
2 tablespoons baking powder	2⅓ cups milk
1½ teaspoons cinnamon	

Cream fat and sugar together until well blended. Add vanilla and continue creaming. Beat eggs and add. Mix well. Sift baking powder, cinnamon, cloves, nutmeg, salt, and flour together and add alternately with milk to first mixture. Beat to thoroughly blend. Turn into greased shallow pan and bake in moderate oven (350° F.) 35 minutes. Serve with any desired fruit sauce. Serves 50.

(3439) TAPIOCA CREAM

4½ quarts milk	5 egg yolks
1¼ cups granulated tapioca	5 egg whites, stiffly beaten
2 cups sugar	¼ cup vanilla
1 tablespoon salt	

Scald milk in double boiler. Add tapioca, 1 cup sugar, and salt. Cook until tapioca is transparent. Beat egg yolks, combine with remaining sugar, and add to first mixture, stirring while adding. Cook 8 to 10 minutes. Fold in egg whites. Remove from heat. When slightly cool, add vanilla. Serve hot, garnished with apricot halves, raspberries, blackberries, blueberries, cherries, strawberries, or pineapple chunks. Serves 50. Other tapioca puddings, suitable for large gatherings, are described in the dessert section. They include tapioca custard pudding (No. 2491), apple tapioca (No. 2492), chocolate tapioca (No. 2493), coffee tapioca (No. 2494), meringue tapioca (No. 2495), and Indian tapioca (No. 2497). Increase amounts of ingredients to meet requirements.

(3440)   BLUEBERRY BETTY

5 quarts stewed blueberries (No. 49)	2 teaspoons nutmeg
4 quarts bread crumbs	3½ quarts water or blueberry juice
3½ cups brown sugar	1⅛ cups fat
3 teaspoons cinnamon	4 tablespoons lemon juice

Cover bottom of greased pans with a layer of crumbs. Add a layer of blueberries, a layer of crumbs and repeat until all are used. Have crumbs on top. Dissolve brown sugar in blueberry juice. Add spices and lemon juice and pour over mixture. Melt fat and pour over top. Bake in a moderate oven (350° F.) 45 minutes. This may be served with hard sauce (No. 3105), lemon (No. 3129), or vanilla sauce (No. 3149), plain or whipped cream. Cake crumbs may be substituted for bread crumbs. Serves 50.

(3441)   PUMPKIN PIE

3¼ quarts mashed pumpkin (No. 1864)	5 cups brown sugar
4 quarts milk	2 tablespoons cinnamon
16 eggs, separated	1 tablespoon ginger
	1 tablespoon salt

Mix pumpkin with milk and well-beaten egg yolks. Combine with sugar mixed with spices and salt. Fold in the stiffly beaten egg whites. Pour mixture into pie pans, lined with plain pastry (No. 2701). Bake in hot oven (450° F.) 10 minutes. Reduce the heat to 350° F. and bake 30 minutes. Yield: 8 9-inch pies.

(3442)   APPLE PIES

6 pounds flour	2 tablespoons cinnamon
¼ cup salt	7 pounds sugar
3 pounds shortening	1 cup flour (additional)
16 pounds tart apples	½ cup butter or fat

Mix and sift 6 pounds flour and salt. Cut in shortening with a knife or work in with finger tips. Moisten with enough cold water to hold dough together. Roll to ⅛-inch thickness. Line 15 slightly floured and greased pie pans with dough. Pare, core, and slice apples thin. Add cinnamon, sugar, and 1 cup flour. Mix well. Put in dough-lined pie pans. Dot with ½ cup butter or fat. Cover with top crusts. Moisten edges of dough with water. Press together and trim. Gash top crusts. Bake in quick oven (425° F.) 10 minutes. Reduce heat and continue baking in moderate oven (350° F.) 25 to 30 minutes. Yield: 15 pies.

(3443) CHERRY TARTS

4 quarts canned red sour pitted cherries	¾ cup cornstarch
	50 tart shells (No. 2708)
5 cups sirup from cherries	2½ cups whipping cream
3¾ cups sugar	

Drain cherries. Heat cherry juice to boiling. Sift sugar mixed with cornstarch into boiling liquid. Cook about 10 minutes or until thick. Add cherries and cook 5 minutes. Cool. Fill tart shells. Put one tablespoon whipped cream on center of cherry filling. Recipe makes 50 tarts, each tart shell 2¾ inches in diameter.

(3444) GINGERSNAPS

1 cup molasses	1 teaspoon cinnamon
1 cup shortening	2 teaspoons ginger
1 cup sugar	1 teaspoon salt
1 teaspoon soda	4 cups flour

Heat molasses, shortening, and sugar together until shortening is melted. Cool. Add soda dissolved in 2 tablespoons water. Sift cinnamon, ginger, and salt with part of the flour. Stir into the first mixture and then add the rest of the flour gradually until dough is stiff enough to roll. Chill. Roll on slightly floured board until very thin. Cut with a cookie cutter and bake in a moderate oven (325° F.) 10 to 12 minutes. Yield: 120 cookies.

(3445) PEACH LAYER CAKE

3¼ quarts canned sliced peaches	1 tablespoon lemon juice
	1 quart cream for whipping
1 quart granulated sugar	

Combine peaches, sugar, and lemon juice and let them stand in a cold place until thoroughly chilled. Just before serving, beat the cream until stiff, add the peach mixture and use as filling and topping for plain two-layer cakes (No. 2953), putting filling between the layers and on top of the layers. The peach filling is planned for eight average-sized two-layer cakes. If a plainer filling is desired, use half as much cream for whipping. Serves 50.

(3446)   CHOCOLATE CAKE

1 cup shortening	2 cups milk
6 cups sugar	9 ounces unsweetened
9 egg yolks	chocolate
8 cups flour	1 tablespoon vanilla
2½ teaspoons salt	9 egg whites
4 tablespoons baking powder	

Cream shortening, sugar, and egg yolks together. Mix and sift flour, salt, and baking powder and add alternately with the milk to the first mixture. Add melted chocolate and vanilla and beat thoroughly. Fold in stiffly beaten egg whites. Pour into greased shallow pans and bake in a moderate oven (350° F.) 20 to 30 minutes. When cool cover with any desired frosting. Serves 50.

(3447)   RASPBERRY MOUSSE

3 cups sugar	6 tablespoons lemon juice
7½ cups canned red raspberries	3 cups heavy cream

Boil sugar with 1½ quarts water 8 minutes. Force raspberry pulp and juice through a sieve and add to sirup. Add lemon juice. Blend thoroughly. Place in a freezing unit. Stir every 30 minutes for 1½ hours. Remove and fold in cream, beating 2 or 3 minutes if crystals are large. Return to freezing unit and freeze 2 to 3 hours longer. Loganberries, strawberries, black raspberries, blackberries, peaches, or cubed pineapple may be substituted for red raspberries. Serves 50.

720   NEW AMERICAN COOK BOOK

Foreign Dishes

FOREIGN homemakers, in many ways, have been less fortunate than their American sisters. Many of the finer choices and selections of foods, used casually by every New World housewife, are unobtainable by the poorer or middle classes in other parts of the world. Also, here in America, the very best and most modern in equipment for cooking is available to most women. In many foreign lands only primitive equipment is in use.

Despite those disadvantages foreign meal-designers and cooks have not lagged behind Americans in the production of tasty, health-giving meals. With limited and often poor varieties of foods to work with, the homemakers of Europe, South America, Asia, Africa, and other parts of the world have become expert in the art of seasoning and combining foods for best results. In this chapter are given many of the most widely known foreign dishes, the reputation of which has brought many into common usage in the United States. Throughout this entire book, other foreign recipes, which have become so well known as to be completely Americanized, will be found. Look for them under the names of countries and races in the index.

The American family will appreciate the variety which is introduced into the menu by the occasional use of foreign dishes. These foods also serve an educational purpose by giving the school children a vivid insight into the lives and customs of their cousins across the seas.

(3501)   CHILEAN KIDNEY BEANS

2 medium-sized onions
1 pound ground beef
¼ cup fat
2 teaspoons salt
⅛ teaspoon pepper

2 tablespoons chili powder
2½ cup stewed tomatoes
        (No. 1893)
2½ cups boiled red kidney
        beans (No. 1721)

Chop onions. Cook them and the beef in the fat until lightly browned, stirring often. Add seasonings and tomatoes and simmer gently 1 hour. Add the kidney beans and simmer several minutes more to allow the flavors to blend. Serves 6.

(3502)   CHINESE CHOP SUEY

1 pound shredded meat,
        either 1 kind or in
        combination
¼ cup butter or fat
1 cup peeled and sliced
        mushrooms

¾ cup shredded celery
1 onion, chopped
½ cup chestnuts, sliced
2 cups canned bean sprouts
2 cups white stock
        (No. 502)

Sauté meat in melted butter until well browned. Strain. Return fat to pan and add mushrooms, celery, onion, and chestnuts. Sauté 5 minutes. Add cooked meat, bean sprouts, and stock. Cover and simmer 30 minutes. Serve with boiled rice (No. 107). Serves 6. Poultry, fish, or shellfish may be substituted for meat. Serve soy sauce on the side.

(3503)   CHINESE CHOW MEIN

Serve chop suey (No. 3502) over noodles (No. 2301) which have been fried to a golden brown in deep hot fat (375° F.) and drained on unglazed paper.

(3504)   CHINESE FOO CHOW SCRAMBLE

8-ounce can sliced mush-
        rooms
2½ cups canned bean sprouts
Butter

6 eggs
½ cup cream
½ teaspoon salt
Dash pepper

Drain the liquid from the mushrooms and the bean sprouts, saving it for soup or sauce. Sauté the mushrooms in butter to a light brown. Add the bean sprouts and sauté a few minutes. Beat the eggs with the cream and seasonings for 1 minute. Cook in melted butter until of a creamy consistency, stirring constantly. Place a mound of the mushroom and bean sprout mixture on the plate and serve the scrambled eggs over it. Serves 6.

(3505)   CUBAN BEEF STEW

1 quart canned or strained stewed tomatoes (No. 1893)	¼ teaspoon red pepper
	1 cup boiled spaghetti (No. 2302)
3 chopped onions	1 pound chopped beef
1 teaspoon salt	2 tablespoons butter

Put tomatoes in saucepan. Add onions, salt, and pepper. Mix well. Let stand 1 hour. Add spaghetti and meat. Bring to boil. Reduce heat. Let simmer 30 minutes. Stir in melted butter. Serve hot. Serves 6.

(3506)   DANISH GOULASH

2 pounds top round steak, ¼ inch thick	4 medium-sized onions
¼ cup butter or fat	1 tablespoon brown sugar
⅛ teaspoon pepper	6 small bay leaves
2½ teaspoons salt	4 tablespoons flour

Wipe meat with cold, damp cloth. Cut in ¼-inch cubes. Melt butter in frying pan. Add pepper and 2 teaspoons salt. Add meat and brown on all sides over high heat about 10 minutes. Peel onions. Cut in half, lengthwise. Shave paper-thin and add to browning meat cubes. Continue searing for 5 minutes, stirring constantly. Transfer to kettle. Add 2 cups boiling water, brown sugar, remaining salt, and bay leaves. Cover and bring to boiling point. Reduce heat and let simmer 1 hour. Remove bay leaves. Thicken stew with flour, mixed to a smooth paste with 6 tablespoons cold water. Cook until thickened, stirring well. Serve over hot, mashed potatoes (No. 1835) on hot platter. Serves 6.

(3507) DANISH APPLE CAKE

½ pound macaroons	3 tablespoons butter
(No. 3063)	2½ cups applesauce (No. 34)
3 cups toast crumbs	1 cup heavy cream, whipped

Roll the macaroons. Mix macaroons and toast crumbs. Sauté them lightly in the butter. Pack in layers in a mold alternately with crumbs and applesauce. Allow to harden in the refrigerator. Serve with whipped cream. Peach butter, apricot butter, crushed pineapple, raspberries, loganberries, cherries or practically any canned fruit may be substituted for the applesauce if the fruit is cooked to a sauce consistency.

(3508) DUTCH POTATOES

6 boiled potatoes	Salt—Pepper
(No. 1834)	1 egg
2 tablespoons chopped onion	½ cup milk
1 tablespoon chopped parsley	1 cup buttered crumbs

Drain potatoes and slice thin. Put in layers in greased baking dish, sprinkling each layer with onion, parsley, salt, and pepper. Beat egg and combine with milk. Pour over potatoes. Cover with crumbs. Bake in moderate oven (350° F.) 30 minutes. Serves 4.

(3509) EAST INDIAN CURRY

1 onion, chopped	1½ cups water or stock
¼ cup butter or fat	(No. 501)
3 pounds lean meat, cubed	Salt
1½ tablespoons curry powder	2 tablespoons lemon juice

Sauté onion in butter until lightly browned. Add meat and sauté 5 minutes longer. Add curry and continue cooking until meat is well browned. Add stock and a dash of salt. Cover and simmer until meat is tender, 1½ to 2 hours. Stir in lemon juice. Serves 6. Curries can also be made with fish or shellfish, in which case substitute milk or cream for water or stock.

(3510) ENGLISH CRUMPETS

Mix 1½ cups lukewarm water with ½ teaspoon each of salt and sugar and one teaspoon melted butter. Dissolve ¼ yeast cake in this mixture. Into this stir enough flour to make a very stiff batter. Beat for 10 minutes adding enough lukewarm milk to make batter just stiff enough to pour. Grease shallow muffin rings and place them on a soapstone griddle or a heavy aluminum griddle. Pour the batter into the rings to the depth of ¼ inch. Bake in slow oven (300° F.), not turning until brown on under side, then turn for just a few minutes.

(3511) ENGLISH LEMON CHEESE

6 well-beaten eggs	½ cup lemon juice
2 cups sugar	¼ cup butter

Combine ingredients and cook over hot water, stirring frequently, until thick. Serve in tart shells (No. 2708), as a filling for layer cakes (No. 2953), or as a spread on toast, biscuits, or bread. Yield: 2 cups.

(3512) FINNISH EGGS

Serve poached eggs (No. 207) on boiled rice (No. 107) with tomato sauce (No. 2035).

(3513) FLEMISH MASHED POTATOES

Rub hot boiled potatoes (No. 1834) through a fine sieve. For each cup of potatoes add ½ cup buttermilk, 1 tablespoon butter, and salt and pepper to taste. Beat until thoroughly mixed and light.

(3514) POT AU FEU (FRENCH)

See Recipe No. 521.

(3515) GAUFFRES (FRENCH)

½ pound sifted flour	6 stiffly beaten egg whites
½ teaspoon salt	Powdered sugar
½ teaspoon vanilla	

Mix and sift flour and salt. Add enough water to make a thin batter and blend thoroughly. Stir in vanilla. Fold in egg whites. Heat the gauffre iron and grease it generously. Pour in thin layer of batter, filling all grooves. Bake on both sides over quick heat until golden brown. Remove and sprinkle with sugar.

(3516)   CRÊPES FRANÇAISE (PANCAKES)

1 egg	½ cup milk
2 tablespoons sugar	1 cup flour
½ teaspoon salt	2 tablespoons melted butter

Beat egg, sugar, and salt together. Add milk and flour. Beat until smooth. Add butter. Heat a small frying pan with a little melted butter. When hot, turn in enough batter to just cover bottom. Fry, shaking frequently, until batter is golden brown on bottom. Turn and brown other side.

(3517)   FRENCH LEG OF LAMB, MODERNE

Frenched leg of lamb   French dressing (No. 716)
Salt—Pepper

Have leg of lamb Frenched at the market; that is, have the meat removed from around the end of shank bone. Do not remove the "fell." Season and place leg, cut side up, on rack in open roasting pan. Insert meat thermometer. Pour French dressing over meat. Roast (No. 1390), basting frequently with French dressing for added flavor. Allow ½ to ¾ pound meat per serving.

(3518)   HASSENPFEFFER (GERMAN)

See Recipe No. 1578.

(3519)   SAUERBRATEN (GERMAN)

Cover 3 to 5 pounds of chuck, rump, or round of beef with equal parts of vinegar and water. Add a few bay leaves, a dozen whole cloves, a spoonful of whole black peppers, and a peeled onion. Let the meat stand in the vinegar for 2 or 3 days, turning it so that it will pickle evenly. Remove the meat from the liquid and brown it in hot fat in a heavy kettle. Then slip a rack under it to keep the meat from sticking to the pot, add 1 cup or less of the pickling liquid or water, cover with a close-fitting lid, and cook slowly about 2 hours, or until the meat is tender. Make gravy of the drippings and add 3 or 4 gingersnaps broken into small pieces and stir until smooth. Or, instead of adding gingersnaps, season the gravy with a little ginger and sugar.

(3520) SAUERKRAUT (GERMAN)

See Recipes No. 1740, 1741, 1742, 1743, and 1744.

(3521) HAWAIIAN CURRY

Substitute coconut water for water or stock in recipe for East Indian curry (No. 3509), add ½ cup diced apple or rhubarb when sautéing onion, and stir in ½ cup shredded pineapple with lemon juice.

(3522) HOLLAND BEETS

Heat diced, boiled beets (No. 1726) in a sauce made by boiling together for 1 minute 1 cup water, 3 tablespoons butter, 2 tablespoons flour, 1 tablespoon chopped onion, 1 tablespoon sugar, 2 tablespoons lemon juice, and salt and pepper to taste.

(3523) STUFFED NOODLE ROLLS (HOLLAND)

Roll noodle dough (No. 2301) thin. Cut in 6-inch squares. Spread with a thin layer of sausage meat. Roll as a jelly roll and skewer with toothpicks. Boil 15 minutes in stock (No. 501).

(3524) HUNGARIAN GOULASH

2 pounds beef or veal in any proportion	½ teaspoon paprika
¼ cup butter or fat	4 medium-sized potatoes, diced
2 sliced onions	1 cup canned or strained stewed tomatoes
1 teaspoon salt	(No. 1893)
½ teaspoon pepper	

Wipe meat with cold, damp cloth. Cut in 1-inch cubes. Melt butter in saucepan. Add meat and onions. Sauté until brown. Add salt, pepper, paprika, and tomatoes. Simmer 30 minutes. Add potatoes and more tomatoes or water if necessary. Cook 30 minutes longer. If desired, 1 cup of cream and ½ cup of water can be substituted for tomatoes. Serves 6.

(3525) ITALIAN ANTIPASTO

This is a salad, consisting of hearts of lettuce, capers, tiny green or red peppers, chunks of tuna fish or salmon, anchovies, sardines, strips of pimiento, salami slices, stuffed celery (No. 431), onion slices, radish slices, cole slaw, boiled asparagus tips (No. 1704), hard-cooked egg (No. 202) slices, or any other appropriate vegetables, fish, or meats, generously sprinkled with French dressing (No. 716).

(3526) MINESTRONE (ITALIAN)

1 cup dried beans	1 cup tomato pulp
1½ tablespoons chopped onion	1 cup cabbage, chopped
1 stalk celery, chopped	Salt—Pepper
1 clove garlic, chopped	1 cup cooked macaroni
2 tablespoons chopped parsley	(No. 2302) or boiled rice (No. 107)
¼ cup olive oil	

Soak beans in cold water 10 hours. Add 1½ quarts water. Simmer until tender, adding more water if necessary. Sauté onion, celery, garlic, and parsley in olive oil until brown. Add tomato and cabbage. Season to taste with salt and pepper. Bring to a boil. Add mixture to beans. Add macaroni or rice. Simmer 30 minutes. Serve with grated Parmesan cheese. Serves 6.

(3527) ITALIAN MEAT BALLS

1½ pounds ground beef	1 teaspoon salt
4 cups bread crumbs	½ teaspoon pepper
½ cup seeded raisins	Kettle of meat (No. 501)
1 cup grated Parmesan cheese	or chicken stock
3 eggs	(No. 502)

Mix thoroughly, add water just to moisten all ingredients but stock. Mold into small balls. Drop them in boiling stock and cook until well done, 20 to 25 minutes. If desired meat balls may be fried in sizzling hot fat. Serves 6 to 8.

(3528) VEAL ITALIAN STYLE

2 pounds veal	1 teaspoon salt
1 cup boiled spaghetti	¼ teaspoon pepper
(No. 2302)	⅛ teaspoon red pepper
½ cup sliced, peeled mush-	1 tablespoon butter
rooms	2 tablespoons olive oil

Wipe meat with cold, damp cloth. Cut into small cubes. Heat oil in pan. Add veal and sauté until well browned. Cover veal with spaghetti and mushrooms. Sprinkle with seasonings. Dot with butter. Add ½ cup water. Cover and cook slowly 20 minutes. Serves 6.

(3529) ITALIAN SPINACH

Mix chopped, boiled spinach (No. 1870) with grated cheese and season to taste with salt and pepper. Cover with highly seasoned tomato sauce (No. 2035).

(3530) RAVIOLI (ITALIAN)

Roll out noodle dough (No. 2301) thin. Cut into rounds with a large cookie cutter. Place 1½ tablespoons chopped meat on ½ of each round. Moisten edges of dough with water. Fold over into a half circle and press tightly together. Fry in deep, hot fat (375° F.) until golden brown. Drain on unglazed paper. Or, drop in boiling salted water or stock and cook until they rise to surface. Serve, either fried or boiled, with a strongly seasoned tomato sauce (No. 2035) and sprinkle with chopped parsley.

(3531) ZABAGLIONE (ITALIAN)

6 egg yolks	¼ teaspoon grated cinnamon
⅓ cup sugar	1 cup sweet wine

Beat egg yolks, adding sugar gradually, until firm. Add cinnamon and wine slowly, beating in well. Set bowl in hot water and cook and beat until sugar is dissolved and mixture resembles custard. Serves 8.

(3532) JAPANESE COOKIES

6 egg whites	1½ cups rice flour
¾ cup sugar	⅔ cup melted shortening
1 teaspoon vanilla	

Beat egg whites, adding sugar and vanilla gradually, until stiff. Add flour and shortening slowly, beating after each addition. Drop by spoonfuls on hot, greased baking sheet and spread thin with back of spoon. Bake in moderately slow oven (325° F.) until crisp. Yield: 72 cookies.

(3533)   MEXICAN CHILAQUILES

1 dozen hard, dry tortillas (No. 3534)	2½ cups stewed tomatoes (No. 1893)
4 tablespoons bacon fat or vegetable oil	2 tablespoons chili sauce
1 large onion, chopped	1 teaspoon salt
½ tiny clove garlic, chopped	Pepper
	6 thin slices American cheese

Break each tortilla into 4 or 5 small pieces. Fry in fat until a golden brown. Remove from fat and fry onion and garlic in same fat until lightly browned. Add tomatoes, chili sauce, salt, and pepper and heat to boiling. Then add tortillas and simmer 8 to 10 minutes. Put mixture in a greased baking dish, top with pieces of American cheese, and bake in a hot oven (400° F.) until cheese is melted. Serve hot. Serves 6.

(3534)   TORTILLAS (MEXICAN)

2½ cups steamed hominy (No. 101)	2 tablespoons cold water
1 tablespoon corn meal	1 tablespoon bacon fat

Drain hominy and put kernels through a food chopper, set fine, 3 times. Combine with other ingredients. Form into 12 thin patties. Put between moist cloth. Place a board on top and weight heavily. Chill. Fry on slightly greased griddle until golden brown on both sides.

(3535)   MEXICAN MOLE

3 tablespoons olive oil	1 tablespoon sugar
1½ ounces mole powder	1 teaspoon cocoa
3 cups beef (No. 501) or chicken stock (No. 502)	3 cups chopped, cold, cooked chicken or turkey

Heat oil in pan. Add mole powder. Simmer 3 minutes, stirring constantly. Add stock and simmer 10 minutes, stirring occasionally. Stir in sugar and cocoa. When thoroughly dissolved, add meat. Cover and simmer 35 minutes. Serves 6 to 8.

(3536)   SALMON CHALUPAS (MEXICAN)

1 cup corn meal	1 egg, well beaten
1 cup boiling water	½ pound canned salmon
1 teaspoon salt	½ cup grated cheese

Mix corn meal, boiling water, and salt. Add the well-beaten egg and salmon and form into patties for frying. Fry in deep, hot fat (375° F.). When brown on both sides, sprinkle a tablespoon of grated cheese on each pattie and serve with a "hot" tomato sauce (No. 2035) and onion slices. Serves 4.

(3537)   MEXICAN CHILI CON CARNE

2 pounds chopped beef	1 teaspoon chili powder
1 pound suet	1 quart boiled chili beans
1 teaspoon salt	(No. 1721)

Melt suet in iron kettle. Remove any solid particles. Put in beef, salt, and chili powder. Let simmer 15 minutes. Add chili beans and 1 pint boiling water. Cook 10 minutes more. Serve hot. Serves 6.

(3538)   HOT TAMALES (MEXICAN)

1 3-pound chicken	1 seeded green pepper, cut in
2 teaspoons salt	strips
12 red chili peppers	1 tablespoon flour
3 tablespoons butter or fat	4 cups corn meal
2 sliced onions	1 pound corn husks
2 sliced tomatoes	

Dress chicken and wipe with cold, damp cloth. Disjoint. Cover with boiling water. Add 1 teaspoon salt. Let simmer until tender, about 1½ hours. Open chili peppers. Discard seeds. Boil them until soft. Drain. Force through a sieve. Melt 1 tablespoon butter in pan. In it slightly brown onions, tomatoes, and green pepper. Add chili pulp. Pick chicken meat from bones. Cut in little pieces. Add to pan. Mix flour to a smooth paste with a little cold water and stir into contents of pan. When thick, cover. Simmer slowly 15 minutes, adding a little water in which the chicken was boiled if necessary. Put corn meal in a pan with 2 tablespoons butter, 1 teaspoon salt, and enough boiling water to make a mushlike paste. Beat mixture well with wooden spoon. Add 2½ cups of liquor in which chicken was boiled. Remove ends from corn husks. Dry insides. Spread thinly with corn meal mixture. Add 1 tablespoon of meat mixture and roll up. Fold ends down. Repeat until all ingredients are used. Stack rolls in a steamer. Pour 4 cups boiling water over them. Cover tightly and steam slowly 45 minutes to 1 hour. Serve hot. Beef or veal can be used instead of chicken.

(3539) MEXICAN TAMALE PIE

1 pound ground beef	½ teaspoon black pepper
1 cup seeded raisins	½ teaspoon red pepper
12 stoned olives, sliced	1½ cups corn meal
1 teaspoon salt	1 tablespoon butter or fat

Mix meat, raisins, olives, salt, black pepper, and red pepper. Put in saucepan. Cover with cold water. Bring to boil. Reduce heat and let simmer until tender, about 20 minutes. Stir in 1 tablespoon corn meal. In another pan boil slightly salted water. Stir in balance of corn meal. Add butter. Boil until mixture resembles mush. Line a greased baking dish with slightly more than half of this batter. Pour in meat mixture. Cover with batter. Bake at moderate heat (350° F.) 30 minutes. Serve hot or warmed over at another meal. Serves 6.

(3540) MEXICAN BAKED BEAN LOAF

1 green pepper, chopped	2 cups baked beans
3 onions, chopped	(No. 1708)
2 tablespoons fat	1 cup tomato sauce
4 drops Tabasco sauce	(No. 2035)
1 cup crumbs	

Sauté pepper and onions in fat until lightly browned. Stir in Tabasco. Add beans and tomato sauce. Cook 5 minutes. Turn into a greased baking dish. Top with crumbs. Dot with butter or fat. Bake in moderate oven (350° F.) until crumbs are brown, about 15 minutes. Add more tomato sauce if necessary. Serves 6.

(3541) MEXICAN BEANS

2½ pounds dried pinto beans	½ teaspoon black pepper
(chick peas)	1 pound ground pork, ¼
2 teaspoons fat	salt and ¾ fresh
1 medium onion, chopped	1 teaspoon chili powder
1 clove garlic, minced	1½ cups stewed tomatoes
1 teaspoon salt	(No. 1893)
1 tablespoon prepared	3 bay leaves
mustard	

Wash and soak beans overnight. Drain, cover with hot water, and boil gently 25 minutes. Make 5 to 6 small flat meat cakes from part of the meat. Brown the onions, garlic, and meat cakes in the melted fat. Remove from pan and brown the rest of the meat. Add the flour, salt, bay leaves, pepper, chili powder, to-matoes, mustard, onions, and garlic to meat mixture. Combine with beans and pour into well-greased casserole. Add water or tomato juice, if necessary, to cover beans. Place meat cakes on top and bake in slow oven (275° F.) 3 hours. Serves 6.

(3542) FISH PUDDING (NORWEGIAN)

2 pounds fish, white flesh, chopped fine	2 beaten eggs
¼ cup butter	2 tablespoons flour
½ cup cream	⅛ teaspoon nutmeg
	Salt—Pepper

Combine ingredients and beat vigorously until very light. Turn into greased mold. Set in hot water and bake in moderate oven (350° F.) until firm, about 1 hour. Serve with caper sauce (No. 2040). Serves 6.

(3543) RAGOUT OF LAMB (RUMANIAN)

2½ pounds boned shoulder of lamb	Salt—Pepper
3 tablespoons butter or fat	2 pounds string beans
1 chopped onion	½ cup white wine
1 teaspoon flour	6 medium-sized boiled pota- toes (No. 1834)
2 cups stewed tomatoes (No. 1893)	2 tablespoons chopped parsley
2 cups stock (No. 501)	

Wipe meat with cold, damp cloth. Cut into 1-inch squares. Melt butter or fat in frying pan. Add meat and onion and sauté until lightly browned. Add flour, mixed to a smooth paste with 1 teaspoon cold water. Add tomatoes and stock. Season to taste with salt and pepper. Wash beans and remove tough strings. Pile whole beans over meat. Add wine. Cover and simmer until meat is tender, about 1 hour. Serve hot with boiled potatoes (No. 1834) and sprinkled with parsley.

(3544) RUSSIAN BORSCH

This is a vegetable soup (No. 578), usually made from beef stock (No. 501) with varying diced vegetables and sometimes chopped beef or poultry, or both. When cooking is finished, stir in some heavy sour cream or whip sour cream and use for top-ping on soup.

(3545)   RUSSIAN COLESLAW

Serve coleslaw (No. 786) with a sauce made by beating together 1 part vinegar with 4 parts sour cream and season to taste with salt, paprika, and chopped onion.

(3546) RUSSIAN TSCHÉ WITH PANCAKES

Select about 2 pounds beef brisket and cut in small pieces. Cook the meat in 1½ quarts water 2 hours or until it is almost done. Chop a head of cabbage, slice 3 or 4 onions or leeks and a parsnip, add to the meat broth, and cook until meat and vegetables are tender. Mix 1 tablespoon flour and ¼ cup sour cream, and add to stew. Season to taste with salt and pepper. Serve whole wheat (No. 978), wheat (No. 976), or corn pancakes (No. 983) with tsché. Serves 4.

(3547)   SCANDINAVIAN BEEF

1 pound cold roast beef (No. 1310)	2 tablespoons flour
2 cups brown sauce (No. 2020)	1 tablespoon vinegar
2 tablespoons fat, melted	4 apples, pared, cored, and sliced
	Salt—Pepper—Sugar

Dice slices of beef. Put brown sauce in saucepan and heat slowly. Mix fat and flour to a smooth paste and add to sauce, stirring until well blended. Add vinegar. Add apples. Simmer slowly until apples are tender. Season to taste with salt, pepper, and sugar. Add meat and warm thoroughly. Serves 4.

(3548)   SPANISH RICE WITH BACON

6 slices bacon, diced	2 cups stewed tomatoes (No. 1893)
2 onions, chopped	
1 green pepper, chopped	2 cups boiled rice (No. 107)
¼ teaspoon pepper	1 teaspoon salt

Cook bacon until crisp (No. 1464). Remove from fat. Add onions and green pepper and cook until soft. Add rest of ingredients and simmer gently until heated through. Turn into a serving dish and sprinkle crisp bacon on top. Serves 6.

(3549)   SPANISH BUN

¾ cup shortening	1 tablespoon baking powder
2 cups sugar	1 teaspoon ground cloves
4 well-beaten egg yolks	½ teaspoon ground ginger
4 stiffly beaten egg whites	1 cup milk
4 cups flour	1 cup chopped raisins
¼ teaspoon salt	

Cream shortening and sugar together. Add yolks while cream-ing and then the egg whites. Mix and sift flour, salt, baking powder, cloves, and ginger and add alternately with milk to creamed mixture. Beat well. Stir in raisins. Turn into buttered and floured loaf pan and bake in moderate oven (350° F.) **1** hour.

(3550)   SPANISH LAMB NECK SLICES

6 neck slices of lamb	6 slices tomato
2 tablespoons fat	6 rings green pepper
6 slices onion	¼ cup rice

Brown lamb neck slices on both sides in hot fat. Cook rice (No. 107) in boiling salted water. Drain. Place browned neck slices in an oiled casserole dish. On each slice, put a slice of onion, one of tomato, and the green pepper ring. Fill this with cooked rice. Add ½ cup water, cover, and cook in a moderate oven (350° F.) until the neck slices are done, about 1 hour. Serves 6.

(3551)   SPANISH SPAGHETTI

¼ cup olive oil	1 tablespoon chili powder
1 chopped onion	3 cups boiled, drained
½ teaspoon salt	spaghetti (No. 2302)
⅛ teaspoon pepper	1½ cups grated American
2½ cups stewed tomatoes	cheese
(No. 1893)	¼ cup chopped olives

Heat oil in saucepan. Add onion and sauté until lightly browned. Add chili powder, salt, and pepper. Mix well. Add tomatoes and simmer 20 minutes, stirring frequently. Put alter-nate layers of spaghetti and cheese in a greased baking dish, seasoning each layer with salt and pepper. Add olives and then the sauce, mixing well. Top with a layer of cheese. Bake in mod-erate oven (350° F.) until cheese is melted and slightly browned. Serves 6.

(3552) TURKISH COFFEE

Put into a brass coffee pot the correct number of after-dinner cups of water required. Bring to boiling point. Add 2 teaspoons powdered coffee for each serving. Bring to a boil 3 times. Pour into small cups. Let settle before drinking.

(3553) CUBED LAMB (VIENNESE)

2 pounds lamb shoulder
2 tablespoons lard
2 tablespoons flour
1 cup chopped onions
1 teaspoon paprika
Salt—Pepper

Have lamb cut into 1- to 1½-inch cubes. Dredge in flour and brown in hot lard. Season with onion, paprika, salt, and pepper. Cover with hot water and simmer slowly until tender. Serve on a bed of steamed rice (No. 106). Serves 6.

(3554) VEGETABLE SOUP (VENETIAN)

2 tablespoons olive oil
1 chopped onion
2 cups stewed tomatoes (No. 1893)
1 cup steamed rice (No. 106)
1 cup stock (No. 501)
½ cup boiled lima beans (No. 1717)
½ cup boiled carrots (No. 1745), chopped
½ cup boiled cabbage (No. 1736), chopped
Salt—Pepper
Parmesan cheese

Sauté onion in oil until slightly brown. Add tomatoes, rice, and stock. Heat slowly and let simmer, covered, 25 minutes. Add beans, carrots, and cabbage. Season to taste with salt and pepper. Heat 5 minutes longer. Serve with Parmesan cheese on the side. Serves 6.

Canning and Preserving

C ANNING is a method of using heat and airtight containers to preserve food as nearly as possible in the condition in which it is served when freshly cooked. It is a desirable and economical method of preserving many foods so that their use can be distributed over seasons and to places where they are not available fresh.

The method of canning foods affects the vitamin content to some extent. With the possible exception of vitamin C there may be no serious loss during the canning process, though of course when foods are removed from the cans and reheated before serving, there may be additional loss of vitamins.

None of the minerals in foods need be lost in canning, providing the liquid in which they are precooked is used to fill up the containers and provided the entire contents of the can is served.

THE BOILING-WATER BATH

For processing acid foods, the water bath is the most generally satisfactory method in the home. If water is boiled in an open vessel or in one on which the top is not clamped down tightly, the temperature reached is never higher than the boiling point of water.

The directions for processing in boiling water are based on the boiling point at altitudes of 1,000 feet or less. For altitudes above 1,000 feet the length of processing should be increased 20 percent for each additional 1,000 feet.

In processing fruits and other acid foods in the water bath, be sure that the jars or cans are far enough apart and that the rack on which they are supported is so arranged that the water can circulate freely under and around them.

Have the water in the canner boiling before putting in the cans of food. In order to keep the glass jars from breaking they must be preheated in water or filled with hot food.

When all the containers are in the canner, see that the water comes over the tops at least 1 or 2 inches. Add more boiling water as needed to keep this level.

Count time as soon as the water begins to boil vigorously. Keep the bath boiling constantly during all of the processing period.

As soon as the processing time is up, remove the glass jars from the water one at a time and seal tightly at once.

Tin cans are sealed before they are placed in the water-bath canner and need no further adjustment.

STEAMERS AND OVENS

In canning acid foods, heat may also be applied in a steamer or an oven.

In the steamer, where the steam circulates but is not held under pressure, the temperature surrounding the cans of food may be the same as in the boiling-water bath. It is necessary, however, to maintain a good circulation of steam if this method is to be efficient in processing. In actual practice, the steamer is often used without good circulation of steam and for that reason is unsatisfactory. When the steamer is properly operated, the processing periods for acid foods are the same as in the water bath.

Oven canning refers to the processing of food in glass jars in an oven. The temperatures generally used for the oven are from 250° to 275° F. Even with the oven at these or higher temperatures the food being processed inside the jars is little if any hotter than boiling water. For as steam forms in the jars it forces its way out, and the temperature remains near 212° F. The glass jars can be only partially sealed for oven processing; otherwise the accumulated steam would break the seals or the jars themselves. Tin cans cannot be used in oven canning because of the danger of spreading or bursting the seams.

Processing periods in the oven are about half as long again as in the boiling-water bath because the air in the oven is not so good a conductor of heat as is water.

THE OPEN KETTLE

In the so-called open-kettle method fruits or tomatoes are cooked directly in an open vessel to kill the bacteria. This cooking takes the place of both precooking and processing in the other methods. Water or sirup is added as required, and the food is boiled for several minutes, or until softened if it is firm fruit. It is then quickly filled into sterilized jars, and each one sealed immediately. The jars should be filled to the top to drive out the air.

THE STEAM-PRESSURE CANNER

A steam-pressure canner is required for processing meats, practically all vegetables except tomatoes, and other nonacid foods. Such foods should not be canned at home if a pressure canner is not available. Other methods of preservation should be used to make the products safe, such as drying, pickling, and storing for fruits and vegetables, and curing for meats.

STEPS IN CANNING

Safe canning requires careful attention to every step in the process from the selection of the raw food to the final check-up of the canned products during storage. The following list gives the steps in order:

1. Select good materials. With fruits and vegetables, grade for size and the same degree of ripeness if a uniform product is desired. Wash thoroughly until every trace of soil is removed.

2. Prepare jars or cans.

3. Sirup. Make the sirup for fruits in advance so there will be no delay when it is required.

4. Precooking. Some foods are precooked for a short time before they are packed into the containers.

5. Packing. When using glass jars, remove one jar at a time from the hot-water bath where it has been held. If needed, place a new wet rubber ring in position resting flat on the sealing shoulder of the jar. Pack the containers quickly so that the precooked food remains hot. Use a sufficient proportion of liquid to solids to prevent too dense a pack, and work out the air bubbles with a knife blade or spatula.

6. Exhausting and adjusting covers. Food in glass jars is exhausted, or the air partially removed during processing, because

the jars are not fully sealed. As each glass jar is packed, carefully wipe off the rubber ring to remove any particles of food, and adjust the cap to seal the jar partially and permit exhausting. Place the jars as finished in the canner or where they will keep hot until processing begins. Tin cans packed with precooked food should be sealed at once, while the food is steaming hot, and placed in the canner.

7. Processing. Process at the temperature and for the time indicated in the tables on pages 740, 741, 748, and 758.

8. Cooling. Cool glass jars in air but protect them from drafts. After they are cool, invert, and observe for leakage. Do not attempt to tighten screw caps or screw bands after the jars have cooled. Cool tin cans in cold water, using running water if possible.

9. Reprocessing. If any containers show signs of leakage, they should be opened, the contents heated and repacked in other containers, and processed again as at first.

10. Labeling. Wipe the containers clean and label with the name, the date, and the lot number, if more than one lot was canned on that day.

11. Checking up results. Hold canned products at room temperature for a week or 10 days where they can be examined from time to time to be sure that they are keeping. If any show signs of spoilage, examine all of that lot carefully.

12. Storage. Store canned foods in a cool, dry place, and protect glass jars from the light so that the food will not fade in color.

(3601)   CANNING FRUITS, TOMATOES, AND OTHER ACID FOODS

Fruits, tomatoes, and other acid foods are best processed at 212° F., the temperature of boiling water at sea level. Read carefully the sections under methods and equipment that relate to the handling of acid foods. The boiling-water bath is the most successful way of applying heat for processing foods of this type in the home.

(3602)   SIRUPS

Sirup made with granulated sugar is generally the most desirable sweetening for canned fruits. Cane sugar and beet sugar are equally good. Honey or light-colored sirups are sometimes substituted for part or all of the granulated sugar on the basis of measure for measure, but the results are variable. Brown sugar may carry spoilage bacteria or other impurities and is not recommended for use in canning. It is advisable to prepare the sirup in advance of the time when it will be needed. For home canning the standard proportions are shown in the following table:

Proportions of Sugar and Water for Light, Medium, and Heavy Sirups

Sirup	Sugar to 1 Gallon of Water				Degrees Balling or Percent of Sugar
	Cups	*Quarts*	*Pounds*	*Ounces*	
Light........................	5	1¼	2	2	20
Moderately light..............	8	2	3	10	30
Medium......................	12½	3⅛	5	9	40
Moderately heavy.............	19	4¾	8	6	50
Heavy.......................	28	7	12	8	60

In making the sirup, add the sugar to the water, and dissolve by warming and stirring. Fill a tall cylinder with the sirup at 60° F. and place the saccharometer in it. The reading is taken at the surface of the liquid. The Balling or Brix saccharometers read directly in terms of percentage of sugar. A heavy sirup may be prepared and diluted with water to yield lighter sirups as required. Sirups should be boiled, strained, and poured over the fruit boiling hot.

(3603) CANNING FRUITS WITHOUT SUGAR

Sugar may be added or not as desired in the canning of fruits. The shape, color, and flavor of the fruits are retained better when some sugar is added. Fruits for pie making or for use in diabetic diets are commonly canned without sugar. Juicy fruits, such as berries, cherries, currants, and plums, should be canned in their own juices when sugar is omitted. Water is not required. Extract the juice from the riper fruits by crushing, heating, and straining. Pack the remaining fruits closely into containers without preheating, and add boiling hot juice to cover. Partially seal glass jars; or exhaust tin cans and seal; then process. Or give the fruits a short precooking, as 2 to 4 minutes simmering, pour into containers at once, seal, and process. The less juicy fruits, such as apples, peaches, and pears, when canned without sugar require the addition of water. To preserve the natural fruit flavor use only the smallest quantity of water necessary.

Timetable for Processing Fruits, Tomatoes, and Other Acid Foods

The times given here for processing in the boiling-water bath apply only to places with altitudes of 1,000 feet or less. For all altitudes above 1,000 feet, the time should be increased 20 percent for each additional 1,000 feet.

When half-gallon glass jars are used, add 5 minutes to times given for pint and quart glass jars.

Process the containers immediately after packing.

Cool the food in tin cans in cold water immediately after processing.

Product	Style of Pack	Processing Period in Boiling Water 212° F.	
		Pint and Quart Glass Jars	No. 2 and No. 3 Tin Cans
		Minutes	*Minutes*
APPLES............	Steam or boil to wilt; pack in hot sirup or water.........	15............	10
	Same as above but dry-pack...	20............	15
	Bake or boil whole; pack in hot sirup................	5............	5
	Applesauce, pack hot........	5............	5
APRICOTS..........	Pack raw; cover with hot sirup	25..........	No. 2, 15 / No. 3, 25
	Precook and pack hot........	15............	15
BEETS, PICKLED.....	Pack hot....................	30.,,,,,,,,	....
BERRIES: Blackberries...... Blueberries....... Dewberries....... Huckleberries..... Logan blackberries Mulberries........ Raspberries.......	Pack raw, cover with hot sirup Precook and pack hot........	20.......... / 5............	15 / 5
CHERRIES..........	Pack raw; cover with hot sirup	25..........	20
	Precook and pack hot........	5............	5
CURRANTS..........	Precook and pack hot........	5............	5
GOOSEBERRIES......	Pack raw; cover with hot sirup	20	15
	Precook and pack hot........	5............	5
PEACHES...........	Pack raw; cover with hot sirup	Soft, 25...... / Firm, 35.....	Soft, 20 / Firm, 30
	Precook and pack hot........	15............	15
PEARS.............	Pack raw; cover with hot sirup	....	No. 2, 20 / No. 3, 25
	Precook and pack hot........	20..........	20
PIMIENTOS.........	Pack hot....................	Pint, 40......	No. 0, 30 / No. 1, 30
PINEAPPLES.........	Pack raw; cover with hot sirup	30..........	25

Product	Style of Pack	Processing Period in Boiling Water 212° F.	
		Pint and Quart Glass Jars	No. 2 and No. 3 Tin Cans
		Minutes	*Minutes*
PLUMS..............	Pack raw; cover with hot sirup	20..........	15
	Precook and pack hot........	5............	5
RHUBARB...........	Precook and pack hot........	5............	5
SAUERKRAUT........	Precook and pack hot........	Pint, 25......	No. 2, 15
		Quart, 30....	No. 3, 30
STRAWBERRIES.......	Precook and pack hot........	5............	5
TOMATOES..........	Pack raw..............	45..........	35
	Precook and pack hot........	5............	5
TOMATO JUICE.......	Pack hot..............	No processing	5
FRUIT JUICES: Berries........... Cherries.......... Currants.......... Plums............	Pack at 160° to 170° F. and process in water bath at 180°.	20..........	
FRUIT PURÉES.......	Pack at 160° to 170° F. and process at 212°............	20..........	

(3604)   APPLES

Apples packed raw shrink in canning, so that the containers are not full. This is prevented by precooking before packing. Pare the apples and cut into the sizes desired. If the pieces must stand, to prevent darkening place them in a mild salt and vinegar solution, 2 tablespoons salt and 2 tablespoons vinegar per gallon of water. Precook by boiling 5 minutes in a light sirup (No. 3602) or steam until wilted. Fill into the cans hot and cover with boiling sirup. Pie apples are commonly packed in water or given a solid pack without added liquid. Apples may be baked, as for serving, adding sugar to taste and water if necessary; or they may be boiled whole in sirup. Pack hot in the containers and cover with hot sirup. Windfall or green apples may be made into sauce. Pack boiling hot.

(3605)   APRICOTS

Same as peaches (No. 3611).

(3606)   BEETS, PICKLED

Select beets of uniform size, cut off the tops, but allow at least 1 inch of the stems to remain so that the beets will not bleed and lose color and sweetness. Wash and cook until tender in enough water to cover. For young beets this will require about ½ hour. When tender, plunge into cold water, remove the skins, and when cool, cut in dice or thin slices. Pack into jars, to each pint add ½ teaspoon salt, and fill with a mixture of vinegar and sugar in equal proportions by measure, heated to boiling, so that the sugar is thoroughly dissolved. If this is too acid, dilute the vinegar ¼ with water.

(3607)   BERRIES: BLACKBERRIES, BLUE-BERRIES, DEWBERRIES, HUCKLEBERRIES LOGANBERRIES, MULBERRIES, RASPBERRIES

Gather berries in shallow vessels so as to prevent crushing, and can them as soon as possible. Wash carefully and remove caps and stems. Sort out the smaller and imperfect berries and extract juice from them for making a sirup of medium sweetness. Raspberries and other berries of soft texture keep their shape better for dessert purposes if packed raw, although they tend to rise to the top of the container after processing. Press the raw fruit gently into the containers so they will be well filled, and cover with hot medium sirup (No. 3602). If using tin cans, exhaust for 3 to 5 minutes before sealing. For use in pies and where the appearance of the whole fruit is not so important, precook the berries and pack hot. To each pound of raw berries add ¼ to ½ pound sugar, according to the sweetness of the fruit, stir gently, and boil 3 to 4 minutes. Pack boiling hot.

(3608)   CHERRIES

Cherries may be canned, pitted or unpitted, depending upon the way in which they are to be served. If unpitted, prick them to prevent shrinkage, and save the juice to use in making the sirup (No. 3602). Pack the cherries in hot containers and cover with hot sirup—heavy sirup for sour cherries and medium for sweet. If using tin cans, exhaust for 3 to 5 minutes before sealing. If cherries are pitted, boil them for 5 minutes with sugar to taste, and fill into the containers boiling hot.

(3609)   **CURRANTS**

Same as berries (No. 3607).

(3610)   **GOOSEBERRIES**

Use the method suggested for berries packed raw (No. 3607), substituting heavy for medium sirup (No. 3602). If using tin cans exhaust for 3 to 5 minutes before sealing. Or add a small quantity of water to the gooseberries after they have been sorted and washed, and boil until they are cooked to a pulp. To each quart of this pulp add ½ cup sugar or more if preferred. Heat until the sugar is dissolved, and pack boiling hot into containers.

(3611)   **PEACHES**

To prepare peaches for canning, immerse them in boiling water for about ½ minute or until the skins will slip easily, plunge at once into cold water for a few seconds, remove the skins, cut the peaches into halves, and discard the pits. If a bushel or more of peaches or apricots is to be canned at one time, the skins may be removed in a lye bath. This method is not justified with a small quantity, unless the peaches are so firm that hot water will not loosen the skins. Be careful in using lye for it is a powerful caustic. To peel peaches or apricots with lye, prepare in an agateware or iron kettle a solution of ¼ pound (4 ounces or about 4 level tablespoons) granulated lye of a standard brand in 2 gallons water. Heat to boiling, and while the solution is actively boiling, immerse the peaches or apricots in it in a wire basket until the skin is loosened and partially dissolved. This will usually require 30 to 60 seconds. Remove the fruit, wash it at once in running water, if possible, until skin and lye are removed, and then thoroughly rinse the fruit. A 2-minute dip in a bath with 2 tablespoons each of salt and vinegar to each gallon of water also helps to prevent the fruit from browning. Lye-peeled fruit should be canned immediately. If a thermometer is available it is better to use a stronger lye solution at a lower temperature. An 8 to 10 percent solution containing 1 pound lye to 1½ gallons water heated to 135° to 140° F. (not higher) is recommended. Use light or medium sirup (No. 3602) on peaches, as desired. In making it put in one cracked peach pit for every quart of sirup and strain out before using. Peaches may be packed raw, but a better pack is obtained if the fruit is first simmered in the sirup for 4 to 8 minutes. Do not cook until soft. Pack at once, placing the halves pit side down in overlapping layers. Fill the containers with hot sirup. If the peaches are packed cold in tin cans cover with hot sirup and exhaust the cans for 5 minutes before sealing.

(3612)   PEARS

The quality of Kieffer pears is improved by holding the fruit for 2 weeks after harvest at a temperature of 60° to 65° F. before canning. Peel, cut in halves, and core. To prevent discoloration place the pared fruit in a solution made in the proportion of 2 tablespoons each of salt and vinegar to a gallon of water. Cook in boiling medium sirup (No. 3602) 4 to 8 minutes, according to the size and firmness of the fruit. Pack the pears hot into containers and fill with boiling sirup. If packed cold in tin cans, cover with hot sirup and exhaust for 5 minutes before sealing.

(3613)   PIMIENTOS, RIPE

Select ripe, thick-fleshed pimientos, free from bruises. To remove the skin, immerse the whole peppers in hot cooking oil (290° F.) 2 or 3 minutes, or place them in a hot oven (450° F.) 6 to 8 minutes; then dip quickly into cold water. Slip the skins off, remove stems, and seed cores. The peppers are then soft and pliable. Fold and pack them into the containers, and add ½ teaspoon salt to each pint. Add no liquid because the processing brings out almost enough thick liquor to cover them in the can. If using tin cans, exhaust them for 5 minutes before sealing.

(3614)   PINEAPPLES

Peel, core, and remove the "eyes." Slice crosswise, pack into the containers, and fill with boiling light sirup (No. 3602). Exhaust the tin cans for 5 minutes before sealing.

(3615)   PLUMS

Plums are ordinarily canned whole, and they should be gathered just as they are commencing to ripen. After they are washed, prick each plum to prevent the skin from bursting.

Pack into containers and cover with hot medium sirup (No. 3602). Exhaust tin cans 5 minutes before sealing. Or, if preferred, prepare sauce by cooking the plums with sugar to taste, and, if desired, strain out the pits and skins. Fill into the containers boiling hot.

(3616)   RHUBARB

Select young, tender stalks; trim, wash, and cut into half-inch lengths. Boil until soft in heavy sirup (No. 3602). Or add ¼ as much sugar as rhubarb by measure, and bake until tender in a covered dish. Since rhubarb corrodes tin cans, it is better for home use to pack it in glass. Pack boiling hot into the jars.

(3617)   SAUERKRAUT

Sauerkraut (No. 3698) should be well fermented before it is canned. Heat the sauerkraut to simmering (about 180° F.), but avoid boiling. Fill hot into the containers and pack closely. Cover with the hot sauerkraut juice, leaving ⅛- to ¼-inch head space.

(3618)   STRAWBERRIES

Strawberries are usually more palatable when preserved than canned. In canning this method gives the best results: To each quart of washed and stemmed berries add 1 cup of sugar. Bring slowly to the boiling point and let stand overnight in the kettle. In the morning bring quickly to boiling, and fill into the containers.

(3619)   TOMATOES

Select firm, ripe tomatoes of medium size and uniform shape, free from spots and decay. Put into trays or shallow layers in wire baskets and dip in boiling water for about a minute, according to ripeness. Then plunge quickly into cold water, drain, peel, and core promptly. Pack into the containers as closely as possible. Fill with tomato juice and add 1 teaspoon of salt per quart. If using tin cans, exhaust them 5 to 6 minutes before sealing. Or cut the tomatoes in quarters, heat just to boiling, and pack hot.

(3620)   TOMATO JUICE

To preserve the natural flavor and color in canned tomato juice, use knives of stainless steel and avoid utensils of copper, brass, and iron. Use only fully ripe, firm tomatoes, preferably of bright-red color, as freshly picked from the vines as possible. Discard any with green, moldy, or decayed portions. Wash well, remove cores, and cut into small pieces. The skins may or may not be removed. Handle the tomatoes in quantities of 1 to 2 gallons and avoid delay at any stage of the procedure. Precook the tomatoes at about 170° F. to 180° F., or if a thermometer is not available, simmer until softened. Avoid boiling. Put the softened, hot tomatoes at once through a fine sieve, preferably a bowl- or cone-shaped sieve because it allows the least air to be incorporated in the pulp. If the tomato juice is for infant or invalid use, omit salt; otherwise add ½ to 1 teaspoon salt to each quart. Spices tend to darken the color of tomato juice and change the flavor undesirably; hence it is better to add them at the time of serving. Reheat the juice at once after putting through the sieve. If using glass containers, heat the juice to 190° F. (or just to boiling), pour into the sterilized containers, and seal. No processing is necessary. Invert the bottles while cooling. If tin cans are used, heat the juice 180° to 190° (or to simmering if no thermometer is available), pour into cans, seal, and process. Do not leave head space in either glass or tin containers.

(3621)   FRUIT JUICES FOR BEVERAGES FROM BERRIES, CHERRIES, CURRANTS, AND PLUMS

Use only sound, well-ripened fruit in such quantities that the process can be carried through promptly. To avoid overcooking and to preserve as much as possible of the original flavor and color, check the temperature with a thermometer as the fruit is precooked and the juice pasteurized. Sugar also helps to preserve color and flavor, but it may be omitted if an unsweetened juice is preferred. Wash the fruit, drain, and crush. Add water, if desired, to thin the juice—about ½ cup of water to each pound of fruit. Heat to 170° to 180° F., and hold for several minutes, or until the juice can be separated from the pulp. Extract the juice with a fruit press or strain through several layers of cheese-cloth. A second straining without pressure makes the juice clearer. Add sugar if desired, about ½ to 1 cup of sugar to a gallon of juice. Heat the juice to 160° to 170° and fill into hot, sterilized glass jars or bottles to within ⅛ inch of the top. Seal at once, and lay bottles on their sides in the water bath.

(3622) FRUIT PURÉES

For purées of almost any soft fruit put the cooked fruit through a fine sieve; otherwise proceed as for fruit juice.

(3623) CANNING NONACID VEGETABLES

Nonacid vegetables require processing in the steam-pressure canner at temperatures of 240° and 250° F. If a pressure canner is not available, then drying, brining, or some method of preservation other than canning should be used for these vegetables.

(3624) ASPARAGUS

Select fresh and tender stalks, sort according to size, and wash thoroughly. Tie in uniform bundles, stand upright with tough portion in boiling water, cover tightly, and boil 2 to 3 minutes. Or cut in half-inch lengths, add enough water to cover, and boil 2 minutes in an uncovered vessel. Pack boiling hot into containers, cover with the water in which boiled, and add 1 teaspoon salt to each quart. Or pack raw in no. 2 tin cans, cover with boiling water, and exhaust for 4 to 5 minutes before sealing.

(3625) BEANS, FRESH LIMA

Only young and tender lima beans should be canned; older ones may be dried. Shell, wash, and bring to a boil in water to cover. Pack hot into the containers, cover with hot water, and add 1 teaspoon of salt to each quart.

(3626) BEANS, SNAP

Wash thoroughly and cut into pieces of desired size. Add boiling water to cover and simmer uncovered for about 5 minutes, or until the beans are wilted and will bend without breaking. Pack hot into the containers, cover with hot water, and add 1 teaspoon of salt to each quart.

Timetable for Processing Nonacid Vegetables in the Steam Pressure Canner

The processes given here apply to places with altitudes of 2,000 feet or less. At altitudes over 2,000 feet, add 1 pound pressure for each additional 2,000 feet. Cool tin cans in cold water immediately after processing.

Product	Pint Glass Jars 240° F., or 10 Pounds Pressure	Pint Glass Jars 250° F., or 15 Pounds Pressure	Quart Glass Jars 240° F., or 10 Pounds Pressure	Quart Glass Jars 250° F., or 15 Pounds Pressure	No. 2 Tin Cans 240° F., or 10 Pounds Pressure	No. 2 Tin Cans 250° F., or 15 Pounds Pressure	No. 3 Tin Cans 240° F., or 10 Pounds Pressure	No. 3 Tin Cans 250° F., or 15 Pounds Pressure
	Minutes	Minutes	Minutes	Minutes	Minutes	Minutes	Minutes	Minutes
ASPARAGUS	30		35		30			
BEANS:								
Fresh lima	50		55		40		50	
Snap	30		35		25		30	
Dried kidney or pinto	80		90		70		85	
Soybeans	80		90		70		85	
BEETS, BABY	30		35		30		30	
CARROTS	30		35		30		30	
CORN:								
Whole-grain	60		70		50		65	
Cream-style		75				70		No. 2½, 60
GREENS, INCLUDING SPINACH		60		65		55		
MUSHROOMS	25		35		25		25	
OKRA	35		40		25		30	
OKRA AND TOMATOES	25		35		25		30	
PEAS:								
Green	45		55		40			
Black-eyed	50				40		50	
PUMPKIN		60		75		60		70
SQUASH		60		75		60		70
SWEET POTATOES	95		120		95		115	
VEGETABLE-SOUP MIXTURES	60		70		50		65	

(3627) BEANS, DRIED KIDNEY OR PINTO

Pick over the beans, wash, and soak overnight in a cool place. Drain. Blanch in boiling water for 3 to 4 minutes and drain. Fill at once into containers to about seven-eighths capacity. Cover with boiling water containing 2 ounces each of salt and sugar to the gallon. The sugar may be omitted or replaced by molasses if desired. Small pieces of salt pork may be added.

(3628)   SOYBEANS

Either green or dried soybeans of varieties suitable for table use may be canned. The green soybeans make a better product, however, in both flavor and color. Follow the directions given for kidney beans (No. 3627), except with green beans omit the overnight soaking and do not add sugar. Salt pork may be added if desired.

(3629)   BEETS, BABY

Select young, tender beets preferably of the turnip-shaped varieties. Trim off the tops, but leave on at least 1 inch of the stems and all of the roots to prevent bleeding. Wash thoroughly and scald in boiling water or steam for about 15 minutes until the skins slip easily. After the beets are skinned and trimmed, pack into the containers, add 1 teaspoon of salt to each quart, and fill with hot water. Pickled beets may be processed in the boiling-water bath.

(3630)   CARROTS

Young tender carrots may be canned in the same way as baby beets (No. 3629).

(3631)   CORN

Use only tender, freshly gathered sweet corn. Shuck, silk, and clean carefully. Sweet corn is canned in two styles—whole-grain and cream style. Whole-grain corn is cut from the cob without scraping, while for cream style the corn is given a more shallow cut and the cobs are scraped. For the whole-grain style cut the corn from the cob deeply enough to remove most of the kernels without objectionable hulls. Do not scrape the cobs. Add 1 teaspoon salt to each quart corn and half as much boiling water as corn by weight. Heat to boiling and pack into containers at once. For the cream style, with a sharp knife lightly cut off the tops of the kernels, and with the back of the knife scrape out the pulp. This gives a thick pasty mass with the minimum of hulls. Add 1 teaspoon salt to each quart, and half as much boiling water as corn by weight. Heat to boiling, and fill into containers at once.

(3632)   GREENS, INCLUDING SPINACH

Pick over the greens, discarding any imperfect leaves and tough fibrous stems. Wash carefully in running water or through a number of waters, lifting the greens out each time. To precook, cover the greens with water heated to simmering, not boiling, and cook in an uncovered vessel for 5 minutes, or until the greens are wilted. Pack hot into the containers, taking care not to make too solid a pack and to have sufficient hot liquid to cover the greens. Add 1 teaspoon of salt to each quart. Greens should not be canned in no. 3 tin cans, because of the difficulty of heat penetration.

(3633)   MUSHROOMS

Wash thoroughly, peel mature mushrooms, and drop into water containing 1 tablespoon of vinegar per quart. Precook, place in a wire sieve or colander, cover with a lid to hold the mushrooms under water, and immerse for 3 to 4 minutes in boiling water that contains 1 tablespoon vinegar and 1 teaspoon salt per quart. Fill into containers at once and cover with freshly boiling water. Add 1 teaspoon salt to each quart.

(3634)   OKRA

Only young, tender pods should be canned; older pods should be dried. After the okra is washed, cover with water, bring to a boil, and pack hot into the containers. Add 1 teaspoon of salt to each quart.

(3635)   **OKRA AND TOMATOES**

Use only young, tender okra and sound, ripe tomatoes. Wash the okra and slice crosswise. Wash the tomatoes, remove the skins and cores, and cut into sections. Combine the okra and tomatoes and heat to the boiling point. Pack while hot, and add 1 teaspoon salt to each quart.

(3636)   **PEAS, GREEN**

Use only young, tender peas. Shell, wash, add hot water to cover, and simmer about 5 minutes. Pack hot in pint jars or no. 2 tin cans, cover with hot water, and add ½ teaspoon salt to each pint.

(3637)   **PEAS, BLACK-EYED**

Same as lima beans (No. 3625).

(3638)   **PUMPKIN**

Wash, peel, and cut the pumpkin into 1- to 1½-inch cubes. Add a small quantity of water and simmer until heated through, stirring occasionally. Pack hot into containers, add 1 teaspoon of salt to each quart, and cover with the water in which cooked.

(3639)   **SQUASH**

Same as pumpkin (No. 3638).

(3640)   **SWEET POTATOES**

Where sweet potatoes can be stored successfully, only enough should be canned to take care of the season during which the stored potatoes are not available. Or if in harvesting more are cut with the plow than can be used immediately, they may be canned in order to save them. In this case, precook them slowly in order to develop the sugar. Wash the sweet potatoes thoroughly and boil or steam them until the skins slip off readily. Peel quickly, cut into medium-sized sections, and pack hot into containers. Add 1 teaspoon of salt to each quart and enough boiling water to cover.

(3641)   VEGETABLE-SOUP MIXTURES

The combinations of vegetables for soups may include two or more of the following: Tomato pulp, corn, lima beans, peas, okra, carrots, turnips, celery, onion, pimientos, and sweet and red peppers. Wash and trim the vegetables and cut into small pieces or cubes. Keep the diced carrots and turnips covered with water or weak brine to prevent darkening. Seasonings should be light, and may include sugar, salt, white pepper, dashes of cayenne and garlic, parsley, thyme, and bay leaf. Bring the soup mixture to the boiling point, and pack hot, with sufficient liquid to cover the vegetables and prevent too dense a pack.

CANNING MEATS AND CHICKEN

Beef, veal, mutton, lamb, pork, and chicken may be canned successfully in the home, provided they are processed under steam pressure. The temperatures required for effective sterilization (240° to 250° F., corresponding to 10 and 15 pounds steam pressure) cannot be obtained inside the can or jar except by the use of the steam-pressure canner. The water bath, the oven, and the steamer without pressure are inadequate for canning meats and cannot be used safely.

When glass jars are used, meats should be precooked in the oven or in water before being packed in the container. When tin cans are used, the meat may be precooked in either of these ways and packed hot, or it may be packed raw and the cans exhausted before being sealed.

SALTING

Salt is added to cans of meat as follows: One-half teaspoon to a pint jar, three-fourths teaspoon to a no. 2 can, and 1 teaspoon to a quart jar or no. 3 can. When tin cans are used, place the salt in the cans before packing them with meat. If the salt is placed on top of the meat, the lids sometimes rust.

(3642)   BEEF, FRESH

Select cuts of beef commonly used for roasts or steaks—round, rump, loin, rib, and chuck. Cuts that contain more connective tissue and bone may be canned as stew meat, hamburger, or other products utilizing small pieces or used in soups. Wipe the meat with a damp cloth, remove the bone and gristle, and leave only enough fat to give flavor. If using glass jars, precook in the oven or in water, pack into containers, add salt, cover with broth, and process as directed in table on page 758. If using tin cans, follow the same method, or pack the meat raw and exhaust the cans.

(3643)   BEEF, GROUND (HAMBURGER)

Prepare hamburger by grinding the meat through a plate with 1/8-inch holes. Add 1 cup of salt for each 25 pounds of meat and mix well. Pack the cold meat tightly into tin cans and exhaust the cans until the meat is steaming hot. If canning in glass jars, form the meat into cakes, precook in the oven, pack hot, and cover with broth.

(3644)   BEEF, HASH AND STEW MEAT

One way of utilizing small pieces of meat is to can it for combining later with potato in hash. Cut or chop the meat into uniformly small pieces. Add sufficient water to cover, bring to simmering, and cook several minutes. Pack hot. For use in making stew, cut the meat into 1-inch cubes, cover with boiling water or broth, and simmer until the meat is shrunken and heated through. This requires about 8 to 10 minutes. The color of raw meat will have almost disappeared from the center of the pieces. Pack the drained meat closely into containers, add salt, and cover with boiling concentrated broth.

(3645)   BEEF, HEART AND TONGUE

The tongue and heart are generally used as fresh meat, but they may be canned as follows: Wash the tongue, drop into boiling water and simmer about 45 minutes, or until the skin can be removed. Skin and cut into pieces that will fit into the containers. Reheat to simmering in broth, pack into containers; add salt and broth to cover. Wash the hearts, remove the thick connective tissue, and cut into pieces suitable for packing. Drop into boiling water and simmer 15 to 20 minutes. Pack at once; add salt and broth to cover.

(3646)   BEEF STEW WITH VEGETABLES

Sprinkle the stew meat with salt and white pepper and dredge with flour. Brown the meat in hot beef fat; then add a small quantity of chopped onion and brown. Remove from the heat. Prepare a mixture of tomato pulp and equal parts of diced carrots, diced turnips, and diced potatoes. Add hot water and bring to boiling. Add the meat mixture and more salt and white pepper if needed. Pack hot.

(3647)   BEEF, CORNED

Wash the corned beef, cover with cold water, bring to the boiling point, and drain. Cover the meat again with cold water, bring to the boiling point, then lower the heat and simmer until the meat is thoroughly heated through. Remove the meat from the broth a piece at a time, and while it is still hot cut into smaller pieces, and pack into the containers. Season the broth as desired, with bay leaves, cloves, or nutmeg. Sometimes gelatin softened in a little cold water is added. Pour boiling broth over the meat to cover.

(3648)   CHICKEN AND OTHER POULTRY

For canning select plump, 2-year-old hens, preferably when they are culled from the flock during July and August. Young birds may be canned, but the texture and flavor of the meat is not so good as that from mature birds. Dress the chickens as for cooking, and take particular care not to break the gall bladder because the meat is then unfit for canning. Also remove the lungs, kidneys, and eggs. Cut the chicken into the usual-sized pieces for serving and separate into three piles—the meaty pieces (breasts, thighs, legs, and upper-wing joints), the bony pieces (backs, wings, necks, and perhaps the feet after they have been skinned), and the giblets. The giblets should not be canned with the other meat as they will flavor and discolor it. Also it is better to can the livers alone, and the gizzards and hearts together. Remove the chicken skin or not as desired, and trim off lumps of fat. Too much fat makes chicken difficult to process. Make broth with the bony pieces. Cover with lightly salted cold water, simmer until the meat is tender, and drain off the broth to use as the liquid in canning the meaty pieces. Strip the meat from the bones and can as small pieces or use in making sandwich spread (No. 3649). If desired, add 5 tablespoons granulated gelatin to each quart broth. Moisten the gelatin first with a little of the cold liquid and dissolve in the hot broth. The meaty pieces of chicken may be canned either with or without the bone. With the bone the product is better flavored. Precook in the oven or in water and pack hot. Or exhaust in tin cans until steaming hot. Add salt according to the size of the container. Precook giblets in water and pack hot, or exhaust in tin cans.

(3649)   CHICKEN SANDWICH SPREAD

4 pounds cooked chicken, chopped or ground
1 pound pimientos, cut in small pieces
1 quart chicken broth (No. 511)

1 ½ pounds olives, chopped
½ teaspoon curry powder
1 teaspoon ground mace
1 teaspoon ground mustard
Salt and white pepper, to taste

Combine all of the ingredients, stir, and heat gradually to simmering. Pack hot.

(3650)   CHICKEN-LIVER PASTE

Chicken livers may be made into a paste for sandwiches. Simmer the livers for 10 minutes and drain. Mash with a fork and remove any stringy tissue. Then add a small quantity of finely chopped olives, mayonnaise (No. 701), and dashes of Tabasco sauce and paprika. Stir while heating carefully to prevent scorching. Pack hot.

(3651)   CHICKEN-GUMBO SOUP

Prepare chicken-gumbo soup (No. 516). Pack hot into the containers.

(3652)   CHILI CON CARNE

Use 2 pounds of chili beans or some other pink or red variety. Pick over the beans, wash, and soak overnight in a cool place. Remove thick connective tissue from 5 pounds of lean beef, or beef and pork mixed, and grind coarsely or chop. Add a little chopped garlic, 3 to 5 tablespoons of chili powder, 3 tablespoons of salt, and one-half cup of wheat flour, and mix well with the meat. Cook the mixture in 1 cup hot beef fat until the red color of the meat disappears. Add 2 quarts hot water, cover, and simmer for about 10 minutes. Drain the beans and blanch 5 minutes in boiling water. Drain. Fill cans or jars about one-third full of the hot beans. Add the hot meat mixture to about seven-eighths of capacity, then hot water to fill.

(3653)   LAMB AND MUTTON

Select the fleshy parts and follow the same method as for beef (No. 3642). Can the smaller pieces as stew meat (No. 3644).

(3654)   LIVER PASTE

3 pounds liver	1 medium-sized onion,
1½ pounds fat fresh pork	chopped
2 tablespoons salt	3 eggs
1 teaspoon white pepper	6 tablespoons fine dry
½ teaspoon ground cloves	bread crumbs

½ cup water

Wash the liver thoroughly and remove veins and membranes. Grind the raw liver and pork twice through a plate with ⅛-inch holes, to make it very smooth. Add the seasonings. Beat the eggs well and combine with the bread crumbs and water. Stir all ingredients together until well mixed. Pack into no. 2 cans leaving 1 inch of head space, and exhaust until the paste is heated through to the center of the cans. This requires about 40 to 50 minutes. Remove some of the paste or add a little hot water if necessary so that the cans have the proper head space before sealing.

(3655)   PORK AND BEANS

Pick over white navy beans, wash, and soak in a cool place for about 16 hours, or overnight. Drain. Prepare liquid to cover the beans, using the proportion of 1 quart water, 1 tablespoon salt, and 1 tablespoon sugar (or molasses) to each pound dry beans. Or prepare an equal quantity of tomato sauce, using 3 cups of tomato pulp to 1 cup of water. Add ground spices, cayenne pepper, and chopped garlic or onion, as desired. Cook until thick. Blanch the beans for 2 minutes in boiling water, and drain. Place small pieces of salt pork in a bean pot or other container for baking. Add the beans and additional pieces of salt pork, and cover with the prepared liquid or tomato sauce. Cover the pot and cook the beans in a slow oven (about 250° F.) 1½ hours. Remove the lid and cook ½ hour longer. Pack hot in the containers and cover with the liquid or sauce.

(3656)   PORK, FRESH

The cuts of pork usually canned are the following: Loin; meat from spareribs; head, tongue, and heart in headcheese; loin and lean trimmings in sausage; and liver in liver paste. While the ham and shoulder may be canned, they are generally preserved by curing. Remove excess fat from the meat to be canned and precook by any of the methods described on page 752. Pack hot and process as directed.

(3657)   PORK, HEADCHEESE

Headcheese may be made from a hog's head, tongue, and heart, according to any good recipe but omitting the sage. Pack the headcheese hot into containers. It is better to use tin cans so that the product can be removed in a single piece.

(3658)   PORK SAUSAGE

Follow any tested formula for preparing the sausage, but omit the sage for that gives the sausage a bitter flavor after processing. See that the seasonings and meat are well mixed together. If using tin cans, pack the raw sausage closely into the no. 2 size and exhaust the cans until the sausage is steaming hot. This requires 40 to 50 minutes. Before opening a can heat for a few minutes in boiling water, then slip the contents of the can out in one piece, slice into rounds, and reheat in gravy or in an oven. If glass jars are used, mold the sausage into cakes and precook in a moderate oven (350° F.) 10 to 15 minutes, or until the cakes are slightly browned and the color of raw meat has almost disappeared. Pack into the jars and cover with the drippings or with hot water.

Timetable for Processing Meats and Chicken in the Steam Pressure Canner

At altitudes over 2,000 feet, add 1 pound of pressure for each additional 2,000 feet.

250° F., OR 15 POUNDS PRESSURE

Product	No. 2 Can	No. 2½ Can	No. 3 Can	Pint Glass Jar	Quart Glass Jar
	Minutes	*Minutes*	*Minutes*	*Minutes*	*Minutes*
BEEF:					
Fresh....................	85	110	120	85	120
Ground (hamburger)........	90	115	....	90	120
Hash....................	90	115	....	90	120
Heart and tongue...........	85	110	120	85	120
Stew meat.................	85	110	120	85	120
Stew with vegetables.......	85	110	120	85	120
Corned..................	85	110	120	85	120
CHICKEN AND OTHER POULTRY:					
With bone.................	55	65	70	65	75
Boned....................	85	110	120	85	120
Giblets..................	85	....	....	85	....
Sandwich spread...........	{No. 1, 55 / No. 2, 90	....	....	{½-pint, 65 / Pint, 90	....
Liver paste...............	{No. 1, 55 / No. 2, 90	....	....	{½-pint, 65 / Pint, 90	....
LAMB AND MUTTON...........	85	110	120	85	120
LIVER PASTE................	90	....	....	90	....
PORK:					
Fresh...................	85	110	120	85	120
Headcheese................	90	....	....	90	....
Sausage..................	90	115	....	90	120
RABBIT, DOMESTIC............	85	110	120	85	120
SOUPS:					
Broth, clear..............	25	30	30	25	30
Broth with rice or barley....	35	40	40	35	40
Chicken gumbo.............	65	75	80	65	80
Soup stock................	40	45	45	40	45
VEAL.....................	85	110	120	85	120

240° F., OR 10 POUNDS PRESSURE

Product	No. 2 Can	No. 2½ Can	No. 3 Can	Pint Glass Jar	Quart Glass Jar
CHILI CON CARNE............	120	135	150	120	150
PORK AND BEANS.............	70	80	85	80	90

(3659)   RABBIT, DOMESTIC

Precook and process in the same way as described for chicken (No. 3648).

(3660)   SOUP STOCK AND BROTH
(CHICKEN OR MEAT)

Broth containing small pieces of meat and sediment from coagulated proteins is commonly called soup stock. Clear meat broths for canning should be fairly concentrated but avoid prolonged boiling as it will cause loss of flavor. Also, if meat bones are cooked for a long time under pressure to make broth or soup stock, the broth will have a disagreeable gluey flavor. Remove excess fat from broth or soup stock before canning. Rice or barley may be added to the broth in the proportion of 1 cup of the uncooked cereal to each gallon of clear meat broth. Wash the cereal, boil for 15 minutes in salted water, drain, and rinse with cold water. Bring the meat broth to the boiling point and add the cereal. Season as desired.

(3661)   VEAL

Same as beef, fresh (No. 3642).

FRUITS FOR JELLY MAKING

Two essentials a fruit must have and in proper proportions if it is to be converted into jelly—pectin and acid. These change with the maturity of the fruit, both decreasing as the fruit ripens. Hence, for the best results use a mixture of slightly underripe and ripe fruit, the underripe to furnish pectin and acid and the ripe to contribute flavor and color. The following fruits at the proper stage of maturity have both of these in sufficient quantity: Tart apples (such as Winesap), blackberries, crab apples, cranberries, currants, gooseberries, grapes (wild native grapes and the cultivated varieties such as Concord), plums (wild plums and the Wild Goose type of cultivated varieties), quinces (tart varieties), raspberries (both black and red).

Some fruits, such as ripe apples, most plums, and grapes of the European type cultivated on the Pacific coast, contain sufficient pectin but lack the acidity necessary for jelly making. Other fruits contain enough acid but have insufficient pectin. Sometimes fruit rich in pectin is combined with one rich in acid in order to get the proper proportions for jelly. Combinations of fruits also result in interesting blendings of flavors or colors. The following combinations are suggested: Crab apple with grape, currant with raspberry, gooseberry with raspberry, tart apple with plum, tart apple with quince, quince with cranberry, crab apple with cranberry.

Proportions of Water to Fruit, and of Sugar to Fruit Juice in Making Jellies

Kind of Fruit	Quantity of Water to Each Pound of Prepared Fruit (for Extraction of Juice)	Time of Boiling Fruit to Extract Juice	Quantity of Sugar to Each Cup of Fruit Juice
	Cup	*Minutes*	*Cup*
Apples[1].....................	1...................	20 to 25	¾
Crab apples[2]...............	1...................	20 to 25	1
Blackberries...............	{Firm fruit, ¼......	5 to 10	¾ to 1
	{Very soft fruit, none.	5 to 10	¾ to 1
Black raspberries...........	......"	5 to 10	1
Cranberries................	3...................	5 to 10	¾
Currants...................	¼ or none..........	5 to 10	1
Gooseberries...............	¼...................	5 to 10	1
Grapes such as Concord[3]....	¼ or none..........	5 to 10	¾ to 1
Grapes, wild...............	1...................	5 to 10	1
Plums, Wild Goose type....	½...................	15 to 20	¾
Quinces...................	2...................	20 to 25	¾
Red raspberries............	None..............	5 to 10	1

[1] To make mint-flavored apple jelly, after the jelly stage is reached and just before the sirup is ready to pour into the glasses, tint with green food coloring and add a few drops of essence of spearmint or peppermint.

[2] For spiced crab apple jelly, cook with the sugar and the juice from 8 pounds of fruit, four 2-inch pieces stick cinnamon, and 12 whole cloves tied loosely in a cheesecloth bag.

[3] For spiced grape jelly, cook 6 pounds of Concord grapes with 1 cup of vinegar, 1 tablespoon of cloves, and 5 pieces of 1-inch stick cinnamon. Strain. Proceed with juice as for grape jelly.

EXTRACTING THE JUICE

Boiling the fruit is necessary to extract the pectin in the juice. With normally juicy fruits no more than the minimum of water indicated in the table above should be added. Any excess of water must be boiled away, and prolonged boiling tends to destroy pectin, flavor, and color.

Boil the fruit in a broad, flat-bottomed kettle, and stir to prevent scorching. Crush soft fruits to start the flow of juice. Count time only after the fruit begins to boil. Berries, currants, and grapes need 5 to 10 minutes to cook soft, and apples and quinces

20 to 25 minutes. The time varies with the degree of firmness of the fruit.

Pour the hot cooked fruit at once into a jelly bag. Let the fruit drip. When the dripping has almost ceased, press the jelly bag to obtain all the juice. Clarify the juice by re-straining through a fresh jelly bag wrung from hot water.

Some fruits, such as currants, crab apples, and wild grapes, are so rich in pectin and acid that two extractions of juice can be made from the same lot of fruit. First- and second-extraction juices may then be combined or made into jelly separately as desired.

COMBINING SUGAR AND JUICE

In order to have the best possible product, work with small lots of juice at a time—not more than 8 cups.

Measure the sugar and the juice accurately. Use ¾ to 1 cup of sugar to each cup of juice. Use a good grade of granulated white sugar. Repeated tests have shown that refined beet and cane sugar produce exactly the same results. For second-extraction juices of crab apples, currants, and wild grapes, allow three-fourths of a cup of sugar to each cup of the juice, instead of 1 cup as with the first-extraction juice.

BOILING TO THE JELLY STAGE

Heat the fruit juice and the sugar quickly to boiling, using a large flat-bottomed pan that permits rapid evaporation. Stir only until the sugar is dissolved—no longer.

Boil rapidly until the jelly stage is reached. To test whether or not this moment has arrived, dip a large spoon into the boiling sirup and lift the spoon so that the sirup runs off the side. When the sirup no longer runs off the spoon in a steady stream but separates into two distinct lines of drops, which "sheet" together, stop the cooking.

PECTIN EXTRACTS

Pectin extracts and powders may be used to prepare jelly from well-flavored but pectin-poor fruits which could not otherwise be so utilized. Both extracts and powders may be bought in commercial form. The extract may be made at home (No. 3662 and 3663).

(3662)   HOME-MADE APPLE PECTIN EXTRACT

Select firm apples such as the Ben Davis and Arkansas (Mammoth Black Twig). Summer apples do not have sufficient pectin for such use. Sound culls or apples with surface blemishes are usable. Scrub the apples and cut out the imperfect spots, then slice thin, retaining skins and cores. For each 4 pounds of prepared apples use 4½ pints of water for the first extraction. Place the apples and the water in a large pan so as to allow rapid boiling. Cover and boil 20 minutes. Strain through four thicknesses of cheesecloth until the juice stops dripping. Repeat the process, adding the same quantity of water and boiling and straining as before. The two extractions should amount to 3 quarts. Boil this juice in a pan large enough so that the liquid will be 2 inches deep. Boil rapidly until the juice is reduced to a fourth of its original volume. This usually requires from 30 to 40 minutes. There should be 1½ pints of the concentrated apple juice or pectin extract. If the extract is not to be used at once, pour it while hot into hot sterilized half-pint jars, partially seal, process on a rack in a boiling-water bath for 20 minutes, complete the seal, and store in a cool, dry place. Once the canned extract is opened, it must be used immediately, as it will not keep.

(3663)   HOME-MADE ORANGE OR LEMON
PECTIN EXTRACT

Select oranges and lemons with thick skins. Wash the fruit and remove the yellow rind, using a stainless steel knife in order not to discolor the peel. For each pound of the fresh white peel, use 2 quarts water and 1 tablespoon tartaric acid. Add the acid to the water and stir until dissolved. Put the fresh peel through a meat grinder, using the coarse plate. Place the ground peel in a large flat-bottomed pan to permit rapid boiling and cover with the acid solution. Allow the mixture to stand for an hour or two. Measure the depth of the mixture in the pan. Boil rapidly and stir constantly until the volume is reduced to half. Strain through four thicknesses of cheesecloth. Make two more extractions in this same way, using 2 quarts of water, and 1 tablespoon of tartaric acid to the pomace each time. It is not necessary, however, for the mixture to stand after the first time. Combine the three extractions. There should be about 2½ pints. If the product is to be kept for future use, process it in a boiling-water bath as directed for the apple pectin extract (No. 3662).

(3664)   CHERRY JELLY WITH ADDED PECTIN

½ cup apple (No. 3662) or lemon pectin extract (No. 3663) or ¾ cup orange pectin extract (No. 3663)

2 pounds sour red cherries
½ cup water
2 cups sugar

Wash the cherries thoroughly and remove the stems. Add the water to the cherries, boil 10 minutes, and strain through a jelly bag. This yields about 2 cups juice. Mix the 2 cups juice with sugar and pectin extract. Cook until the jelly stage is reached and pour into hot sterilized glasses.

(3665)   STRAWBERRY JELLY WITH ADDED PECTIN

⅔ cup apple (No. 3662) or lemon pectin extract (No. 3663) or ¾ cup orange pectin extract (No. 3663)

2 pounds strawberries
2 tablespoons water
2 cups sugar

Wash berries thoroughly and remove caps. Add water to berries, boil rapidly a few minutes until berries are soft, and strain through a jelly bag. This yields about 2 cups juice. Mix 2 cups juice with sugar and pectin extract. If the berries are especially lacking in acid, add 1 teaspoon lemon juice to each cup juice. Boil rapidly until jelly stage is reached and pour into hot sterilized glasses.

(3666)   PRESERVES

The standard proportion of sugar varies from ¾ to 1 part by weight of sugar to 1 part by weight of the prepared fruit. To be suitable for preserving, fruits must hold their shape and color, as for example apricots, cherries, citron melon, kumquats, peaches, pears, damson plums, quinces, strawberries, watermelon, tomatoes, and figs. It is better to allow tender fruits to stand over-night in sugar. Or the fruit may be cooked without this pre-liminary treatment and have only enough water added to the sugar to prevent scorching as the mixture begins to cook. Pre-serves are cooked until the sirup is quite thick and the fruit is fairly translucent. The temperature at which this concentration is reached varies from 217° to 223° F., but the temperature test is not always a reliable guide. The temperature varies widely, de-pending on where the thermometer bulb is located in the boiling mass. Glass fruit jars are the most satisfactory containers for pre-serves. The jars should be filled three-fourths full with the pre-served fruit, and then enough of the sirup added to completely fill the containers. They should be sealed while hot.

(3667) CHERRY PRESERVES

Select sour red cherries. Discard any imperfect ones. Wash and drain. Remove stems and pits without tearing the fruit need-lessly. For each pound of pitted cherries use ¾ to 1 pound sugar. Combine the fruit and sugar in alternate layers and let them stand 8 to 10 hours or overnight before cooking. Or, if pre-ferred, add the sugar and ¼ cup water for each pound of the fruit and cook it at once. Whether or not the fruit has been allowed to stand with the sugar, it must be stirred carefully while it is being heated to the boiling point. Boil rapidly until the sirup is somewhat thick, taking care to prevent scorching. Pour at once into hot sterilized jars and seal.

(3668) CITRON MELON PRESERVES

Select a slightly underripe melon, wash, and pare off the green rind. Cut the melon into half-inch slices and separate the inner and outer portions. These two portions must be handled sep-arately throughout the preserving process because of the differ-ence in their texture, and they should be packed in separate jars. Cut each portion into half-inch cubes and remove the seeds. Weigh the prepared fruit, and to each pound allow 1½ quarts water, three-fourths pound sugar, one-half lemon, thinly sliced, and, if desired, one or two pieces gingerroot. Boil the citron melon in the water about 25 minutes, or until tender. Add the sugar and boil 1 hour. Add the lemon and the ginger and con-tinue to boil until the sirup "sheets off" the spoon in the jelly test. Fill hot sterilized jars with the preserves and seal.

(3669) PEACH PRESERVES

Any variety of white or yellow peach of good dessert quality will make satisfactory preserves if chosen at the firm-ripe stage. Wash and pare the peaches. Either leave them whole or cut them into uniform pieces such as halves, quarters, or eighths. To each pound of prepared fruit allow ¾ to 1 pound sugar. Combine the fruit and the sugar in alternate layers and let stand 8 to 10 hours or overnight before cooking. Or add the sugar and one-fourth cup water for each pound of the fruit and cook at once. In either case stir carefully while heating to boiling. Boil rapidly until the sirup is somewhat thick, stirring constantly to prevent burning. Pour at once into hot sterilized jars and seal.

(3670) PEAR PRESERVES

The Kieffer pear is a variety commonly used for preserving because it holds its shape and has a good flavor. It is important to allow the fruit to reach the firm-ripe stage. If possible, store Kieffer pears for 2 or 3 weeks at 60° to 65° F. to obtain the best qualities for preserve making. Wash, pare, and cut the fruit into uniform pieces, as quarters or eighths, depending upon the size of the fruit; then core. To each pound of prepared fruit allow ¾ to 1 pound sugar. Combine the fruit and the sugar in alternate layers and let stand 8 to 10 hours or overnight before cooking. Or cook at once with the sugar and one-fourth cup water to a pound of fruit. Whichever method is used, stir carefully while heating to the boiling point. Boil rapidly until the sirup is somewhat thick, stirring constantly to prevent burning. Pour at once into hot sterilized jars and seal.

(3671) GINGER PEAR PRESERVES

A modification of pear preserves (No. 3670) may be made by the addition of gingerroot and lemon. After paring and coring the fruit, cut it into small uniform pieces. For each pound of fruit use ½ to ¾ pound sugar, 1 to 2 pieces gingerroot, and ½ lemon, thinly sliced. Combine the sliced pears and sugar in alternate layers and let them stand 8 to 10 hours or overnight before cooking. Boil the lemon about 5 minutes in only enough water to cover. Add the lemon with what water remains and the gingerroot to the pear and sugar mixture. Boil rapidly and stir constantly until the fruit is clear and of a rich amber color. Pour at once into hot sterilized jars and seal.

(3672)   DAMSON PLUM PRESERVES

Wash the fruit, drain, and prick each plum in three or four places. For each pound fruit use ½ cup water and ¾ to 1 pound sugar. Dissolve the sugar in the water and bring to boiling. Add the plums and boil gently until the fruit is clear and tender and the sirup sheets from a spoon. Pour into hot sterilized jars and seal.

(3673)   QUINCE PRESERVES

Allow the fruit to ripen until it is yellow but still firm. Wash the fruit, pare, cut into quarters, and core. For each pound of prepared fruit use 1¾ cups water and ¾ pound sugar. Dissolve the sugar in the water and boil 5 minutes. Add the fruit and boil slowly 1 to 1½ hours. Stir occasionally to prevent burning. As soon as the fruit becomes tender and of a clear, reddish color and the sirup reaches the jelly stage, pour into hot sterilized jars and seal.

(3674)   STRAWBERRY PRESERVES

Method 1.—Select large, firm, tart berries. Wash, drain, and remove caps. For each pound fruit use 1 pound sugar. Combine the fruit and the sugar in alternate layers and let stand 8 to 10 hours or overnight before cooking. While heating to boiling, stir carefully. Boil rapidly 15 to 20 minutes or until the sirup is somewhat thick, taking care to prevent burning. Remove the scum. Pour at once into hot sterilized jars and seal.

Method 2.—In this method the smaller, less-perfect berries are picked out to be used for juice. Crush these berries, then stir them while cooking them about 3 minutes. Strain. To each pound choice prepared berries allow ¼ cup juice and 1 pound sugar. Add the sugar to the juice, stir, and heat slowly until the sugar is entirely dissolved. Drop the berries into the sirup, simmer 3 to 5 minutes, then boil rapidly 10 to 15 minutes, or until the fruit is somewhat clear. Remove the scum. Allow the preserves to stand about 8 hours or overnight in a glass or porcelain bowl. Fill hot sterilized jars ¾ full with the drained berries, without reheating them. Boil the sirup rapidly until fairly thick, or to 221° F. Pour the hot sirup over the berries and seal.

(3675)   TOMATO PRESERVES

Select firm, small, yellow or red pear-shaped tomatoes. Wash and drain. If a tomato preserve without skins is desired, dip the tomatoes into boiling water, then into cold water, and remove the skins before starting the preserving process. The tomatoes must then be handled with extra care to prevent their going to pieces. To each pound tomatoes allow ¾ cup water, ¾ pound sugar, ¼ lemon, thinly sliced, and 1 piece gingerroot. Boil the lemon 5 minutes in part of water. Boil the remainder of water with the sugar 5 minutes to make a sirup. Add tomatoes, gingerroot, lemon, and the liquid in which the lemon was cooked. Boil until the tomatoes are clear and the sirup somewhat thick. Remove the scum; then pour the preserves at once into hot sterilized jars and seal.

(3676)   WATERMELON PRESERVES

Select thick watermelon rind and trim off the outer green skin and the pink flesh, leaving only the greenish-white part. Cut into ½- or 1-inch cubes and weigh. For each 4 pounds of the prepared rind, prepare 2 quarts limewater containing 2 tablespoons lime (calcium oxide). Let the melon stand in the limewater 2½ hours to make it crisp. Drain and place in clear water 1 hour. Drain and boil 1½ hours in fresh water. Drain again. To each 4 pounds of the prepared watermelon rind, weighed before the limewater treatment, allow 4 quarts water, 4 pounds sugar, 2 lemons, thinly sliced, and, if desired, 4 small pieces gingerroot. Boil the lemon 5 minutes in ½ cup water. Boil the rest of the water with the sugar 5 minutes to make a sirup. Add the watermelon and the gingerroot to the sirup. Boil about 1 hour. When the sirup thickens, add the lemon and the water in which it was cooked. Continue to boil, stirring constantly, until the sirup is somewhat thick and the melon is clear. Pack at once into hot sterilized jars and seal.

(3677)   AMBER MARMALADE

Select an orange, a grapefruit, and a lemon—each smooth, thick-skinned, and free from blemishes. Remove the peel, slice it very thin, add a quart of cold water, and parboil 5 minutes. Drain off the water, add a quart of fresh water, parboil again, and drain. Add water a third time and parboil. Cut the fruit pulp into thin slices and remove the seeds and rag. Combine the sliced pulp with the drained parboiled peel. To each pressed measure of this mixture of fruit pulp and parboiled peel, add twice that quantity of water and boil rapidly about 40 minutes. Then weigh or measure this mixture and to it add an equal weight or measure of sugar. Add ⅛ teaspoon salt. Boil the fruit mixture and the sugar rapidly 25 minutes, or until it thickens and becomes amber-colored. Stir the mixture as it cooks down, to prevent scorching. Let the marmalade stand in the kettle long enough for the shreds of peel to distribute themselves uniformly throughout the jellied juice—that is, until it is slightly cooled. Stir and pour into hot sterilized jars and seal; or pour into hot sterilized jelly glasses and cover with paraffin.

(3678)   SOUR, OR SEVILLE, ORANGE MARMALADE

Use 2 pounds sour oranges (about 6 medium-sized), 2 quarts water, 3 pounds sugar, and ½ teaspoon salt. Select from the oranges two with clear skins and remove the peel. Slice the peel very thin and cover with water. Boil until tender, adding more water as it boils away. Change the water frequently if the bitter flavor is objectionable. Peel the other oranges, discarding the peel. Boil the pulp in the 2 quarts water until very soft and then strain through a bag with pressure. Re-strain without pressure. Mix this juice with the drained peel, sugar, and salt, and boil until the jelly stage is reached. Let stand in the kettle until slightly cool, then stir, and pour into hot sterilized jars and seal; or pour into hot sterilized jelly glasses and cover with paraffin.

(3679)   SWEET ORANGE MARMALADE

Select four oranges and four lemons with smooth thick skins free from blemishes. Limes may be substituted for all or part of the lemons. Wash the fruit, remove the peel, and slice it very thin. Cover the sliced peel with cold water and boil until tender, adding more water as it boils away. Change the water frequently if the bitter flavor is objectionable. Cut the fruit pulp into thin slices, and remove the seeds and rag. Combine the sliced pulp with the parboiled peel. To each pressed measure of this mixed fruit pulp and parboiled peel, add twice the quantity of water, and ⅛ teaspoon of salt. Boil rapidly 25 minutes. Then weigh or measure this mixture and to it add an equal weight or measure of sugar. Boil 15 minutes or until the jelly stage is reached. Allow the marmalade to cool slightly, stir, and pour into hot sterilized jars and seal; or pour into hot sterilized jelly glasses and cover with paraffin.

(3680)   GREEN TOMATO MARMALADE

Wash green tomatoes, trim, and cut into small pieces or slices. To 4 pounds of the prepared tomatoes allow 2 pounds sugar, ½ teaspoon salt, and 5 lemons. Remove the peel of the lemons, cut it into thin slices, and boil for 5 minutes in 1 cup of water. Discard the water and repeat the parboiling if the bitter flavor in the rind is not desired. Slice the lemon pulp and remove the seeds. Combine the tomatoes, sugar, salt, sliced lemon, and drained peel. Heat slowly and stir until the sugar is dissolved. Continue stirring and boil 1 hour, or until the mixture is somewhat thick and the fruit clear. Pour at once into hot sterilized jars and seal.

(3681)   JAMS

Jams are made from crushed fruits cooked with sugar until the mixture is more or less homogeneous and thick. Well-ripened, yet sound berries and soft-fleshed fruits like apricots, peaches, and plums make good jam. The standard proportion of sugar varies from ¾ to 1 part by weight of sugar to 1 part by weight of the prepared fruit.

(3682)   APRICOT OR PEACH JAM

Wash the fruit carefully; then dip it into boiling water about ½ minute or until the skins slip easily. Plunge it at once into cold water a few seconds, remove the skins, cut the fruit into halves, and discard the pits. To each pound prepared apricots allow ¾ pound sugar and 2 tablespoons lemon juice. To each pound peaches allow ¾ to 1 pound sugar and omit the lemon juice. Crush the fruit, combine with the sugar in alternate layers, and let stand until some of the juice is extracted, that is about 3 or 4 hours. Then heat slowly until the sugar is dissolved, stirring meanwhile. Bring to a boil and cook, stirring constantly, until the fruit is clear and the jam somewhat thick. Pour into hot sterilized jars and seal.

(3683) BLACKBERRY AND OTHER BERRY JAM

Wash the berries carefully, drain, and remove the caps and stems. To each pound prepared fruit allow an equal weight sugar. Crush the berries and bring slowly to a boil, stirring constantly. Add the sugar and boil until the fruit mixture has thickened to jellylike consistency. Stir throughout the cooking. Pour into hot sterilized jars and seal. If the seeds in blackberries and black raspberries are objectionable, boil the fruit for a few minutes, then put through a fine sieve to remove the seeds before weighing the fruit and adding the sugar.

(3684) CURRANT AND RED RASPBERRY JAM

Wash and drain the fruit. Remove the currants from the stems. Combine 2 pounds currants with 1 pound red raspberries, and crush. Add an equal weight of sugar. Heat slowly until the sugar is dissolved, stirring constantly. Continue stirring while cooking 10 to 15 minutes, or until the jelly stage is reached. Pour into hot sterilized jars and seal.

(3685) PLUM JAM

Select plums of a tart variety. Wash the fruit and drain. To each pound fruit allow ¾ pound sugar and 1 cup water. Boil the plums in the water 10 to 15 minutes, or until the skins are tender. Add sugar and stir, while boiling, until the jelly stage is reached. Pour into hot sterilized jars and seal.

(3686) STRAWBERRY AND PINEAPPLE JAM

Wash the strawberries, drain, and remove the caps. Wash the pineapple and remove the top. Cut the pineapple into ½-inch slices. Pare the slices, remove the eyes, then cut into ½-inch cubes. Prepare 2 pounds strawberries for every pound pineapple. For each 2 pounds strawberries, use 1½ pounds sugar, and for each pound pineapple, 1 pound sugar. Heat slowly the pineapple and its equal weight of sugar, stirring until the sugar is dissolved. Then bring to a brisk boil and cook 10 minutes, stirring constantly. Add the strawberries and their quota of sugar. Stir while boiling for 15 to 20 minutes or until the jam is somewhat thick. Pour into hot sterilized jars and seal.

(3687)   STRAWBERRY AND RHUBARB JAM

Wash the strawberries, drain, and then remove the caps. Cut young tender rhubarb into inch pieces, taking care not to remove the skin. For each pound strawberries use a pound rhubarb. To each 2 pounds combined fruits, allow 1½ to 2 pounds sugar. Cover the rhubarb with a part of the sugar and allow it to stand an hour or two to extract the juice. Crush the strawberries, mix with the remaining sugar, and combine with the rhubarb. Heat slowly until the sugar is dissolved, stirring meanwhile. Continue the stirring while boiling 15 to 20 minutes or until the jam is somewhat thick. Pour into hot sterilized jelly glasses and seal with paraffin or put into glass jars and seal.

(3688)   CRANBERRY CONSERVE

Pick over the cranberries and discard any that are specked or soft. For 2 pounds sound cranberries use 1 cup raisins, 2 oranges, 3 cups sugar, ¼ teaspoon salt, and 1 pint water. Wash the berries and the raisins. Peel the oranges and discard the seeds. Combine the fruits and the orange peel, and chop. Add the sugar, salt, and water. Boil, stirring constantly, about ½ hour or until the jelly stage is reached. Pour at once into hot sterilized jelly glasses and seal with paraffin or put into glass jars and seal.

(3689)   GRAPE CONSERVE

Use slip-skin grapes such as the Concord. Wash and drain the grapes and then remove them from the stems. To 4 pounds prepared grapes allow 2 pounds sugar, 1 cup seedless raisins, 1 orange, 1 cup nut meats, and 1 teaspoon salt. Slip the skins from the grapes and keep them separate from the pulp. Peel the orange and discard the seeds. Chop the orange pulp and peel fine. Also chop the nuts fine. Boil the grape pulp, stirring constantly about 10 minutes, or until the seeds show. Press through a sieve to remove the seeds. To the grape pulp add sugar, raisins, orange, and salt. Boil rapidly, stirring to prevent scorching, until the mixture begins to thicken. Add the grape skins and boil 10 minutes longer or until somewhat thick. Stir in the chopped nuts, pour at once into hot sterilized jelly glasses and seal with paraffin or put into glass jars, and seal.

(3690)   RHUBARB CONSERVE

Select young, tender rhubarb, and wash, drain, and weigh it. To each pound rhubarb allow 2 pounds sugar, 1 orange, 2 lemons, 1 cup blanched almonds, and ¼ teaspoon salt. Without removing the skin, cut the rhubarb into small pieces. Remove the peel from the orange and the lemons, parboil it 5 minutes in 1 cup water, then drain. Discard the seeds from the orange and the lemons and chop the pulp and the parboiled skins fine. Chop fine the blanched almonds. Combine all ingredients except the almonds. Heat the mixture slowly until the sugar is dissolved. Boil rapidly, stirring constantly, until somewhat thick. Add the almonds, pour at once into hot sterilized jelly glasses or into glass jars and seal.

(3691)   FRUIT BUTTERS

For fruit butters the pulped fruit is cooked with sugar until the mixture has a homogeneous thick consistency that is soft enough to spread easily when cold. The fruits most commonly used for butters are tart apples, apricots, grapes, peaches, pears, plums, and quinces. Apple butter made with cider has an especially good flavor. Other combinations are apples and grape juice, apples and plums, and apples and quinces, to give desirable blendings of flavor and color. Use only sound, ripe fruit or firm portions of windfalls or culls. Wash the fruit thoroughly and prepare it as follows:

Apples: Pare and slice. Use equal measures fruit and cider, or a 50-50 mixture cider and water.

Apricots and peaches: Scald; remove skins and pits. Crush fruit and cook in own juice.

Grapes: Remove from stems, crush, cook in own juice.

Pears: Quarter; remove stems but not cores and skins. Add half as much water as fruit.

Plums: Crush and cook in own juice.

Quinces: Cut into small pieces, and remove blossom ends but leave cores and skins. Add water, using from ½ to equal quantities water to fruit.

Cook until the fruit is soft, stirring constantly. Press through a colander, then through a fine sieve to remove all fibrous material and give a smooth consistency. The quantity of sugar varies according to taste, but the usual proportion is half as much sugar as fruit pulp. Add ¼ to ½ teaspoon salt to each gallon butter. Boil rapidly and stir constantly to prevent burning. As the butter cooks down and becomes thicker reduce the heat to prevent spattering. When the butter is thick, test by pouring a small quantity on a cold plate. Cook until no rim of liquid separates around the edge of the butter. Stir in spices as desired; for example, 1 to 2 teaspoons mixed ground spices to the gallon of butter. Use only fresh spices and just enough to give a delicate flavor without obscuring the natural fruit flavor. Or if a light-colored butter is desired, add whole spices tied loosely in a cheese-cloth bag while the butter is cooking. Pour the butter while boiling hot into sterilized containers and seal. These can be used as sandwich spreads or as fruit, fish, meat, vegetable, or dessert sauces.

Brining and Pickling

(3692) **CUCUMBER PICKLES**

Because of their shape, firmness, or keeping quality some varieties of cucumbers, notably Chicago Pickling, Boston Pickling, and Snow's Perfection, are better adapted for making pickles than others. Cucumbers to be pickled should retain from ⅛ to ¼ inch of their stems, and they should not be bruised. If dirty they should be washed before brining. They should be placed in brine not later than 24 hours after they have been gathered. Cucumbers contain approximately 90 per cent of water. As this large water content reduces materially the salt concentration of any brine in which they are fermented, it is necessary to add an excess of salt at the beginning of a fermentation in the proportion of 1 pound for every 10 pounds cucumbers. The active stage of cucumber fermentation continues for 10 to 30 days, depending largely on the temperature at which it is conducted. The most favorable temperature is 86° F. Practically all the sugar withdrawn from the cucumbers is utilized during the stage of active fermentation, at the end of which the brine reaches its highest degree of acidity. During this period the salt concentration should not be materially increased; for, although the lactic bacteria are fairly tolerant of salt, there is a limit to their tolerance. The addition of a large quantity of salt at this time would reduce their acid-forming power just when this is essential to a successful fermentation. Salt, therefore, should be added gradually over a period of weeks.

(3693)   SALT PICKLES

Salt pickles, or salt stock, are made by curing cucumbers in a brine which should contain not less than 9.5 per cent of salt (approximately 36° on the salinometer scale) at the start. Not only must the brine be kept at this strength, but salt should be added until it has a concentration of about 15 per cent (60° on the salinometer scale). If well covered with a brine of this strength, the surface of which is kept clean, pickles will keep indefinitely. Proper curing of cucumbers requires from six weeks to two months, or possibly longer, according to the temperature at which the process is carried out and the size and variety of the cucumbers. Pack the cucumbers in a 4-gallon jar and cover with 6 quarts of a 10 per cent brine (40° on salinometer scale). At the time of making up the brine, or not later than the following day, add more salt at the rate of 1 pound for every 10 pounds of cucumbers used—in this case 1 pound and 3 ounces. Cover with a round board or plate that will go inside the jar, and on top of this place a weight heavy enough to keep the cucumbers well below the surface of the brine. At the end of the first week, and at the end of each succeeding week for five weeks, add ¼ pound salt. In adding salt always place it on the cover.

(3694)   SOUR PICKLES

After pickles have been processed sufficiently (No. 3692), drain and cover them at once with vinegar. A 45 or 50 grain vinegar usually gives all the sourness that is desirable. If, however, very sour pickles are preferred, it would be well to use at first a 40 or 45 grain vinegar, and after a week or 10 days transfer the pickles to a vinegar of the strength desired. As the first vinegar used will in all cases be greatly reduced in strength by dilution with the brine contained in the pickles, it will be necessary to renew the vinegar after a few weeks. If this is not done and the pickles are held for any length of time they may spoil. The best containers for sour pickles are stone jars, or, for large quantities, kegs or barrels. Covered with a vinegar of the proper strength, pickles should keep indefinitely.

(3695)   SWEET PICKLES

Cover the cured and processed cucumbers (No. 3692) with a sweet liquor made by dissolving sugar in vinegar, usually with the addition of spices. Depending upon the degree of sweetness desired, the quantity of sugar may vary from 4 to 10 pounds to the gallon of vinegar, 6 pounds to the gallon usually giving satisfactory results. The chief difficulty in making sweet pickles is their tendency to become shriveled and tough, which increases with the sugar concentration of the liquor. This danger can usually be avoided by covering the pickles first with a plain 45 to 50 grain vinegar. After one week discard this vinegar, which in all probability has become greatly reduced in strength, and cover with a liquor made by adding 4 pounds of sugar to the gallon of vinegar. If a liquor containing more than 4 pounds of sugar to the gallon is desired, it would be best not to exceed that quantity at first, but gradually add sugar until the desired concentration is obtained. A sugar hydrometer readily indicates the sugar concentration. A reading of 42° would indicate a concentration of approximately 6 pounds of sugar to the gallon of vinegar. Spices are practically always added in making sweet pickles. The effect of too much spice, especially the stronger kinds, like peppers and cloves, however, is injurious. One ounce of whole mixed spices to 4 gallons of pickles is enough. As spices may cause cloudiness of the vinegar, they should be removed after the desired flavor has been obtained.

(3696)   DILL PICKLES

The fermentation of pickles is much more rapid in a brine containing 5 per cent of salt than in one containing 10 per cent. Pickles fermented in brine are usually flavored with spices, chiefly dill herb, which gives them their common name. Place in the bottom of the jar a layer of dill and ½ ounce mixed spice. Then fill the jar, to within 2 or 3 inches of the top, with washed cucumbers of as nearly the same size as practicable. Add another half ounce of spice and layer of dill. It is a good plan to place over the top a layer of grape leaves. In fact, it would be well to place these at both the bottom and top. They make a very suitable covering and have a greening effect on the pickles. Pour over the pickles a brine made as follows: Salt, 1 pound; vinegar, 1 pint; water, 2 gallons. Never use a hot brine at the beginning of a fermentation. The chances are that it would kill the organisms present, thus preventing fermentation. Cover with a board cover or plate with sufficient weight on top to hold the cucumbers well below the brine.

If the cucumbers are packed at a temperature around 86° F., an active fermentation will at once set in. This should be completed in 10 days to 2 weeks, if a temperature of about 86° F. is maintained. The scum which soon forms on the surface and which consists usually of wild yeasts, but often contains molds and bacteria, should be skimmed off. After active fermentation has stopped, it is necessary to protect the pickles against spoilage. This may be done in one of two ways: (1) Cover with a layer of paraffin. This should be poured while hot over the surface of the brine or as much of it as is exposed around the edges of the board cover. When cooled this forms a solid coating which effectually seals the pickles. (2) Seal the pickles in glass jars or cans. As soon as they are sufficiently cured, which may be determined by their agreeable flavor and dark-green color, transfer them to glass jars, and fill either with their own brine or with a fresh brine made as directed. Add a small quantity of dill and spice. Bring the brine to a boil, and, after cooling to about 160° F., pour it over the pickles, filling the jars full. Seal the jars tight and store in a cool place.

(3697)   MIXED PICKLES

Onions, cauliflower, green peppers, tomatoes, and beans, as well as cucumbers, are used for making mixed pickles. All vegetables should first be cured in brine. For making mixed pickles, very small vegetables are much to be preferred. If larger ones must be used, first cut them into pieces of a desirable and uniform shape and size. Place in the bottom of each wide-mouth bottle or jar a little mixed spice. In filling the bottle arrange the various kinds of pickles in as neat and orderly a manner as possible. The appearance of the finished product depends largely upon the manner in which they are packed in the bottle. Do not completely fill the bottles. If sour pickles are desired, fill the bottles completely with a 45-grain vinegar. If sweet ones are wanted, fill with a liquor made by dissolving 4 to 6 pounds of sugar in a gallon of vinegar. Seal tight, and label properly.

(3698)   SAUERKRAUT

For making sauerkraut in the home, 4 or 6 gallon stone jars are considered the best containers, unless large quantities are desired, in which case kegs or barrels may be used. Select only mature, sound heads of cabbage. After removing all decayed or dirty leaves, quarter the heads and slice off the core portion. For shredding, one of the hand-shredding machines which can be obtained on the market is much the best, although an ordinary slaw cutter or a large knife will do. In making sauerkraut the fermentation is carried out in a brine made from the juice of the cabbage which is drawn out by the salt. One pound of salt for every 40 pounds of cabbage makes the proper strength of brine to produce the best results. The salt may be distributed as the cabbage is packed in the jar or it may be mixed with the shredded cabbage before being packed. The distribution of 2 ounces of salt with every 5 pounds of cabbage probably is the best way to get an even distribution. Pack the cabbage firmly, but not too tightly, in the jar or keg. When full, cover with a clean cloth and a board or plate. On the cover place a weight heavy enough to cause the brine to come up to the cover. If the jar is kept at a temperature of about 86° F., fermentation will start promptly. A scum soon forms on the surface of the brine. As this scum tends to destroy the acidity and may affect the cabbage, it should be skimmed off from time to time. If the jar is kept at 86° F., fermentation should be completed in 10 days.

(3699) CUCUMBER MUSTARD PICKLES

8 large cucumbers	2 cups sugar
4 cups vinegar	1 tablespoon mixed whole
2 tablespoons mustard seed	spice

Peel cucumbers, remove seeds, and cut into long strips. Salt lightly and let stand 24 hours. Drain well. Mix vinegar, sugar, mustard seed, and spice and pour over the cucumbers. Cook until soft. Pack into clean, hot jars and seal at once.

(3700) BREAD AND BUTTER PICKLES

6 quarts sliced medium cucumbers	1 cup salt
1½ quarts vinegar	½ cup mustard seed
6 cups sugar	1 tablespoon celery seed
6 onions, medium-sized, sliced	¼ to ⅓ teaspoon cayenne pepper

Combine cucumbers, onions, and salt and let stand 3 hours. Drain. Combine seasoning and vinegar and boil. Add cucumbers and onions. Heat to simmering and pack hot. Be careful to avoid boiling as that makes pickles soft. Pack while hot in clean jars and seal immediately.

(3701)   GREEN TOMATO PICKLES

1 peck green tomatoes, sliced	1 dozen onions, sliced
1 ounce black pepper	1 ounce whole cloves
4 cups sugar	1 ounce mustard seed
1 ounce whole allspice	2 quarts vinegar
1/4 ounce ground mustard	3/4 cup salt

Mix tomatoes with 1/2 cup salt and onions with 1/4 cup salt.
Let stand overnight, drain. Tie spices in bag and place into a
kettle with the vinegar and sugar, heat to the boiling point, add
tomatoes and onions and let simmer slowly 20 minutes. Pack into
clean, hot jars. Seal immediately.

(3702)   CHOW-CHOW

1 gallon chopped cabbage	1 gallon vinegar
1 dozen chopped onions	2 pounds sugar
1/2 dozen chopped green peppers	1/2 cup ground mustard
1/2 gallon chopped green tomatoes	6 tablespoons white mustard seed
1/2 dozen chopped red bell peppers	3 tablespoons celery seed
	1 tablespoon cloves
	Salt

Put cabbage, onions, green peppers, tomatoes, and red peppers
in alternate layers in an enamel pan. Sprinkle each layer with
salt and top with a complete covering of salt. Let stand 12 hours.
Drain. Put vinegar, sugar, mustard, mustard seed, and celery
seed in enamel kettle. Tie cloves in cheesecloth and add to mixture. Bring to boiling point. Add vegetable mixture and simmer
slowly until all are tender, about 1/2 hour. Remove cloves. Pack
mixture into hot, clean jars. Seal at once.

(3703)   CHILI SAUCE

4 quarts chopped and peeled tomatoes	3 tablespoons salt
	1/2 cup sugar
2 cups chopped onions	1 tablespoon white mustard seed
1 cup chopped sweet red pepper	1 teaspoon cinnamon
1 cup chopped green pepper	1 teaspoon allspice
1 small hot, red pepper	2 1/2 cups vinegar

Combine the vegetables, salt, and sugar, and cook until the
mixture begins to thicken. Add vinegar and whole spices, in bag,
and cook until the mixture becomes a thick sauce. Pour into hot

Sweet Potato Pie

1/4 cup butter
1/2 cup sugar
3. egg

1/3 cup milk
1/2 teaspoon salt
1 cup mashed sweet potatoes

1/2 cup water
1 1/2 tablespoon butter

jars and seal immediately. Drain juice from vegetables before adding vinegar. This will shorten the cooking period.

(3704) **PICCALILLI**

1 peck green tomatoes	⅔ cup sugar
5 pounds cabbage	½ pound mustard seed
6 sweet peppers	2 tablespoons celery seed
4 medium-sized onions	1 tablespoon ground
1 cup salt	horseradish
3 pints vinegar	

Chop and mix tomatoes, cabbage, sweet peppers, and onion with salt and let stand 12 hours. Mix vinegar, sugar, mustard seed, celery seed, and horseradish. Bring to boiling point. Add vegetables and warm through. Pack into hot, clean jars. Seal immediately.

(3705) **CHUTNEY**

24 ripe tomatoes, medium-sized	1 pound seedless raisins
	1 cup celery, cut fine
6 onions, medium-sized	2 quarts vinegar
3 red peppers	3 cups sugar
3 green peppers	Salt
12 tart apples	

Chop vegetables first and then the apples. Cut celery. Combine ingredients and cook chutney until it is thick and clear. Pour immediately into clean, hot jars, and seal at once.

(3706) **APPLE CHUTNEY**

2 quarts apples	1 small onion
1 quart brown sugar	1 ounce black mustard
2 quarts cider vinegar	seed
2 pounds seeded raisins	2 ounces ground ginger
1 ounce white mustard seed	1 tablespoon salt
	2 chopped red peppers

Wash, peel, and core the apples. Cook them with the brown sugar and vinegar until they are smooth. When the mixture is thick, place it in a crock and add raisins, chopped fine, onion, white and black mustard seed, ginger, salt, and red peppers. Mix the ingredients thoroughly, heat them, and let them stand over night. In the morning place the chutney in jars and seal them.

(3707)   PEACH CHUTNEY

4 quarts peaches	¼ pound white mustard
5 cups vinegar	seed
½ cup chopped onion	2 ounces scraped ginger-
½ cup sugar	root
¼ pound raisins	1 ounce red peppers

1 ounce garlic

Peel peaches and remove stones. Add 2 cups vinegar to each 4 quarts peaches and cook until soft. Add another cup of vinegar, chopped onion, sugar, raisins, white mustard seed, ginger-root, red peppers, and garlic. Mix ingredients well and add 2 cups vinegar. Boil mixture 15 minutes. Pack into clean, hot jars and seal at once.

(3708)   TOMATO CATCHUP

½ peck tomatoes	2 teaspoons celery salt
3 red peppers	2 teaspoons ground
2 medium-sized onions, cut	mustard
fine	1 tablespoon whole allspice
2 tablespoons salt	1 tablespoon cloves
⅓ cup sugar	1 tablespoon cinnamon
2 cups vinegar	1 teaspoon paprika

Cook tomatoes, peppers, and onions together without adding water. Press mixture through strainer, and measure pulp. To pulp (4 quarts) add the salt, sugar, and spices. Place whole spices in a bag during the cooking and remove bag before pouring the catchup into jars. Ground spices, except paprika, will darken catchup. Long, slow cooking also gives a dark color. Cook ingredients together, except vinegar, rapidly for 1 hour, add vinegar, and cook mixture until it is thick. Seal in clean, hot jars. It should be bright-red in color.

(3709)   CRANBERRY SAUCE

Wash and pick over cranberries. Boil in an equal measure of medium sirup (No. 3602), without stirring, until the skins pop open, about 5 minutes. Pack hot into sterilized jars and seal at once.

(3710)   FRUIT FOR SALAD

A combination of light-colored fruits makes an attractive pack and it is a convenient product to have at hand, since it is ready to serve as fruit cocktail, salad or dessert. For fancy packs the fruit may be packed in alternate layers, or arranged in other attractive designs. Pleasing combinations are (1) Green gage plums, pears, white grapes. (2) Peaches, pears, blue plums. (3) Pineapples, kumquats, figs. Pack cold into hot jars; cover with sirup (No. 3602) made with 3 parts sugar to 2 parts water; partly seal and process 20 minutes in a hot-water bath. Seal immediately.

(3711)   QUINCES

Quinces should be well ripened for canning. Wipe with a damp cloth to remove the "fuzz." Peel and cut into pieces of convenient size, boil gently in a moderately heavy sirup (No. 3602) until fruit is tender. Pack the fruit into hot jars so that the proportion of sirup to fruit is greater than for pears (No. 3612) or peaches (No. 3611). Seal immediately.

(3712)   CRANBERRY JUICE

4 cups cranberries   4 cups water
$\frac{2}{3}$ cup sugar

Boil 4 cups cranberries in 4 cups water until skins burst, about 5 minutes. Strain juice through cheesecloth bag. Do not squeeze bag. Put juice in kettle, bring to boiling point, add $\frac{2}{3}$ cup granulated sugar and boil 2 minutes. Fill hot jars to overflowing and seal immediately.

(3713)   GRAPE JUICE (COOKED)

Use clean well-ripened but not over-ripe grapes. Pick over and wash grapes. Place in kettle, barely cover with water and boil until seeds are free. Strain through cheesecloth bag without squeezing. Measure the juice and replace on fire and bring to boiling point. Add $\frac{1}{2}$ cup sugar to each quart juice and let the mixture boil 5 minutes. Fill hot jars to overflowing and seal immediately.

(3714)   GRAPE JUICE (UNCOOKED)

Wash and stem firm, ripe grapes. Measure and place 1 cup grapes into clean, hot quart jar. Add 1 cup sugar. Fill jar to overflowing with boiling water and seal immediately. Invert jar for a few hours before storing. Will be ready for use in about 6 weeks.

(3715)   PINEAPPLE JUICE

An excellent juice for fruit drinks, ices or sauces, may be made from the cores, eyes and skins of pineapples, which are often discarded. Cover cores and skins with cold water and cook slowly in a covered kettle 30 to 40 minutes. Strain the mixture through a jelly bag. Measure the juice, heat it and add ⅛ as much sugar as juice. Boil rapidly 10 minutes. Fill clean, hot jars to overflowing and seal. This juice may be used in equal proportions with tart apple juice for jelly; ¾ as much sugar as juice should be allowed.

(3716)   FRUIT VINEGARS OR "SHRUBS"

Dissolve 2 cups sugar in 1 cup vinegar, heat to boiling, and pour over 2 quarts ripe berries—strawberries, raspberries, or blackberries. Let stand 1 hour or more, stirring at intervals. Allow the juice to drip through a jelly bag, bring to boil, and pour into clean, hot jars and process 10 minutes in a hot-water bath canner. Remove from canner and seal.

(3717)   BRUSSELS SPROUTS AND CABBAGE

Wash and boil 10 minutes in an open kettle. Add salt to cooking water in proportion of 1 level teaspoon salt to 1 quart water. Pack hot into clean jars, fill with cooking water, partly seal, and process for 40 minutes in a steam-pressure cooker at 10 pounds or 1½ hours in a hot-water bath. Remove from canner and seal at once.

(3718)   CAULIFLOWER AND BROCCOLI

Soak 1 hour in a cold brine made in the proportion of 1 tablespoon salt to 1 quart water. This will remove any lurking insects and help to prevent discoloring later in the cooking process. Boil 3 minutes, pack quickly into hot jars, add 1 teaspoon salt to each quart, fill with cooking water, partly seal and process for 40 minutes in a steam-pressure cooker at 10 pounds or 1½ hours in a hot-water bath. Remove from canner and seal at once.

(3719)   CORN ON THE COB

Remove husk and silk. Boil cob 5 minutes. Pack into hot 1-quart jars. Add 1 teaspoon salt to each quart and fill with cooking water. Partly seal and process 70 minutes in a steam-pressure cooker at 10 pounds or 3½ hours in a hot-water bath. Seal immediately. Allow ⅓ more time for processing 2-quart jars.

(3720)   EGGPLANT

Peel and cut into ¼- to ½-inch slices. Boil 3 minutes. Pack into hot jars. Fill with cooking water and process 60 minutes in a steam-pressure cooker at 10 pounds or 2½ hours in a hot-water bath. Seal immediately. Do not add salt.

(3721)   KOHLRABI, SALSIFY AND TURNIPS

Sort and grade for uniform size. Wash and scrub with a stiff vegetable brush. Scrape, if kohlrabi and turnips are old. Boil 15 minutes. Slice or pack whole into hot jars. Add 1 level teaspoon salt to each quart, fill with cooking water, partly seal and process for 45 minutes in a steam-pressure cooker at 10 pounds, or for 2 hours in a hot-water bath. Remove from canner and seal immediately.

(3722)   PARSNIPS

Sort and grade for uniform size. Wash and scrub with a stiff vegetable brush. Scrape if parsnips are old. Boil 15 minutes. Slice or pack whole into hot jars. Add 1 level teaspoon salt to each quart, fill with cooking water, partly seal and process for 45 minutes in a steam-pressure cooker at 10 pounds, or for 2 hours in a hot-water bath. Remove from canner and seal immediately.

(3723)   BELL PEPPERS

Can with the skin on. Wash and remove the seed pod. Boil 5 minutes. Flatten and pack tight in hot jars. Add 1 teaspoon salt to each quart. Fill with cooking water and process 15 minutes in a steam-pressure cooker at 10 pounds or 45 minutes in a hot-water bath. Seal immediately.

(3724)   SUCCOTASH

Cut fresh corn from cob. Boil 5 minutes, add to the corn an equal quantity of young, tender shelled beans, which have been boiled 5 minutes. Pack quickly and loosely, into hot jars, add 1 teaspoon salt to each quart, fill jar with cooking water, partly seal and process 70 minutes in a steam-pressure cooker at 10 pounds, or for 3 ½ hours in a hot-water bath. Remove from canner and seal immediately.

(3725)   TOMATOES

Scald, peel and core, cut into pieces, add salt to taste, boil 20 minutes, pack into clean, hot jars, and seal immediately.

(3726)   TOMATOES AND OKRA

Cut the okra into thin slices and cook gently with the tomatoes until tender. Pack immediately into clean, hot jars, add 1 teaspoon salt to each quart, partly seal, and process for 40 minutes in a steam-pressure cooker at 10 pounds, or 1 hour in a hot-water bath. Remove from canner and seal immediately.

(3727)   FISH

Fish, for canning, should be absolutely fresh. As soon as fish are caught it is well to kill them with a knife and let the blood run out. In scaling fish it is easier to remove the scales if the fish is dipped into boiling water. If skin is very tough, remove skin and wash the fish clean. Remove entrails and the dark membrane that in some fish covers the abdominal cavity. For small fish the backbone may be left in. For larger fish remove the backbone and use it with what meat adheres to it, for making fish chowder. For the softer-fleshed fish such as mackerel, trout, whitefish, mullet, etc., split the clean fish. Do not remove back-bone. Cut fish into jar-length pieces and soak in brine (½ pound salt to 1 gallon water) 60 minutes. Drain. Pack into hot pint jars, alternating heads and tail ends. The skin side should be next to the glass. The fish should reach to the top of the jar. Submerge the open jar into a kettle of hot brine (½ cup salt to 1 gallon water). Boil 15 minutes. Remove jar and invert to drain 5 minutes. Partly seal and process 100 minutes in steam-pressure cooker at 10 pounds or 3 hours in hot-water bath. Remove from canner and seal immediately.

(3728) SALMON, SHAD, AND OTHER FIRM-FLESHED FISH

Scale fish, wash, cut open, remove entrails, thoroughly wash, wipe dry and cut into jar-length pieces. Soak in brine (½ pound salt to 1 gallon cold water), 60 minutes. Drain 10 minutes. Pack raw into clean, hot pint jars. Add 1 level teaspoon salt. Do not add water. Partly seal and process for 100 minutes in steam-pressure cooker at 10 pounds or for 3 hours in hot-water bath. Remove from canner and seal immediately.

(3729) CLAMS AND OYSTERS

Use only fresh clams and oysters. If clams are muddy, wash before opening. After opening, discard all discolored clams. In canning oysters be sure they are absolutely fresh, have not soured and contain no oysters that are spoiled. It is therefore best to open them by hand and absolutely refuse any which have the shell partly open. Pack into hot clean jars. Fill jar to within ½ inch from top with the clam or oyster liquid. If not enough, fill with hot brine made in the proportion 1 teaspoon salt to 1 quart water. Partly seal and process 80 minutes in steam-pressure cooker at 10 pounds or 3 hours in hot-water bath. Remove from canner and seal immediately.

(3730) LOBSTERS

Plunge live lobsters into boiling salted water (1 tablespoon to each quart of water). Boil rapidly 4 minutes, then simmer 15 minutes. Remove and dip lobsters into cold water, drain, remove meat from shell. Blanch meat 1 minute in water to which lemon juice has been added (3 tablespoons lemon juice to 1 quart water). This makes the meat firm and prevents discoloration. Pack meat into clean, hot jars. Add 2 or 3 tablespoons salt brine made by dissolving ½ cup salt in 1 quart water. Process 80 minutes in steam-pressure cooker at 10 pounds or for 3 hours in hot-water bath. Remove from canner and seal immediately.

(3731)   CRAB MEAT

Place live crabs into a large kettle of rapidly boiling water. Boil 5 minutes. Remove crabs and wash in cold water. Crack shell and pick out the meat, being careful to remove all particles of shell. Wash crab meat in a cold brine made in proportion of 1 teaspoon salt to 1 quart water. Drain and pack into clean, hot jars, partly seal and process 80 minutes in a steam-pressure cooker at 10 pounds or 3 hours in a hot-water bath. Remove from canner and seal immediately.

(3732)   SHRIMP

Shrimp should be canned when absolutely fresh. Wash in 2 or 3 clear cold waters. Drain. To each gallon water, add 1 cup salt and when boiling, drop in washed shrimp. Boil 10 minutes. When cold, remove shell by tearing open on the upper side beginning at the head. Pack into clean, hot pint jars. Add ½ teaspoon salt. Boiling water may be added if desired or the dry pack in which no water is added may be used. Partly seal and process 70 minutes in the steam-pressure cooker at 10 pounds or 3 hours in the hot-water bath. Remove from canner and seal immediately. Remove intestinal canal which runs the entire length of the back by scraping with point of paring knife before serving.

(3733)   CLAM BROTH

Open fresh clams and place them with their liquid in a kettle. Add enough cold water to cover clams. Add a few stalks of celery, cut fine. Boil 10 minutes. Season with salt and pepper to taste, and add 1 level tablespoon butter for each 50 or 60 clams. Strain and pour while hot into clean, hot jars. Partly seal and process 100 minutes in a steam-pressure cooker at 10 pounds or 3 hours in a hot-water bath. Remove from canner and seal immediately.

(3734)   CLAM CHOWDER

24 clams, chopped fine
2 quarts hot water
2 medium, white onions, sliced
2 stalks celery, finely chopped
2 leeks, cut fine
2 slices pork or bacon, cut into small pieces

3 large potatoes, peeled and diced
1 teaspoon salt
$\frac{1}{8}$ teaspoon pepper
3 large tomatoes, peeled and cut fine
$\frac{1}{4}$ teaspoon thyme
1 teaspoon finely chopped parsley

Heat the pork or bacon and fry the onions, celery and leeks in the fat. Add the liquid from the clams, water, and potatoes. Boil 10 minutes. Add clams, tomatoes, salt, pepper, and thyme. Boil mixture 10 minutes. Add the parsley, and, while hot, pour into clean, hot jars. Partly seal and process 100 minutes in a steam-pressure cooker at 10 pounds or 3 hours in a hot-water bath. Remove from canner and seal immediately. When serving, equal amounts of butter and flour may be creamed together and added as thickening to the heated chowder.

(3735)   FISH CHOWDER

5 pounds potatoes
5 pounds fish (without bones)
$\frac{3}{4}$ pound salt pork
$\frac{1}{2}$ pound onion

2 quarts fish stock (No. 504)
2 tablespoons salt
$\frac{1}{2}$ teaspoon black pepper
$\frac{1}{4}$ pod hot red pepper

Cut the pork and potatoes in small cubes. Chop the onions. Cut fish in 1-inch pieces. Heat the pork until deep yellow. Add onions and cook until tender but not brown. Add fish, stock, potatoes, salt, and pepper. Boil 5 minutes and pour into hot jars, partly seal, and process 100 minutes in steam-pressure cooker at 10 pounds or 3 hours in hot-water bath. Remove from canner and seal immediately.

(3736)   MINT JELLY

Wash mint and chop fine. To each cup of chopped mint add $\frac{1}{4}$ cup sugar and $\frac{1}{4}$ cup water, and let stand for several hours, or overnight. Bring to boiling point, then strain. Combine sugar and apple juice, using $\frac{2}{3}$ cup sugar to 1 cup apple juice. Cook and test for jelly, and when the jellying point is obtained, add green vegetable coloring and 1 or 2 tablespoons prepared mint juice for each quart apple juice.

(3737)   PEANUT BUTTER

2 quarts Spanish peanuts   2 tablespoons salt
4 quarts Virginia peanuts

Roast peanuts uniformly brown. Cool, remove the red skins and tiny hearts or germs. Grind, add salt and grind twice again so salt will be well distributed. Use finest plate of meat grinder. Pack into pint jars. Fill the jars as full as possible, completely seal, and process by simmering (180° F.) 1 hour in hot-water bath.

(3738)   MINCEMEAT

2 pounds lean beef   1 nutmeg, grated
1 pound chopped suet   1/2 teaspoon ground mace
4 pounds tart apples   2 oranges
6 cups sugar   2 lemons
3 pounds currants   1/2 pound citron
2 pounds raisins   1 tablespoon salt

Stew beef in as little water as possible until quite tender. Cool and chop into fine pieces. Add beef suet, chopped fine, and apples pared, cored and chopped, sugar, currants, raisins, spices, orange and lemon juice, grated rind of the oranges and of 1 lemon, chopped citron, and salt. Mix thoroughly and cook 1 hour. Pack in clean jars. Seal immediately and store in a cool place.

(3739)   MOCK MINCEMEAT (GREEN TOMATO)

1 peck green tomatoes   1/2 cup water
  chopped   1 teaspoon ground cloves
3 pounds brown sugar   2 teaspoons nutmeg
2 pounds raisins   Grated rind of 1 orange
1 cup suet   3 cupfuls chopped apples
2 tablespoons salt   3 lemons (pulp and juice
2 teaspoons ground   only) or 1/3 cup vinegar
  cinnamon

Chop or slice tomatoes, sprinkle salt over them and allow to stand for 1 hour. Drain and discard juice. Cover with cold water. Place over fire and boil for 5 minutes. Drain off liquid, add suet and ½ cup water, return to fire and simmer 20 minutes. Stir in sugar and boil until dissolved. Add other ingredients and boil rapidly until thick, about 20 minutes. Pack into clean, hot jars and seal immediately.

(3740)   **CRAB APPLE HONEY**

Wash crab apples, remove cores and any defective spots, but do not pare. Cut apples into small pieces or run through a food chopper. Place apples in a preserving kettle with water to cover. Boil 10 minutes. Measure the pulp and add ¾ as much sugar as pulp. Cook the mixture until it is clear, and has a jelly-like consistency. Seal in clean, hot jars.

(3741)   **NUTS**

Various nut meats such as pecans, walnuts, hickory nuts, etc., can be canned and kept in perfect condition for several months. Use large unbroken halves which are in perfect condition. Pack into hot jars which have been thoroughly sterilized, add no liquor, partly seal jars and process for 10 minutes in steam-pressure cooker at 5 pounds pressure. Remove from canner and seal immediately. Or after packing, place caps loosely on the jars and set in pan of hot water. Heat for 10 minutes. This is to exhaust the air and prevent the nut meats from becoming rancid. Remove from pan and seal immediately. Then process for 10 minutes in steam-pressure cooker at 5 lbs. pressure or for 20 minutes in the hot-water bath.

Chop or slice tomatoes, sprinkle salt over them and allow to stand for 1 hour. Drain and discard juice. Cover with cold water. Place over fire and boil for 5 minutes. Drain off liquid, add sliced and ½ cup water, return to fire and simmer 20 minutes. Stir in sugar and boil until dissolved. Add other ingredients and boil rapidly until thick, about 20 minutes. Pack into clean, hot jars and seal immediately.

Candies

Nuts and Confections

HOMEMADE candy, if the fundamental rules are mastered, can equal in quality, taste, and appearance the finest candies made by professionals. The most important of these rules are as follows:

1. Use a candy thermometer. It provides much greater accuracy than the cold-water test.

2. Do not stir creamy candies after sugar has dissolved.

3. Cook candy in pans with perfectly smooth insides.

4. Cool creamy candies before beating.

5. Stir cooking taffies and brittles only enough to prevent burning.

6. Brush down sugar crystals on side of pan with a fork, wrapped in cheesecloth and dipped in cold water.

7. Wrap caramels in wax paper as soon as they are cold.

8. To keep fudge and penuchi, store in tightly covered containers.

Candy sirup is cooked to one of five stages, depending on the kind of candy being made. Those stages, with their corresponding temperatures are as follows:

Soft Ball	236° to 240° F.
Firm Ball	242° to 248° F.
Hard Ball	250° to 265° F.
Brittle	270° to 290° F.
Very Brittle	295° to 310° F.

(3801)   CHOCOLATE FUDGE

2 cups sugar
⅔ cup milk
2 tablespoons corn sirup
2 tablespoons butter or fat

3 ounces unsweetened
  chocolate, broken in
  small pieces
1 teaspoon vanilla

Put sugar, milk, sirup, and chocolate in a saucepan. Stir until sugar is dissolved. Cook slowly until the temperature reaches 236° F. or until the mixture forms a soft ball when a little is dropped into cold water. Remove from heat. Add butter. When cooled to lukewarm, add vanilla. Beat until thick. Pour into a shallow, greased pan. Chill. Cut into squares when firm.

(3802)   PENUCHI

½ cup evaporated milk
2 cups brown sugar
2 tablespoons butter or fat

1 teaspoon vanilla
⅛ teaspoon salt
1 cup broken nut meats

Combine milk and sugar. Cook slowly, stirring only until sugar is dissolved, until 236° F. is reached, the stage at which a drop of the mixture will form a soft ball when dropped into cold water. Add butter or fat. Cool slightly. Add other ingredients and beat until creamy. Pour into a greased pan. Chill.

(3803)   SANDWICH FUDGE

Turn layer of freshly made fudge (No. 3801) into shallow pan. Top with a layer of freshly made penuchi (No. 3802). Chill.

(3804)   MOLASSES FUDGE

1 cup granulated sugar
1 cup brown sugar
½ cup cream
¼ cup molasses

¼ cup melted butter
2 ounces unsweetened
  chocolate, grated
1½ teaspoons vanilla

Combine sugar, brown sugar, cream, molasses, and butter. Bring to a boil and boil 2 minutes. Add chocolate. Boil 5 minutes longer, stirring until well blended and, then, only enough to prevent burning. Remove from heat. Add vanilla. Stir until creamy. Turn into buttered pan. Chill.

(3805)   VANILLA FUDGE

Omit chocolate from recipe for chocolate fudge (No. 3801) and increase vanilla to 1½ teaspoons.

(3806)   CHOCOLATE COCONUT FUDGE

After beating chocolate fudge (No. 3801), stir in ½ cup shredded coconut.

(3807)   CHOCOLATE NUT FUDGE

After beating chocolate fudge (No. 3801), stir in 1 cup broken nut meats.

(3808)   RAISIN FUDGE

Add ½ cup chopped nuts and ½ cup chopped raisins to recipe for chocolate fudge (No. 3801) after beating.

(3809)   CHOCOLATE MARSHMALLOW FUDGE

Make chocolate fudge (No. 3801). After beating, pour ½ into greased pan. Slice several marshmallows, lengthwise, and arrange on top of fudge. Top with fudge remaining in saucepan. Chill. When firm, cut into squares.

(3810)   BUTTERSCOTCH

¼ cup molasses	1 tablespoon vinegar
2 cups brown sugar	½ cup butter

Combine molasses, sugar, and vinegar. Bring to boiling point, stirring only until sugar is dissolved. Boil 2 minutes. Add butter. Cook to 290° F. or until sirup becomes brittle when dropped in cold water. Turn into greased, shallow pan. Cool. Cut into small rectangles. Chill.

(3811)   VANILLA CARAMELS

2 cups sugar	1½ cups milk
1 cup brown sugar	⅓ cup butter or fat
1 cup light corn sirup	¼ teaspoon salt
1 cup condensed milk	1½ teaspoons vanilla

Cook sugar, corn sirup, condensed milk, and milk together in a saucepan, stirring constantly until the sugar is dissolved. Cook slowly, stirring occasionally to prevent burning, until the temperature is 248° F., or until mixture forms a firm ball when tested in cold water. Remove from fire, add butter, salt, and vanilla and mix well. Pour into a greased pan. When cold remove from pan, cut in cubes and wrap each caramel in waxed paper.

(3812) CHOCOLATE CARAMELS

Add 5 ounces melted, unsweetened chocolate, cut into small pieces, to recipe for vanilla caramels (No. 3811) before cooking.

(3813) COFFEE CARAMELS

Substitute 1½ cups coffee (No. 301) for milk in recipe for vanilla caramels (No. 3811) and omit vanilla.

(3814) NUT CARAMELS

Add ⅔ cup broken nuts to recipes for vanilla (No. 3811) or chocolate caramels (No. 3812) after cooking.

(3815) CLUB CARAMELS

Make chocolate (No. 3812) and vanilla-nut caramels (No. 3814). Pour one batch into chilling pan and top with other.

(3816) MOLASSES COCONUT CHEWS

½ cup corn sirup
½ cup molasses
1 tablespoon vinegar

2 tablespoons butter
2 cups shredded coconut

Combine sirup, molasses, vinegar, and butter. Place over low flame and stir until mixture boils. Continue boiling to 240° F. or until a small amount of sirup becomes brittle in cold water. Remove from fire, add coconut. Drop from two forks on greased surface. Chill.

(3817)　　OPERA CREAMS

1½ cups sugar	2 tablespoons butter or fat
3 ounces unsweetened	1 teaspoon vanilla
chocolate, grated	1 cup cream

Put sugar, cream, and chocolate in saucepan. Stir until dissolved. Cook slowly until temperature reaches 236° F. or until the mixture forms a soft ball when a little is dropped into cold water. Add butter. When cooled to lukewarm, add vanilla. Beat until thick. Drop from spoon onto wax paper. Chill.

(3818)　　PEPPERMINT CREAMS

Melt fondant (No. 3169) over boiling water until it is liquid enough to drop from spoon, adding a few drops of hot water if necessary. Flavor with oil of peppermint. Stir until creamy. Drop from teaspoon on wax paper. Chill.

(3819)　　CHOCOLATE CREAMS

Form fondant (No. 3169) into small balls, cones, or any desired shape. Chill 2 hours. Dip into melted, unsweetened chocolate. Do not have the chocolate any warmer than necessary. Set dipped balls on wax paper. Chill.

(3820)　　NUT BRITTLE

2 cups nuts	¼ teaspoon soda
2 cups granulated sugar	1 teaspoon vanilla
¼ teaspoon salt	

Heat the sugar gradually in a frying pan. Stir constantly with the bowl of the spoon until a golden sirup is formed. Remove from the fire and stir in quickly the salt, soda, and vanilla. Pour the sirup over a layer of nuts in a greased pan. When cold, crack into small pieces.

(3821)　　MAPLE NUT BRITTLE

2 cups nuts, broken in pieces	¾ cup water
1½ cups maple sugar, cut in pieces	2 tablespoons butter or fat
1½ cups light corn sirup	¼ teaspoon salt

Brown nuts in the oven. Cook sugar, sirup, salt and water together in a saucepan, stirring until the sugar is dissolved. Add butter or fat. Continue cooking without stirring until the temperature is 290° F., or until sirup becomes brittle when tested in cold water. Add nuts and pour on an inverted greased pan in a very thin sheet. Do not scrape the bottom and sides of the saucepan. Break into pieces.

(3822)   **COCONUT BRITTLE**

Substitute shredded coconut for nuts in recipe for maple nut brittle (No. 3821).

(3823)   **NOUGAT**

2 cups sugar	1 teaspoon vanilla
½ cup corn sirup	1 cup chopped nuts
3 stiffly beaten egg whites	¼ cup candied cherries

Combine 1 cup sugar, ¼ cup corn sirup, and ½ cup water. Stir until sugar is dissolved. Boil until temperature reaches 248° F. or until a firm ball is formed when a little of the mixture is dropped into cold water. Pour sirup over egg whites slowly and beat until cool. While beating, make a duplicate sirup with the remaining sugar and corn sirup and ½ cup water. When cooking is finished, pour slowly into cool mixture, beating while adding. When cool, beat in vanilla, nuts, and cherries. Turn into buttered pan. Chill overnight. Cut and wrap in wax paper.

(3824)   **MOLASSES MINT TAFFY**

2 cups molasses	⅛ teaspoon salt
2 teaspoons vinegar	½ teaspoon soda
1½ tablespoons butter or fat	7 drops oil of peppermint

Cook molasses and vinegar in a saucepan slowly, stirring constantly, until the temperature is 270° F., or until sirup becomes brittle when tested in cold water. Remove from fire and add butter or fat, salt, and soda. Stir until mixture ceases to foam. Pour into a greased pan. When cool enough to pull, pour the peppermint in the center of the candy and draw the corners toward the center. Remove from pan and pull until light in color and firm. Roll into a thin rope. Cut in pieces and wrap in waxed paper.

(3825) MOLASSES TAFFY

Omit oil of peppermint from recipe for molasses mint taffy (No. 3824).

(3826) BLACK WALNUT OR BUTTERNUT MOLASSES TAFFY

1 cup nuts, finely chopped	½ teaspoon cream of tartar
1½ cups sugar	4 tablespoons butter or
½ cup molasses	other fat
1½ cups water	⅛ teaspoon salt
2 tablespoons vinegar	¼ teaspoon soda

Boil the sugar, molasses, water, vinegar, and cream of tartar to the soft-crack stage (270° F.). Add the fat, salt, and soda and pour into a greased pan. When cool enough to handle, pull until light in color. Add the nuts, and work them into the mass by kneading and pulling. Pull into strips the desired thickness and cut into pieces about 1 inch long with scissors. If desired, wrap pieces in wax paper.

(3827) LOLLIPOPS

2 cups sugar	Appropriate vegetable
⅛ teaspoon cream of tartar	coloring
Any desired flavoring	

Combine sugar and cream of tartar with ⅔ cup water. Stir until sugar is dissolved. Boil until a temperature of 290° F. is reached or until a drop of mixture will become hard when dropped into cold water. Remove from heat. Add flavoring and coloring. Pour into greased pans or molds. When partly cooled, insert wooden sticks. Chill.

(3828) MEXICAN KISSES WITH CANDIED CHERRIES

Substitute ½ cup chopped candied cherries for an equal quantity of nuts in recipe for penuchi (No. 3802). After beating, drop by teaspoons onto wax paper. Chill.

(3829)   CHOCOLATE COCONUT KISSES

3 egg whites
1½ cups sifted confec-
        tioners' sugar
1 tablespoon sifted flour

½ cup shredded coconut
1 teaspoon vanilla
1 7-oz. bar semi-sweet
        chocolate, cut in pieces

Sift flour and sugar. Beat egg whites until they stand in peaks. Gradually sprinkle sugar and flour mixture over egg whites, beating constantly. Add vanilla, chocolate and coconut. Drop by teaspoonfuls on greased cookie sheet and bake at 450° F. 10 minutes. Yield: 4 dozen kisses.

(3830)   CHOCOLATE MARSHMALLOWS

¼ pound milk chocolate
32 marshmallows

Fresh grated coconut

Place chocolate in saucepan and heat slowly until chocolate is melted. Quickly dip marshmallows into chocolate, roll at once in coconut, and place on buttered plate. Chill.

(3831)   SALTING AND ROASTING NUTS

The flavor of some mild-flavored nuts, such as almonds, hickory nuts, Persian (English) walnuts, and filberts, may be developed by either roasting or frying. This makes them more desirable for use in baked products, such as nut breads, cakes, and cookies. For ice creams and candies the addition of salt to the fried or roasted nuts is a further improvement. For ½ pound of shelled and blanched almonds or of shelled, unblanched, raw peanuts or filberts, allow 1 quart of fresh cooking oil. In a kettle adapted for deep-fat frying, heat the oil to a temperature of 300° F., or until a cube of bread browns in 5 or 6 minutes. Place the nut kernels in a sieve that is deep enough to prevent them from floating over the top, and lower them into the hot fat. After 6 or 7 minutes, or as soon as the nuts are light brown, remove them from the fat. They continue to cook for a few minutes afterward. Spread them on absorbent paper. While they are still hot, pat them gently with the paper to remove the excess fat, and sprinkle with salt. Do not fry more than one kind of nuts at a time, because some kinds of nuts cook more rapidly than others.

(3832)   BLANCHING NUTS

Blanching is a means of removing the skin from kernels of almonds and other nuts that have a smooth surface. Peanut skins slip off easily after the nuts are roasted, and other nut kernels that have a tender skin, such as pecans, hickory nuts, butternuts, black walnuts, and Persian (English) walnuts, do not need to be blanched for most uses. Only nuts with a smooth surface can be blanched satisfactorily. To blanch almonds pour boiling water over them and hold at simmering temperature (185° F.) about 3 minutes. Remove them and drain off the water. The skins will then come off easily when pressed with the thumb and forefinger at the pointed end of the nut. Spread the blanched kernels on absorbent paper and dry overnight at ordinary room temperature. To blanch Brazil nut and filbert kernels prepare in an agateware or iron kettle (never aluminum) a lye solution, using 2 level tablespoons of granulated lye to each gallon of water. Heat to the boiling point, and immerse the kernels until the skins loosen. This will take from 1 to 2 minutes. Rinse and remove the skins while the kernels are still warm. Wash thoroughly in cold water and dry thoroughly 12 to 16 hours or overnight.

(3833)   GLACÉ NUTS

1½ cups nuts, salted or unsalted
2 cups sugar

¼ teaspoon cream of tartar
1 cup hot water
⅛ teaspoon salt

Mix the sugar, cream of tartar, hot water, and salt in a small saucepan and place over a hot fire. Stir until the sugar has dissolved. Let the sirup boil until it reaches a temperature of 293° F., or the hard-crack stage. Remove from the fire at once and place in a pan of hot water while dipping the nuts. Hold nuts separately with tweezers or on a long pin, and dip in the sirup to cover. Place dipped nuts on waxed paper to dry. Reheat the sirup carefully if it becomes too thick.

(3834)   DIPPED NUTS

Melt fondant (No. 3169) over hot water, turning it from time to time, but avoiding stirring. When the whole mass has become mobile but still thick, remove from the hot water and start dipping. Hold each nut separately with tweezers and dip into the fondant, drain, and place on waxed paper. If the fondant becomes too thick it may be reheated. The fondant-covered nuts as well as the plain nuts, either raw or roasted, may be coated with chocolate in the following way: Break dipping chocolate in small pieces and place in a shallow dish over hot water. As soon as the chocolate begins to soften, remove from the hot water, and stir with the fingers until it is all melted. Dip the candies or nuts into the chocolate until coated, and place on waxed paper to chill and dry.

(3835)   SPICED NUTS

1¾ cups nut kernels	¼ cup cinnamon
2 cups confectioners' sugar	2 teaspoons ginger
½ cup cornstarch	1 tablespoon ground cloves
2 teaspoons salt	1 egg white
1 teaspoon nutmeg	2 tablespoons cold water

Sift together three times the sugar and other dry ingredients. Beat the egg white slightly and add the cold water. Put the nuts in a wire strainer and dip into the egg mixture until each nut is well coated. Drain. Roll the nuts in a part of the spice mixture. Spread the spice mixture ¼ inch thick in a shallow pan and place the nuts on this, separating each one. Cover with the rest of the spice mixture and bake in a slow oven (250° F.) 3 hours. Remove from the oven and sift. Save the spice mixture to use again.

(3836)   NUT LOAF

3 cups sugar	1 cup broken nuts
1 cup milk	1 teaspoon vanilla

Combine sugar and milk. Stir until sugar is dissolved. Cook slowly until temperature reaches 236° F. or until the mixture forms a soft ball when a little is dropped into cold water. Remove from heat and let cool. When almost cold, add vanilla and beat vigorously until creamy. Turn out on board and knead, adding nuts gradually, until firm enough to hold shape. Form into a loaf. Set on waxed paper. Chill.

(3837)   MARZIPAN

1 cup almond paste	2 cups confectioners'
1 egg white	sugar
¼ teaspoon salt	

Beat the egg white and mix with the almond paste. Add the salt and enough sugar to make the mixture stiff enough to handle. Knead 10 to 15 minutes and place in a covered earthenware or glass dish. After about 24 hours the marzipan is ready to mold. Color with vegetable colors and mold into small shapes of fruits or vegetables, such as pears, apples, or carrots, using angelica for stems.

(3838)   GLACÉ FRUITS AND NUTS

Berries, small piece of fruit, or whole nut meats	2 cups sugar
	½ cup corn sirup

Mix sugar with corn sirup and 1 cup water. Bring to boiling point, stirring only until sugar is dissolved. Cook to 290° F. or until sirup becomes brittle when dropped in cold water. Remove from heat and place pan in very hot water to keep sirup from hardening. Drop in berries, fruits, or nuts. Skim out and chill on wax paper.

(3839)   CANDIED ORANGE, LEMON, OR GRAPEFRUIT PEEL

Cook thin strips of thin peel, with all white removed, 5 minutes in sirup made for glacé fruits and nuts (No. 3838).

(3840)   CANDIED BERRIES OR FRUITS

Simmer small fruits or pieces of large fruits 5 minutes in sirup made for glacé fruits and nuts (No. 3838).

(3841) CHOCOLATE-COATED CANDIED APPLES

3 tart, firm apples	½ cup water
1 cup sugar	¼ teaspoon salt
1 cup honey	Chocolate for dipping

Boil together the sugar, honey, water, and salt for a few minutes. Wash, core, and pare the apples, cut into half-moon shaped pieces about $\frac{1}{2}$ inch thick, drop into the sirup, and cook rapidly until the apples are transparent and practically all the sirup is absorbed. Lift onto waxed paper to dry. Break up cake chocolate, made especially for dipping candies, and put into a shallow dish over hot water. As soon as the chocolate begins to soften, remove from the hot water, and stir the chocolate with the fingers until it is all melted. Dip the pieces of apple into the melted chocolate until well coated, and place on waxed paper to dry. Pack the apple candies in layers between sheets of waxed paper.

(3842) DATES AND PRUNES STUFFED WITH FONDANT

Remove stones and replace with fondant (No. 3169) and 1 whole nut meat to each fruit.

(3843) POPCORN BALLS

$1\frac{1}{4}$ cups sugar	1 tablespoon butter or fat
$1\frac{1}{4}$ cups brown sugar	$3\frac{1}{2}$ quarts popped corn
$\frac{1}{2}$ cup light corn sirup	(No. 138)
$\frac{2}{3}$ cup water	$1\frac{1}{4}$ teaspoons salt

Put sugar, brown sugar, sirup, and water in a saucepan, stirring until sugar is dissolved. Add butter or fat and continue cooking, without stirring, until the temperature 240° F. is reached, or until mixture forms a soft ball when tested in cold water. Put popped corn in a large bowl and sprinkle with salt. Pour the hot sirup over it and mix thoroughly. Shape in small balls, wrap in wax paper.

(3844) BOILED CHESTNUTS

Blanch (No. 3832). Cover with boiling, salted water. Cover pan and simmer until tender, from 10 to 15 minutes. Drain. Mash to a paste or grind. Season to taste with butter, salt, and pepper.

(3845)   NUT PATTIES

2 cups sugar	1 teaspoon vanilla
1¼ cups water	2 squares unsweetened
2 tablespoons light corn	chocolate, melted
sirup	

Combine sugar, water, and corn sirup. Place over low flame and stir constantly until sugar is dissolved and mixture boils. Cover and cook 3 minutes. Remove cover and continue boiling, without stirring, until a small amount of sirup forms a soft ball in cold water (238° F.). Wash down sides of pan occasionally with damp cloth. Pour out on cold, wet platter or poreclain table top, or on greased surface. Cool to lukewarm (110° F.). Work with paddle or spatula until white and creamy. Add vanilla and knead until smooth. Shape in ball. Make indentation in top and pour about ¼ of chocolate into it. Knead until chocolate is blended. Repeat until all chocolate is used. Store in tightly covered jar to ripen for several days before using. If fondant begins to dry out, cover with damp cloth. Shape fondant in small balls. Flatten balls slightly and press half walnut meat into each. Makes 3 dozen 1-inch patties.

(3846)   COCONUT CHERRY DIVINITY

2 cups sugar	½ can moist, sweetened
⅔ cup water	coconut, toasted and
½ cup light corn sirup	crumbled
2 egg whites, stiffly beaten	¾ cup candied cherries,
1 teaspoon vanilla	thinly sliced
Dash of salt	

Bring ½ cup sugar and ⅓ cup water to a boil and boil until a small amount of sirup forms a slightly firm ball in cold water (240° F.). While this mixture is boiling, bring remaining sugar and water and the corn sirup to a boil and boil until a small amount of sirup forms a hard ball in cold water (252° F.). Remove first sirup (240° F.) from fire and cool slightly. Pour slowly over egg whites, beating constantly until mixture loses its gloss (1½ minutes). Then add second sirup (252° F.) slowly, beating as before. Fold in vanilla, salt, coconut, and cherries, and turn immediately into greased pan, 8 x 8 inches. Cool until firm. Cut in pieces, 1½ x 1 inches. Roll in additional toasted coconut, if desired. Makes 3½ dozen pieces. Broken pecan meats, chopped dates or raisins may be substituted for candied cherries in this recipe.

(3847)   COCONUT FONDANT BALLS

2 cups sugar	1¼ cups water
2 tablespoons light corn sirup	1 teaspoon vanilla
	Moist, sweetened coconut

Combine sugar, water, and corn sirup. Place over low flame and stir constantly until sugar is dissolved and mixture boils. Cover and cook 3 minutes. Remove cover and continue boiling, without stirring, until a small amount of sirup forms a soft ball in cold water (238° F.). Wash down sides of pan occasionally with damp cloth. Remove from fire and pour out on cold, wet platter or porcelain table top, or on greased surface. Cool to luke-warm (110° F.). Work with paddle or spatula until white and creamy. Add vanilla and knead until smooth. Store in covered jar to ripen for several days. Add 1 cup chopped coconut to fondant. Knead and shape into balls about 1 inch in diameter. Roll balls in additional coconut, plain or delicately tinted. Makes 6 dozen balls. This recipe may be varied by using toasted, shredded coconut or by kneading 1 cup finely chopped raisins or dates into fondant.

(3848)   PINEAPPLE KISSES

2 egg whites	1 dozen canned pineapple
½ cup granulated sugar	gems
½ teaspoon vanilla or almond extract	Slivered almonds or chopped walnuts

Beat egg whites until stiff. Add sugar gradually and continue beating. Add flavoring. Rinse off cookie sheet, leaving the surface damp. Cover cookie sheet with a piece of unglazed brown paper. About 2 inches apart, spread 1-inch rounds of meringue. Top each round with a well-drained pineapple gem and then cover each gem with meringue. Sprinkle with slivered almonds or chopped walnut meats. Bake in a slow oven (300° F.) 45 to 50 minutes. Yield: 1 dozen kisses.

Wine Service

WINE, like music, eludes complete definition or description; and like music, its play upon the emotions covers a wide range of influence. As jazz may cause a music-lover to wince with spiritual pain, so may coarse wine cause the epicure to shudder with shock. That old, mellow wine awakens dreams of inexpressible romance in sensitive people is common knowledge; why it does, no man has ever understood.

Man's chemical organization attracts or repels certain wines, hence no expert can with assurance affirm that any particular good wine is better than another. To a normally healthy person, however, there is fair certainty that some wine, taken with food and in moderation, will contribute materially to health. This is especially true of adults with increasing age; for wine acts as a mild stimulant on the digestive organs and is a solvent for pasty accumulations that are prone to clog the intestines and retard elimination.

There has evolved a standard formula for wine service with meals which may be followed with assurance that it is at least conventional and "stylish." It probably represents, also, insurance against combinations that might result in an upset stomach.

THE WINE-COURSE DINNER

Hors d'œuvres—Sherry, Dry.
Sea Foods—Chablis or Moselle, Dry. (Champagne is considered "ultra" with this course in certain high social circles in the United States, but it is not sanctioned by seasoned epicures.)
Soup—Sherry, Dry. (Omit if wine has been served with hors d'œuvres.)
Fish—Dry Sauterne, Moselle, or Rhine.
Entree—Bordeaux, Red.
Roast—Medoc, Red.
Dessert—Champagne.
Coffee—Cordial or Brandy.

TEMPERATURES FOR SERVING

Temperature is important. Wines too cool or too warm lose their best taste.
Do not mix ice with any wine.
Red wines are best at a temperature of 65 degrees.
White wines, excepting champagne, are best at 45-50°.
Champagne and other sparkling wines should be chilled in a bucket of chopped ice for 20 to 30 minutes before serving. Do not immerse the neck of the bottle. Sparkling wines deteriorate if they are cooled and not used. Avoid double cooling.
The store of wines should be kept, bottles on sides, in a cool cellar.

SERVING THE COCKTAIL

The cocktail should be served as an appetizer—before the meal and always with the food-bit. Served just before the meal, the food-bit with the cocktail takes on the character of a special *hors d'œuvre,* with toast or cracker combinations, and may be followed by the regular hors d'œuvre.
The sweet cocktail should not be served just prior to the meal. The tart or "dry" cocktail properly precedes the meal.

(3901) BRANDY COCKTAIL

    1 ice cube
    2 ounces brandy
    3 dashes curaçao

Mix. Stir. Strain and serve. Serves 1.

[3902] SIDECAR

    8 ounces brandy
    4 ounces lemon juice
    4 ounces cointreau
    Cracked ice

Shake together. Strain into cocktail glasses. Serves 6.

(3903) SOUTHERN MINT JULEP

    2 teaspoons sugar
    Mint leaves
    3 ounces brandy
    Dash of rum
    Fresh fruit slices

Put sugar in tall glass. Add enough water to dissolve sugar. Add small pieces of mint leaves and crush. Add cracked ice and brandy. Stir thoroughly. Add more mint leaves. Sprinkle with sugar. Add rum. Fill glass with cold water. Garnish with sprig of mint leaves and fruit slices. Serves 1.

(3904) TOM AND JERRY

    3 eggs
    ¼ cup sugar
    6 ounces Jamaica rum
    12 ounces brandy
    Milk
    Nutmeg

Separate eggs. Beat whites until stiff. Add sugar gradually, beating thoroughly. Beat yolks until watery and combine with whites. Divide mixture equally between 6 tall glasses. Put 1 ounce Jamaica rum and 2 ounces brandy in each glass. Fill glasses with milk. Mix thoroughly by pouring back and fourth between glasses several times. Sprinkle with nutmeg. Serves 6.

(3905) DAIQUIRI COCKTAIL

    12 ounces rum
    ¼ cup powdered sugar
    Juice of 3 lemons or 3 limes
    Cracked ice

Mix ingredients in shaker. Shake 25 times. Strain into cocktail glasses. If desired, grenadine to suit taste may be added. Serves 6.

(3906) DRY MANHATTAN COCKTAIL

    12 ounces rye or Irish whisky
    6 ounces Italian vermouth
    ½ teaspoon angostura bitters
    Ice
    6 cherries
    6 segments of lemon slices

Mix whisky, vermouth, bitters, and ice in shaker. Shake 10 times. Put 1 cherry in each cocktail glass. Strain mixture into glasses. Garnish with lemon. Serves 6.

(3907) SWEET MANHATTAN COCKTAIL

    12 ounces rye or Irish whisky
    6 ounces Italian vermouth
    6 ounces French vermouth
    ½ teaspoon gum sirup
    Ice
    6 cherries
    6 segments of lemon slices

Mix same as dry Manhattan cocktail (No. 3906). Serves 6.

(3908) WHISKY MINT JULEP

Substitute whisky for brandy in recipe for southern mint julep (No. 3903) and omit rum.

(3909) OLD FASHIONED COCKTAIL

    1 lump sugar
    2 tablespoons water
    2 dashes angostura bitters
    2 dashes curaçao or absinthe
    1 ice cube
    2 ounces whisky
    ½ slice orange
    ½ slice lemon

Put sugar in old fashioned cocktail glass. Add water, bitters, and curaçao or absinthe. Mash sugar until dissolved. Add ice cube. Pour in whisky. Garnish with orange and lemon. Serves 1.

(3910) WHISKY SOUR

    12 ounces whisky
    ¼ cup powdered sugar
    Juice of 3 lemons or 3 limes
    Cracked ice

Mix ingredients in shaker. Shake 30 times. Strain into tall glasses.

(3911) HOT TODDY

    1 lump sugar
    2 tablespoons hot water
    1 piece stick cinnamon, ½ inch long
    1 piece lemon peel
    2 ounces rye or Scotch whisky
    Hot water

Dissolve sugar in 2 tablespoons hot water in serving glass. Add other ingredients and hot water to taste. Stir. Serves 1.

(3912) WARD EIGHT

    2 ounces rye whisky
    1 tablespoon grenadine
    1 teaspoon powdered sugar
    Juice of 1 lemon
    Cracked ice

Mix ingredients in shaker. Shake 10 times. Strain into 8-ounce glass. Serves 1.

(3913) BRANDY PUNCH

1 quart brandy
1 pound powdered sugar
2 ounces curaçao
2 ounces grenadine
Juice of 8 lemons
Juice of 4 oranges
1 quart carbonated water

Set punch bowl in a bed of ice. Put all ingredients in bowl and stir until cold and sugar is dissolved. Yield: 40 small punch servings.

(3914) CHAMPAGNE PUNCH

1 quart champagne
1 pint carbonated water
2 ounces curaçao
2 ounces brandy
2 ounces maraschino
¼ pound sugar
Slices of fruit

Set punch bowl in a bed of ice. Mix all ingredients but fruit slices in bowl. Add fruit. Stir until cold. Yield: 20 small servings.

(3915) WINE PUNCH

3 pints wine
3 ounces curaçao
1 quart carbonated water
3 ounces lemon juice
¼ pound powdered sugar
Fruit slices

Set punch bowl in a bed of ice. Mix all ingredients but fruit slices in bowl. Stir until cold. Garnish individual servings with fruit slices. Orange, lemon, and grapefruit are the usual fruits used. Yield: 40 small servings.

(3916) BRONX COCKTAIL

6 ounces dry gin
6 ounces French vermouth
6 ounces orange juice
Cracked ice

Mix in shaker. Shake 25 times. Strain into cocktail glasses. Serves 6.

(3917) GIN BUCK

1 ice cube
2 ounces gin
Juice and peel of ½ lemon
Ginger ale

Put ice cube in tall glass. Add gin, lemon juice and peel, and fill with ginger ale. Stir gently. Serves 1.

(3918) GIN FIZZ

Cracked ice
12 ounces gin
¼ cup sugar
Juice of 3 lemons or limes
Carbonated water

Mix ice, gin, sugar, and fruit juice in shaker. Shake 30 times. Strain into highball glasses. Fill with carbonated water. Serves 6.

(3919) GOLDEN FIZZ

Add 1 egg yolk per drink to recipe for gin fizz (No. 3918), putting it into shaker before any other ingredient.

(3920) GIN RICKEY

Ice cube
2 ounces gin
Juice of 1 lime
Carbonated water

Put ice, gin, and juice into 8-ounce glass. Fill with carbonated water. Stir gently. Serves 1.

(3921) DRY MARTINI COCKTAIL

12 ounces gin
6 ounces French vermouth
¼ teaspoon orange bitters
Cracked ice
6 olives

Mix gin, vermouth, bitters, and ice in shaker. Shake 12 times. Put 1 olive in each of 6 cocktail glasses. Strain in mixture. Serves 6.

(3922) SWEET MARTINI COCKTAIL

12 ounces gin
3 ounces Italian vermouth
3 ounces French vermouth
Cracked ice
6 olives
6 dashes lemon juice

Mix gin, vermouths, and ice in cocktail shaker. Shake 12 times. Put 1 olive and 1 dash lemon juice in each of 6 cocktail glasses. Strain in mixture. Serves 6.

(3923) PINK LADY

12 ounces gin
6 tablespoons grenadine
6 egg whites
Cracked ice

Mix ingredients in shaker. Shake 25 times. Strain into cocktail glasses. Serves 6.

(3924) SILVER FIZZ

12 ounces gin
¼ cup powdered sugar
2 tablespoons lemon juice
2 tablespoons lime juice
6 egg whites
Cracked ice
Carbonated water

Mix all ingredients except carbonated water in shaker. Shake 25 times. Strain and pour into 6 8-ounce glasses. Fill glasses with carbonated water. Serves 6.

(3925) SLOE GIN COCKTAIL

12 ounces sloe gin
½ teaspoon French vermouth
¼ teaspoon orange bitters
Cracked ice

Mix in shaker. Shake 10 times. Strain into cocktail glasses. Serves 6.

(3926) SLOE GIN FIZZ

Substitute sloe gin for dry gin in recipe for gin fizz (No. 3918).

(3927) TOM COLLINS

12 ounces gin
¼ cup powdered sugar
Juice of 6 lemons
Cracked ice
Carbonated water

Mix gin, sugar, lemon juice, and cracked ice in shaker. Shake 15 times. Strain into 6 8-ounce glasses. Add carbonated water to taste. Serves 6.

(3928) SHERRY AND EGG COCKTAIL

Put a whole egg into a wine glass, being careful not to break yolk. Fill with sherry. Serves 1.

(3929) APPLEJACK COCKTAIL

12 ounces applejack
3 ounces lemon juice
3 ounces grenadine
Cracked ice

Mix in shaker. Shake 30 times. Strain into cocktail glasses. Serves 6.

(3930) CHAMPAGNE COCKTAIL

1 lump sugar
Angostura bitters
1 ice cube
2 ounces champagne
Slice orange
Slice lemon

Put sugar in cocktail glass. Saturate with bitters and crush. Add ice cube. Add champagne. Stir gently. Garnish with fruit slices. Serves 1.

(3931) CRÈME DE MENTHE

Pack a cocktail glass with crushed ice. Fill with crème de menthe. Serves 1.

(3932) BRANDY EGGNOG

2 ounces brandy
1 ounce rum
1 tablespoon powdered sugar
1 cup milk
1 egg
Cracked ice
Nutmeg

Mix all ingredients but nutmeg in shaker. Shake 40 times. Strain into glass and sprinkle with nutmeg. Serves 1.

(3933) POUSSE CAFÉ

1 ounce raspberry sirup
1 ounce maraschino
1 ounce vanilla
1 ounce curaçao
1 ounce yellow chartreuse
1 ounce brandy or cognac

Pour ingredients, one at a time, into glass. Use extreme care so that they will not mix but will remain in layers.

(3934) WHITE CARGO

12 ounces gin
2 cups vanilla ice cream (No. 2547)

Put ingredients into cocktail shaker. Shake 15 times. Serves 6.

(3935) HOT RUM

2 ounces rum
1 lump sugar
Juice of 1 lemon

Put ingredients in 10- or 12-ounce glass. Fill with hot water. Stir to dissolve sugar. Serves 1.

(3936) BOBBY BURNS COCKTAIL

2 ounces Scotch whisky
1 ounce Italian vermouth
1 teaspoon benedictine
1 ice cube
Lemon twist

Put whisky, vermouth, benedictine, and ice in cocktail glass. Stir. Garnish with lemon twist.

Design and Equipment for a Kitchen

~~~~~~

THE big kitchen—often the largest room in a house—is no longer considered essential or even desirable. Streamlining applies to kitchens just as it does to automobiles, airplanes, or locomotives. The larger the kitchen, the more steps required to do the cooking.

Every good kitchen should have either window or outside-door openings on opposite sides of the room. A cross draft will make it easier to keep odors and fumes from other parts of the house. The floor and walls should be pleasing in appearance with surfaces that are easily kept clean. Lights should be installed at points where the most time is spent and should be placed so that they will not glare into the eyes.

In general, meal-serving routine is about the same in every home and at every meal. The principal steps in the process are:

1. Assembly and preparation of raw food
2. Cooking
3. Serving
4. Clearing away
5. Dishwashing
6. Putting away and cleaning up

Every piece of equipment in the kitchen should be placed with that routine in mind. Small tools and utensils should be stored as close as possible to where they are used most frequently. The equipment listed below should be in every kitchen. Each piece is classified according to the step in the above routine where it is used the most. *A place for everything and everything in its place* is a motto that should be in the mind of every homemaker. Time wasted seeking misplaced articles signifies inefficiency.

ARTICLES USED IN THE ASSEMBLY AND PREPARATION OF RAW FOOD

Containers for foods, seasonings, etc.
2 1-pint bowls, earthenware or glass
2 ½-pint bowls, earthenware or glass
1 1-quart bowl, earthenware or glass
1 2-quart bowl, earthenware or glass
2 1-cup measures
1 2-cup measure
1 4-cup measure
Flour can and dredger
Bread box
Salt container and dredger
Cake box
6 cans for sugar, flour, etc.
Grater
Potato ricer
Apple corer
Ball cutter
Lemon borer
Chopping knife
Food chopper
Shears
Meat cleaver
Skewers
Carving knife
Bread knife
Grapefruit knife
Spatula
Meat knife
4 steel forks
3 kitchen knives
Paring knife
2 biscuit cutters
2 fancy cookie cutters
1 2-quart pitcher with cover
1 1-quart pitcher with cover
Meat grinder

Chopping bowl
Bread board
Chopping board
Pastry board
Rolling pin
Funnel
3 tablespoons
3 teaspoons
Can opener
Corkscrew
Ice pick
Rotary beater
Small strainer
Medium strainer
Wire egg beater
Flour sieve
Colander
1 ½-pint ladle
2 wooden spoons
1 brush for vegetables
Angel cake pan
Spring-form pan
1 1-gallon kettle
1 2-quart kettle
1 1-quart kettle
1 1-pint saucepan
1 ½-pint saucepan
2 roasting pans
1 1-quart baking dish
8 custard cups
1 butter dish
1 2-quart baking dish
1 2-layer-cake pan
2 9-inch pie plates
2 bread pans
2 muffin pans
2 biscuit pans
Oilsilk or cheesecloth bags for leafy vegetables
Gelatin molds
Tart pans
Cookie sheets
2 wooden spoons

1 2-tine fork
Bottle opener
Funnel
Pastry bag

Pastry blender
Parchment paper
Knife sharpener

ARTICLES USED IN COOKING

1 1-pint double boiler
1 1-quart double boiler
1 coffee percolator
1 coffee pot
1 tea pot
1 tea kettle
1 omelet pan
4 frying pans
1 frying kettle and basket
1 pancake turner
1 toaster
4 potholders

Dutch oven
Candy thermometer
Fat thermometer
Meat thermometer
Oven thermometer
Timer or clock
Draining spoon
Asbestos mats
Vegetable tongs
Waffle iron
Pressure cooker
Preserving kettle

ARTICLES USED IN SERVING

Set of china
Set of glassware
Silver service
Carving fork and knife

Trays
Electric roaster
Chafing dish
Cake cooler

ARTICLES USED IN CLEARING AWAY

Rubber plate scraper
Garbage bags

Garbage pail
Oilsilk food bags and bowl covers

ARTICLES USED IN DISH WASHING

Bottle brush
Dishpan
Soap and scouring materials
Steel wool

Wire drainer
Dish cloths
Dish towels
Glass towels

ARTICLES USED IN PUTTING AWAY AND CLEANING UP

Paper towel rack
Sink brush
Stove brush
Floor brush
Broom
Long-handled mop and pail

Pail
Long-handled scrub brush
Oil mop
Dry mop
6 floor cloths
Roller towels

MISCELLANEOUS UTENSILS

Clock
Refrigerator thermometer
Scales

Ice bag
Mallet
Ice cream freezer

COMPLETE MEAL COOKER

COVERED KETTLE and DUTCH OVEN

Easy-pouring, no-drip spout. New type hinge-less cover will not drop off when pouring.

Flat bottoms for quick and efficient heating on all types of ranges.

Pressure Cooking

GENERAL RULES

1. Know your cooker. Study and follow manufacturer's directions.
2. Prepare food in the usual way. Place trivet in pressure saucepan if recipe calls for it. Season now or later.
3. Fill pan not over two-thirds to three-quarters full of solid food to avoid clogging steam outlet. Leave room for cover adjustment in case of inside closure.
   (a) Fill no more than half full of soup, liquids, or when cooking cereal.
4. Add water called for. Use a minimum of one-fourth cup. Do not have water come over rack unless a boiled or stewed effect is desired.
5. Place cover, and seal according to type of pan used.
6. Place over high heat with steam vent open. Be sure a steady flow of cold air with steam is coming out of vent. This takes from 2 to 4 minutes, according to size of cooker and temperature of liquid and food.
7. Close steam vent as directed for type of cooker used.
8. Count cooking time from when the indicator, weight or gauge shows number of pounds pressure required.
9. Reduce heat to where it will maintain this pressure.
10. When cooking time is up, remove from heat and reduce pressure according to manufacturer's directions. Foods tend to overcook if allowed to stand in cooker after cooking period.
11. After pressure has been completely reduced, remove lid.

ADAPTING HOME RECIPES TO PRESSURE COOKING

No material on pressure cooking will tell you how to prepare all your favorite recipes. Here are a few suggestions to help you adapt your own.
1. Find instructions for a similar food or recipe in instruction book and read carefully.
2. Reduce the amount of liquid in your recipe to the quantity indicated for pressure cooking.
3. Correspondingly, reduce amount of seasoning, since you have less liquid to dilute it. Use one-fourth less fat.
4. Adapt your recipe to time and pressure indicated for similar food or recipe.

Note this time and pressure on your recipe for further use and reference. You may want to correct it for next time; note this also.

ADJUSTMENT TO ALTITUDE

No adjustment is needed for altitudes below 2,000 feet. Above this, add 1 pound pressure for each additional 2,000 feet above sea level. Do not increase processing time.

STERILIZING

The pressure saucepan is perfect for sterilizing baby bottles, nipples and utensils. It may also be used for sterilizing surgical, dental or other instruments.

To sterilize, place the rack in the pan, and add 1½ cups of water. Place bottles on rack and cover. Turn to vent. Place on high heat until steam escapes for five minutes. Then set gauge at 15 lbs. When steam escapes, allow 10 to 20 minutes for sterilizing. Be sure that heat is high enough to maintain pressure.

After sterilizing, cover tops of bottles and place nipples in sterile, covered glass jar until used.

CANNING WITH PRESSURE SAUCEPAN

Several of the pressure saucepans have been designed for canning on a small scale. It is advisable to follow manufacturer's booklet for canning instructions.

Here are a few general rules:

1. Use only those pans with weights which indicate the pounds of pressure and give you a choice of 5, 10, or 15 lbs.

Note: Karen 1 = 5; 2 = 7½ lbs.; 3 = 10 lbs.; 4 = 12½ lbs.; 5 = 15 lbs.

2. Use 2 inches of water.
3. Exhaust saucepan for 2 minutes before bringing it to pressure.
4. Bring up to required pressure. Start timing as soon as pressure is reached. Reduce heat to maintain that pressure. Process required number of minutes. When time is completed, remove pan from heat and allow it to cool normally. Do not cool quickly.
5. Can only 3 pints at a time, unless manufacturer states otherwise.
6. Refer to the bulletin issued by the United States Department of Agriculture for time and pounds pressure.

MEATS AND POULTRY

MEAT	*Minutes to Cook after Pressure Is Reached*	*Amount of Water*	*Pounds Pressure*
Corned Beef	15 to 20 per lb.	2 cups	10
Beef—hamburgers	5*	1 tablespoon	10
Beef—short ribs	45 to 50	½ cup	10
Beef—rolled	14 to 18 per lb.	¼ cup	10
Beef—Pot Roast	15 to 17 per lb.	¼ cup	10
Beef—Swiss Steak	25 to 30*	¾ cup	10
Beef Stew	20 to 25	¾ cup	10
Chicken, Fried	15 to 20*	½ cup	10
Chicken, Fricassee	30 to 35	2 cups	10
Chicken, boiled	30 to 35	2 cups	10
Chicken Stew	30 to 35	2 cups	10
Ham, slice	20	⅓ cup	10
Ham, Picnic	60	1 cup	10
Lamb Stew	25*	1 cup	10
Meat Loaf	30*	¼ cup	10
Pork Shoulder Roast	15 to 18 per lb.	⅓ cup	10
Spareribs	25*	½ cup	10
Pork or Veal Steak	12 to 15	⅓ cup	10
Veal Stew	20	1 cup	10
Veal Roast	12 to 15 per lb.	⅓ cup	10

* If marked with an asterisk (*), heat should be reduced immediately. If not marked, allow pressure to reduce naturally.

Brown most meats first, to enhance flavor and appetite appeal. Use a small amount of hot fat, and, if you like, brown right in the pressure saucepan to save the juice.

With a pot roast the vegetables may be added the last part of the cooking period by reducing the pressure quickly, adding vegetables and bringing up to pressure. Refer to vegetable chart for time required to cook the vegetables.

FROZEN VEGETABLES

Vegetables—All frozen vegetables except corn on the cob, kale and spinach may be cooked frozen or defrosted. Separate all vegetables before cooking.	Minutes to Cook after Pressure Is Reached	Amount of Water	Pounds Pressure
Asparagus cuts..........................	3 to 4	½ cup	5
Beans, green or wax.....................	6*	½ cup	5
Beans, lima.............................	4 to 5	½ cup	5
Broccoli................................	4 to 5*	½ cup	5
Brussels Sprouts........................	3 to 4*	½ cup	5
Carrots and Peas.......................	2 to 3*	½ cup	5
Cauliflower.............................	3 to 4*	½ cup	5
Corn (cut).............................	1 to 2	½ cup	5
Corn on cob............................	2½ to 3*	½ cup	5
Mixed vegetables.......................	2½ to 3*	⅓ cup	5
Peas...................................	2 to 3*	½ cup	5
Spinach...............................	1	⅓ cup	5

* If marked with an asterisk (*), heat should be reduced immediately. If not marked, allow pressure to reduce naturally.

CEREALS AND PASTES

FOOD	Minutes to Cook after Pressure Is Reached	Amount of Water	Amount of Food	Pounds Pressure
Pearl Barley, soak overnight..	10	2½ cups	½ cup	15
Corn Meal...................	10	4 cups	1 cup	15
Hominy Grits...............	12 to 15	3 cups	½ cup	15
Rice........................	7*	1½ cups	1 cup	5
Noodles....................	6	3 cups	1 cup	5
Macaroni...................	6	3 cups	1 cup	5
Spaghetti..................	8*	3 cups	1 cup	5

* If marked with an asterisk (*), heat should be reduced immediately. If not marked, allow pressure to reduce naturally.

DRIED VEGETABLES

DRIED VEGETABLE	Minutes to Cook after Pressure Is Reached		Amount of Water for 1 Cup of Vegetable	Pounds Pressure
	Soaked	Not Soaked		
Beans (Pea)................	20	45	3 cups	15
Beans (Kidney)..............	35	1¼ hours	3 cups	15
Beans (large Limas)..........	35	1 hour	3 cups	15
Beans (small Limas).........	30	45	3 cups	15
Beans (Navy)...............	35	1¼ hours	2 cups	15
Beans (Great Northern)......	20	45	2 cups	15
Peas (Split)................		15	2 cups	15
Lentils....................	20	40	2 cups	15

FRESH VEGETABLES

VEGETABLES (Prepare in the Usual Way)	Minutes to Cook after Pressure Is Reached	Amount of Water	Pounds Pressure
Asparagus	1½ to 2*	⅓ cup	15
Beans, green whole	3 to 3½*	⅓ cup	15
cut up	2½ to 3*	⅓ cup	15
Beans, wax	2½ to 3*	⅓ cup	15
Beans, lima	3 to 3½	⅓ cup	15
Beets, sliced	4 to 5	¼ cup	15
Beets, whole	12 to 15	½ cup	15
Broccoli	2½ to 3*	¼ cup	15
Brussels Sprouts	3 to 3½*	½ cup	15
Cabbage, quartered	6 to 8*	¾ cup	15
Cabbage, shredded	2 to 3*	½ cup	15
Carrots, whole	3 to 4	⅓ cup	15
Carrots, sliced	2 to 2½	¼ cup	15
Cauliflower, whole	5 to 6*	⅓ cup	15
Cauliflower, flowerettes	2 to 2½*	⅓ cup	15
Celery, whole stems	4	¼ cup	15
Celery, cut in ½-inch pieces	2½ to 3	¼ cup	15
Corn on cob	5 to 6*	⅓ cup	15
Corn off cob	3 to 4*	¼ cup	15
Kale	4 to 5*	¼ cup	15
Okra, sliced	3 to 4*	¼ cup	15
Onions, sliced	3 to 4	¼ cup	15
Onions, whole medium	7 to 10*	½ cup	15
Parsnips, sliced	2 to 3*	½ cup	15
Peas	2 to 3*	¼ cup	15
Potatoes, whole, medium	15 to 17*	¾ cup	15
Potatoes, cut up	8	½ cup	15
Potatoes, sweet, quartered	6 to 8*	⅓ cup	15
Potatoes, sweet, halved	10 to 12*	⅓ cup	15
Spinach	1½ to 2*	¼ cup	15
Sauerkraut	8 to 9	¼ cup	15
Squash, Hubbard	6 to 8*	¼ cup	15
Tomatoes, whole	1 to 2	¼ cup	15

* If marked with an asterisk (*), heat should be reduced immediately. If not marked, allow pressure to reduce naturally.

SAVORY CHICKEN

3 lb. chicken
Salt and pepper
2 tablespoons butter
1 cup water

1 cup sliced mushrooms
1 medium onion, sliced
1 bay leaf
3 cloves

Disjoint chicken as for frying; season with pepper and salt. Brown in cooker with 2 tablespoons of butter. When chicken is thoroughly browned, add 1 cup water, sliced mushrooms, onion and spices. Cook at 10 lbs. for 15 minutes. Reduce pressure immediately. Remove chicken, thicken gravy and serve over hot biscuits. Serves 4 to 5.

STEAMED FISH PUDDING

1½ lbs. fresh or frozen fish fillets	½ teaspoon salt
2 tablespoons butter	¼ teaspoon paprika
½ cup hot milk	2 teaspoons lemon juice
1 cup fine soft bread crumbs	2 eggs

Remove all bones and skin from the fish. Then put the fish through the food chopper twice using the medium-sized blade. Add the butter to the milk; pour over the bread crumbs; add the salt, paprika, lemon juice and combine with the fish. Separate the eggs; beat the whites stiff and the yolks until creamy. Add the yolks to the fish mixture and stir thoroughly. Fold in the whites. Turn into a greased mold; tie waxed or parchment paper over the top. Put rack in pressure saucepan, then add 1¼ cups hot water. Close the saucepan. Cook at 15 lbs. pressure for 15 minutes. Reduce pressure immediately. Unmold and surround with cream sauce containing shrimp, if desired.

JIFFY MEAT BALLS

½ lb. ground beef	¼ teaspoon poultry seasoning
½ lb. ground pork	1 egg, beaten
¼ cup grated, raw potato	¼ cup milk, heated
2 tablespoons grated onion	2 tablespoons flour
1½ teaspoons salt	2 tablespoons shortening
⅛ teaspoon pepper	1 cup meat stock
Dash of nutmeg	

Have meat ground three times. Combine with raw potatoes, onion, salt, pepper, nutmeg, poultry seasoning, egg and milk. Mix until mixture is smooth. Shape into small balls. Roll lightly in flour. Heat pressure saucepan, add shortening, brown meat balls and add meat stock. Place cover on cooker. Cook at 15 lbs. pressure for five minutes. Reduce pressure immediately.

SPAGHETTI WITH MEAT SAUCE

2 tablespoons fat	1 teaspoon chili powder
1 lb. ground beef	⅛ teaspoon cayenne pepper
1 large onion, chopped	⅛ teaspoon curry powder
½ cup chopped celery	4 cups water
1 green pepper, diced	2 teaspoons salt
2 teaspoons salt	8-oz. package spaghetti
1 6-oz. can tomato paste	1 3-oz. package grated Parmesan
1 cup tomato juice	Cheese

Heat pressure saucepan and add fat. Brown ground beef. Add onion, celery, green pepper and salt. Combine tomato paste, tomato juice, chili powder, cayenne pepper and curry powder and pour over ingredients in saucepan. Mix well. Cook 10 minutes at 10 lbs pressure. Cool saucepan at once. Remove meat sauce and keep hot. Bring water to boil in saucepan. Add 2 teaspoons salt and spaghetti. Stir. Cook 8 minutes at 5 lbs. pressure. Reduce pressure. Drain spaghetti and rinse in hot water. Pour sauce over spaghetti on serving plates. Sprinkle with cheese. Serves 5.

Vitamins—Menu Planning—
Scientific Feeding Simplified

THE clever homemaker should know that her meals do more for her family than satisfy hunger and please tastes. She should have full understanding that the bodies of all members of her family are composed of many substances, combined in such manner as to form skin, blood, muscles, bones, hair, gland secretions, and all other component parts of the human machine.

She realizes that each of those she loves so well are constantly exhausting those substances in many ways—by exertion, by growing, by the normal functions of the organs, elimination, and respiration, and in other ways. Her task, as the menu planner of the home, is to restore those lost substances in the proper quantities and form.

If she does her task well, she is amply recompensed when she sees healthy complexions, strong teeth, happy smiles, and unimpaired vigor and vitality. Her well-done dietary work also pays huge dividends in the form of smaller doctor's bills, in less frequent colds and minor ailments, in sunny dispositions, and in vigorous mental reactions.

How can the new homemaker, ambitious though she may be, learn the truths necessary to the proper feeding of a family?

How can the good food be told from the bad?—the worthwhile from the useless? Fundamentally the problem is simple.

Every bit of food taken into the body does either one of three things:

1. It goes into the building of new bone and tissue.

2. It supplies energy and the substances for gland secretions.

3. It merely passes through the digestive and elimination organs without effect or in a manner which assists or disturbs the proper functioning of those organs.

The foods which supply energy are fats and carbohydrates, the latter term including starch and sugar.

The foods which list the proper regulation of the digestive and elimination organs are roughage and inorganic salts.

The foods which build bone and tissue are proteins and those with high mineral content (inorganic salts).

One other class of food needed for healthy, happy bodies is vitamins.

For the menu planner of the average home, where none of the members require any special dietary treatment prescribed by a good physician, the one important rule to remember is:

Serve one food from each of the three classifications at least once every day to every member of the family and, if possible, at every meal.

What foods supply these necessary articles for the adequate diet? The answer to that question, too, is simple.

Proteins necessary for the maintenance of life, for growth, and for the replacement of worn-out tissues. The average person uses too much protein. Taken to excess, the body is unable to split up this food completely into harmless end-products; instead, certain irritating substances are produced which have a harmful action on vital organs of the body, particularly the kidneys. Proteins are obtained particularly from **meats, eggs, milk, cheese, fish, poultry, nuts, leguminous vegetables,** such as **peas** and **beans,** the **gluten of wheat,** and **other cereals.**

Mineral Foods (Inorganic Salts—Roughage. Calcium, phosphorus, and **iron).** The amounts required are very small but are of great importance. They are found in various foods containing proteins and in **fruits** and **green vegetables.** The latter articles of food are also the source of alkaline ash which forms basic (alkaline) compounds useful in overcoming a tendency to "acidosis" (a condition of lessened alkalinity of blood) caused by the average diet. Green vegetables furnish "roughage," which is essential to insure normal elimination. Green vegetables are relatively low in food value, containing approximately 7% carbohydrates and a large amount of water: Asparagus, string beans, cabbage, cauliflower, celery, onions, spinach, tomatoes, turnips, lettuce, eggplant, bread, meats, milk, eggs, and cereals.

Carbohydrates are derived from the **sugars** and **starches.** With the fats, they are the principal sources of energy and heat. The carbohydrates are consumed in the body much as coal is burned in a stove, the energy produced giving the power to perform work as well as heat to keep the body warm. The most common sources of carbohydrate foods are the various **sugars, candies, molasses, desserts, honey, fruits, potatoes, rice, wheat,** cereals, peas, potatoes, kidney beans, and lentils.

Fats serve the same purpose as carbohydrates for food. Any excess of fat that is eaten, over the requirements for heat and energy, is stored away under the skin and in various organs of the body. Fat has the highest heat value and is served in the most concentrated form of any food. A small part of butter has the same food value as a potato. Fat is the most difficult food for the body to digest and consume. The energy of fat is released slowly and those who eat fats excessively become sluggish mentally and physically. The chief souces of fat are **butter, cream, fat meat, bacon, lard, nuts, egg yolk, olive and other oils.**

Menu Planning the Vitamin Way

The Simplified Shortcut to Menu Planning. It is no longer necessary for the housewife to balance her menus by means of calculation of quantities of Proteins, Minerals, Fats, Carbohydrates, and Vitamins contained in the various foods. For **if the Vitamins are provided in proper quantities, in food, the diet will be balanced and adequate.**

As a simple key to selection—menu planning—the vitamin way, there are three simple steps:

1. **To know the daily minimum of Vitamin requirements** for the individual. See **Table A** following.
2. What is the *loss* of Vitamins *in cooking.* See **Table B** following.
3. **What Vitamins** are contained in various **foods.** See **Table C** following.

By the use of these three tables, the selection of food for a balanced diet may be worked out with confident assurance. Note that vitamin requirements are minimum, and bear in mind that an average intake of vitamins cannot do harm, as the system either rejects or stores surpluses, according to its practical needs.

[The publishers have in preparation, for early publication, a complete Vitamin Cook Book, which gives the vitamin content of each recipe, thus doing away with the necessity for any calculation whatsoever by the housewife.]

A. RECOMMENDED DAILY VITAMIN REQUIREMENTS

	VITAMIN A Internat'l. Units	VITAMIN B1 Internat'l. Units	VITAMIN C Internat'l. Units	VITAMIN D Internat'l. Units	VITAMIN G Sherman Units
Men..................................	5,000	650	1,500	600	850
Women..............................	5,000	500	1,500	600	850
Pregnant or Nursing Women...........	7,500	665	2,500	800	1,000
*Children............................	3,500	350	1,200	700	600

* The term *Children* covers the ages 6 to 12 years. Vitamin requirements of children over 12 years of age are taken as equivalent to those of an adult.

Vitamin requirements vary somewhat according to size, sex, age and activity. For all practical purposes, however, the above figures representing the average requirements, may be safely used. Illness affects vitamin requirements. Consult your physician.

The above daily requirements are recommended for the attainment of the abundant health which is every individual's goal—rather than the mere prevention of deficiency diseases.

B. ESTIMATED LOSSES OF VITAMINS IN COOKING

COOKING PROCESS	VITAMIN "A" % OF LOSS	VITAMIN "B1" % OF LOSS	VITAMIN "C" % OF LOSS	VITAMIN "D" % OF LOSS	VITAMIN "G" % OF LOSS
Baking.......	10%	15% (with acid †) 5%	80% (with acid †) 40%	No Loss	40% (with acid †) 20%
Boiling.......	No Loss	In acid solution † 0 In water 20% In water 50% In alkaline solution (soda) 40%	In acid solution † 15% In water *20% In water 50% In alkaline solution (soda) 80%	No Loss	In acid solution † 0 In water *10% In water 50% In alkaline solution (soda) 40%
Broiling......	25%	40%	80%	No Loss	40%
Canning......	No Loss	No Loss	10%	No Loss	No Loss
Frying.......	25% Butter has 100% Loss	30%	80%	No Loss	40%
Roasting......	25%	50%	80%	No Loss	40%
Sauteing......	Butter has 50% Loss 25%	30%	80%	No Loss	40%

* Boiled Rapidly.   † Using lemon, tomato, vinegar, etc.
These cooking losses must be deducted from vitamin content in Table C.

C. TABLE OF ESTIMATED VITAMIN CONTENT OF COMMON FOODS

THE following table, unlike others of its kind, is figured in ordinary kitchen weights and measures and requires no further interpretation. It will be found useful as a basis for judging *relative* vitamin values of foods and as a guide in marketing and menu-planning. It will also serve as a key for computing the vitamin value of recipes other than those in this book.

Variety, soil, climate, maturity, preservation and storage of foods all affect vitamin content, hence foods do not have a fixed vitamin value, but rather a range of values. For practical purposes, however, it is customary to put single vitamin values on common foods. The single values in the table which follows, result from a correlation of the most recent and reliable summaries, and are, in the opinion of the editors, the most representative figures obtainable.

FOOD	Quantity	(I. U.) A	(I. U.) B1	(I. U.) C	(I. U.) D	Sherman Units (S. U.) G
Alfalfa, lean meal, dried............	1 cup, 4 oz.	18,000	—	—	—	500
Almonds, shelled.................	10 nuts	10	10	—	—	—
Almonds, shelled.................	1 cup	150	150	—	—	—
Apples, raw.....................	1 med.	75	23	200	—	20
Apples, dried...................	1 med.	—	—	—	—	—
Apples, baked..................	1 med.	60	20	40	—	12
Apples, juice...................	1 cup	—	—	125	—	—
Apples, sauce..................	1 cup	120	40	320	—	36
Apricots, fresh.................	1 med.	1,840	4	25	—	16
Apricots, fresh.................	1 cup	9,200	23	115	—	80
Apricots, canned...............	1 cup	9,200	13	58	—	80
Apricots, dried.................	1 cup	12,000	70	90	—	160
Artichokes, French.............	1 med.	250	70	300	—	8
Artichokes, Jerusalem..........	1 med.	—	46	200	—	—
Asparagus, blanched (white).......	1 cup	68	83	1,508	—	10
Asparagus, green................	1 cup	960	116	1,600	—	80
Asparagus, canned, (incl. liquid) white........................	1 cup	—	110	120	—	—
Avocado......................	1 med.	200	70	400	—	110
Bacon, raw.....................	1 strip	—	5	—	—	4
Bacon, broiled crisp..............	1 strip	—	3	—	—	2
Bacon, fried....................	1 strip	—	1	—	—	—
Banana, raw....................	1 med.	375	25	200	—	40
Banana, baked..................	1 med.	300	25	80	—	24
Barley, whole grain.....	1 tblsp.	—	25	—	—	—
Barley, pearled.........	1 tblsp.	—	—	—	—	—
Barley, whole grain.............	1 cup	—	345	—	—	—
Barley, pearled.................	1 cup	—	15	—	—	—
Beans, baked w. pork, comm........	1 cup	15	150	—	—	—
Beans, baked, without pork, comm....	1 cup	15	70	—	—	—
Beans, kidney, dried.............	1 cup	—	345	—	—	—
Beans, lima, fresh..............	1 cup	1,150	264	1,380	—	230
Beans, lima, dried.............	1 cup	230	402	—	—	—
Beans, navy, dried, baked........	1 cup	—	391	—	—	—
Beans, string, (snap) fresh.......	1 cup	2,300	57	690	—	92
Beans, string, cooked w. soda.......	1 cup	2,300	29	—	—	—
Beans, string, canned..........	1 cup	2,300	32	345	—	—
Beans, soy, white, dried.........	1 cup	—	500	—	—	480
Beans, soy, green, dried.........	1 cup	—	970	—	—	480
Beans, soy, black, dried..........	1 cup	1,800	200	—	—	480
Beans, wax, butter or yellow.......	1 cup	820	60	320	—	75
Bean sprouts..................	1 cup	10	20	975	—	92
Beef, lean.....................	1 lb.	230	300	—	60	392
Beer..........................	1 glass, 6 oz.	—	4	—	—	—
Beets, diced...................	1 cup	140	48	400	—	25
Beet tops (same content as Chard)...						
Blackberries, fresh................	1 cup	230	10	300	—	—
Blueberries....................	1 cup	150	21	160	—	7
Bone marrow..................	4 oz.	930	—	—	—	—
Bouillon, commercial (beef or chicken)	1 cube	—	—	—	—	—
Brains, calf.....................	1 lb.	—	371	1,300	—	585
Bran (see Wheat)................						
Brazil nuts.....................	1 nut	—	9	—	—	—
Brazil nuts....................	1 cup	20	700	—	—	—
Bread, Boston brown.............	1 slice	—	12	—	—	7
Bread, crumbs, (enriched bread)......	1 cup	—	70	—	—	9
Bread, French or Vienna...........	1 slice	—	—	—	—	—
Bread, raisin...................	1 slice	—	—	—	—	—
Bread, white, enriched............	1 slice	—	23	—	—	3
Bread, rye.....................	1 slice	—	18	—	—	—
Bread, toast or melba (white)......	1 slice	—	—	—	—	—
Bread, white (with water)..........	1 slice	—	5	—	—	3
Bread, white (with milk)..........	1 slice	—	7	—	—	20
Bread, whole wheat, 100%.........	1 slice	—	40	—	—	12
Broccoli......................	1 cup	8,000	45	1,600	—	150
Brussel sprouts.................	1 cup	1,100	50	1,800	—	—
Butter	1 square	200	—	—	6	—
Butter	1 tblsp.	300	—	—	9	—
Butter	1 cup	4,800	—	—	150	—
Butter........................	1 oz.	600	—	—	18	—

FOOD	Quantity	(I. U.) A	(I. U.) B2	(I. U.) C	(I. U.) D	Sherman Units (S. U.) G
Buttermilk........................	1 cup	—	35	40	—	103
Cabbage, raw, white...............	1 cup	—	50	2,000	—	15
Cabbage, raw, green...............	1 cup	100	50	3,000	—	30
Cantaloupe (See Melon, musk).......						
Carp.............................	1 lb.	—	—	—	—	55
Cashew nuts, shelled..............	5 nuts (½ oz.)	19	—	—	—	9
Cashew nuts, shelled..............	1 cup	570	—	—	—	270
Carrots, fresh.....................	1 med.	1,350	16	80	—	16
Carrots, fresh, raw, diced..........	1 cup	2,700	32	160	—	32
Carrots, fresh, cooked, diced........	1 cup	2,700	26	148	—	29
Carrots, canned...................	1 cup	2,700	13	60	—	—
Cauliflower.......................	¼ hd. (3 oz.)	25	50	1,500	—	35
Cauliflower.......................	1 cup	50	100	3,000	—	70
Caviar...........................	1 tblsp.	—	—	—	—	—
Celery, fresh, blanched (white).....	1–7″ stalk	5	5	50	—	—
Celery, fresh, blanched (diced)......	1 cup	20	20	200	—	—
Celery, fresh, green...............	1–7″ stalk	500	5	50	—	5
Celery, fresh, green, (diced)........	1 cup	2,000	20	200	—	20
Celery, fresh, green, (chopped)......	1 tblsp.	125	2	13	—	1
Chard............................	1 cup	20,000	30	1,120	—	75
Chard............................	1 lb.	45,712	64	2,560	—	176
Cheese, American Cheddar, grated....	1 cup	1,713	11	—	—	210
Cheese, American Cheddar, grated....	4 oz.	2,285	15	—	—	280
Cheese, Camembert................	4 oz.	3,750	—	—	—	—
Cheese, Cottage, (skim milk).......	1 tblsp.	70	—	—	—	22
Cheese, Cottage, (skim milk).......	1 cup	910	—	—	—	286
Cheese, Cream, full...............	4 oz.	2,000	—	—	—	84
Cheese, Parmesan, grated...........	1 cup	800	24	—	—	500
Cheese, Pimento (processed)........	1″ cube	500	—	—	—	—
Cheese, Roquefort.................	1″ cube	850	—	—	—	—
Cheese, Swiss.....................	4 oz.	2,000	12	—	—	175
Cheese, Swiss, processed...........	4 oz.	2,000	—	—	—	—
Cherries, fresh, Bing..............	1 med.	8	1	23	—	—
Cherries, fresh, Bing..............	1 cup	160	20	460	—	—
Cherries, fresh, Royal Anne........	1 med.	13	1	23	—	—
Cherries, fresh, Royal Anne........	1 cup	390	30	690	—	—
Cherries, canned..................	1 med.	10	1	20	—	—
Cherries, canned..................	1 cup	320	32	640	—	—
Chestnuts........................	1 med.	—	12	—	—	—
Chestnuts........................	1 cup	—	144	—	—	—
Chicken, light....................	1 lb.	—	138	—	—	40
Chicken, dark....................	1 lb.	—	230	—	—	100
Chicken, liver....................	1 lb.	3,000	150	2,100	200	115
Chicory (same content as Endive).....						
Chives...........................	1 tspn.	—	—	40	—	—
Chocolate, unsweetened............	1 sq. (1 oz.)	18	—	—	—	—
Chocolate, milk..................	1 oz.	—	3	—	—	—
Clams............................	1 clam	13	1	18	—	12
Clams............................	1 cup	462	14	255	—	175
Cocoa, powdered..................	1 tblsp.	—	2	—	—	—
Cocoa, (as beverage w. milk).......	1 cup	237	22	48	6	45
Coconut, shredded, fresh...........	1 tblsp.	—	1	10	—	5
Coconut, shredded, fresh...........	1 cup	—	16	160	—	80
Coconut, milk, fresh...............	1 cup	—	—	140	—	—
Cod Liver Oil (U. S. P. Stand.)......	1 tblsp.	6,500	—	—	950	—
Cod..............................	1 lb.	12	136	—	—	92
Cod, salted.......................	1 lb.	—	—	—	—	—
Coffee (as beverage)...............	1 cup	—	—	—	—	—
Collards..........................	1 cup	10,000	100	10,000	—	200
Corn, sweet, white (Gentleman).....	1 ear, 6″	33	30	133	—	—
Corn, sweet, white (Gentleman).....	1 cup	100	90	400	—	—
Corn, canned, white...............	1 cup	100	70	300	—	—
Corn, yellow......................	1 ear, 6″	330	30	133	—	20
Corn, yellow......................	1 cup	1,000	70	400	—	35
Corn, yellow, canned..............	1 cup	1,000	70	300	—	—
Corn oil (refined).................	1 cup	—	—	—	—	—
Cornflakes (not enriched)..........	1 cup	—	—	—	—	—
Cornmeal, white..................	1 cup	—	143	—	—	—
Cornmeal, yellow.................	1 cup	1,200	110	—	—	46
Cornstarch.......................	1 cup	—	—	—	—	—

FOOD	Quantity	(I. U.) A	(I. U.) B2	(I. U.) C	(I. U.) D	Sherman Units (S. U.) G
Corn sirup	1 cup	—	—	—	—	—
Cottonseed oil (refined)	1 cup	—	—	—	—	—
Cowpeas, dry	1 cup	150	690	—	—	230
Crabs, (meat, fresh)	¼ lb.	—	195	10	—	133
Crab meat, canned	1 cup	—	175	5	—	115
Crackers, Graham	1 cracker	—	8	—	—	—
Crackers, Graham, crumbs	1 cup	—	128	—	—	—
Crackers, all others	—	—	—	—	—	—
Cranberries, fresh	1 cup	70	—	400	—	—
Cranberries, juice	1 cup	—	—	300	—	—
Cranberries, sauce	1 cup	56	—	300	—	—
Crawfish	1 lb.	—	—	276	—	—
Cream, light (coffee) 20% fat	1 cup	1,024	32	—	20	—
Cream, heavy (whipping) 40% fat	1 cup	2,112	26	—	28	—
Cucumbers, fresh	1 large	20	110	720	—	2
Currants, black, fresh	1 cup	—	11	4,400	—	—
Currants, red, fresh	1 cup	—	16	1,100	—	—
Dandelion greens	1 cup	18,000	36	1,400	—	150
Dates, fresh	1 med.	9	3	—	—	3
Dates, fresh	1 cup	153	51	—	—	51
Dates, dried	1 med.	4	2	—	—	—
Dates, dried	1 cup	84	42	—	—	—
Doughnuts	1 med.	—	—	—	—	—
Duck	1 lb.	—	—	718	—	—
Eels	1 lb.	10,500	55	—	—	57
Eggplant	1 slice, ½"	23	14	116	—	11
Eggplant, diced	1 cup	92	56	464	—	44
Eggs, whole	1 med.	900	19	—	16	85
Eggs, white	1 med.	—	—	—	—	45
Eggs, yolk	1 med.	900	19	—	16	35
Eggs, soft cooked	1 med.	900	19	—	16	76
Eggs, hard cooked	1 med.	900	19	—	16	72
Endive	1 stalk, 6"	1,900	23	135	—	45
Escarole, (same content as Endive)						
Farina, light	1 cup	—	2	—	—	—
Farina, dark	1 cup	—	84	—	—	7
Farina, enriched	1 cup	—	276	—	—	200
Figs, fresh	1 med.	30	10	15	—	20
Figs, fresh, chopped	1 cup	150	50	75	—	100
Figs, dried	1 med.	19	7	—	—	8
Figs, dried	1 cup	133	49	—	—	56
Fish, (see Cod, Eels, Flounder, Haddock, Halibut, Herring, Mackerel, Perch, Salmon, Sardines, Shad, Smelt, Sole, Trout and Tuna.)						
Fennel	1 cup	—	—	1,062	—	—
Flounder	1 lb.	—	—	—	—	32
Flour, buckwheat, sifted	1 cup	—	300	—	—	—
Flour, rye	1 cup	—	214	—	—	—
Flour, white, enriched	1 cup	—	139	—	—	—
Flour, white, enriched	1 tblsp.	—	9	—	—	—
Flour, white, whole, unbleached	1 cup	—	160	—	—	—
Flour, white, patent (pastry)	1 cup	—	30	—	—	—
Flour, white, plus germ	1 cup	—	58	—	—	—
Flour, soy bean	1 cup	—	555	—	—	—
Fowl	1 lb.	—	218	—	—	221
Garlic	1 clove	—	—	20	—	—
Gelatin	1 tblsp.	—	—	—	—	—
Gelatin dessert	1 cup	—	—	—	—	—
Ginger ale	1 glass	—	—	—	—	—
Gingerbread	1 piece	—	—	—	—	—
Goose	1 lb.	—	—	1,200	—	—
Gooseberries, fresh, green	1 cup	760	56	680	—	—
Grapefruit	½ med.	—	40	1,500	—	20
Grapefruit, juice, fresh	1 cup	—	45	2,000	—	20
Grapefruit, juice, canned	1 cup	—	45	2,000	—	20
Grapes, fresh	½ bunch (25-30)	—	20	75	—	10
Grape juice	1 cup	—	15	60	—	60
Guava, fresh, stoned	1 med.	200	14	1,500	—	2

FOOD	Quantity	(I. U.) A	(I. U.) B1	(I. U.) C	(I. U.) D	(S. U.) G
Grouse, roasted....................	1 lb.	—	660	—	—	—
Haddock, finnan haddie............	1 lb.	—	23	—	—	—
Halibut...........................	1 lb.	—	138	—	—	280
Ham, cured.......................	1 lb.	—	2,187	—	—	—
Ham, fresh (see Pork).............						
Hazelnuts.........................	1 med.	5	10	—	—	—
Hazelnuts, shelled................	1 cup	230	506	—	—	—
Heart, beef.......................	1 lb.	—	600	10	—	1,350
Heart, lamb.......................	1 lb.	—	600	10	—	—
Heart, pork.......................	1 lb.	—	920	310	—	170
Herring...........................	1 lb.	1,200	—	—	8,500	315
Hichory nuts......................	1 med.	—	5	—	—	—
Hickory nuts......................	1 cup	—	260	—	—	—
Hominy (made from white corn)....	1 cup	—	—	—	—	—
Honey............................	1 cup	—	—	—	—	—
Horse radish, grated..............	1 tblsp.	—	—	350	—	—
Huckleberries.....................	1 cup	—	—	1,600	—	—
Ice cream, comm., w. skim milk.	8 oz.	—	15	60	—	—
Ices, fruit, commercial............	8 oz.	—	—	—	—	—
Jam..............................	1 cup	—	—	—	—	—
Jelly.............................	1 cup	—	—	—	—	—
Junket powder (renet).............	8 oz.	—	—	—	—	—
Kale.............................	1 cup	10,000	24	1,440	—	400
Kidney, beef or calf..............	1 lb.	5,000	390	—	—	1,600
Kidney, lamb.....................	1 lb.	4,000	375	—	—	—
Kidney, pork.....................	1 lb.	—	825	1,300	—	3,000
Kohlrabi..........................	1 cup	—	16	1,200	—	—
Kumquats.........................	1 med.	—	—	135	—	—
Lamb, chops, lean................	1 lb.	—	448	—	—	528
Lard.............................	1 cup	—	—	—	—	—
Leek.............................	1 stalk	17	8	140	—	—
Leek.............................	1 cup	119	56	980	—	—
Lemons...........................	1 med.	—	20	1,100	—	—
Lemons, juice.....................	1 tblsp.	—	2	150	—	—
Lemons, rind, grated..............	1 tblsp.	—	3	375	—	—
Lentils, dried.....................	1 cup	180	250	—	—	200
Lettuce, Romaine.................	1 leaf, 9"	650	2	10	—	5
Lettuce, Romaine....	1 av. head	13,000	40	200	—	100
Lettuce, leaf, green...............	1 leaf	600	5	35	—	10
Lettuce, iceberg, outer leaf........	1 leaf	250	4	20	—	3
Lettuce, iceberg, inner head........	Entire	180	80	360	—	68
Lettuce, iceberg, whole head.......	Entire	600	80	360	—	68
Lima beans (see Beans)............						
Limes............................	1 med.	100	—	400	—	—
Limes, juice......................	1 tblsp.	25	—	100	—	—
Liver, beef.......................	1 lb.	58,000	400	3,200	200	4,725
Liver, calf.......................	1 lb.	74,000	—	3,000	37	—
Liver, lamb.......................	1 lb.	55,000	630	2,400	100	4,080
Liver, mutton.....................	1 lb.	65,000	650	2,600	125	5,525
Liver, pork.......................	1 lb.	44,000	750	2,400	200	4,150
Lobster...........................	1 med.	—	—	—	—	—
Loganberries......................	1 cup	—	—	1,600	—	—
Loganberries, juice................	1 cup	—	—	1,260	—	—
Macaroni.........................	1 cup	—	—	—	—	—
Macaroons........................	1 macaroon	—	—	—	—	—
Mackerel.........................	1 lb.	800	136	—	4,800	1,000
Mangoes..........................	1 med.	1,500	30	600	—	20
Maple sugar......................	1 piece	—	—	—	—	—
Maple sirup......................	1 cup	—	—	—	—	—
Margerine, without "A" added.....	1 tblsp.	—	—	—	—	—
Margerine, with "A" added........	1 tblsp.	500	—	—	—	—
Margerine, with "A" added........	1 cup	8,000	—	—	—	—
Marmalade, orange...............	1 tblsp.	—	—	—	—	—
Marshmallow......................	1 marsh.	—	—	—	—	—
Mayonaise, comm.................	1 tblsp.	30	—	—	—	—
Melon, Musk, Rocky Ford.........	½ med.	770	73	1,200	—	80
Melon, Honeydew.................	½ med.	—	—	1,420	—	—
Milk, condensed..................	1 cup	720	160	—	20	—
Milk, evaporated, irradiated, and un-diluted.........................	1 cup	1,058	35	62	68	300

FOOD	Quantity	International Units				Sherman Units (S. U.) G
		(I. U.) A	(I. U.) B1	(I. U.) C	(I. U.) D	
Milk, raw	1 cup	350	36	88	10	101
Milk, pasteurized	1 cup	350	29	80	10	101
Milk, skim	1 cup	17	15	—	—	80
Milk, malted	1 cup	—	250	—	—	380
Molasses, commercial	1 cup	—	—	—	—	—
Mushrooms	1 med.	—	10	—	—	—
Mushrooms, fresh	1 cup	—	100	—	—	—
Mushrooms, canned	1 cup	—	90	—	—	—
Mussels	1 cup	—	—	276	—	—
Mustard greens	1 lb.	92,000	207	6,500	—	675
Mutton	1 lb.	—	276	—	—	425
Nectarines, yellow, fresh	1 lb.	4,800	—	480	—	—
Noodles	1 cup	—	—	—	—	—
Nuts, mixed	1 cup	211	273	—	—	63
Oatmeal, quick-cooking	1 cup	—	476	—	—	95
Oats, rolled	1 cup	—	500	—	—	250
Oats, whole grain	1 cup	—	587	—	—	117
Okra	1 lb.	1,840	184	1,380	—	800
Okra	1 pod	46	5	35	—	20
Olives, green, chopped	1 cup	892	10	—	—	—
Olives, ripe, Mission	1 cup	782	10	—	—	—
Olive oil, refined	1 cup	—	—	—	—	—
Oleomargerine (see Margerine)						
Onions, spring	1 med.	500	—	75	—	—
Onions, mature	1 med.	—	10	160	—	30
Onions, mature, chopped	1 tblsp.	—	2	25	—	5
Onions, mature, chopped	1 cup	—	24	300	—	60
Oranges	1 med.	175	25	825	—	15
Oranges, juice, fresh	1 cup	625	62	825	—	15
Oranges, juice, canned	1 cup	625	62	550	—	—
Oranges, rind, grated	1 tblsp.	87	18	225	—	3
Oysters, raw	1 cup	345	172	12	12	16
Papaya	8 oz.	5,750	58	1,970	—	1,380
Paprika		—	—	Exc.	—	—
Parsley, chopped	1 tblsp.	1,000	—	222	—	—
Parsnips	1 cup	—	100	1,035	—	—
Parsnips	1 med.	—	84	900	—	—
Peaches, fresh, white	1 med.	—	5	160	—	—
Peaches, fresh, yellow	1 med.	900	28	70	—	—
Peaches, canned, white	1 cup	—	—	120	—	—
Peaches, canned, yellow	1 cup	2,500	64	105	—	—
Peaches, dried, yellow	1 cup	6,000	—	—	—	—
Peanuts, unroasted, shelled	1 cup	50	438	240	—	200
Peanuts, roasted, shelled	1 cup	—	200	—	—	—
Peanut butter	1 tblsp.	9	62	—	—	33
Peanut butter	1 cup	144	1,000	—	—	528
Pears, fresh, raw	1 med.	50	5	60	—	5
Pears, fresh, cooked	1 cup	112	10	120	—	11
Pears, dried, cooked	1 med.	5	2	3	—	10
Pears, canned	1 med.	—	—	—	—	5
Pears, juice	1 cup	—	—	—	—	—
Pears, fresh, raw	1 cup	2,000	275	900	—	172
Peas, dried, green	1 cup	2,400	300	—	—	253
Peas, canned	1 cup	2,000	194	276	—	100
Pecans, shelled	1 med.	6	5	—	—	3
Pecans, shelled	1 cup	460	350	—	—	230
Peppers, green	1 med.	1,500	69	2,000	—	40
Peppers, red	1 med.	7,000	10	2,700	—	14
Peppers, green, chopped	1 tblsp.	150	7	200	—	4
Peppers, red, chopped	1 tblsp.	700	1	270	—	1
Perch	1 lb.	—	—	—	—	105
Persimmon	1 med.	2,550	—	400	—	—
Pickles, all varieties	1 med.	—	—	—	—	—
Pigeon	1 lb.	—	—	920	—	—
Pimientos	1 med.	3,500	5	1,350	—	7
Pimientos	1 cup	28,000	40	10,800	—	56
Pineapple, fresh	1 slice, ½"	100	20	325	—	50
Pineapple, canned	1 slice, ½"	90	7	275	—	35
Pineapple, canned, shredded	1 cup	100	24	300	—	10
Pineapple, juice	1 cup	200	70	700	—	20

FOOD	Quantity	International Units				Sherman Units
		(I. U.) A	(I. U.) B1	(I. U.) C	(I. U.) D	(S. U.) G
Pistachio nuts, shelled.............	1 nut	4	—	—	—	—
Plums, fresh......................	1 med.	180	12	50	—	5
Plums, canned..................	1 med.	100	7	50	—	—
Plantains........................	1 med.	500	25	200	—	40
Pomegranate.....................	1 med.	—	—	450	—	—
Pomegranate, juice, canned.	1 cup	—	—	—	—	6
Popcorn, freshly popped.............	1 cup	500	—	—	—	—
Pork, lean.......................	1 lb.	—	2,136	—	—	456
Potatoes, old, white...............	1 med.	80	50	400	—	40
Potatoes, new, white.............	1 med.	80	75	500	—	40
Potatoes, yellow (sweet)............	1 med.	7,000	60	800	—	60
Prawns, boiled....................	1 lb.	4,400	80	—	—	150
Prunes, uncooked, raw.............	1 med.	98	—	20	—	—
Prunes, cooked..................	1 med.	73	—	2	—	—
Prunes, uncooked, raw.............	1 cup	1,470	—	300	—	—
Prunes, cooked.................	1 cup	1,080	—	224	—	—
Pumpernickel (see Bread, rye).......						
Pumpkin.........................	1 cup	380	30	120	—	12
Quinces.........................	1 med.	—	—	220	—	—
Rabbit, stewed...................	1 lb.	—	138	—	—	92
Radishes........................	1 cup	—	40	800	—	20
Raisins..........................	1 cup	112	84	—	—	52
Raspberries, fresh................	1 cup	270	18	660	—	—
Raspberries, canned..............	1 cup	270	10	200	—	—
Raspberries, juice................	1 cup	270	10	150	—	—
Rhubarb, fresh...................	1 cup	230	18	360	—	—
Rhubarb, canned.................	1 cup	200	16	50	—	—
Rice, brown......................	1 cup	—	120	—	—	50
Rice, polished, white..............	1 cup	—	—	—	—	7
Rice, polishings..................	1 cup	—	1,700	—	—	—
Rice, wild.......................	1 cup	—	460	—	—	50
Rice, ground.....................	1 cup	—	28	—	—	—
Rutabagas, white.................	1 cup	—	35	900	—	—
Rutabagas, yellow................	1 cup	60	35	900	—	—
Rye (whole grain)................	1 cup	—	210	300	—	—
Sago............................	1 cup	—	—	—	—	—
Salad dressing, French............	1 cup	—	—	—	—	—
Salad dressing, mayonnaise........	1 tblsp.	30	0.5	—	—	—
Salmon, fresh....................	1 lb.	2,000	50	—	5,280	—
Salmon, canned, red..............	1 cup	750	80	—	1,650	150
Salmon, canned, pink.............	1 cup	100	10	—	1,440	120
Salsify..........................	1 cup	—	—	350	—	—
Sardines, canned in oil............	4 oz. can	400	35	—	1,500	—
Sauerkraut, fresh, uncooked........	1 cup	—	—	320	—	—
Sauerkraut, fresh, cooked..........	1 cup	—	—	60	—	—
Sauerkraut, fresh, canned.........	1 cup	—	—	180	—	—
Sauerkraut, juice, fresh...........	1 cup	—	—	640	—	—
Sauerkraut, juice, old.............	1 cup	—	—	160	—	—
Scallions (see Onions, spring).......						
Scallops.........................	1 cup	—	—	—	—	—
Shad, fresh......................	1 lb.	—	—	—	—	—
Shad, roe........................	1 lb.	9,200	500	—	—	—
Shallot (stem and bulb)...........	1 cup	—	—	690	—	—
Shrimp, fresh....................	1 cup	—	—	—	345	—
Shrimp, canned..................	1 cup	—	—	—	325	—
Smelt...........................	1 lb.	—	—	—	193	—
Sole............................	1 lb.	—	112	—	—	—
Soy beans (see Beans).............						
Soy sauce........................	1 tblsp.	—	—	—	—	1
Spaghetti (see Macaroni)...........						
Spinach, fresh, raw..............	1 lb.	90,000	207	5,850	—	598
Spinach, canned..................	1 cup	40,000	69	2,300	—	—
Squash, summer (white)...........	1 cup	690	32	138	—	62
Squash, winter, (Hubbard, yellow)...	1 cup	7,000	32	138	—	62
Strawberries, fresh...............	1 cup	—	—	2,900	—	—
Strawberries, canned..............	1 cup	—	—	1,500	—	—
Sugar, white, gran.-loaf-pwdr.......	1 cup	—	—	—	—	—
Sugar, brown....................	1 cup	—	—	—	—	—
Sugar, maple....................	1 cup	—	—	—	—	—
Sweetbreads, beef or lamb..........	1 lb.	—	480	—	—	1,208

FOOD	Quantity	(I. U.) A	(I. U.) B1	(I. U.) C	(I. U.) D	Sherman Units (S. U.) G
Sweet potatoes (see Potatoes)........						
Sirup, cane..........................	1 cup	—	—	—	—	—
Sirup, corn..........................	1 cup	—	—	—	—	—
Sirup, maple........................	1 cup	—	—	—	—	—
Sirup, sorghum.....................	1 cup	—	—	—	—	—
Tangerines........................	1 med.	280	22	560	—	7
Tapioca............................	1 cup	—	—	—	—	—
Tea (as beverage)...................	1 cup	—	—	—	—	—
Tomato catsup......................	1 cup	—	—	—	—	—
Tomatoes, fresh....................	1 med.	3,000	60	450	—	16
Tomatoes, canned..................	1 cup	7,200	50	480	—	66
Tomato juice, canned..............	1 cup	7,064	60	650	—	10
Tongue, beef or sheep.............	1 lb.	—	415	—	—	—
Turnip, white......................	1 cup	—	24	1,200	—	24
Turnip, yellow.....................	1 cup	40	24	1,200	—	24
Tripe...............................	1 lb.	—	92	—	—	—
Trout, fresh water.................	1 lb.	—	132	—	—	—
Tuna fish, fresh...................	1 lb.	920	—	—	2,000	100
Tuna fish, canned..................	1 cup	460	—	—	1,000	45
Turkey.............................	1 lb.	—	218	—	—	221
Turtle..............................	1 lb.	—	—	580	—	—
Turnip greens......................	1 lb.	46,000	180	13,800	—	550
Veal...............................	1 lb.	—	412	—	—	552
Vegetable Marrow (see Squash, white)						
Vinegar............................	1 cup	—	—	—	—	—
Walnuts, English (shelled, chopped)..	1 nut	7	10	—	—	—
Walnuts, English (shelled, chopped)..	1 cup	200	300	—	—	—
Walnuts, Black (shelled, chopped)...	1 nut	9	7	—	—	—
Walnuts, Black (shelled, chopped)...	1 cup	260	220	—	—	—
Watercress.........................	1 bunch	4,000	56	880	—	—
Watercress.........................	1 leaf	800	1	18	—	—
Watermelon........................	1 slice (3/4"x6")	—	40	300	—	25
Wheat, cereals, bran...............	1 tblsp.	85	28	—	—	—
Wheat, cereals, cracked............	1 tblsp.	—	25	—	—	7
Wheat, cereals, farina, light........	1 tblsp.	—	—	—	—	—
Weat, cereals, farina, dark.........	1 tblsp.	—	7	—	—	7
Weat, cereals, germ...............	1 tblsp.	15	192	—	—	33
Weat, cereals, middlings plus (15 % germ)........................	1 tblsp.	50	65	—	—	7
Wheat, cereals, puffed (not enriched)	1/2 cup	—	—	—	—	—
Wheat, cereals, rolled..............	1 tblsp.	—	26	—	—	7
Wheat, cereals, seminola...........	1 tblsp.	30	7	—	—	—
Wheat, cereals, shredded...........	1 bisc.	4	20	—	—	33
Wheat, cereals, whole grain........	1 tblsp.	—	24	—	—	7
Wines, grape.......................	1 glass, 6 oz.	—	8	—	—	70
Yeast, bakers', compressed.........	2 oz. cake	—	100	2	—	456
Yeast, bakers', dried...............	1/2 oz. cake	—	70	—	—	157
Yeast, brewers', fresh..............	2 oz. cake	100	220	—	—	283
Yeast, brewers', dried..............	1/2 oz. cake	—	322	—	—	133

Note: Where dashes occur in the foregoing table (—), the vitamin content is either *insignificant, completely lacking* or *cannot be indicated by any reliable value at this writing*.

Values are for raw foods, except those specifically designated as cooked.

Values should be taken as applying to foods that are reasonably fresh. Allowance should be made by the homemaker for fruits and vegetables which are known to have been stored for a considerable period.

Menu Planning

FAMILIES with an unlimited allowance for food may wish to follow the Liberal Diet outlined in this chapter. It contains generous amounts of fruits, vegetables, eggs, lean meat, milk, and a moderate amount of cereals, fats, and sugars. It provides abundantly the nutrients needed by young and old for the enjoyment of buoyant health.

Those with a less liberal food budget will find the pattern for a Moderate Cost diet helpful. The quantity of milk is the same as in the liberal diet but there are less of eggs and lean meat and more of cereals and fats. Also expensive "extras" are omitted. The homemaker selects fruits and vegetables that are in season and moderately priced. She chooses less expensive cuts of meat, and she makes up in skillful preparation and serving what her menus lack in luxury.

The Minimum Cost Diet is a design for healthful meal planning suited to families with a minimum amount to spend on food. In order to meet all nutritional needs at lowest possible cost, large amounts of cereal products are used. Naturally the day-to-day variety is limited. In a diet of this type, evaporated milk may be used for cooking. Skim milk may be used for drinking purposes, provided the absence of butter fat is compensated for. Margarines, fortified with Vitamins A and D, may substitute for butter at a lower cost without a sacrifice of food value. The limited meat expenditure is devoted to meat sundries—liver, heart, kidneys, etc., also the less tender cuts of meat ground into hamburger.

The **Restricted Diet** presented here is for emergency use only. While it provides sufficient vitamins to prevent the deficiency diseases, it does not contain enough of them to assure good health over an indefinite period. In a diet as limited as this, every penny must be spent with consideration of the food value it will buy. Because the same foods must be used again and again, variety must be achieved by varying their manner of presentation.

A PLAN FOR A LIBERAL DIET

($3,000 or over annual income)

A liberal diet, as its name implies, provides very generously for all of the food requirements. It contains an abundance of fruits and vegetables, eggs, and lean meat, as well as a generous allowance of milk, along with moderate quantities of cereals, fats, and sugars. This combination of foods allows for better-than-average nutrition, because it provides more than amply for the items necessary for growth, health, and general well-being. At the same time, it offers an assortment pleasing to the eye and the palate, and allows for a great deal of variety from meal to meal.

A WEEK'S MENU FOR A LIBERAL DIET

MONDAY

BREAKFAST

Sliced oranges
Hot cereal (No. 101) (children)
Soft-cooked eggs (No. 202)
Whole-wheat toast (No. 988)
Milk (children)
Coffee (No. 301) (adults)

LUNCH OR SUPPER

Cream of potato soup (No. 563)
Toast
Avocado salad (No. 838) with French
dressing (No. 716)
Milk (children)

DINNER

Baked ham (No. 1448) with raisin
sauce (No. 2055)
Sweet potatoes, any style
Brussels sprouts (No. 1735)
Hot biscuits
Waldorf salad (No. 820)
Honey cake (No. 2946)
Milk for all

TUESDAY

BREAKFAST

Grapes, melon, or berries
Cereal (children)
Scrambled eggs (No. 209)
Toast (No. 988)
Milk (children)
Coffee (No. 301) (adults)

LUNCH OR SUPPER

Carrot and bell pepper salad
(No. 791)
Sharp cheese
Bran muffins (No. 1054) with jelly
Cocoa (No. 310) for all   Cake

DINNER

Cold sliced ham with relish
Creamed celery (No. 1762)
Buttered beets (No. 1726)
Baked peach halves (No. 58)
Crusty rolls (No. 1046)
Milk (children)

WEDNESDAY

BREAKFAST

Bananas   Crisp flaked cereal
Bacon (No. 1464)
Toast and marmalade
Milk (children)
Coffee (No. 301) (adults)

LUNCH OR SUPPER

Creamed vegetables (No. 1914) with
hard-cooked eggs (No. 202)
Stewed okra (No. 1809)
Whole-wheat toast   Pineapple
Milk for all

DINNER

Stuffed lamb shoulder (No. 1392)
Creamed new potatoes (No. 1844)
Buttered cabbage (No. 1736)
Bread and butter
Hot apple tarts (No. 2814) with
cream
Milk (children)

THURSDAY

BREAKFAST

Baked apples (No. 36) with raisins
Hot cereal (No. 101) (children)
Griddle cakes (No. 976) with maple
sirup
Milk (children)
Coffee (No. 301) (adults)

LUNCH OR SUPPER

Minced lamb sandwiches (No. 3301)
Cabbage carrot salad (No. 790)
Stewed dried apricots (No. 42)
Milk for all

DINNER

Baked cheese fondue (No. 2212) with
tomato sauce (No. 2035)
Buttered peas (No. 1823)
Boiled potatoes (No. 1834)

Toast

Fruit shortcake (No. 964) with
whipped cream
Milk (children)

FRIDAY

BREAKFAST

Orange and pineapple juice
Hot cereal (No. 101) (children)
French toast (No. 991) with jelly
Coffee (No. 301) (adults)

LUNCH OR SUPPER

Cream of spinach soup (No. 567)
with croutons (No. 2105)
Bacon (No. 1464) sandwiches, toasted
Ice-box cookies (No. 3067)
Milk (children)
Hot tea (No. 306) (adults)

DINNER

Vegetable soup (No. 578)
Scalloped salmon (No. 1188) or fresh
fish, any style, with pickle
Green beans (No. 1712)
Whole-wheat muffins (No. 1052)
Fruit-juice gelatin (No. 2420)
Milk (children)

SATURDAY

BREAKFAST

Stewed apricots (No. 42)
Hot cereal (No. 101) (children)
Poached eggs (No. 207) on toast
Milk (children)

LUNCH OR SUPPER

Vegetable soup (left-over)
Fruit salad (No. 819)
Cream cheese
Whole-wheat crackers
Milk for all

DINNER

Sirloin steak (No. 1301) or calf's
liver and bacon (No. 1500)
French-fried potatoes (No. 1836)
Broiled tomatoes (No. 1895)
Parker House rolls (No. 1030)
Blackberry flummery (No. 2466)
Milk (children)

SUNDAY

BREAKFAST

Grapefruit or other fruit in season
Hot cereal (No. 101) (children)
Waffles (No. 938) with honey
Sausage (No. 1469)
Milk (children)
Coffee (No. 301) (adults)

DINNER

Roast chicken with savory stuffing
(No. 1525)
Baked yams (No. 1885)
Creamed asparagus (No. 1705)
Head lettuce salad (No. 758)
Ice cream with strawberry preserves
(No. 3674)
Milk (children)

SUPPER

Mixed green salad (No. 760)
Potato chips (No. 1862)
Olive and nut sandwiches (No. 3306)
Cookies and fruit
Milk (children)
Coffee (No. 301) or tea (No. 306)
(adults)

A PLAN FOR A MODERATE-COST ADEQUATE DIET
($2,000 to $3,000 annual income)

The so-called moderate-cost adequate diet is well described by its name. For a reasonable amount of money it provides all of the different nutrients in sufficient quantities to keep adults and children in good nutritional condition, with a surplus for safety. It contains the same quantity of milk as the liberal diet, but less of vegetables, fruits, eggs, and lean meat, and more cereals and fat.

There is not so much difference in food value between a liberal diet and a moderate-cost diet, as outlined here, as there is in the selection of foods within each group and in the amount of money that can be spent for relishes, garnishes, whipping cream, and other special items. Such additions contribute to the attractiveness of a meal, but they increase the cost of the food budget considerably in the course of a week. The homemaker who wishes to set a moderate-cost table can with a little ingenuity provide her family with meals fully as attractive as the liberal-cost meal. In marketing she will select moderate-priced fruits and vegetables that combine well in flavor and color, and will by skillful preparation make the food appealing without expensive extras.

A WEEK'S MENU FOR A MODERATE-COST ADEQUATE DIET

MONDAY

BREAKFAST

Sliced bananas
Ready-to-eat cereal
Muffins and jam
Milk (children)
Coffee (No. 301) (adults)

LUNCH OR SUPPER

Split-pea soup (No. 557)
Buttered toast (No. 988)
Apple and pimiento salad on lettuce
(No. 831)
Milk (children)
Hot tea (No. 306) (adults)

DINNER

Meat scallop (No. 1610)
Baked sweet potatoes (No. 1885)
Coleslaw (No. 786)
Bread and butter
Prune pie (No. 2752)
Milk for all

TUESDAY

BREAKFAST

Cereal (children)
Apples fried in bacon drippings
(No. 39)
Whole-wheat toast
Milk (children)
Coffee (No. 301) (adults)

LUNCH OR SUPPER

Bacon (No. 1464) (adults)

Poached eggs (No. 207) (young (children)

Fried sweet potatoes (No. 1884)

Bread and butter

Sliced oranges   Milk for all

DINNER

Braised beef liver (No. 1505)

Creamed potatoes (No. 1844) or hominy (No. 101)

Buttered spiced carrots (No. 1745)

Hard rolls (No. 1046)

Butter

Creamy tapioca pudding (No. 2490)

Milk (children)

Coffee (No. 301) (adults)

WEDNESDAY

BREAKFAST

Hot cereal (No. 101) with raisins

Soft-cooked eggs (No. 202)

Toast (No. 988)

Milk (children)

Coffee (No. 301) (adults)

LUNCH OR SUPPER

Potato salad (No. 780)

Whole-wheat bread and butter

Left-over creamy tapioca pudding with canned or stewed fruit (No. 2490)

DINNER

Roast stuffed spareribs (No. 1428) (adults)

Scrambled eggs (No. 209) (young children)

Baked yellow squash (No. 1878)

Whole-wheat muffins (No. 1052) and butter, marmalade

Milk for all

THURSDAY

BREAKFAST

Oranges   Hot cereal (No. 101)

Buckwheat cakes (No. 976) with maple sirup

Milk (children)

Coffee (No. 301) (adults)

LUNCH OR SUPPER

Corned-beef hash (No. 1357) or kidney stew (No. 1496)

Relish   Rye bread and butter

Cocoa (No. 310) for all

DINNER

Macaroni and cheese (No. 2306)

Baked onions (No. 1814) in tomato sauce (No. 2035)

Bread and butter

Spiced apples (No. 82)

Milk (children)

Coffee (No. 301) or tea (No. 306)

FRIDAY

BREAKFAST

Tomato juice

Scrambled eggs (No. 209)

Raisin toast   Milk for all

Coffee (No. 301) (adults)

LUNCH OR SUPPER

Corn chowder (No. 547)

Toasted rolls

Oatmeal cookies (No. 3068)

Milk (children)

Coffee (No. 301) (adults)

DINNER

Baked creamed oysters (No. 1263) or broiled fish (No. 1101)

Broccoli (No. 1734)

Potatoes, any style

Cheese biscuits (No. 1021)

Lemon-gelatin pudding (No. 2418)

Milk (children)

Coffee (No. 301) or tea (No. 306)

SATURDAY

BREAKFAST

Stewed prunes (No. 71)
Browned mush (No. 132) and jelly
Toast (No. 988), if desired
Milk for all
Coffee (No. 301) (adults)

LUNCH OR SUPPER

Stewed tomatoes (No. 1893)
Fried potatoes (No. 1839)
Toast (No. 988)
Jam or jelly
Cocoa (No. 310) for all

DINNER

Boston baked beans (No. 1708) and
brown bread (No. 936)
Vegetable slaw (No. 787)
Citrus-fruit cup (No. 414)
Milk for all
Coffee (No. 301) (adults)

SUNDAY

BREAKFAST

Berries, melon, or other fruit in season
Cereal   Crisp bacon (No. 1464)
Cinnamon rolls (No. 1036)
Milk for all
Coffee (No. 301) (adults)

DINNER

Stewed chicken (No. 1537) with rice
(No. 107)
Green beans (No. 1712)
Hot biscuits
Ice cream with fruit sauce
Milk (children)
Coffee (No. 301) (adults)

SUPPER

Tomato and cottage cheese salad
(No. 774)
Currant jelly
Whole-wheat toast
Cocoa (No. 310) for all

A PLAN FOR A MINIMUM-COST ADEQUATE DIET
($1,000 to $2,000 annual income)

The plan for a minimum-cost adequate diet gives the cheapest combination of foods that it is desirable to use for an indefinite period. In order to meet all nutritional needs as cheaply as possible, this diet has a large quantity of cereal products and milk as its basis. Just enough of vegetables, fruits, eggs, and lean meats are used to supply vitamins, minerals, and protein not adequately furnished by bread and milk, and enough of fats and sweets are included to round out the calories.

The choice among the different kinds of foods is considerably limited by cost, and careful selection among the most nutritious of the less expensive kinds is essential. There can be very small variety in any one meal or from day to day when the cost of a well-rounded diet is kept at the minimum. The cost of this suggested diet, according to average city prices in 1941, was about $9.15 a week for a family of four, $4.85 for a family of two, and $15.50 a week for a family of seven.

A WEEK'S MENU FOR A MINIMUM-COST ADEQUATE DIET

MONDAY

BREAKFAST

Sliced oranges (adults)
Orange or tomato juice (young children)
Hot whole-wheat cereal (No. 101)
Toast (No. 988)
Marmalade
Milk (children)
Coffee (No. 301) (adults)

LUNCH OR SUPPER

Boiled beans (No. 1721)
Poached eggs (No. 207) (young children)
Bread and butter
Stewed prunes (No. 71)
Milk (children)
Coffee (No. 301) (adults)

DINNER

Meat loaf (No. 1603)
(ground beef or liver)
Scalloped potatoes (No. 1847)
Buttered beets (No. 1726) with beet tops (No. 1727)
Bread and butter
Hot gingerbread (No. 2938)
Milk (children)
Coffee (No. 301) (adults)

TUESDAY

BREAKFAST

Rolled oats (No. 101)
Tomato or orange juice (young children)
French toast (No. 991) and molasses
Milk (children)
Coffee (No. 301) (adults)

LUNCH OR SUPPER

Vegetable hash (No. 1919) with rice (No. 107)
Bread and butter
Left-over gingerbread
Tea (No. 306) (adults)
Milk (children)

DINNER

Cold meat loaf (No. 1603)
Crusty fried potatoes (No. 1839)
Creamed turnips (No. 1910)
Bread and butter
Milk (children)

WEDNESDAY

BREAKFAST

Hot whole-wheat cereal (No. 101)
Griddle cakes (No. 976) and molasses
Tomato or orange juice (young children)
Milk (children)
Coffee (No. 301) (adults)

LUNCH OR SUPPER

Creamed chipped beef (No. 1359) or corned beef (No. 1358)
Potatoes boiled in jackets (No. 1834)
Whole-wheat toast
Milk (children)

DINNER

Scrambled eggs (No. 209) or egg salad (No. 879)
Quick-cooked cabbage (No. 1736)
Bread and butter
Hot coffee cake (No. 1001)
Milk (children)
Tea (No. 306) (adults)

THURSDAY

BREAKFAST

Stewed dried peaches (No. 60)
Corn-meal mush (No. 132) and milk
Bread or toast (No. 988)
Jam or jelly
Milk (children)
Coffee (No. 301) (adults)

LUNCH OR SUPPER

Navy bean soup (No. 534)
Bread and butter
Apple and pimiento salad (No. 831)
with cooked dressing (No. 737)
Cocoa (No. 310) for all

DINNER

Tuna fish rarebit on toast (No. 2205)
Soft-cooked eggs (No. 202) (young
children)
Boiled potatoes (No. 1834)
Bread pudding with raisins
(No. 2473)
Milk (children)

FRIDAY

BREAKFAST

Rolled oats (No. 101) and milk
Tomato or orange juice (young
children)
Browned mush (No. 132) and
molasses
Milk (children)
Coffee (No. 301) (adults)

LUNCH OR SUPPER

Hashed-brown potatoes (No. 1842) or
potato soup with onions (No. 564)
Raw carrot sticks
Bread and butter
Crisp peanut cookies (No. 3070)
Milk for all
Tea (No. 306) (adults)

DINNER

Creamed fish (No. 1118) and maca-
roni (No. 2302)
Stewed tomatoes (No. 1893) and
onions (No. 1810)
Muffins   Jelly
Milk (children)
Hot tea (No. 306) (adults)

SATURDAY

BREAKFAST

Hot cereal (No. 101) and milk
Tomato or orange juice (young
children)
Poached eggs (No. 207) on toast
(No. 988)
Milk (children)
Coffee (No. 301) (adults)

LUNCH OR SUPPER

Cottage cheese
Coleslaw (No. 786) or sliced tomatoes
in season
Toast (No. 988)
Jam or jelly
Milk or cocoa (No. 310) for all

DINNER

Lima beans (No. 1717) with salt pork
Baked apples (No. 36)
Bread and butter
Milk (children)
Hot tea (No. 306) (adults)

SUNDAY

BREAKFAST

Johnnycakes (No. 1000)
Butter
Cereal with raisins and milk
Tomato or orange juice
Milk (children)
Coffee (No. 301) (adults)

DINNER

Shoulder pork chops (No. 1430)
Candied sweet potatoes (No. 1883)
Creamed spinach (No. 1871)
Bread and butter
Sliced bananas
Milk (children)
Tea (No. 306) or coffee (No. 301)
(adults)

SUPPER

Peanut butter sandwiches
(No. 3307)
Raw-carrot sticks or shredded raw
cabbage
Chocolate pudding (No. 2500)
with milk or cream
Milk (children)
Coffee (No. 301) (adults)

A PLAN FOR A RESTRICTED DIET FOR
EMERGENCY USE
($1,000 or less annual income)

This restricted-diet plan is for emergency use only, because it may not provide a sufficient surplus of protective foods (milk, eggs, tomatoes, and green vegetables) to insure good health over an indefinite period. Because of the very limited quantity of the protective foods possible within the price limits, exceedingly careful and wise choice must be made from among the cheapest, most nutritious foods. Every penny must be spent with consideration of the food value it will purchase. The variety of foods that can be chosen at this level of spending is extremely limited, but palatable meals can be served by varying the method of preparing the same kinds of food when they must be repeated often. Even with its shortcomings, this is a better diet for the money than would be obtained by choosing foods at random.

A WEEK'S MENU FOR A RESTRICTED DIET

MONDAY

BREAKFAST

Hot cereal (No. 101) with milk
Tomato juice (young children)
Toast (No. 988)
Coffee (No. 301) (adults)

LUNCH OR SUPPER

Baked (No. 1708) or boiled beans
(No. 1721) with salt pork (adults)
Eggs, any style (young children)
Bread   Milk (children)

DINNER

Onion soup (No. 553) with cheese
and toast (No. 988)
Fried potatoes (No. 1839)
Bread

TUESDAY

BREAKFAST

Pancakes (No. 976) with molasses
Bread
Tomato juice (young children)
Milk (children)
Coffee (No. 301) (adults)

LUNCH OR SUPPER

Hot cracked-wheat cereal (No. 101)
with milk

Bread   Milk (children)

DINNER

Hominy (No. 101) and sausage
(No. 1469) or braised liver and
potatoes (No. 1505)

Boiled kale (No. 1795) or stewed tomatoes (No. 1893)

Bread   Milk (children)

WEDNESDAY

BREAKFAST

Hot cracked-wheat cereal (No. 101)
with milk

Cornbread (No. 928)

Tomato juice (young children)

Coffee (No. 301) (adults)

LUNCH OR SUPPER

Potato soup (No. 564) (with onion
to season)

Stewed prunes (No. 71)

Bread and butter

DINNER

Bean purée (No. 535) with tomatoes

Bread   Milk (children)

THURSDAY

BREAKFAST

Hot cereal (No. 101) with milk

Toast (No. 988)

Tomato juice (young children)

Coffee (No. 301) (adults)

LUNCH OR SUPPER

Fried potatoes (No. 1839) and
hominy (No. 101) with onion

Bread

Eggs, any style (young children)

Milk (children)

DINNER

Whole-wheat chowder with carrots,
potatoes, and onions (No. 615)

Bread

Cupcakes (No. 3012) or doughnuts
(No. 966)

FRIDAY

BREAKFAST

Oatmeal (No. 101) with milk

Pancakes (No. 976)

Tomato juice (young children)

Coffee (No. 301) (adults)

LUNCH OR SUPPER

Cheese mush (No. 135)

Boiled potatoes (No. 1834)

Raw-carrot sticks or shredded raw
cabbage

Bread and butter

Milk (children)

DINNER

Fried eggs (No. 203)

Mashed-potato cakes (No. 1856)

Bread   Milk (children)

SATURDAY

BREAKFAST

Whole-wheat cereal (No. 101) with
milk

Toast (No. 988)

Tomato juice (young children)

Coffee (No. 301) (adults)

LUNCH OR SUPPER

Cottage cheese

Chopped raw vegetables

Bread   Milk (children)

DINNER

Hominy soup (No. 613)

Stewed prunes (No. 71)

Bread and butter

SUNDAY

BREAKFAST

Browned mush (No. 132) and sirup
Bread
Tomato juice (young children)
Cocoa (No. 310) for all

DINNER

Salmon croquettes (No. 1190)
Raw cabbage
Whole-wheat bread
Cookies
Coffee (No. 301) (adults)

SUPPER

Hot milk toast (No. 990) or bread
and milk
Applesauce (No. 34)

TWO WEEKS' MENU FOR WARM AND HOT WEATHER

MONDAY

BREAKFAST

Blueberries   Cold cereal
Milk or cream
Broiled bacon (No. 1464)
Toast (No. 988)
Marmalade
Coffee (No. 301)

LUNCH OR SUPPER

Tuna fish or salmon
Cheese biscuits (No. 1021)
Potato chips (No. 1862)
Fruit salad (No. 819) with pineapple
dressing (No. 748)
Tea (No. 306)   Milk

DINNER

Minced lamb en casserole (No. 1404)
Radishes
Steamed rice (No. 106)
String beans (No. 1712)
Romaine salad (No. 760) with tar-
ragon dressing (No. 739)
Baked custard (No. 2402) with cara-
mel sauce (No. 3109)
Coffee (No. 301)

TUESDAY

BREAKFAST

Cantaloupe   Flaked cereal
Milk or cream
Sautéed lamb kidneys (No. 1494)
Toast (No. 988)
Marmalade
Coffee (No. 301)
Cocoa (No. 310)

LUNCH OR SUPPER

Cream of tomato soup (No. 570)
String bean salad (No. 802)
Sardine sandwiches (No. 3302)
Sliced peaches
Cupcakes (No. 3012)
Tea (No. 310)   Milk

DINNER

Broiled steak (No. 1301)
French fried potatoes (No. 1836)
Baked stuffed tomatoes (No. 1898)
Endive salad (No. 762) with celery
dressing (No. 741)
Rolls or biscuits
Blueberry pudding (No. 2466) with
foamy sauce (No. 3104)
Coffee (No. 301)

WEDNESDAY

BREAKFAST

Fresh apricots   Flake cereal
Milk or cream
Poached eggs (No. 207) on toast
(No. 988)
Coffee (No. 301)
Cocoa (No. 310)

LUNCH OR SUPPER

Cheese fondue (No. 2212)
Carrot and cabbage salad (No. 790)
Mayonnaise (No. 701)
Sour milk biscuits (No. 1014)
Peach jam (No. 3682)
Milk   Iced tea (No. 307)

DINNER

Cream of watercress soup (No. 581)
Beefsteak hash (No. 1328) with
mushroom sauce (No. 2039)
Boiled potatoes (No. 1834)
Baked corn (No. 1778)
Pineapple sherbet (No. 2574)
Nut cookies (No. 3086)
Coffee (No. 301)

THURSDAY

BREAKFAST

Sliced watermelon
Omelet (No. 208)
Toast (No. 988)
Marmalade
Coffee (No. 301)
Cocoa (No. 310)

LUNCH OR SUPPER

Creamed beef (No. 1359) on toast
(No. 988)
Tomato salad (No. 759)
Sugar cookies (No. 3075)
Iced cocoa (No. 311) or milk

DINNER

Chicken chop suey (No. 1554)
Corn fritters (No. 1777)
Crisp rolls
Asparagus salad (No. 797)
Peach shortcake (No. 964)
Coffee (No. 301)

FRIDAY

BREAKFAST

Blueberries
Hominy (No. 101)
Shirred eggs (No. 211)
Bran muffins (No. 1054)
Coffee (No. 301)
Cocoa (No. 310)

LUNCH OR SUPPER

Rice croquettes (No. 112) with cheese
sauce (No. 2008)
Peas (No. 1823)
Popovers (No. 951)
Waldorf salad (No. 820)
Whipped cream dressing (No. 738)
Iced cocoa (No. 311)   Milk

DINNER

Cream of asparagus soup (No. 530)
Broiled mackerel (No. 1174)
Scalloped potatoes (No. 1847)
Swiss chard (No. 1892) or beet tops
(No. 1727)
Sliced cucumbers
Cottage pudding (No. 2480) with
lemon sauce (No. 3129)
Coffee (No. 301)

SATURDAY

BREAKFAST

Oranges   Flaked cereal
Bacon (No. 1464)
Coffee ring (No. 1004)
Coffee (No. 301)
Cocoa (No. 310)

LUNCH OR SUPPER
Italian spaghetti (No. 2328)
Heart of lettuce salad (No. 758)
Biscuits   Raspberries
Milk   Iced Tea (No. 307)

DINNER
Cream of pea soup (No. 558)
Veal cutlets (No. 1366)
Mashed potatoes (No. 1835)
Boiled carrots (No. 1745)
Chocolate layer cake (No. 2954)
Coffee (No. 301)

SUNDAY
BREAKFAST
Pears   Flaked cereal
Waffles (No. 938) and honey
Coffee (No. 301)
Cocoa (No. 310)

DINNER
Roast duck (No. 1556)
Currant jelly   Celery
Roast potatoes (No. 1838)
Brussels sprouts (No. 1735)
Lettuce salad (No. 758)
Vanilla ice cream (No. 2547) with
fresh strawberries
Coffee (No. 301)

SUPPER
Jellied vegetable salad (No. 816)
Scotch scones (No. 1029)
Olives
Sliced peaches and cream
Marble cake (No. 2961)   Milk
Cocoa (No. 310)

MONDAY
BREAKFAST
Blackberries
Ready-to-eat cereal
Poached eggs (No. 207) on toast
(No. 988)
Coffee (No. 301) Cocoa (No. 310)

LUNCH OR SUPPER
Cheese soufflé (No. 2211)
Fried tomatoes (No. 1894)
Graham muffins (No. 1056)
Strawberry jam (No. 3686)
Milk   Iced cocoa (No. 311)

DINNER
Rolled flank steak (No. 1332)
Potato puffs (No. 1859)
Cabbage (No. 1736)
Cucumber salad (No. 766)
Huckleberry pie (No. 2739)
Cheese   Coffee (No. 301)

TUESDAY
BREAKFAST
Cantaloupe
Bacon (No. 1464) and eggs (No. 203)
Toast (No. 988)
Coffee (No. 301)
Cocoa (No. 310)

LUNCH OR SUPPER
Corn chowder (No. 547)
Egg plant au gratin (No. 1788)
Bran muffins (No. 1054)
Honey
Cocoa (No. 310)   Milk

DINNER
Meat balls (No. 1604) with steamed
rice (No. 106)
String beans (No. 1712)
Baked stuffed tomatoes (No. 1898)
Watercress salad (No. 761)
Peach basket turnover (No. 2542)
Coffee (No. 301)

WEDNESDAY
BREAKFAST
Orange juice
Ready-to-eat cereal
Spanish omelet (No. 247)
Corn muffins (No. 1055)
Coffee (No. 301) Cocoa (No. 310)

LUNCH OR SUPPER

Broiled sandwich (No. 3327)
Asparagus salad (No. 797)
Mayonnaise (No. 701)
Strawberries and cream
Nut cookies (No. 3086)
Milk   Iced cocoa (No. 311)

DINNER

Boiled salmon (No. 1181) with
horseradish sauce (No. 2038)
Lyonnaise potatoes (No. 1843)
Beets (No. 1726)
Green salad (No. 760)
Bread and butter
Macaroon custard pudding
(No. 2409)
Coffee (No. 301)

THURSDAY

BREAKFAST

Plums   Hominy (No. 101)
Egg fluff (No. 266)
Toast (No. 988)   Marmalade
Coffee (No. 301)

LUNCH OR SUPPER

Creamed chicken (No. 1545) on toast
(No. 988)
Biscuits
Currant jam (No. 3684)
Iced cocoa (No. 311)
Pecan cakes (No. 3073)

DINNER

Cream of tomato soup (No. 570)
Veal loaf (No. 1371) with mushroom
sauce (No. 2039)
Scalloped potatoes (No. 1847)
Peas (No. 1823)
Biscuits
Grapefruit and pear salad (No. 828)
Coffee (No. 301)

FRIDAY

BREAKFAST

Strawberries and cream
Codfish balls (No. 1139)
Toast (No. 988)
Coffee (No. 301)
Cocoa (No. 310)

LUNCH OR SUPPER

Egg salad (No. 879)
Fruit muffins (No. 1058)
Cocoa (No. 310)
Caramel custard (No. 2404)

DINNER

Broiled bluefish (No. 1128)
Baked stuffed tomatoes (No. 1898)
French fried potatoes (No. 1836)
Cucumber salad (No. 766)
Cherry pie (No. 2722)

SATURDAY

BREAKFAST

Pears   Ready-to-eat cereal
Soft-cooked eggs (No. 202)
Muffins   Coffee (No. 301)
Cocoa (No. 310)

LUNCH OR SUPPER

Scalloped left-over fish (No. 1117)
Baking powder biscuits (No. 1012)
Tomato salad (No. 759)
Iced tea (No. 307)   Cookies

DINNER

Braised sweetbreads (No. 1515) on
toast (No. 988)
Creamed potatoes (No. 1844)
Baked summer squash (No. 1878)
Heart of lettuce salad (No. 758)
Molasses cake (No. 2967) with
whipped cream
Coffee (No. 301)

TWO WEEKS' MENU FOR COOL AND COLD WEATHER

SUNDAY

BREAKFAST

Orange juice
Sausages (No. 1469)
Baked potatoes (No. 1837)
Griddle cakes (No. 976) and maple sirup
Coffee (No. 301) Cocoa (No. 310)

DINNER

Roast beef (No. 1310) with Yorkshire pudding (No. 2103)
Roast potatoes (No. 1838)
Baked squash (No. 1878)
Olives   Currant jelly
Asparagus salad (No. 797)
Thousand Island dressing (No. 719)
Butterscotch pie (No. 2771)
Coffee (No. 301)

SUPPER

Shrimp newburg (No. 1274)
Sweet pickles
Scotch scones (No. 1029)
Canned peaches
Chocolate layer cake (No. 2954)
Tea (No. 306)

MONDAY

BREAKFAST

Baked apples (No. 36)
Hot cereal (No. 101)
Shirred eggs (No. 211)
Muffins   Coffee (No. 301)
Cocoa (No. 310)

LUNCH OR SUPPER

Cream of tomato soup (No. 570)
Macaroni and cheese (No. 2306)
Fruit salad (No. 819) with pineapple dressing (No. 748)
Tea (No. 306)   Milk

DINNER

Shepherd's pie (No. 1609)
Boiled carrots (No. 1745)
Spinach salad (No. 800) with French dressing (No. 716)
Clover leaf rolls (No. 1044)
Spanish cream (No. 2429)
Coffee (No. 301)

TUESDAY

BREAKFAST

Oranges   Oatmeal (No. 101)
Bacon (No. 1464)
Bran muffins (No. 1054)
Peach jam (No. 3682)
Coffee (No. 301)
Cocoa (No. 310)

LUNCH OR SUPPER

Corn chowder (No. 547)
Cabbage and carrot salad (No. 790)
Parker House rolls (No. 1030)
Stewed peas (No. 1823)
Peanut cookies (No. 3070)

DINNER

Baked Virginia ham (No. 1448)
Potato soufflé (No. 1861)
Creamed parsnips (No. 1914)
Chutney (No. 3705)
Rice pudding (No. 2485) with raisins
Coffee (No. 301)

WEDNESDAY

BREAKFAST

Stewed prunes (No. 71)
Hot cereal (No. 101)
Scrambled eggs (No. 209)
Toast (No. 988)   Marmalade
Coffee (No. 301)
Cocoa (No. 310)

LUNCH OR SUPPER

Left-over ham soufflé (No. 1607)
Baking powder biscuits (No. 1012)
Waldorf salad (No. 820)
Tea (No. 306)   Milk

DINNER

Lamb Chops (No. 1396)
Candied sweet potatoes (No. 1883)
Scalloped cabbage (No. 1738)
Mint jelly (No. 3736)
Pumpkin pie (No. 2753)
Cheese   Coffee (No. 301)

THURSDAY

BREAKFAST

Bananas   Ready-to-eat cereal
Griddlecakes (No. 976) and honey
Coffee (No. 301)
Cocoa (No. 310)

LUNCH OR SUPPER

Egg and spinach en casserole
(No. 261)
Grapefruit and pear salad (No. 828)
Cereal muffins (No. 1059)
Tea (No. 306)   Milk

DINNER

Braised liver (No. 1505) with bacon
(No. 1464)
Mashed potatoes (No. 1835)
Baked stuffed onions (No. 1815)
Heart of lettuce salad (No. 758) with
Russian dressing (No. 725)
Dutch apple cake (No. 2535) with
lemon sauce (No. 3129)
Coffee (No. 301)

FRIDAY

BREAKFAST

Grapes
Corn-meal mush (No. 132)
Omelet (No. 208)
Toast (No. 988)
Coffee (No. 301) Cocoa (No. 310)

LUNCH OR SUPPER

Cream of potato soup (No. 563)
Baked macédoine (No. 1922)
Stewed apricots (No. 42)
Oatmeal cookies (No. 3068)
Tea (No. 306)   Milk

DINNER

Baked stuffed haddock (No. 1157)
Potato puffs (No. 1859)
Spinach and egg (No. 1872)
Celery salad (No. 779)
Steamed chocolate pudding
(No. 2500)
Custard sauce (No. 3103)
Coffee (No. 301)

SATURDAY

BREAKFAST

Grapefruit
Hot cereal (No. 101)
Toast (No. 988)
Marmalade   Coffee (No. 301)
Cocoa (No. 310)

LUNCH OR SUPPER

Creamed left-over haddock
(No. 1118)
Baked potatoes (No. 1837)
Corn-meal muffins (No. 1055)
Peach jam (No. 3682)
Tea (No. 306)   Milk

DINNER

Baked beans (No. 1708)
Steamed brown bread (No. 936)
Pineapple and cheese salad (No. 823)
Marble cake (No. 2961)
Coffee (No. 301)

SUNDAY

BREAKFAST

Grapefruit
Fried scallops (No. 1269)
Waffles (No. 938) and sirup
Coffee (No. 301)   Cocoa

DINNER

Roast chicken (No. 1525) with chest-
nut stuffing (No. 2075)
Celery
Cranberry sauce (No. 54)
Potato puffs (No. 1859)
Cauliflower au gratin (No. 1758)
Heart of lettuce salad (No. 758)
Vanilla ice cream (No. 2547) with
chocolate sauce (No. 3107)
Coffee (No. 301)

SUPPER

Welsh rarebit (No. 2202)
Baking powder biscuits (No. 1012)
Stewed apricots (No. 42)
Hermits (No. 3045)
Cocoa (No. 310)   Milk

MONDAY

BREAKFAST

Apples   Hot cereal (No. 101)
Crisp bacon (No. 1464)
Toast (No. 988)
Coffee (No. 301)
Cocoa (No. 310)

LUNCH OR SUPPER

Egg croquettes (No. 220) with cheese
sauce (No. 2008)
Muffins   Jam
Tea (No. 306)   Milk

DINNER

Left-over chicken pot pie (No. 1541)
Cranberry sauce (No. 54)
Sweet potato croquettes (No. 1890)
Scalloped cabbage (No. 1738)
Grapefruit salad (No. 828)
Cottage pudding (No. 2480) with
chocolate sauce (No. 3107)
Coffee (No. 301)

TUESDAY

BREAKFAST

Bananas   Flaked cereal
Fried smelts (No. 1206)
Corn-meal muffins (No. 1055)
Jam or jelly
Coffee (No. 301)
Cocoa (No. 310)

LUNCH OR SUPPER

Chicken soup (No. 513)
Salmon salad (No. 858) with cooked
dressing (No. 737)
Waffles (No. 938) and maple sirup
Tea (No. 306)   Milk

DINNER

Veal cutlets (No. 1367)
Boiled potatoes (No. 1834)
Eggplant au gratin (No. 1788)
Celery
Bread and butter
Cranberry sauce (No. 54)
Lemon meringue pie (No. 2772)
Coffee (No. 301)

WEDNESDAY

BREAKFAST

Sliced oranges
Cooked cereal (No. 101)
French omelet (No. 208)
Toast (No. 988)   Jam
Coffee (No. 301)
Cocoa (No. 310)

LUNCH OR SUPPER

Baked green peppers (No. 1832),
stuffed with left-over veal and
tomatoes
Sweet potato biscuit (No. 1018)
Applesauce (No. 34)
Molasses cake (No. 2967)

DINNER

Curried lamb with rice (No. 1408)
Vegetable fritters (No. 1923)
Chutney (No. 3705)
Lettuce salad (No. 758)
Roly-poly pudding (No. 2518) with
foamy sauce (No. 3104)
Coffee (No. 301)

THURSDAY

BREAKFAST

Stewed figs (No. 55)
Ready-to-eat cereal
Bacon (No. 1464)
Toast (No. 988)
Coffee (No. 301)
Cocoa (No. 310)

LUNCH OR SUPPER

Oyster chowder (No. 588)
Whole-wheat muffins (No. 1052)
Cabbage and carrot salad (No. 790)
Doughnuts (No. 966)   Milk
Tea (No. 306)

DINNER

Beef kidney stew (No. 1496) with
dumplings (No. 954)
Candied sweet potatoes (No. 1883)
Asparagus (No. 1704) with béarnaise
sauce (No. 2032)
Cranberry sauce (No. 54)
Celery
Chocolate soufflé (No. 2453) with cus-
tard sauce (No. 3193)
Coffee (No. 301)

FRIDAY

BREAKFAST

Stewed prunes (No. 71)
Codfish balls (No. 1139)
Muffins   Coffee (No. 301)
Cocoa (No. 310)

LUNCH OR SUPPER

Cheese soufflé (No. 2211)
Biscuits   Jam
Tea (No. 306)   Milk

DINNER

Filet of sole (No. 1148) with tartar
sauce (No. 2044)
Potato soufflé (No. 1861)
Baked stuffed tomatoes (No. 1898)
Bread and butter
Romaine salad (No. 760) with horse-
radish dressing (No. 740)
Orange layer cake (No. 2957)
Coffee (No. 301)

SATURDAY

BREAKFAST

Bananas
Hot cereal (No. 101)
Scrambled eggs (No. 209) and bacon
(No. 1464)
Toast (No. 988)
Coffee (No. 301)
Cocoa (No. 310)

LUNCH OR SUPPER

Ham salad (No. 873) with cooked
dressing (No. 737)
Baking powder biscuits (No. 1012)
Cake   Tea (No. 306)
Milk

DINNER

Pork chops and sweet potatoes en
casserole (No. 1433)
Baked squash (No. 1878)
Tomato jelly salad (No. 815)
Apple fritters (No. 37) with lemon
sauce (No. 3129)
Baking powder biscuits (No. 1012)
Coffee (No. 301)

Entertainment

~~~~~~

Menus for Special Occasions

GUEST DINNERS WITH SERVANT

Canapés   Bouillon (No. 505)

Filet of sole (No. 1148) with tartar
sauce (No. 2044)

Roast capon (No. 1526)

Creamed peas (No. 1826) in timbale
cases (No. 2710)

Dinner rolls (No. 1045)

Cranberry sauce (No. 54)

Green salad (No. 760)

Orange ice (No. 2594)

Coffee (No. 301)   Mints

Mock lobster bisque (No. 597)
Crackers

Baked ham (No. 1448)

Spinach timbales (No. 1874)

Boiled potatoes (No. 1834)

Sautéed mushrooms (No. 1801)

Hard rolls (No. 1046)

Jelly   Pickles

Mixed green salad (No. 760)

Cherry tarts (No. 2819)

Coffee (No. 301)

GUEST DINNERS WITHOUT SERVANT

Fruit cup (No. 414) with crushed
candy mints

Stuffed pork chops (No. 1435)

Baked corn (No. 1778)

Roast sweet potatoes (No. 1885)

Endive salad (No. 762) with
French dressing (No. 716)

Gingerbread (No. 2938) with
whipped cream

Coffee (No. 301)

Oysters on the half-shell (No. 422)
Consommé (No. 507)

Planked steak (No. 1305)

Hearts of lettuce salad (No. 758)

Dinner rolls (No. 1045)
Celery

Fruit mousse (No. 2602)

Coffee (No. 301)

Mints

Salted nuts (No. 3831)

BRIDGE LUNCHEONS

Tomato juice cocktail (No. 417)
Cheese straws (No. 2234)
Curried chicken with rice (No. 1552)
Glazed pineapple rings (No. 67)
Artichoke hearts (No. 1701)
Chutney (No. 3705)
Ripe olives
Biscuits
Marmalade
Tomato and fig salad (No. 777)
Mayonnaise (No. 701)
Strawberry mousse (No. 2604)
Fruit sauce
Ice box cookies (No. 3067)
Coffee (No. 301)

Waldorf pear salad (No. 821)
Banana bran muffins (No. 1063)
Caramel custard (No. 2404)
Tea (No. 306) with lemon

———

Sliced baked ham (No. 1455) with
raisin sauce (No. 2055)
Baked apples (No. 36)
Boiled potatoes (No. 1834)
Green beans (No. 1712)
Carrots (No. 1745)
Gingerbread (No. 2938) with
whipped cream
Tea (No. 306)
Coffee (No. 301)

GUEST LUNCHEON WITH SERVANT

Cream of mushroom soup (No. 551)
Sweetbreads béchamel (No. 1520)
Stuffed mashed potatoes (No. 1860)
Asparagus (No. 1704) with hollandaise sauce (No. 2022)
Lettuce and cucumber salad (No. 760)
French dressing (No. 716) or mayonnaise (No. 701)
Parker House rolls (No. 1030)
Mock nesselrode pudding (No. 2427) with whipped cream
and maraschino cherries
Salted almonds (No. 3831)
Coffee (No. 301)

GUEST LUNCHEON WITHOUT SERVANT

Fruit cocktail (No. 414)
Chicken pie (No. 1539)　　　　Julienne potatoes (No. 1840)
Scotch scones (No. 1029)
Currant jelly　　　　Romaine salad (No. 760)
Meringue cake
Coffee (No. 301)　　　　Salted nuts (No. 3831)
Cookies　　　　Mints

SUPPER PARTIES

Chicken à la king (No. 1547)
Jellied tomato salad (No. 815)
Assorted sandwiches
Fruit cake (No. 2935)
Coffee (No. 301)

Salmon salad (No. 858)
Watercress sandwiches (No. 3306)
Cranberry ice (No. 2589)
Cookies
Coffee (No. 301)

Chow mein (No. 3503)
Fried noodles
Banana omelet (No. 249)
Rice croquettes (No. 112)
Kumquat (No. 3666) or apricot preserves (No. 3666)
Tea (No. 306)

BUFFET SUPPER OR LUNCHEON

Chilled pineapple juice
Shrimp and eggs (No. 1278)
Toast (No. 988)
Black currant jam (No. 3684)
Devil's food layer cake (No. 2923)
Coffee (No. 301)

BUFFET SUPPER

Tomato cups (No. 465)
Relishes   Cottage cheese
Baked ham (No. 1448) with horseradish sauce (No. 2038)
Stuffed mashed potatoes (No. 1860)
Corn pudding (No. 1776)
Lima bean salad (No. 801)
Assorted breads and crackers
Assorted cookies   Coffee (No. 301)   Tea (No. 306)

PICNIC LUNCHES

Cold ham and tongue
Potato salad (No. 780)
Pickles
Buttered rolls
Coffee (No. 301) in thermos bottle
Fruit
Cake

Cold fried chicken (No. 1533)
Watercress sandwiches (No. 3306)
Vegetable salad (No. 795)
Egg and olive sandwiches
(No. 3304)
Coffee (No. 301) or tea (No. 306)
Orange layer cake (No. 2957)

CAMPFIRE PICNICS

Broiled bacon (No. 1464) sandwiches
Scrambled eggs (No. 209)
Roasted corn (No. 1766)
Coffee (No. 301)
Fruit   Cake

Broiled steak (No. 1301)
Baked potatoes (No. 1837)
Rolls
Doughnuts (No. 966)
Coffee (No. 301)

WEDDING BREAKFAST

Fruit cup (No. 414)
Sweetbread grill (No. 1514)
French fried potatoes (No. 1836)
Parker House rolls (No. 1030)
Jelly   Ice cream
Wedding cake (No. 3011)
Coffee (No. 301)

NEW YEAR'S DINNER

Pineapple juice
Roast fresh ham (No. 1429)
Tart applesauce (No. 34)
Mashed sweet potatoes (No. 1882)
Baked onions (No. 1814)
Endive salad (No. 762) with roquefort French dressing (No. 734)
Assorted bread
Mince pie (No. 2743)
Coffee (No. 301)

WASHINGTON'S BIRTHDAY DINNER

Cream of tomato soup (No. 570)
Baked ham slice (No. 1455)
Sweet potatoes (No. 1881)
Glazed pineapple rings (No. 67)
Creamed cauliflower (No. 1756)
Ginger ale salad (No. 842)
Baking powder biscuits (No. 1012)
Peach cobbler (No. 2534)
Coffee (No. 301)

LINCOLN'S BIRTHDAY DINNER

Celery
Pork chops (No. 1435)
Corn stuffing (No. 2070)
Roast potatoes (No. 1838)
Creamed onions (No. 1813)
Asparagus salad (No. 797), built in log cabin shape
Baked apples (No. 36)
Coffee (No. 301)

VALENTINE SUPPER

Consommé (No. 507)
Heart-shaped croutons (No. 2105)
Chicken à la king (No. 1547)
Heart-shaped toast (No. 988)
Green peas (No. 1823)
Raw vegetable salad (No. 765) with carrots, radishes, etc.,
cut in shape of hearts and arrows
Rolls Cherry sherbet (No. 2577)
Heart-shaped cookies Punch

ST. PATRICK'S DAY DINNER

Grapefruit halves (No. 12) with mint
Irish stew (No. 1406)
Clover leaf rolls (No. 1044)
Cottage cheese in green pepper rings (No. 809)
Pistachio ice cream (No. 2568)
Cake Coffee (No. 301)

EASTER DINNER

Fruit cup (No. 414)
Roast leg of lamb (No. 1390) Mint sauce (No. 2046)
Creamed potatoes (No. 1844)
Green peas (No. 1823)
Watercress salad (No. 761) French dressing (No. 716)
Lemon chiffon pie (No. 2781)
Coffee (No. 301)

MOTHER'S DAY DINNER

Tomato juice
Baked hamburg (No. 1321)
Creamed potatoes (No. 1844)   Buttered green beans (No. 1712)
Lettuce salad (No. 758)
Thousand Island dressing (No. 719)
Chocolate mint ice cream (No. 2558) with chocolate sauce (No. 3107)
Coffee (No. 301)

FATHER'S DAY DINNER

Celery   Olives
Broiled steak (No. 1301)
Fried onion (No. 1811)
Shoestring potatoes (No. 1840)
Vegetable salad (No. 765)
Apple pie (No. 2714) with vanilla ice cream (No. 2547)
Coffee (No. 301)

JULY 4 PORCH SUPPER

Pickles   Olives   Radishes
Platter of sliced, cold meats
Au gratin potatoes (No. 1845)
Tomato aspic (No. 815) with cottage cheese
Strawberry shortcake (No. 2999) with whipped cream
Coffee (No. 301)

HALLOWE'EN DINNER

Pineapple juice   Canapés
Chicken fricassee (No. 1540)
Hot rolls
Asparagus tips (No. 1704) in hollandaise sauce (No. 2022)
Corn pudding (No. 1776)
Cherry jelly (No. 3664)
Pumpkin ice cream (No. 2569)
Hallowe'en cookies (No. 3083)
Coffee (No. 301)

HALLOWE'EN BUFFET SUPPERS

Shrimp wiggle (No. 1275)
Preserved apricots (No. 3605)
Artichoke heart salad (No. 812)
Hamlets (No. 1462)
Potato chips (No. 1862)
Apple compote (No. 38)
Sponge cake (No. 3003)
Coffee (No. 301)
Cider

Sausages (No. 1469) and mush-
rooms (No. 1801)
Hot biscuits
Mustard pickle (No. 3699)
Vegetable salad (No. 795)
Biscuits
Mulled cider (No. 363)
Pumpkin tarts (No. 2830)
Coffee (No. 301)

THANKSGIVING DINNER

Fruit cocktail (No. 414)
Celery   Olives
Cream of corn soup (No. 545) with crisp crackers
Roast turkey (No. 1560) with chestnut stuffing (No. 2075)
Mashed potatoes (No. 1835)
Baked stuffed onions (No. 1815)
Cranberry sauce (No. 54)
Bread and butter
Pumpkin pie (No. 2753)
Cheese   Coffee (No. 301)
Nuts   Mints

CHRISTMAS DINNER

Oysters on the half-shell (No. 422)
Stuffed celery (No. 431)   Ripe olives
Cream of mushroom soup (No. 551)
Bread sticks (No. 995)
Roast goose (No. 1559) or duck (No. 1556) with fried apples (No. 39)
Candied sweet potatoes (No. 1883)
Creamed cauliflower (No. 1756)
Dinner rolls (No. 1045)   Currant jelly
Hearts of lettuce salad (No. 758)
French dressing (No. 716) or mayonnaise (No. 701)
Mince pie (No. 2743)
French ice cream (No. 2548)
Nuts   Mints   Coffee (No. 301)
Assorted candies

CHURCH OR GRANGE SUPPERS

Potato salad (No. 3410)
Cold baked ham (No. 1448)
Cornbread (No. 3414)
Chocolate cake (No. 3446) with
whipped cream
Coffee (No. 3403)

Chicken à la king (No. 3427)
Baking powder biscuits (No. 3415)
Hearts of lettuce (No. 758) with
Russian dressing (No. 725)
Strawberry shortcake (No. 964)
Coffee (No. 3403)

Macaroni and cheese (No. 3437)
Parker House rolls (No. 1030)
Tomato gelatin salad (No. 3413)
Apple pie (No. 3442)
Coffee (No. 3403)

Pinebark stew (No. 3424)
Baked beans (No. 3431)
Asparagus salad (No. 797)
Ice cream and cake
Coffee (No. 3403)

SCHOOL BOX LUNCHES

Cream of tomato soup (No. 570)
in thermos
Egg salad sandwich (No. 3304)
Ripe banana
Cookies

Tomato sandwiches on whole-wheat
bread (No. 3306)
Baked apple (No. 36)
Cookies
Milk

Egg sandwiches on whole-wheat
bread (No. 3304)
Celery
Applesauce (No. 34)
Milk

Cottage cheese sandwich on
brown bread (No. 3303)
Jelly sandwich (No. 3307)
Apple
Milk

WORKERS' BOX LUNCHES

Vegetable soup (No. 578) in
thermos bottle
Broiled bacon (No. 1464) sandwiches
on whole-wheat bread
Doughnut (No. 966)
Apple
Milk

Minced ham sandwich on white bread
(No. 3301)
Swiss cheese sandwich on rye bread
(No. 3303)
Whole tomato
Apple dumpling (No. 958)
Coffee (No. 301) in thermos bottle

Salmon and lettuce sandwiches
(No. 3302)
Potato chips (No. 1862)
Orange
Cookies
Milk

Weight Regulation through Diet

~~~~~~

THE same essential food elements that are needed by the normal individual to sustain life are needed by the person who is reducing weight. In order to lose weight, however, instead of adding fat to the diet, it must be the fat of the body that is consumed.

As fat is difficult to consume there must be added to the diet a sufficient quantity of carbohydrate to use up the fat lost by weight reduction and also the fat that is eaten. If there is not sufficient carbohydrate added a condition of acidosis (lessened alkalinity of the blood), perhaps of a serious degree, can result. To prevent such acidosis there must be added at least one part of sugar or starch for each part of fat in the diet or of fat lost by weight reduction. The higher the percentage of carbohydrate to the fat the less likelihood there is of unpleasant symptoms. However, since carbohydrate foods also can cause fat accumulation in the body, it is necessary that the diet be as free as possible of fats so that the carbohydrates eaten can be reduced to an amount only sufficient to balance the body fat lost as weight.

The fat person requires only a low calorie diet to sustain life because the fat layer under his skin acts as an insulating layer allowing a comparatively slow heat loss. Consequently, it does not require a diet of very high caloric value to cause the further deposit of fat which is eaten, but is not needed. Therefore, a strict diet, that is, one which requires the body to use up the surplus body fat as fuel, must be very low in food value. About one-half of the average daily requirement of 2,500 calories usually is sufficient, the remaining amount to be derived from the fat lost by the body weight. *To Reduce Body Weight,* therefore, it is necessary to:

(1) Eat as little fat as possible. Remember that fat contains

twice the food value of other foods by weight; avoid pork, butter, oil dressings, rich cheese, cream, fried foods, rich soups.

(2) Limit the carbohydrate foods to the combined amounts of fat contained in your food and lost by weight reduction. Take the carbohydrate in form of "low percentage" articles, such as fresh fruits (excepting bananas, very sweet apples, pears, or cherries), and green vegetables. Avoid pies, pastries, preserves, candies, and ice cream. Limit the amount of bread and potatoes.

(3) Take ample protein in form of skimmed milk, buttermilk, very lean meat, cottage cheese.

The following gives an idea how you may eat and lose weight. The diet list is well balanced and you cannot possibly starve by following it.

BREAKFAST

Cup coffee, with milk and, if desired, one lump sugar.

Fresh fruit, preferably an orange or one-half grapefruit, or two peaches, or two slices pineapple, or one-half small cantaloupe, or one tart apple.

Two eggs, not fried, or prepared with butter or milk.

Bread or toast (4 x 4 x ½ inches) very thinly buttered. Instead of bread, one-half saucer of oatmeal or breakfast food may be substituted, with enough milk to moisten the cereal.

LUNCH

Clear soup, bouillon, or consommé, without vegetables, thickening, or bread crumbs.

Lean meat or fish or chicken (no pork) about 3 ounces—or an ordinary small portion.

One potato (2½ x 1½ inches) or a small saucer of beets, peas, beans, green corn, or sweet potato.

One slice bread (4 x 4 x ½ inches) thinly buttered.

One variety of green vegetable (a small saucerful).

Fresh fruit, and a small cup of black coffee.

DINNER

Clear soup, or six small oysters, or six small clams. Lean meat or fish or chicken (no pork) about 3 ounces.

One potato (2½ x 1½ inches) or a small saucer of beets, peas, beans, green corn, or sweet potato.

One slice bread (4 x 4 x ½ inches) thinly buttered.
One variety of green vegetable (a small saucerful).
Lettuce.
Fresh fruit and a small cup of black coffee.

This diet is well balanced and will keep the body in good condition until the proper weight is reached. When you have reduced your weight to the desired figure the diet may be slightly increased, but the increase must be done slowly and must be carefully checked by weighing yourself at least once a week. The best plan is to cut down slowly the amount of meat and to increase slowly the bread and potato allowance.

A FEW DON'TS ON DIET

(1) **Don't** drink too much water with your meals. The best time to drink water is early in the morning before breakfast, between meals, or on retiring.

(2) **Don't** reduce the amount of carbohydrate to the point that you are not properly consuming the fats in your food and the fat lost from your own body.

(3) **Don't** use drugs of any kind for reducing weight. There are some drugs that will reduce weight but their use is attended with so much danger that they should be taken only under a physician's instructions.

(4) **Don't** use alcohol.

(5) **Don't** start out too enthusiastically; will power and persistence count for more in a long race than enthusiasm.

(6) **Don't** swallow food before it is thoroughly masticated. By chewing your food for a long time you will more easily appease your appetite—it's good for the digestion and helps deceive the stomach as to the quantity of food consumed.

(7) **Don't** try the various fad cures for obesity. Some of them are dangerous.

(8) **Don't** let your appetite deceive you into believing that the diet is weakening you. It is well to remember that the treatment is usually more successful when carried out under the supervision of a skilled physician—but this is not essential except in extreme cases of obesity or when the heart is diseased or the kidneys are in bad condition.

(9) **Don't** eat between meals or after your third meal. If you get very hungry between meals, try a cup of weak tea (unsweetened) or a glass of real buttermilk (not buttermilk made of whole milk).

(10) Don't forget that the individual temperament plays an important part in the treatment. Persons who are high-strung and nervous will generally reduce faster, while the more phlegmatic, easy-going person may require a more restricted diet to produce results.

(11) Don't think that because your parents were stout you cannot reduce. Overeating and lack of exercise are much more potent causes.

(12) Don't take liberties with the diet table if you expect to get results. A strict adherence to its general principles is essential if any good is to be accomplished.

UNDERWEIGHT DIET

If your weight is below what is proper for your age and height, it is advisable to try to increase by eating more nutritious foods, such as milk and eggs, cereals with plenty of cream, plenty of bread and butter, and as much starchy food as you can digest without discomfort, such as potatoes and other vegetables.

How to Carve
and Serve

CARVING sets are available in almost any size with blades from 5½ to 9 inches long. Satisfy your taste with any of the various shapes and kinds of handles; but remember, of first importance is the quality of the steel, a blade that will take and hold a keen edge. Most carving needs can be met with the standard set and the steak set.

Standard carving set consists of a knife, fork, and steel. The knife has an 8- to 9-inch blade. There is a guard on the fork for protecting the hand when cutting toward the fork. With this set you can do all-round carving of roasts and fowl.

Steak set consists of a knife with a 6 or 7-inch blade and matching fork which may or may not have a guard. This set is used to carve all steaks and is a convenient size for small roasts and small fowl.

Roast meat slicer and carver's helper are often preferred for carving large roasts. The roast meat slicer has a long flexible blade, especially suited to cutting large thin slices. A large roast is easily steadied with the carver's helper, which has widely spread tines.

STEELING THE KNIFE

The steel is used to true the blade and keep the edge in perfect condition. Although there is a technique to handling the steel, it is easily mastered with practice.

Hold the steel firmly in the left hand, thumb on top of the handle, with the point upward and slightly away from the body. Place the heel of the blade against the far side of the top of the steel. The steel and the blade should meet at a slight angle, about 25 degrees. Bring the blade down across the steel toward the left hand with a quick swinging motion of the right wrist and forearm. The entire blade edge should pass lightly over the steel. Bring the knife into position again but with the blade against the near side of the steel. Repeat the same motion, passing the blade over the steel. Alternating from side to side, a dozen strokes will true the edge.

CARE OF THE TOOLS

To get the full cooperation of your carving set you must give it good care. Keep it separated from other cutlery so the knife will not be dulled or nicked. A good blade needs only occasional sharpening but it should always be steeled before using. Well kept tools add to a carver's confidence.

STANDING RIB ROAST

When a standing rib roast is purchased, the meat retailer will, on request, remove the short ribs and separate the backbone from the ribs. The backbone can then be removed in the kitchen after roasting. This makes the carving much easier, as only the rib bones remain. The roast is placed on the platter with the small cut surface up and the rib side to your left.

Either the standard carving set or the roast meat slicer and carver's helper can be used on this roast. With the guard up, insert the fork firmly between the two top ribs. From the far outside edge slice across the grain toward the ribs. Make the slices ⅛ to ⅜ inch thick. Release each slice by cutting close along the rib with the knife tip.

After each cut, lift the slice on the blade of the knife to the side of the platter. If the platter is not large enough, have another hot platter near to receive the slices. Make sufficient slices to serve all guests before transferring the servings to individual plates.

ROLLED RIB ROAST

The roast is placed on the platter with the larger cut surface down. Use the standard carving set or the slicer and carver's helper. With the guard up, push the fork firmly into the roast on the left side an inch or two from the top. Slice across the grain toward the fork from the far right side. Uniform slices of ⅛ to ⅜ inch thick make desirable servings.

As each slice is carved, lift it to the side of the platter or to another hot serving platter. Remove each cord only as it is approached in making slices. Sever it with the tip of the blade, loosen it with the fork and allow it to drop to platter.

Because of the difficulty of carving shoulder and rump cuts they are often boned and rolled at the market. All are sliced across the face in the same way as the rolled rib, but since many of them make a long roll you will find carving easier with the roast lying horizontally on the platter.

PORTERHOUSE STEAK

Contrary to most carving rules a steak is carved with the grain. A steak need not be cut across the grain because the meat fibers are tender and already relatively short. Use the steak set, a blade of 6 or 7 inches.

Holding the steak with the fork inserted at the left, cut close around the bone. Then lift the bone to the side of the platter where it will not interfere with carving. With the fork in position, cut across the full width of the steak. Make wedge-shaped portions, widest at the far side. Each serving will be a piece of the tenderloin and a piece of the large muscle. Serve the flank end last if additional servings are needed.

In order to protect the cutting edge of the knife, as well as the platter, a board cut to fit the center section of the steak platter is almost a necessity when carving a steak.

BLADE POT-ROAST

The blade pot-roast contains at least part of one rib and a portion of the blade bone. The long cooking process softens the tissues attached to the bones, therefore the bones can be slipped out easily before the roast is placed on the table. Either the steak set or the standard carving set may be used for carving the pot-roast.

Hold the pot-roast firmly with the fork inserted at the left and separate a section by running the knife between two muscles, then close to the bone, if the bone has not been removed. Turn the section just separated so that the grain of the meat is parallel with the platter. This enables you to cut the slices across the grain of the meat. Holding the piece with the fork, cut slices of ¼ to ⅜ inch thick. Separate the remaining sections of the roast; note the direction of the meat fibers and carve across the grain. Two or three slices, depending on size, are served to each person.

BAKED WHOLE HAM

The ham is placed on the platter with the fat or decorated side up. The shank end should always be to the carver's right. The thin side of the ham, from which the first slices are made, will be nearest or farthest from the carver, depending on whether the ham is from a right or a left side of pork.

Use a standard carving set or the slicer and carver's helper on the baked ham. Insert the fork and cut several slices parallel to the length of the ham on the nearest side. Turn the ham so that it rests on the surface just cut. Hold the ham firmly with the fork and cut a small wedge from the shank end. By removing this wedge the succeeding slices are easier to cut and to release from the bone. Keep the fork in place to steady the ham and cut thin slices down to the leg bone. Release slices by cutting along bone at right angles to slices. For more servings turn the ham back to its original position and slice at right angles to the bone.

PORK LOIN ROAST

It is much easier to carve a pork loin roast if the backbone is separated from the ribs. This is done at the market by sawing across the ribs close to the backbone. The backbone becomes loosened during roasting.

The standard carving set is preferred for carving the pork loin, although a smaller size may be used. Before the roast is brought to the table remove the backbone by cutting between it and the rib ends. The roast is placed on the platter so that the rib side faces you. This makes it easy to follow the rib bones, which are the guides for slicing. Make sure of the slant of the ribs before you carve, as all the ribs are not perpendicular to the platter.

Insert the fork firmly in the top of the roast. Cut close against both sides of each rib. You alternately make one slice with a bone and one without. Roast pork is more tempting when sliced fairly thin. In a small loin each slice may contain a rib; if the loin is large it is possible to cut two boneless slices between ribs. Two slices for each person is the usual serving.

ROAST LEG OF LAMB

The leg of lamb should be placed before the carver so that the shank bone is to his right and the thick meaty section, or cushion, is on the far side of the platter. Different roasts will not always have the same surface uppermost because of the difference in right and left legs. However, this does not affect the method of carving.

A standard carving set is a convenient size for this roast. Insert the fork firmly in the large end of the leg and carve two or three lengthwise slices from the near thin side. Turn the roast so that it rests on the surface just cut. The shank bone now points up from the platter. Insert the fork in the left of the roast. Starting at the shank end slice down to the leg bone. Parallel slices may be made until the aitch bone is reached. One-quarter to ⅜ inch is a desirable thickness. With the fork still in place, run the knife along the leg bone releasing all the slices.

LAMB CROWN ROAST

A lamb crown roast is made from the rack, or rib section, of the lamb. A pork crown is made from the rib sections of two or more loins of pork. Either cut is carved in a method similar to that of the pork loin roast.

Use a standard carving set. Move to the side of the platter any garnish in the center which may interfere with carving. Dressing can be cut and served along with the slices. Steady the roast by placing the fork firmly between the ribs. Cut down between the ribs, allowing one rib to each slice. Lift the slice on the knife blade, using the fork to steady it.

CARVING OTHER CUTS

Center cut ham slice—Divide into thirds and turn one of the sections on its side. Make slices the desired thickness across the grain. Carve other sections in the same way. The bone must be removed from the end section before slicing.

Cushion lamb shoulder—This cut is boneless and easy to carve. Cut slices about ⅜ inch thick through the meat and dressing.

Picnic shoulder—Procedure is almost identical with that of the baked ham. Take slices from the smaller meaty side; turn the shoulder to stand on this surface. Slice to bone starting at shank end. Release slices by cutting along bone.

Beef tongue—Slice off excess tissue and cartilage from the large end of the tongue. Continue making thin, even and parallel slices. This gives lengthwise slices from the small end of the tongue.

Half ham (shank end)—Remove the cushion section, turn it on the cut side, and make slices beginning at the large end. For further servings from the remaining section, separate it from the shank by cutting through the joint; remove bone, turn and slice.

Beef brisket—Place on the platter with the round side away from you. Trim off excess fat. Make slices in rotation from three sides. Slices should be thin and at a slight angle. Carving in this way makes all cuts across the grain.

POULTRY

Place bird on platter with legs pointing to carver's left. Insert carving fork into leg with one tine in drumstick and other in second joint. With knife cut around hip joint. Use fork as a lever to bend leg back. Lay leg down flat. Insert knife between tines of fork. Probe for joint and knife will pass through it. Thrust fork into bird and slice breast thinly. Slice meat from second joint and serve slices of both dark and white meat to each person. If necessary, for more portions, turn the bird on platter, carved side down, and remove other leg in same manner as first. The wings are removed same as legs.

Setting the Table

THERE are three basic requirements, all of which must be observed if a meal is to serve its twofold purpose of giving health and pleasure. First, it must be planned to contain all chemicals necessary to bodily health. Secondly, it must be tasty and, thirdly, it must be properly served in as pleasant surroundings and in as attractive a style as available equipment and general conditions make possible.

The first requisite for good service of meals is that hot dishes should be *hot* and cold dishes *cold*. The various items which make up any single dish should be chosen if possible for their color combinations. Everyone knows what one or two splashes of well-chosen brilliance does to a solid-colored gown. The same principle applies to garnishing dishes. Parsley, radishes, tomato slices, pineapple rings, mayonnaise, golden croutons, and the myriad of other popular garnishes are the corsages or bright ribbons of good meals.

The well-appointed table provides a proper backdrop for good eating. Whether served on snowy linen, gay oilcloth, or on dainty, lace doilies, through which gleams the brilliant luster of highly polished wood, lovely and efficient service adds to the value of meals.

Practically every home has the means for perfect service. It is not necessary to "keep up with the Browns" in the matter of china, silverware, and linen. Many homemakers, with ordinary essentials, supplemented by exquisite taste together with daintiness and cleanliness, far surpass the table settings of others with superior equipment.

The fundamental rules for fine table service are:

1. All utensils and dishes must be arranged with geometrical precision. A general feeling of order is the goal sought.

2. Every utensil which may be needed should be on the table to avoid delays.

3. Silverware and china should be polished as brightly as possible.

4. Cracked or chipped dishes should never be used. Besides being ugly, they are a distinct health menace.

5. Linen should be immaculate. It is far better to eat off doilies than from the most beautiful of tablecloths with a single spot.

6. Never use flowers for a centerpiece unless they are fresh.

7. Allow at least 20 inches for each place at the table.

8. Every place should be set with a plate. The knife should be at the right of the plate, with the sharp edge of the blade inward. The fork should be at the left with the tines pointing upward. The water glass should be 2 or 3 inches above the knife blade and the bread-and-butter plate should be just above the fork, with the butter knife across its plate. The napkin may be placed either on the place plate or at the left of the fork. Spoons are placed at the right of the knife and are arranged from *right to left*, in their order of use. Additional forks are placed at the left, from *left to right*, in the order of use.

CHINA

Today, among homemakers who entertain often, there are two schools of thought with reference to the use of china. One school believes that chinaware of a single pattern should be used throughout the meal. A more daring school, but one which also is in wide vogue, serves each course on china of different patterns. To the homemaker with a wide variety of lovely serving pieces the latter method often brings unexpected pleasure to her guests.

GLASSWARE

Exquisite glass is coming more and more into use as one of the most decorative departments in the service of meals. The wide range of design, the graceful curves, the brilliant gleams of diamondlike splendor, and the vast variety of color-tints now available in glassware can be used to impart almost any desired mood to the formal or informal meal.

SILVERWARE

Lovely silverware, faultlessly polished, will add to the enjoyment of your meals. Never before have such beautiful designs been available to the homemaker on a limited budget. The finest sets in the service of kings and queens are now duplicated at prices within the reach of all. In selecting silverware, dignity, as well as beauty, should be considered. It is advisable to purchase silverware that is not high style in order that lost or damaged pieces may be replaced. All other table-service articles of silver—pitchers, bowls, spoons, ladles, forks, and the various types of servers for special purposes—should also be selected for beauty, dignity, and comfort. Your silverware deserves care. It should be carefully packed away after using in order to minimize scratches as far as possible and to keep it shiny.

TABLE LINEN

Snowy-white linen damask has remained for centuries as the richest of all table coverings for meals of great splendor. It is suitable and proper for use at every meal under almost any circumstances. For many meals, including the formal, all-lace cloths, laid directly on a highly polished table, are also exquisite. For informal meals the homemaker with good taste can let her choice of table coverings run riot. She may completely cover her table with brilliant pastel shades, woven in many interesting patterns, or she may expose proudly the luster of shining wood, accented by the use of lace doilies, strips, or runners, tastefully arranged. All cloths which completely cover the table should hang over all sides 10 to 15 inches.

Napkins should always exactly match the tablecloth. Large ones, 28 x 28 inches, are proper for formal dinners but ones much smaller are proper for all other occasions.

DECORATIONS AND CENTERPIECES

Flowers in lovely vases or bowls and candles in silver holders are the most favored of table decorations and are in good taste at almost every meal. Whatever the decorations, they should be arranged with a definite plan in mind. Are they to add dignity, gaiety, or beauty? Select and arrange them accordingly. For cozy, small meals the decorations should not tower so high as to obstruct vision across the table. At large state dinners where

Breakfast Table for Two Adults and Two Children
Mugs and Porringers at Either Side for the Children

The Service for Luncheon

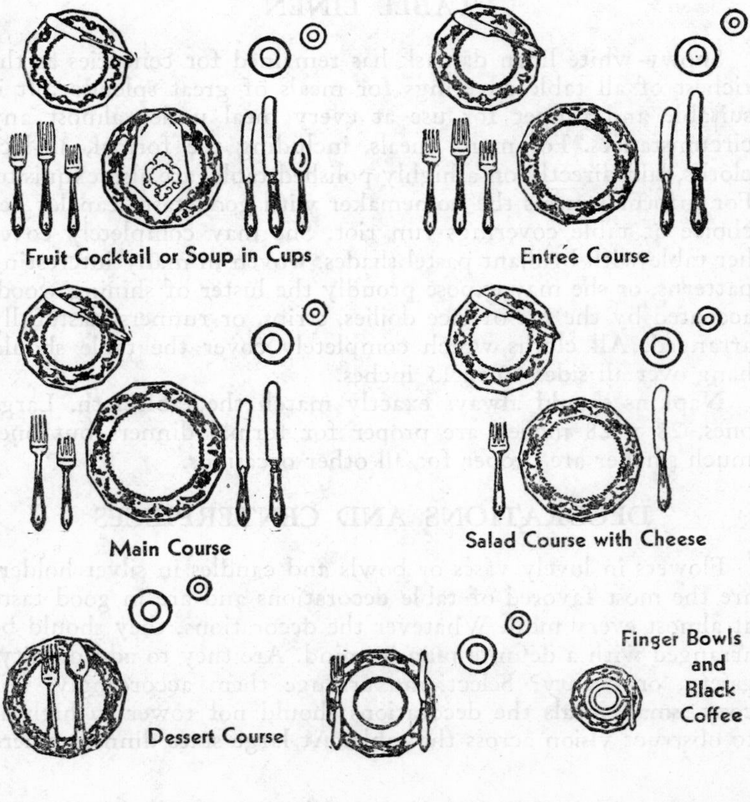

Fruit Cocktail or Soup in Cups

Entrée Course

Main Course

Salad Course with Cheese

Dessert Course

Finger Bowls and Black Coffee

The Service for Dinner

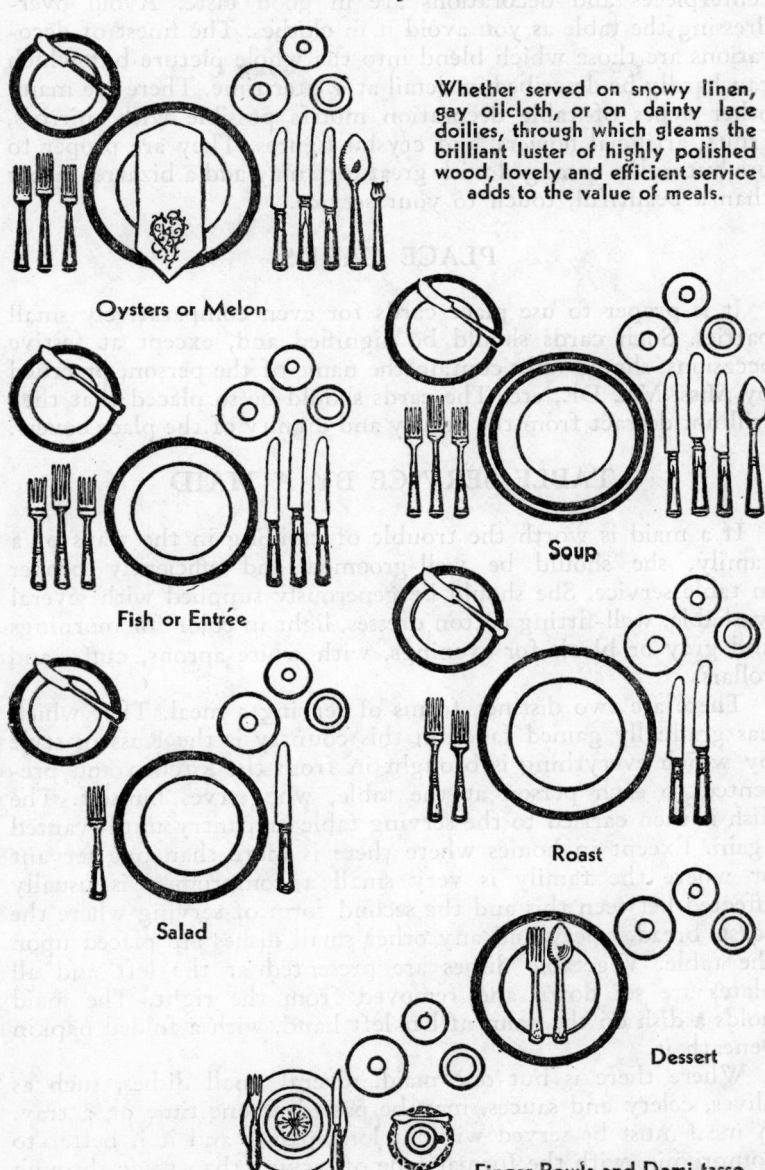

Whether served on snowy linen, gay oilcloth, or on dainty lace doilies, through which gleams the brilliant luster of highly polished wood, lovely and efficient service adds to the value of meals.

Oysters or Melon

Soup

Fish or Entrée

Roast

Salad

Dessert

Finger Bowls and Demi-tasse

it is only possible to converse with immediate neighbors, taller centerpieces and decorations are in good taste. Avoid over-dressing the table as you avoid it in clothes. The finest of decorations are those which blend into the whole picture but which can hardly be described in detail at a later time. There are many other types of table decoration motifs possible with mirrors, fruits, artificial flowers, and crystal figures. They are proper to use but unless arranged with great care may add a bizarre, rather than a beautiful, touch to your service.

PLACE CARDS

It is proper to use place cards for even comparatively small parties. Such cards should be dignified and, except at festive occasions, should only contain the name of the person, preceded by Miss, Mr., Dr., etc. The cards should be so placed that they will not detract from the beauty and dignity of the place covers.

TABLE SERVICE BY A MAID

If a maid is worth the trouble of training in the ways of a family, she should be well-groomed and efficiently proper in table service. She should be generously supplied with several washable, well-fitting cotton dresses, light in color for mornings and gray or black for evenings, with white aprons, cuffs, and collars.

There are two distinct forms of serving a meal. That which has gradually gained favor in this country is the Russian style by which everything is brought in from the kitchen and presented to each person at the table, who serves himself. The dish is then carried to the serving table or pantry until wanted again. Except in homes where there is more than one servant or where the family is very small a compromise is usually effected between this and the second form of serving where the roast, bread, celery and any other small dishes are placed upon the table. Vegetable dishes are presented at the left and all plates are set down and removed from the right. The maid holds a dish on the palm of her left hand, with a folded napkin beneath it.

Where there is but one maid, several small dishes, such as olives, celery and sauces, may be passed at one time on a tray. A meal must be served without long pauses and it is better to compromise with the formal code of serving than to go through the agony of seeing the last relative or guest supplied just as the first one finishes.

THE FORMAL LUNCHEON

Each place is laid with a service plate and with the necessary knives, forks, and spoons with the exception of the dessert fork and spoon. A small napkin, matching the table cover, is folded on the service plate. A bread-and-butter plate with a small butter knife is placed at the left, just above the forks. Butter may be on the plate but it is better to have it served by the waitress while the first course is being eaten. The water glass is on the right, 2 inches from the tip of the knife.

The first course—soup, seafood cocktail, or hors d'oeuvre—is served as soon as all are seated and is placed on the service plate. This plate remains until the main course when it is replaced by a warm plate. Except just before dessert, when the table is being crumbed, there is always a plate before each guest.

When the dessert is served, everything else is removed from the table but confections and nuts. The dessert dish, prepared in the kitchen, is served with the necessary silver. The finger bowl, sometimes decorated with small flower blossoms or rose petals, with doily underneath, is placed on the dessert plate.

THE FORMAL DINNER

A place at the dinner table is set very much as it is for luncheon except that there is no bread-and-butter plate, some extra knives or forks are seen and the napkin is a large one to match the cloth. If there are any other beverages to be served than water, the extra glasses are arranged in a semicircle to the right of the water glass.

For a dinner of more than eight it is almost necessary to have two maids and a double service, each dish of food being exactly duplicated. For a small dinner use the divided dish in which two vegetables can be offered at one time. Each dish when it is brought in is passed first to the hostess.

If there are two maids one serves one side of the table and the other the opposite side and usually they vary the ends at which they begin so that one guest is not every time left until the last. At a formal dinner things are passed but once; at a smaller affair they may be passed twice.

How to serve the meat course is entirely a matter for individual choice. If a hostess abides by the letter of the law of fashion the roast is carved in the kitchen, then skillfully put together again so that its appearance is not harmed. It is then brought in and offered to each guest who serves himself. But even with a retinue of servants some households prefer to have the carving done at table, and there is no good reason why this should not be done.

THE LARGE TEA

The formal reception as a form of entertaining has been relegated to the past along with bustles and hips and ping-pong and has been replaced by the jollier, less formal afternoon tea. This may be of any proportions from the two or three intimates gathered together over a small tea table to the large affair introducing a society bud.

For the larger functions the dining-room table is laid with a pretty cloth, the tea service is at one end, and if men are invited, a service of coffee is surely at the other. (If just women are coming, chocolate might be provided instead.) If the time is summer, the table is usually out on the veranda or on the lawn, and the tea becomes an even less formal affair.

For an indoor tea, the shades are drawn and the table is lighted with candles. There is a handsome centerpiece of flowers, and both on the table and the sideboard or buffet are small dishes of various kinds of candies and salted nuts so that a guest may help herself. Dishes of small and delicious sandwiches and cakes are either on the table within easy reach or they are passed by maids or by friends who are assisting.

The tea or coffee service is presided over by an intimate friend of the hostess who usually knows most of the guests and says something agreeable to them as they pause beside her.

Herbs and Spices

W HETHER you are going to use an eighth of a teaspoonful of spice or a full tablespoon depends largely
upon one's own individual preference. In the matter
of seasoning there is no better rule than "season to taste." Your
neighbor may find that half a teaspoon of mustard added to the
cream sauce satisfies her palate; you may prefer a full teaspoon,
and you are both entitled to your preference. Moreover, the difference in amount will have no effect upon the chemistry of
cooking. If you were to use one egg where a recipe calls for two
you might run into trouble, but not so with spices. There you
have a free hand, with your own judgment and taste as the sole
determining factor.

Recipes that have been handed down from an earlier, lustier
generation usually show this need for individual decision. They
simply read "add pepper, mustard and paprika" or "spice with
cinnamon, clove and nutmeg." Modern recipes that are built
around exact, level measurements for their uniform perfection
usually indicate a definite amount of the seasonings. These
amounts are the home economists' ideas of what will please the
average person. Rarely should they be decreased if any overtone
of seasoning is to be evident in the finished dish. In many cases
they may be doubled or tripled to give greater character to the
recipe.

Over-seasoning, however, must be guarded against as well as
under-seasoning. The result should be such that people say
"What *have* you put in to give this delicious flavor?" rather
than "Um, you've got ginger in this, haven't you?" Subtlety
should be the keynote—make the results alluringly mysterious
and never obvious or blatant.

To prolong the flavor and aroma value of spices, whole as
well as ground, they should always be kept tightly covered when
not in actual use. The minute that the nose test shows that they
have lost their strength they should be replaced with fresh spices.

TABLE OF HERBS AND SPICES

Name	Description and Source	Food and Other Uses
ALLSPICE *Pimento Officinalis*	Pea-sized fruit of a West Indian tree. Flavor resembles a blend of cinnamon, nutmeg and cloves —hence its name.	*Whole*—pickling, preparation of meats, gravies, boiling fish. *Ground*—baked goods, puddings, relishes, some fruit preserves. Used in West Indian cordial, Pimento Dram. Used powdered as moth preventive and scent for stored clothing.
ANISE *Pimpinella Anisum*	Fruit of a small plant grown in southern Europe, also Tunis, India and Chile. Is much used in flavoring licorice.	Sprinkled on coffee-cakes, sweet rolls, etc. Good for cookies and candies. Added to sweet pickles. Widely used to make the cordial Anisette. Use one teaspoon powdered, to pint of warm milk for sleep-producing nightcap. Used to flavor some cough medicines. Almost *all* licorice products are flavored with anise.
BAY LEAVES *Folia Lauris Nobilis*	Aromatic leaves of species of laurel tree. Comes from eastern Mediterranean countries.	Used in pickling, stews, spiced vinegars, soups. Combines well with fish, boiled or in chowder. Use with any tomato mixture. One bay leaf whole or broken flavors a whole tomato casserole or a can of tomato soup. A decoction of the leaves is a healing wash for some skin troubles. The famous "laurel leaves" which crowned Greek heroes were bay leaves.
CAKE SPICE	A blend of spices.	Useful in mincemeat and dark spice cakes. Added to household incense, greatly intensifies its fragrance.
CARAWAY SEED *Carum Carui*	Dried fruits of biennial plant. Is grown in northern Europe, notably Holland.	Use in rye bread, sauerkraut, new cabbage, sprinkle on French fried potatoes; on pork, liver, kidneys before cooking. Mix with cream or other soft cheeses for canapé spread and celery stuffing. Pearl with sugar for confection. Add to popcorn balls. Caraway Seed is *THE* important ingredient in the cordial Kümmel.
CARDAMOM SEED *Elettaria Cardamomum*	Small brown seeds which grow enclosed in a pod varying from ¼ to 1 inch in length. Grown in Malay Archipelago, India, Ceylon, etc.	*Whole* (in pod) used in Mixed Pickling Spices. Decorticated (pod removed)—a seed to each demi-tasse or in Turkish coffee. *Ground* flavors Danish pastry, bun breads, coffee cakes, sliced oranges. Improves the flavor of Grape Jelly. Spicing wine; disguising taste of medicines. Among Oriental people, chewed to sweeten the breath. New York bars furnish Cardamom to kill liquor breath. Grandmother used to chew them in church, like peppermints.

Name	Description and Source	Food and Other Uses
CASSIA *Cinnamomum Cassia*	Commonly called "cinnamon" because the flavors resemble each other, but from a botanically different plant. The part used as spice is the bark which is peeled off and cleaned.	*Whole* — pickling, preserving, flavoring puddings, stewed fruits. Serve with clove-stuck lemon slices in hot tea. Used in hot wine drinks. *Ground*—baked goods often in combination with allspice, nutmeg and clove. The principal mincemeat spice. Combine with mashed sweet potatoes; and with sugar for cinnamon toast. Dust on fried bananas. Used to flavor tobacco products, including snuff.
CASSIA BUDS	From Cassia tree of Malay Archipelago, China.	Used in pickling. Chewed to sweeten the breath.
CAYENNE *Capsicum Minimum*	Small red peppers ground fine. Grown mainly in Africa.	Good with meats, fish, sauces, used in moderation. A pinch helps *all*, even sweet soufflés. Use with care, in egg dishes. The real antidote for flatness. The ground product is poured into ant nests to drive ants away. Some dog-trainers shake it on rugs and other spots to discourage animals. A stimulant for the stomach.
CELERY SALT	Made by combining ground Celery Seed with salt.	Good with fish, boiled or fried eggs, potato salad, etc. Valuable in salad dressings. Particularly fine in tomato and kraut juices, in bouillon.
CELERY SEED *Apium Graveolens*	A minute seed-like fruit. Grown in many countries, including France, India, Holland and the United States.	Good with fish, potato salad, tomato dishes, tomato soup. Mix with cream cheese colored with paprika for canapés and spreads. Used in pickling and salad dressings. Superb in Irish stews. Making a HIT in hamburgers.
CHILI PEPPERS *Capsicum Frutescens*	Small, elongated pods are grown in Japan. Mexico, California, the Carolinas and Louisiana produce other kinds.	Mexican varieties are basic for chili powder; used whole in pickling. Always present in pickling spices. One or two chilis (broken) cooked with soup, stews or fish chowder much improves the quality. Seeds produce ornamental bushes of convenient size for growth indoors.
CHILI POWDER	Made from Mexican Chili Peppers and blended spices. Can be secured either mild or "hot."	For such Mexican dishes as chili con carne Good in shell fish and oyster cocktail sauces; for boiled and scrambled eggs, gravy and stew seasoning, canned corn. Chili flavored hot dogs and bologna are tops.
CINNAMON *Cinnamomum Zeylanicum*	Aromatic bark of cinnamon tree. Mostly from Ceylon.	See Cassia. Try sticks in Ski Balls; hot, sweet, strong tea with clove-stuck lemon slices plain or spiked. Use *long* sticks for tall drinks. Flavors medicines, chocolate. Makes "tea."

Name	Description and Source	Food and Other Uses
CLOVES *Eugenia Caryophyllata*	Nail-shaped flower bud of the stately clove tree. Originally found only in Netherlands East Indies. Now also grown in Madagascar and Zanzibar.	*Whole*—for pork (ham) roasts; pickling of fruits, spiced sweet sirups. *Ground*—baked goods, chocolate puddings; potato soup, bortsch, stews. Stud lemon slices with cloves for tea. Pomanders: Stud oranges with cloves. Roll in mixture of equal parts powdered orris root and cinnamon. Wrap in tissue for a few weeks; shake off powder. For fragrance and moth repellent.
CORIANDER *Coriandrum Sativum*	Dried fruit of a small plant. Resembles a white peppercorn. Grown in Southern Europe and India, but mainly in Morocco.	*Whole*—in mixed pickles. Use 1 teaspoon to apple pie with nutmeg and cinnamon; a few seeds with a bit of ginger root, a whole clove, a few mustard and allspice seeds, a bay leaf in pea soup. Add to gingerbread batter, to cookies, cakes, biscuits, poultry stuffings, mixed green salads, frankfurter rolls. *Ground*—in sausage making; to flavor buns; to rub on fresh pork; to flavor gin. Crush one seed in each demitasse. Favors hot dogs.
CUMIN (also spelled Cummin) *Cuminum Cyminum*	Small dried fruit resembling caraway seed in shape. Comes from Mediterranean islands, Morocco, and India.	An ingredient in curry and chili powders. Boil seeds briefly and pound for cooking use. Rice and saffron dishes need generous cumin flavor. Good in soups, cheese, pies, stuffed eggs. For canapés, mix chutney with snappy cheese and garnish with cumin seed. One of the oldest known spices. Used in Cornwall for ritualistic tithe-paying.
CURRY POWDER	A blend of several spices. Native to India, but increasingly popular in the United States.	Used for curry sauce, in currying meat, fish, eggs. Makes a good cream soup with chicken-stock base. (One teaspoonful to one can of tomato soup.) Try a dash in French dressing; fine in scalloped tomatoes, clam and fish chowders.
DILL SEED *Peucedanum Graveolens*	Small dark seed of dill plant. Imported from its native India.	Used for pickling. Use a pinch in sauerkraut, salads, in soups, especially bortsch and bean; in fish and meat sauces, in gravies, in spiced vinegars, green apple pie. As "tea" relieves stomach discomfort. Such "dill water" was official in the British Pharmacopaeia.
FENNEL *Foeniculum Vulgare*	Small seed-like fruit with flavor somewhat like Anise.	Used with boiled fish; also in pastries. Popular in Scandinavian cooking. Its anise-like flavor enlivens apple pie. Popular in sweet pickles. Used to flavor many candies and liqueurs, and in soap manufacturing.

Name	Description and Source	Food and Other Uses
FINES HERBES	Chop separately ½ onion, 2 scallions, 2 sprigs parsley, ½ small leek, 1 tablespoonful leaf marjoram.	Stews, soups, meat and fish stuffings. Garnishing. Excellent in omelets, butter sauce for fish, especially mackerel. Grilled meats. Mix with prepared mustard for cold cuts. Seasoning for invalid's broth.
GARLIC SALT	Fresh garlic with salt. A powerful vegetable harnessed to do no more than desired.	A vitalizing food. Tops with tomato juice and any meat or vegetable dish. Puts zest into French dressing or salads.
GINGER *Zingiber Officinale*	Root of a tuberous plant grown mainly in Jamaica, B.W.I., West Africa, India and the Orient.	*Cracked*—chutneys, conserves, pickling. Stew with dried fruits, applesauce, etc. *Ground*—cakes, especially gingerbread, Indian pudding, pumpkin pie, cookies. Many canned fruits benefit by a dash of ginger, especially canned pears. Powdered Jamaica Ginger is a remedy for stomach ills. Flavors ginger ale, ginger beer. *Tonic*—Ginger Tea.
MACE *Myristica Fragrantis*	Arillus or fleshy growth between the nutmeg shell and outer husk; orange-red in color. Flavor resembles nutmeg. From Netherlands East Indies and Grenada, B.W.I.	*Blades*—especially good with fish sauces; pickling, preserving. Excellent in stewed cherries. Add a blade to Welsh rarebit. One blade, chopped, flavors fruit jellies, gingerbread batter. Chop fine and add to biscuit dough for service with fruit salad. *Ground*—essential in fine pound cakes, contributes a golden tone and exotic flavor to all yellow cakes. One teaspoon to 1 pint whipped cream cuts oiliness, increases delicacy. Valuable in all chocolate dishes. A dash in oyster stew is good. Perfume and incense ingredient. Used to flavor medicine. Sachet bags of ground mace with linen impart fresh fragrance.
MARJORAM *Origanum Marjorana*	Herb of the mint family. Imported mostly from France and Germany and Hungary.	*Leaf*—delicious with lamb, sprinkled over while cooking. In combination with other herbs makes stews, soups, sausage products, etc. unexpectedly appetizing. Also in poultry seasonings. There is a stimulating freshness to the aroma of marjoram which may explain the preference of Queen Bess for perfumes containing it.
MIXED WHOLE SPICE	An assortment of a dozen or more whole spices, used chiefly in pickling.	Used in the pickling and preserving of meats, vegetables, relishes, etc. Also, to savor stews and gravies. A tablespoonful with boiling beets and cabbage imparts the gourmet touch.

Name	Description and Source	Food and Other Uses
MUSTARD White *Brassica Alba* Black *Brassica Nigra*⎱	Small seed, widely cultivated but imported mainly from England, Europe and the Orient. Some good varieties are now grown in the U. S. A.	Most popular U. S. Condiment. *Whole*—used to garnish salads, pickled meats, fish and hamburgers. *Dry*—(also known as Mustard Flour)—flavors meats, sauces and gravies. Used in white sauce for fish. *Prepared*—(blended with other spices and vinegar)—sandwiches and hot dogs are incomplete without it. Ham and no mustard—unthinkable. Mustard flour, mixed with water to a paste makes curative plasters. A tub of warm water + mustard = the "Mustard bath" so helpful in treating colds and fatigue. There are other medicinal uses for Mustard.
NUTMEG *Myristica* *Fragrans*	The kernel of a fruit also known by that name. Grown in Netherlands East Indies and British West Indies.	*Whole*—to be grated as needed. *Ground*—used in baked goods, sauces, puddings. Good sprinkled over certain vegetables such as cauliflower. Merges well with spinach. Topping for eggnog and custards. Sprinkle on fried bananas, on bananas and berries with cream. Use in sweet potato soufflé. The best spice flavoring for doughnuts and many alcoholic and nonalcoholic beverages. Nutmegs are sometimes carved into charms and pins.
ONION SALT	Fresh onion combined with salt and dried.	Used wherever a mild onion flavor is wanted, such as sauces, meats, gravies, chicken sandwiches. Ideal for that touch of perfection to a cup of consommé. Reaches the peak of satisfying usefulness in hamburgers. Particularly good in ground-meat dishes.
OREGANO	Known also as Mexican Sage. Grown in Mexico.	Used principally in making chili powder, for chili con carne. A good seasoning for varying the flavor of pork dishes. See marjoram. Rub a little between the hands, letting it fall on an omelet or boiled eggs. Note the resulting distinctive flavor harmony.
PAPRIKA or Sweet Pepper, usually made from *Capsicum* *Annum*	A sweet red pepper, ground after seeds and stems have been removed. Spain and Hungary are the chief producers.	Mild flavor good with shellfish, fish, salad dressings. Used lavishly as a garnish, also with sweet corn on the cob. Mix with butter to make paprika butter. For canapés mix with cream cheese and celery seed. Enriches the flavor and color of catchup and other tomato condiments; also tomato juice. An excellent source of the "resistance" Vitamin C, a necessity for good tooth health.

Name	Description and Source	Food and Other Uses
PEPPER *Piper Nigrum*	Most generally used of all spices. A small round berry picked before ripe which grows on a climbing vine. The Netherlands East Indies and India are the chief sources of supply. *White pepper* is the mature berry with the outer hull removed. Less pungent than the black.	*Whole*—(Black and White)—Used in pickling, soups and meats. *Ground*—(Black and White)—Used in meats, sauces, gravies; many vegetables are improved by a sprinkling of pepper. Important in curing "Virginia" style hams. The assertive ingredient in preparing pastrami. *Ground*—Sprinkled in floor cracks and around any area to be protected from insects, black pepper is an effective repellent. Used in soap making and carnation perfumes. Spread lavishly on rugs to be stored or in woolens, is a moth-repellent used throughout the world.
POPPY SEED *Papaver Rhoeas*	Seed of the poppy plant. Imported from Holland. About 900,000 seeds to the pound.	Topping for breads, rolls and cookies. Mix 1 pound ground seed with ½ pound sugar and 1 cup milk. Boil 10 minutes, stirring constantly. When cool spread on pastry dough, dot with butter. A valuable edible oil pressed from Poppy Seed is used for margarine, salads, etc.
POULTRY SEASONING	A mixture of herbs and spice.	For poultry, veal and pork stuffings. Fine also for fish stuffings. Much liked with paprika also in meat loaf. Mixed with fritter batter yields a neat biscuit for service with poultry.
PUMPKIN PIE SPICE	A blend of spices.	For pumpkin cookery and in spiced cookies. Varies gingerbread, cookies and breakfast buns. For that "something new" French fry slices of raw pumpkin. Dust lightly with the spice.
ROSEMARY *Rosmarinus Officinalis*	A spiky herb, rather sweetish. Grows in southern Europe.	Sprinkle on beef before roasting. Combine with basil and marjoram for *herb garni* especially in turtle soup. Use in lamb dishes, in soups and stews. Flavors fish and meat stocks. Combines well with gin drinks. Europeans stuff pillows with rosemary often mixed with pine needles "for remembrance." Said to insure faithfulness. A pint of boiling water poured on 1 ounce of rosemary makes a fine hair wash.
SAGE *Salvia Officinalis*	Leaf of a low-growing herb. Choicest comes from Yugoslavia. Also Greece	Used in meat stuffings, head cheese, various pork products, particularly sausage. Steeped in hot water makes a medicinal tea to abate colds. Sage + American Cheese = Sage Cheese.

Name	Description and Source	Food and Other Uses
SAFFRON *Crocus Sativus*	Tiny stigma of a crocus-like flower. Takes 225,000 to make a pound. Grown in Mediterranean areas. Three stigmata to each flower. Over 70,000 blossoms needed per pound.	Used principally for the pleasant yellow color it imparts. Saffron rolls and buns are a delight to Latin palates. Most highly esteemed in "Arroz Con Pollo" the famous Chicken-Rice dish of Spain. Was strewn for its perfume in the Roman baths and before Nero on his entrances to the city.
SAUSAGE SEASONING	A blend of herbs and spices.	Used in sausage making and is good in meat loaf, veal, birds, and similar dishes. Mixed with fritter batter to make an herb bun to serve with fresh ham and other roasted pork.
SAVORY *Satureia Hortensis*	Herb of the mint family. Grown in many climates. Imported from Germany.	Often combined with other herbs to flavor meats. Use in scrambled eggs, in salads, in soups. Used like rosemary to stuff pillows.
SESAME SEED *Sesamum Indicum*	Small honey-colored seed, grown in Turkey, India and the Orient. Not much left for import after native consumption is taken care of.	Baked on rolls, breads and buns a rich toasted nut flavor is developed. The source of sesame oil. Principal ingredient in Oriental candy known as halvah.
SWEET BASIL *Ocymum Basilicum*	Annual plant cultivated in Western Europe. Grows elsewhere. Leaves and tender stems, cleaned and dried.	Famed as seasoning for tomato paste and turtle soups. Also use in tomato dishes, cooked peas, squash and string beans. Venerated by the Hindus; planted outside their temples and homes to insure happiness.
THYME *Thymus Vulgaris*	Garden herb, grown in temperate climates. Much imported from France. Leaves and tender stems, cleaned and dried.	Used in stews, soups, and stuffings for poultry. Often used with other herbs. Outstandingly good in clam and fish chowders. Yields an element called thymol, important in the compounding of cough remedies.
TURMERIC *Curcuma Longa*	A root of the ginger family. Has a rich appetizing odor, and is bright yellow in color. Grown in India.	Blending to a most appetizing flavor turmeric and mustard have long travelled together. These two spices in varying proportions are ideal for pickles and almost every meat and egg dish. Turmeric paper made by dipping paper into a turmeric solution for alkalinity tests. Used dissolved in water for tinting unvarnished floors in the tropics.

Canned Foods

SEASONINGS and sweetening are used in cooking, likewise in canning. The canner usually seasons lightly so that the housewife may add other seasoning to suit her individual taste. Various canned foods, of course, are made on a recipe basis that gives the food a distinctive flavor and seasoning.

Most vegetables are canned in water, to which salt, or salt and sugar have been added. Others, like corn, may be canned in vacuum without the addition of water or other liquid. Tomatoes are canned without the addition of water and usually without the addition of salt. Pumpkin is canned without the addition of water, and without salt. Sweet potatoes are canned both with and without sirup. Corn and peas are generally seasoned with salt and sugar. Vegetables for special diets are canned without seasoning.

Fruits are sometimes packed unsweetened, but most fruits are packed in sirup, and the sweetness of the sirup may be shown on the label by the terms, "Medium," "Heavy," and "Extra Heavy."

Heavy sirup is the usual amount of sweetness. In household terms it is sufficient for ordinary table service and may vary from 30 per cent to 55 per cent, depending upon the natural sweetness and acidity of the fruits. Some fruits require the addition of more sugar than others to bring them to the desired sweetness.

SAFETY

From the standpoint of safety, food may be left in the open can if the same care is given to it that would be given to any cooked food, that is, if it is kept covered and in a cool place, preferably in a refrigerator. The Bureau of Home Economics of the U. S. Department of Agriculture, in a news release entitled, "Oh Sure! You Can Keep It in the Can," said, "it is just as safe to keep canned food in the can it comes in—if the can is cool and covered—as it is to empty the food into another container."

Can sizes used for various products naturally differ with the character of the product. The canner also tries to supply sizes meeting the various consumer requirements. In recent years the industry has carried on a successful program to simplify and standardize the can sizes in use. Those used in greatest number, and their approximate capacity in terms of cupfuls are as follows:

Can name	Contents in cups
No. 1 (Picnic)	1¼
No. 300	1¾
No. 1 Tall	2
No. 303	2
No. 2	2½
No. 2½	3½
No. 10	13

THE LABEL AS A GUIDE

The label is the immediate guide for the canned food shopper. Labels have been, and are being, improved so as to furnish you with definite, practical information that enables you to find the kind of product in the style of pack and size of container best suited to your particular purpose.

The net contents of the can must always be stated on the label in terms of weight or volume.

Variety information is given because each variety of a food has characteristics—flavor, texture, color, etc.—which set it off from others and which adapt it to your tastes and preferences or the use you intend to make of it. Clingstone and freestone peaches, white and yellow corn, sweet and sour cherries, sweet and early June peas, Bartlett and Kiefer pears, red and pink salmon,—these are examples of how variety information is helpful.

Style of pack means much to the shopper who knows just how she wants to use the food. For example, are the peaches canned whole, in halves or in slices; are the apricots peeled or unpeeled; are the pears whole unpeeled or peeled halves; is the asparagus in long spears or in salad tips; are the green beans whole, cut, or in asparagus style; are the beets whole, cut, diced, sliced or shoestring; is the corn cream or whole kernel? Label answers to these questions help you make your choice.

Size of pieces in the can may also be indicated by terms such as "Tiny," "Small," "Medium," or "Large," for green lima beans, or peas, or mushrooms, or by "Mixed sizes" where the product is not graded for size.

Color may be shown by such terms as "White," "Green," "Green tipped," or "Green tipped and white," such as used for asparagus; "Green" or "Green and white" for lima beans; "White" or "Golden" for corn.

Seasonings may be indciated by such terms as "Salt added," "No salt added," "Sugar added," or "No sugar added."

WISE BUYING

Read the label to make sure that the food purchased meets the need for which it is intended, because there is a style of pack to fit every need, and usually food to be used in a casserole or mixed salad is not the same style of pack as would be used as a garnish or if it were to be served uncombined.

Buy the can size that fits the number to be served, or buy in large cans and keep the unused portion in the refrigerator. The method of buying that will be most satisfactory will depend on the system of housekeeping.

It is economical to buy by the case or dozen cans, if storage space permits.

Whenever the supply on hand is used, replace it before being inconvenienced by not having it replenished.

Keep advised on new products by observing the stocks on the shelves and by talking with the grocer in order to insure variety in meal planning.

Freezing

LARGE numbers of modern homemakers can remember when they lived with iceboxes in their kitchens instead of refrigerators. Many, many more can remember the days before they lived with the miracle of frozen foods. Freezers have become an indispensable part of today's kitchen and the wise housekeeper uses them to maximum efficiency. They solve the problem of leftovers, of long-time food storage, of having available out-of-season foods at all times of the year, of having to shop and cook frequently when one is short of time, and they let the housekeeper buy when various foods are priced lowest during the year.

Proper use of a freezer starts with its purchase, whether as an individual unit or part of a refrigerator. Obviously, the capacity (measured in cubic feet) you choose depends on your family size. It is wise to figure approximately 3 cubic feet per family member. If heavy use is to be made of the freezer, a large allowance per person should be made.

You may buy a freezer-refrigerator combination, or a separate freezer unit, depending on your cubic-foot requirements and the floor space available for the unit. If you buy a separate freezer, you will have a choice of upright or chest models. Each has its advantages. The chest models are usually available in larger capacities and are more economical to run. Their principal disadvantages are that they require more floor space than the upright models and are harder to clean and to keep in order. Upright freezers use less floor space and are not only relatively easy to clean but lend themselves to more orderly maintenance. That is, food is easier to store in such a way that the housekeeper uses "old" food first and puts new food last.

Nowadays, freezers are also available in frost-free as well as regular models. Frost-free models do not have to be defrosted, but they should be emptied and washed out at least twice a year. Non-frost-free models should be defrosted and cleaned on a regular schedule, according to manufacturer's instructions. Frost-free models are more costly than those which ice up.

When purchasing any type of freezer, be clear about all details, such as emergency use in power failures, warranties on parts and food spoilage, service contracts, etc.

Once you have bought your freezer, you must consider the problem of proper working materials to assure maximum satisfaction from this most useful appliance. An adequate supply of various wrapping materials and containers, together with marking pencils, labels, and tape, is essential. The principal criteria for packaging materials are the ability to keep air and moisture out, and to retain moisture within the food being stored. These fall into several categories:

Freezer-weight aluminum foil which shapes tightly to the food and prevents the formation of air pockets;

Transparent cellophane-type wrapping paper which also shapes itself closely to the food, aiding easy identification of the food;

Plastic (polyethylene) bags which are flexible and transparent;

Freezer paper which must be sealed with freezer tape;

Various containers made of wax or plastic-lined materials, of aluminum, of plastic materials, or of glass. These are available in many sizes and shapes, and should be selected according to the form of the food being stored; that is, whether solid, liquid, combination of solid and liquid, etc.

All packages should be labeled and dated, and stored promptly. Labeling and dating are aids in assuring that you use "old" foods first, and that you do not store food too long. The following is a guide to storage times. Keeping foods longer than these recommended periods will result in loss of flavor.

Beef (chopped)	up to 4 months
Cooked and baked foods	up to 6 months
Frankfurters	up to 3 months
Fruits and vegetables	up to 12 months
Ham	up to 2 months
Ice cream	up to 2 months
Meat (beef, lamb, veal)	up to 12 months
Pork (fresh), fowl, fish	up to 4 months
Soups	up to 6 months

Once food has been frozen, a general rule to follow is not to refreeze it after it has been thawed. If it still retains ice crystals and is only partially thawed, it can be refrozen. Raw food which is thawed and then cooked can be refrozen, in its cooked state.

Be sure to freeze in quantities you will use at one time, and do not freeze too much at one time or your freezer will not function properly.

FREEZING VEGETABLES

General Rules

1. Use garden-fresh vegetables which are young and tender.
2. Before freezing, wash in cold water and cut into a uniform size which lends itself to easy packaging and, later, serving.
3. Blanch before freezing, according to time noted for vegetable, in boiling water, cool and chill immediately after removing from boiling water. Use a gallon of water to 1 pound of vegetables.
4. Drain well and package.

Cooking frozen vegetables takes about half as long as cooking them fresh. All except corn-on-the-cob, which should be thawed first, can easily be cooked by placing in a small amount of boiling, salted water and covering until just tender.

FREEZING FRUITS

General rules

1. Use only sound, fully ripe fruits.
2. Freeze as soon as possible after picking.
3. Wash all fruits thoroughly.
4. Decide on the use you will have for the fruit—whole, sliced, puréed, and whether you will pack whole or in syrup, so that you set up your preparations accordingly.
5. Use any moisture-tight, rigid container.
6. Avoid using metallic implements, like iron and tin. They can give a metallic flavor. Try to use aluminum or glassware.
7. Since many fruits darken rapidly after peeling (a prerequisite for all fruit freezing), work with small quantities at a time to prevent spoilage.
8. Although most fruits should be packed in sugar or sugar syrup, there are some, like apples, plums, rhubarb, cranberries, gooseberries, strawberries, and currants, which can be frozen without any type of sugar.
9. Ascorbic acid can be added to fruit to prevent darkening, in a quantity of ½ teaspoon of ascorbic acid to each quart of syrup or each cup of dry sugar. It should be added just prior to final packing.

Vegetable	Preparation	Blanching Time	Chilling Time	Suggested Wrapping
asparagus	break tough ends, wash, sort; cut or leave as spears	2 min.	2 min.	polyethylene* bags
broccoli	wash, trim, cut lengthwise	2 min.	2 min.	polyethylene bags
Brussels sprouts	trim, wash, sort according to size	3 min.	3 min.	polyethylene bags
corn-on-the-cob	husk, wash, sort	2 min.	3 min.	polyethylene bags
whole kernel corn	husk, wash	2 min.	3 min.; then cut kernels off cob	polyethylene bags
green beans, wax beans	remove ends, cut into 2″ pieces or French cut	2 min.	2 min.	polyethylene bags
carrots	wash, dice, slice or cut Julienne	2 min.	2 min.	polyethylene bags
lima beans	shell, wash, sort	2 min.	2 min.	polyethylene bags
green peppers	wash, remove stem and seeds; freeze whole or halve or slice	1 min.	1 min.	polyethylene bags
peas	shell, wash	1 min.	1 min.	polyethylene bags
spinach	wash, remove stems	1 min.	1 min.; chop if desired, after chilling	polyethylene bags
squash	wash, slice	2 min.	2 min.	polyethylene bags

* Polyethylene bags may be placed in waxed containers which lends themselves to easy labeling and more convenient freezer storage than irregularly shaped bags.

10. In using a dry sugar pack, mix sugar and fruit gently in quantities of ½ to ⅓ cup of sugar per quart of fruit, depending on sweetness desired and use of fruit (for pies, cooking, etc.).

11. In using a sugar-syrup pack, there are four weights of syrup to make, according to the type of fruit and quantity of syrup desired.

Light syrup—50 percent solution (1 part sugar to two parts water).

Medium syrup—75 percent solution (1½ parts sugar to two parts water).

Heavy syrup—100 percent solution (2 parts sugar to two parts water).

Extra-heavy syrup—125 percent solution (3 parts sugar to two parts water).

Fruit	Preparation	Type of Pack
apples	wash, peel, core	sugar pack or medium syrup
apricots	sort, wash, halve, pit	sugar pack or medium syrup
blackberries, boysenberries	sort, remove stems and leaves, wash	sugar pack or medium or heavy syrup
blueberries, huckleberries	sort and wash	medium syrup
cherries (sour)	stem, sort, wash, pit	sugar pack or extra-heavy syrup
cherries (sweet)	stem, sort, wash, pit	sugar pack or medium syrup
cranberries	stem, sort, wash	medium syrup
melons	seed, peel, slice, cube or ball	light syrup
peaches	wash, pit, peel	sugar pack or medium syrup
plums	whole or halves	no sugar or syrup
rhubarb	wash, trim, cut, heat in boiling water 1 min., cool	unsweetened or medium syrup
strawberries	sort, wash, hull	unsweetened, sugar pack or medium syrup

When using frozen fruits, thaw only right before use and serve ice cold.

Cooked fruits, such as applesauce, stewed rhubarb, and other puréed fruits, can be cooked as you usually do and frozen in the same type of container you would use for raw fruits. No additional sugar or syrup need be added.

FREEZING MEATS AND POULTRY

General rules

1. Select, fresh, good-quality meats and fowl.
2. Package in quantities only large enough for a meal at a time so that you do not defrost more than you need for one meal.
3. Wrap tightly.
4. You may or may not thaw (in refrigerator or at room

temperature) before cooking meat. Pork *must* be completely thawed before cooking. If you do not thaw before cooking, you must allow more cooking time, but this is sometimes necessary if a meal is put together late in the day. Ground meat must also be thawed in advance, unless you have been foresighted enough to shape it into patties and season it before freezing.

5. Do not stuff poultry before freezing.

FREEZING FISH AND SEA FOOD

General rules

1. Clean and cut fish into portions of desired size and wrap in freezer paper as for meat.

2. All seafood except crabs and lobsters may be simply washed and frozen raw, either shelled or unshelled, in freezer containers.

3. Crabs and lobsters should be cooked as usual, the meat removed from the shells and packed in containers for freezing.

4. When using, thaw only enough to separate into individual pieces. Then, cook promptly as usual or serve raw.

FREEZING COOKED AND BAKED FOODS

General rules

1. Packaging is important. Plan to use containers in which food can be reheated whenever possible.

2. Package in moisture-proof containers.

3. Chill foods before freezing.

4. Do not keep over-long. Try to use up your cooked foods within 2-3 months after preparation.

5. Do not refreeze cooked foods.

The mealtime variety a homemaker can achieve with frozen precooked foods is limited only by her imagination and taste. Here are only a few suggestions of the kinds of cooked and baked foods that your freezer can hold.

Soups—All clear soups freeze well and are easily thawed over low heat to serving temperature. Creamed soups may either be thawed in a double boiler or, preferably, the cream or milk should be added after thawing. Potatoes should not be frozen in soup. They should be cooked in the soup afterward.

Creamed dishes should be undercooked and cooked rapidly, then frozen. They should not contain hard-cooked egg whites, which become leathery on defrosting. Reheat in a double boiler.

Fish should be prepared and cooked as usual, and frozen in

casseroles or regular freezer containers. Casseroles should be defrosted in the oven and other dishes heated in a double boiler.

Meats and poultry should be prepared as usual and be undercooked rather than too well done. They should be chilled and packaged and frozen promptly. If they are casserole dishes, they can be prepared and oven-defrosted in the casserole. Otherwise they should be heated in a double boiler. Roasts can be left whole, packaged, and sliced before serving, after being defrosted in the refrigerator or at room temperature and heated to taste.

Potatoes can be frozen in several ways:

1. French fried—fry and drain as usual, package and freeze. Defrost in a 400° oven for 5-8 minutes.

2. Baked—stuff, prepare as usual but do not brown. Freeze in freezer foil. When using, thaw, uncover, and place in shallow baking dish and heat at 325° in the oven for 25 minutes.

3. Candied sweet potatoes—prepare as usual, pack in freezer container. To use, it is not necessary to thaw, but heat either in a double boiler or in a covered baking dish in a 350° oven.

Sandwiches and canapes are easily frozen by preparing as usual and wrapping tightly. To use, defrost at room temperature for 2 to 3 hours. Do not freeze lettuce, celery, tomatoes, cucumbers, jelly, mayonnaise, hard-boiled egg whites, water cress.

Breads should be baked as usual, cooled, wrapped, and sealed. They should be defrosted in the refrigerator or at room temperature. Rolls and muffins should be thawed in slow ovens (250°).

Cakes should be baked as usual, cooled, wrapped, and sealed. They may be defrosted at room temperature or in a slow oven (300°). If they are iced, they should be frozen before wrapping or the wrapping will spoil the icing. Iced cakes cannot be defrosted in the oven.

Cookies can be frozen baked or unbaked. You can bake as usual, cool, pack with freezer paper between layers in the container and thaw at room temperature when using. Or you can pack the dough in freezer containers, seal, and when using, defrost at room temperature until the dough is soft enough to roll and cut for cookies, then bake as usual.

Pies and pastries are generally better frozen unbaked. They should be prepared as usual, not baked, and frozen at once. Then they can be baked as they are defrosted, in a very hot oven (400°-450°) for 20 minutes and a moderate oven (325°-310°) until done, generally for another 25 minutes. If you bake before freezing, you can thaw in the refrigerator or at room temperature or heat in a 375° oven.

Outdoor Cooking

N OT too many years ago, cooking outdoors was almost exclusively reserved for sportsmen and campers. But this has changed as Americans have discovered the fun and pleasure in outdoor meals.

As outdoor cooking has become more popular, so have the equipment diversified and the menu-planning expanded. It would be impossible to describe all the equipment and utensils available, and obviously, the range of what you can cook outdoors is limited only by your own imagination.

EQUIPMENT

The size of your basic investment in cooking equipment should be determined by the use you plan to make of it. Elaborate cooking obviously demands more elaborate equipment than one-dish gear, and you must judge your needs as to size of meals planned, frequency of use, etc., before making an investment. Some types of outdoor cooking equipment available are:

(1) Bucket broilers which are inexpensive and lightweight, making them very suitable for carrying along to picnics.

(2) Oriental charcoal broilers are more expensive but are also lightweight. The grills are adjustable and the heat can be regulated in them.

(3) Vertical broilers hold the meat in a center grill with the hot coals on either side, so that the meat is cooked on both sides simultaneously while the fat drips off.

(4) Round charcoal grills in one form or another rank among the most popular types. They vary in price from the simple, inexpensive types with adjustable grills to more complex ones with shields, turntable adapters, hoods, etc.

(5) Rectangular "smoking" grills operate on the same principle as the ordinary charcoal grill but have hoods which close

to form an oven and, with the fire deflected from the grill by a plate, the food cooks in a smoking oven.

(6) Various circular and rectangular grills have further refinements of electric rotisseries, with single or multiple spits and other conveniences (places for towels and mitts, for cooking tools, for charcoal, etc.).

In addition, the outdoor cook should be equipped with such items as a

Carving board	Carving set	Protective mitts
Cutting board	Barbecue fork	Barbecue turner
Fire tongs	Barbecue spoon	

Don't forget such other essentials as an automatic coffee maker to plug in near your grill, an ice buffet to keep cubes handy for cold drinks, and a bottle opener.

BUILDING A CHARCOAL FIRE

Store your charcoal briquets in a dry place. Start your fire about 30 minutes before cooking time so that it is ready to use when you need it. The most common way to start a fire is to pour liquid starter over a pyramid of briquets, let stand for 30 seconds, and then ignite them. For even grilling, spread the coals evenly over the entire firebox.

A fast-start method is to soak a few briquets in liquid starter for 10-15 minutes in a large juice or two-pound coffee can, remove the briquets with tongs, heap them in a mound together with a few untreated briquets, and light up. This method will halve the time it takes the coals to become ashey and right for cooking. Caution: Keep the can of liquid starter covered and well away from the flame.

If you need more coal, add it around the edge of your hot coals so that you do not cut down on your heat.

BARBECUED MEATS

(1) Remove from refrigerator and have at room temperature before cooking.

(2) Use a meat thermometer for roasts and other large cuts.

(3) Preseason with garlic, seasoned salt, or any other chosen flavoring at least an hour before cooking to get maximum seasoning flavor.

(4) Trim off as much fat as possible to avoid flame flare-ups.

Chicken Ole'

Ingredients

1 tbsp. vegetable oil
1 lb. boneless, skinless
  chicken breast, cut
  into strips
1 can (15 oz.) tomato sauce
1 can (16 oz.) whole kernel
  corn, drained
1 can (4 oz.) chopped
  green chilies
1 1/2 tsp. **Chili Powder**
1 tsp. **Onion Powder**
  Tortilla chips
  Shredded Cheddar
  cheese

Directions

1. Heat oil in large skillet over medium-high heat. Add chicken and cook 5 minutes, stirring frequently.
2. Add tomato sauce, corn, chilies, Chili Powder, and Onion Powder. Bring to a boil. Reduce heat to medium-low and cook 10 minutes, stirring occasionally.
3. To serve, spoon over tortilla chips and top with cheese.
Makes 4 servings.

Developed by the
Kitchens of McCormick/Schilling

9772211

McCORMICK Schilling

Chicken Ole'

Chicken Ole'

Ingredients

1 tbsp. vegetable oil
1 lb. boneless, skinless chicken breast, cut into strips
1 can (15 oz.) tomato sauce
1 can (16 oz.) whole kernel corn, drained
1 can (4 oz.) chopped green chilies
1 1/2 tsp. **Chili Powder**
1 tsp. **Onion Powder**
Tortilla chips
Shredded Cheddar cheese

Developed by the
Kitchens of McCormick/Schilling

Directions

1. Heat oil in large skillet over medium-high heat. Add chicken and cook 5 minutes, stirring frequently.
2. Add tomato sauce, corn, chilies, Chili Powder, and Onion Powder. Bring to a boil. Reduce heat to medium-low and cook 10 minutes, stirring occasionally.
3. To serve, spoon over tortilla chips and top with cheese.
   Makes 4 servings.

Chicken Ole'

(4001)   **STEAK**

Use 2-inch-thick slices of sirloin, club, T-bone or chuck steak. Broil to brown color when coals are right. Turn over, salt and pepper browned side to taste, and continue to cook until done to your satisfaction.

(4002)   Before broiling steak, preseason with garlic or seasoned salt or brush with butter and cook as in (4001).

(4003)   **MARINATED STEAK**

6 pounds 1-inch round   1 cup salad oil
    shoulder steak   1 cup wine vinegar
12 cloves peeled garlic   ¼ cup Worcestershire sauce
    salt and pepper

Insert 4 cloves of garlic in each piece of steak and salt and pepper generously. To make marinade, combine salad oil, vinegar and sauce. Pour over steaks and marinate overnight in refrigerator. Grill over hot coals about 15 minutes on each side or until done to taste, basting with marinade.

(4004)   **CHUCK STEAK**

4 pounds ½-inch chuck steak   ½ teaspoon pepper
2 medium onions   1 clove garlic, minced
    finely chopped   ½ teaspoon dried basil leaves
½ cup olive oil   1 can (1 lb) tomatoes,
½ teaspoon salt   undrained

Combine all ingredients except steak. Marinate steak in mixture 4-5 hours before broiling. Grill on hot coals to taste, basting frequently with marinade.

HAMBURGERS

Note: If you have no skillet or broiler basket, spread aluminum foil over the grill.

(4005)   Prepare in your normal way, and grill over coals to desired rareness.

(4006)   HAMBURGER SPECIALS

2 pounds ground chuck	Pepper to taste
½ cup minced onions	Soft butter
2 teaspoons seasoned salt	

Combine all ingredients except butter, shape into patties, spread with butter and grill to taste. Makes 8 servings.

(4007)   HAMBURGERS DELUXE

2 pounds chopped chuck	Pepper to taste
°or sirloin	1 clove minced garlic
2 eggs	2 green onions, sliced
2 teaspoons salt	1 cup fresh bread crumbs

Combine all ingredients except onions and form into patties. Grill to taste and serve on warm hamburger rolls with sliced onion topping. Makes 12 servings.

(4008)   SPICY BEEFBURGERS

3 pounds ground beef	1 tablespoon prepared mustard
4 tablespoons catsup	1 cup chopped onion
3 tablespoons salt	½ cup fat

Sauté the onions in the fat until just brown. Combined browned onions with other ingredients and shape into patties of desired thickness and broil or fry. You can vary the flavor of this dish by using various other sauces with the recipe.

(4009)   CHEESEBURGERS

You may use any of the above hamburger recipes (4005, 4006, 4007, 4008) to make a delicious cheeseburger, simply by topping the burgers with slices of cheese the last few minutes they are on the grill. Most people prefer sharp, tangy cheese, and you can vary the taste of your cheeseburgers by selecting different types of cheese for your topping.

(4010)   BARBECUED FRANKFURTERS

1 dozen frankfurters	½ teaspoon seasoned salt
1 cup seasoned tomato sauce	1 teaspoon Worcestershire
1 tablespoon lemon juice	sauce

Combine all ingredients except frankfurters in a sauce pan and bring to a boil. Add the frankfurters and simmer until thoroughly cooked (about 10 minutes). Serve with sauce.

Alternately, you can grill the frankfurters separately and baste them with the sauce frequently, serving them with any sauce remaining. These frankfurters can be eaten on or off rolls. Makes 6 servings.

(4011)   CHEESEFURTERS

Split franks and insert a strip of cheese down the length of each. Anchor with toothpicks and wrap in aluminum foil. Grill and serve in the foil. Cooking time, about 5 minutes on each side.

(4012)   BARBECUED SPARERIBS

Pork or beef spareribs can be laced on a spit for rotisserie cooking or grilled slowly over hot coals. In either case, they should be basted frequently with barbecue sauce. Allow approximately 1 pound of ribs per person, and cook until tender. Some good barbecue sauces follow.

(4013)   TANGY BARBECUE SAUCE

1 cup catsup	1 medium onion, chopped
1 cup water	2 tablespoons prepared mustard
1 teaspoon salt	2 tablespoons fat

Sauté onions in fat until tender and golden. Add all ingredients, mix thoroughly.

(4014)   RANCH SAUCE

1 tablespoon Worcestershire sauce	1 cup water
3 dashes Tabasco sauce	¼ cup vinegar
1 cup seasoned tomato sauce	¼ cup horseradish

Combine all ingredients. Heat to boiling and allow to simmer ½ hour.

BARBECUED CHICKEN (OR TURKEY, DUCK, ROCK CORNISH HENS, CAPON)

These must all be cooked on a spit if cooking whole and if you are using a barbecue sauce, you must baste frequently. Barbecuing any type of whole bird involves the additional work of trussing it properly—tying the feet together, tying the wings to the body, and tying up the body.

(4015) **GLAZED CHICKEN**

2-3 pound whole broilers
1 cup pineapple juice
1 cup brown sugar
½ cup ginger

½ cup salad oil
2 teaspoons salt
½ teaspoon pepper

Brush birds inside and out with salad oil and season with salt and pepper. Truss and skewer. Grill slowly. When skin is well-browned, brush with pineapple glaze made of pineapple juice, brown sugar, ginger. Broil about 10 minutes longer.

(4016) **GRILLED CHICKEN**

2-2½ pound broilers, split and disjointed so that birds stay flat during broiling.

½ cup salad oil
salt and pepper to taste

1 clove garlic

Rub chickens with garlic, brush with salad oil, season with salt and pepper. Grill underside first. When inside is well browned, turn, brushing skin side first with salad oil. Grill until done.

(4017) **BAKED CHICKEN**

2-3 pound broilers,
    cut into eighths
2 cups salad oil
salt and pepper to taste

1 8-oz. box corn flakes,
    finely ground
garlic powder

Season corn flakes with salt, pepper, and garlic powder. Season each piece of chicken with salt, pepper, and garlic powder, dip into salad oil and then into corn flakes, making sure that each is completely covered with flakes. Place servings (2 to 3 pieces of chicken) into a foil bag made by folding aluminum foil around them and either bake in a very hot oven (425°) for 25 minutes on each side or grill over hot coals for same length of time. Serve on foil.

(4018) GRILLED FISH

2 pound fish (trout, bass, flounder, bluefish)	1 cup melted butter ¼ cup lemon juice

Grill fish for ½ hour on well-oiled aluminum foil, brushing frequently with melted butter. Turn only once, after 15 minutes. Serve with lemon juice to taste. Makes 3 servings.

(4019) BROILED FISH FILLETS

2 pounds fillets of perch, sole or flounder ¼ cup butter, melted	salt and pepper to taste ¼ cup chopped parsley

Add salt and pepper to melted butter, brush over fish. Broil on foil about 5 minutes on each side, sprinkle with parsley and serve. Makes 6 servings.

(4020) FISH 'N CHEESE

2 pounds fillets of perch, sole, or flounder 6 slices American cheese	¼ cup melted butter salt and pepper to taste

Add salt and pepper to melted butter. Brush over fillets on both sides. Make "sandwiches" of two fillets and a slice of cheese each. Place each "sandwich" on to a square of aluminum foil and fold over and turn over edges to make a bag. Grill over coals about 5 minutes on each side. Serve on foil.

(4021) KABOB COOKOUT

5 1-inch lamb steaks cut in 1-inch cubes 1 pound frankfurters cut in 1-inch pieces Dill pickles cut in 1-inch slices	1 cup catsup 2 teaspoons prepared mustard 2 tablespoons Russian dressing 2 teaspoons vinegar

Combine vinegar, dressing, catsup and mustard. Thread skewer alternately with lamb, frankfurter and pickle. Roast over hot coals for 15 minutes, turning and basting frequently with barbecue sauce.

(4022)   DELLY KABOB

1 pound salami, cut in 1-inch cubes	½ pound mushrooms, trimmed
½ pound Swiss cheese, cut in 1-inch cubes	2 large tomatoes, sliced
2 large onions, sliced	Barbecue sauce as in (4021)

Alternate all ingredients on skewer, roast over hot coals for 15 minutes, turning and basting frequently with barbecue sauce.

(4023)   POTATOES FROM A CAN

If you are limited in grilling space, here's an easy way to prepare baked potatoes—suitable also for use on a regular stove.

Scrub medium baking potatoes, place in a tall coffee can with the lid on loosely, and bake until tender, rolling the can occasionally to turn the potatoes. Serve after cutting crisscross on top and seasoning with salt, pepper and butter.

(4024)   BAKED POTATOES IN FOIL

Scrub medium-sized baking potatoes and wrap each in aluminum foil. Bake until done (45-60 minutes), turning them from time to time. Potatoes are cooked when soft to the touch. When they are ready, cut open crosswise and top with the traditional butter and seasoning (milk optional) or one of the following toppings.

(4025)   TANGY POTATO TOPPING

1 cup crumbled blue cheese   ½ cup sour cream

Combine ingredients and spoon onto potatoes.

(4026)   CHEESE TOPPING

Sprinkle grated Parmesan cheese on top of potatoes. Repeat briefly or grill if desired.

(4027)   COTTAGE CHEESE TOPPING

1 cup cottage cheese   1 cup sour cream

Blend ingredients and spoon onto potatoes.

(4028)   CRUSTY SLICED POTATOES

Scrub potatoes and cook in jackets in salted water until done. Peel, slice, and brown in oil until crusty all around. Season with salt and pepper, and serve piping hot.

(4029)   EASY FRENCH FRIES

Warm frozen french fries over grill either by spreading on a square of aluminum foil or by shaking in a corn popper or strainer until properly heated.

(4030)   ROASTED CORN

Husk and clean ears of corn. Wrap each ear in aluminum foil, first brushing with butter and seasoning with salt and pepper. Roast over hot coals for 20 minutes, turning frequently. Serve on foil.

(4031)   ROASTED CORN IN HUSKS

Strip back husks from each ear of corn, clean off all corn silk and fold husks back around ears of corn. Line up corn on grill over hot coals and roast until husks are dry and brown (about 20 minutes), turning ears several times. Break off husks, season with salt and pepper, and serve.

Meat or fish and vegetables are only the beginning of your outdoor meal. Once you have learned to handle your cooking equipment, you will want to experiment with more elaborate dishes and meals. You will find that many skillet foods can easily be prepared outdoors on a grill, and you can choose your favorites to vary your menu.

One dish that is almost a necessity for any outdoor meal is a salad. Starting on page 151 of this book, you can choose from a variety of recipes the one which is right for your meal.

Your other necessity is bread. If you are serving hamburgers or hot dogs, you will use appropriate rolls. Otherwise, again, you have a choice of breads from the entire section starting on page 200 of this book.

Blender Foods

TODAY'S homemaker lives in an age when shortcuts and household accessories make easy a previously difficult job, or make possible a feat that was ordinarily impossible for the average housewife in the past.

Not the least of these accessories is the blender, an electrical appliance that chops, grates, shreds, minces, mixes, whips, and liquefies foods. Its proper use can open whole new worlds of cooking experience to the housekeeper.

BUYING A BLENDER

There are several brands of blender on the market, most having the same basic design features. As in every other appliance, you should shop with care, remembering your particular requirements for use.

1. If you wish to use your blender to prepare baby foods, give serious consideration to the type which can be completely dismantled and sterilized.

2. Make sure the blender you select has a heavy base that anchors firmly to your working surface. Avoid the too-light models which can slide and be dangerous to use.

3. Be sure to select a model that has at least two speeds. Many foods can be prepared only at low speeds and if you buy a one-speed, high-speed mixer, you have limited its potential value to you in advance of using it.

4. Select a base color scheme or design that fits your kitchen décor.

WHAT NOT TO EXPECT FROM YOUR BLENDER

We've already told you the magic a blender can work in your kitchen, but there are some things it just can't do either safely or successfully.

1. Large ice cubes will bend a blender's blades. Chop them up first before placing in your blender.

2. Cream will whip only at low speed. If you have only a high-speed blender, don't try to use it for whipped cream.

3. Forget about whipping egg whites in your blender. It just doesn't do the job successfully.

4. Don't plan on working with large pieces of food or large quantities of food. The blades can't move fully in either case. You may still have to resort to your grinder or mixer for more satisfactory performance in either case.

USING YOUR BLENDER

Your blender will serve you well as long as you use and care for it properly. Your basic rule for use is that you must follow the manufacturer's directions at all times.

1. Make sure your blender is set firmly on its base before turning on the motor. Disaster can result if it is tipped.

2. Make sure you place the cover on the blender after the ingredients are in and before you start the motor. It is helpful to keep your hand on the cover when you turn the motor on, to prevent splashing which sometimes occurs, and to prevent accidental tilting. Both can happen with the first surge of power in the appliance.

3. In working with liquids, never fill more than ¾ full, and use high speed.

4. You can leave the motor on when adding liquids, but never use a spatula or other tool while the motor is on.

5. Wait until the blades stop turning before removing the cover.

6. In blending solids, use high and low speeds alternately with complete stops in between to push food down with a spatula from the sides and into the path of the blades. The degree of fineness you get will depend on how much you repeat this pushing procedure.

7. Divide in advance if you want coarser textures, and use low speeds for short times.

8. Blenders cannot work with large quantities at one time. Too much food will clog the blades and prevent them from rotating properly, if at all. The heavier the food, the more you will have to come down to the three-quarter-full maximum capacity for liquids. If you need more than the blender will turn out at one time, you must empty the prepared food from it, and repeat.

(4101)   GRAHAM CRACKER CRUST

16 Graham crackers   ½ teaspoon cinnamon
½ cup sugar   ¼ cup melted butter

Break 5 Graham crackers at a time into blender. Cover and blend at high speed for 5 seconds. Empty crumbs into bowl. Repeat until all crackers are crumbled. Add remaining ingredients, stir until crumbs become moistened, then press into 8-inch buttered pie plate.

(4102)   CRACKER CAKE

1 cup nut meats   ½ cup shortening
32 Graham crackers   or soft butter
2 tablespoons flour   1 cup sugar
¼ teaspoon salt   3 eggs
2 teaspoons baking powder   ¾ cup milk

Grate nut meats in blender and empty into mixing bowl. Crumb crackers, 6 at a time and add to nuts; stir in flour, salt, baking powder. Into blender put shortening, sugar, eggs, and blend on low speed for 20 seconds. Slowly add milk and blend 10 seconds more. Pour into dry ingredients and stir until mixed. Fill 2 8-inch greased layer cake pans with mixture and bake in 350° oven for 30 minutes. Cool, serve with frosting or whipped cream.

(4103)   APPLE-RAISIN STUFFING

8 slices bread   Salt and pepper to taste
2 large apples,   ½ teaspoon marjoram
    sliced and cored   ½ teaspoon thyme
1 cup seedless raisins   ½ cup melted butter

Crumb bread, one slice at a time. Empty into bowl. Fill container to top with apples, add water to cover. Blend on high speed for 3 seconds. Drain, and add to crumbs. Stir in raisins, remaining ingredients. Stuffs a 5-6 lb. bird.

(4104)   GRATED CHEESE

Hard cheese such as Parmesan may be grated in your blender by first dicing cheese, then blending at high speed 3 or 4 seconds.

Once grated, cheese tends to go rancid quickly, so it is best to grate only what you need and store hard cheese in chunks.

(4105)   GRATED SWISS OR CHEDDAR CHEESE

Cheeses which are high in oil content require the addition of a few chunks of fresh bread to keep the action free-moving. Blend ½ thin slice and 1 cup diced cheese on high speed for 3 seconds. Stop motor, clean sides of container, then blend on high for 3 more seconds.

(4106)   PECAN BUTTER

¾ cup pecan halves
½ cup coarsely cut celery
¼ teaspoon salt
⅛ teaspoon pepper
½ cup soft butter (1 stick)

Grate nuts on high speed for 2 seconds, add remaining ingredients. Blend on high speed for 30 seconds.

(4107)   CHOCOLATE ICE CREAM

¼ cup sugar
½ cup water
1 6-oz. package semi-sweet chocolate chips
3 egg yolks
1½ cups heavy cream

In small saucepan combine the sugar and water. Bring to boil and let boil for 3 minutes. Put resulting syrup and chocolate chips into blender container. Blend on high speed for 20 seconds. Add egg yolks, then blend 10 seconds more. Fold mixture into heavy whipped cream. Freeze in refrigerator tray covered with waxed paper for 2 to 3 hours.

(4108)   CHOPPED CABBAGE

Slice ¼ medium head cabbage into container. Add 3 cups water or enough to almost cover cabbage. Turn motor on high and blend only 2 or 3 seconds. Pour mixture into sieve and let drain.

(4109) COLE SLAW

1 small onion, quartered	½ green pepper, cut in strips
1 small carrot, diced	Chopped cabbage
4 sprays parsley	(see #4108 above)

Put first 4 ingredients into container and blend with short on-off action of motor for 2 seconds. Drain and add to chopped cabbage. Add salt and pepper to taste and moisten with mayonnaise thinned with lemon juice or a little vinegar. Serves 4.

(4110) HAM HASH

1 slice bread	½ cup milk
2 oz. diced cheese	1 egg
2 cups diced cooked ham	¼ teaspoon dry mustard
½ small onion	¼ stick butter
½ green pepper,	(2 tablespoons)
cut into strips	

Tear bread and blend for 5 seconds on high speed. Set aside. Grate cheese on high speed for 5 seconds, and add to bread crumbs. Shred ham ½ cup at a time for 5 seconds each time. Put ham in casserole dish. Blend remaining ingredients except for butter together in high speed for 6 seconds. Pour over ham. Sprinkle with cheese and bread crumbs mixture, dot with butter, bake in preheated 350° oven for 20 minutes. Garnish with water cress if desired.

(4111) POTATO PANCAKES

2 eggs	¼ cup parsley clusters
1 slice medium onion	2 cups diced raw potatoes
1 teaspoon salt	¼ cup flour

Blend eggs, onion, salt, parsley and 1 cup potatoes on high speed for 2 seconds. With motor still on, uncover container and add flour and remaining potatoes. Turn motor off as soon as potatoes are in. Pour batter onto hot greased griddle and cook on both sides until brown. Makes 8 pancakes.

(4112) POTATO PURÉE

1 thin slice small onion	½ cup leftover or canned
½ cup canned chicken broth	potatoes
or homemade chicken stock	

Blend onion and broth on high speed for 5 seconds. Add
potatoes and blend for 10 seconds more. To thicken, add more
potatoes, small amounts at a time. This purée is perfect as a basis
for creamed soups or as a thickening agent. For example, the
recipe given below is for a basic vegetable soup using this purée.

(4113)   BASIC VEGETABLE SOUP

Potato purée as in #4112   ¼ cup parsley clusters
1 cup chicken broth   ½ teaspoon salt
1 cup cooked leftover   1 cup cream
    vegetables

Put all ingredients except cream into container and blend for
a few seconds only. With motor on add cream, but stop motor
immediately when all the cream has been added. Heat in saucepan over simmering water, or serve cold. Serves 6.

(4114)   MAYONNAISE

1 egg   2 tablespoons vinegar
½ teaspoon dry mustard   1 cup salad oil
½ teaspoon salt

Combine first four ingredients in blender with ¼ cup oil, at
low speed. Immediately uncover container and with motor running pour in remaining oil. As soon as all the oil is added, flick
motor on high for 2 seconds, then off. Makes ¼ cup.

If your blender has only one speed, add all the oil at once,
pouring very quickly in a thick, heavy stream.

(4115)   CHOCOLATE BUTTER CREAM
FROSTING

1 package (6 oz.) semi-sweet   1 teaspoon vanilla
    chocolate bits   1 stick soft butter
¼ cup boiling water   or margarine
4 egg yolks

Empty chocolate bits into blender container and add boiling
water. Blend on high speed for 20 seconds. Add egg yolks and
vanilla, turn motor onto high. With motor on, drop in butter.
Blend for 15 seconds, or until smooth.

(4116)   LIME FILLING FOR PIE

1 tray crushed ice cubes   ½ cup sugar
⅔ cup hot water   6 oz.-can partially defrosted
2 envelopes plain gelatin   limeade

Blend hot water and gelatin on high speed for 40 seconds. Add
sugar. Blend for 2 seconds more to dissolve sugar. Add limeade,
turn motor on high and add 2 cups crushed ice or enough to
bring liquid to top of container. Blend for about 10 more seconds,
until all the ice is dissolved. Pour filling into Graham cracker
crust (#4101). Serves 6.

(4117)   FROZEN SHERBERT

3 oz. concentrated fruit juice   2 cups crushed ice
2 tablespoons sugar

Put ingredients into container and turn motor on high. As
mixture freezes around the blades, they may stop churning. With
a rubber spatula, carefully work mixture free, continue to blend
for at least 1 minute. Serves 2.

(4118)   CLAM DIP

1 7½ oz. can minced clams,   ¼ teaspoon salt
drained   1 tablespoon cut chives
¼ cup juice from clams   or green onion tops
6 oz. cream cheese   6 drops Tabasco

Place all ingredients together in blender and turn speed on
high for 10 seconds, or until smooth.

(4119)   CRANBERRY-ORANGE MUFFINS

1 cup fresh or defrosted   3 tablespoons soft butter
cranberries   or shortening
1 cup milk   ⅔ cup sugar
Thin yellow rind of one   ½ teaspoon salt
orange   2 cups sifted flour
1 egg   3 teaspoons baking powder

Put all ingredients except flour and baking powder into container. Blend on high speed for 5 seconds, or until cranberries

are finely chopped. Pour over flour and baking powder mixture and stir just to moisten flour. Empty into greased muffin cups and bake in preheated 400° oven for 25 minutes. Makes 1½ doz.

(4120)   SOUR CREAM CHEESECAKE

2 eggs
½ cup sugar
2 teaspoons vanilla
1½ cups sour cream

1 lb. soft cream cheese,
    cut into pieces
2 tablespoons melted butter

Put first four ingredients into blender container. Blend on high speed for 15 seconds. With motor on, add remaining ingredients, and blend for 15 seconds more. Pour into Graham cracker crust (see #4101) and bake in preheated 325° oven for 30 to 40 minutes, or until set in center. Filling will still be very soft, but will firm up as the cake cools. Chill thoroughly.

(4121)   CHEESE RAREBIT

⅓ cup hot milk
1 cup diced cheddar cheese
1 tablespoon flour
½ teaspoon dry mustard

¼ teaspoon salt
Dash pepper
1 tablespoon soft butter

Blend all ingredients together on high speed for 10 seconds. Heat over simmering water and serve on buttered toast.

(4122)   CHEESE SOUFFLÉ

1 cup diced cheese
2 tablespoons butter
4 tablespoons flour
¼ teaspoon dry mustard
½ teaspoon salt

5 egg yolks (set whites aside
    for later use as indicated
    below)
1 cup hot milk

Put all ingredients into blender and turn motor on high speed for 15 seconds. Pour into saucepan and cook over low heat, stirring until smooth and thick. Fold in 5 stiffly beaten egg whites and pour into 1½-qt. soufflé dish. Bake in preheated 375° oven. Serve at once.

(4123) BASIC FRENCH DRESSING

½ cup cider or wine vinegar, or lemon juice
1½ cups salad oil

1 teaspoon salt
¼ teaspoon peppercorns
½ teaspoon dry mustard

Blend all ingredients together for 20 seconds, first on low speed, then on high. Makes 1 pint. This dressing may be flavored by the addition of any of the following ingredients:

½ cup crumbled blue cheese
½ teaspoon curry powder
6 sprigs fresh mint

¼ cup parsley clusters and ½ teaspoon marjoram or oregano

(4124) CHICKEN SALAD SPREAD

¼ cup mayonnaise (see #4114)
1 canned pimiento, quartered
¼ green pepper
1 stalk celery

¼ teaspoon salt
3 drops Tabasco
1 cup cooked diced chicken
1 thin slice small onion

Blend all ingredients together on high speed for 30 seconds, stopping to stir down if necessary.

(4125) SWEET BUTTER

1 cup heavy cream
½ cup ice water

Blend cream in container until whipped. Add ice water and continue blending on high speed for 1 to 2 minutes, until butter forms. Pour into small sieve to drain.

Listed below are some equivalents which you can expect to get from use of your blender.

2 slices bread = 1 cup bread crumbs
8 crackers = ½ cup cracker crumbs
6 squares chocolate = 1 cup grated chocolate
1 cup dry cheese = ⅞ cup grated cheese

1 medium carrot, diced = ½ cup shredded carrot
⅔ cup sliced celery = ½ cup shredded celery
¼ medium head cabbage = 2 cups chopped cabbage
½ cup diced cooked meat plus 3 small cubes bread = ¾ cup shredded meat

Miscellaneous Appliances

CASSEROLES, CHAFING DISHES, MIXERS, ETC.

THE number and variety of time-saving kitchen appliances on the market today have influenced cooking methods to such an extent that it is no longer necessary for the average housewife to spend hours or even days preparing a "soup to nuts" dinner. The most elegant meal can be prepared almost entirely at the table with the aid of a chafing dish, for instance; creamy whipped potatoes or a frothy dessert can be served in seconds through the efficiency of a mixer; the number of pans involved in cooking has even been reduced by the pressure cooker and rotisserie to the minimum. Even many interesting foreign recipes, once too complicated and time-consuming for American kitchens, can now be adapted to party or everyday use through modern appliances.

An important thing to remember in purchasing a kitchen appliance is its capacity in relation to your family and your expected needs. It's a good idea to remember that a slightly larger size than what you would consider suitable is better than a unit that is too small for company use.

ROTISSERIE

Rotisserie cooking is not only a little faster than oven roasting, but has the added advantage of requiring no basting. The rotation effect assures even cooking, with little loss of natural juices. It is important that the meat be at room temperature before starting to cook it, and that it be exactly centered on the spit. Beef, ham, chicken, even turkey, can be cooked in this manner, either indoors or, if you have barbecue equipment, outdoors. And of course, kabobs add an exotic touch to any meal, prepared as follows.

(4201)   KABOBS

Select quick-cooking foods like lamb or filet steak, tomatoes, green peppers, mushrooms, canned potatoes, onions. When used in alternating combinations, make certain that all pieces of food are approximately the same size, and leave a tiny amount of space between pieces so that the heat gets to all sides. During cooking, pour small amount of melted butter or margarine over the vegetables on the skewer. Motorized skewers may be purchased, and although they are quite handy, the turning can nevertheless be done by hand to reach the same effect. When kabobs are done, push off a few pieces at a time onto a plate, using a 2-tined fork to prevent squashing the tender vegetables.

PRESSURE COOKER

Pressure cookers are so varied in use, although alike in the basic principle, that it is best to follow the directions that come with the type of unit you have. Some general recipes follow.

(4202)   ROUND STEAK DINNER

2 lbs. round steak, cut in ½-in. cubes	1 clove garlic
2 tablespoons flour	1 3-oz. can mushrooms, drained
1½ teaspoons salt	1 8-oz. can tomato sauce
2 tablespoons fat	2 teaspoons Worcestershire sauce
½ cup chopped onion	½ cup sour cream
½ cup chopped celery	

Roll meat in flour and salt. Brown in hot fat in cooker. Add remaining ingredients except sour cream, and cook 10 minutes at 15 pounds pressure. Reduce pressure quickly under cold running water. Stir in sour cream, and serve over rice or mashed potatoes.

(4203) CHICKEN AND CREAM GRAVY

1 2-3 lb. broiler-fryer, cut in pieces	2 small onions, sliced
	2 bay leaves
Seasoned flour (2 teaspoons salt, 2 teaspoons paprika, ½ cup flour)	¼ cup chopped celery leaves
	1 teaspoon salt
	Dash pepper
¼ cup fat	Milk as required
1 cup water	⅓ cup flour

Roll chicken in seasoned flour and brown in hot fat in pressure pan. Add water, onions, bay leaves, celery leaves, salt, and pepper and cook at 15 pounds pressure 15 to 20 minutes. Allow pressure to go down normally, then remove chicken and strain broth. Add enough milk to broth to make 3 cups. Shake 1 cup of this liquid with flour and return to pressure pan with rest of liquid. Cook, stirring constantly until thick. Pour over chicken. Serves 4.

(4204) MEAT BALLS

1½ lbs. ground beef	¼ cup chopped onion
½ cup uncooked rice	1 can condensed tomato soup
1 teaspoon salt	½ cup water
¼ teaspoon pepper	

Combine meat, rice, salt, pepper, onion and shape into small balls. Blend soup and water and heat in pressure pan till bubbly. Add meat balls. Cook at 15 pounds pressure for 10 minutes, then let pressure go down normally. Serves 6-8.

CHAFING DISH

The chafing dish is undoubtedly one of the most elegant additions to your cooking convenience. Its widespread use on social occasions should not, however, limit it to purely party-time events. It can be a time-saver for you, and is also handy for keeping kitchen-prepared foods or such dishes as stews or soups warm at the table and ready for quick "seconds."

Chafing dishes provide heat in one of two main ways: fuel or electricity. The fuels used are generally either sterno or alcohol, with sterno being considered the safer of the two. If children are going to be present when you use your chafing dish, certainly sterno would be the wiser choice. However, sterno heat does not have the intensity or flexibility of alcohol.

Electric chafing dishes are similar to electric skillets, and offer very little flexibility in cooking, since the heating coils stay hot even when the heat is turned off. An asbestos pad is recommended as a protection against too much heat.

(4205) CHICKEN BALLS HORS D'OEUVRES

1½ cups cooked chicken	¼ teaspoon curry powder
¼ cup India relish, well drained	¼ teaspoon salt
	dash cayenne pepper
1 egg, beaten	½ cup cheese-cracker crumbs
⅓ cup fine dry bread crumbs	2 tablespoons butter

Grind chicken and mix with remaining ingredients except cracker crumbs and butter. Form into 1-inch balls and roll in cracker crumbs. Heat butter in blazer pan of chafing dish. Sauté balls until lightly browned. Serve with toothpicks.

(4206)   LOBSTER STEW

2 tablespoons butter	2 cups light cream
3 tablespoons flour	2 6½-oz. cans lobster meat
1 teaspoon salt	¼ cup chopped parsley
½ teaspoon white pepper	

Heat butter in blazer pan of chafing dish. Blend in flour, salt, pepper. Gradually stir in cream; continue to stir until thickened and smooth (10-12 minutes). Add lobster meat and simmer 5 minutes. Stir in parsley. Serves 4.

(4207)   FONDUE BOURGUIGNONE

This Swiss specialty has become increasingly popular in the United States, and can be served with the condiments suggested below or with your own additions and variations. Although the meat is usually cooked at the table in oil in a special fondue pot, you can adapt the original recipe to your chafing dish as follows:

2 lbs. lean tenderloin or filet of beef	½ lb. butter
	⅔ cup olive oil

Cut beef into ¾-inch cubes. Heat oil and butter over highest flame in your chafing dish. Each member of the meal then cooks his own meat to the desired condition, using a long fork to dip the meat in the oil and butter. When ready, the meat may then be rolled in any or all of the ingredients below, as desired.

Bearnaise Sauce	Chopped garlic
Remoulade Sauce	Mustard
Curry Sauce	Tabasco Sauce
Chopped parsley	Applesauce
Chopped onion	Horseradish

(4208)   HUNGARIAN VEAL CHOPS

4 1-inch thick veal chops	1 teaspoon salt
1 cup yogurt	½ teaspoon pepper
1 teaspoon dill	¼ cup finely chopped onion
1 teaspoon paprika	

Trim excess fat from chops. Blend yogurt with seasonings and pour over chops. Let stand at room temperature 2-3 hours, then remove chops and dry well. Save marinade. Heat excess fat in blazer pan of chafing dish; sauté onions in the fat, then push onions to one side and sauté chops in the fat until browned on both sides. Pour marinade over chops, cover and simmer about 30 minutes. Makes 4 servings.

CASSEROLES

Casserole dishes can be simple or complicated, festive or informally served when time to eat and clean up afterward is at a premium. A casserole can be a delicate mixture as in the Crabmeat Dinner below, or hale and hearty Beef and Noodles (see #4210).

Many casserole dishes are equipped with a stand and warming candle so that they may be kept hot at the dinner or buffet table. These are recommended, although not absolutely necessary. Any Pyrex dish with a cover may be used as a casserole dish.

(4209)   CRABMEAT DINNER

1 cup crabmeat, drained	⅓ cup chopped onion
1 cup soft bread crumbs	¼ cup sliced green olives
1 cup mayonnaise	¾ teaspoon salt
¾ cup milk	½ cup buttered soft bread
6 hard-cooked eggs	crumbs for topping

Break crabmeat in chunks and mix with next 7 ingredients. Place in casserole dish and top with buttered bread crumbs. Bake at 350° for 20-25 minutes.

(4210)　BEEF AND NOODLE CASSEROLE

1 lb. chopped onions
½ lb. mushroom caps
¼ lb. butter
1 teaspoon Worcestershire
　sauce
1 teaspoon thyme
1 cup red wine
1 12-oz. can peeled tomatoes

2 cloves chopped garlic
1 lb. flat steak,
　cut in long strips
1 box green noodles
1 cup white sauce
1 cup grated Parmesan
　cheese

Brown onions and mushrooms in butter for 5 minutes. Add Worcestershire, thyme, wine, tomatoes, garlic and meat and simmer for about 1 hour. Cook noodles. Alternate layers of noodles and layers of above in casserole dish. Spread white sauce on top and sprinkle with cheese. Bake in 350° oven ½ hour. Serves 8.

(4211)　OVEN HASH

1½ cups coarsely ground
　cooked beef
1 cup coarsely ground
　potatoes
½ cup coarsely ground onion
¼ cup chopped parsley
1 teaspoon salt

Dash pepper
2 teaspoons Worcestershire
　sauce
1 6-oz. can evaporated milk
⅓ cup slightly crushed
　corn flakes
1 tablespoon melted butter

Lightly mix all ingredients except corn flakes and butter. Put in greased 1-qt. casserole dish. Combine corn flakes and butter and sprinkle over top. Bake in 350° oven 30 minutes. Serves 4.

(4212)　MACARONI AND CHEESE

1½ cups elbow macaroni,
　cooked
3 tablespoons butter
　or margarine
3 tablespoons flour
2 cups milk
½ teaspoon salt

Dash pepper
¼ cup minced onion
2 cups shredded Cheddar
　cheese
6 tomato slices
4 slices bacon

Melt butter. Blend in flour and then add milk gradually. Stir until thick and add remaining ingredients except tomatoes and bacon. Continue to stir until cheese is melted. Combine with macaroni and put into 1½-qt. casserole dish. Arrange tomato slices and then lay bacon strips across top. Bake in 350° oven about 45 minutes, or until bubbly and browned.

(4213)   HUNGARIAN NOODLES

2½ cups noodles, cooked
1 cup cottage cheese
1 cup sour cream
¼ cup chopped onion
1 clove garlic

1 tablespoon Worcestershire sauce
Dash Tabasco sauce
½ teaspoon salt
Dash pepper

Combine noodles with remaining ingredients in greased 10×6×1½″ casserole dish. Bake in 350° oven 25-30 minutes. Serves 6.

ELECTRIC FRYING PAN

The electric frying pan is a welcome addition to any kitchen where space is a problem or ventilation is poor, since it can be used at the table and it saves heating up the stove or oven, especially desirable in hot months. Many are now able to be immersed in water completely, for more convenient cleaning, and several have heating coils in the cover which make it ideal for pot roast and similar meat dishes. Its size and depth add to its convenience, since vegetables such as corn and asparagus can easily be boiled in the electric skillet if a large saucepan is not available. Its major feature, of course, is the even distribution of heat over the cooking surface, ensuring near-perfect cooking of such delicate foods as eggs and rare steak.

ELECTRIC MIXER

Electric mixers are available in standard models or portable units. The latter are handy for beating eggs or potatoes, cake mixes, or anything which requires short mixing times, and can be stored in a drawer or cabinet easily, thus saving counter space. However, they are not really suitable for all-purpose use or for mixing anything that requires longer mixing times, since the portable model is tiring to hold and just does not have the power or variations in speed required for larger jobs.

The standard models will perform a variety of chores in the kitchen. Most of them have a revolving base on which to sit the mixing bowl, so that the ingredients are evenly mixed. Attachments for mixers are many, ranging from juicers to knife sharpeners.

Cooking for Two

YOUNG brides and, in fact every woman who cooks for two, have a very real problem in household management. Selection and purchasing of foods is far more difficult than in a larger family and what to do with left-overs is a real bugbear.

Most recipes in this book can be reduced in amounts of ingredients to make dishes for two. However, some forms of food are entirely barred to the twosome which cannot afford to throw away left-overs.

In meats, such appetizing articles as roasts, poultry for roasting, or cuts with a large proportion of bone or fat are out of the question for two persons. In this department, purchases must be limited to those articles which can be bought equally well in small quantities—ground meat, steaks, chops, sausages, broilers, and the various meat sundries, such as livers, sweetbreads, etc.

Vegetables, although they cannot be purchased as cheaply in small quantities, nevertheless can be served equally well in families of two. Prepare them exactly according to instructions, reducing quantities. Because water will cook out at a faster rate where the quantity used is small, it may be necessary to slightly increase the proportion of liquid used.

Most desserts can be reduced efficiently to serve two and should be made in individual cups or ramekins if possible. Cakes can be baked in small pans and, of course, biscuits, muffins, rolls, or cookies can be made satisfactorily in any quantity, large or small.

Canned foods are a great help in solving the problem of meals for two. They are available in small cans that are just enough for two, so that there will be no left-overs.

Although the problem is different, the bride can prepare and serve dishes and meals equally as appetizing and health-promoting as those of her sisters with big families. If she has a husband who likes salads, she has an opportunity to display great artistic talent.

Cooking in High Places

~~~~~~

THE homemakers who live at altitudes above 3,000 feet have a problem not faced by those who reside at or near sea level. Although about one-third of the United States lies in that high range, it is the most sparsely settled area, containing some 5,000,000 people.

The woman in a high place finds quickly that her principal cooking problems are in the fields of bread and cake making, boiling foods, preserving, and candy making.

At sea level water boils at 212° F. At Denver water boils at 202° F. Accordingly, it requires a longer time to cook foods in boiling water there than it does in New York or Boston or any other place at sea level.

In the field of candy making this throws the usual instructions completely off. The various testing stages, such as soft-ball, come at lower temperatures as the altitude increases.

In the field of baking serious conditions develop, which affect, not only the home cook, but also commercial bakers. To achieve good results it is necessary to change the quantities of almost all ingredients, particularly shortening, baking powder, sugar, and liquid from the quantities used at sea level.

Several exhaustive studies of cooking at high altitudes have been made and the homemaker in high places who aspires to do well should secure some of the best pamphlets on the subject. They include:

Vegetable Cookery at High Altitudes by Emma J. Thiessen, University of Wyoming.

Baking Quick Breads and Cakes at High Altitudes by Marjorie W. Peterson, Colorado State College.

Baking Angel Food Cake at Any Altitude by Mark A. Barmore, Colorado State College.

Preparing and Baking Yellow Sponge Cake at Different Altitudes by W. E. Pyke and Gestur Johnson, Colorado State College.

KEY TO PRONUNCIATION

a
- ā: māke, lāte, sāy, abrogate (ab' rō gāt).
- â: bâre, pârent, where (hwâr).
- a: at, map, fat, afford, elephant, vocal.
- ä: färm, fäther, cär, psälm.
- a: ȧsk, dȧnce, laugh (lȧf).
- *a*: sof*a*, banan*a*, pajam*a*, Cub*a*.

c
- s: cereal (sē' rē-al).
- k: cat (kat), cabbage (kab' ij).

ch: chat, charm, cherub.

e
- ē: ēqual, feet (fēt), see (sē), mēre, cē' rē al, edition (ē di' shun).
- e: let, bend, elect, violent, novel.
- ĕ: fingĕr, racĕr, thĕ (usually not stressed).

g
- g: go, grand.
- j: gem (jem), edge (ej).

i
- ī: bīte, fire, mīght.
- i: it, pin, him, obvious (ob' vi us).

j: jelly, jury, judge (juj).

n: seance (sā ä*n*s).

ng: song, uncle (ung' kl).

o
- ō: gō, coat (kōt), vōte, sew (sō), sōlarium.
- ô: ôrder, all (ôl), hôrse, dôg, gône, lôft, bought (bôt).
- o: lot, not, knock, romp, what (hwot), om' i cron.
- oi: oil, voice.
- o͞o: no͞on, do (do͞o), ro͞ot.
- oo: good, foot, could (kood).
- ou: out, sound.

s
- s: so, sell, silly, ceiling (sēl' ing).
- sh: she, nation (na' shun), sure (sho͞or).
- z: is (iz), surprise (sûr prīz'), dogs (dôgz).

h
- *th*: *th*ere, brea*th*e.
- th: thin, thorough.

u
- ū: ūse, mūte, few (fū), execūte.
- û: tûrn, her (hûr), cûrse, permanent (pûr' m*a* nent): usually stressed.
- u: up, but, abrupt, under, focus, nation (nā' shun).
- ü: menü.

x
- gs: exist (egs-ist').
- ks: execute (eks' ē cūt).
- z: Xenophon (zen-   )

' : primary accent or stress.

916

PRONOUNCING DICTIONARY OF FOREIGN COOKING TERMS

(Key to Pronunciation on Opposite Page)

A

agneau (à nyō') [Fr.] Lamb.

à la (ä lä) [Fr.] After the style of; in the fashion of.

à la broche (ä lä brōsh') [Fr.] Cooked on a spit.

à la carte (ä lä kärt') [Fr.] According to the menu.

à la mode (ä lä mōd') [Fr.] Designating a pot roast, larded before braising and simmered in the vegetables forming the sauce; designating pie covered with a serving of ice cream; in the usual manner.

allemand, allemande (àl mänd') [Fr.] German; velouté sauce with cream and the yolk of eggs added.

anglais, anglaise (äng'glä, äng' gläz) [Fr.] English.

antipasto (än tē päs'to) [It.] Hors d'oeuvres.

apéritif (à pä rē tēf') [Fr.] A liquor used as an appetizer.

aspic jelly (as'pik jel'i) [Fr.] A savory jelly, used for garnishing.

au (ō) [Fr.] With or in, as potatoes *au gratin,* potatoes with cheese.

au beurre fondu (ō bûr fon dōō') [Fr.] With melted butter.

au beurre roux (ō bûr rōō') [Fr.] With browned butter.

au bleu (ō blû') [Fr.] Fish cooked in stock with a litle wine added.

au four (ō fōōr') [Fr.] Cooked in an oven.

au gratin (ō gra tan') [Fr.] Dishes covered with a cheese sauce and browned.

au jus (ō zhü') [Fr.] With gravy or natural juices.

au lait (ō lä') [Fr.] With milk or cream.

au maigre (ō mä'gēr) [Fr.] Dishes without meat, as Lenten dishes.

au naturel (ō na tü rel') [Fr.] Cooked simply.

aux (ō) [Fr.] With, as *aux choux,* with cabbage.

B

baba (bä bä') [Fr.] A light cake made with yeast.

bain-marie (ban ma rē') [Fr.] A vessel containing small pans in which sauces, etc., are kept hot.

bard, barder (bärd, bär dä') [Fr.] To cover the breasts of poultry or game with slices of bacon before roasting.

beignet (bän'yä) [Fr.] A fritter.

beurre (bûr) [Fr.] Butter.

beurre noire (bûr nwár') [Fr.] Browned butter.

blanc (blank) [Fr.] White.

blanch, blanchir (blanch, blänch-ēr') [Fr.] To parboil or to scald.

blanquette (blän ket') [Fr.] A mince of white meat served with velouté or similar sauce; also, a white fricassee.

boeuf (bûf) [Fr.] Beef.

bombe glacé (bônb gla sä') [Fr.] A frozen dessert molded in round form.

bordelais, bordelaise (bôr d lä', bôr de läz') [Fr.] From Bordeaux or its environs.

borsch (bôrsh) [Rus.] A soup or ragout containing beets.

bouchée (boo shā') [Fr.] A small
patty of light pastry, sufficient for
a mouthful.

boudin (boo dan') [Fr.] An entrée
prepared with quenelle or finely
minced or pounded meat.

bouilli (boo yē') [Fr.] Beef stew,
served with sauce.

bouillon (boo yon', bool'yun) [Fr.]
Broth.

bouquet-garni (boo ke gar nē')
[Fr.] A tied bunch of herbs or
vegetables.

bourgeoise, à la (boor zhwaz', ä lä)
[Fr.] Family style; simply.

braise (brāz) [Fr.] To cook in a
covered pan with various hot vegetables and bacon.

Brie (brē) [Fr.] A soft cheese.

brioche (brē ōsh', brē'ōsh) [Fr.] A
light French yeast bread.

brochette, en (brō shet', än) [Fr.]
Broiled on a skewer.

brut (brüt) [Fr.] Dry, said of wines;
no sugar added.

C

cabobs (ka bobs') [Hind. and Pers.]
See kabobs.

café (ka fā') [Fr.] Coffee.

café au lait (ka fā ō lā') [Fr.] Coffee
with cream.

café noir (ka fā nyär') [Fr.] Black
coffee.

canapé (ka na pā') [Fr.] A small
piece of fried bread, toast, or pastry
served with hors d'oeuvres or
savories.

cannelon (kan lôn') [Fr.] A small
roll of pastry filled with mince.

caramel (kar'a mel) [Fr.] Browned
sugar or sugar boiled until it turns
dark brown: used for coatings or
for coloring.

carte du jour (kärt' du joor') [Fr.]
Menu for the day.

casserole (kas'e rōl) [Fr.] A stewpan in which food is cooked and
served.

caviar (kav'i är) [Fr.] Sturgeon roe,
prepared as a relish.

champignon (sham pin'yun) [Fr.]
A mushroom.

chantilly (shän tē yē') [Fr.] With
whipped cream.

chapon (sha pôn') [Fr.] Capon.

chartreuse (shär trûz') [Fr.] Mold
of fruit, jelly, or savory mixture.

chaud-froid (shō frwa') [Fr.] A
cold sauce used for coating game,
meat, or fish.

chile con carne (chē'lä kon kär'nā)
[Sp.] A Mexican dish of minced
red peppers and meat, with beans.

chili (chil'ē) [Sp.] Tropical American herb yielding cayenne pepper.

chili sauce (chil'ē sôs) [Sp.] A
spicy sauce of tomatoes and peppers.

chou (shoo) [Fr.] Cabbage.

choucroute (shoo kroot') [Fr.] Pic
kled cabbage; sauerkraut.

compote (kom'pōt) [Fr.] Fruit
stewed in sirup; also, a rich stew
of game or poultry.

confiture (kon'fi tūr) [Fr.] Jam or
fruit preserve.

consommé (kon so mä') [Fr.] Clear
soup.

coquille (kō kēl') [Fr.] A shell or
anything served in a shell or a
shell-like mold.

cordon bleu (kōr dôn blū') [Fr.]
An excellent cook.

court bouillon (kōrt boo yon',—
bool'yun) [Fr.] Fish stock.

crème (krām or krem) [Fr.] Cream.

crêpe (krāp) [Fr.] A pancake.

crevette (krē vet') [Fr.] A shrimp;
shrimp color.

croissant (krwä sän') [Fr.] A half-
moon shaped piece of fried bread
or pastry.

croquette (krō ket') [Fr.] A savory
mince of fish, meat, poultry, or
game, made into a small mold,
egged and breadcrumbed, and fried.

croustade (kroo stad') [Fr.] A case
or shell of bread, potato, or rice
in which a mince or other filling
is served.

cuisse (kwis) [Fr.] A leg of chicken.

D

dal, dhal (däl) [Hindu] An Indian split pea or lentil.

dariole (dà ri ōl') [Fr.] A small cup-shaped mold holding a mince; a pâté.

darne (därn) [Fr.] A middle cutlet of fish.

daube (dōb) [Fr.] A stew of minced meat or fowl.

de, d' (dē or dĕ, d) [Fr.] Of.

demitasse (dem'i tas *or* -täs) [Fr.] A small cup of black coffee; literally, half a cup.

dhal. *See* **dal.**

diable (dyä'bl) [Fr.] Sharp; highly seasoned; deviled.

d'Uxelles (dü sel') [Fr.] A mixture of parsley, mushrooms, shallots, etc., used for flavoring sauces or purées, or as a forcemeat.

E

éclair (ā klâr') [Fr.] A pastry shell filled with whipped cream or custard.

en brochette (än brō shet') [Fr.] Broiled on a skewer.

en coquille (än kō kēl') [Fr.] In a shell.

en papillotte (än pap'i lōt) [Fr.] Served with paper frills or on greased paper.

entrée (än'trā) [Fr.] A hot or cold dish served between main dinner courses.

entremets (än'trē mä) [Fr.] Dressed vegetables, or hot or cold sweets, served as second course of a dinner.

escalop, escallop (es kol'up) [Fr.] To bake in a sauce of cracker or bread crumbs, butter, etc.

escargot (es kàr gō') [Fr.] A snail.

espagnole (es pa nyōl') [Fr.] A brown sauce.

estragon (es'tra gon) [Fr.] Tarragon oil.

F

farce (fàrs) [Fr.] A forcemeat or stuffing.

farci, farcie (fàr sē') [Fr.] Stuffed, as an olive or a pepper.

fines herbes (fēn zĕrb') [Fr.] Chopped herbs, used for seasoning, stuffing, or garnishing.

flambé (flän bä') [Fr.] Served covered with flaming spirits.

flan (flan) [Fr.] An open fruit or custard tart.

fleuron (flû rôn') [Fr.] A small piece of pastry used for garnishing.

foie gras (fwà grä') [Fr.] Goose's liver.

fondant (fon'dant) [Fr.] A kind of icing.

fondue (fon dōō') [Fr.] Melted, usually with reference to cheese dishes.

forcemeat (fōrs'mēt) Meat used for stuffing.

frangipane (fran'ji pān) [Fr.] Confectioners' custard.

frappé (frà pä') [Fr.] Iced; frozen.

fricandeau (frik'an dō) [Fr.] A filet of veal, larded and braised.

fricandelles (frik an del') [Fr.] Very small pieces of game or meat, usually braised.

fricassee (frik a sē') [Fr.] White stew.

frijoles (frē'hōlz) [Sp.] A Mexican dish consisting of beans cooked with oil, tomatoes, and chili.

froid (frwä) [Fr.] Cold.

fromage (frō màzh') [Fr.] Cheese.

G

galantine (gal'an tēn) [Fr.] Boned and stuffed meat or poultry served cold with sauce, or glazed.

galette (ga let') [Fr.] French roll or bun.

garniture (gär'ni tūr) [Fr.] Garnishing.

gâteau (gà tō') [Fr.] A round, flat cake.

gefüllte fish (ge fil'te fish) [Heb.] Stewed or baked fish, stuffed with a mixture of fish flesh, bread crumbs, eggs, and seasoning.

gelée (zhē lā') [Fr.] Jelly.

gibier (zhi byā') [Fr.] Game.

glace (glàs) [Fr.] Ice; a frozen dessert.

glacé (gla sā') [Fr.] Frozen; iced or glazed.

glaze (glāz) Stock boiled to a jelly.

godiveau (gō dē vō') [Fr.] A kind of forcemeat.

grillé, grillée (grē yā') [Fr.] Broiled; grilled.

H

hâché (hä shā') [Fr.] Cold meat minced or cut into small pieces and warmed in sauce.

haricot (har'i kō) [Fr.] String bean; also, a ragout of meat and vegetables.

haricots verts (à rē kō vâr') [Fr.] Green string beans.

hâtelet (hä te lā') [Fr.] Silver skewer, used for decorating meat or fish dishes.

homard (ō mâr') [Fr.] Lobster.

hors d'oeuvres (ôr dû'vr) [Fr.] Appetizers; dainty, savory dishes served before soup.

huitre (wē'tr) [Fr.] An oyster.

J

jambon (zhän bôn') [Fr.] Ham.

jardiniere (jär di nēr') [Fr.] Garnish of vegetables; stew of vegetables.

julienne (jōō li en') [Fr.] Garnish of vegetables cut into fine shreds.

jus (zhü) [Fr.] Gravy; juice.

K

kabobs (ka bobs') [Hind. and Pers.] Small pieces of meat fixed on a skewer, braised or curried.

kirsch, kirschwasser (kirsh, —'väs ēr) [Ger.] Cherry cordial.

knäckebröd (k'nak'e brûd) [Swed.] A flat, hard, rye bread.

kuchen (kōō'chen) [Ger.] Cake.

L

lait (lā) [Fr.] Milk.

laitue (lā tü') [Fr.] Lettuce.

langue (läng) [Fr.] Tongue.

lapin (là pan') [Fr.] A rabbit.

larder (lär'dēr) To lard.

lardoon, lardon (lär dōōn', lär'don) A piece of bacon used for larding.

liaison (lē ā zôn') [Fr.] Mixture of egg and cream used for thickening white sauces and soups.

lyonnaise (lī o nāz') [Fr.] Prepared with chopped onions.

M

macédoine (mas à dwän') [Fr.] A mixture of fruits or vegetables cut into small pieces or diced; also fruits set into molds of jelly.

macon (mā'kun) [Eng.] Synthetic bacon, made from mutton.

maigre (mā'gēr) [Fr.] Meatless, as a Lenten dish.

maître d'hôtel, à la (mâ'tr dō tel', ä lä) [Fr.] Hotel style; also, a type of sauce which is served on grills.

marinade (mar i nād') [Fr.] A mixture of herbs and oil, wine, or vinegar, in which fish or meat is soaked to render it tender and full of flavor.

marmite (mär mēt') [Fr.] Stock pot.

marron (mar'on) [Fr.] A chestnut.

marrons glacés (mà rôn glà sā') [Fr.] Chestnuts, coated with sugar or sirup.

matelote (mat'elot) [Fr.] A fish stew.

minestrone (mē na strō'na) [It.] A thick, rich vegetable soup with barley.

mirepoix (mēr pwà') [Fr.] Preparation of vegetables, herbs, and bacon, used for braising or as a foundation for soups or sauces.

mousse (mōōs) [Fr.] A light, spongy mixture.

N

navarin (nà và ran') [Fr.] Mutton or lamb stewed with turnips.

noir, noire (nwär) [Fr.] Black.

normande sauce (nôr mänd′ sôs′) [Fr.] A white sauce containing cream, wine, egg yolk and the liquor of fish, oysters, and mushrooms.

nouille (nōō′y) [Fr.] A noodle; a paste made of flour, water, and eggs.

O

oeuf (ûf) [Fr.] An egg.

P

pailles (pä′y) [Fr.] Straws; potatoes cut into strawlike slices and fried.

pain (pan) [Fr.] Bread.

panada (pa nä′da) [Sp.] A paste of flour and water or soaked bread.

panure (pà nür′) [Fr.] Bread crumbs used to cover croquettes.

panurette (pà nür et′) [Fr.] Preparation of grated rusks, usually coral color.

papillote (pap′i lōt) [Fr.] Greased paper; a paper frill.

paprika (pap′ri ka) [Hung.] Red pepper

Parmesan (pär me zàn′) [It.] A hard, dry Italian cheese made from skimmed milk.

pâté (pä tä′) [Fr.] Pie, pastry, or paste.

pâté de foie gras (pä tä′ dĕ fwä grä′) [Fr.] A paste of goose livers.

patisserie (pa tis′ĕr i) [Fr.] Pastry.

pêche (pesh) [Fr.] A peach.

petite marmite (pĕ tĕt′ màr mĕt′) [Fr.] A brown soup stock served with vegetables, poultry, meat, etc.

petits fours (pĕ tĕ fōōr′) [Fr.] Little cakes.

petits pois (pĕ tĕ pwä′) [Fr.] Green peas.

pièce de résistance (py es dĕ rä zēs tàns′) [Fr.] The main course or dish of a meal.

pimento (pi men′tō) [Sp.] Allspice; pimiento.

pimiento (pē myen′tō) [Sp.] Red, Spanish peppercorns.

pimola (pi mō′la) An olive stuffed with pimiento.

piquant, piquante (pē′kant) [Fr.] Sharp, pungent.

pizza (pēt′sa) [It.] A pastry of raised dough, covered with anchovy or cheese sauce.

pois (pwä) [Fr.] Peas.

poisson (pwä′sôn) [Fr.] Fish.

pommes (pum) [Fr.] Apples.

pommes de terre (pum dĕ tàr′) [Fr.] Potatoes.

potage (pō tazh′) [Fr.] Soup.

pot-au-feu (pô tō fû′) [Fr.] A dish of broth, meat, and vegetables boiled in a pot.

potpourri (pō pōō rē′) [Fr.] A stew of various meats and spices.

poulet (pōō le′) [Fr.] Chicken.

pousse-café (pōōs kà fä′) [Fr.] An after dinner cordial with various liqueurs in layers.

praline (prä′lēn) [Fr.] Flavored with burnt almonds.

purée (pū rä′) [Fr.] A pulp of mashed or sieved fruit or vegetables; meat or fish that has been pounded or sieved; thick soup.

Q

quenelle (ke nel′) [Fr.] Forcemeat or meat, fish, game, or poultry, pounded, rubbed through a sieve, and formed into balls or fancy shapes, poached or fried.

R

ragout (ra gōō′) [Fr.] A rich, highly-seasoned stew.

ramekin, ramequin (ram′ē kin) [Fr.] A mixture served in small paper or china cases, either oval or round.

ravioli (rä vyô′lē) [It.] Squares of dough pressed together over a filling of cheese, spinach, or meat, steamed and served with a sauce.

réchauffé (rä shō fä′) [Fr.] Warmed over.

réchauffer (rä shō fä′) [Fr.] Reheat; warm over.

relevé (rē le vā′) [Fr.] A joint; a dish that replaces another.

ris de veau (rē′ d′ vō′) [Fr.] Calf's sweetbreads.

rissole (rē sôl′) [Fr.] A mixture of minced fish, meat, poultry, or game enclosed in paste, egged and bread-crumbed, and fried.

rôti (rō tē′) [Fr.] Roast.

rôtisserie (rō tē s′rē′) [Fr.] A restaurant featuring broiled and barbecued meats.

roux (rōō) A preparation of flour and butter used for thickening soups and sauces.

S

salade (så làd′) [Fr.] Salad.

salmi (sal′mi) [Fr.] A hash made with game.

sauté (sō tā′) [Fr.] Deep fried in a little fat.

sauterne (sō tûrn′) [Fr.] A sweet, white wine.

sippet (sip′et) A small slice of toasted or fried bread used as a garnish.

smörgåsbord (smûr′gōs bōrd) [Swed.] Hors d'œuvres.

socle (sok′l) [Fr.] A stand made of rice or bread on which to serve poultry, game, meat, etc.; sometimes made of ice or sugar and used for sweet dishes or ices.

sorbet (sôr′bet) [Fr.] A half-frozen ice, flavored with wine; frozen punch.

soubise (sōō bēz′) [Fr.] A smooth onion pulp served with entrées or a thick onion sauce.

soufflé (sōō flā′) [Fr.] A very light mixture, either sweet or savory; puffed.

spumone, spumoni (spōō mō′nå, spōō mō′nē) [It.] Italian ice cream.

suprême (sü prâm′) [Fr.] A rich, white sauce made of chicken or veal stock, to which cream has been added.

T

tamale (ta mä′lē) [Sp.] A Mexican dish of minced meat and corn meal, seasoned with red pepper, wrapped in corn husks, dipped in oil and steamed: usu. called *hot tamales.*

tamis (tam′is) [Fr.] Cloth used for straining soups or sauces.

tartare (tär târ′) [Fr.] A cold mayonnaise sauce, flavored with gherkins, capers, and herbs.

tarte (tärt) [Fr.] Tart; pie.

tartelette (tär t′ let′) [Fr.] A little tart.

tartine (tär tēn′) [Fr.] A slice of bread or a bread and butter sandwich.

timbale case (tim′bal kās′) [Fr.] A case or shell of fried batter in which creamy desserts are served.

tourte (tōōrt) [Fr.] A tart baked in a shallow tin.

truffle (truf′l) [Fr.] A kind of fungus, growing underground, similar to a mushroom: used in seasoning and as a garnish.

turban (tûr′ban) [Turk.] An ornamental entrée of forcemeat or filet of poultry, game, or fish.

tutti-frutti (too′tē frōō′tē) [It.] Mixed fruits, either fresh or crystallized.

V

veau (vō) [Fr.] Veal.

vert, verte (vâr, vârt) [Fr.] Green.

viande (vē ànd′) [Fr.] Meat.

vichy (vē shē′) [Fr.] Mineral or carbonated water.

vol-au-vent (vō lō vän′) [Fr.] Light, puffed pastry shapes filled with ragout of chicken and sweetbread.

W

wurst (woorst) [Ger.] Sausage.

Z

zest (zest) A rind of lemon or orange.

Index